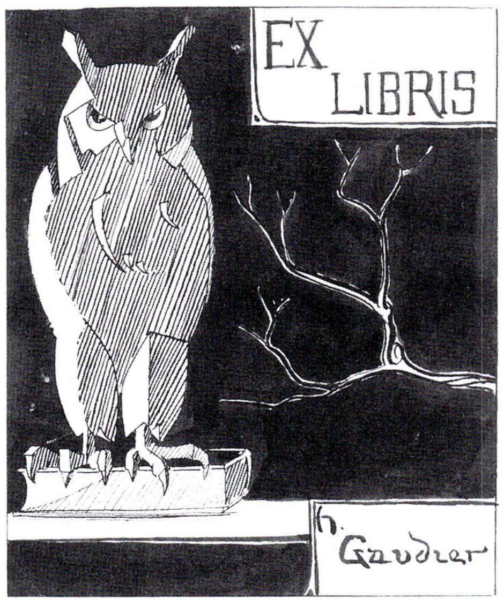

GAUDIER-BRZESKA
LIFE AND ART

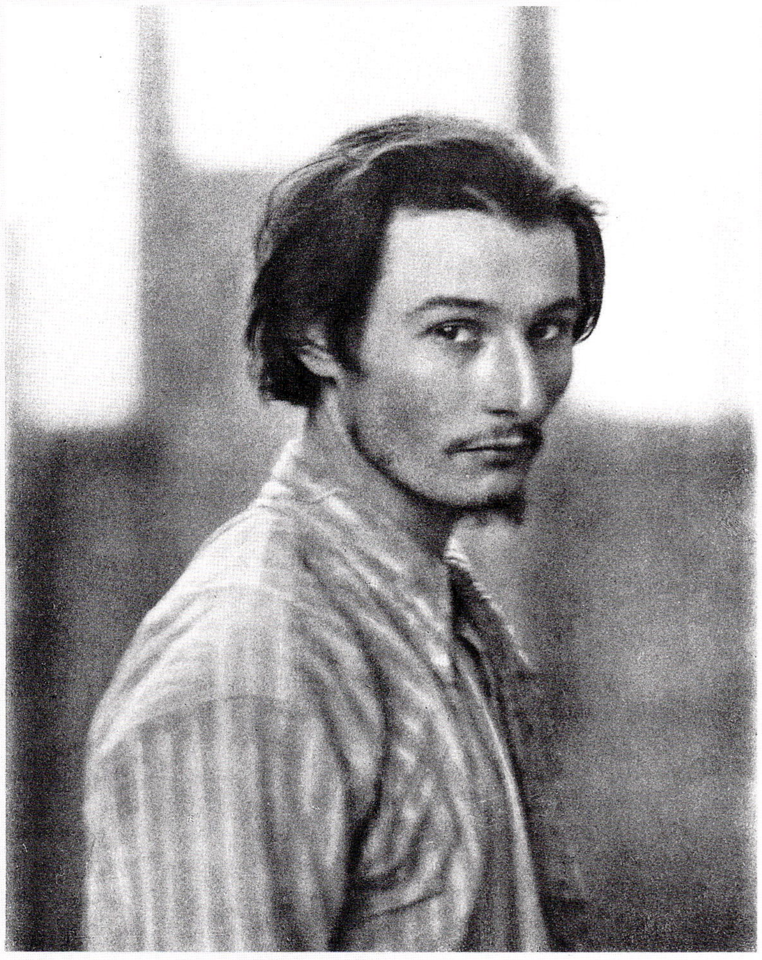

EVELYN SILBER

GAUDIER-BRZESKA

LIFE AND ART

PHOTOGRAPHS BY DAVID FINN

With a Catalogue Raisonné
of the Sculpture

*295 illustrations, 16 in colour,
168 in duotone*

THAMES AND HUDSON

The publishers are especially grateful
to Iris and B. Gerald Cantor
for their generous support of this publication.

1 (half title) *Ex Libris Design with Owl*, 1907–8
2 (frontispiece) Henri Gaudier-Brzeska. Photograph by Walter Benington

British Library Cataloguing-in-Publication Data
A catalogue record for this book is available from the British Library

ISBN 0-500-09261-3

Printed and bound in Singapore by C.S. Graphics

CONTENTS

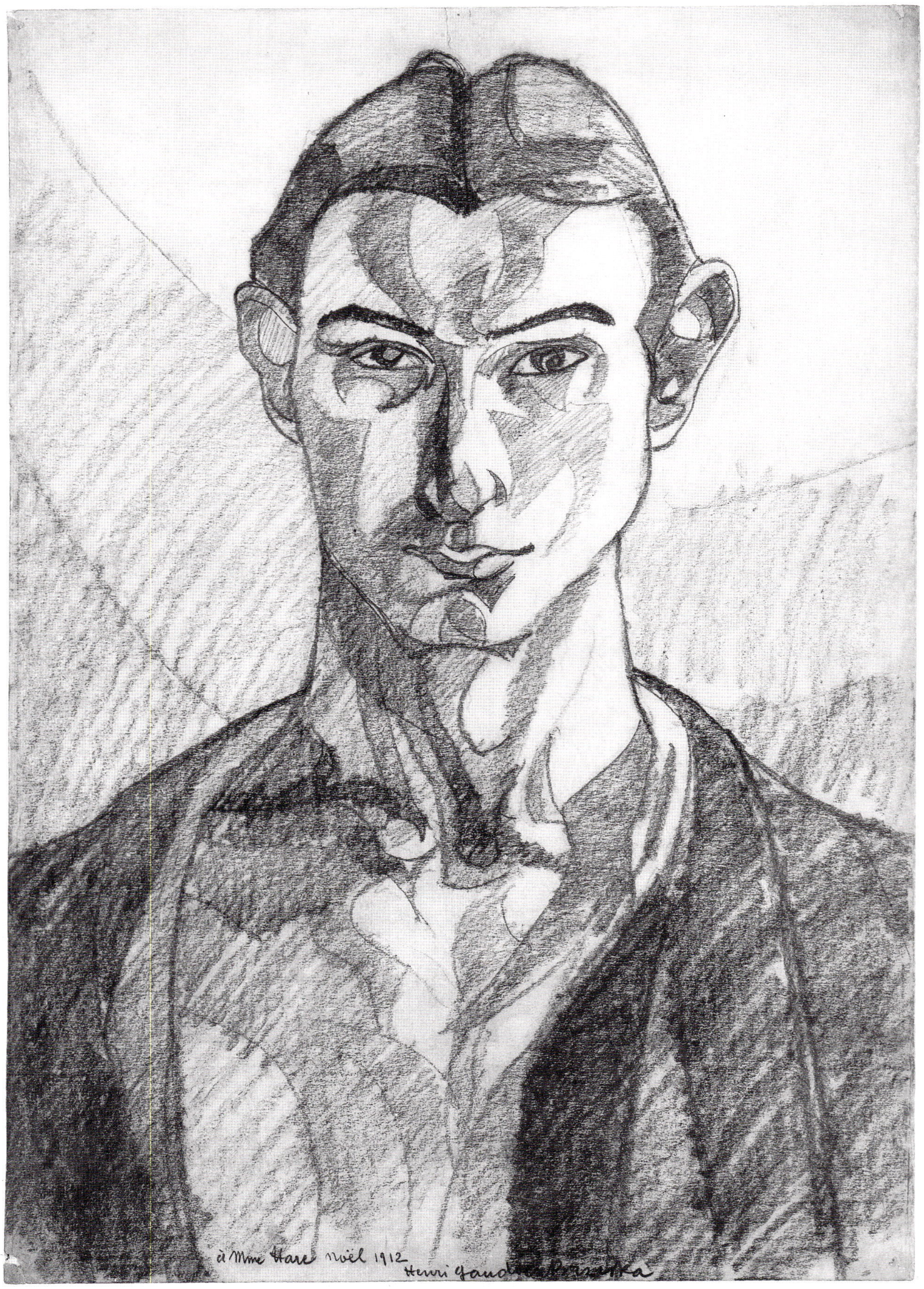
à Mme Hare Noël 1912

INTRODUCTION

There died a myriad,
And of the best, among them,
For an old bitch gone in the teeth,
For a botched civilization.
Ezra Pound,
Hugh Selwyn Mauberley IV

Six million men died during the First World War, but the loss of the brilliantly talented young was especially poignant; their early achievements tantalizingly suggested a wealth of possible futures forever denied. A few artists and writers escaped direct engagement through conscientious objection, poor health or employment in ancillary activities. But the majority saw action. The casualties – physical and mental – among the British 'war poets' are well known. But within the pre-war groups of modernist artists, the losses had a disproportionately savage impact since these young men were most often their energizing force. The Munich Blaue Reiter (Blue Rider) group, the Cubists, Futurists and Vorticists were all decimated. Franz Marc and August Macke in Germany, the sculptor Raymond Duchamp-Villon and the poet and critic Guillaume Apollinaire in France, the sculptor Umberto Boccioni in Italy, the philosopher and critic T. E. Hulme and the sculptor Henri Gaudier-Brzeska in Britain, were just a few of the casualties from within the European avant-garde.[1]

Henri Gaudier-Brzeska, the youngest of these, was twenty-two when he enlisted in August 1914 and twenty-three when he was killed while serving as an infantry sergeant in the French army at Neuville St Vaast, on 5 June 1915. He was little known outside a small, London-based group of artists, writers and collectors and was completely unknown in his native France. But within his immediate circle, which included such diverse figures as the writers Ezra Pound and Ford Madox Ford, the sculptor Jacob Epstein, the painters Wyndham Lewis, Nina Hamnett and Roger Fry, there was a shared conviction of his outstanding gifts. Pound expressed his sense of a more than personal loss in a letter: 'Gaudier-Brzeska has been killed at Neuville St Vaast, and we have lost the best of our young sculptors and the most promising. The arts will incur no worse loss in the war than this is. One is rather obsessed with it.'[2]

Gaudier-Brzeska's reputation has therefore largely been constructed posthumously through his writings and those of his companion Sophie Brzeska, from the memoirs of his friends and through the labours of artists and art historians working within the variously framed readings of Modernism. His work took time to be appreciated; before 1930 the Victoria and Albert Museum, the Tate Gallery and the Contemporary Art Society had acquired only a handful of his sculptures and drawings, most of which were gifts. However, with the publication of books about him by Ezra Pound (1916), H. S. (Jim) Ede (1930 and 1931) and Horace Brodzky (1933), and the gradual appearance of his work in national and regional collections, Gaudier-Brzeska was recognized as a key figure in the pre-war transformation of British art. Though few artistic careers of significance have been shorter, he produced a remarkable amount – about 120 sculptures of which at least 70 are extant, and more than 2000 works on paper including pastels. The diversity and quality of his work revealed his sensitivity to the competing claims of Post-Impressionism, Primitivism, Fauvism, Cubism, Futurism and Vorticism, of which he was a central figure.

3 *Self-Portrait*, inscribed 'à Mme Hare Noël 1912'

To Frank Dobson, Henry Moore, Barbara Hepworth and John Skeaping, for whom carving direct was a central tenet of their work, Gaudier-Brzeska, more than Jacob Epstein and Eric Gill, was a pioneer and role model. He had taken risks and succeeded in the face of all kinds of adversity. Unlike Epstein and Gill, who were still active in the Twenties, Gaudier-Brzeska's image had not been tainted for the younger generation of sculptors by later evolutions in the direction of his work.

His carvings, though small in scale, were monumental in the lucidity of their volumes; they exemplified a high degree of craftsmanship and a sophisticated understanding of the history of sculpture, yet were dominated neither by their materials nor past models. They were adventurous in their variety from near abstraction to a seemingly intuitive organic unity. His work opened up possibilities which he himself had not had time to develop. He had also written pithily and with astonishing verve about the nature of sculptural form. His *Vortex* essay in *Blast* in 1914 (reprinted here on pp. 279–82) demonstrated his 'amazing faculty for synthesis'; it 'put the whole history of sculpture in three pages'.[3] Its epigrammatic opening, often quoted, acquired the incantatory force of a rallying cry for modern sculpture:

> Sculptural energy is the mountain.
> Sculptural feeling is the appreciation of masses in relation.
> Sculptural ability is the defining of these masses by planes.

Gaudier-Brzeska achieved neither fame nor fortune in his lifetime but the mythology which has gathered around him would befit a far longer-lived and more publicly known artist – a Modigliani, Epstein or Picasso. When Ede's *Savage Messiah* was published the revelatory quality of Gaudier-Brzeska's letters was compared with those of Van Gogh. This book is not a biography but it is impossible to detach his art entirely from the circumstances of his life, so closely were they interwoven. The very brevity of his career begs the question of just what he achieved and why his work has survived. Why should an untrained artist, who had only a troubled three-year career, have attracted a lasting following and had not one but half a dozen books devoted to him? Was there more to it than promise and the advocacy of Pound and Ede? Has his stature as an artist been unfairly boosted or obscured by the mythic power of the life?

This book will attempt to unravel the facts and re-created legends of Gaudier-Brzeska's life; it will seek to examine how these stories relate both to prevailing ideas about the artist and the English art world at the beginning of the twentieth century. Many photographs have been specially taken for this book by David Finn to show Gaudier-Brzeska's sculpture with an attention to detail and a sensitivity to light and surface which has not been possible in any previous book on the sculptor in English.[4]

The catalogue establishes a tentative chronology based on the fragmentary documentation available and supplies information on the making of individual works. However, a purely chronological approach does not seem the most illuminating means of exploring the diversity of his sculpture and drawings as he constantly tested out ideas and put images and lessons learnt into practice. Many of Gaudier-Brzeska's contemporaries – Archipenko, Picasso, Lipchitz, Duchamp – spent ten years or so wrestling with the dissolving tradition of sculptural practice and building up new sculptural languages for themselves; in Gaudier-Brzeska's work this process, so far as it went, took three years. It was not a neat linear development, more a see-saw in the ongoing dialogues between classicism and modernism, representation and abstraction, nature and concept.

However, it was his adventurous sense of three-dimensional form, the instinctive directness with which he used his materials and his inventive wit which made him an artist whose work yields lasting pleasure. It is my hope that this book will contribute to the understanding of his art and the delight of those who see it.

Author's note

By 1911, Gaudier had adopted the name of his companion, Sophie Brzeska. Thereafter his signature was 'Gaudier-Brzeska'. He is referred to in contemporary accounts as Gaudier, Gaudier-Brzeska or simply Brzeska. In the interests of clarity, he is referred to here as Gaudier throughout. Brzeska therefore refers only to Sophie Brzeska.

Gaudier's letters to Brzeska, Mrs Hare and his parents were generally written in French, while his letters to Kitty Smith and other English correspondents were in English. Neither the original letters to Dr Uhlemayr nor copies have been available to the author. From the excerpts of Gaudier's letters to him reproduced by Cole and from the comments Gaudier wrote on drawings sent to him, these letters were in both French and German. Gaudier's letters are quoted in the excellent translations made by Jim and Helen Ede, supplemented by my translation of omitted passages from the originals. Though some of Brzeska's stories were in Polish, her 'Détails pour Matka' and her Journal 'A ta très chère mémoire' were written in French. Brzeska is quoted in my translation.

ABBREVIATIONS

AAA – Allied Artists' Association

Brodzky – Horace Brodzky, *Henri Gaudier-Brzeska*, London 1933

Brodzky, *Drawings* – Horace Brodzky, *Gaudier-Brzeska Drawings*, London 1946

Cole (1978) – Roger Cole, *Burning to Speak: The Life and Art of Henri Gaudier-Brzeska*, Oxford, 1978

Cole (1995) – Roger Cole, *Gaudier-Brzeska. Artist and Myth*, Bristol 1995

Cork, *Vorticism* – Richard Cork, *Vorticism and Abstract Art in the First Machine Age*, 2 vols., London, 1946

Ede, *Life* – H. S. Ede, *A Life of Gaudier-Brzeska*, London, 1930

Ede, *SM* – H. S. Ede, *Savage Messiah*, London, 1931

Levy – M. Levy, *Gaudier-Brzeska: Drawings and Sculpture*, New York, 1965

Matka (Orléans), *Matka* (CUL) – Brzeska's autobiographical writings, variously headed 'Détails pour Matka' and 'A mon fils adopté', are now split between Orléans, Musée des Beaux-Arts MO 93.2.1 (1910–11) and Cambridge University Library Add. ms. 8554 (1911–15).

Journal – Brzeska's *Journal* (July 1915 – November 1922) is among the Gaudier-Brzeska Papers (Essex University Library).

Pound – Ezra Pound, *Gaudier-Brzeska. A Memoir*, London, 1916. Unless otherwise stated the edition cited is Marvell Press, Hessle, 1960.

Secrétain – Roger Secrétain, *Un sculpteur "maudit": Gaudier-Brzeska 1891–1915*, Paris, 1979

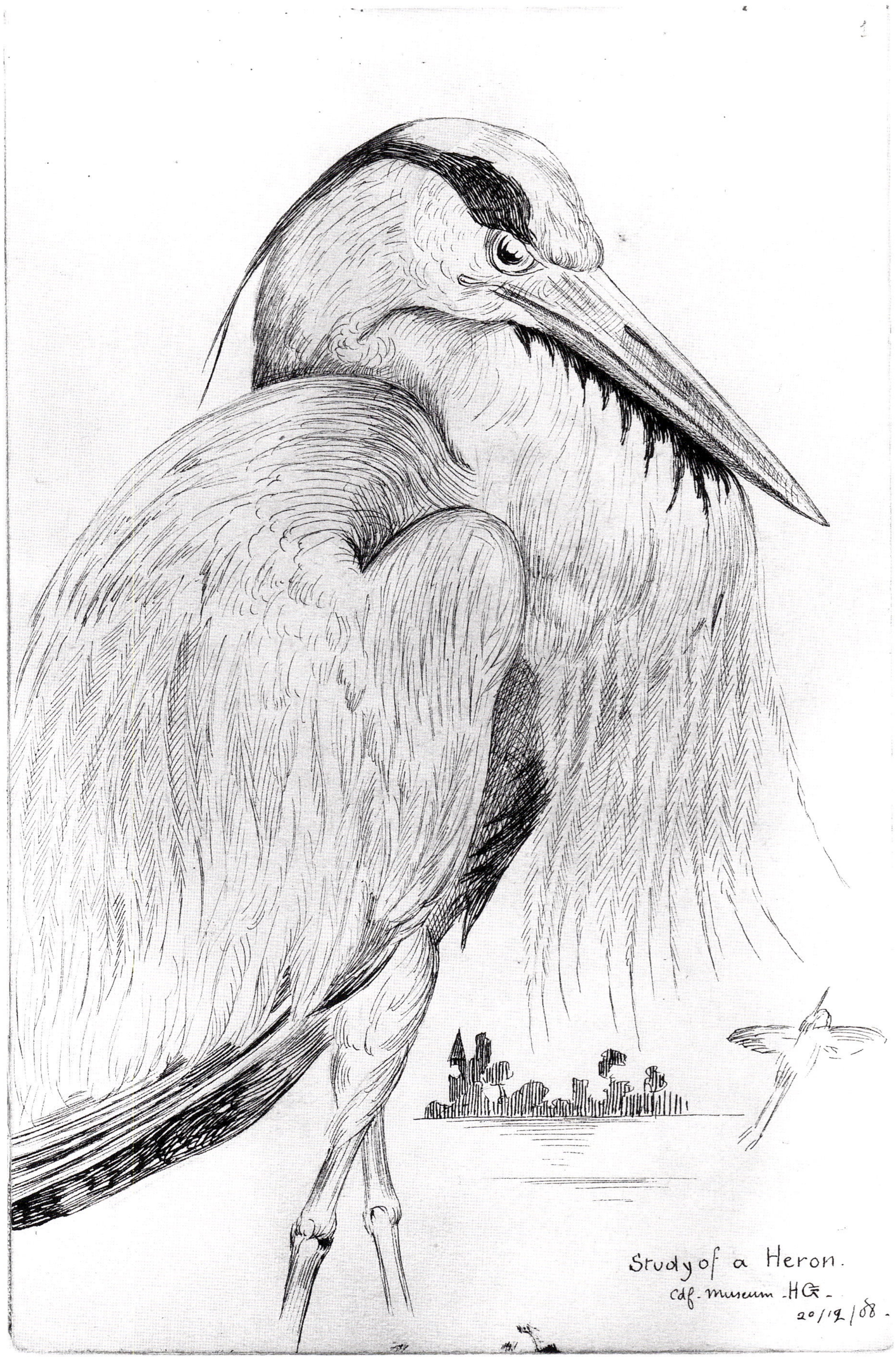

4 *Study of a Heron*, 1908

PART ONE: THE LIFE OF GAUDIER-BRZESKA 1891–1915

1

St Jean de Braye and Orléans 1891–1907

In April 1891 the joiner Germain Gaudier and his wife Marie-Alexandrine Bourgoin moved to St Jean de Braye. It was a village of some 400 houses and fewer than 2,000 people just north-east of Orléans and a couple of kilometres from the River Loire. Though still rural, surrounded by vineyards and farms, St Jean de Braye was, like many of the villages on the Seine depicted by the Impressionists a few years earlier, in the throes of change as France became increasingly urban and industrialized. Vomimbert, where the Gaudiers settled, was a district of new houses on the edge of the village, and the place lay close enough to Orléans itself to be increasingly absorbed into the economic and social life of the historic town, of which it is now a suburb.

Both families had roots going back generations in northern France and carpentry seems to have been their hereditary craft.[1] Gaudier *père* originally came from Sougy, 20 kilometres north of Orléans, where his father had also been a joiner. There was even an oral tradition that an ancestor had taken part in the building of Chartres Cathedral.[2] The couple had been living only a few miles away at Vennecy, east of Orléans, where they had met when Germain Gaudier came to work for Marie-Alexandrine's father, a wheelwright, and where they had married on 3 October 1887. At St Jean de Braye they moved into a neat detached house at Vomimbert, a little distance from the village on the Pithiviers road (fig. 6).

The year they moved, on 4 October, their first child was born and named Henri Alphonse Séraphin Marie Gaudier. There followed two daughters – Henriette, born in 1893, and Renée in 1899. Comparatively little is known about their family life. Madame Gaudier remains an enigmatic figure; physically she was a thin ruddy-faced woman who spoke the local *patois*.[3] Gaudier *père* seems to have been an upright but strict, moody man of conventionally patriotic outlook, who made a reasonable but modest living from his craft, using a wooden shed attached to the house as his workshop. He also did a little drawing and painting, his skills being called on by local groups to paint the decorative backdrops for the entertainments they staged.[4] Among the children's most constant experiences would have been the sights, sounds and smells of a carpenter's workshop and their father's activity designing, accurately shaping and joining timber to meet the requirements of his clients.

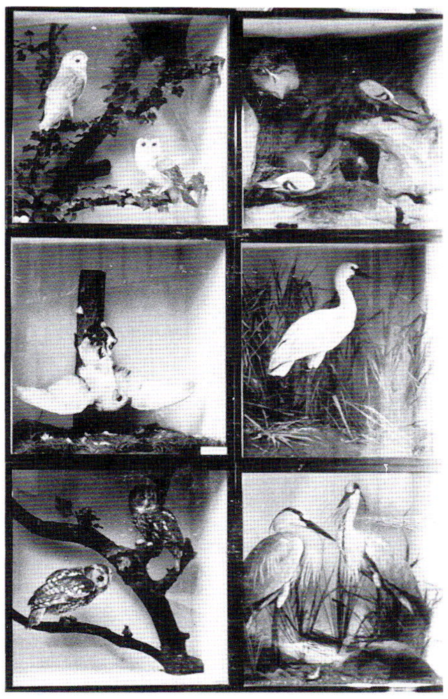

5 Ornithological displays at the old Cardiff Museum. Heron visible bottom right. Early 20th century

Germain Gaudier was also a knowledgeable and, by all accounts, observant naturalist who knew 'the name of all the flowers, the trees, the animals, the birds, everything he saw'.[5] There was much to see within walking distance of their home – in the Charbonnière woods only a kilometre to the north, and by the Loire only a little further to the south. The river was host to masses of migrant birds as well as to a rich indigenous population. The young Henri acquired a keen interest in nature and made collections as well as drawing; when he went at the age of fifteen to stay with the Smith family in Bristol, their daughter Kitty, several years younger than Gaudier, was impressed by his knowledge of the birds and

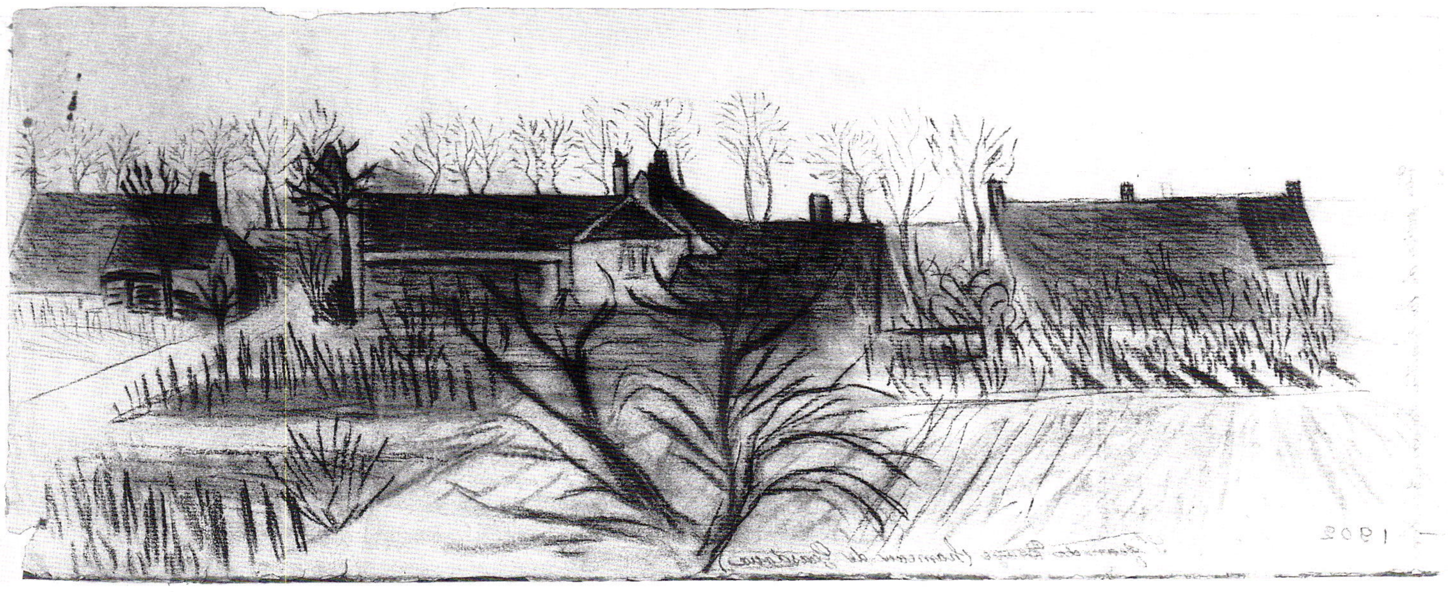

6 *View from Bedroom Window, St Jean de Braye*, 1902

animals around St Jean de Braye and by the collection of moths and butterflies he had brought with him.[6] He told her he spent his school holidays fishing and wandering alone in the woods watching the wildlife.[7] Many of the early drawings he kept and over which he had taken most pains were of birds and animals copied from other works of art or from museum specimens (fig. 4) and in 1912 he would still describe himself as 'a passionate naturalist'.[8]

Given the predominantly rural character of the village and the family tradition, it is likely that at first little more was expected than that Henri Gaudier would follow in his father's footsteps. He would acquire pride in his skill and the family's artisan tradition but would remain within the close-knit, highly conformist parameters of life in a provincial French community. However, by the time he took his first communion at the age of twelve, it had become apparent that, in addition to a talent for drawing, he was highly intelligent. He went on to the more competitive environment of the nearest école normale supérieure, the Ecole municipale professionelle (soon to become the Ecole Benjamin Franklin) in Orléans. The teaching at the school was academic but it was devoted neither to a classical education like the Lycée nor to art training like the local Ecole des Beaux-Arts; technical skills, including shorthand and languages, predominated.[9] Successful pupils went on to clerical and junior managerial jobs in public service and business.

Gaudier soon distinguished himself; he received nine commendations in the honours list in his first year, achieved his school certificate with a special prize for English in 1906, and the following year won one of the highly competitive national bursaries for two years' work-study abroad.[10] Curiously none of these prizes was for drawing, yet he drew obsessively, not only in the margins of his schoolbooks but in sketchbooks filled with observations of everyone and everything around him, including copies of newspaper illustrations and prints, and his own room.

A sketch of Gaudier's bedroom in Orléans dating from 1907 (fig. 7), probably shortly before he left for England, contains at first sight the clutter of souvenirs, jumble and favourite images that one might expect in any schoolboy's room; a closer look reveals objects which already foreshadow many of his later preoccupations. Alongside the globe and a model of the Eiffel Tower are prints after Dutch and Italian Old Masters and a dramatic shipboard scene. The head of a woman on the chest of drawers may conceivably have been his own work rather than a purchased cast. However, the array is dominated by the natural world – a cockle shell, a mounted kingfisher on a branch and a bat with outspread wings, as well as a powerful image of a tiger's head which is either his own watercolour of May 1907 or the print after the late nineteenth-century Chinese painting from which he had copied it.[11] However, surviving drawings from this period are rare, for Gaudier tore nearly everything up. When his father reproached his destructive behaviour he replied, 'What matters is that I have done them. If I kept them I'd be tempted to do them again and that would be lazy.'[12]

In spite of being the eldest child, the only son and showing such promise, Henri's relationship with his parents does not seem to have been particularly affectionate. He told Sophie Brzeska that he had always been in revolt: 'even when I was a child I would fight my parents until they had to give in.'[13] At all events his mother seems to have given most of her affection to the older of his two sisters, Henriette. Later Gaudier was to agree with Sophie Brzeska that neither of them had done well with their

7 *The Bedroom, St Jean de Braye, c.* 1906–7

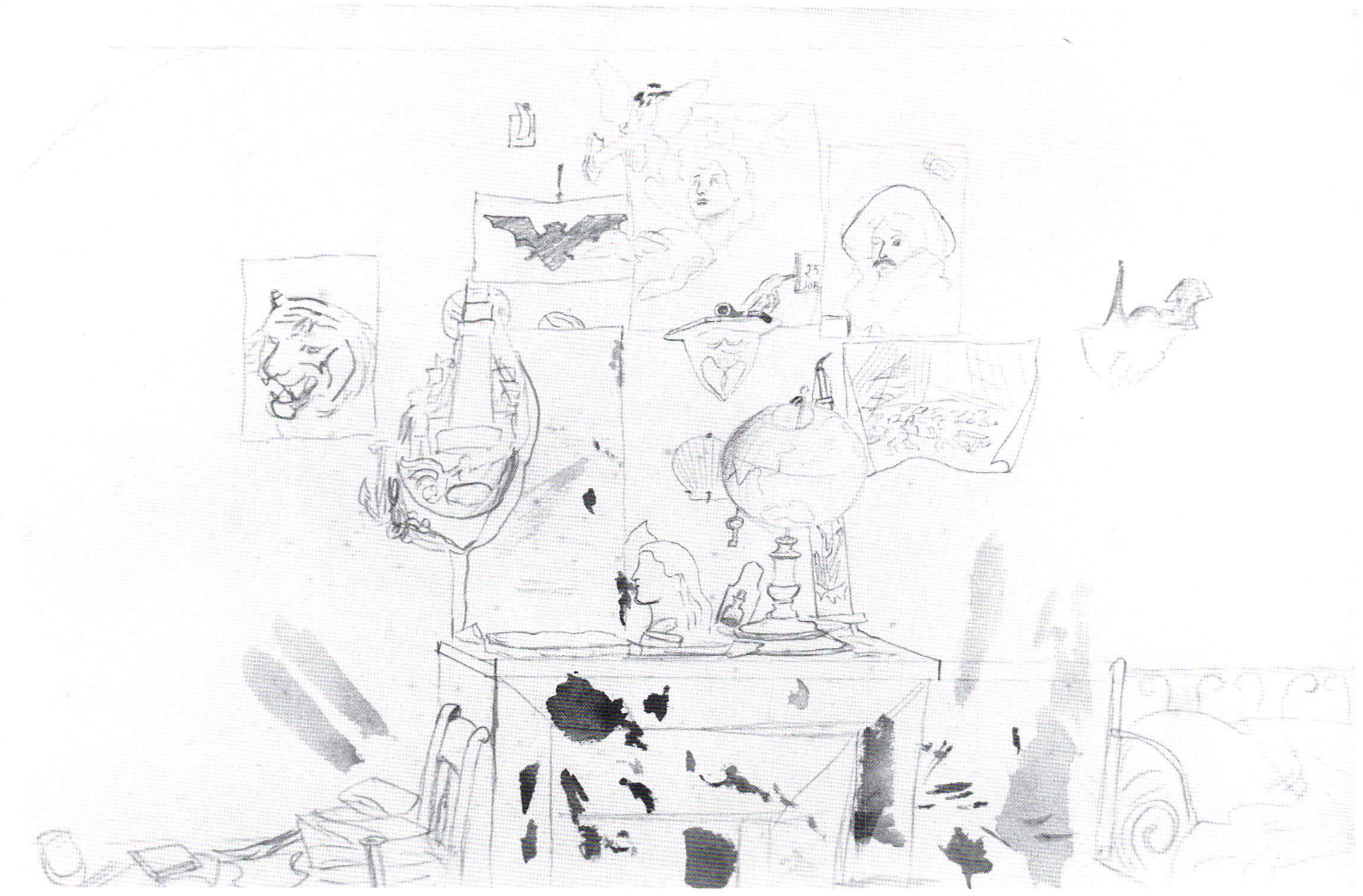

mothers, both being monsters.[14] The relationship between Germain Gaudier and his son was much closer; Henri's ingenuity with materials and his keen observation and enjoyment of nature seems to have stemmed from his father. But the relationship seems also to have been quite combative. His father encouraged him to argue his views forcefully and, as he grew older, their disputes became fiercer; Gaudier seems to have told Sophie that he was frequently beaten until one time, when he was fourteen, he had fought back kicking and biting, after which he was let be.[15] Gaudier's best early portrait, and one of very few to lack a satirical edge, was of his father (*cat.* 2). Germain Gaudier's interest in Henri's drawing certainly did not mean that he viewed his mania for it as anything other than a hobby; he now expected his clever son to go into business in Paris with all the prestige that life in the capital conferred.[16]

In the summer of 1906 Gaudier's academic prowess won him a two-month visit to London and the following year he was awarded one of the prized national bursaries worth 3,000 francs to study business methods abroad.[17] At first it seems Mr Gaudier opposed his son taking up his scholarship. To have been abroad at all was comparatively rare in France at this time.[18] For someone who had probably travelled very little, the notion of his son going abroad alone for two years must have been alarming and of dubious value, as well as signifying his separation from family tradition. But the bursary was aimed at training for a commercial career and the English, by common consent, excelled at business, whatever other suspicions a Frenchman might cherish about them. In July 1907 Gaudier left for England.

The fifteen-year-old who now left home was an energetic, slight, wiry youth with an intense, alert gaze. His world had previously been circumscribed by small town life, the natural beauty of the surrounding countryside and the patriotic dignity of Orléans, its cathedral and its association with Jeanne d'Arc whose heroic equestrian figure by Foyatier dominated the Place du Martroi. Paris was only an hour or two's train journey away and we may guess that Gaudier already knew the city a little. It would have been hard to be unaware of the political tensions still aroused by the Dreyfus case and its aftermath, of political ferment, anarchist attacks and assassinations taking place in France and throughout Europe. Fear of Germany was not far from the surface of events whether viewed from France or England; reports of the fleet, of exercises and manoeuvres were frequent. However such matters would have been more or less remote from his personal experience. Going off alone to study and live abroad gave them far greater immediacy. If Gaudier left France as a bright schoolboy he returned two years later as a precociously well travelled youth whose personality, ideas and ambitions had assumed independent, well defined form.

2

Bristol and Cardiff 1907–9

Nothing is known about Gaudier's first visit to London during the summer of 1906, where he stayed or what he did. We can only surmise that it would probably have been largely a holiday spent practising his English in a family setting. He would have experienced the doubtful pleasures of *cuisine à l'anglaise*, learnt to get about by tram, omnibus and by underground and would have visited some of the usual sights – the Thames, the Houses of Parliament, the Tower of London, the South Kensington museums, the British Museum in Bloomsbury, the National Gallery in Trafalgar Square and perhaps the Tate Gallery on Millbank where British and contemporary art could be seen. He would have encountered the English mania for sport – Henley, Goodwood, cricket – and perhaps glimpsed the social and economic divide between the urban rich and poor, upper and working classes, which would have been more dramatically apparent in the Edwardian metropolis than in Orléans.

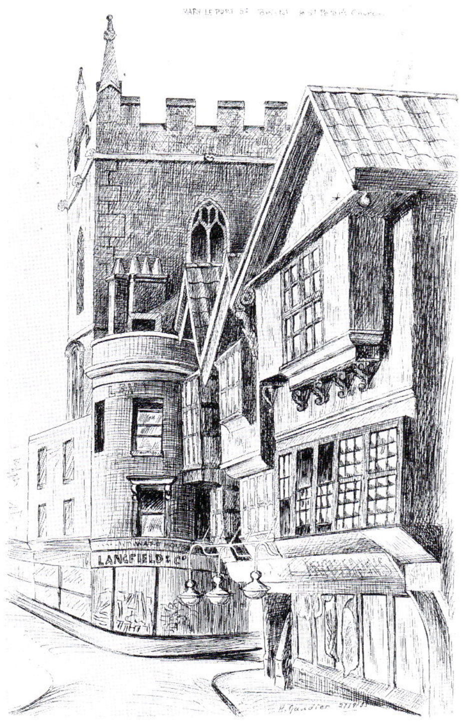

8 *St Peter's Church, Mary-le-Port, Bristol,* 1907–8

When he returned to England to take up his government bursary a year later in September 1907, his time was far more structured; he spent a full academic year at Merchant Venturers' Technical College in Bristol, an established contact for these prize-winning students, though Gaudier was the only French student that year. He was lodged comfortably *en famille* with one of his teachers, George Smith, at 24 Cotham Grove, Bristol. He was able to visit Bath, Somerset and Wales, to join the family on bicycle rides in the country as well as studying and drawing (fig. 8). He retained warm memories of the Smith family and continued to correspond with their daughter Kitty for the rest of his life.[1]

In September 1908 he moved on to less homely lodgings at 29 Claude Road, Cardiff, while he worked for a small coal export company, Fifoot, Ching & Co., who had already received two previous French scholarship winners.

It is during this period that certain aspects of his personality – strength of purpose, unconventionality and humour – first begin to come into focus through the eyes of others. Mr Ching perceived that 'commerce was not his forte and that he should be bound to leave it at the first possible chance.' He was 'somewhat Bohemian, and just a little casual, which was perhaps to be expected in a lad of his nature, but he was the kind of boy that one would have expected, if necessary, to have lived in a garret whilst he got on with his life's work as he felt it to be.'[2] He was getting by more than adequately on the minimum amount of the work he was supposed to be doing, while spending all his spare time drawing. Alfred Hazell, an employee at Ching's on whom Gaudier made a lasting impression, recalled more than twenty years later, 'Henri Alphonse Seraphim Mari [sic] Gaudier, he called himself, and … spent virtually all of his time drawing, with a special passion for pen and ink pictures of bits of old churches, and Ruskin was his guide.'[3] Ching himself gave him credit for rather more work when he looked back in 1929 to the seventeen-year-old Henri Gaudier's time at his business:

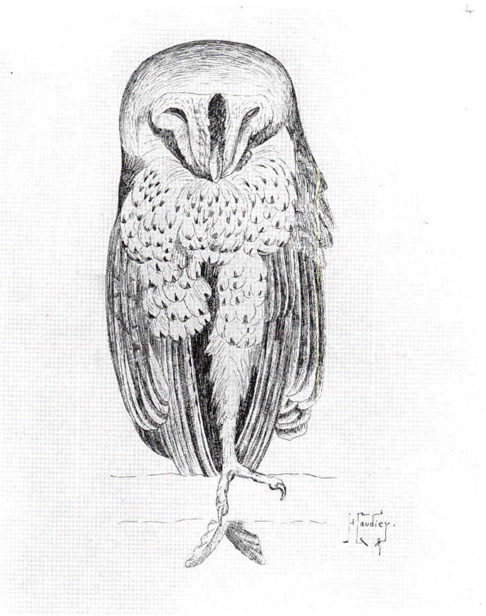

9 *Barn Owl*, 1909

> whilst he excellently fulfilled the duties allotted to him, one could easily notice that his mind was not altogether in his work. Art undoubtedly occupied the greater part of it and in his spare moments he was everlastingly, pencil or pen in hand, sketching some little incident that appealed to him … During his lunch-hours he periodically walked across to the Docks and brought back with him a small sketch of perhaps the bow of a boat or the pine end of a crane or tip.[4]

He also used the natural history displays in the Cardiff Museum for his studies of birds and it was doubtless close proximity to serried ranks of mounted specimens (fig. 5) which inspired a whimsical drawing, now sadly lost, but still cherished in the late Twenties by Ching: 'a taxidermist with one hand to his nostrils while holding up with the other what appears to be a stoat evidently sent him for treatment, whilst at his feet a "tabby" rubs its head in a very lifelike manner.'

Nuremberg and Munich 1909

ON 12 APRIL Gaudier left Cardiff to say farewell to the Smiths before travelling to London. There he seized the opportunity to do some drawings after the Parthenon frieze in the British Museum before setting out for Nuremberg on 16 April (fig. 10). After three days' train journey he reached the home of Dr Uhlemayr and his family at 9-3 Schlüsselfelderstrasse.[5] Gaudier was far more reserved about Germany than about Britain; soon after his arrival, he wrote to his parents that, lovely though Nuremberg was, he preferred England and 'if ever the English go to war with the Germans, I shall be on their side and will be delighted every time these "pointed helmets" get the worst of it.'[6] Some of his sketches of German life are also informed by social unease (fig. 11).

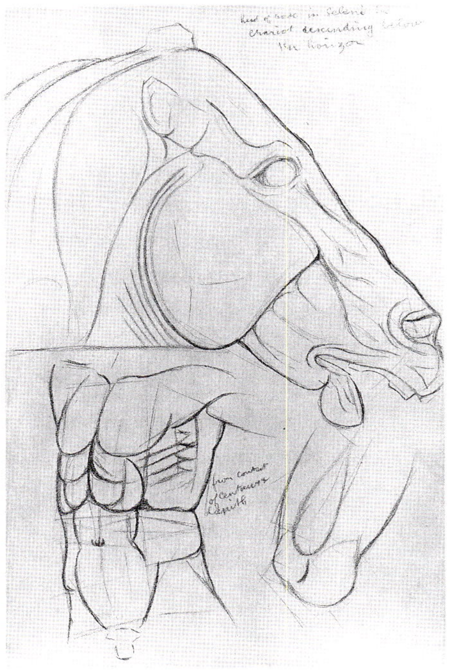

10 *Drawings after the Parthenon Frieze*, 1909

However, the Uhlemayrs were another hospitable family. Gaudier assured his parents, 'I am very friendly with the people of the house', and gave a vivid glimpse of them as they interrupted their lunch to rush out onto their balcony and then into the street to stare amazed, along with most of the rest of the population, at a Zeppelin flying over the town *en route* from Friedrichshaven to the Alps.[7] The children, Gunther and Walter, were too young to provide the kind of companionship he had found in Bristol with the Smiths but Dr Uhlemayr, though of modest origins – one of twelve children of 'a mountain peasant' – was a cultured man interested in art. 'I frequently discuss art and civilization with the Doctor: "Kultur" they call it here', he told his parents and, judging from the frequency of his references to classical art, this formed the substance of much of their discussions, though they also discussed Gaudier's own paintings and drawings. '[He] is a very nice gentleman,' he wrote to Kitty Smith in June, 'Also a nature lover and an art-critic.'[8]

It is unlikely that Gaudier attended formal classes or worked in a business while in Nuremberg, though he was later to claim that he had; there are no hints of it in his letters to his parents or Kitty Smith. Probably the main aim of the visit was to learn German, which he did with alarming rapidity. Many years later Dr Uhlemayr recalled:

It was amazing how quickly he learnt German. He could understand everything after a fortnight, and was fairly good at talking, so that one could converse with him about everything in German. We were surprised at his talent for languages, and his extraordinary gifts and mental richness were also evident. I discussed art and cultural questions with him and found in him an astonishing understanding for all problems of this sort. He obviously felt that he was helped by his conversations with me ... He took up my opinions greedily, without however making himself a slave to them, but on the contrary worked them around in his way and used them as elements in his own view of life ... For as long as he was here, he wanted to be a painter, and he practised indefatigably at it. More often he said when alone that he doubted he was destined to be a painter and thought that drawing would be his only art; at the same time he said he actually was a sculptor. So the genius in him struggled for clarity.[9]

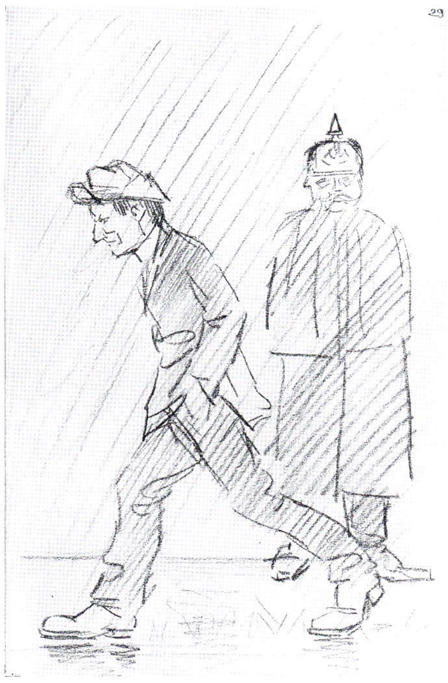

11 *German Street Scene*, 1909

This *Wanderjahr* acted as a catalyst, expanding Gaudier's understanding of art and stimulating him to look at museums, churches and works of art in earnest.[10] The churches of St Sebald and St Lorenz and the Nationalmuseum contained outstanding examples of late fifteenth- and early sixteenth-century carving in wood and stone by Adam Kraft, Veit Stoss and Peter Vischer the Elder. These he certainly studied for one of his surviving sketchbooks which includes, alongside drawings of castles and landscapes of the surrounding area, a drawing after Peter Vischer's self-portrait from the St Sebald Shrine (figs. 12, 13).[11]

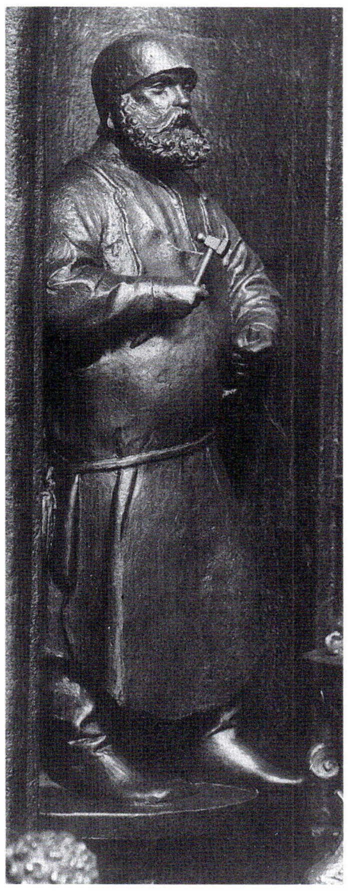

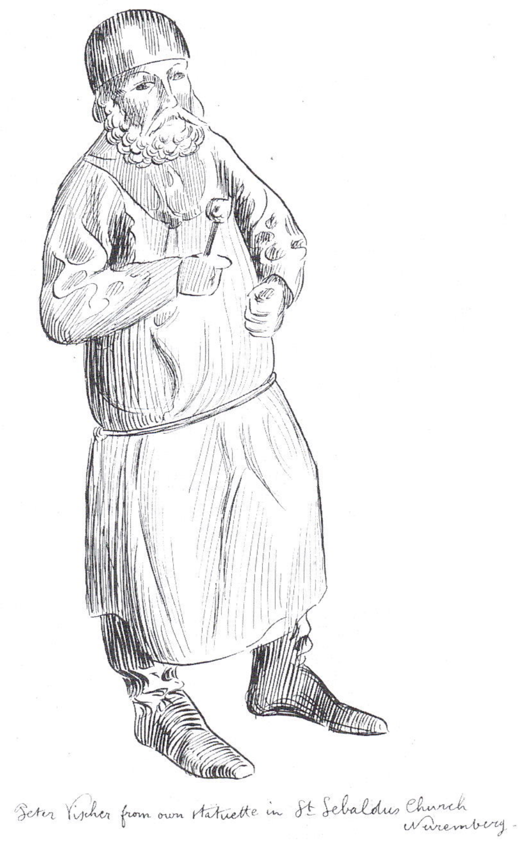

12 Peter Vischer, *Self-Portrait* from St Sebald's Shrine, Sebalduskirche, Nuremberg

13 *Peter Vischer, Self-Portrait from St Sebald's Shrine, Sebalduskirche, Nüremberg*, 1909

However, by early July he was writing to Kitty Smith that he had exhausted the possibilities of Nuremberg – 'I can find nothing new to me here' – and was about to move to lodgings in Munich.[12] Despite the relative brevity of his time in Nuremberg, the visit there and above all making the acquaintance of Dr Uhlemayr were of lasting importance. The cultured Uhlemayr's openness to discussion of serious topics and the breadth of his interests made him a person with whom Gaudier could share his thoughts, receiving from him the understanding and moral support he was losing at home as his aspirations parted company with those of his parents. During the following year and intermittently thereafter, it was to Dr Uhlemayr that Gaudier confided his artistic ambitions.

Gaudier spent about eight weeks in Munich, from mid-July to mid-September. His lodgings at 56 Barerstrasse were well chosen; not far from the artists' quarter of Schwabing, they were practically next door to the Alte Pinakothek. He seems to have spent much of his time exploring museums, galleries and libraries, revelling in the cultural wealth of the city.

During the later nineteenth century Munich had acquired a reputation as a city for art and artists second only to Paris. Even by 1909 when it had been overtaken as German art capital by Berlin and its art market was in crisis, there was still a tremendously busy and varied artistic life. In 1900 Wassily Kandinsky, Franz Marc and Paul Klee had attended the Munich Academy.[13] Contemporary painting, sculpture, illustration and decorative art could also be seen in beautifully produced magazines, *Jugend* and *Simplicissimus*, both of which were published in Munich. Thomas Mann, writing in 1902 with the intimacy of a resident, confidently placed art at the heart of the city's life:

> Every fifth house had studio windows blinking in the sun … Little shops that sold picture-frames, sculptures and antiques there were in endless number; in their windows you might see those busts of Florentine women of the Renaissance, so full of noble poise and poignant charm … If you looked into the windows of the book-shops your eyes met such titles as *Interior Decoration Since the Renaissance*, *The Renaissance in Modern Decorative Art*, *The Book as a Work of Art*, *The Decorative Arts*, *Hunger for Art*, and many more. And you would remember that these thought-provoking pamphlets were sold and read by the thousand and that the discussion of these subjects were the preoccupation of all the salons … Art flourished, art swayed the destinies of the town, art stretched above it her rose-bound sceptre and smiled. On every hand obsequious interest was displayed in her prosperity, on every hand she was served with industry and devotion. There was a downright cult of line, decoration, form, significance, beauty.[14]

There was much else to see, from the royal residences and the Englischer Garten to the famous bronze foundry. The museums were amazingly rich thanks largely to the Wittelsbach collections, with antiquities in the Glyptothek, applied arts in the newly built Bayerisches Nationalmuseum and Old Master paintings, drawings and engravings in the Alte Pinakothek. Modern works, executed after 1800, were on show in the Neue Pinakothek, Germany's first gallery of international contemporary art; and regular exhibitions made a huge range of local and

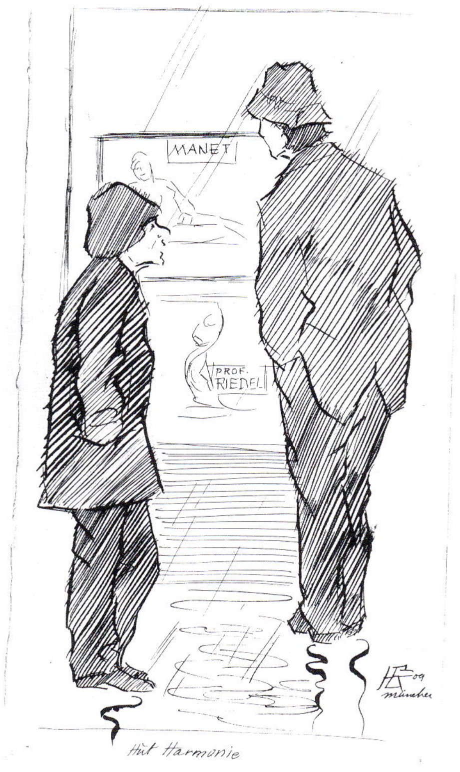

14 *Hüt Harmonie* (Hat Harmony), 1909

foreign contemporary art available.[15] Apart from the one-man shows, such as the Van Gogh exhibition which took place just after Gaudier left, there had for years been huge exhibitions of contemporary art held mostly in Munich's equivalent of London's Crystal Palace, the Glaspalast, and smaller, more selective shows in the galleries of the Munich Secession group.

By 1909, however, the Secession had long since gone into decline; like so many breakaway exhibiting societies it was the product of a particular generation of artists and lost its radical vigour as its members aged.[16] Wassily Kandinsky was just establishing a new group, the Neue Künstlervereinigung, whose members were to hold their first exhibition before the end of the year; amidst the artistic inertia of the city, he reported the foundation of the group as one of the more hopeful recent events, along with the rehanging of many important pictures in the Alte Pinakothek by the new director, Hugo van Tschudi, and a large loan exhibition, *Japan und Ostasien in der Kunst*, which drew on public and private collections all over Germany.

It is unlikely that Gaudier, to whom all this was new, was so critical. Though some of his satirical drawings seem to allude to the contested territory between traditional art teaching and modern art, he lacked the experienced cynicism of Kandinsky who had been working and trying to exhibit in Munich off and on for nearly ten years. From his surviving correspondence there is little indication that contemporary art engaged his attention. Gaudier summed up his feelings two weeks before his return to 'the sweetness of home life' in a letter to Kitty Smith on 31 August:

> On the whole I am very pleased with the town. The life is particularly attractive here, and the picture galleries, libraries, royal collections of engravings have proved so useful to me that I am now so far in art as to be able to go in for illustration as soon as I am in Paris.[17]

The spiky rhythm and strong diagonal hatching of his pen drawings (fig. 14) at this time suggest that he had been studying the types of drawing which appeared in *Simplicissimus* in order to prepare himself for his intended métier, but the following week he wrote of his hopes to work as a draughtsman in a publisher's office such as Hachette or Colin and of his determination to avoid a solely commercial existence: 'As for pure commerce I could not stay three months, I have not got the least sparkle of Jewish spirit, I ought to have borrowed some at the MVTC [Merchant Venturers' Technical College] there's plenty of it there.'[18]

3

Paris 1909–10

After no more than a fortnight at home in September 1909 he moved to Paris and a rented room at 14a rue Bernard-Palissy in Montparnasse, close to the boulevard St Germain and the Luxembourg Gardens with their profusion of sculpture and the Museum with its collections of recent works of art. It was the first time he had really lived alone without an amiable family to keep an eye on him and someone else to take care of domestic chores. He had few contacts at first and his hopes of a job as a draughtsman had been dashed. He was working as a correspondence clerk and translator for Colin which took up ten hours each day. Soon he detested it, as he told Dr Uhlemayr:

> The misery of commerce, though tempered by art, is the enemy of pleasure ... The exigencies of life compel man to obtain money. Commerce provides this but I cannot face it and since art doesn't bring any money I am inclined to abandon this life of a middleman robber which repels me and will do all that I can to learn some craft which will dissipate the idea that to produce nothing during the day is to waste my time. But I have decided nothing ... if I have a trade, I shall still need art ... One thing I can absolutely decide, it is the only thing I can cut off at once, namely to give up commerce for some craft work. I am going to learn the technique of sculpture in wood for cabinet-making. I shall give next month to do this and it is with this I hope to earn my daily bread and not by fleecing the masses. When I face the beauty of nature I am no longer sensitive to art, but in the town I appreciate its myriad benefits – the more I go into the woods and the fields the more distrustful I become of art and wish all civilization to the devil; the more I wander about amidst filth and sweat the better I understand art and love it; the desire for it becomes a crying need.[1]

He resigned from Colin's only a week or two later, telling Kitty Smith that it was 'because of the fierce rapaciousness and lust of lying of tradesmen'.[2] But instead of finding craft work he joined C. P. Goerz, a big German firm manufacturing gunsights, cameras and lenses who marketed their goods throughout Europe. Again the work held little attraction. 'I am supposed to execute all correspondence work and sell cameras to the people who want them,' he told Kitty Smith unenthusiastically. 'I find commerce a kind of torture to me.'[3]

Montparnasse had long been an area favoured by artists, especially sculptors. Mercié, Falguière and Bartholdi had all had studios there and Rodin and Bourdelle were among the best known current inhabitants. Modigliani was living in the boulevard Raspail and later rue Danzig; Archipenko also lived there. Brancusi's spartan quarters were in the rue de Montparnasse, Matisse's apartment and studio were in the boulevard des Invalides. But Gaudier seems to have had little, if any, contact with artists and studios.

After work he would escape to the tranquillity of the Bibliothèque Ste Geneviève, as he told Kitty Smith:

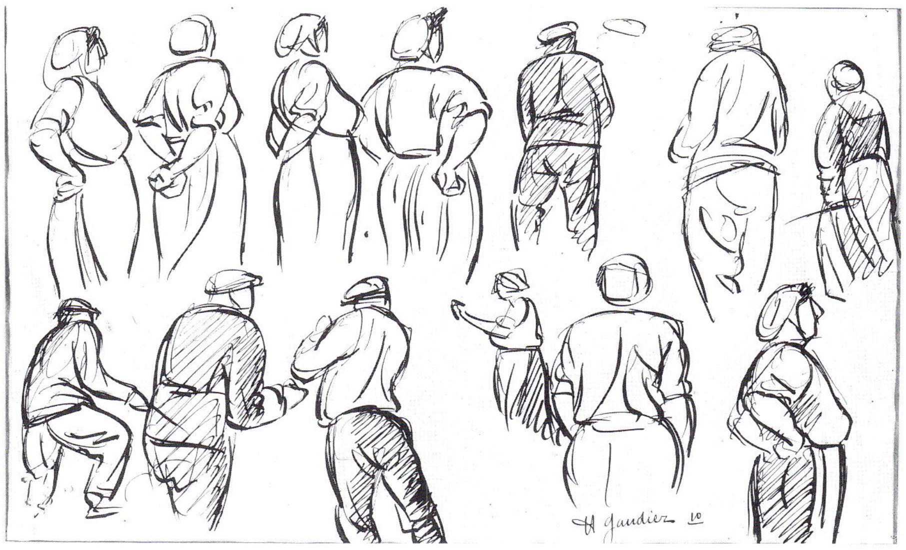

15 *Studies of Men and Women*, 1910

> The day's work is not so long and does not want much strength. The night's work is more pleasant because it is for one's own profit and requires the whole intellect. There is a library not far from my lodgings and every evening you could find me working there between 7 and 10. Then I come home where nobody is waiting for me and as my only friend find the big old stick I used to take with me when I went for long walks. And then, the friends that are dead but can come to life again – in this series are Shakespeare, Ruskin and many others German, French and Spanish, in fact they are so numerous that I cannot pay enough attention to them.[4]

Gaudier may have been laying on the misery of life in Paris a little thick; one can infer from Gaudier's letters that Kitty, working as a shop assistant in the depths of the country, wistfully envisioned Gaudier leading a glamorous life enlivened by 'the nice girls of Paris'. The following year, writing to her from London, he chided her for lamenting her unexciting village life and assured her he disliked the city and was only there for the libraries and museums.[5] Nevertheless one gets a strong sense of his isolation, impatience and depression at the life he was leading as well as his unswerving determination and rapidly expanding intellectual awareness.

His notebooks and sketchbooks reveal not only observations from everyday life (fig. 15), but also the disciplined intensity of his studies – art, philosophy, anatomy – all directed towards his self-education in art. A notebook headed 'Le Chaos', begun in April 1910, announces on its opening page, 'This book belongs to Henri Gaudier who intends to fill it with sketches and drawings'; even the almost Dadaist cover image of a nude bearded cyclist with a mallet on a string trailing from his waist ('Phidias goes to the Acropolis to sculpt the Parthenon figures, riding a magnificent bicycle') seems intended to remind him that even the greatest works of art were made by daily toil and are thus not impossibly remote aspirations. He did numerous candid studies of the heads of his fellow readers: heads, in profile, angled or full-face, are sketched in soft pencil, conté crayon or pen and ink, some gone over in black ink with a brush. All establish solidly on the page the structure and mass of the head with strong diagonal hatching. All are placed unhesitatingly and without erasures. Even now he was an unsparing critic of others, scribbling an

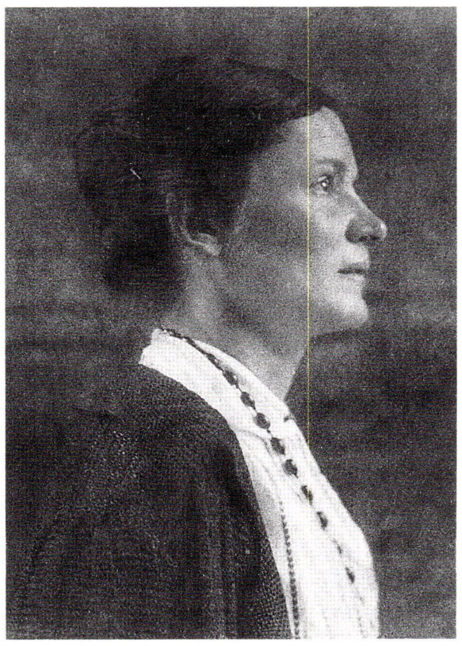

16 Sophie Brzeska (photographer unknown)

angry outburst against one unfortunate acquaintance, a German woman: 'A painter who needs an eraser to draw shouldn't be allowed to have materials but should pass them to talented artists who are dying for lack of money.'[6]

It was during this period of increasing desperation with his work and his life, around April–May 1910, that he got to know another solitary habituée of the library, Sophie Brzeska, a thirty-eight-year-old Polish woman (fig. 16). She was accustomed to sit at the same table in the library, a slight, inconspicuously dressed woman with delicate features and expressive large, dark eyes. Her nervous intensity of mood and occasional significant glances attracted the attention of her neighbours. Gaudier also attracted her attention for he was making sketches of her; he was, she confided in her 'journal', 'as beautiful as an angel (but one acquainted with sin)'. He had wonderful eyes which sparkled with intelligence. She felt drawn to him in spite of his poor clothes, grimy collar and dirty hands.[7] Eventually a request to see his sketchbook led to hours-long conversations in the street or in the nearby cafés. Quite rapidly there came to be friendship, trust and increasing affection between them. She visited Gaudier's room and saw his attempts at clay busts and his drawings; at first he lied to her, pretending that he worked in a sculptor's studio and only later admitting that he was working with others on textile designs.[8] They went together to the Louvre, to the Luxembourg Gardens and further afield to the Vallée de Chèvreuse.[9] The 'Chaos' sketchbook contains the first drawings of Sophie Brzeska and passages from her favourite poetry, Baudelaire's *Les Fleurs du Mal*.

Like him, she cherished artistic ambitions and had already written several short stories unseen by anyone, while eking out her friendless and impoverished daily existence. Tormented by memories of her unhappy childhood, the personal rejections she had suffered, the humiliation of her jobs as a teacher or governess, and finally despairing of her future health and sanity, she had been contemplating suicide before they met. Both were volatile, impatient and discontented. Each seems to have found in the other someone whose intelligence and talent were repressed by circumstance. Naturally talkative and full of fiercely held opinions, both had lacked someone with whom to debate on equal terms. They shared a sharply subversive and observant wit and a scathing contempt for dull bourgeois conformity. Yet their temperaments and background were in other respects in complete opposition. Brzeska was a pessimist, burdened by her past, while Gaudier looked ever hopefully to the future. To her world-weary cynicism and fragile sense of self-worth he presented youthful resilience, driving energy, ambition and apparent self-confidence. At her insistence their relationship was to be platonic; she would be as a mother or sister to him.[10] Though Gaudier was to find this increasingly difficult to sustain, her initial impact on him was overwhelming. Her mixture of intelligence, flirtation, half-bullying affection and touchy independence seems to have answered his need for maternal love and intelligent companionship and to have boosted his confidence in his ability to become an artist. In him, at least to begin with, Brzeska thought she had finally found someone whom she could safely love, care for and trust to treat her with a candour and honesty she demanded.

Within a few weeks of their meeting Gaudier had reached the decision that he must become a sculptor. In late May he wrote to Dr Uhlemayr:

> I have taken a great decision – I am not going to do any more colour work but will restrict myself entirely to the plastic. I have never been able to see colour detached from form, and this year, after doing a few studies in painting, I noticed that the drawing and the modelling were all I have been concerned with. I have put by the brushes and the tubes and have snatched the chisel and the boaster – two simple instruments which most admirably second the most wonderful of modelling tools, the human thumbs. This and clay are all I need now, with charcoal or red chalk and paper. Painting is too complicated with its oil and pigments, and is too easily destroyed. What is more, I love the sense of creation, the ample voluptuousness of kneading the material and bringing forth life, a joy which I never found in painting for as you have seen I don't know how to manipulate colour, and as I've always said, I'm not a painter, but a sculptor. It may surprise you that I can be content with confining myself to this one branch of art, leaving all others untouched. Yet sculpture is the art of expressing the reality of ideas in the most palpable form. It makes plain, even to the eyes of fools, the power of the human mind to conceive ideas, and demonstrates in cold lucidity all that is fervent, ideal and everlasting in the soul of man.
>
> You will have noticed that civilizations begin with sculpture and end with it; painting, music, letters are later refinements … For my part I see quite clearly that I don't wish to wield the brush any longer, it's too monotonous and one cannot feel the material near enough; paints sticks well to the hairs of the brush and sings on the canvas, one appreciates its fertile texture, but the sensuous enjoyment is far greater when the clay slips through your hands, when you can feel how plastic it is, how thick, how well bound together, and when you can see it constantly bringing forth.
>
> I am now right in the midst of Bohemia, a queer and mystic group but happy enough, there are days when you have nothing to eat, but life is so full of the unexpected that I love it as much as I used to detest the stupid and regular life of commercial employment.[11]

It was also to Uhlemayr that he confided his new relationship:

> I have such a lot of things to tell you, but things quite different from those I have already talked about – I refer to the effect of love on one's working power. Would you believe it, I am in Love! I see that you already picture me with some 'backfisch' strolling in the 'Boul Mich', or whispering sweet nothings in secluded corners around the Pantheon. You are wrong; the woman I love is thirty years old – you smile – I love her with a purely ideal love, it is a flow of sensation which you must feel, since words are too coarse a medium to convey it. She is Polish – Brzeska is her name. I met her in the Library where I go to work each evening. I've done several sketches of her, and thus we got to know each other. She is a poet, and her ideas on the family, society and Western civilization are the same as ours; she has an entirely independent nature, simply and naturally, has a beauty à la Baudelaire – and might have stepped out of *Fleurs du Mal*. She is lithe and simple, with a feline carriage and enigmatic face, the fine character of which reflects her most intimate thought – planes combining in the most surprising manner, impressions of

age and youth in alarming contrast. In a word we are both as mad as hatters. Would you believe it last Sunday we talked from eight in the morning until three in the afternoon without noticing how the time had passed. I told her of my ideas about Art for Art's sake, and she explained hers on the basis of a society founded on motherhood undertaken freely and with open eyes. We parted about four o'clock, and I came home and at once set to work. I was so thrilled that I did a great bust that evening to give her the next morning, as she had asked me for a bit of sculpture.[12]

To his parents he was much more secretive about his affair and stopped writing altogether for a while; in late June, he finally wrote to set their minds at rest after a worrying hiatus:

Dear Parents,
I have just seen Mr Maurice – it seems you are anxious about me, and you think that I have run away abroad. I am safe and sound in Paris, and hope to be here for some time yet. I've only changed my job. I went away from Goerz without giving notice because they would have made me stay fifteen extra days. I have now got a job as a draughtsman for materials and carpets. I work ten hours a day and get sixty centimes an hour, I believe, I haven't been told yet, and even if I only get two francs a day I am relatively happier, and I can no longer think why I was such an ass as ever to go in for trade. I know that you will be annoyed by this, but do for goodness' sake get it into your heads that I am an artist and that nothing else holds any interest for me. At figures I am an absolute nincompoop, and in commercial life one must be interested in figures and in money. I shall stay here long enough to learn the tricks of the trade, and then I think I shall go and work in Poland or in Russia. Please don't write me nasty letters about this. With all the will in the world I cannot conscientiously do any kind of work, other than that of a sculptor in wood. Apart from this job I work very hard at my modelling; the drawing here doesn't require any intellectual energy, and when I get home I am still fresh and keen. I am free on Saturday afternoons and Sundays, which is excellent.
Love to all
H. Gaudier[13]

His new job, as a draughtsman in a firm producing textiles and carpets, was far less well paid but at least it was a step in the right direction, however hard it was going to be to follow his chosen path:

I always want to become more than that, an artist, and to become that I must work much – and ever. That's why I have not time left to write to my friends. As I am not earning much now I must get practice as a wood carver, I am just making a big huge frame in order to be able of getting more money. When I have worked thus a few years and have got a small sum I shall take up a studio and make one or two statues, and when the money is gone I shall begin again. Life seems much more interesting that way than doing always the same work, typewriting and everything ... There is huge stock of misery and hard times waiting for me in the way I want to lead my life, but I like it a hundred times better than to die for every breath in an office, obeying Jews all the time, and it wants too much decision, thievishness and wickedness. I cannot consider life so seriously as to be always compelled to tie myself down to material things and events, I want more freedom because I am proud.[14]

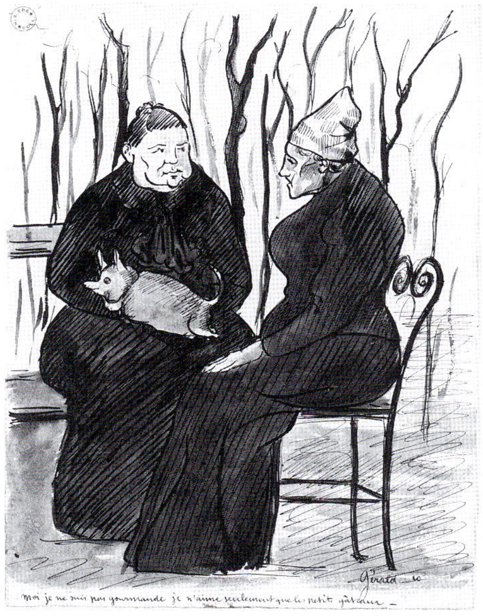

17 *'Moi je ne suis pas gourmande je n'aime seulement que les petits gâteaux'* ('I'm not really greedy, I only like *small* cakes'), 1910

His increasingly anarchistic socialist views – he told Uhlemayr he was delighted that an illustrated anarchist review, *Les Hommes du Jour*, was now being published in Paris – were bringing him to the fringes of political activism.[15] During the same period he was putting forward a critique of Taine's deterministic philosophy, countering that many artists, far from embodying the *Zeitgeist*, were in opposition to society's norms. To his parents he did not use these political arguments but pleaded for art in the interests of his own happiness, and reiterated his total lack of interest in figures and money. His vision of being an artist was severely practical; it would involve poverty, dedication and hardship.

He described himself at this time mixing with a bohemian and cosmopolitan crowd, of Russians, Germans and Poles, both in the library and nearby cafés. Certainly he was articulating increasingly radical views and submitted drawings to two of the leading satirical magazines, *Rire* and *Charivari*, signing himself the English-sounding 'Gerald', though none appear to have been published (fig. 17). As he told Dr Uhlemayr in November, he was acutely aware of his immaturity:

> One's line lacks snap and vigour, and one's outlook is narrow, there is a want of coherence. There are parts which seem free and original, and others which seem full of outside influences and childishness. The editors see this clearly enough, and it is better for their paper, but it sometimes drives me to despair. Still, one has to sacrifice oneself a bit.[16]

Other sacrifices led to a breakdown in his health through a combination of malnutrition, anaemia and overwork. While Brzeska sought rural peace at Royan at the mouth of the Gironde estuary, north of Bordeaux, Gaudier returned home to St Jean de Braye, staying several months to regain his strength. Brzeska moved into a cottage nearby in Combleux. He modelled several portraits in clay, including a carefully characterized one of his father (*cat.* 2, pl. 4), perhaps intended to demonstrate his talent and seriousness of purpose. However, while Gaudier's father appears at first to have been reasonably sympathetic to his ambitions and his relationship, his mother was uncompromisingly hostile; on the sole occasion when she visited the cottage at Combleux she made it clear, according to Brzeska, that she thought Gaudier's ambition to be an artist was shameful and ridiculous.[17]

Scandalous rumours began to circulate in the neighbourhood, culminating in a police visit to Brzeska's cottage after an anonymous letter had denounced her as a prostitute. Furious, Gaudier fired off a letter full of spleen to Dr Uhlemayr, inveighing against the turpitude and decadence of his countrymen and vowing to leave the country. They both returned to Paris and separate lodgings on the Left Bank. After some fruitless job hunting and long debate, Gaudier persuaded Brzeska that they should go to England. There, with his fluent English and less competition for work, he was convinced he would be able to sell his drawings. There was another reason: his two years of military service were due to start the following year, and there was talk of a possible war with Germany. Since he was a small boy, Gaudier had dreamed that he would die in war.[18]

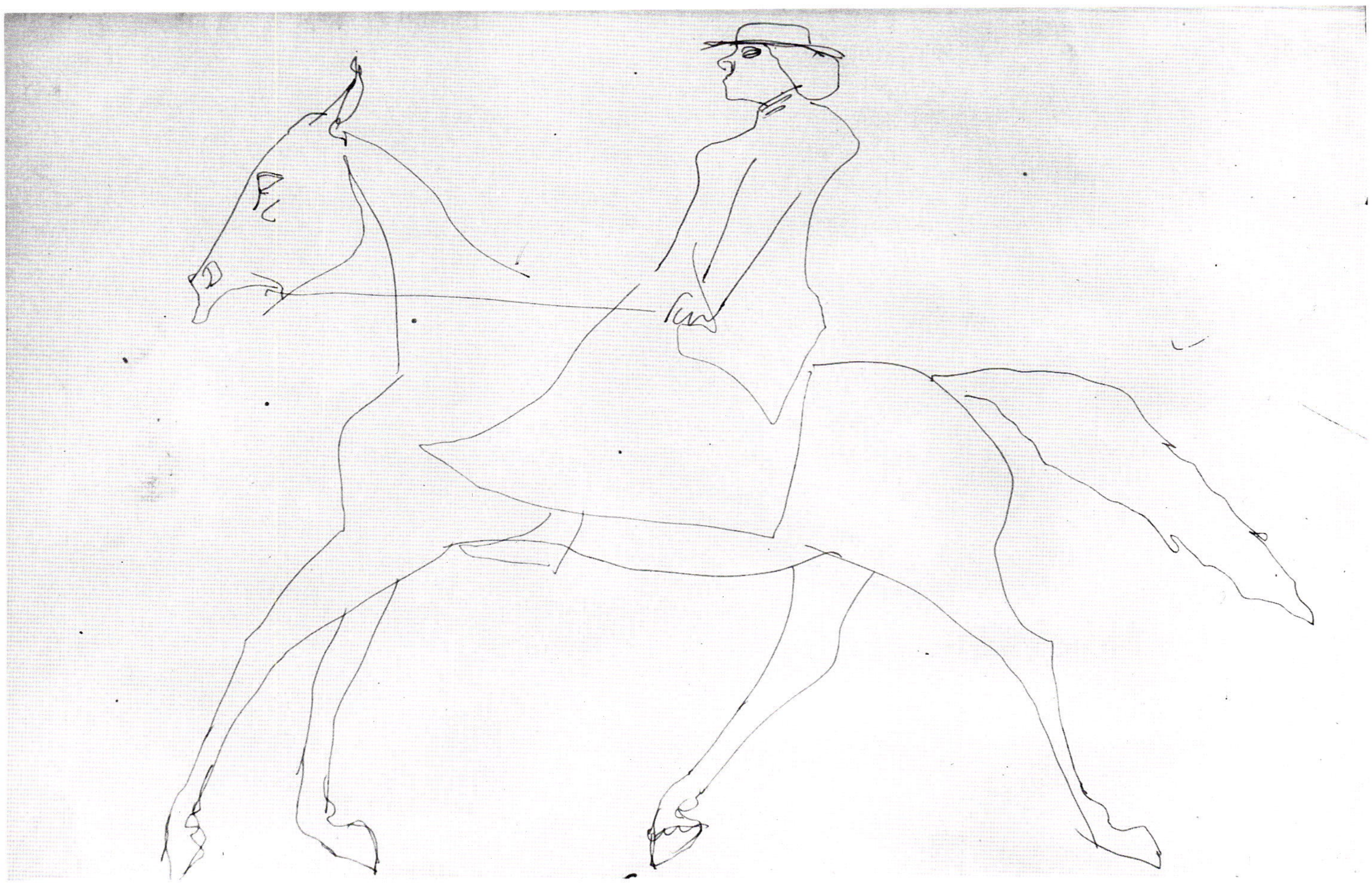

18 *Rotten Row*, c. 1913

19 *A Whitechapel Jewess*, 1912

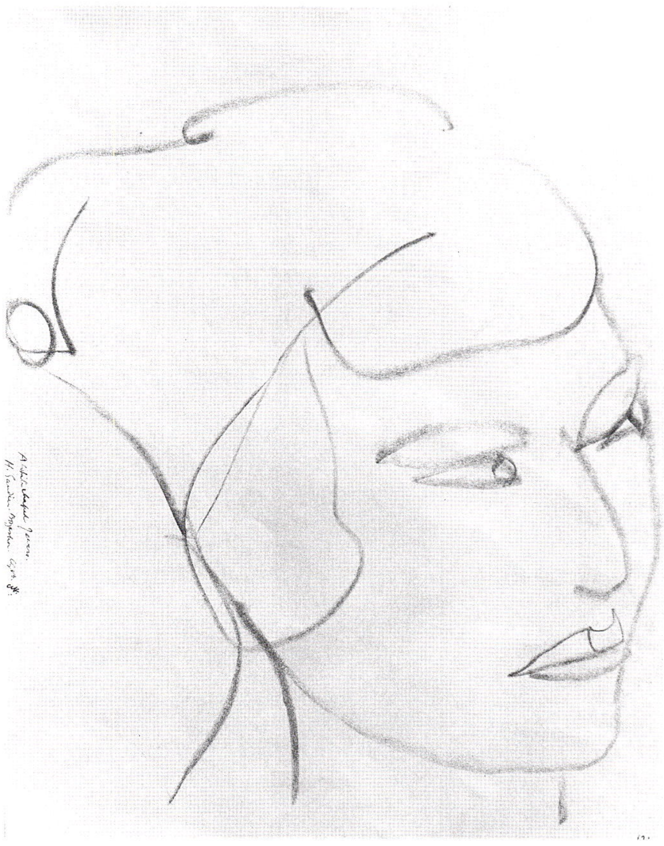

4

London 1911–14

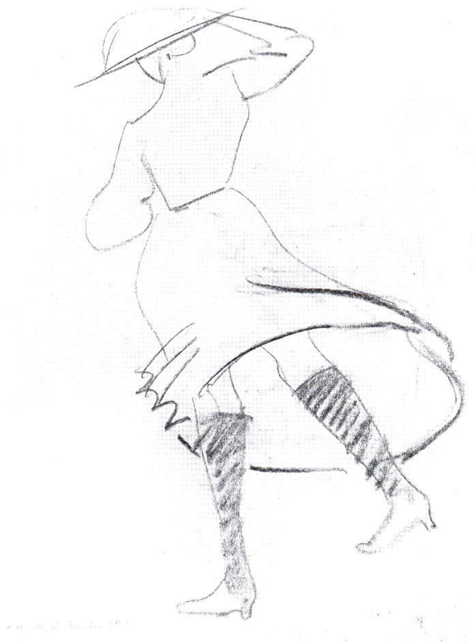

20 *Girl with Skirt Blowing*, *c.* 1912

In January 1911 Gaudier moved to London with Sophie Brzeska, whose name he now added to his own. By presenting themselves as Franco-Polish brother and sister they rendered their co-habitation socially acceptable while also giving symbolic expression to their emotionally charged but unconsummated relationship. They had apparently not lived together in Paris; now, isolated in London with little money and no work, their differences of age and temperament soon began to tell. They moved from one set of cheap, unsatisfactory lodgings in Kensington to another: Edith Road in January, then Sterndale Road. Brzeska, who detested noise, sought above all else clean, tranquil surroundings, while Gaudier cared for nothing but a space he could use as a studio. The ideal of a clean, quiet set of rooms with two bedrooms and space enough for Gaudier to work at his art was apparently unobtainable on their meagre budget.

Gaudier's optimism about finding artistic work was soon dashed. Brzeska evokes Gaudier's frustrated efforts in *Matka*:

> I've knocked on every door. First at the marble and stone sculptors, then at the sculptors who work in wood. Then at the studios of designers and textile manufacturers. I've written to anyone advertising for postcard designs and paper bags; I've shown caricatures and drawings at newspaper offices. There's nowhere I haven't tried to get my foot in the door. And there's nothing! Nothing![1]

In March, to prevent further seepage from Brzeska's savings, he took a clerical and translating job for £6 a month with a timber importer, Wulfsberg & Son, who had offices in St Mary Axe in the City. It was merely a stopgap. Something would soon turn up. In the meantime his schemes ranged from the severely practical to the quixotic. A notebook begun on 5 April 1911 contains pages of colour notes and sketches, made that very day, for floral wallpapers in monochrome, three, five or seven colours, intended for Sanderson's at Chiswick.[2] There are ideas for cartoon captions and a whole list of suitable commercial topics for poster design – chocolate, cocoa, coffee, mustard, sugar, collars, blouses, ties, shoes, razors and soap. Still on the same day he planned a *Gesamtkunstwerk* of architecture, precious marbles and paintings entitled *Matka*, the title of Brzeska's never-completed autobiographical novel. With its three doors of love, birth and death and its frescoed scenes comprising everything from landscape ('sunset and ships on the Loire') to classical figures, cavalcades and battles, all with colour schemes suggested, this temple was an escapist fantasy, a sign of all that art stood for and which seemed so utterly beyond reach. He was to continue working for Wulfsberg for more than two years.

In April Brzeska left London for Felixstowe to take a teaching job. Though she disliked the work, it enabled her to escape from the noisy city and from the strain of life with the nineteen-year-old Gaudier whose

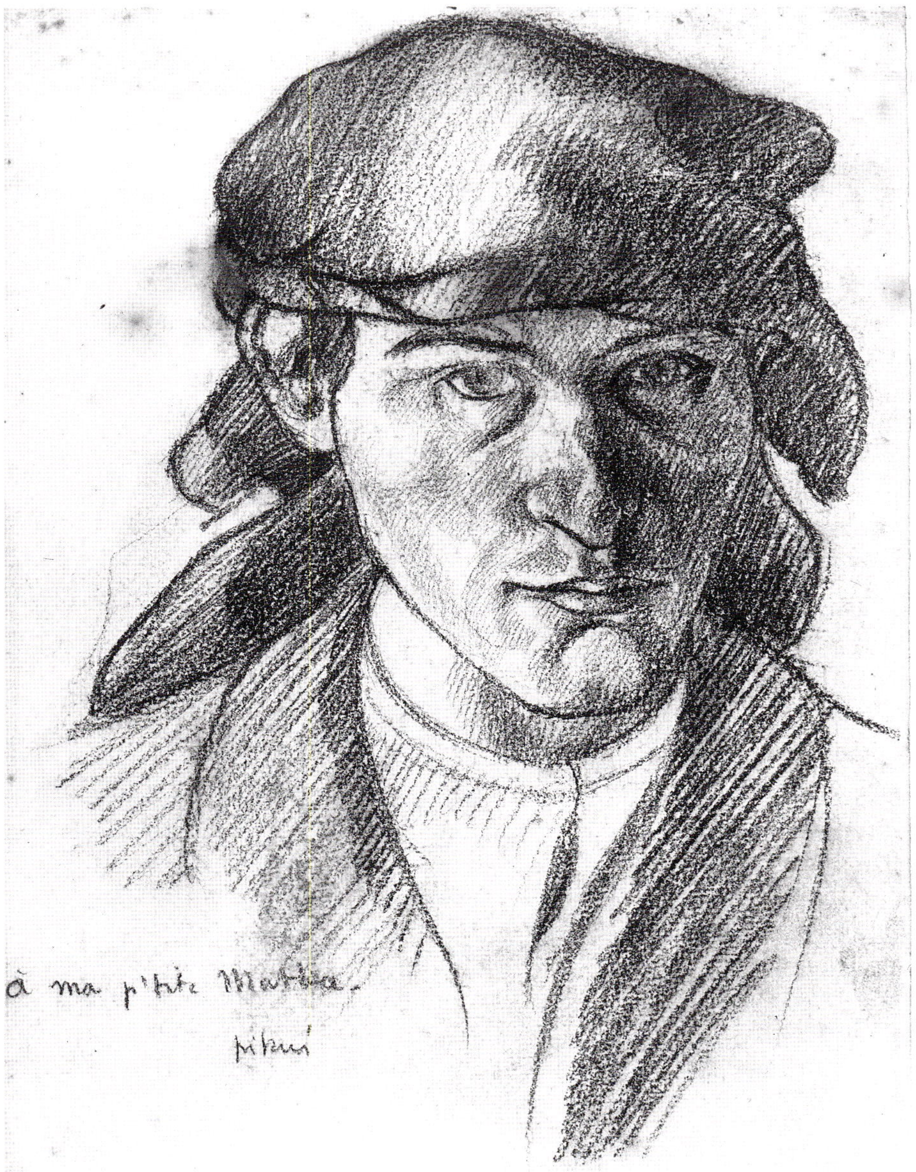

21 *Self-Portrait*, 1912

energy far outstripped her own. She might be able to get on with her writing in tranquil surroundings. They wrote to each other twice or more a week and Gaudier's side of the correspondence – the only part of it to survive – is reproduced in edited form by Ede.[3] It gives a vivid insight into the emotional seesaw of their relationship and of Gaudier's states of mind as excitement over something he had seen or read and the surge of work which went with these discoveries was succeeded by sexual longing, exhaustion and nervous irritability.[4] They met for a few days' holiday at Burnham-on-Crouch in late June before Gaudier returned to town to find new lodgings. His first choice was so bad that they moved after two weeks to 45 Paultons Square, Chelsea, where they remained until early 1912.

Throughout 1911 they remained claustrophobically isolated by their foreignness, poverty, intransigent intellectual pride and by their mutual disdain for the emotional restraint and propriety of the English petite bourgeoisie. Dependent exclusively upon each other, they struggled with the exigencies of daily life and Gaudier's determination to spend every spare minute and penny on his art. During his lunch-hour he would go and draw in the heart of the Jewish community, in Whitechapel markets and library (fig. 18). At weekends he would draw in the park, in the streets, by the river, anywhere there were people and stimulation to be found in capturing them in charcoal, pencil or conté crayon (figs. 19, 20). Visiting parks and museums, especially the South Kensington and British Museums, was their main leisure pursuit. In late September they formed a brief friendship with a Veronese, Arrigo Levasti, whom they met on their museum wanderings. He was invited to visit, but the relationship ended abruptly when he departed unannounced for Italy in December. It was the first of many disillusioning experiences as quick, intense friendships, begun with wild hopes of intellectual and spiritual sympathy, turned just as fast to coolness or enmity.

Their relationship developed a recurrent pattern of violent arguments and brief periods of affectionate calm. Brzeska with her thwarted literary ambitions, poor health and highly strung, acutely self-conscious temperament, rebelled constantly against the physical privations and hostile otherness of life in England. Gaudier, equally frustrated in his intellectual and artistic ambitions, and prone to assert his frequently changing opinions without compromise or excuse, was equally volatile. His desire to establish a relationship of complete intimacy with Brzeska was repeatedly thwarted by her deep-seated anxieties for her own physical and mental well-being; her insistence on a platonic, almost maternal relationship exacerbated his frustration, even while he remained in many ways filially dependent upon her, little 'Pikus' to her 'Mamus' (fig. 21). Brzeska confided her anxieties about him in *Matka*:

> What worries me most about Pik's character is how changeable his opinions are and how completely thoughtless he when he is mistaken. He never has any doubts about anything, it's either positive or negative. To hear him talk you would think he was always right. When you know him better you can't believe more than half of what he says. He's either completely right or completely wrong. It bothers me that I've come to the conclusion that the more confident Pik is in putting forward some idea, fact or belief, the less sure he is of himself.[5]

During the autumn his estrangement from his parents became complete after he refused to return to France for military service. A letter from Louis Gallouédec, Mayor of St Jean de Braye, reproached him for his unpatriotic behaviour, for the pain he was causing his father and for ingratitude after the lavish scholarship he had received. Turning on the emotional pressure, he reminded Gaudier that he would be barred from returning to France even in the case of family illness and that, when his talent brought him success, as it was sure to do, he might have to make a humiliating public act of contrition. In his furious reply Gaudier announced his intention of becoming a naturalized Englishman in two years and of going to Germany to work if he could not work in Paris. More reasonably he proposed to repay the cost of his bursary not in military service but in art.[6] Yet despite his anger he continued to write and send presents to his younger sister, Renée, praising her drawings, sending her paints and advising her how to improve.[7]

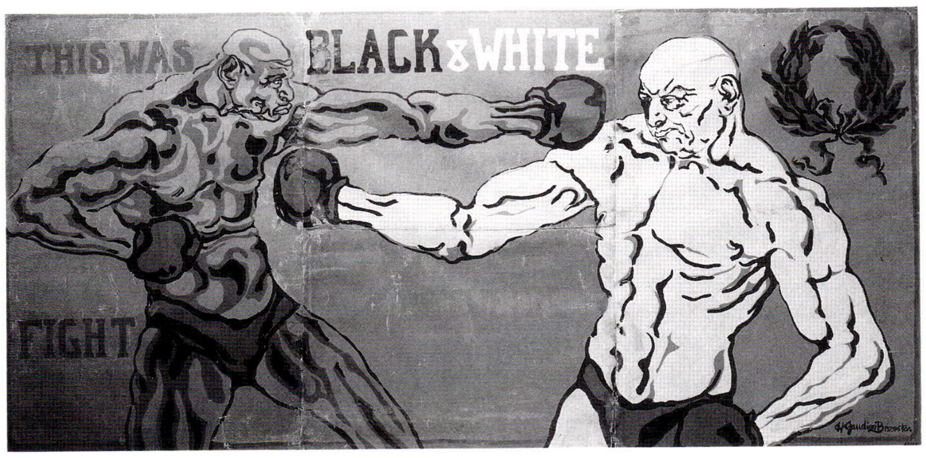

22 *Poster Design for Black & White Whisky*, 1911–12

He suffered frequent headaches and wrote to Brzeska in Folkestone that he often became overwrought. Then, as on future occasions, Brzeska encouraged him to go to prostitutes and gave him money but, as he made clear to her, they provided an occasional and unsatisfactory release from tension.[8] He wanted her. Most of their rare moments of peaceful pleasure in each other's company occurred in the relaxing surroundings of Richmond Park which became a favourite refuge.

Through all this Gaudier remained absolutely determined on living as an artist. He jotted down names and addresses of those who might possibly purchase or commission designs and made a number of poster designs painted full-size, apparently unaware that such designs were scaled up for commercial use (fig. 22). As he had told Kitty Smith the previous summer, he was 'a very stern boy always thinking of clay, stones, chisels and bodies to sculpt and considering everything else as second rate matter':

> I have become a sort of monk who, instead of directing all his acts towards the strengthening of his faith, directs them towards the strengthening of his art ... and I must be very severe with myself if I want to succeed – I may not live to enjoy life only, but first of all to work, and this at any price, even if suffering and pain come from it. They have come already and will come on again, but I must be glad all the same.[9]

23 King's Road, London, *c.* 1901

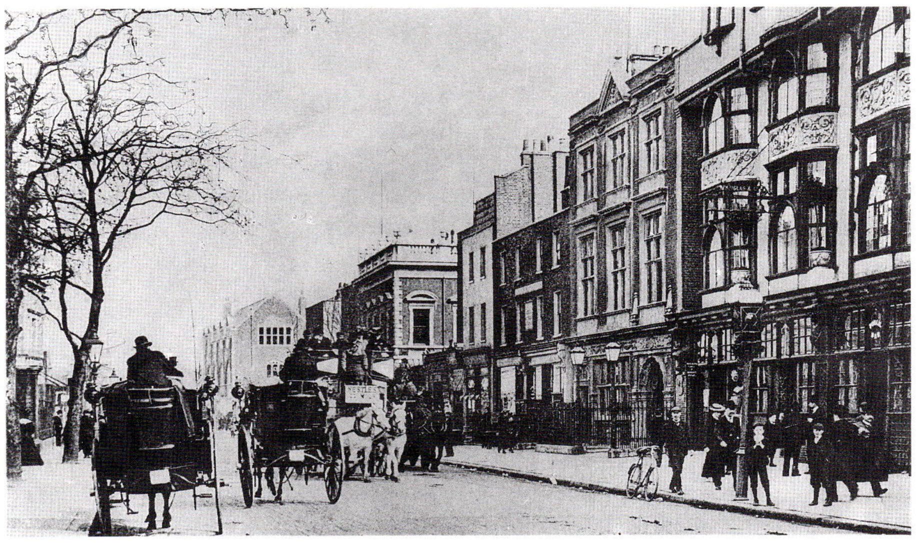

5

The Breakthrough 1912

In January 1912, Gaudier finally managed to make contact with someone in the swim of London cultural life through a frank, even desperate, appeal to the writer Haldane Macfall whose article on 'The Theatre and the Puritan' in the *English Review* led Gaudier to judge him a kindred spirit.

> Your letter in this month's number of the English Review has awoken in me a craving to make your acquaintance. It is very hard to find here someone who looks at life in the broader sense – in a manner freed from all prejudice and who dares say that Art is a vital need – I came to London a year ago and though I have not missed one opportunity to come near to anybody whom I thought would be worth knowing I have not so far succeeded. You are well able to understand the kind of loneliness and self-disgust that has overcome me, the more because I am suffering from uncongeniality – I work hard at my branch of art unfortunately only in the spare-time left me by an every-day attendance to a shipbroker's office. Not later than yesterday I was baffled by that Puritanism against which you write – I had prepared posters and the editor sent me back – saying they were too original – that people do not want expression, character but mediocre prettiness and that my productions were too distorted for his purpose – If I am not mistaken it appears hopeless for anyone to do anything original here when necessity is compelling.
>
> The man began a lengthy speech to try and induce me not to paint any nude figures or give any expression to anyone of them not to frighten the customers – I do not despair because of that neither do I intend to change my own ideas about drawing and decoration – the only thing I wish for just now is to have somebody to talk to in a frank and open manner – too great an isolation spoils me undoubtedly and you would be very kind indeed if you would allow me to see you one of these evenings when you are free.
>
> Yours respectfully
> H. Gaudier[1]

Macfall had made an impassioned plea for the place of art in civilized life, adumbrating ideas he later set out in his book, *The Splendid Wayfaring*:

> We live a mean little day, so petty indeed that most men – honest fellows – deem themselves as having lived who go to their graves the narrow life-long slaves of a paltry wage, content to have earned that wage, as though earning a wage was life! … But the largest and widest life is for him who dares the fullest adventure – who has become a partaker in all that life can give. And by the Arts alone shall he know the fullest life; and by the lack of the Arts shall he know the meanest.[2]

In reality Macfall's engagement with the arts was of an easy-going salon variety which paled beside Gaudier's all-out commitment. A retired army officer in his fifties, Macfall painted and exhibited a little but he was primarily a writer and reviewer (pls. 5, 6). His interests in the theatre, book design and illustration brought him to the edges rather than the turbulent centre of London's artistic life. He was more engaged in the art of the past than the present, having written books on Whistler, Boucher, Fragonard, Vigée-LeBrun and eighteenth-century French pastels, as well as an eight-volume history of painting, published the previous year. His friends were mostly well-off literary people like himself. They included a novelist, Henry Harding, his fellow critic and editor, Thomas Leman Hare and his French wife, the magazine editor Holbrook Jackson, army friends such as Major Raymond-Smythies, the young Enid Bagnold, daughter of an army officer, who was just then studying at Sickert's school, and her close friend, the brilliant young designer and illustrator Lovat Fraser (figs. 26, 27) whose work Macfall promoted.[3]

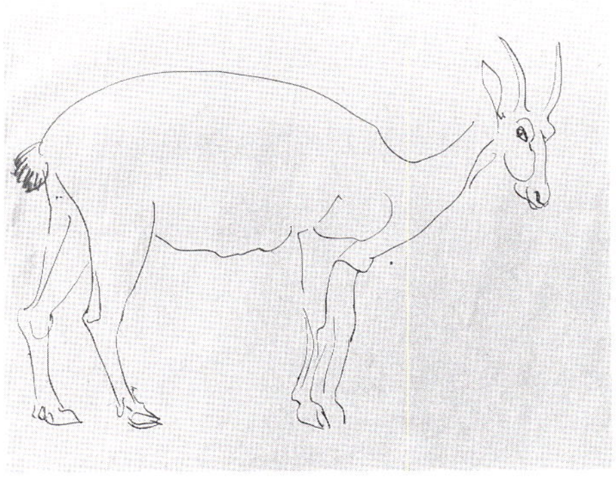

24 *Antelope,* 1912–13 (fig. 25 offset on verso)

Through Macfall, Gaudier finally gained entry into a literary and artistic circle who could provide some of the stimulus and approval he craved and who could introduce him to a wider circle of potential patrons. In early February, just as Gaudier and Brzeska were preparing to move to new lodgings at 12 Redburn Street in Chelsea, the Hares arrived on their doorstep with an immediate commission – a sculpture of Maria Carmi in her famous role as the Madonna in Rheinhart's *The Miracle* which was playing at Olympia (*cat.* 9, pl. 14); later they visited the studio and purchased a small plaster *Maternity* (*cat.* 16, pl. 15). Macfall was encouraging Gaudier to have a one-man show but he held back, well aware that he did not have nearly enough to exhibit. During the spring and early summer, Macfall, Smythies and Bagnold sat for portraits (*cat.* 11, 12, 17), a disconcerting experience as Bagnold recalled:

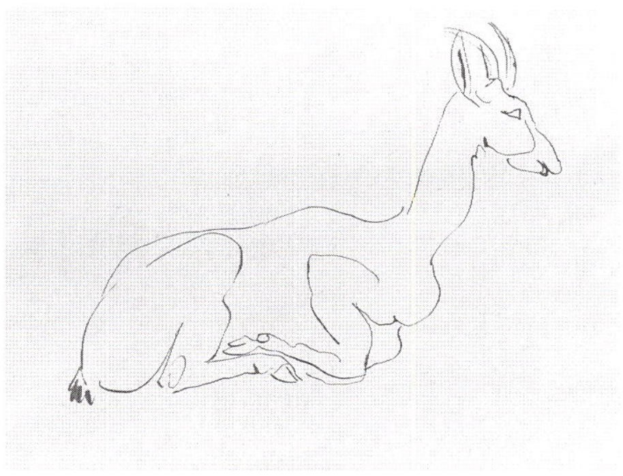

25 *Seated Antelope* 1912–13

> While I sat still, idle and uncomfortable on a wood chair, Gaudier's thin body faced me, standing in his overall behind the lump of clay, at which he worked with feverish haste. We talked a little, and then fell silent; from time to time, but not very often, his black eyes shot over my face and neck, while his hands flew around the clay. After a time his nose began to bleed, but he made no attempt to stop it; he appeared insensible to it, and the blood fell on his overall. At last, unable to stand it any longer, I said: 'Your nose is bleeding.' He replied: 'I know. You'll find something to stop it in that bag on the wall.'[4]

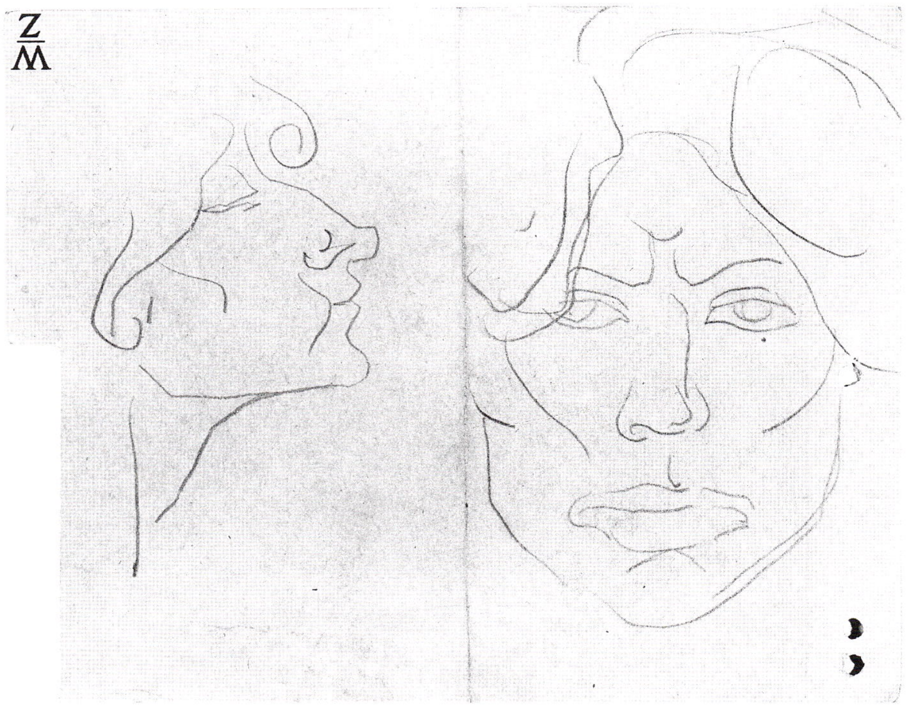

26 *Profile of Sophie Brzeska and Portrait of Lovat Fraser,* 1912

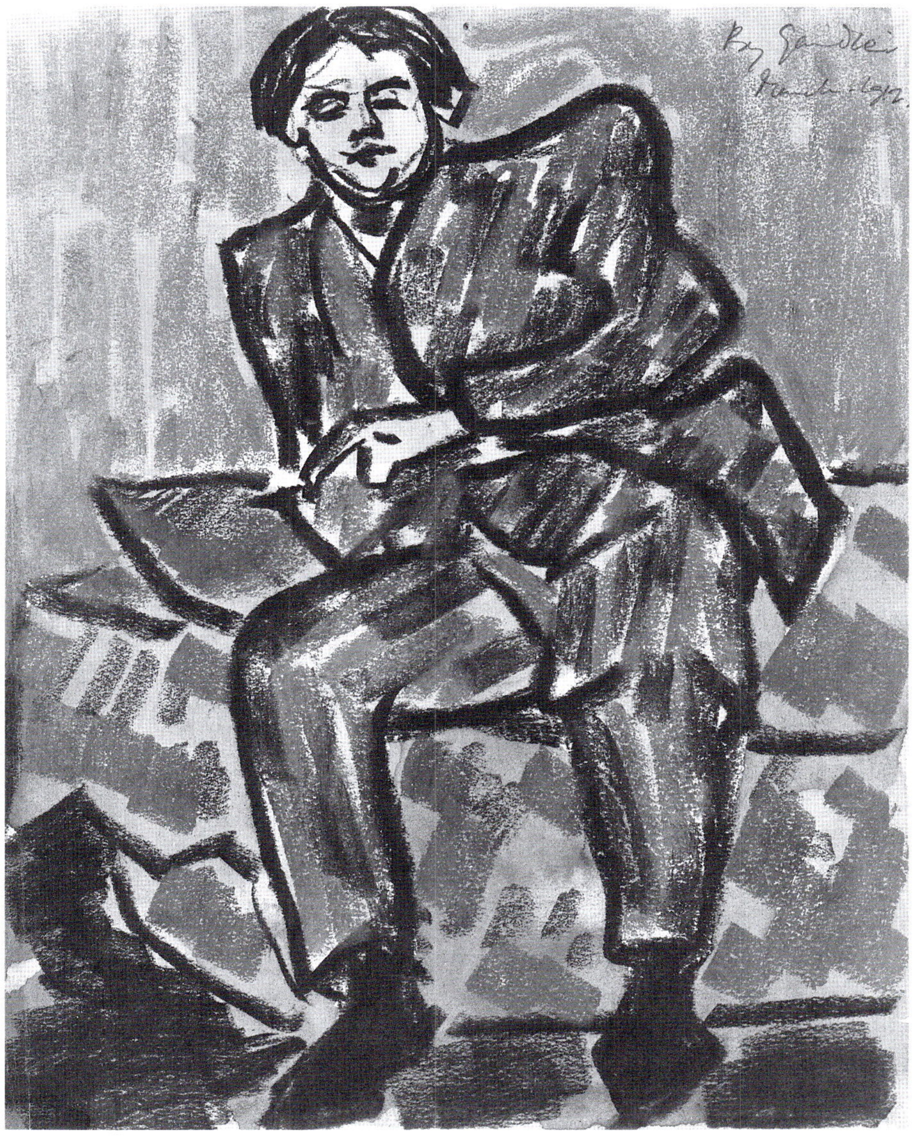

27 *Lovat Fraser*, 1912

Lovat Fraser, a fellow artist of about his own age but with the advantages of wealth and a family sympathetic to his ambitions, proved a good friend. He was especially generous with contacts for models, materials and presents of tickets for Regents Park Zoo which enabled Gaudier to spend hours at weekends making pen drawings – executed so rapidly the ink was often still wet on the last sketch as he started a new one – of deer, antelopes, elephants, birds and baboons (figs. 24, 25). In keeping with Lovat's taste Gaudier made him a painted plaster *Ornamental Mask* (*cat.* 31, pl. 28) and a painted plaster *Jungle Cat* (*cat.* 26, pl. 13), as well as using paint left over from the mask to decorate Fraser's studio.

As Brzeska's writings reveal, his new friends' enthusiasm for his work often stopped short of an actual commission; the portraits he modelled of them were Gaudier's own suggestion done for the price of the clay and casting in plaster; only Smythies' portrait (*cat.* 12, pl. 7) was cast in bronze. Even the Hares' commission for *The Madonna of 'The Miracle'* remained in plaster, far from the remunerative edition of one hundred bronzes originally proposed to him. Further, the relatively easy

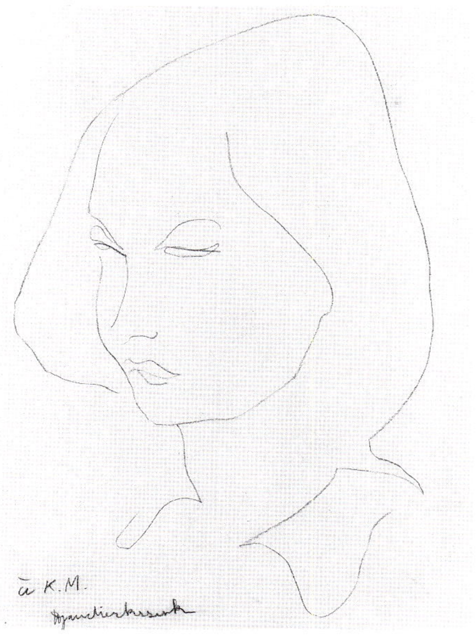

28 *Katherine Mansfield*, 1912

circumstances of their lives and the lengths to which Gaudier and Brzeska went to conceal their extreme poverty meant that some failed to grasp how important a modest purchase could be to the artist's morale and survival. Others were defeated by Gaudier's pride; they would offer to buy drawings, only to have him insist on giving them.

On the other hand, Gaudier made new friends and contacts during the latter part of 1912 and early 1913, many of which came about directly or indirectly through Macfall. It was probably Macfall, a founder member of the Cabaret Theatre Club, also known as the Cave of the Golden Calf, who first took Gaudier there, even before it had officially it opened in June 1912; he seems to have seen Jacob Epstein at work on his painted plaster columns decorated with the heads of hawks and camels.[5] He would also have seen Spencer Gore and Charles Ginner's brightly coloured primitivist murals of tiger and deer-hunting, designs by Wyndham Lewis and Eric Gill's priapic *Golden Calf* designs. Shortly before this he had visited Epstein's Cheyne Walk studio and seen his Assyrian-inspired and directly carved *Oscar Wilde Tomb* (fig. 67). Epstein's name would undoubtedly have been known to him. Since the revelation of his over-lifesize nude figures carved for the Strand headquarters of the British Medical Association in 1908, he had been a controversial figure, spoken of in some circles as the leading advanced sculptor then working in England. The Polish-American Epstein was, like Gaudier, an outsider and an artist way in advance of polite and popular tastes. Though eleven years older than Gaudier, Epstein and his Scots wife, Margaret Dunlop, had to struggle to make ends meet and lived an improvisatory bohemian existence far closer to Gaudier's own than Macfall's or Fraser's.

Gradually, as he began to broaden his circle of friends and to meet more painters and sculptors who had to try and make a living from their art alone, Gaudier grew far more critical of the conservative taste and bourgeois dilettantism of Macfall's circle. In a letter to Brzeska in November 1912, he contrasted the 'dandified' Lovat Fraser's elegant surroundings with Epstein's:

> There is an enormous difference between old Epstein's place and that of Fraser & Co. – Little Epstein, dirty and dusty and covered with plaster, sitting on the sill of his window, cutting at marble. In the room, two bunks mean and miserable (like Pikus' chair), one bigger than the other – a little table, very small, and nothing else. No picture nor image, nothing on the large white walls, only the torso of a woman, half-broken, in a corner.[6]

Another Macfall contact was the collector and artist Julian Lousada, who subsequently commissioned a group celebrating the Russian ballet production of *The Firebird* (*cat.* 18, pl. 11–12). Lousada suggested that Gaudier send some of his drawings to J. D. Fergusson for possible publication in the new magazine, *Rhythm*, of which Fergusson was Art Editor and John Middleton Murry the Editor. The review was Bergsonian in tone, and had a declared policy of asserting the centrality of rhythm in all art forms. Further, it counted a number of young Paris-based artists among its contributors, including Dunoyer de Segonzac, Otto Friesz, André Derain and Pablo Picasso. In addition to a preoccupation with the latest theatre design and dance, the journal carried up-to-date coverage of theory and practice in the visual arts; in the Spring 1912 issue an article by M. H. Sadler, 'After Gauguin', discussed the Fauvism of Derain and Kandinsky's *Über die Geistige in der Kunst*; Dunoyer de Segonzac's Cubistic semi-abstract painting *Boxers* (1911) was reproduced. Gaudier sent eight drawings and introduced himself somewhat diffidently:

> I had the pleasure of seeing you when you were over here at your exhibition – of my work you have – as far as I know – only seen a coloured statuette of a virgin at Mr J. Hare's – this may help you to recall me to your mind.[7]

Soon afterwards, Murry and Katherine Mansfield sought an introduction to Gaudier through Macfall and promptly invited him to contribute drawings to the September and October issues. The outline bird and figure drawings reproduced did not represent his latest or most ambitious work but they at least placed his name alongside that of leading foreign and British artists, and in a distinctly modernist framework. The October issue, for instance, contained an open-minded review by Raymond Drey of the Autumn Salon in Paris, during which he picked out the Cubists as the most interesting contemporary grouping; noting Picasso's absence with regret, he praised Roger de la Fresnaye's *Cardplayers* and *Bathers*, Le Fauconnier's *Les montagnards attaqués par des ours* and, above all, Kupka's *Amorpha fugue in two colours*: 'Every line and curve suggests rhythmic motion and virility.'[8]

A brief, intense friendship developed between Gaudier, Brzeska, Mansfield and Murry during the summer of 1912 leading up to the September issue. Gaudier drew them both (fig. 28) and began work on a modelled portrait of Murry (*cat.* 21).[9] Plans were even made for Brzeska to stay with them at their rented house near Chichester but the relationship ended acrimoniously before the eagerly anticipated issue of *Rhythm* had even appeared, after Gaudier discovered Mansfield's acute antipathy for Brzeska.[10] Murry was alarmed by a threatening visit from Gaudier and 'George' Banks, a theatrical designer and fellow contributor to *Rhythm*, and the unfinished portrait bust was later pelted to destruction by Gaudier, Brzeska and Horace Brodzky.[11]

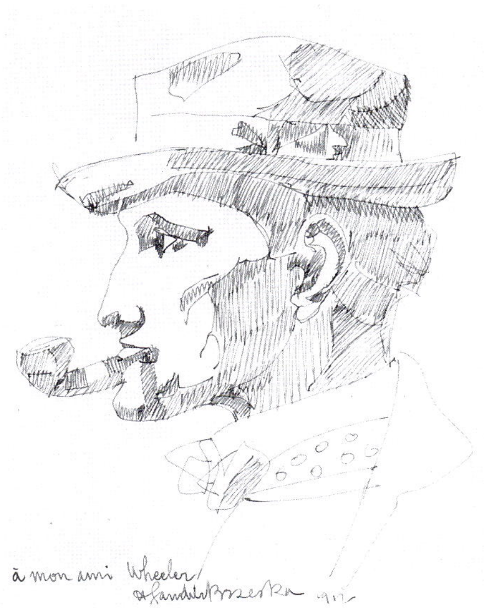

29 *Portrait*, probably of Ewart Wheeler, 1912

There were other new friends of increasingly advanced literary and artistic taste strategically placed to make his work known – Edward Marsh, civil servant, collector and impresario of the Georgian poets, the collector Sidney Schiff, the American writer John Cournos, Dan Rider, at whose bookshop in St Martin's Court he was able to exhibit drawings and the occasional sculpture, and where he met the journalist Frank Harris and the actor Ewart Wheeler (fig. 29). At the same time Gaudier was able to keep abreast of contemporary developments in Europe and continue to learn more about the art of the past through the art magazines available at the South Kensington Museums; in a letter to Uhlemayr he rejoiced that his linguistic ability made him one of the few reading Italian, German, French, Spanish and Dutch periodicals there.[12]

During Brzeska's four-month absence from October to January 1913, living at Frowlesworth and then at Dodford, near Bromsgrove, to write and restore her health, the tempo of Gaudier's work accelerated. Huge quantities of pen, charcoal and conté drawings, now increasingly assured and springy in their vigorous economy of line, date from this period (fig.

31). During November he attended evening classes in life drawing (fig. 30) working from models who ranged from 'a beautiful youth with a wrestler's loin cloth of black silk bordered with a lovely Indian stuff' and 'a girl, without a rag' to a man 'old, brutal with a great belly' and 'a poor little Italian workman'. He found other models in unexpected places. Ewart Wheeler's brother, Charles, was a Birmingham manufacturer interested in the possibility that Gaudier might make some sculptural decorations for electric radiators. He was also sports-mad; Gaudier agreed to make statuettes of a wrestler and bather for him to have cast. Though only the *Wrestler* (*cat.* 32) was made, and this was never cast, being far too large for its intended purpose, he introduced Gaudier to the London Wrestling Club where he revelled in the athletic physique and movements of the wrestlers (figs. 48–50, 77). A large number of zoo drawings also date from this period; several notes to Lovat Fraser either thank him or ask him for more tickets for Regents Park Zoo. With the help of Mrs Hare he began looking for a studio where he could work with greater freedom and carve.[13] Yet in spite of all this activity he cannot have been entirely neglecting his employer, for on 7 December he also agreed a further one-year contract with Wulfsberg at the increased salary of £10 a month.

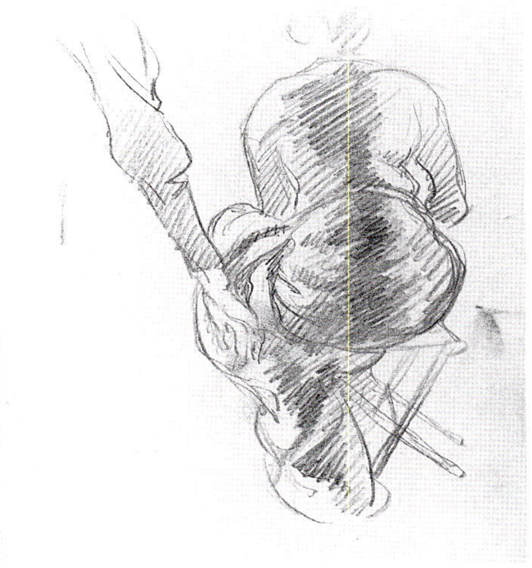

30 *The Life Class*, 1912

In January 1913 he acquired a studio for the first time, Studio 5 at 454a Fulham Road, where one of his neighbours was an experienced journeyman sculptor, Aristide Fabrucci, who produced quality copies of recognized works.[14]

> It's as if I have been transported from hell to heaven and I feel completely inspired, burning with creative fire. It is so peaceful, so tranquil after the hellish noise of Redburn Street. Ideas come flooding into my mind. I have thousands of projects for different sculptures. I am working on three – I have just finished one of them and and making sketches for lots more. It is so good in the studio ...[15]

The artist Horace Brodzky was one of his first visitors, having been invited to supper out of the blue by a letter from Gaudier who had

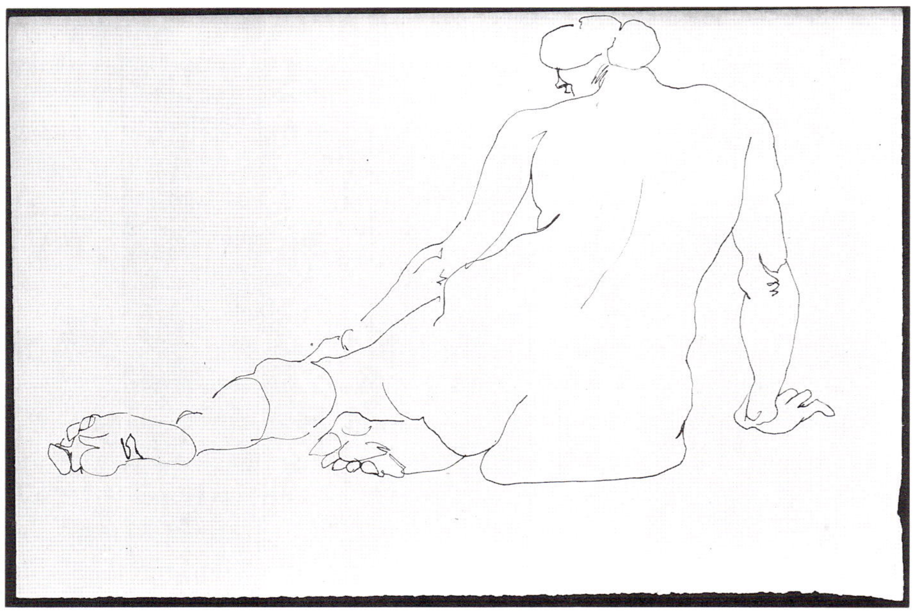

31 *Reclining Female Nude*

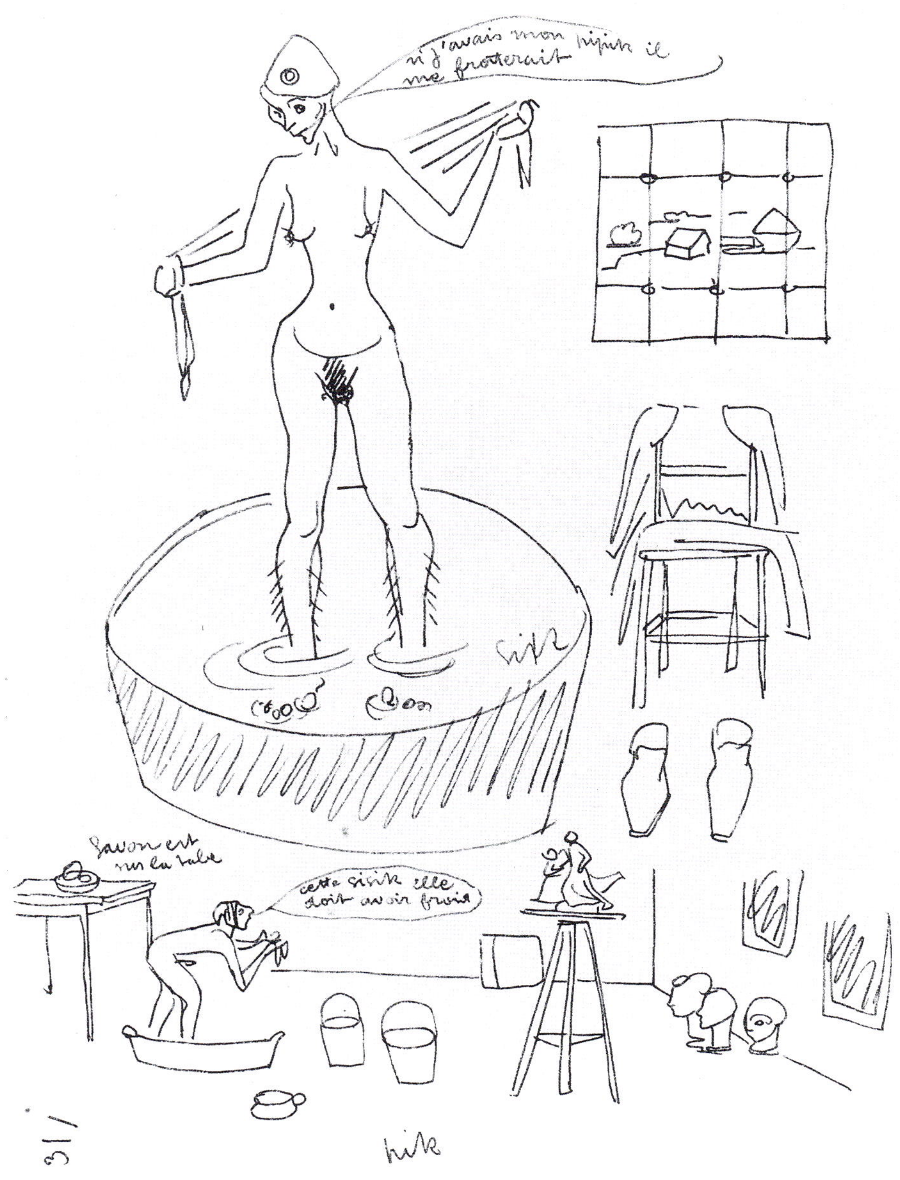

32 Gaudier, bathing in London, imagines Sophie bathing at Dodford, in a drawing accompanying a letter, 31.10.12

admired one of his illustrations for the *Art Chronicle*. He retained an indelible memory of the 'little fellow, quite a boy, dirty and unkempt and smiling' who greeted him at the gas-lit studio; it 'contained the barest of necessities, working benches, a table and a few odd chairs' and was in a state of disorder with dirt, stone dust and the appalling stench of Gaudier's less than fresh *pot-au-feu*. 'On the walls I noticed two or three huge painted posters, possibly seven or eight feet high. These were rejected originals of posters submitted. In these the nude predominated, both male and female. One was for Black and White whisky' (fig. 22).[16] Other early visitors to the studio were Edward Marsh, Rupert Brooke, Frank Harris, Alfred Wolmark and John Cournos. During the spring Harris, Wolmark and Brodzky all sat for portraits (*cat.* 45–47, fig. 46).

Though still not much better off than before, the studio set Gaudier free of the practical constraints of working at his lodgings which he gave up. Though continuing to model portraits, he also began to carve in stone

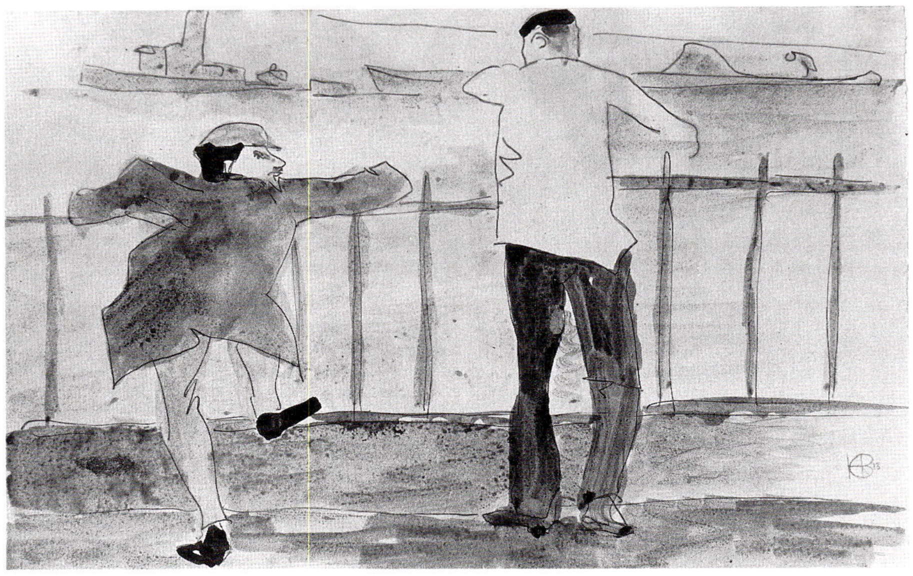

33 *The Sea Front*, signed 'HGB 1913'

and by March was reporting to Lovat Fraser that he was 'making as many reliefs as I can'.[17] Stones he bought, begged or stole, usually making do with irregularly shaped offcuts. Happily there were several monumental masons' yards in Fulham and Vauxhall not far from his studio. He often made his own tools on a forge borrowed from Fabrucci and from spindles provided by Raymond Drey. Drey was editor of the *Manchester Playgoer* but was able to obtain spindles through his contacts in the cotton industry.[18] However, he had met Gaudier through 'George' Banks when all three were contributors to *Rhythm*.

Despite the brighter outlook in his artistic life he missed Brzeska (fig. 32). Soon after a four-day visit to Dodford for Christmas he began to per-

34 *Stags*, 1913

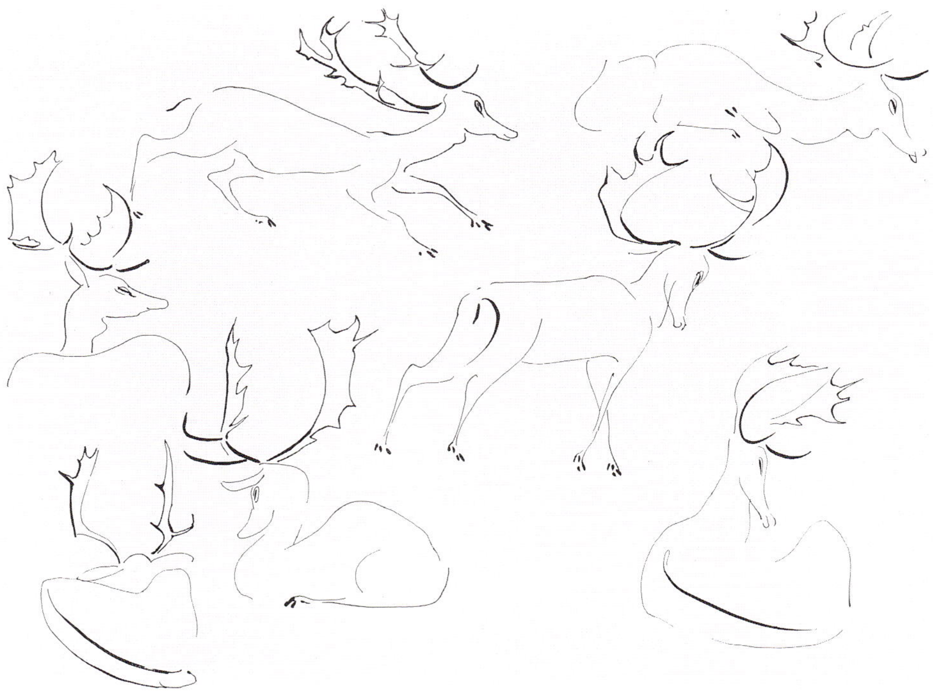

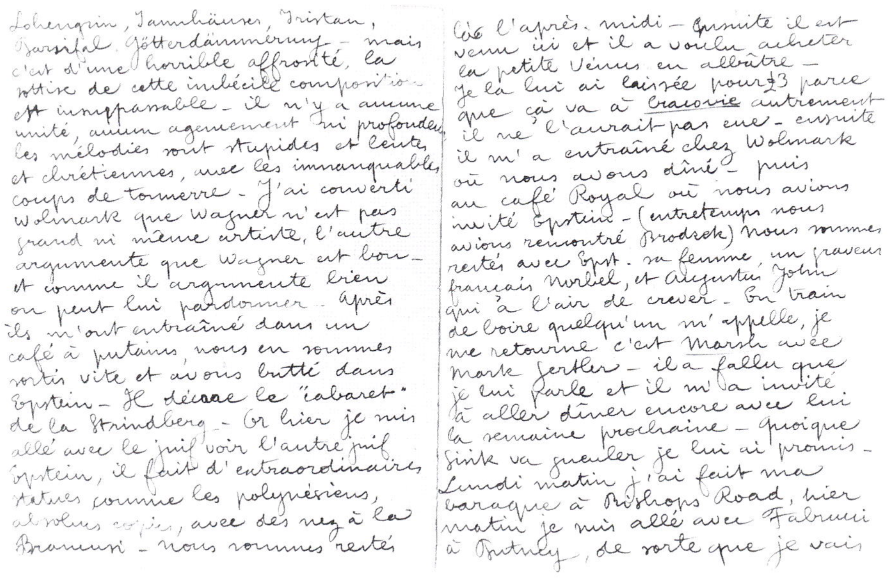
Lohengrin, Tannhäuser, Tristan,
Parsifal, Götterdämmerung – mais
c'est d'une horrible affronté, la
sottise de cette imbécile composition
est incomparable – il n'y a aucune
unité, aucun agencement ni profondeur,
les mélodies sont stupides et lentes
et chrétiennes, avec les immanquables
coups de tonnerre – J'ai converti
Wolmark que Wagner n'est pas
grand ni même artiste, l'autre
argumente que Wagner est bon –
et comme il argumente bien
on peut lui pardonner – Après
ils m'ont entraîné dans un
café à putains, nous en sommes
sortis vite et avons butté dans
Epstein – Il décore le "cabaret"
de la Strindberg – Or hier je suis
allé avec le juif voir l'autre juif
Epstein, il fait d'extraordinaires
statues comme les polynésiens,
absolues copies, avec des nez à la
Brancusi – nous sommes restés
toute l'après-midi – ensuite il est
venu ici et il a voulu acheter
la petite Vénus en albâtre –
je la lui ai laissée pour £3 parce
que ça va à Cracovie autrement
il ne l'aurait pas eue – ensuite
il m'a entraîné chez Wolmark
où nous avons dîné – puis
au café Royal où nous avions
invité Epstein – (entretemps nous
avions rencontré Brodzek) nous sommes
restés avec Epst. sa femme, un graveur
français Norbel, et Augustus John
qui a l'air de crever – En train
de boire quelqu'un m'appelle, je
me retourne c'est Marsh avec
Mark Gertler – il a fallu que
je lui parle et il m'a invité
à aller dîner encore avec lui
la semaine prochaine – quoique
Sisik va gueuler je lui ai promis –
Lundi matin j'ai fait ma
baraque à Bishops Road, hier
matin je suis allé avec Fabrucci
à Putney, de sorte que je vais

35 Excerpt from a letter from Gaudier to Brzeska, 8.10.13

suade her to return to London. She did so in February, lured by Gaudier's misleading evocations of the comfort of the studio. Apart from the damp, dust and general squalor, the lease was for a workshop not a residence. Brzeska found acceptable rooms in Bishops Road, but from her own writings it becomes apparent that Gaudier was most frequently to be found at the studio, often staying to work late into the night before falling asleep in his deckchair. In September they left for a holiday at a boarding house by the seaside at Littlehampton (fig. 33) but they rowed continually. Harmony was briefly restored during a day trip to Arundel Park where Gaudier produced some of his most inspired studies of deer (fig. 34), but he was bored and desperate to get back to London where he had many new friends and an urge to work which he could now indulge to the full, having resigned from his job in the summer. After only a week he returned to town, leaving Sophie at Littlehampton for a further fortnight, during which she found a companion in a young Frenchwoman, Marie Borne, who was teaching there.

The letter he wrote to Brzeska a few days later evokes the exciting and varied life he was leading, and which very obviously largely excluded her (fig. 35). He had been to a Wagner concert, visited Wolmark and met a Jew from Kraków who bought his alabaster *Venus* (*cat.* 50), spent an afternoon with Epstein who was 'making some extraordinary statues which are absolute copies of Polynesian carvings, with noses like Brancusi'. That very evening they went on to the Café Royal: 'on the way we met Brodzky. We sat with Epstein, his wife … and Augustus John who looked as if he would explode. While we were drinking someone called out to me and I turned round to see Marsh with Mark Gertler. I had to talk to him and he invited me to dine with him next week. I accepted.'[19]

He had also got wind of a new cheaper studio; within a couple of days of his return he had gone with Fabrucci to see a large railway arch workshop, at 25 Winthorpe Road, Putney (figs. 36, 37). Apart from the trains rumbling overhead it was a backwater with only a few houses at the end of the road and a nearby livery stable; they agreed to rent the arch between

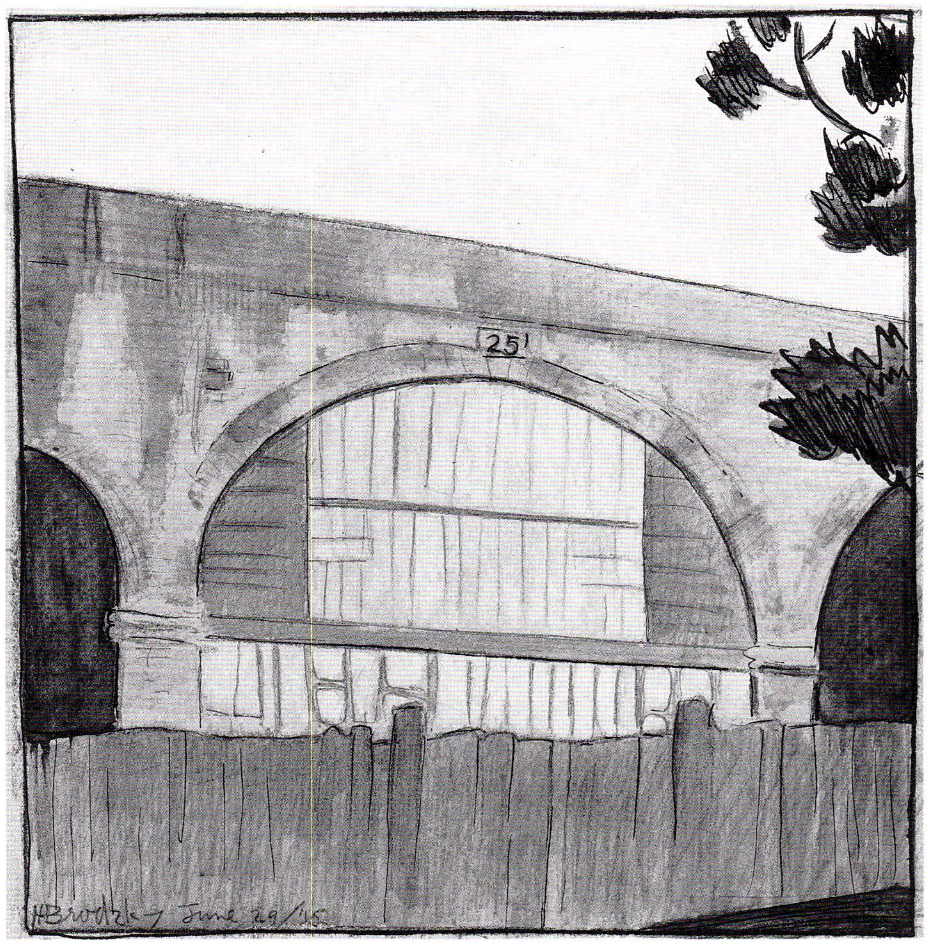

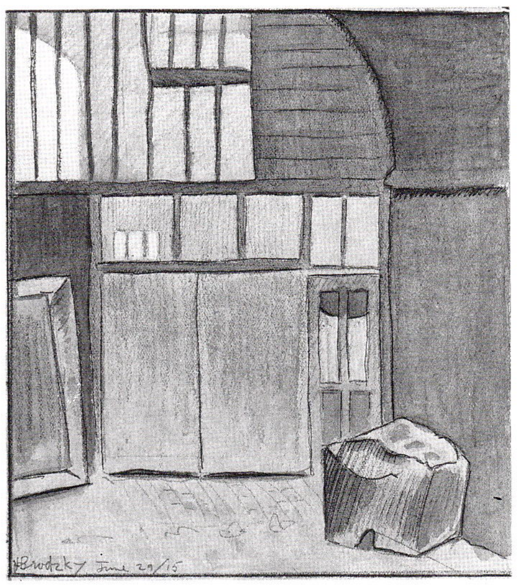

36, 37 Horace Brodzky, *Exterior* (left) and *Interior of Gaudier-Brzeska's Studio, 25 Winthorpe Road, Putney, 29 June, 1915*

them and Gaudier helped Fabrucci to build a partition down the middle.[20] Though it was damp and hard to heat in cold weather, 'it was a good, workman-like place with a concrete floor, well lit by windows at each of its quadrant-shaped ends ... [It] contained nothing designed for comfort. Benches, a portable furnace for tempering his chisels, a couple of decrepit chairs and a small stove were all its furniture ... On the inside of the double doors the Gaudier-Brzeska phallic monogram was painted, six foot high, in heavy black lines.'[21]

Another cause of eagerness was the knowledge that he could spend more than early mornings, evenings and weekends there. He had resigned from Wulfsberg sometime during July or August, thus giving up his steady ten pounds a month to try once again to be a full-time artist. Confidence to take this drastic step almost certainly derived from the encouragement of friends and the heady experience of exhibiting sculpture in a major exhibition for the first time. At the huge Allied Artists' Salon at the Albert Hall in July, he exhibited his portraits of Brodzky, Macfall and Wolmark, *Firebird* (*cat.* 18, pls. 11–12), *The Madonna* (*cat.* 9, pl. 14) and the *Wrestler* (*cat.* 32, pls. 37, VIII). All were modelled works, though he had been carving for some months, but they were nevertheless innovative and striking enough to seize the attention of the young American poet and cultural entrepreneur Ezra Pound (fig. 39), who was visiting the exhibition with his future mother-in-law, Olivia Shakespear.

Pound was wrestling with the pronunciation of the artist's name when Gaudier appeared and introduced himself before vanishing just as abruptly. Other contacts followed – with artists in Sickert's circle such as Spencer Gore (from whom Gaudier acquired a cat), Robert Bevan and Stanislawa de Karlowska whose Polish origin immediately endeared her to Brzeska. Gaudier was probably a guest at some of Sickert's Fitzroy Street gatherings during the autumn. According to Brzeska it was also at the Albert Hall that he met the young painter, Nina Hamnett, with whom he soon developed a close relationship (fig. 38). As fellow artists and free spirits, they posed nude for one another and Hamnett was the model for several of his most sensuous works, the exquisite bronze *Dancer* (*cat.* 58, pls. 68–70) and the three *Torsos* (cat. 59–61, pls. 71, 73, 76). Brzeska, though she developed a grudging respect for Hamnett, was also jealous of her. She suspected that Gaudier could find with Hamnett the sexual fulfilment which Brzeska had long denied him.[22]

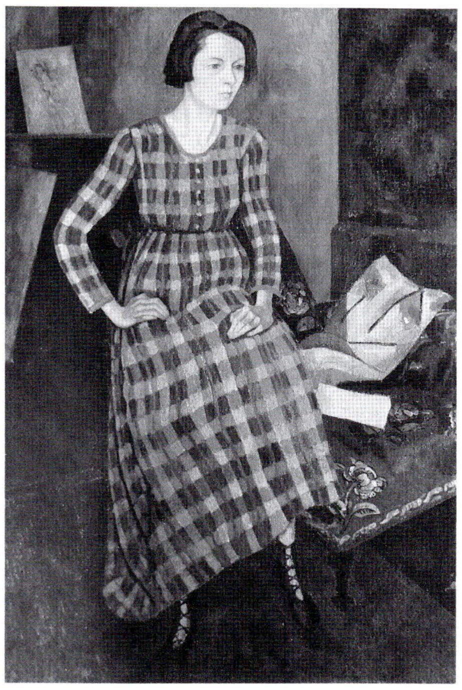

38 Roger Fry, *Portrait of Nina Hamnett*, 1917

These new contacts were all the more important because he exhibited little during the autumn; he had nothing in the Post-Impressionist and Futurist exhibition at the Doré Galleries in October and nothing in the exhibition *The Camden Town and Others* at Brighton; a plaster of *The Madonna*, unsold at £40, was exhibited in the Royal West of England Academy in Bristol and there was a dispute over payment for his gilded plaster *Golden Figure* (*cat.* 33) after it was sold from the Grosvenor Gallery during the International Society of Sculptors, Painters and Gravers exhibition. Visits from potential patrons as well as friends now became an occasional feature of life at the studio, though sales of anything other than drawings were rare. The leather manufacturer and friend of Wolmark, Alfred Kohnstamm, visited the studio and pondered long on *Maternity*, priced at £40, before deciding regretfully that it was too expensive for him.[23] Two important visitors in September were Paul Morand, secretary to the French Ambassador and son of the Director of the Musée des Arts Decoratifs, and the Ranee of Sarawak; he sought to interest them in *Singer* (*cat.* 51, pls. 56, IV). Nothing came of the meeting with Morand and the Ranee only purchased some drawings for ten pounds.[24]

A more remunerative contact was Roger Fry to whom Hamnett introduced him. Fry had set up the Omega Workshops in Fitzroy Square as a means of bringing together artists and designers to undertake a variety of collaborative decorative projects in return for regular payment. Gaudier could already have seen work by some of the participants including Fry, Henri Doucet, Spencer Gore, Wyndham Lewis and Edward Wadsworth at the London Salon. He was carving busily during the autumn and does not seem to have done much work at Fitzroy Square, but he entered into the spirit of the enterprise by making designs of a marquetry tray (*cat.* 67, pl. 102) and possibly painting a box, designing some vases, and modelling the little *Cat* (*cat.* 65, pl. 103). As Winifred Gill recalled, 'He never actually worked there but we sold drawings of his and small pieces of sculpture on commission and he looked in fairly often, probably to see if we owed him anything and to bring in fresh stuff. He never stayed long.'[25] Several sculptures, including the alabaster *Boy*, the marble *Cat*, *Maternity* and the *Watercarrier* were deposited there for sale and advance payments probably assisted with the purchase of new stones. Ezra Pound, by now a regular visitor, suggested in his *Memoir* that two other important carvings, *Boy with Coney* (*cat.* 76, pls. 104, VI) and *Stags* (*cat.* 77, pls. 113–16), were also carved during the autumn of 1913, not long after *Torso* (*cat.* 60, pl. 73).

By the end of 1913, in spite of having sold very little, Gaudier was becoming known as a promising talent within the most advanced groups of artists working in London. He had yet to come out with a personal creed or with a group of works which would unequivocally ally him with one group or another. Partly because of this he was in the unusual position of being on friendly terms not only with Pound, Lewis, Wadsworth and Epstein, but also with Fry's circle and the Camden Town artists, each of whom may have wished to persuade him to their 'cause'.

Artist of the Avant-Garde

DURING 1914 Gaudier began to consolidate his nascent reputation. His association with Omega led to his inclusion in the second Grafton Group Show at the Alpine Gallery in January 1914, alongside Fry, Vanessa Bell, Duncan Grant, William Roberts and Nina Hamnett. Here, for the first time he exhibited a group of carvings – *Watercarrier* (*cat.* 74, pl. 117), the alabaster *Boy* (*cat.* 56, pl. 75), the stone *Crouching Fawn* (*cat.* 62, pl. 80), *Cat* (*cat.* 70, pl. 89) and *Redstone Dancer* (*cat.* 69, pls. 97, XI). His election to the London Group the following month, with more votes than any of his fellow candidates, was eloquent testimony to the support he enjoyed from several factions. Sickert had just resigned from the Group, unable to tolerate the inclusion of Epstein and Lewis whose work recently exhibited at Brighton he considered pornographic; in March both Wolmark and Brodzky were rejected, and of all those nominated only Stanley Spencer was successful.[26] The first London Group show in March included a striking selection of primitivizing direct carvings by Epstein and Gaudier: Gaudier's carvings ranged from the naturalism of the white marble *Maternity* and *Torso* to the primitivism of *Redstone Dancer* and the two alabaster groups, *Boy with Coney* and *Stags*, while Epstein showed two of his series of carvings of birds and the controversial *Female Figure in Flenite* (fig. 90).

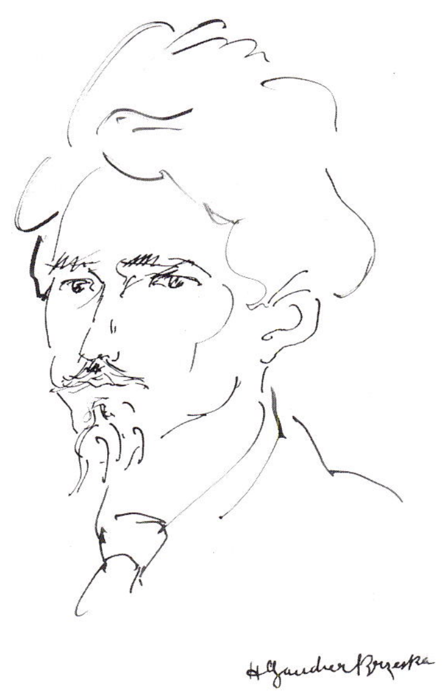

39 *Portrait of Ezra Pound, c.* 1913

In addition to being elected to the new London Group Gaudier was also chosen as chairman of the artists' committee for the London Salon; Wolmark was a member, as were Lucien Pissarro and several of the Camden Town Group, Robert Bevan, Harold Gilman, Charles Ginner and Renée Finch, a French protegée of Sickert who became a good friend and confidante to Sophie Brzeska. During the spring Gaudier became increasingly associated with Pound, Lewis and the Rebel Art Centre which Lewis established in March 1914 after a bitter split with the Omega Workshops; Gaudier himself did not part company with Omega until June or July. He was seeing a great deal of Pound; having helped him out with a 'rush job' to produce a presentation casket for the poet Wilfred Scawen Blunt's Peacock Dinner in January 1914 (*cat.* 72, pl. 100), Gaudier spent the best part of two months carving a monumental stone portrait in phallic form (*cat.* 79, pls. 119–22, IX, fig. 45). Among Pound and Lewis's associates in the rapidly evolving Vorticist group were Edward

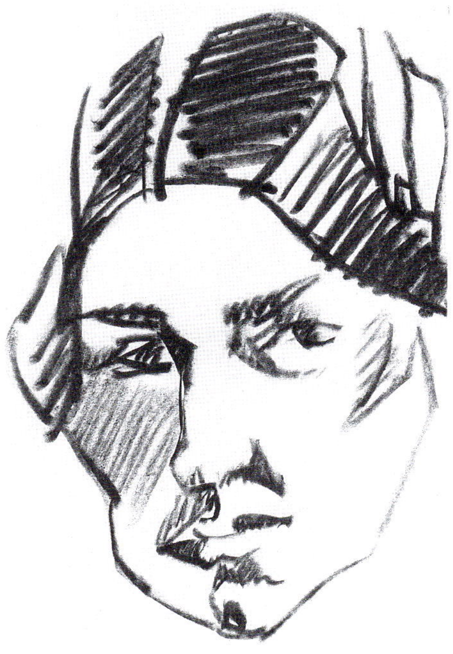

40 *Wyndham Lewis*, 1913–14

Wadsworth, William Roberts, Kate Lechmere, David Bomberg, Frederick Etchells, the philosopher T. E. Hulme and Jacob Epstein. Even before the publication of Gaudier's seminal essay 'Vortex Gaudier-Brzeska' in *Blast* in July, he had begun to acquire greater assurance as a writer on art, reviewing the London Salon for *The Egoist* in May. Modelling himself on Apollinaire's reviews in the *Mercure de France*, he wrote incisively, with tremendous verve and a positively Gallic relish for the hyperbole, cut and thrust of the battle between artistic groupings.

In May, thanks in part to the payment of cartage by the exhibition organizers, Gaudier's work was prominent in a wide-ranging show of nearly 500 works at the Whitechapel Art Gallery, *Twentieth Century Art: A Review of Modern Movements*. Compared with Epstein's two bronzes, neither representing his recent work, and a Modigliani stone head – the only other sculptures on show – Gaudier's six pieces made an impressive impact.[27] The bronze *Firebird* represented his 'older' work; *Maternity*, *Figure*, *Cat* and the marble *Fawn* represented his more naturalistic direct carvings. *Head of Ezra Pound*, with its self-conscious primitivism and high degree of formal abstraction, may have formed a focus for the dozen or so works by Lewis, Etchells, Bomberg, Wadsworth, Roberts and Nevinson which represented the ideas of the new breakaway group.

Gaudier's public affiliation with the Rebel Art Centre and the disparate but increasingly abstract work carried out by its associates was confirmed during June, seemingly precipitated by the misguided attempt by Nevinson and Marinetti to claim the members of the group as adherents of Futurism. Gaudier was one of the signatories, along with Atkinson, Bomberg, Pound, Roberts, Lewis, Wadsworth and others, of a letter to the *Observer*, published on 14 June 1914. An angry response to the Futurist Manifesto published the previous week, it echoed the barracking to which Marinetti and Nevinson had been subjected on 12 June during a Futurist event at the Doré Gallery: about ten of the rebels including Lewis, Epstein, Wadsworth and Hulme attended, but Gaudier appears to have been at the forefront, heckling in voluble French and English throughout and even correcting Nevinson's pronunciation of 'Vortickists'.[28]

Gaudier's masterly condensed history of sculpture, 'Vortex Gaudier Brzeska', which provided one of the clearest statements of artistic intent produced by the loose alliance of artists, writers and poets, must have been written very shortly thereafter, just in time to be the last article in the launch issue of *Blast* in July (see pp. 279–82). Wyndham Lewis organized a celebratory dinner for the launch at the Dieudonné Restaurant on 15 July; Gaudier, who paid with a *Fawn* carving (*cat.* 84) as he could not afford the ten-shilling fee, 'spent a good part of the meal speculating on the relation of planes nude of one of our guests (Amy Lowell)', Pound recalled, 'though this was kept to our own particular corner.'[29]

Unfortunately all this activity did not mean that Gaudier was earning much from his work. In March 1914, after he had sold nothing at the London Group, Sophie Brzeska noted bitterly that he had earned only £47 19s 0d over the previous six months, far less than what Wulfsberg would have been paying; of this £24 12s 0d had been spent on materials and exhibition fees, leaving only £23 7s 0d or less than £4 a month to contribute to the household budget and causing a heavy drain on Sophie's savings. Even Gaudier agreed that he would have to get a job soon if sales did not improve.[30]

There were other strains on their partnership as Gaudier's increasing self-confidence, nourished by acceptance, praise from his new friends and by his rising status in literary and artistic circles, reduced his emotional dependence on Brzeska. Her maternal care and continued refusal of any greater intimacy irritated him more and more. He frequently dismissed her criticisms of his friends, his behaviour and his latest work – his 'Brancusi egg-heads' and 'champagne corks' – and led his own life.[31] Sophie herself was angered by his attitude and began to consider returning to France. After a brief visit to Littlehampton in June she returned to London and made plans to increase her income and get some congenial company by letting rooms to Mlle Borne and her sister for the summer. In the event the sister, apprehensive of the international situation, never arrived from France, and Mlle Borne soon became a cause for anxiety as Gaudier moved rapidly from surly reluctance to evident pleasure in her company, inviting her to the studio, taking her to social gatherings and even to the moving pictures. (pls. 158, 159)[32]

41 *Self-Portrait with Mallet and Chisel*, c. 1913

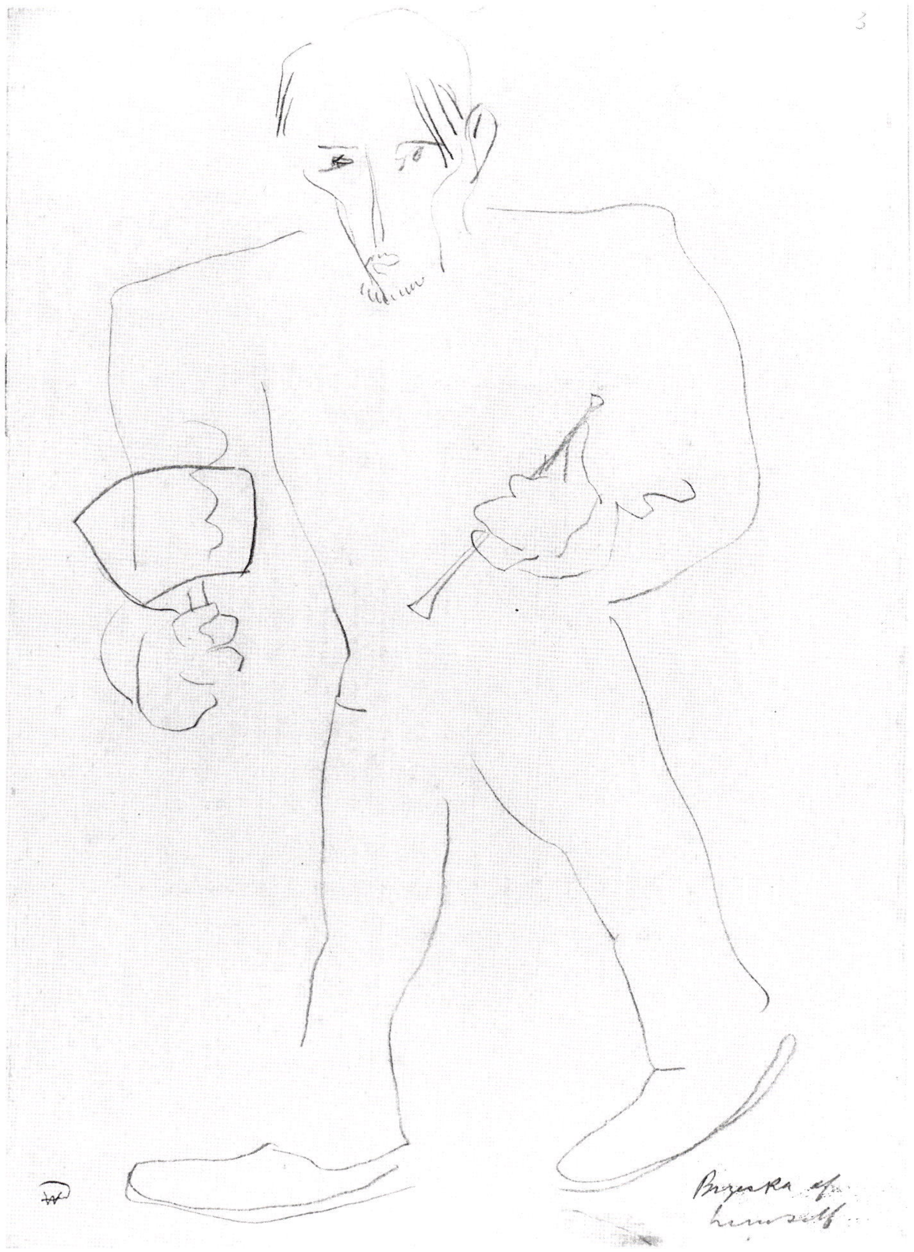

6

War – 'la Patrie en danger'

THE OUTBREAK of war in August 1914 put an abrupt halt to all plans. Gaudier had been insisting in the face of Brzeska's gloomy certainty that the politicians would manage to avoid it.[1] Amidst the prevailing jingoism and forecasts that the war would be over by Christmas, many young men feared that if they did not join up promptly the whole show would be over before they could 'do their bit'. T. E. Hulme, Stanley Spencer, David Jones, Paul and John Nash were among those who enlisted during the first month. But while some like Hulme, who was already in the Territorials, relished the prospect of war, many of Gaudier's friends were part-American or Polish, and some – notably Pound and Epstein, both American-born – initially carried on as if nothing was happening.

The impending invasion of France was quite another matter. Marie Borne hastened to join her family. Gaudier, roused to a frenzy of anti-German feeling by news of the destruction of his grandfather's house and of the bombardment of Reims Cathedral, determined to return to France and enlist immediately.[2] He reviewed his affairs, drawing up a list of work and a 'will' leaving everything to Brzeska, and returned to France to enlist.[3] There were emotional scenes at Charing Cross as many friends, including the Epsteins, Cournos, Lewis, Hulme and Aldington, came to see him off. Sophie was distraught. Melodrama turned to farce at Boulogne where he was promptly arrested as a deserter for evading military service and locked up. Resourceful as ever, he escaped from the guard-house the same day, managed to get aboard a ferry and turned up in London to general astonishment. During the ensuing weeks he regularized his position with the French authorities, did a little work left unfinished and saw his friends, many of whom tried to discourage him from going a second time. He ignored them, as he did Brzeska who feared to see Gaudier's own foreboding that he would die in war come true. Gaudier's almost euphoric mood was witnessed by D. L. Murray, who often attended Hulme's Soho Square gatherings:

> One of the most tragic memories of my love [sic] is of Hulme and young Gaudier-Brzeska, the one about to complete the formalities of enrolment in to the British army, the other already registered in the French army, sitting in the study at Soho Square on a sunny afternoon of August 1914, chanting their joy at the prospect of going to war. To say it was a 'pic-nic' to them would be inadequate; it was more like a nuptial eve. Gaudier in particular was bubbling over with delighted anticipation.[4]

The poet Richard Aldington, one of those who saw him off, recalled him 'in high spirits, assuring us repeatedly that he would bring back the Picassos from Düsseldorf ... we walked together, across Hyde Park and Kensington Gardens on his last day in London, and he told me gravely that being in prison had entirely changed his views on art – he was going to abandon the modern style entirely, and follow the Greeks. He even offered to do a classical statue of me as the youthful Hercules.'[5]

On 5 September 1914, aged twenty-two, he returned to France, enlisted in the French army as a private and on 20 September, after less than three weeks training, was sent to the Craonne sector not far from Reims. At first, as he wrote to the Hares, he found the trench-digging, marching and countermarching much harder than the actual fighting; he found the exchange of fire exhilarating.[6] From his reports over the next few months and his rapid promotion, he showed courage and resource. In the intervals between dangerous patrols and reconnaissance from the trenches, he continued to ponder his work, even making a few small objects from materials to hand and sending a couple of drawings to Wadsworth (fig. 42).[7]

Before the end of 1914 he wrote 'Vortex Gaudier-Brzeska' for the second issue of *Blast*; here, Gaudier, the countryman, artist and thinker reflected soberly on the ultimate triviality of war and contrasted his personal experience with the enduring patterns of nature, landscape, the roots of three-dimensional form and perception:

> I have been fighting for two months and I can now gauge the intensity of Life. Human masses teem and move, are destroyed and crop up again. Horses are worn out in three weeks, die by the roadside. Dogs wander, are destroyed, and others come along.
>
> With all the destruction that works around us nothing is changed, even superficially. Life is the same strength … The bursting shells, the volleys, wire entanglements, projectors, motors, the chaos of battle do not alter in the least the outlines of the hill we are besieging. A company of partridges scuttle along before our very trench … This war is a great remedy. In the individual it kills arrogance, self-esteem, pride …
>
> My views on sculpture remain absolutely the same, it is the vortex of will, of decision, that begins.
>
> I shall derive my emotions solely from the arrangement of surfaces, I shall present my emotions by the arrangement of my surfaces, the planes and lines by which they are defined.
>
> Just as this hill where the Germans are solidly entrenched gives me a nasty feeling, solely because its gentle slopes are broken up by earth-works, which throw long shadows at sunset. Just so shall I get feeling, of whatever definition, from a statue according to its slopes, varied to infinity.
>
> I have made an experiment. Two days ago I pinched from an enemy a Mauser rifle. Its heavy unwieldy shape swamped me with a powerful image of brutality. I was in doubt for a long time whether it pleased or displeased me. I found I did not like it. I broke the butt off and with my knife I carved in it a design, through which I tried to express a gentler order of feeling, which I preferred. But I will emphasize that my design got its effect (just like the gun had) from a very simple composition of lines and planes.[8]

It is a powerful and brilliantly succinct passage in which Gaudier's aesthetic of volumes, planes and the fall of light becomes the reassuring core of a philosophy in which the war, however terrible, can be seen as peripheral.

He corresponded with many long-standing and more recent friends and patrons – Kitty Smith, Brzeska, Macfall, the Hares, Pound, Mrs

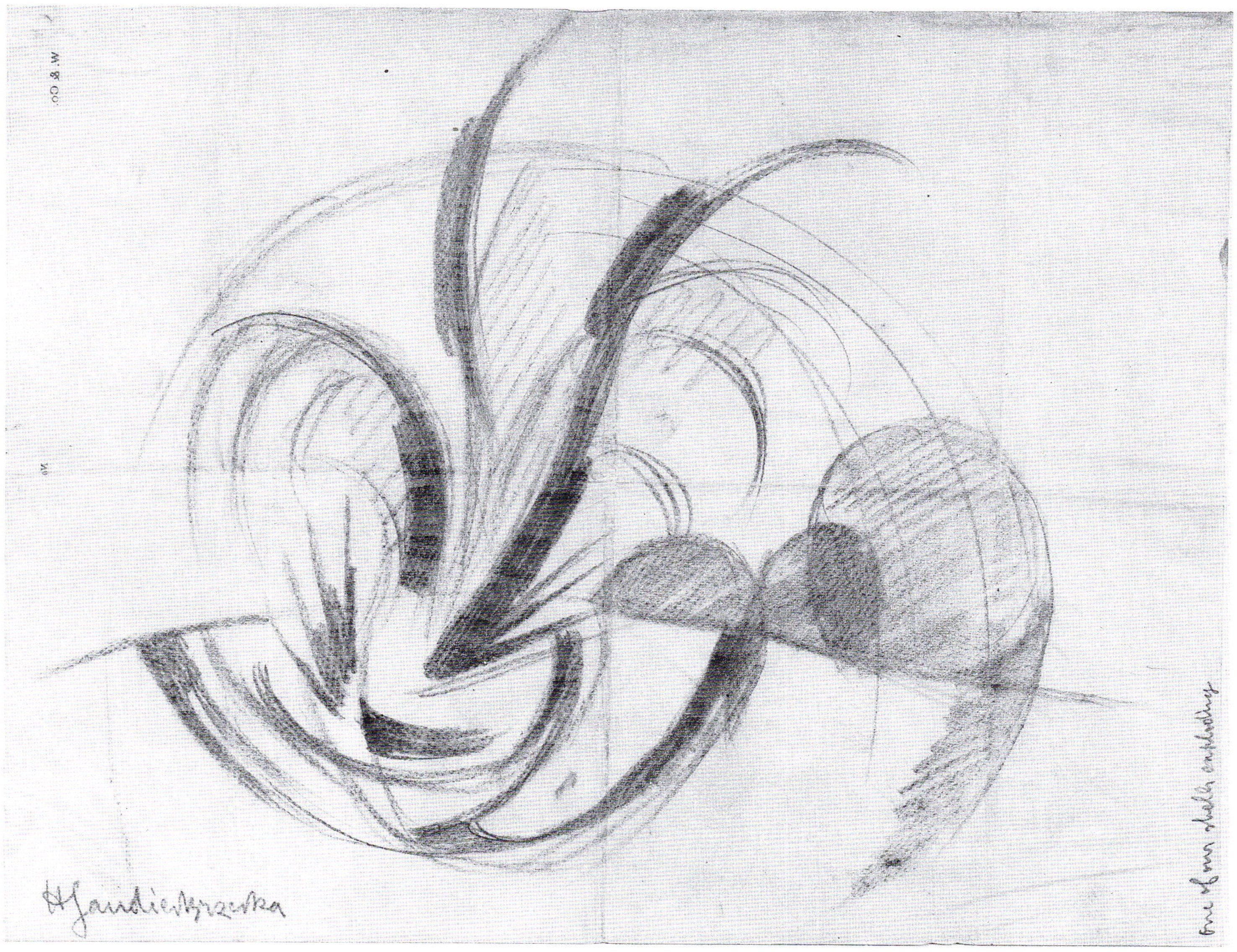

42 *One of Our Shells Exploding*, 1915

Shakespear, Cournos, Wadsworth, the Bevans and the Schiffs who had bought *Dancer* – who sent him news, recent magazines and more material comforts. He also re-established contact with his parents who now forgave his previous dereliction of patriotic duty. Undoubtedly the hard life he had led for the past few years had toughened him; he was more used to cold, discomfort and sporadic rations than many of his comrades. Unlike the restraint of so many letters from the front, Gaudier's gave unemotional, frank and often hair-raising accounts of life and death in the front line. To Kitty Smith he wrote in February 1915 expressing sympathy at the death of someone they had both known, adding:

> I have lost all my French friends already & I have only miraculously escaped until now. Once we attacked the boches in the night & we had to fight for an hour and a half on either side of a big road – at a distance of 15 yards. We left 48 chaps on the ground out of some eighty & where I was with my squad of 12 we came back three … I hope the luck may last but I am quite prepared to lose my life. We see here nothing but death and desolation – the villages

> are burnt & the fields are covered with German corpses. We do not bury them because their comrades bombard us if they see our parties digging graves – so that one gets accustomed to the idea of dying and it has nothing very dreadful.[9]

Even in April 1915 after more than seven months in the trenches he could tell her during an interval, 'I am enjoying the war – to me it's a fine sport though there are miseries like rain and vermin.'[10] Twice slightly wounded and twice promoted – to corporal and then to sergeant – he was preparing to continue officer training when he was killed by a single bullet in the forehead while taking part in a sortie at Neuville St Vaast on 5 June 1915.

Post Mortem

HIS DEATH, though not entirely unexpected, profoundly affected his friends. In a private act of remembrance Brodzky drew the abandoned studio (figs. 36, 37). As Wyndham Lewis, himself serving in a gun battery, expressed it:

> This little figure was so preternaturally *alive*, that I began my lesson then: a lesson of hatred for this soul-less machine, of big-wig money-government, and these masses of half-dead people, for whom personal extinction is such a tiny step, out of half-living into non-living, so what does it matter?[11]

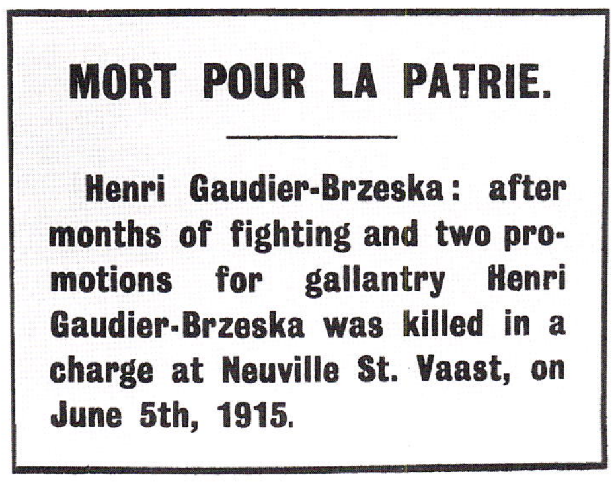
MORT POUR LA PATRIE.

Henri Gaudier-Brzeska: after months of fighting and two promotions for gallantry Henri Gaudier-Brzeska was killed in a charge at Neuville St. Vaast, on June 5th, 1915.

43 Obituary notice from *Blast*, July 1915

John Cournos wrote, 'There was a legend among us that dear Gaudier could not die. Because it is hard to believe that a man so gifted with genius, so abundantly endowed with aliveness, should come upon our earth merely to die by a bullet – his work undone, his creative secret untold.'[12] Epstein wrote to John Quinn, 'I feel a sympathetic and keen intelligence is gone'.[13] His death passed unnoticed in the daily newspapers and almost its first announcement was the panel published in *Blast* in early July (fig. 43). Over the following months several tributes appeared in the small-circulation magazines dedicated to contemporary art and literature to which his friends often contributed. Ford Madox Hueffer's tribute formed part of his rebuke to an intemperate critic of *Blast* who ventured to allude to Gaudier's death as some kind of joke. Of his sculpture he offered no opinion – 'he had carried his experiments far enough to make one say that he was a fine fellow; as a student of his art he had an erudition and a turn of phrase that I never heard equalled.' His tribute set the record straight by describing Gaudier's determination to enlist, his distinguished military record and then evoking the quality of his thoughts and his writing by quoting – without *Blast*'s typographic flourish – a passage from his last essay, 'Vortex Gaudier-Brzeska', written from the trenches.[14]

Ezra Pound was deeply affected, not merely by the immediate loss of a friend who was also one of the key figures in Vorticism, but by the death of a visionary creator who took on an increasingly complex mythic status in Pound's own imagination over succeeding years.[15] After the Second World War, from his asylum room, he told Wyndham Lewis that his serious interest in politics and economics dated from Gaudier's death.[16] His *Gaudier-Brzeska: A Memoir* (1916) was his most often revised and reissued book.[17] Open and coded references to Gaudier recur in the *Cantos* whose composition spanned most of Pound's career before during and after the Second World War. In the most explicit reference,

the lake of bodies, aqua morta,
of limbs fluid, and mingled, like fish heaped in a bin,
and here an arm upward, clutching a fragment of marble

And Henri Gaudier went to it,
        and they killed him,
And killed a good deal of sculpture. (Canto 16)

Pound's tone is matter-of-fact, almost flippant. By Canto 47 Gaudier's death has assumed the power to the regenerate and inspire the poet through their shared participation in Eleusinian rites asserting the symbiosis of creativity, birth and death in the cycle of the seasons.

As for Sophie Brzeska, she had lost the only person she held dear. While Gaudier was at the front, she had stayed on at their old lodgings; she also spent some time with the Camden Town painters, Robert Bevan and his wife, Stanislawa de Karlowska, a fellow Pole, as well as with the French painter Renée Finch. For a while she taught at a school in Sussex and then, finding this unendurable, rented a cottage in a nearby village and gave French lessons for a family who lived some five miles away. In his last letter to her, Gaudier had asked her to marry him and her angry, scolding reply added the burden of remorse to her grief.[18]

After Gaudier's death, broken to her as he had requested by Mrs Bevan, Brzeska returned to London. Even those of Gaudier's friends who had disliked her rallied round, though she angrily refused T. E. Hulme's well meant but tactless offer of a sum of money in recognition of her years of care for Gaudier.[19] In 1917 she rented a small cottage, 'The Cot' at Wotton-under-Edge near Gloucester, where she lived in seclusion, though Nina Hamnett wrote and visited her in April 1918.[20] She confided her remorse, her memories and thoughts to her journal, headed, 'A ta très chère mémoire'. Her one thought was to protect the work her 'brother' had entrusted to her. She deeply distrusted those who now suddenly took an interest in it, especially the American collector John Quinn; unknown to her he had, with the encouragement of Augustus John and Ezra Pound, been seeking to buy Gaudier's work before his death. Now, assisted by Pound, he was trying to buy Gaudier's work in quantity. Her resentment also focused on those who had, she felt, exploited Gaudier's naive generosity, helping themselves to drawings and acquiring his sculpture for a pittance. Only the Bevans and Sidney Schiff won her respect for their disinterested sympathy. She agreed to lend many works to the Leicester Galleries for the *Memorial Exhibition* in June 1918, though she was tormented by distrust of the dealers, by disappointment at the paucity of perceptive reviews and by Pound's interpretation of Gaudier in the exhibition catalogue for which he had supplied the preface but which she felt she should have written.[21]

Gradually her behaviour became more erratic. Tolerated eccentricity became confusion and verbal aggression. During a visit to London she ended up being arrested and spending several days in the Paddington Infirmary; a misunderstanding with Lucien Pissarro's family whom she was visiting in Hammersmith led her to storm out of the house only to become hopelessly disorientated en route to Hampstead where the Bevans expected her for supper.[22] She wandered about all night, talking and swearing, and was eventually picked up by the police from an ABC café near Paddington Station. Rescued from custody by Mrs Bevan, she returned to Wotton where her condition gradually deteriorated.

> From time to time Sophia still came to London, saw de Karlowska, and haunted those places where she and Henri used often to be seen … she is remembered as a forlorn creature, dragging herself around, wretchedly dressed and shod – a most pitiable spectacle.[23]

She became increasingly subject to obsessions and paranoid delusions which she recounted at length in her *Journal*; she had never liked the English and her animosity now became acute. Her fears and sense of being trapped in alien territory were exacerbated by her inability to replace the lost identity papers which would have allowed her to leave England for France or Poland. De Karlowska arranged a meeting for her with the Polish Consul so that she could replace her passport and return to Poland but her behaviour convinced him she was mad and he was unable to issue papers.[24] After failing to turn up for appointments at the Victoria and Albert Museum, where some of Gaudier's work was being stored at her request, she wrote to the museum authorities, 'I must inform you that I am being kept in England as a sort of prisoner of state – for crimes committed by others I suppose.'[25] Eventually her increasingly violent public manifestations of mental illness – the fate she had feared for many years – caused the local authorities to take action. Her *Journal* comes to a sudden halt on 2 November 1922. On 9 November Sophie Suzanne Gaudier-Brzeska was certified insane and committed to the County Mental Hospital in Gloucester. Despite a healthy bank balance she was classified as a 'pauper lunatic'. The officer in charge recalled her as 'a very bad case indeed … during the three years she was with us we were unable to elicit any reference to her past life.'[26] She died of bronchial pneumonia on 17 March 1925. Identified in the death certificate as an authoress, aged 45 years, she received a pauper's funeral and was buried in an unmarked grave in Gloucester City Old Cemetery.[27]

7

Myths and Realities

'Our story will become a legend – one of those beautiful, pure legends which lift up one's heart to God'

(Brzeska's *Journal*, 5.6.18)

Like his contemporary, Modigliani, Henri Gaudier's bohemian lifestyle and early death has given rise to an extensive mythology, rich in anecdotes and in its almost operatic storyline of tragically unfulfilled genius and tormented love. The tone of bohemian melodrama is evoked in the titles of several books on the artist – H. S. Ede's *Savage Messiah*, Roger Sécretain's *Un sculpteur "maudit"* and Roger Cole's *Burning to Speak*. The projection of this public Gaudier *persona* began soon after his death with the publication of Ezra Pound's *Gaudier-Brzeska: A Memoir* in February 1916. Pound's jumbled and deeply felt tribute acclaimed Gaudier as a savant, 'a sort of modern Cellini', a 'great spirit' and 'a great artist'. Its distribution was limited and its impact weakened by Pound's overtly polemical stance as one of the promoters of Vorticism.[1] Far more influential in its public impact was the biographical treatment in H. S. Ede's *A Life of Gaudier-Brzeska* (1930), enthusiastically reviewed in London and New York and reissued in a cheaper edition in April 1931 under a new title, *Savage Messiah*. Ede's book has become a classic which is still in print; the image of the artist as 'Savage Messiah' and the immediacy of his evocation of the passionate relationship between Henri Gaudier and Sophie Brzeska has been far more significant than any subsequent art historical appraisal in assuring his fame and extending it beyond the boundaries of academic study into theatre, film, musical and dance. Their relationship was the acknowledged source for the artist and writer protagonists in the 1934 play *The Laughing Woman* by Gordon Daviot.[2] Wyndham Lewis based the character of Victor Stamp, the tragic artist protagonist of his 1937 novel *Revenge for Love*, in part on Gaudier.[3] It inspired Ken Russell's 1971 film, *Savage Messiah*, where their relationship acquired all the overtones of the Sixties youth-led counter-culture. These later interpretations used the notion of artist as protagonist less for its own sake than to invoke the appeal of an unconventional *vie de bohème* and to endow a tragic love story with sub-plot.

The facts of his life fitted so neatly the paradigm of the tragic genius as it has been constructed in Western culture from Thomas Chatterton to James Dean: coming from an unpropitious background where his talent was greeted with hostility rather than encouragement, he seemed self-made; he displayed precocious brilliance and an unswerving sense of mission; his chronic poverty and disregard for comfort could be seen as emblematic of his fanatical dedication to his art; undismayed by the continual rebuffs and lack of comprehension of his work, his inherent qualities and disturbing but charismatic presence eventually attracted the recognition of his peers; though he sold little, he had just begun to achieve critical recognition when he succumbed to what appeared a predestined but avoidable fate. The passionate but unconsummated relationship with Sophie Brzeska could be seen as profoundly ambivalent in its effects though typically it has been viewed almost exclusively for its negative effects upon him, adding another dimension to the disadvantages he had to overcome and the lack of fulfilment that seemed to be his fate. Finally there was the double tragedy of Gaudier's death and Brzeska's lingering descent into insanity.

However this is too simplistic a view of a complex and multi-layered process through which the canonic image of Henri Gaudier-Brzeska has evolved. Responsibility for the Gaudier myth has generally been assigned to Pound and Ede, but this is to overlook the character of the source material and Gaudier's own collusion in the creation of a fictive self as 'bohemian artist' and 'primitive' or 'savage', labels which themselves stem from Romantic and late nineteenth-century conceptions of the artist.[4] Gaudier's letters, Brzeska's writings and the memoirs of friends provide supporting evidence for the creation of this persona by Gaudier and his circle. The subsequent shaping of Gaudier's life and reputation must also be seen in the context of Modernism and accompanying transformations in the definition of sculpture. It is worth trying to disentangle some of the strands of these rival, complementary accounts both for the light they shed on the artist's personality and for an insight into the relative value given to different sources for the construction of the artist's life.

The brevity and relative obscurity of Gaudier's career means that the useful evidence of exhibition reviews, critical appraisals and interviews are largely absent. Almost the sole sources are Gaudier's surviving letters and Brzeska's unpublished writings (on which Ede's *Savage Messiah* and Sécretain's *Un sculpteur "maudit"* were largely based). Additionally there are the published memoirs of Gaudier by Pound and Brodzky and the passing references in the later autobiographies of others who knew him, such as Enid Bagnold, John Middleton Murry, Jacob Epstein, Richard Aldington and John Cournos.

Gaudier was himself the source of many stories about his early life which he related to Brodzky and Pound among others. His most obvious fiction, designed as a cover for their co-habitation in England, was that of Henri and Sophie as Franco-Polish brother and sister. Gaudier became 'Gaudier-Brzeska' though Sophie was usually addressed as Mlle Brzeska. Privately Gaudier was entertained by the readiness with which the story was accepted and at once gave rise to certain assumptions in his listeners; in November 1912, he wrote to Sophie after attending a little salon in Hampstead as the guest of the Wilshires, American friends of Macfall:

> I have been telling the tallest stories. The Americans called me Brzeska, and several of the French when they heard that I was 'polonais' said to me that I spoke French and English like a Russian, and several others who had thought I was Italian saw very clearly from my type and my walk that I was Slav. What fools! What asses![5]

Although the secret was not especially closely kept – they quickly confided their real relationship to Katherine Mansfield and John Middleton Murry – it was widely believed and absorbed into the canon of biographical information.[6] Gaudier's obituary in *Colour* described him as 'born in France of Franco-Polish parents'.[7] Macfall recalled his impression that Gaudier's mother was the daughter of a Polish head of state.[8] John Cournos, too, perpetuated the belief that Gaudier was part Polish and identified aspects of his temperament with his origin.[9] Even Brodzky,

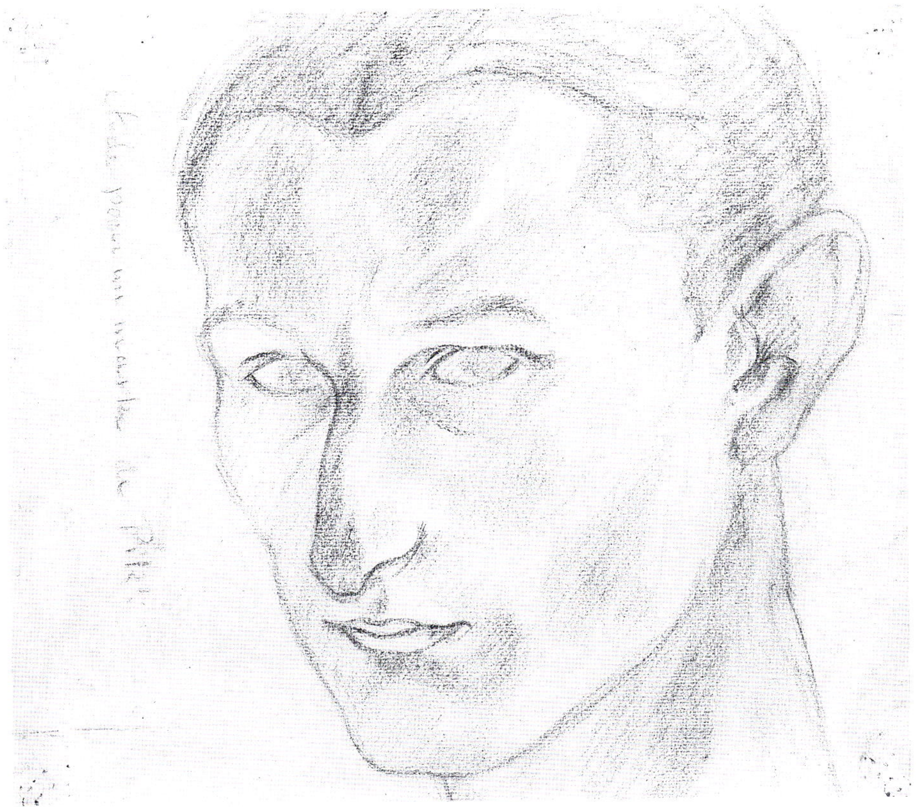

44 *Self-Portrait* inscribed 'Etude pour un maske de Pik' ('Study for a mask of Pik'), 1911–12

himself of Polish origin though he did not speak the language, accepted the story – 'I always addressed him as Brzeska'.[10] Pound undoubtedly knew the truth; after Gaudier's death it was through his urging that the leading French *littérateur* Rémy de Gourmont wrote the only tribute to be published in France. Pound's own text refers to Gaudier's birth and upbringing in St Jean de Braye, his respect for his father's craftsmanship as a joiner, and his scholarships while also perpetuating the family legend that 'Gaudier's ancestors had been masons and stone carvers for generations and had worked on the cathedral of Chartres.'[11]

Gaudier embroidered other stories around his childhood and youth, intertwining fact and fiction about his experiences in Bristol and Germany. Pound retold the tale Gaudier had told Brodzky of his boyhood travels: 'Gaudier's wanderings afoot about Europe had taken place between his ninth and fourteenth year.'[12] The account Gaudier gave Brodzky seems to have been still further ornamented; he claimed he had worked at road-mending by day while attending the local *gymnasium* in the evening during his precocious *Wanderjahr*, that he had been ill-treated in Bristol and that he had worked as a 'ghost' to a humorous illustrator while in Paris.

His friends knew him as a storyteller; it was part of his charm. Even if he sometimes used the stories to entertain them and to ridicule pretension, they were left in doubt of the border between truth and invention. Pound relished Gaudier as 'the best fun in the world, whether he was inveighing against the softness of modern customs, or telling tales of his life', though he was aware that much of what he was told was greatly exaggerated; of the road-mending story, he commented 'Possibly he may have, for a day or two or to provide a stray night's lodging'. But he appears to have credited other stories:

> when he was in Munich he was part of a Rembrandt factory. He used to go to the ghetto and draw types: the sweep, the vigour, the faces. Then a Swiss used to take the drawings up to the pinakoteka and carefully daub them *à la Rembrandt*, studying the mannerisms, all the ways of lighting the hands, etc., etc. And then a German took them and put on the tone of time, tea-leaves, etc., and then they were sold to a Jew ... Thus they made new Rembrandts, not doubtful copies or 'originals of which copies are at the Hermitage.[13]

Brodzky gives a similar account: 'Brzeska was also a manufacturer of "Old Masters", including Rembrandts, and he knew the uses of stale coffee and prune juice and other concoctions used in the production of the *patine* of time.'[14] Both Ede and Sécretain cite the story, the latter with a hint of scepticism.[15] There may be a germ of truth in it somewhere but there is no support in extant letters or sketchbooks. His many life drawings of people at work date from 1910 and it was in Whitechapel that he made his drawings of Jewish people.

Even the reasons for Gaudier's departure from France were doctored, conveniently avoiding the banalities of his parents' disapproval of Brzeska and his reluctance to do military service; his involvement on the fringes of the Hervé riots and the questioning of Brzeska by the Orléans police were conflated into a tale combining elements of *Tosca*, an anarchist-style assassination and student riots against the police. Though Brzeska too made up stories to conceal their extreme poverty, she demanded mutual honesty in her relationship with Gaudier and was wounded when she discovered that he often lied to her, mostly about unimportant matters; when she challenged him, 'he tells me that lying is very interesting and indispensable for an artist – I don't believe it.'[16]

The freedom with which Gaudier fictionalized his origins as well as some of his most extreme behaviour suggest something more than *épatisme* or youthful exuberance: perhaps a lack rather than an overabundance of confidence, an urge to play to his audience and a need to live up to a particular idea of bohemian artistic identity. This may have led him to flout authority and most social norms, even at the cost of alienating those from whom he most desperately sought recognition. As a poor foreigner and one of the few among his contemporaries with neither family wealth, university nor art school behind him, Gaudier had good reason to feel insecure and, after a year of isolation in London, to be sensitive to being an outsider even among the émigré poets and artists who made up many of his new acquaintances. Once he had begun to move in circles outside Macfall's cosy and slightly dilettante English group, most of his new friends – Wolmark, Brodzky, Epstein, Cournos, Pound, Lewis – were also operating at the margins of mainstream British society and culture. Gaudier's self-dramatization exaggerated and reinforced his position as an outsider, asserting his extra difference and otherness in a milieu where flouting conventions was a matter of pride. His adoption of a fictitious past was far from unique; Pound had been known to exaggerate his

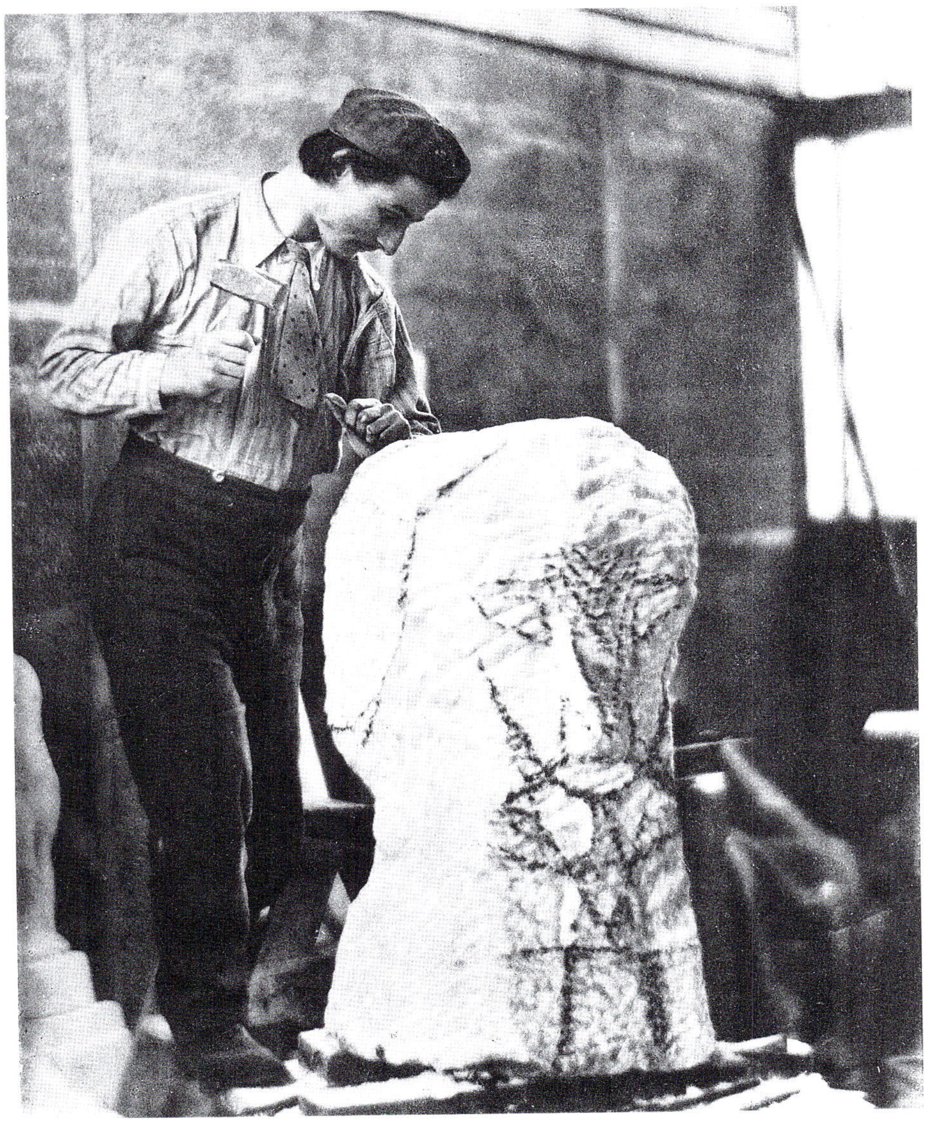

45 Gaudier carving *Head of Ezra Pound*, spring 1914. Photograph by Walter Benington

mid-Western origins in Hailey, Idaho by claiming that he had been born in a pioneer shack.[17]

The affectation of a self-conscious *persona* was not a new phenomenon, but it is particularly noticeable that during this period of the emergence of Modernism many leading artists and writers marked themselves out through carefully constructed, highly self-conscious identities – the painter Augustus John, the journalist, confessional writer and con-artist Frank Harris, his closest associates in the Rebel Art Centre, Wyndham Lewis and Ezra Pound. As Douglas Goldring recalled, 'Both of them at that period, in clothes, hairdressing and manner, made no secret of their calling ... Pound contrived to look "every inch a poet", while I have never seen anyone so obviously a "genius" as Wyndham Lewis.'[18] Dress and grooming or lack of it were intended not only to mark out the artist's difference from the rest of society but also to contrast with the effete dandyism of the previous generation of 'greenery-yallery' artists; Gaudier was certainly aware of the distinction, contrasting the gentlemanly aesthetic air of Lovat Fraser's studio with the workmanlike austerity and casual poverty of Epstein's.[19]

Almost since childhood Gaudier had been preoccupied with the idea of being an artist but, in the absence of the formative contacts of art school and under the pressure of daily office work, his role models would have been largely imaginary or derived from books and magazine articles. He had identified himself as an artist in the relative privacy of his notebooks if not to his parents; there are no fewer than five completely different signatures in his 1908–9 sketchbook, ranging from 'HG' and 'H Gaudier' in several calligraphic styles to 'HASM Gaudier'.[20] The following year, at about the same time that he began to discuss his ambitions with Dr Uhlemayr, he fantasized a splendid future for himself within the artistic establishment as a winner of the 'prix d'honneur', depicting his painting, *L'Etre Nouveau* (a nude woman seated on a nude man's lap against a sunset landscape) being worshipped by Rodin, his current idol.[21] However, during 1910, as his distaste for commercial life became more focused he began to see the free life of the artist as the antithesis of the corrupt urban life of commerce.[22] By the time he left Munich he seemed determined to pursue a career as an illustrator and, from the efforts he made to sell his drawings to the satirical magazines *Rire* and *Charivari* as well as the *épatisme* of many of his private sketches, he seems to have been developing an increasingly confrontational idea of the relationship between an artist and society. Forain was the artist he cited to Dr Uhlemayr as an example of someone whose criticisms of society became more bitter the more success he enjoyed. He was also a profound admirer of the graphic artists who deployed mordant wit and superb technique in pictorial satirical journals such as *L'assiette au beurre*.[23] Increasingly anarchistic, anti-authoritarian convictions frame his definition of the artist's role. Pound commented, 'He accepted himself as "a sort of modern Cellini." He did not *claim* it, but when it was put to him one day, he accepted it mildly, quite simply, after mature deliberation.'[24]

Gaudier took this self-conscious definition of himself as an anti-authoritarian, anti-bourgeois artist to considerable extremes in his everyday behaviour. Brzeska repeatedly describes incidents illustrating his disregard for her efforts to maintain at least a facade of cleanliness and gentility in their lodgings. Brzeska herself was, on political, literary and social grounds, fiercely anti-bourgeois – 'les sales bourgeois' is one of her favourite phrases – but she set great store by neat, clean surroundings and a minimum level of comfort to which Gaudier was completely indifferent, not just in sleeping in a deckchair in his studio but in neglecting to wash himself or care for what he ate: 'As for me, I am an artist – an artist must live in a bohemian way', Sophie reported him declaring.[25] Even to his friends and fellow artists such behaviour was disconcerting. The poet Richard Aldington, his literary sparring partner in the debate about the merits of classical sculpture, recalled:

> He was probably the dirtiest human being I have ever known and gave off horrid effluvia in hot weather. One summer day he came to see us in our small flat; so we prudently placed him on a couch at one end of the room and ourselves retired to the other. Who should come in but Ford [Madox Hueffer], who had been at a fashionable luncheon, and wanted to display his shiny topper and formal morning clothes with a carnation. Unluckily he had to sit

> beside Gaudier and soon left. The next morning Ford gave me a paternal lecture on my wickedness in letting such a creature to be in the same room with HD [Hilda Dolittle, his future wife]. It was, he said, not done.[26]

Even Brodzky, who was equally poor though less radical in his views, was torn between entertainment and irritation at some of Gaudier's pointedly bohemian gestures:

> One evening we were going to dine in Soho, and I had decided to take him to my favourite restaurant, where he could behave as much like a workman as he chose.
>
> But as soon as we arrived, a single glance from Brzeska [i.e. Gaudier] and he baulked at the door. His objection to white napery had now become more than a fad. He was a real crank about it. This place was anything but a *de luxe* place, but I could not get him to enter. He objected to the tablecloths. It was too *bourgeois* ... we could not find any restaurant to suit him. He was as obstinate as a mule. So I asked him what we were going to do. 'Buy something,' he said, 'some bread, cheese, salame. We can eat it out here.'
>
> I went into a nearby shop and bought a full length of a long French loaf, had it split down the centre, and sandwiched with cheese and salame. The loaf was then divided in two, half for each. Here was our fine Soho meal!
>
> I handed Brzeska his portion saying, 'We can't eat this stuff walking about.' 'Then let's sit down' said the savage. And so we sat down at the corner of Old Compton Street and Dean Street with our backs to the wall, whilst our legs stretched out in front of us and hindered passers-by ... Brzeska laughing at the discomfort of the people passing by who had to dodge our upturned boots, and hurling 'Bloody bourgeois!' at anyone who looked disapprovingly at us.[27]

Gaudier's appearance and behaviour prompted animal nicknames and recurrent references to him as a primitive or savage; in Bristol the younger Smiths had called him 'Goat' for his wiry energy and as a pun on his name; when Brodzky, seeing the chaos of the studio and Gaudier devouring hunks of meat from his malodorous casserole, called him a 'Red Skin', Gaudier replied that his colleagues in the Paris textile design firm had called him 'the Indian'.[28] To Pound, on first encountering him in the upper galleries of the Albert Hall during the 1913 Allied Artists' show he was 'like a well-made young wolf or some soft-moving, bright-eyed wild thing.'[29] Aldington, reviewing *Blast*, identified his behaviour with his work, characterizing him as 'a wild, unkempt barbarian ... the sort of person who would dye his statues in the gore of goats if he thought it would give them a more virile appearance ...'[30] Gaudier clearly enjoyed playing up to this image of himself, so much so that his 'primitivism' seems to have been at least as much about his own behaviour as it was about the formal or raw emotional qualities of his carvings. Brodzky, for whom Gaudier 'the savage' was a kind of running gag in their friendship, recalled Gaudier's half-playful fascination with the South Seas, his Maori-style greenstone *Charm* (*cat.* 85, pls. 130, XIII) which for a few weeks he wore round his neck on a string, his talk of the sexual freedom of life there, of their body ornaments and how he teased Sophie by pretending to pierce his ears for elaborate primitive-style earrings with a chisel.[31]

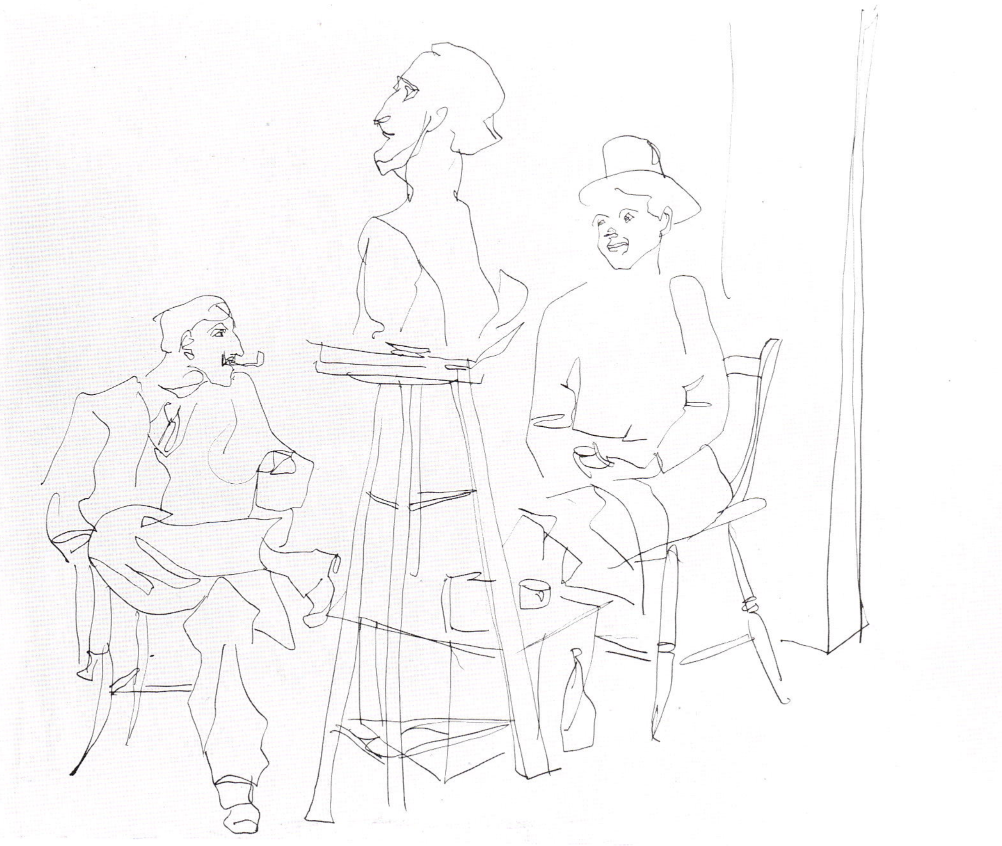

46 *The Studio of Gaudier-Brzeska: Horace Brodzky and Sophie Brzeska Looking at the Bust of Brodzky*, 1913

The evocative title 'savage Messiah', with its overtones of authority, destiny and sacrifice, actually originated in one of these joking sallies as told by Brzeska. It was on one of Gaudier's noisy homecomings that she remarked ironically to Brodzky (who was awaiting his return with her having spent some hours working on her portrait):

> 'Here comes the savage messiah!'
>
> Seeing him come in Brodzky leapt from his chair, picked up his hat and hung it high on a nail behind the door.
>
> 'Why these precautions with your hat?' I asked him, laughing. 'Because it's the only one I've got and I must safeguard it from the destructive instincts of the master of the house. He could reduce it to the same state as his own and I saw that new only a month ago.'[32]

It is scarcely credible that Gaudier would have been so much liked and missed had he been a mere youthful poseur. Many of his friends and acquaintances struggled to express his peculiar lithe grace, quickness, mental toughness, restlessness and nervous vigour and his contradictory qualities of aggression and gentleness, humour and penetrating intensity. His was a stimulating but disturbing presence. Many of the stories told about him can also be read as ways of conveying the hyper-reality, that quality of superabundant energy and 'aliveness' which they all lamented after his death. Middleton Murry, whose brief friendship with Gaudier ended with a tremendous row, nevertheless recalled that Gaudier and D. H. Lawrence were the two people he had known who seemed to possess a *daimon*, a genius which made them appear different not in degree but in kind from everyone else.[33] Even the thirty-two-year-old Pound, poet and entrepreneur of the new, and not one easily given to humility, conveys a curious sense of deference at their first meeting: 'I knew that many things would bore and disgust him, particularly my rather middle-aged point of view, my intellectual tiredness and exhaustion, my general scepticism and quietness.'[34] Brodzky described him at their first meeting as

> a little fellow, quite a boy, dirty and unkempt and smiling … peaky faced and anything but the romantic artist of fiction, a most unattractive and unimpressive figure. I had expected to see an adult and exotic foreigner more in keeping with the double-barrelled name, and here was an insignificant youngster greeting me.[35]

Yet this belied his intensity; as the novelist and playwright Enid Bagnold later recalled, 'Gaudier was like a dagger in the midst of us. He had a hungry face (we did not know how hungry) and a mind made of metal. He talked like a chisel and argued like a hammer'.[36] She recalled an evening at Haldane Macfall's:

> One night we came from the Macfalls', Dolly [Tilden, her flatmate], Gaudier, and Lovat [Fraser] and I, and we were again on a Tube railway station. Though we still expected it, the last train had gone. It was winter and a wind like a wolf galloped down the Tube tunnel. We stood in its passage, Gaudier talking. He did not drop a subject when he had added a little to it. He did not throw a word in here and there, and make a crisp sentence sum up a bale of thought. What had been talked of a quarter of an hour before at Macfalls' was still being followed up. Gaudier, his long front hair hanging in a string down the side of his white brow, was throwing his future and his past and his passion into the discussion. We lazier English stood and shivered, and tried to back out of the wind. Gaudier felt our bodies moving, grouped, away from him, and I remember as he talked, and his eyes and pale face shone, he put out his thin arms and surrounded us and held us fast in the wind so that our edging movements should not distract him.[37]

The borderline between myth and reality is often blurred. Contemporary testimony may be equally unreliable, as the famous story of Gaudier's first meeting with Epstein in 1912 illustrates. Pound's anecdote appears to have gone the rounds of the Café Royal already:

> Frank Harris told Brodzky the following tale of Gaudier's first carving in stone. Gaudier aetatis suae XVIII or thereabouts, met Epstein, who said, mustering the thunders of god and the scowlings of Assyrian sculpture in to his tone and eyebrows,
>
> 'UMMHH! Do … you cut … direct … in stone?'
>
> 'Most certainly!' said Gaudier, who had never yet done anything of the sort.
>
> 'That's right,' said Epstein: 'I will come around to your place on Sunday.' So Gaudier at once went out, got three small stone blocks and by working more or less night and day had something ready by Sunday.[38]

This story is relayed as fact by several commentators though even Pound signals its doubtful status by adding, 'This may very well have happened', and by comparing it as a topos of the birth of artistic genius with Vasari's story of the boy Michelangelo knocking the teeth out of his 'Antique' head of an old faun in the Medici sculpture garden. When Epstein read in Pound's *Gaudier-Brzeska: A Memoir* the alleged account of his and Gaudier's first meeting, he overlooked Pound's claim that he had the story from Harris and thought Gaudier himself had told it to Pound, commenting cryptically, 'this was very characteristic of him'.[39] But what was characteristic? That he should have bluffed out of pride and then worked non-stop to be ready for the visit? Or that he recognized Gaudier's characteristic humour and powers of invention in a story which bore at best a tangential relation to the actual events? Interviewed by Arnold Haskell in 1929, Epstein said that 'he took to carving after admiring a work he saw in my studio one day'.[40]

After Gaudier's death his work and artistic aims became an area contested by opposing camps of 'modernists', each attempting to define his 'real work' and assert a conclusive direction for his art. Pound, whose *Memoir* was published within months of Gaudier's death, and who had known him for just a year, hastened to annexe him for Vorticism, a movement of which he himself was one of the main animators. His text, reproducing Gaudier's published work, notably the 'Vortex' essay and his letters from the trenches, is essentially about the Gaudier he knew. His account and outline list of works focuses on the most primitivizing, hard-edged and abstracted carvings and drawings, dismissing the naturalistic work and almost everything before they met in the latter part of 1913 as early, unimportant work. His polemical stance is highlighted by the fact that he and his wife owned one of Gaudier's most naturalistic works, *Torso 1* (*cat.* 60) as well as *Samson and Delilah* (*cat.* 57).[41] His belligerent appropriation of Gaudier for Vorticism immediately aroused the ire of his friends outside the Pound-Lewis axis, for whom Gaudier's recent work represented a passing phase of youthful experiment. Roger Fry, judging Pound 'too emphatic and overbearing in the statements of claims for himself, his dead friend and their associates', advised readers to 'turn to the admirable series of reproductions and there judge for himself the importance of Brzeska's work.' In Fry's opinion, Gaudier was 'seeking to create a classic art, one of purely formal expressiveness':

> It was only natural however that the experiments of Cubism and its offshoot Vorticism should attract him, and in a few pieces of sculpture he tried to treat organic forms with a system of plasticity derived from mechanical objects so as to give them the schemes of planes and their surfaces the same kind of relations that appear in the planes of machinery.
>
> However useful this attempt may have been as an exercise in the problem of plane relations reduced to their simplest terms, I cannot think that the work was in line with Gaudier's special gifts and artistic temperament.
>
> Brzeska himself recognised this in his later conversations with me and states in one of his letters that he intends to return to organic forms.[42]

To Macfall, Pound and his friends were 'loose-mouthed, self-advertising mediocrities' who had 'sucked the dead lad's blood like the ghouls they are'.[43] On his return from wartime service he willingly sent anything

he could to support Brodzky's memoir drafted in 1919.[44] Brodzky's book was intended as a riposte to 'the jumble of inaccuracies and mass of Vorticist propaganda' produced by Pound and 'the Rebel Art Centre coterie'; 'some of his "friends" do him a great injustice by allowing him such a mediocre intellect as to suppose that he could produce nothing but geometrical absurdities'.[45] Like Fry, Brodzky sought to reclaim Gaudier as a classical artist whose 'real work' was represented by *Dancer* and *Torso 2*. When Brodzky prepared his final text in 1932–33 he toned down his criticisms of Pound; he could also look to Picasso, Epstein and other artists who were working in representational, more naturalistic styles during the Twenties as well as to the new generation of direct carvers, Dobson, Moore, Hepworth and Skeaping (see pp. 138–140). Pound and Brodzky claimed to give a view of Gaudier authenticated by the intimacy of their relationship with him.[46] Both could assert the extra cameraderie that comes from shared professional understanding. Yet, as we have seen, matters were not so simple.

H. S. (Jim) Ede never met Gaudier, only discovering his work when it arrived in his office at the Tate Gallery after Sophie Brzeska's death.[47] However, he too could claim to write from a uniquely privileged position, since he alone had access to all Brzeska's writings and to Gaudier's letters to her, as well as to the mass of drawings and sculptures. He was also able to contact many people who had known the artist and his companion. *Savage Messiah* appears to chronicle Gaudier's development as an artist and his and Sophie's relationship in a peculiarly intimate, unmediated way, with Ede himself as mere translator and narrator of a true story told in the words of the protagonists:

> any remarks about them in no way denote my own feeling, but entirely those of Henri Gaudier and Sophie Brzeska ... My authority for what I have written has mostly been a diary kept by Miss Brzeska, whose statements I have checked with letters from Henri Gaudier and by conversations with people who knew them both.[48]

This somewhat disingenuous statement distances Ede from Pound's and Brodzky's openly partisan accounts. However, it is misleading to take Ede's claims to self-effacing objectivity entirely at face value; though he was an excellent translator and a highly sympathetic writer, he nevertheless makes a number of tacit assumptions, above all in his definition and use of Brzeska's 'diary'. Ede uses Brzeska's writings freely, usually in paraphrase, though he often quotes direct speech given apparently verbatim in the 'diary'.

The definition of Brzeska's writings is itself problematic; the term 'diary', employed by nearly all writers on Gaudier, is inadequate.[49] The poet W. B. Yeats spotted this at once; on first reading *Savage Messiah*, he doubted the existence of the 'diary' but finally came to the conclusion not only that it existed but also that Sophie might actually be a great novelist.[50] A diary suggests contemporaneity and the regular chronicling of events. While the *Journal* covering the years after Gaudier's death does contain regular dates, Brzeska's texts covering the period from 1910 to 1915 are episodic in structure; the sections are usually numbered but not

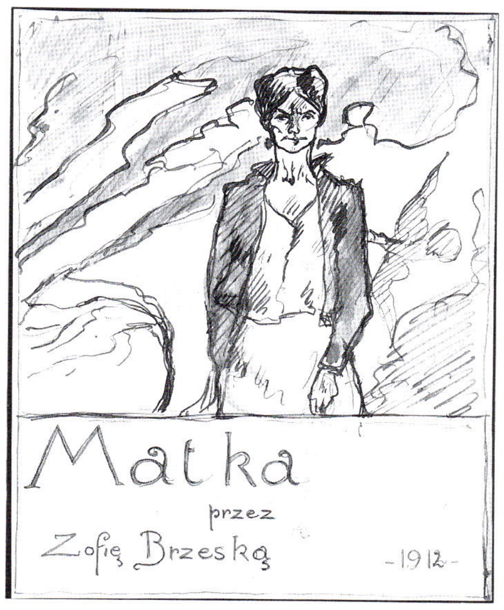

47 Design for book jacket for *Matka*, 1912

dated and the consistency of the writing and ink colour suggests that several sections were written at a time. Although they include accounts of events which can be verified and dated from Gaudier's letters or given credence by other external evidence, many of the events described and conversations given in direct speech were being recounted weeks or even months later.[51] The mass of foolscap manuscript, parts water- or mud-stained with sporadic numbering and displaced inserts, falls into two broad sections: 'Détails pour Matka', a draft autobiographical novel called *Matka*, one of Brzeska's own pet names (fig. 47), interspersed with other sections headed 'A mon fils adoptif'. It is less a diary than a memoir-cum-novel with confessional episodes in which invented and actual conversation and narrative often become indivisible.

Long before Brzeska met Gaudier she had been writing short stories in Polish and English which were thinly disguised accounts of her own childhood and the miseries of her life as a governess (Pleurette) in France, Italy, Poland and the United States.

It is still in the character of Pleurette that Brzeska describes meeting Henri Gaudier (Prince Ailé) at the Bibliothèque Ste Geneviève in the first section of *Matka*, though she soon adopts Pik and Sisik or Mamus, the names they called each other. There are some remarkably cool reflections on herself and Gaudier:

> Am I merely destined to play a rôle in Pik's life, perhaps mentioned in the annals on the great men of the twentieth century as a woman who exerted a certain influence on the genius sculptor? No, that would be too weird.[52]

During the section covering 1912, real names alternate with thinly disguised puns, loaded with contemptuous humour: Updown or Down for Haldane Macfall, Mr Bonny or Mr Yellow for Leman Hare, Colonel Squeeze for Major Smythies, Mr Fox for Macfarlane Cocks, Dumpling for the round-faced Lovat Fraser, Lord Southrock for Lord Northcliff, Mr Worthing and Mandarine Puppet for Middleton Murry and Katherine Mansfield, and Packhall or Sackhold for Enid Bagnold. Brzeska had a sharp eye and tongue for appearance and details of social interraction and an apparently vast memory for dialogue, with pages devoted to the give-and-take of her conversations or arguments with Gaudier and others. Though at times painfully honest in analysing and criticizing her own prejudices, she made no pretence of objectivity and much of what she wrote seems to have been coloured by her anger, unhappiness and insecurity. It is both profoundly autobiographical and angrily feminist in its emphasis on the humiliations and marginalization experienced by women in their family, social and working lives.

Two doom-laden premonitions, all the more terrible for being fulfilled by events, recur throughout the account – Gaudier's premonition that he will die young in war and Brzeska's own awareness of mental instability and her fear of madness. She recognized that she had a difficult temperament and often put people off either by pouring out her feelings and assuming an intimacy they were unable to return or by jealousy of attention paid to Gaudier which threatened to exclude her. None of her stories was ever published and their rejection by Murry and Pound wounded her fragile self-esteem and further prejudiced her against them.

Her bitterness was only increased by the patronizing chauvinism she perceived in the way she was treated by Gaudier's literary and artistic friends, and by Gaudier himself, whenever she tried to discuss literature or art with them. Gaudier had at first applauded and encouraged her approach:

> It is no use for Mamus to waste herself in theories, for she lies to herself all the time. All that she says consciously is at war with her talent, which comes from her unconscious self ... You write what you know about, what you have lived – you blame yourself for only writing your Trilogy because you have suffered, and because that so burns within you that you cannot choose but tell it. So much the better, for had you not this living idea you would do nothing, you would write historical stupidities without any life.[53]

Two years later, soon after the rejections of her work, he was urging her to write less autobiographically and less stridently, referring to 'ton propaganda du féminisme' (your feminist propaganda).[54]

Contemporary and later memoirs as well as Brzeska's own writings reflect the varying ways in which Katherine Mansfield, Enid Bagnold, Ezra Pound, Jacob Epstein and others reacted against her: as Epstein recalled, she 'was intensely and morbidly jealous of all his friends'.[55] Critics have noted that she will always be cast as an unreliable witness.[56] However, her testimony is valuable because her overriding interest was in Gaudier of whose actions and behaviour she was a loving but exacting judge. Moreover, she observed him not only in domestic privacy but also in social settings or in the studio with almost all his new friends. Many of the conversations she reports ring true, being consistent with views which can be verified from letters or published statements. She was not especially perceptive about Gaudier's art, being chiefly concerned that he should make some money; she remained staunchly classical in taste, much preferring the portraits and works such as *Dancer* and the *Torso* to the 'egg-headed', Brancusian and more abstract works which she thought unsaleable and done merely to court approval and attention.

The painful intimacy of Brzeska's work comes through in Ede's account. It formed an important part of the book's appeal as the reviews indicate: Frank Rutter judged, 'Since the publication of the letters of Van Gogh there has been no more vivid and intimate revelation of an artist's life.'[57] For the *Observer* reviewer,

> The story of Gaudier's meeting with the astonishing Sophie Brzeska in Paris, of their life together in London, of the young artist's return to his own country for war service and his tragic death is told with the economy of reverence; there are numerous letters, almost painfully revelatory and intimate. Queerer love story there can scarcely be and the absorbed reader's only doubt will be whether he has the right to know so much about it.[58]

Yet the mainspring of Ede's work and, it might well be argued, of his entire interpretation of Gaudier's life was the extraordinary, secret hope expressed by Sophie Brzeska herself. On 5 June 1918, the third anniversary of Gaudier's death, while the Memorial Exhibition was still on at the Leicester Galleries, Brzeska reflected on the potentially exemplary and ideal character of her relationship with Gaudier:

> It is inconceivable that our story won't live on, that it won't move those who know only base physical passion. Our story will become a legend – one of those beautiful, pure legends which lift up one's heart to God. It's a great consolation to me. And even if the Devil's pitiless malice prevents me from constructing the work I envision – and it remains unpublished – even then I won't give up hope because I have faith that our legend as it stands is already a work which will at least teach those who are already on the right road.[59]

Savage Messiah also significantly inflated evaluations of Gaudier's work for public consumption. Hitherto an artist of interest only to a handful of artists and critics, Gaudier became an artist 'who, with Brancusi and Picasso, helped to clear the cobwebs from the fundamentals of art for many but less gifted practitioners throughout Europe.'[60]

Brzeska's writings were among the papers and works of art acquired by Ede from the Brzeska Estate and, as he often said, they would have been destroyed, simply thrown away as worthless, had he not preserved them. Many have speculated on how Gaudier's work might have developed had he lived and how the shape of British or European sculpture might have been changed. We may more fruitfully ask what Gaudier's reputation would now be if all Brzeska's writings and Gaudier's own notebooks had been destroyed. *Savage Messiah*, if written at all, would have taken a very different approach and a different title. Would Gaudier's handful of disparate but daring carvings have had significance only for a few sculptors of the Twenties and Thirties like Frank Dobson and Henry Moore who, finding Pound's book or later seeing his work, found him a source of private inspiration? Would his reputation have depended upon the scholarly revival of interest in Vorticism which took place in the Sixties and Seventies? Ede's text, in the spirit of Brzeska's private hope, has exercized an enduring influence not only on other art forms but also on real life. In 1941, the painter Arshile Gorky, writing to his future wife, extensively plagiarized Gaudier's letters to Sophie in *Savage Messiah*, and the words were long taken for his own.[61]

The most obvious effects of the myths which have enshrouded Gaudier have been to focus on his personal life and early death – the might-have-beens rather than looking at what he actually did – and to make him a pawn in the battles for Modernism. But the stories told about him can also provide insights which may deepen our understanding of his work. His arrogant self-assurance, intelligence and chameleon-like changes of style and opinion can be seen as evidence not only of youthful talent, but possibly also as strategies to cover insecurity; his antic outbursts, posturing and dogmatic eloquence in debate were almost as important as his work in helping him to obtain acceptance and prominence within the contemporary avant-garde.

1 Sophie Brzeska, pastel

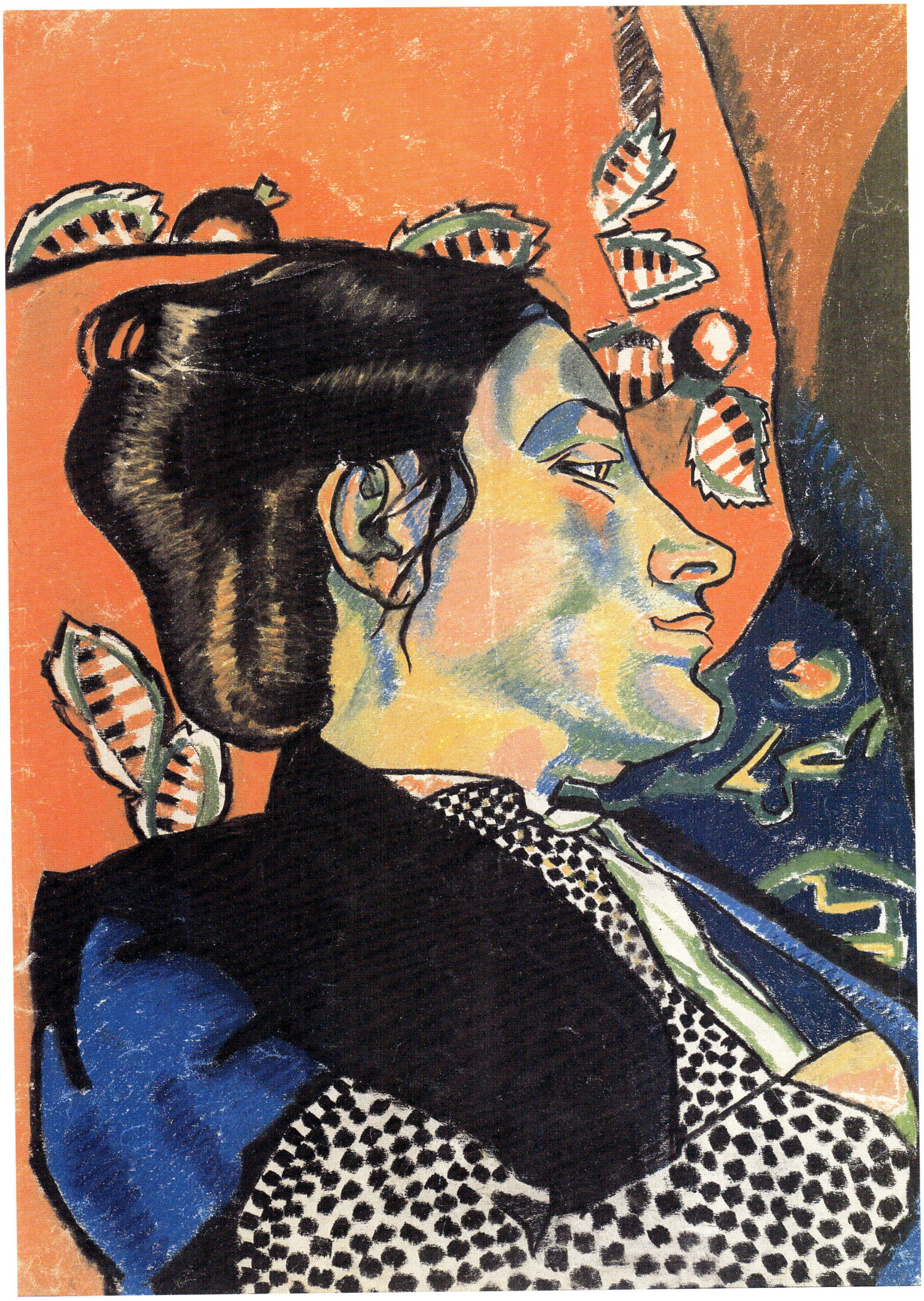

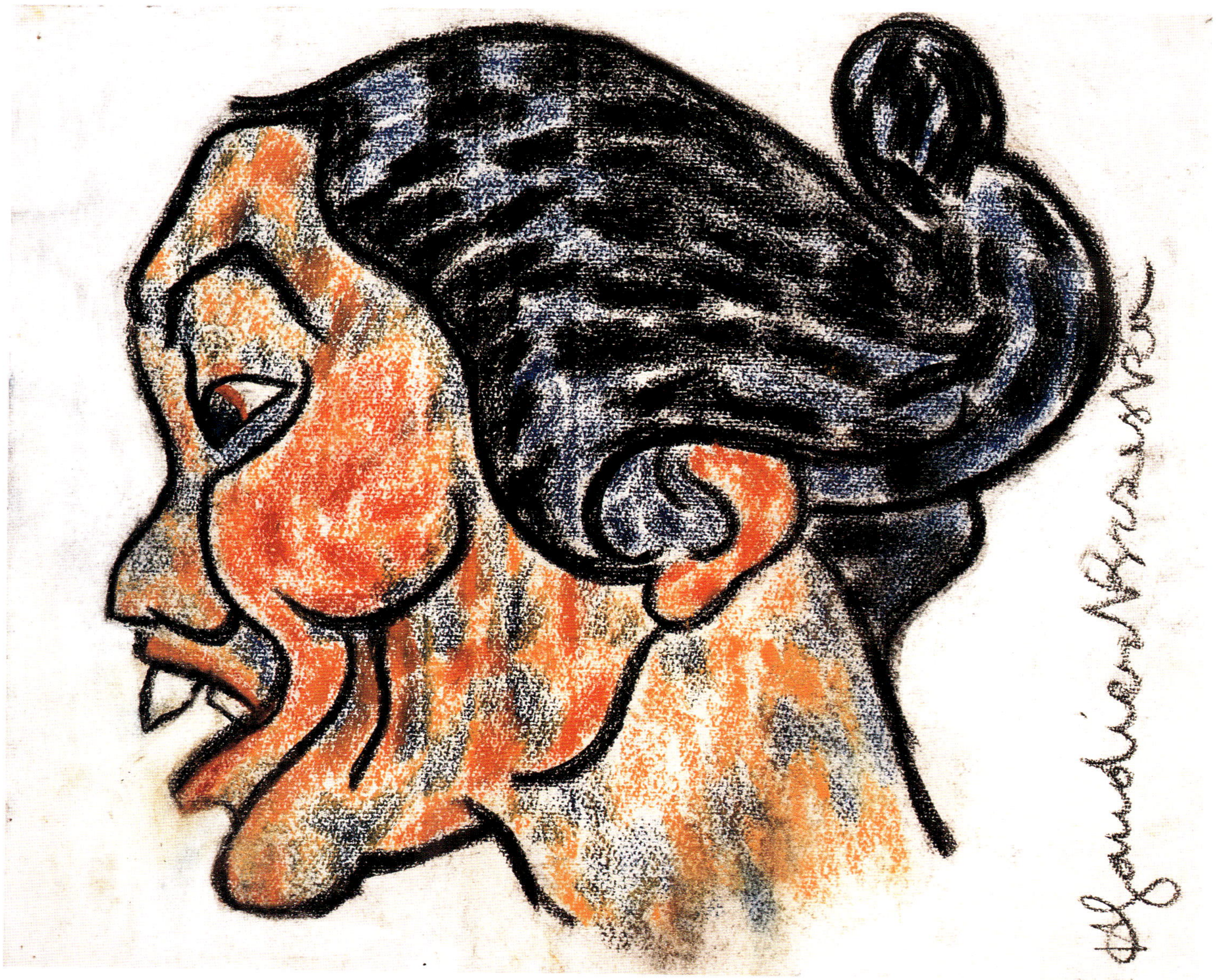

II Japanese Head, charcoal and pastel

III Head of an Idiot (*cat.* 30)

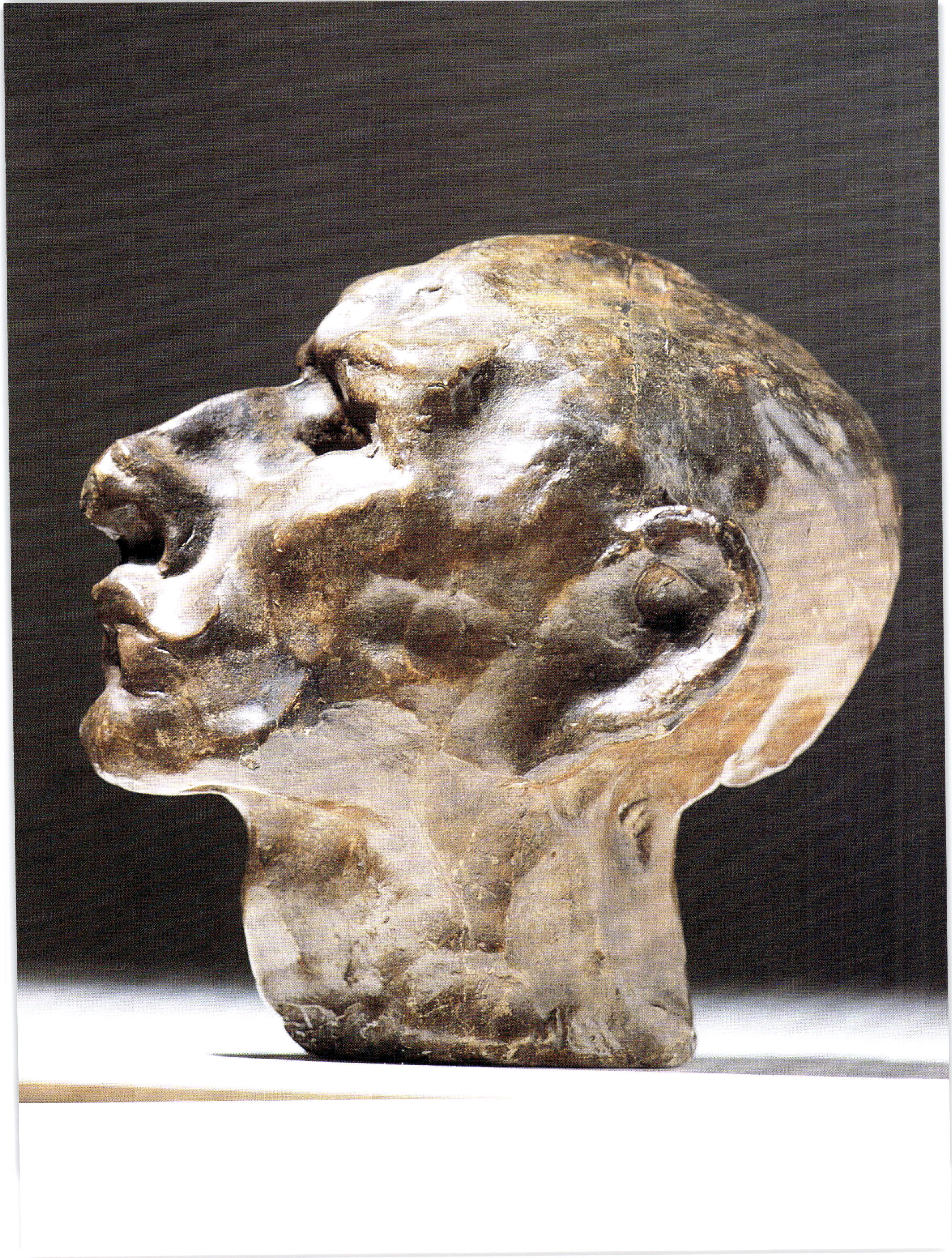

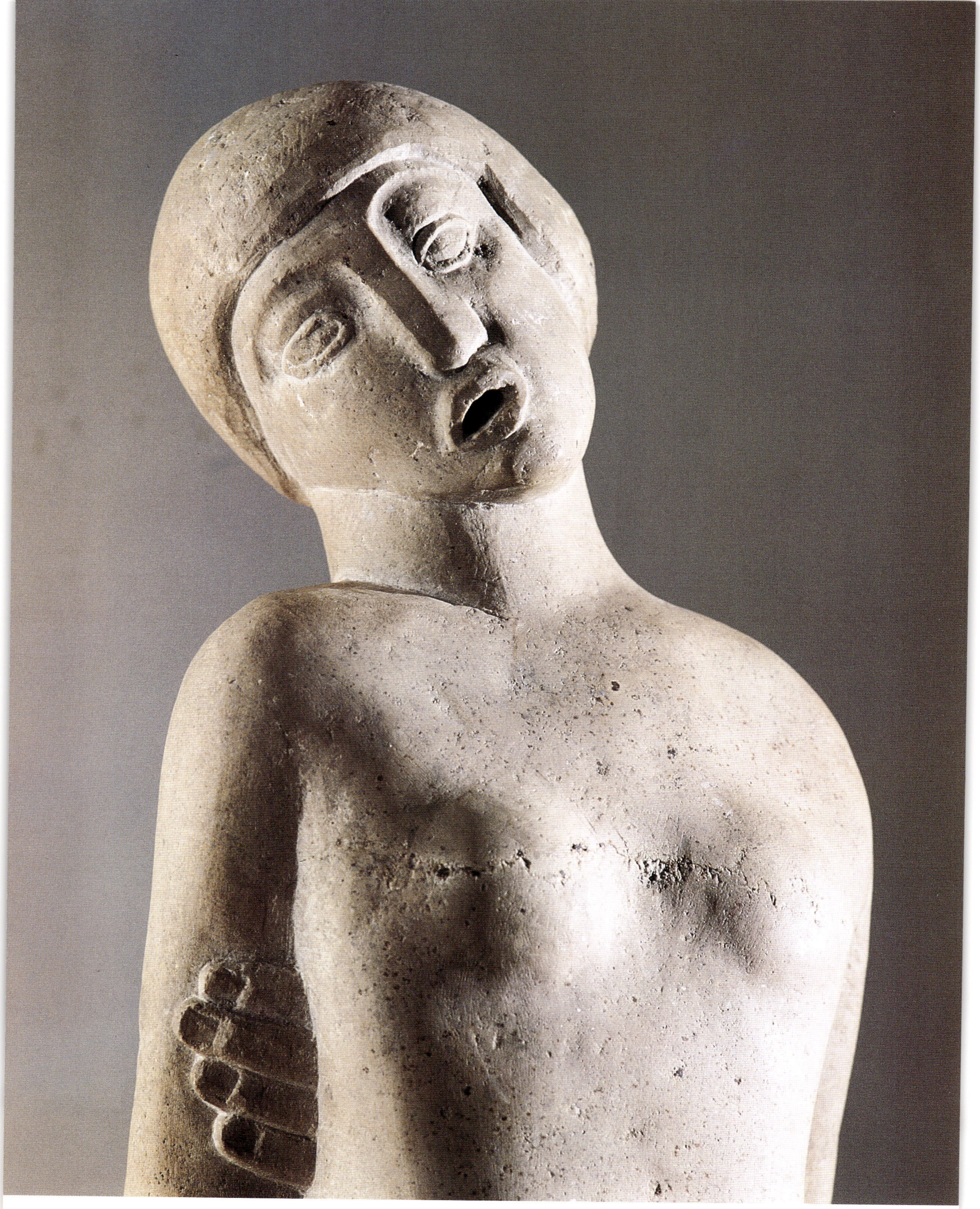

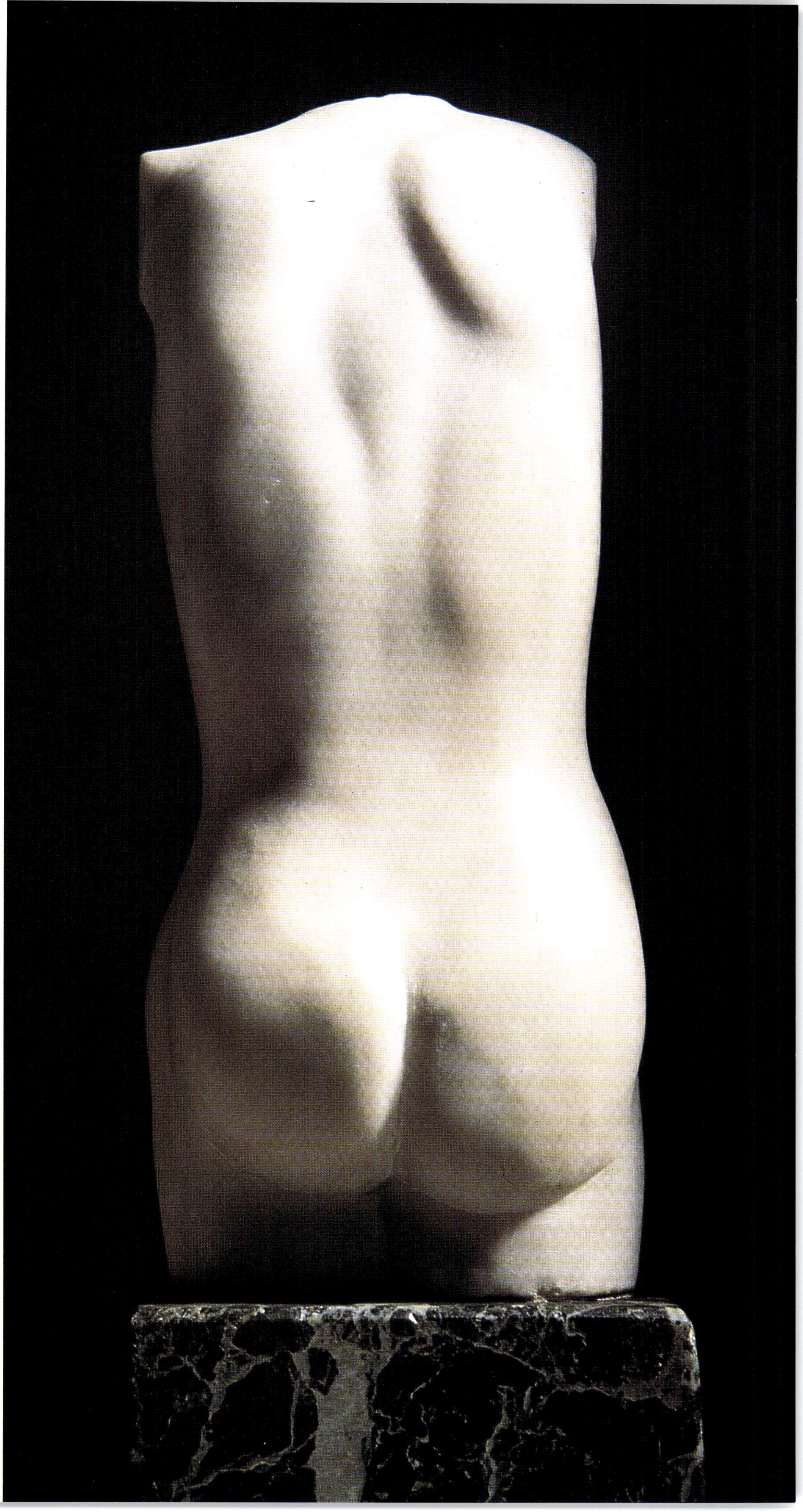

IV Singer (*cat.* 51)

V Torso I (*cat.* 61)

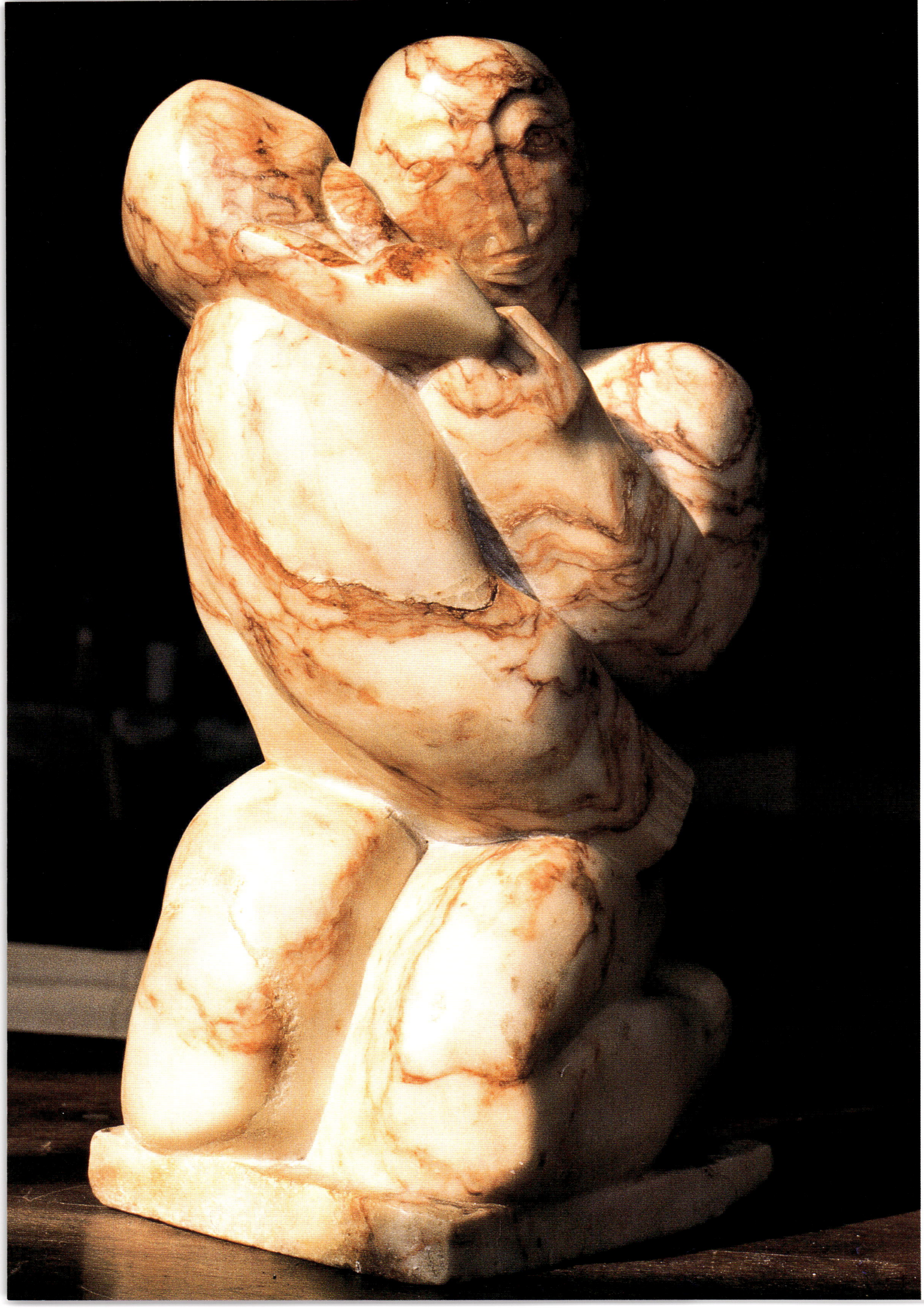

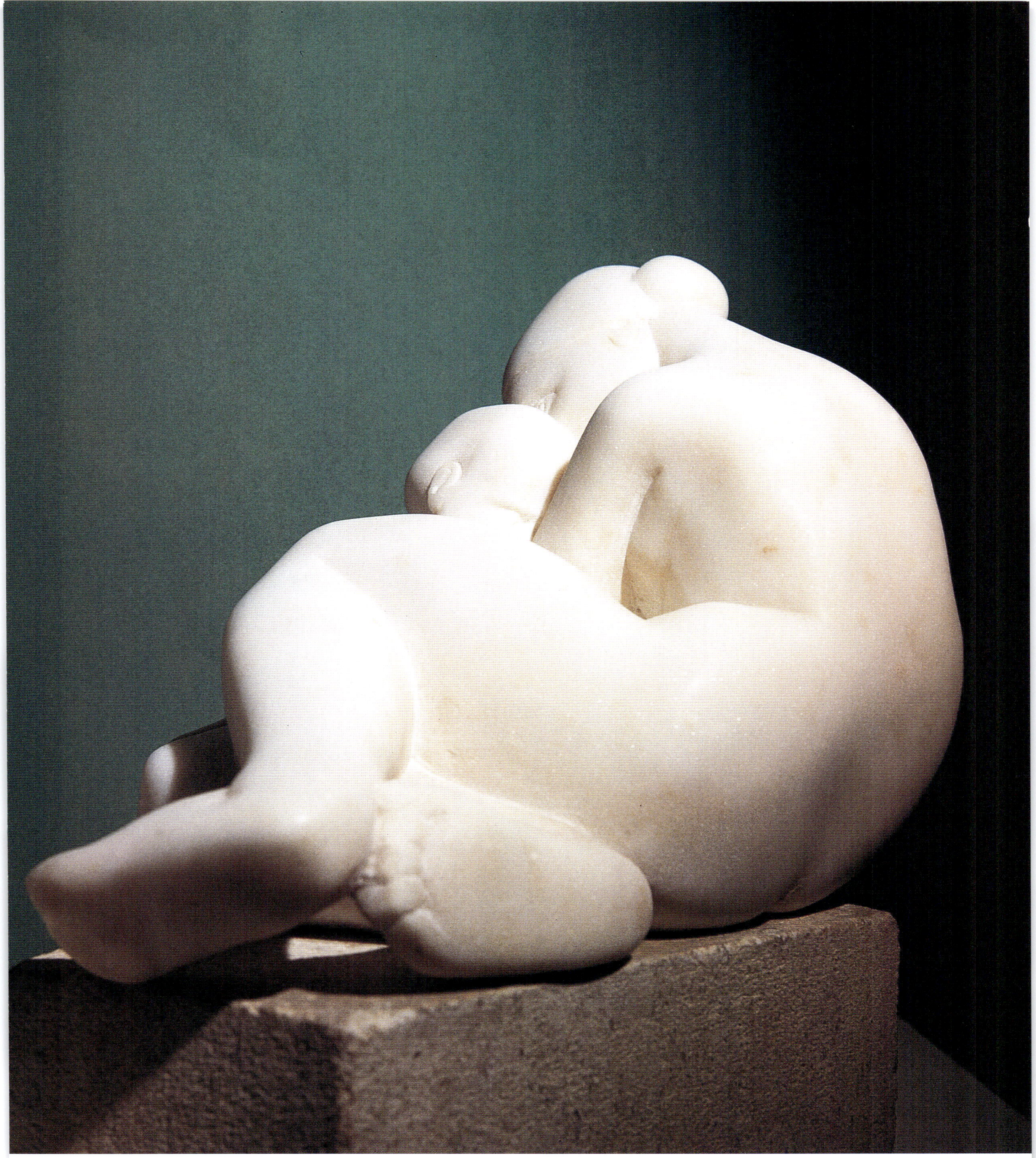

VII Maternity (*cat.* 64)

VI Boy with a Coney (*cat.* 76)

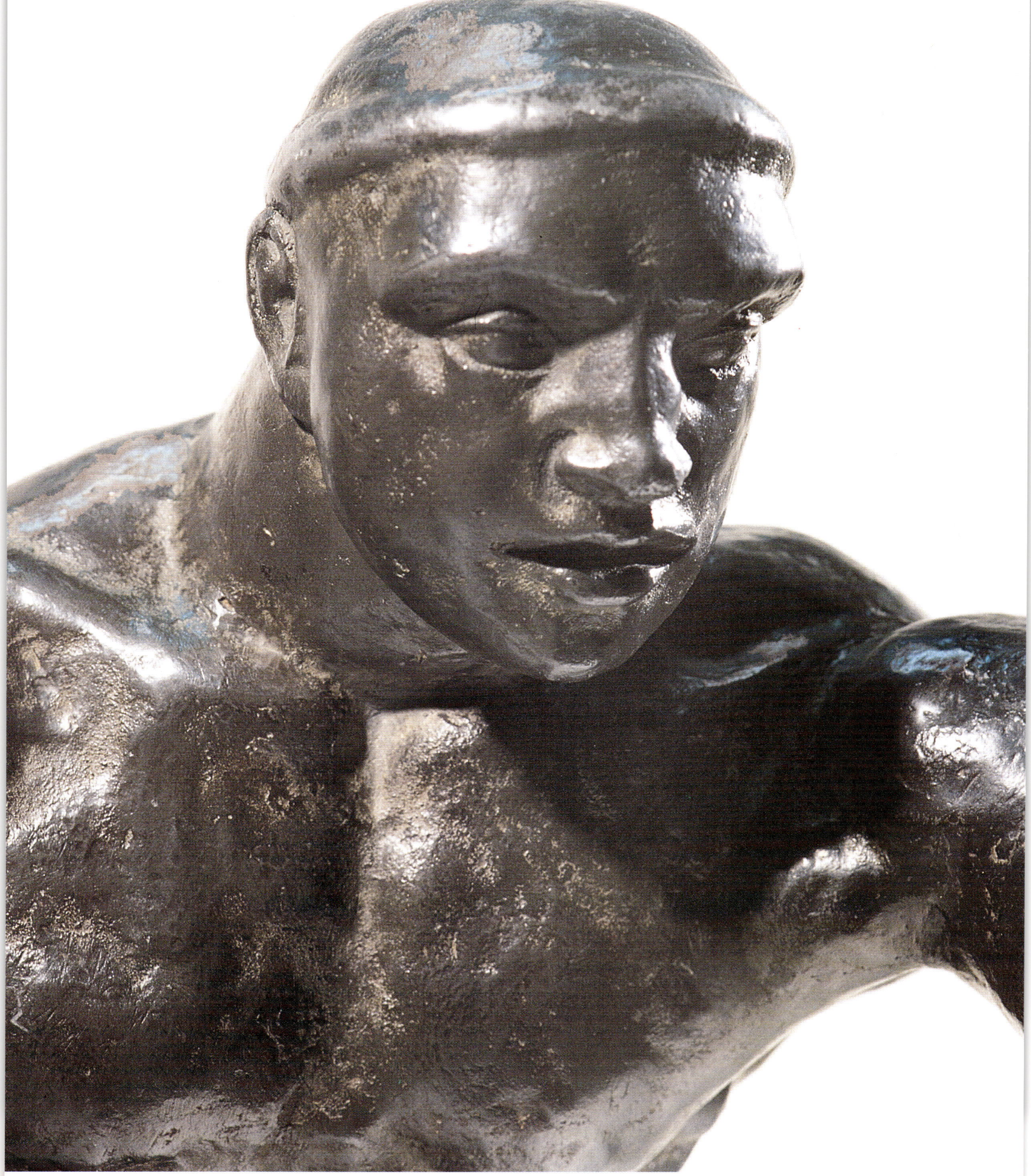

VIII Wrestler (*cat.* 32)

8

The Shaping of the Artist

During the autumn of 1912 Gaudier attended a twice-weekly evening class in life drawing. The model would take several poses, each held for between ten and fifteen minutes during the two-hour class. For Gaudier this was not the promised 'quick sketch'; 'I should have liked to have a model who didn't pose at all, but did everything he wanted to, walked, ran, danced, sat, etc.'[1] Typically he worked with frenetic intensity, producing vast numbers of studies in the unforgiving medium of stylographic pen which yielded a thin, even line. He would move around to realize the pose from several different angles, often making more than a dozen studies in which the mass, balance and presence of the figure are conveyed through line alone without any ground line or shading (figs. 48–50).[2] His relish for the opportunities the class provided was offset by his irritation at the painstaking slowness of his fellow students (fig. 51):

> The people in the class are so stupid, they only do two or three drawings in two or three hours, and think me mad because I work without stopping – especially while the model is resting, because that is much more interesting than the poses. I do 150 to 200 drawings each time, and that intrigues them no end.[3]

This, so far as we know, was the only art class he ever attended but Gaudier was already an accomplished draughtsman and not in the least diffident about the individuality of his approach. The economy of line and speed of coordination implicit in his drawing method resembled graphic reportage rather than the precise modulations of line and tone taught in most European art-schools. They are reminiscent of Rodin's methods; his habit of drawing models in movement around the studio derived from the technique taught him by Lecoq de Boisbaudran, who encouraged his students to draw rapidly while looking at the model rather than the paper. The method, focused on essentials, was conducive to capturing movement so that the trained spontaneity of the draughtsman mirrored that of the model.

Gaudier was undoubtedly aware of Rodin's drawings and on more than one occasion drew figures in movement round the studio, but his method was also the product of years of snatched opportunities when he drew whatever was close at hand.[4] His practice predisposed him to value contemporary life, the casually unposed figure, the natural rather than the idealized body.

Among Gaudier's early drawings, the studies of birds are those which mostly clearly signal his talent and had most personal meaning. Mounted specimens in the natural history galleries of the Cardiff Museum stimulated a series of highly finished pen drawings; the *Study of a Heron* (fig. 4) and *Golden Eagle* (Cambridge, Kettle's Yard) both date from December 1908.[7] During a visit to the small zoo in Victoria Park, Cardiff, on 2 January 1909, he produced sketches of a crow's head, barbary ducks, a ringed turtle dove and a cat as a well as a study of a barn owl asleep on a

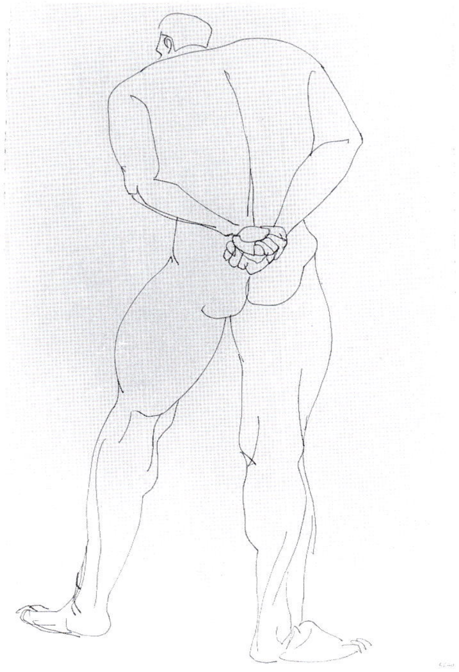

48 *Male Nude Study*, back view, 1912–13

perch which he worked up in pen and ink (fig. 9). Dramatically composed on the page, stylishly inscribed and signed, the format and technique of these highly finished studies is plainly based on engraved plates. They can be seen as the first indication that Gaudier was beginning to seek an identity for himself as an artist and foreshadow the prominence of bird and animal studies in his later drawings and sculptures.

Drawing themes from the natural world occupied as important a place in Gaudier's self-education as did copying after the Antique and Old Masters in the conventional training of most young artists. Not that Gaudier neglected the art of the past, but his path was serendipitous; once his enthusiasm for medieval art and architecture had faded he turned to the Antique, making drawings after the Parthenon frieze (fig. 10) and the works of Antiquity in the Munich Glyptothek and the Louvre.

In May 1910, he could write to Dr Uhlemayr, an admirer of Antique art, 'I begin to understand the Greek and pagan antiquity, which I now prefer to the Gothic. For a long time I have been obsessed by Ruskin and the English; now I have finished with them as with Christian philosophy …'.[8] He sent Uhlemayr a study for a sculpted Prometheus (fig. 53) clearly based on Antique and Michelangelesque models to demonstrate the increased strength of his drawing, and produced a number of studies for an elaborate sculptural group on the theme (the hero is surrounded by female figures rather than abandoned to the predatory eagle alone on his rock).[9] This and other contemporary sketches for sculptural groups reflect transitory enthusiasm, inspired largely by his admiration for Rodin, for monumental public sculpture. His study of the *Gates of Hell* is reflected in several sculptures such as *Head of an Idiot* (*cat.* 30, pl. 25) and *Workman Fallen from a Scaffold* (*cat.* 29, pl. 29) but his letters also reflect the profound impression made on him by the naturalism of *Man with a Broken Nose* (fig. 61), *St John the Baptist* (fig. 52) and *Elle qui fut la belle heaulmière* (She who was once the helmet-maker's beautiful wife). His political views and his concurrent studies of contemporary graphic art were contributing to his rejection of Christian, literary, mythological and historical subjects in favour of a realistic art of the present. In the Gothic, he conceded, Christianity had produced great art but he would undertake no more Christian subjects – 'martyrs being slaughtered like sheep.'[10]

> I admire Michelangelo's 'Slave' for its magnitude, because its heroism, creative energy, astonishes me; the Samothrace 'Victory' because its poetry pleases my sense; but I don't really understand one or the other … I can't look

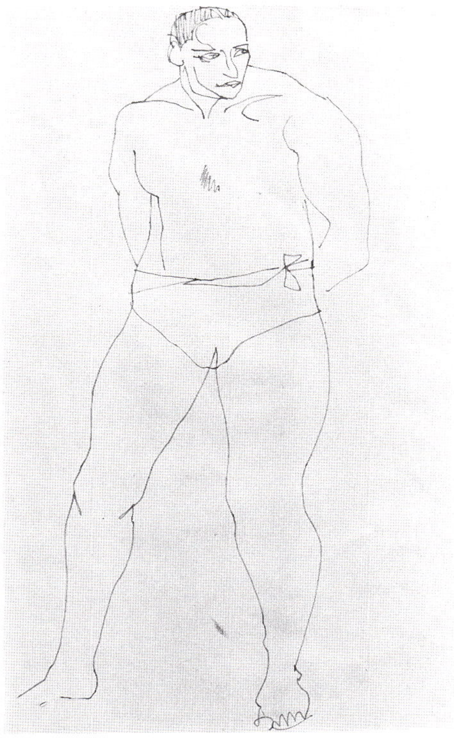

49 *Male Nude Study*, front view, 1912–13

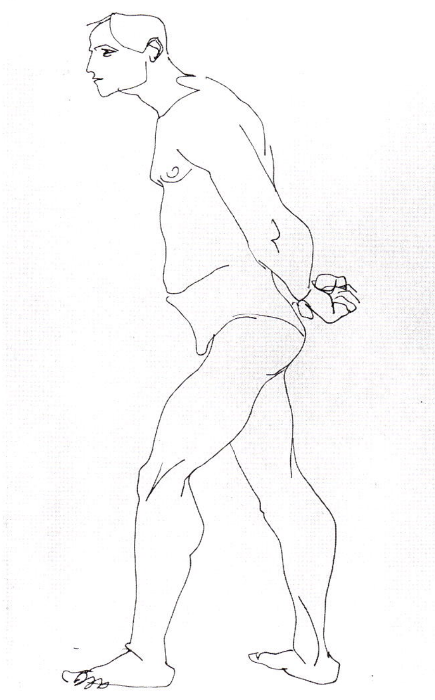

50 *Male Nude Study*, side view, 1912–13

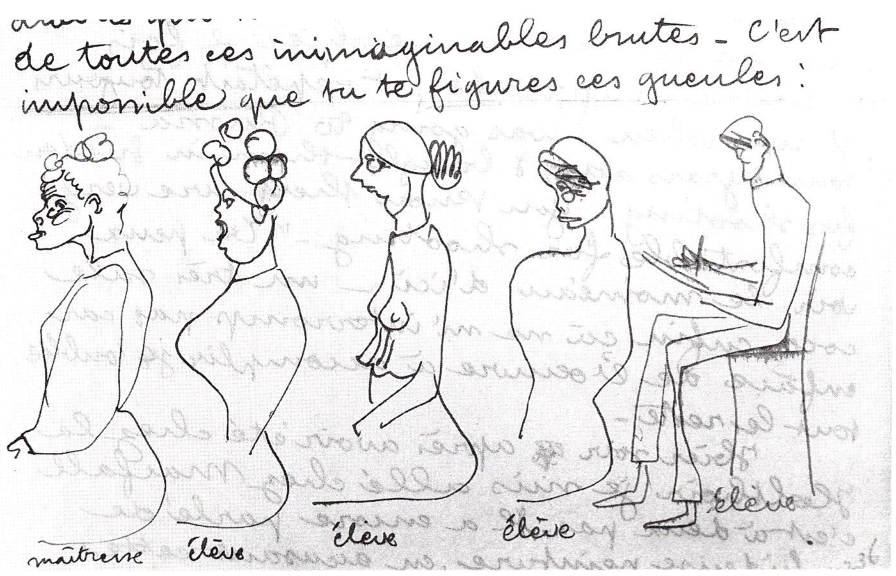

51 The life drawing class, in a letter from Gaudier to Brzeska, 17.11.12

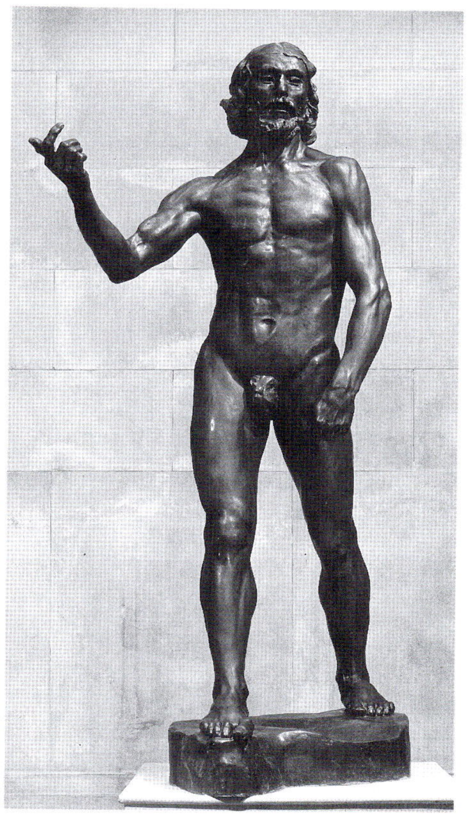

52 Auguste Rodin, *St John the Baptist*, 1879–80

> at them for long without getting tired; but Rodin's 'John the Baptist' on the other hand, would hold me for days on end ... A St John by Rodin is a subject, an old woman is a subject, a man with a broken nose is a subject, everything is a subject; but it has no need to be an old woman dressed up in the garb of mythology ... In my opinion the St John is more beautiful than the Venus de Milo ... he is a beggar who walks along, who speaks and gesticulates – he belongs to my own time, is in my epoch, he has a twentieth-century workman's body just as I see it and know it ... Art should be seen in the present, looked for in the present, and not in the past... Artistic vision, sensation if you like, is not called forth because some picture is labelled 'The Battle of Hermann', in which Romans and Germans kill each other, but by some beautiful form which it contains.[11]

Increasingly he identified realism, however ostensibly ugly – as in Rodin's 'old woman' – with beauty. The apparent artlessness of the movement and gesture in the striding *St John* (fig. 52) complemented his own habitual practice of sketching ordinary people at work (fig. 15); they move and stand casually in soft worn clothes which mould the wearer whose solidity and physical coordination is captured with swift strokes of the pen. The freedom and boldness of these drawings and the growing confidence of the pen drawings he made of his fellow readers at the Bibliothèque Ste Geneviève contrast with the painstaking refinement of the earlier bird studies and mark his accelerating technical development. It is less the execution of individual drawings which impresses than the consistent quality of observation married to hand-eye coordination and the immediate synthesis of the image.

Illustrations and cartoons, made in the hope of publication in one of the satirical journals, were based on these street sketches, but were also deeply influenced by his study of graphic artists; he had a print by Steinlen and a Toulouse-Lautrec poster on the wall of his room in Paris, and expressed admiration for the work of political cartoonists, such as Gavarni and Daumier. In May 1911 he wrote excitedly of a visit to the Victoria and Albert Museum:

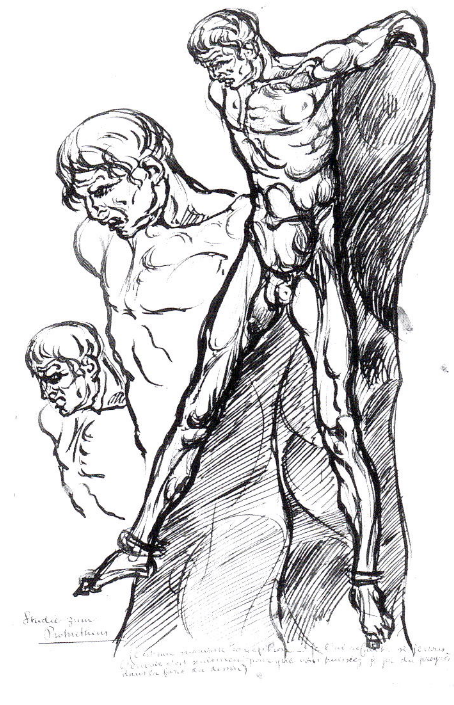

53 *Study for Prometheus*, 1910

> When I tired of drawing Michelangelo – about eight o'clock – I went to see the Goyas. He is a Spanish painter – the first since Rembrandt who knew how to use aquatint with mastery. He did three series of engravings [sic]: 'Los Capricos', 'Los Desastres de la Guerra' and 'La Tauromáquia'. Last night I only looked at the first two series ... although they are, for the most part, very scrupulous studies of life and movement, they are, at the same time, real drawings, and are all impregnated with a very strong philosophy and sarcasm. In the 'Capricos', for instance, he has drawn the most outrageous things: an old woman, fat, abominable, naked, held by devils who carry her in the air, and underneath he has written: '¿Adonde va Mama?' [Where's mother going?] ... 'Y se le quema la casa' [And he's burning the house down]. That's absolutely the most comical print I've seen ... The words he uses are so short, so strong, and so intimately connected with the drawings that it is impossible not to be bowled over with admiration ... The drawing is magnificent, and I believe that the best draughtsmen in this manner – Goya, Daumier, Gavarni, Toulouse-Lautrec, Phil May, Keene, Forain, Belcher – have been, or are still, the profoundest thinkers.[12]

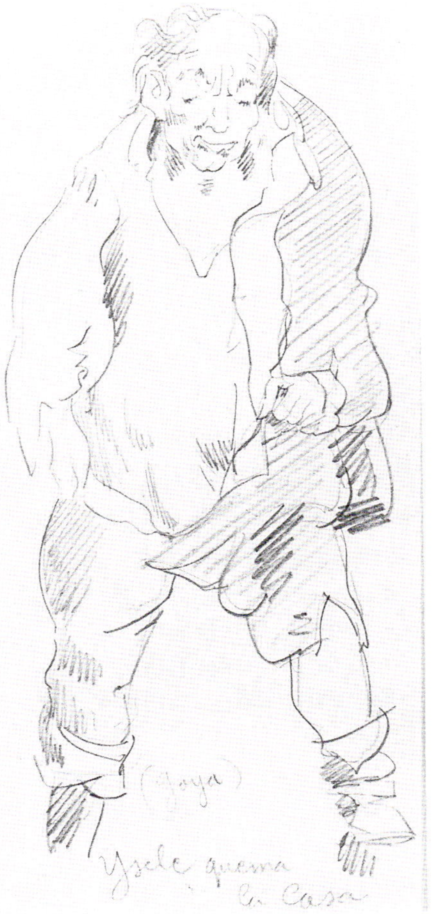

54 After an etching by Goya, *Y se le Quema la Casa*, 1911

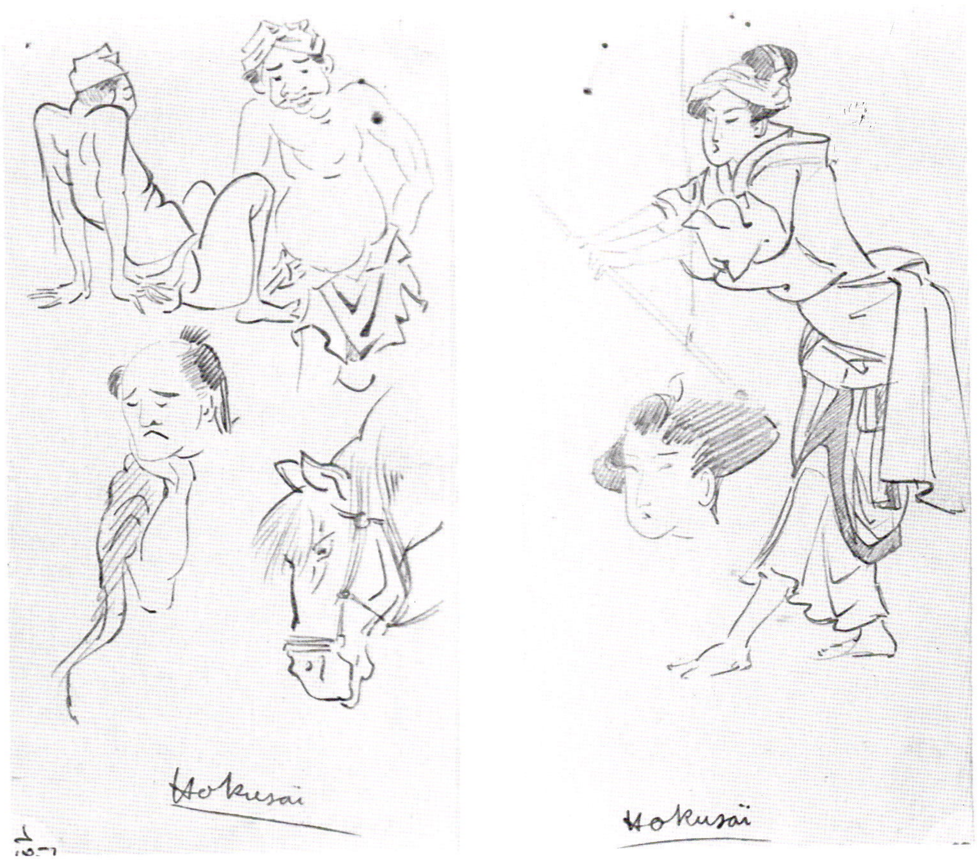

56 Sketches after Hokusai, 1911

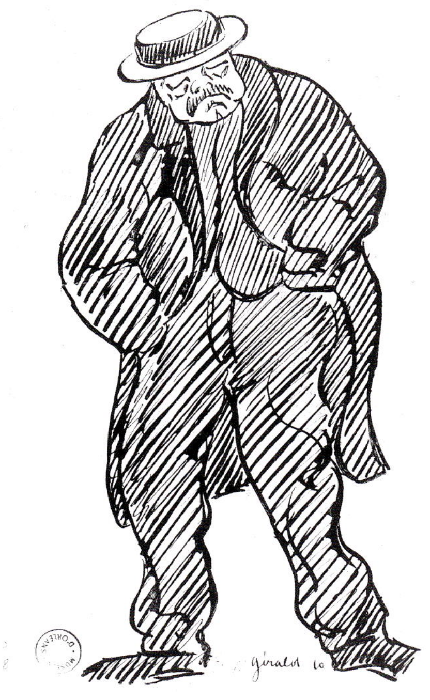

55 *Old Man*, signed 'Gérald 10'

Gaudier drew repeatedly from two of the most naturalistic genre-like scenes in the set of etchings – the menacing, unsteady figure of the drunken peasant's lurching movement and hunched shoulders, *Y se le Quema la Casa* (fig. 54) – and the bare-bottomed boy being beaten by his angry mother for breaking a kitchen pot (*Si quebró el Cantaro*).[13] The pose of the drunkard bears an uncanny resemblance to one of Gaudier's satirical drawings of the previous year (fig. 55) and the straddled forward movement of the drunkard is close to that of Rodin's *St John the Baptist* but with ignominy and ridicule rather than nobility of action the predominating theme.

During the same period – for the sketches come from the same small sketchbook – Gaudier was picking out figures, facial expressions and the characteristically springy linear rhythms from prints of Hokusai's *Fifty-three Stations of the Tôkaidô Highway* (fig. 56), also on show at the Museum.[14] Unlike the artists of Whistler's or Van Gogh's generation, for whom *kabuki* and landscape prints had provided inspiration for new compositional and decorative effects, Gaudier chose naturalistically posed, active figures from these panoramic views of street life, using them as a kind of displaced life drawing.

Undoubtedly these drawings were important for the evolution of a naturalistic art rooted in everyday experience and imbued with expressive energy. But Gaudier was becoming equally sure that form and mass rather

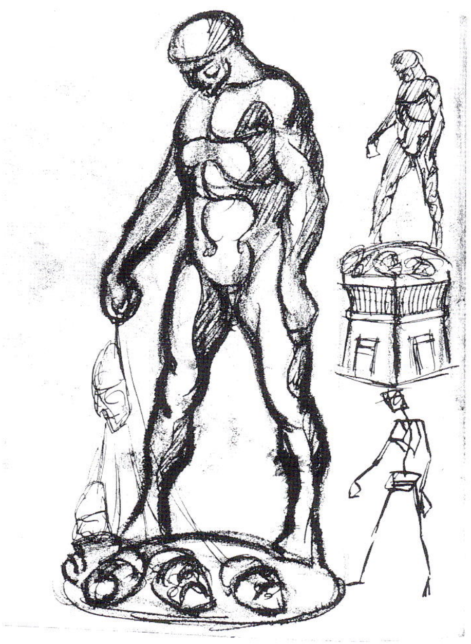

57 Study after *Marchand des Masques*

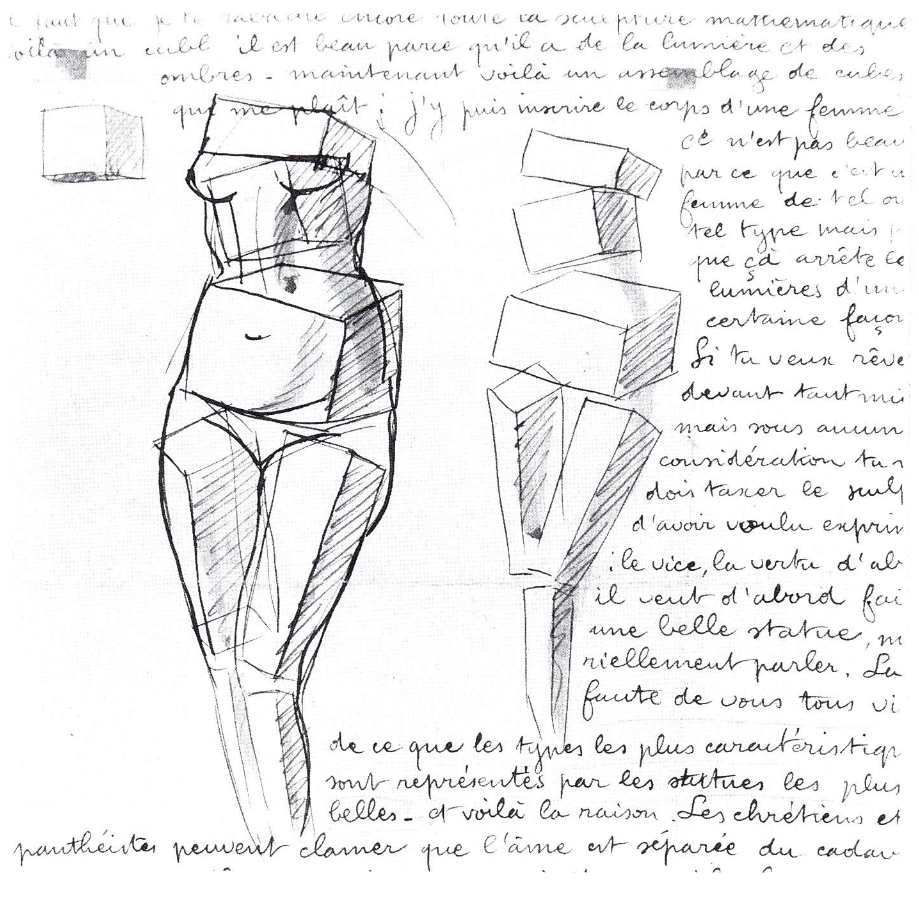

59 Sketch in a letter from Gaudier to Brzeska, 3.6.11

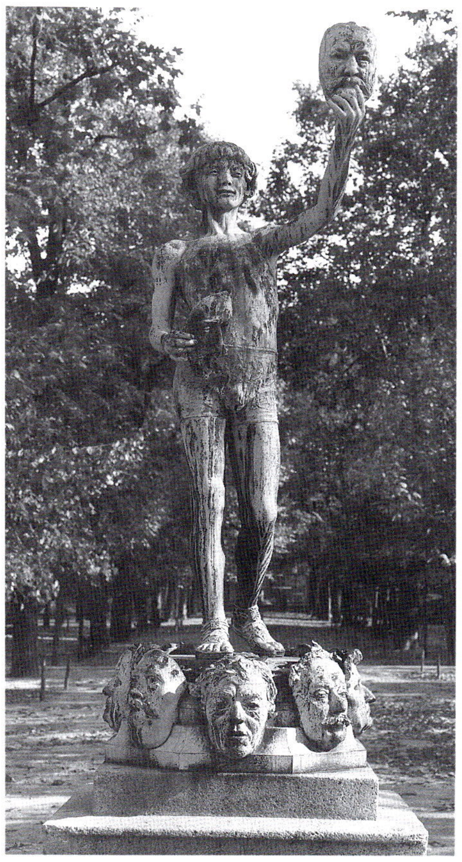

58 Zacharie Astruc, *Marchand des Masques*, 1883

than subject matter, colour and line must be the basis for his aesthetic philosophy. In part this was a natural evolution from his working method; a curious hybrid pen and charcoal drawing, probably dating from 1910, which reworked Zacharie Astruc's *Marchand des Masques* from the Luxembourg Gardens, replaces Astruc's slender, somewhat effete figure with a powerfully muscled Rodinesque nude who bestrides the masks in a pose strongly reminiscent of *St John the Baptist* (figs. 57, 58). The rapid pen sketch to the lower right of the sheet illustrates his method for establishing the weight and balance of the figure though a simple geometric diagram. He described this method: 'instead of drawing the fellow straight off … I draw square boxes, adjusting the sizes, one for each plane, and then, suddenly, by joining the boxes with a few little lines, they see the statue emerge' (fig. 59).[15] During April 1911 when he wrote this he was drawing from the Victoria and Albert Museum's casts of Michelangelo's *Dying Captive*. The notes he made in his sketchbook illuminate his growing understanding of three-dimensional form:

> draw the main masses within the larger planes,
> draw the smaller planes within the larger masses
> draw the smaller masses within the smaller planes and render form in terms of small masses by the most attentive, accurate study of all the planes.
> I think working this way leads to splendidly truthful detail always contained within a more imposing composition which is at the same time created by it.

> Line is a purely imaginary thing. It only exists in drawing to contain the planes of the mass which receive light and create shadow. These planes are the essence of artistic sensation and line only serves as their frame. The artist who aims for purity of line and adjusts the planes accordingly is mistaken – he making the painting fit the frame and not the frame the painting. That's why I hate Ingres, Flaxman and the Pre-Raphaelites – and all modern sculptors except Dalou, Carpeaux, Rodin, Bourdelle and a few others.[16]

This logical approach to formal coherence, working from the larger masses and their definition through planes to the smaller, was to be the method he adopted and developed during 1912–13 in works such as his portrait of Horace Brodzky (*cat.* 47, pl. 52) and which was profoundly to affect his carvings. Only a few weeks later he paraphrased the passage to Brzeska:

> I do not wish a system of aesthetics ... based on so absurd and illusory a thing as line. Line is a bar, a limit, an infraction on liberty, a slavery, while mass is free, and can be multipled infinitely, treated in a thousand ways. It leaves me free, and on top of all that, it is true, it exists.[17]

He was unmerciful in his critique of even the most commonly revered works which failed this test: the Venus de Milo was

> no more than a line enjoyed by pigs – an enormous stomach ... without lumps, without holes, without hardness, without angles, without mystery, and without force ... What hands could be more abominable than those of the Venus of Cnidos: tapering hands, butter fingers which flow without joints, without phalanges, without tendons, and with which she hides her 'cucu', that marvellous thing, that wonderfully divine delight? I loathe Praxiteles, for, he, better than any other, has rounded the angles and levelled the depressions: stumps of marble very polished, very sweet ... but these are not men, only well oiled corpses one has set up; and they give pleasure because they are corpses, they are not forms which can give a local rhythm, do not evoke the base or the sublime, have no vibrating life-force; and that is why all the Greeks, with the exception of Phidias, of Polycletus and of Lysippus, are nothing but vulgar hewers of marble.[18]

Though he acknowledged the greatness of the Greeks in the balance of masses and in their study of planes and rhythms, he would not follow 'their ramblings, sweet lines, suave mouths, little feet, big breasts, no'.[19] In his own work, he asserted, one would see not the flabby Academic 'woman with big breasts' but 'her bones and muscles'.[20]

When Gaudier wrote this in mid-1911 his convictions were still some way ahead of his practical experience; he had made few nude studies other than self-portraits and drawings after other works of art; though the evidence is scant he appears to have modelled heads for the most part rather than complete figures.[21] However, the following year his life drawings (figs. 48–50) reveal the consistency and clarity of his purpose and his ability to practise what he preached; the structure of bone, muscle and sinew underlying the softness of the surface flesh is always implicit so that the perception of weight, thrust, pivot and articulation emerge clearly in the drawings without any support or camouflage from ground lines or cast shadows. Though many of his life studies were taken from amply proportioned models the underlying structure is never lost and the mass of flesh has a taut density (figs. 31–70).

Gaudier's references to 'local rhythm' and 'the life force' signal the influence theoretical writings, especially those of Henri Bergson, were exerting on the development of his aesthetics and on his politics. At the library he might sketch his fellow readers and make drawings and notes on anatomy, but he was also reading widely: Baudelaire, Nietzsche, Taine and Bergson, as well as English, Russian and Spanish literature, articles on Jewish identity and capitalism, periodicals such as the socialist-anarchist and anti-militarist *la guerre sociale*. The validation these works conferred on his abhorrence of commerce and his conviction of the artist's differential status complemented the contemporaneity and dogmatic, even satirical realism which attracted him in art.

Writing to Uhlemayr on his nineteenth birthday, he offered an incisive critique of Hippolyte Taine's influential *Philosophie de l'Art*, lectures originally given at the Ecole des Beaux-Arts in 1869 and widely published. He had little patience with Taine's scientific determinism, which explained the arts through their environment and considered that each age had its appropriate art form expressing its dominant characteristics. Forain, Gaudier countered, was reacting against the customs and manners of his contemporaries and became more rather than less critical as he got older and richer.[22] Gaudier's bohemianism has a distinctly moral and political bias. His Nietzschian and Romantic vision of the artist transcending and in opposition to most social norms by virtue of his gifts was complemented by radical political views which were emphatically anti-industrial, anti-commercial, often casually anti-semitic and anti-militaristic. He had been caught up in the Hervé riots while still in Paris. In London he went to hear Keir Hardie speak, sketching him as he did so and, hearing that the leading anarchist Prince Kropotkin lived in the city, expressed a desire to make a portrait of him.[24] In London he continued to read *la guerre sociale* as well as more literary periodicals such as *Revue des deux mondes*.

Not surprisingly in view of the already anti-classical, naturalistic and intuitive bias of Gaudier's thinking about the nature of art, Bergsonism was the philosophy with which he seems to have felt the deepest and most lasting sympathy. At this period Henri Bergson's influence extended far beyond a narrowly academic audience; he had become a international celebrity whose public lectures at the Collège de France in Paris were packed to the doors. The Catholic writer Charles Péguy, Gaudier's fellow townsman and close contemporary, described the crowds who flocked to Bergson's lectures in 1902:

> elderly men, women, young girls, many young men, Frenchmen, Russians, foreigners, mathematicians, naturalists ... students in letters, students in science, medical students ... engineers, economists, lawyers, laymen and priests ... poets, artists ... well known bourgeois types, socialists, anarchists.[25]

His broad appeal related in part to the poetically visual imagery and sheer eloquence with which he expounded his philosophy, qualities which also attracted theorists of art such as Apollinaire and Metzinger. Gaudier read Bergson's influential *Evolution créatrice* (1907) straight after his contemptuous dismissal of Taine, in October 1910, finding it 'so profound that I must study it carefully and … meditate about it' before being able to discuss it.[26] A few months later Gaudier was asserting the pervasive role of rhythm in all art forms:

> The great thing is:
> That sculpture consists in placing planes according to a rhythm
> That painting consists in placing colours according to a rhythm
> That literature consists in placing stories according to a rhythm
> That music consists in placing sounds according to a rhythm.[27]

For Bergson the world was in a state of continual flux in which all forms of life had their own rhythms of growth and interraction; he made no radical separation between the temporal and the spatial, introducing concepts of duration and 'extensity' as part of the ever-moving dance of existence which, he argued, is grasped intuitively rather by than systematic or conceptual analysis. For the individual, the consciousness too would be constantly changing in response to awareness of the interrelatedness of things and of the ongoing interraction of experience and memory. Bergson insisted on the interdependence of the antithetical elements of inert matter and life with its slow build-up and explosive expenditure of energy. Comparing human and animal life, he contrasted the 'somnambulism of instinct', the automatism of routine, with the rational capacity of man.

Two years later a letter to Brzeska highlights the compatibility of Bergson's theories of constant flux with Gaudier's own fast-changing perspective. Bergson's theories validated his own experience; 'for a conscious being, to exist is to change, to change is to mature, and to mature is to re-create oneself indefinitely.'[28]

> Life, according to Bergson and the later philosophers, is simply intuition of the passing moment, and time, which flows continually, eternally, makes itself known by change … I look at things a great deal and I draw a great deal. I notice how everything differs, mingles with and knocks up against everything else. I am never sure what I think is true, still less that what I have thought or said is true; and I can't bring myself to sacrifice new ideas, quite different from those I had yesterday, just because the old ones happened to have the honour of passing through my head and I advocated them ferociously.[29]

The definition of art which followed in the next letter is pure Bergson:

> the world is positive, real … [Bergson] emphasizes intuition as more valuable than reason – for reason is scientific and leads to the absurd… As to my ideas about art I am perpetually modifying them … art is the interpretation of the emotions, and consequently of the idea. For this emotion I recognize as necessary only the discipline of technique, and at the moment I think the idea comes better the more the technique is simple and limited; on the other hand I fully recognize that the more you limit your technique, the greater danger you run of falling into mannerism, which is the negation of all the emotion which we experience in front of nature.

> Again in this emotion I see three divisions, linear emotion, produced by the rhythm of outlines and strokes, sculptural emotion, rendered by the balance of masses, such as are revealed by light and shade, and lastly, pictorial emotion, produced by various coloured pigments.[30]

Gaudier's response to Bergsonism echoes other artists within the European avant-garde, Matisse and the Fauves, the early theorists of Cubism, Gleizes and Matzinger, and J. D. Fergusson and the circle who contributed to *Rhythm*, the journal founded by Fergusson and Murry in 1911. However, Bergsonism also meant different things to different people; for the Simultanists and Cubists it opened up the possibility of a painting being much more than a single perception of a moment in time; it could evoke many interpenetrating states of consciousness and perception akin to the complexity of life itself. For the Futurists, duration might be more suggested by multiple images evoking a sequence of movement. In Gaudier's work as in that of the Fauves and the German Expressionists, indebted to Nietzsche and Bergson, to express intuitive and primal behaviour was to return to man's animal rather than rational nature. However, Gaudier would probably first have encountered Bergson's ideas in periodicals, in conversation with his fellow readers at the Bibliothèque Ste Geneviève and 'the queer mystic group' he mixed with in the cafés in 1910 rather than through direct contacts with artists, at least before his association with *Rhythm* in 1912.[31]

Ironically, the aspect of Gaudier's intensive self-education about which least is known is his contact with and knowledge of contemporary art and artists in Munich and Paris, during a period when his understanding of art remained confined to paper while his appreciation of sculpture was almost exclusively theoretical. In Munich and in Paris during early 1910 he may have visited some artists' studios but there is no evidence that he attended an atelier nor had he much spare time in which to do so. Through the mischance of timing and a mixture of ignorance and diffidence Gaudier seems to have narrowly missed meeting some of the artists and seeing much of the work which was subsequently to shape the course of modernism. In January 1909 Kandinsky had established a new grouping of young artists, the Neue Künstlervereinigung München (NKVM) which was to be the forerunner of Die Blaue Reiter (Blue Rider group). The NKVM artists shared an ambition to go beyond naturalism and mood painting to express a more subjective and emotional inner world:

> We start with the thought that the artist, besides the impressions which he receives from the outer world, from nature, also ceaselessly gathers together experiences of an inner world, and searches for artistic forms which will express the mutual interaction of all these experiences, forms which must be cleansed of the incidental in order to give forceful expression only to the necessary – he searches, in short, for artistic synthesis.[32]

Since the NKVM's first exhibition only took place in December, several months after his return to France, it is doubtful whether Gaudier got to meet any of the artists involved or heard about the new group's aims. He had little natural sympathy with mystical subjectivism, whether that of the neo-Impressionists or that expressed in Kandinsky's *Of the Spiritual in Art*.[33] Even during the height of his involvement with Vorticism when an excerpt from Kandinsky's treatise was being reproduced in *Blast*, and his own drawings and sculptures were becoming increasingly abstract, he remained hostile to his paintings, which to his eye lacked structure, and to his writings which he dismissed as 'twaddle'.[34] On the other hand Franz Marc's paintings of animals in landscape, such as *Yellow Cow*, stemmed from an outlook far closer to Gaudier's; in a letter in April 1910, Marc explained, 'I am seeking … a feeling for the organic rhythm in all things, a pantheistic empathy into the shaking and flowing of the blood in nature, in trees, in animals, in the air… I see no happier means to the "*animalization* of art", as I would like to call it, than the animal picture.'[35]

Gaudier's awareness of the contemporary European avant-garde is far more likely to have derived primarily from the great Parisian Salons. He was back in Paris in time for the 1909 Salon d'Automne and it seems almost inconceivable that someone of his omnivorous appetite would have missed the opportunity. There he could have spotted work by Kandinsky if he was not absorbed in examining the sculpture on show. In 1909, as well as the numerous established sculptors like Carpeaux, Bourdelle and Maillol, he could see works by the Futurists Severini, Balla and Boccioni, a *Tête d'enfant* by Brancusi, two works by Duchamp-Villon and paintings by Matisse. At Druet in November there were fifty-two paintings by Van Gogh and, over the following year, Cézanne, Vallotton, Toulouse-Lautrec, Bonnard, Vlaminck, Matisse, Derain, Manet, Manguin and Redon were among the artists exhibiting at the dealers.[36] It is fairly unlikely that Gaudier would have seen the huge Gauguin retrospective at the 1905 Salon d'Automne but his works were relatively accessible at the dealers and there were small shows at Vollard's and Galerie E. Blot while Gaudier was in Paris.

This was also a period of enormous and diverse creative activity in the evolution of Cubism though Picasso's and Braque's work remained largely unexhibited. However, there is no evidence that Gaudier was aware of Cubism at this time; he would have missed the 1910 Salon d'Automne where the nascent Cubist group made their public debut (with paintings by Gleizes, Metzinger, Le Fauconnier, Léger among others, and early, pre-Cubist sculptures by Duchamp-Villon and Archipenko) since he spent October and November in Orléans.

Though Gaudier learned more about Cubism in England than he had in Paris, it has been suggested that he was in direct contact and even studied with one artist soon to emerge as one of the great innovators of the period, Alexander Archipenko. In an interview given during the Sixties, Archipenko claimed he had known Gaudier in Paris in 1911.[37] Gaudier was then in England, but they could have met during 1909–10; Archipenko too was living in Montparnasse and frequenting the studios at La Ruche in the boulevard Raspail; quite a few Slavs used the Bibliothèque Ste Geneviève and Gaudier mentions 'a queer mystic group' of Bohemians he was meeting in a tantalizing letter to Dr Uhlemayr in April 1910.[38] However, neither Gaudier's notebooks nor Brzeska's writings, which cover the months following her meeting with Gaudier in some detail, contain even a hint of such an encounter, and the Archipenko Papers do not cover this early period.

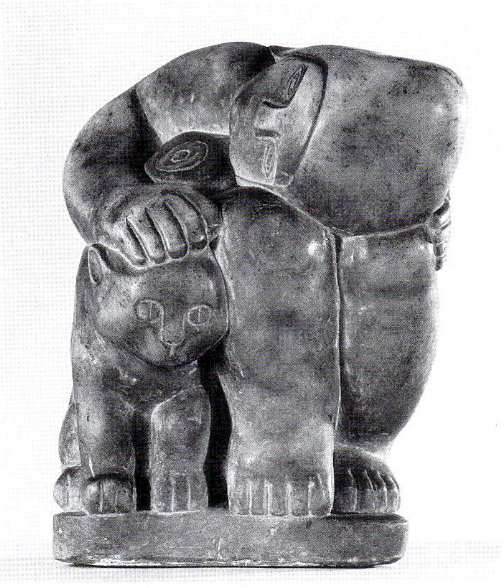

60 Alexander Archipenko, *Woman with Cat*, 1910

The plausibility of contact beyond the purely social therefore rests on the striking comparisons which can be made between works by Archipenko such as *Woman with Cat* and *Mother and Child*, generally dated 1910–11 (fig. 60), and Gaudier's work of several years later.[39] Both carvings are block-like, the figures so tightly interwoven that the larger enfolds and envelops the smaller; faces are broad with stylized eyes and short flat noses. Though only a brief phase in the Russian's work, they anticipate the monumental figure style of his close friend Léger. But they also prompt comparisons with carvings produced by Gaudier in 1913–14; elements of *Woman and Cat* seem to be echoed in the head of *Singer* (*cat.* 51, pl. 56), the composition and conception of *Boy with Coney* (*cat.* 76, pl. 104) and the enveloping intimacy of *Maternity* (*cat.* 64, pls. 83, VII).[40] The child in Archipenko's *Mother and Child* clings limpet-like to its mother's breast in a relationship which immediately invokes comparisons with Gaudier's *Caritas* (*cat.* 75, pl. 108). Gaudier might have seen works of this type if he visited Archipenko's studio. However, in practical terms he was then still very much a beginner. In mid-1910, after he had made the crucial decision to be a sculptor and told Dr Uhlemayr he had decided to learn woodcarving for furniture-making in order to get into some art-job (see p. 20), he gave a terracotta self-portrait to an Italian wood sculptor living in Paris, possibly to repay him for professional advice.[41] At the same time his letters and extant work still reflect his admiration for Rodinesque naturalism and bravura modelling. Later, in 1913, he was aware of Archipenko's more recent, semi-abstract work. It seems rather more likely that both were responding separately to similar Gauguinesque and 'primitive' sources in their search for new formally coherent languages.

It was in England rather than in Paris or Munich that Gaudier absorbed the significance of much that he had seen and encountered more directly the full range of work by Futurists, Cubists and Fauves. It was in England that he went beyond the private experiments in modelling represented by the startlingly accomplished portrait of his father and studies of local people. Gaudier's powers of observation and assimilation and the diversity of his interests were astonishing. Mark Gertler, less than a year younger than Gaudier, viewed the maelstrom of competing theories, schools and factions with caution and amused detachment; in September 1912, then twenty and still a student at the Slade, he described to Dora Carrington how he 'went out and saw more unfortunate artists. I looked at them talking art, Ancient Art, Modern Art, Impressionism, Post-Impressionism, Neo-Impressionism, Cubists, Spottists, Futurists, Cave-dwelling, Wyndham Lewis, Duncan Grant, Etchells, Roger Fry! I looked on and laughed to myself'.[42] Nothing could be more different from Gaudier's daring willingness to learn new languages and his omnivorous appetite to appraise, try out, amend or reject each philosophy and style.

9

Gaudier the Modeller

In spite of Gaudier's bold talk in 1910 of taking up the chisel and thinking only of stones and sculptures, it was largely through modelling that he developed his sculptural technique. However, during his first year in England he barely touched clay and confessed to Haldane Macfall in January 1912 that he was hungry for modelling, but also aware that 'I have for years been studying character almost to the exclusion of rhythm and composition and confined myself to the drawing of people's faces'.[1] Portraiture dominated his modelled work of 1912–13 but, through pieces such as *Firebird* (*cat.* 18, pl. 11–12), *Workman Fallen from a Scaffold* (*cat.* 29, pl. 24), *Jungle Cat* (*cat.* 26, pl. 13) and *Wrestler* (*cat.* 32, pl. 37), he developed an intensely expressive technique, still Rodinesque, but owing nothing to individual characterization and everything to composition and rhythm. Until 1913 nearly all his sculpture was modelled and he continued to use clay to try out ideas; when the Lousadas, who commissioned *Firebird*, visited the studio, their young son Anthony was entertained by being shown 'a number of little figures in clay kept damp under little paper bags'.[2] Clay was also the medium for several classicizing later pieces – *Dancer* (*cat.* 58, pl. 68) and *Mlle Borne* (*cat.* 105, pl. 157). However, as he became increasingly committed to carving he began to use leather-hard clay and plaster as cheap carving media – in *Wrestlers* relief (*cat.* 66, pl. 87), *Men with Bowl* (*cat.* 98, pl. 146), *Maquette for a Bird Bath* (71, pl. 149) and his *Maquettes for Garden Vases* (*cat.* 99, 100, pls. 150, 148).

Portraits

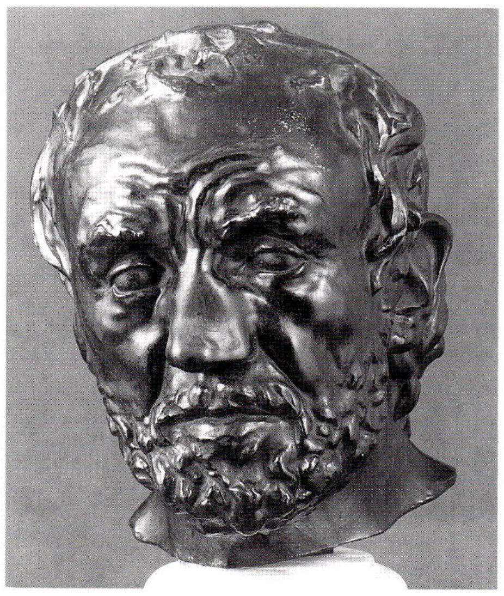

61 Auguste Rodin, *Man with a Broken Nose*, 1864

Portraits frame Gaudier's oeuvre; they dominate his early sketchbooks and account for most of his sculpture before 1913. Although he had moved away from traditional portraiture by early 1914 and the *Head of Ezra Pound*, he returned to it in one of his last works, the soberly classical *Mlle Borne*.

Many of Gaudier's earliest drawn portraits – those that fill the sketchbooks made at the Bibliothèque Ste Geneviève – were made without the usual complicity between model, artist and spectator since they were 'stolen' from intent readers. These unposed models bent over their books enabled him to concentrate on cranial structure, foreshortening and unconscious expressions.[3] Whether drawn with a pen or in conté crayon they are delineated by decisive curving lines and vigorous parallel hatching which give mass to even the most rapid sketch. They are often caricatural as were several of his earliest modelled heads – *Chican* (*cat.* 4) and the *So-called Portrait of Madame Gaudier* (*cat.* 3, pl. 2).

In this context the *Portrait of Monsieur Gaudier* (*cat.* 2, pl. 4) has the painstaking gravity of a diploma piece, which in a way it was since it may well have been intended to demonstrate his talent to his parents. Few of Gaudier's other portraits – even the drawn self-portraits – are so straightforwardly naturalistic and none is so physically detailed or intense. The rhythmic unity of hair and moustache with the weathered lines of the face and the degree of finish reflect Gaudier's study of the French realist tradition represented by Dalou, Meunier and Rodin, recalling especially his *Man with a Broken Nose* (fig. 61).

Gaudier's first commissioned work, *The Madonna of 'The Miracle'* (*cat.* 9, pl. 14), was a portrait of a kind since it was intended to commemorate the performance of Maria Carmi in Max Reinhardt's celebrated production. But, within the strict limits imposed by the role, it also provided the opportunity for composition and rhythm which Gaudier had craved. Reinhardt's *The Miracle* was the hit of the winter season; the Hares, so Brzeska tells us, had already seen it eight times. The wordless spectacle of medieval pageant-cum-morality play with its elaborate costumes, ingenious stage effects and huge cast, was staged in the vast auditorium of Olympia. In fact the sheer scale of the arena made features and expressions hard to see; *Punch* joked that the Knight, the romantic lead, needed opera glasses to discern the beauty of the nun he was about to lure from her divine calling across the vast space of the 'cathedral'. Far from being a highly characterized figure, *The Madonna*, a miraculous sculpted image which comes to life, conformed to the conventions which this dramatic conceit required. Making the Madonna one of the protagonists of the action caused a certain *frisson* and the press made much of the 'Botticelli' beauty, dignity and spiritual presence of the mysterious woman playing the role under the pseudonym of Maria Carmi (fig. 62).[4] In a eulogistic review following her last performance in early February 1912, Sir Claude Phillips commented, 'those who have seen this artist can never forget the beautiful humility and yet the loftiness of her demeanour, the intensity of her all-pervading sorrow, of her all-embracing love'.[5]

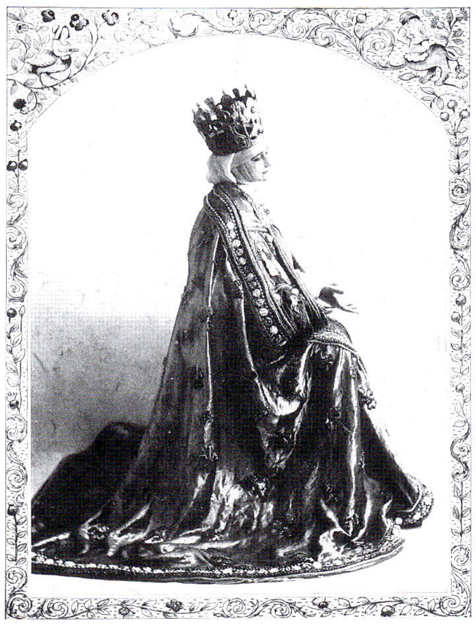

62 'Maria Carmi' as the Madonna in *The Miracle*, from *The Sketch*, 31 January 1912

Gaudier did not think much of it: 'My impression of *The Miracle* is that neither the music nor the drama interest me, but I find good character in the actors: Carmi, Ridley and the one who acts the devil's part – but I fail to see much unity of thought in it.' To Haldane Macfall he deplored the poor taste of its 'motley spectacular effect'.[6] Despite or perhaps because of his familiarity with northern European polychrome sculpture, he seems to have had some difficulty with the staged conceit of a 'Madonna' sculpture; Brzeska recorded how at first he drew horses, monks and devils (all employed in active roles) before eventually getting down to making some studies of the Madonna.[7] Indeed the largely static figure enveloped in robes and ornately decorated mantle appeared to offer more scope for a study of drapery than a portrait. Production photographs reveal how faithfully he followed the Madonna's staged posture, even to the pathetically outstretched hands from which the 'sculpted' Christ Child has been stolen during the action of the play. His solution was to seize on the basically pyramidal composition offered by the pose to establish a compositional balance between the immobile enthroned figure and the axial movement implied by the inclined head with its immense crown. The drapery is summarily indicated with fingered runnels rather than folds suggesting that the essential mass and planes, not detail, were the sculptor's concern. The pyramidal mass of the robes and exaggeratedly stagey crown are set off against the serenity of the face which, by contrast, is delicately modelled. Though the projected bronze casts were never made and the original plasters remained with the Hares, the sculpture was well received when exhibited at the Allied Artists' in 1913 and reviewed there as a portrait.[8]

The portraits of *Haldane Macfall* (*cat.* 11, pl. 5), *Major Smythies* (*cat.* 12, pl. 7) and *Enid Bagnold* (*cat.* 17, pl. 8) were his own speculative gambit. He had neither enough work nor sufficient reputation to make the solo exhibition Macfall urged him to seek. In May when he announced that Major Smythies was coming the following day to sit for his portrait, Sophie Brzeska asked if Smythies had commissioned it, only for Gaudier to reply: 'No, it was I who suggested it to him. I must do some of these mugs for nothing in order to build up a reputation.'[9] Modelling portraits of acquaintances enabled him to test and improve his modelling technique in a genre where he felt most confident and from which he might reasonably anticipate payment and recognition. Enid Bagnold affirmed this approach when recalling the arrangements for her own portrait; 'Gaudier asked if he could model my head. Not as a compliment but lacking a sitter.'[10]

For the most formal of the three portraits, that of Macfall, he adopted a traditional Renaissance format, though the very broad shoulders are cut off without the arms being even suggested. The high collar and bow tie reinforce the sitter's formality but the characterization is reticent and the modelling hesitant, especially round the eyes. We may infer the existence of many previous modelled portraits made in Paris and Orléans from Brzeska's writings and the artist's *List of Works*, but he was out of practice and it is doubtful whether he had previously made a portrait which mattered so much; it had to impress its sitter who, however, had to intervene to rescue it from the artist's impulse to destroy it.[11] *Smythies* and *Enid Bagnold* are more smoothly and decisively modelled, with the eyes deeply recessed so that the shadow created enhances their vitality. The element of parody pervading the portrayal of Smythies and the more subtle humour apparent in the heroicized, self-confident poise of Bagnold's head suggest that, in the delicate three-way collusion of the portrait genre, the viewer is being invited to share the sculptor's ambivalent feeling towards his sitters. This suggestion is supported by Sophie's evocation of the risible impression made by Major Smythies, whom she nicknamed 'Colonel Squeeze':

> He is about fifty, and a real bizarre mixture. Quite small and well proportioned but, in spite of his neat figure, his face is scarlet, full and undulating. He has a grandfatherly air, almost that of an old man so, in spite of his carrying himself like a man of energy and decision – a real professional officer – one takes him for a soft old fool. He could be a veteran 'paterfamilias' whose only purpose in life is to make sure he has a worthy wife to parade on his arm and whose sole preoccupation is to get his four daughters nicely married. It's hilarious that that's the impression he gives because he isn't and never has been married.[12]

Gaudier's portrait captures his slightly puffed-up expression and air of bourgeois rectitude. Smythies himself was delighted with the portrait, paying for its casting in bronze and devoting great care to its placing in his rooms.

Enid Bagnold created an altogether more favourable first impression;

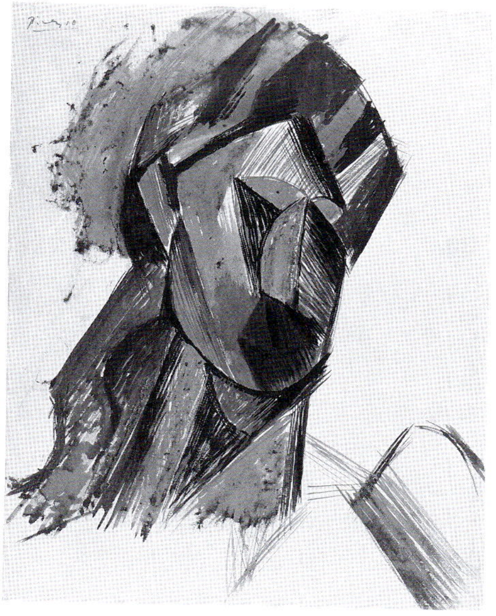

63 Pablo Picasso, *Head of a Woman*, 1909

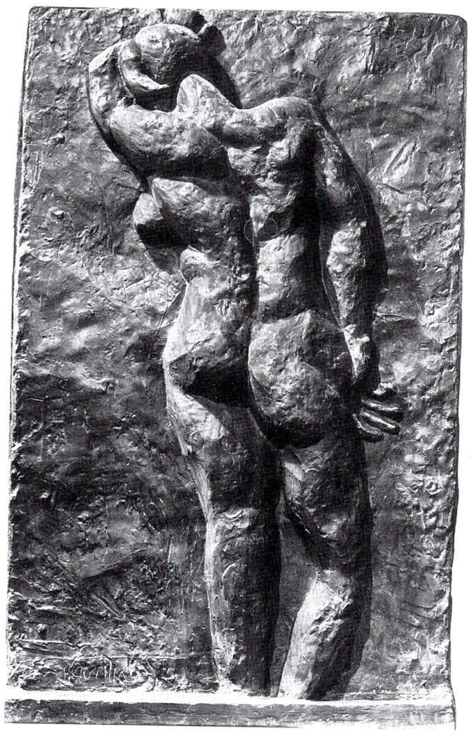

64 Henri Matisse, *Back 1*, 1909

Brzeska described her as 'une belle jeune fille de taille magnifique ... les yeux perspicaces et vifs' ('a beautiful young girl with a magnificent figure ... with clear, lively eyes').[13] Her portrait is infused with a monumental presence and self-assurance so powerful that the head and massive columnar neck suggest the embodiment of some goddess or virtue.

The rhetorical and dramatic possibilities of portraiture are more fully explored in the busts of *Horace Brodzky* (*cat.* 47, pls. 48) and *Alfred Wolmark* (*cat.* 46, pl. 46). Though both were impoverished immigrant artists like himself, struggling for recognition, their postures and expressions signify pride, authority and, in Wolmark's case, tremendous intensity of thought. Both busts are openly indebted to the tradition of heroic portraiture and the topos of moody Romantic genius. The arrogant tilt of the heads and monumentality of both figures are strongly reminiscent of Rodin's *Balzac* (fig. 66) and Bourdelle's portraits of *Ingres* and *Beethoven*. The gravity of the genre is insidiously undermined by humour in the *Portrait of Brodzky*; the caricatural tendency already apparent in *Smythies* resurfaces in the slight exaggerations of eyebrow, eyes and moustache, in the playful inclusion of the inverted nipples, created by impressing some machine-made button or stud, and the incised figures of a nude man apparently fleeing from a woman. Brodzky's own account of the sittings underlines the light-hearted playacting which counterpointed Gaudier's obsessive activity.[14]

The portraits are staging posts in a rapid journey of technical exploration, though they are consistent in their lack of fussy, additive modelling and tricks of variable surface texture. The earlier portraits were modelled more by hand than by tools; the skull of *Major Smythies* presents a slightly dimpled surface of fingertip touches as the clay was pressed and evened out. The soft unevenness of the transition from eye socket to shadowed depth is achieved principally by thumb and finger pressure rather than by gouging with spatula or knife. Tools were used more extensively on the face where cleanly edged planes accentuate the modelling of the cheeks, nose and jowls. A few months later the monumental character of the busts of *Wolmark* and *Brodzky* – broader masses and facetted planar rhythms – is achieved by cutting the moist clay. The stylized curves and planes of the hair and combs in the *Portrait of Enid Bagnold* foreshadow this approach, while the lost *Bust of Frank Harris* (*cat.* 45, pl. 44) seems a transitional work with the face modelled with numerous small, less crisply defined facets.

The angular facetting, most marked in the crisp geometry of *Wolmark*'s bowtie and hair, almost certainly reveals Gaudier's first response to Cubism and the unitary simplifications of form in Matisse's early sculpture. In addition to any works he may have seen in Paris he would have had recent memories of Roger Fry's 1912 Post-Impressionist exhibition, which included early Cubist drawings by Picasso with their very sculptural division of the head into broadly facetted masses (fig. 63, three states of Matisse's *Head of Jeannette* and his plaster *Back 1* (fig. 64). Gaudier described both his portraits as 'Cubique' but the facetting of form is relatively superficial; it can be seen as the logical continuation of Gaudier's own prescription for the construction of sculpture through broad masses defined by planes, a method already apparent in the portrait of *Enid Bagnold*; it is very far from the radical restructuring of the head using multiple viewpoints with their implication of spatial and temporal duration which characterized Cubist portraiture.

Notwithstanding the relative superficiality of their Cubism, the busts of Brodzky and Wolmark were formally and expressively daring; portraits by 'advanced' contemporaries such as Epstein and the Swedish American David Edstrom – then a regular exhibitor at the London Salon and an artist whom Macfall recalled Gaudier admiring – were in a far more reserved, traditional vein;[15] one of Epstein's more adventurous pre-War portraits, *Lady Gregory*, 1910, was quite tightly and smoothly modelled; nevertheless the alert, brisk poise of the head had prompted her nephew, Sir Hugh Lane, to exclaim, 'Poor Aunt Augusta. She looks as if she could eat her own children.'[16] It was therefore unsurprising that, when Gaudier made his public debut with the three portrait busts and three other modelled pieces at the London Salon in July 1913, their formal inventiveness and vitality were lost on the critics who saw in them merely an insincere exaggeration of mood and a desire to shock. A conservative critic, Sir Claude Phillips, characterized Gaudier as 'overbold and recklessly defiant':

> The too frequently astonished but now no longer very astonishable citizen will hardly be startled from his calm by the fierce, uncouth versions of the human countenance, perhaps because he cannot quite bring himself to believe in the agitated mood either of the portraitist or the portrayed.[17]

P. G. Konody, otherwise relatively sympathetic to the new tendencies, was equally scathing:

> M. Henri Gaudier-Brzeska is somewhat hard to follow in his busts of Brodzky, Wolmark and Haldane Macfall, the first two of which are executed in a kind of frenzied cubism that is certainly calculated to attract attention, but fails as much in conveying a sense of the sitter's character and appearance as the more normally treated head of Mr Macfall. The artist's failure in portraiture is the more surprising as his 'Madonna', a portrait statuette of Maria Carmi in 'The Miracle', provides unmistakeable evidence of rare ability.[18]

Gaudier himself appears to have rated these portraits highly; in a passage of *Matka*, dateable by its context to autumn 1913, Gaudier, taunted by Brzeska for his failure to attract patronage and accused of a lack of originality, retorts:

> Well, at least I have achieved something. I would already be judged among the great sculptors, even on the work I have done so far. The portrait of Smythies is as good as any of Rodin's portraits. Brodzky and Wolmark are perhaps better and completely original in technique.[19]

There are numerous drawings and pastels of these sitters. Though they capture with extreme economy salient features of physique, posture or expression they often bear an elliptical relationship to the finished sculptures and were not necessarily preparatory studies. Many have the appearance of entertaining caricatures (fig. 65) and on at least one occasion at Macfall's home, Lovat Fraser, Gaudier and Bagnold made

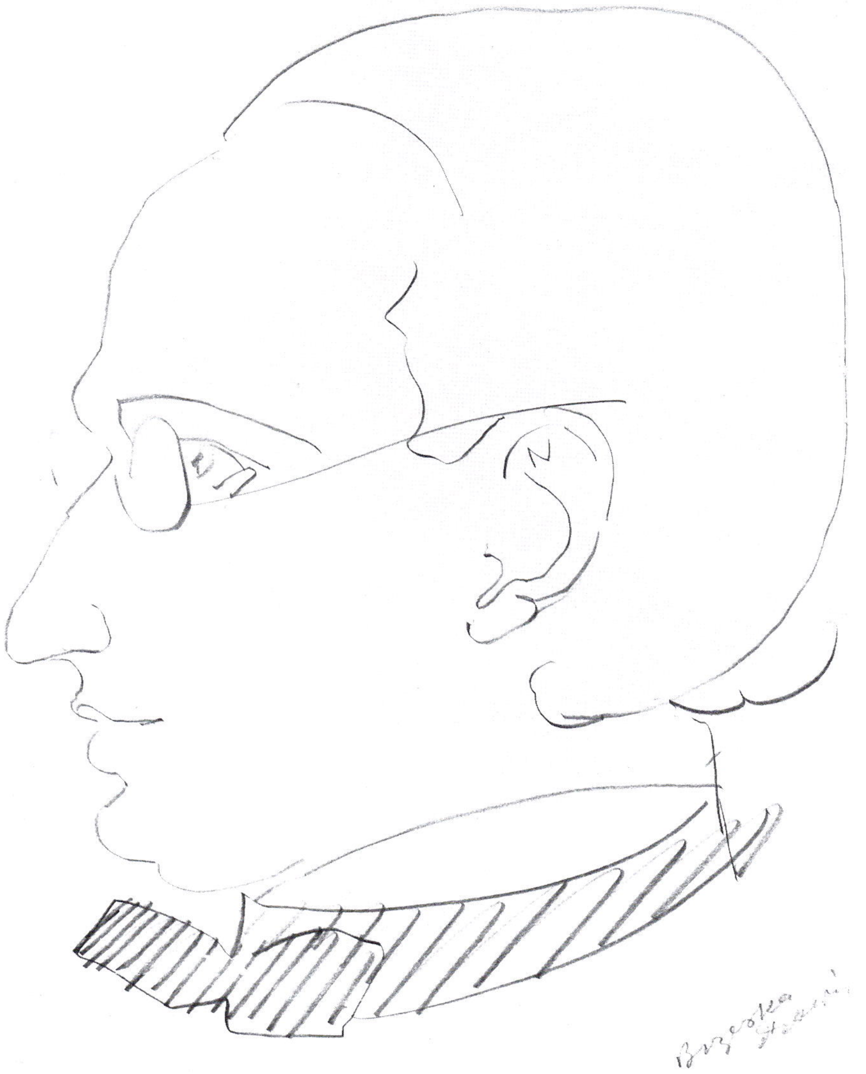

65 *Portrait of Alfred Wolmark*, *c.* 1913

caricatures of each other with paper and pencils supplied by Fraser specially for the purpose.[20] Brodzky's craggy features recur throughout 1913 in portrait drawings, nude studies, three pastels and three sculptures, all of which emphasize his long, strong-jawed face, round eyes, moustache and distinctive Roman-nosed profile; the fine pencil drawing (pl. 49), with its Cézanne-like patches and arcs of diagonal hatching to mark the planes of face, hair and beard, is far less like the Brodzky portrayed in the bronze bust than the quick, bold caricature (pl. 50) or the pastel portraits where Gaudier used a Fauve-inspired palette of saturated colours to create planes analogous to those in the bust.[21] On the other hand, a fine profile drawing of Alfred Wolmark in a bow tie (fig. 65), one of several likely studies for the bust, serves also to highlight its Romanticism. An old friend, Geoffrey Konstam, remembered Wolmark during the Twenties and Thirties as 'a small, dapper, bespectacled man with an outsize head and a flowing mane'.[22] While not entirely ignoring the painter's neatness, the sculpture suggests an almost Michelangelesque *terribilità* through the

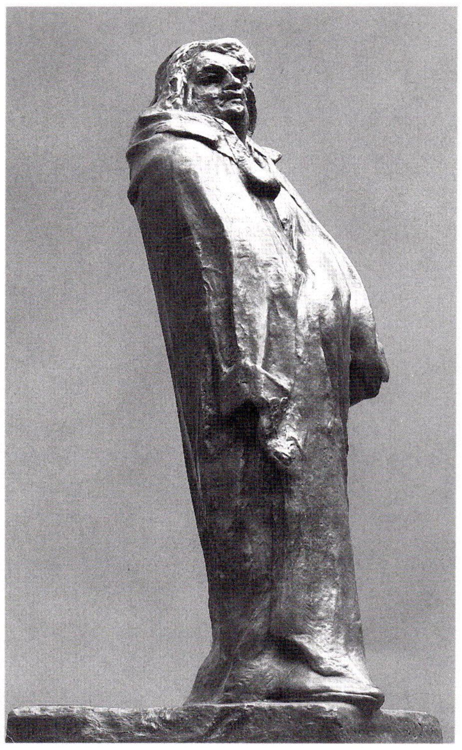

66 Auguste Rodin, *Balzac*, 1898

aggressive pose and the imposing volumes of the head and mane of hair. Wolmark was a daring colourist whose bold simple compositions and Fauvist application of flat areas of saturated, high-keyed colour perceptibly influenced Gaudier's pastel portraits. Gaudier's treatment of Wolmark, like Rodin's of Balzac, seems intended to embody the boldness of his artistic personality.

Despite their stylistic daring, these portraits reveal Gaudier still concerned with individual characterization and with Romanticism as the key to expressive intensity. Notwithstanding their Cubist motifs they can be seen as part of Gaudier's continuing apprenticeship with Rodin. This is especially apparent in the fluent surface modelling and emotional extremes of his exquisite study *Head of an Idiot* (*cat.* 30, pl. 25) and the clay sketch, *Workman Fallen from a Scaffold* (*cat.* 29, pl. 24). However, the shadow of Rodin has entirely vanished from his last portrait, *Mlle Borne* (*cat.* 106, pls. 157, 160). After the abstracted forms of Gaudier's Vorticist work and even the repose of *Seated Woman* (pl. 154), the naturalistic classicism of *Mlle Borne* comes as a surprise. The two preparatory drawings (pl. 158, 159) capture her withdrawn profile and slightly apprehensive expression with tender exactitude. The unusual absence of mockery complements the hints in Brzeska's writings that the relationship between her friend and the artist had become closer than she had expected or wished. Yet the drawn and still more the sculpted portrait are curiously lacking in intimacy. Compared with any of his previous portraits, the bronze is suavely classical, its smooth finish effectively obliterating the traces of process. The monumental scale of the head, the columnar neck and the blank treatment of the eyes refer back quite consciously to classical prototypes. The result is a curiously distanced portrait despite the naturalism of the nose, mouth, chin and brow line. Conceivably the sculpture was modelled from the drawings rather than from the sitter herself.

Gaudier's skill and originality as a sculptor in stone and the unequivocal praise for direct carving expressed in his articles for *The Egoist* and *Blast* in 1914 have coloured subsequent judgments of his modelled work; the painter Horace Brodzky, an unstinting admirer both of Gaudier's graphic style and of his more naturalistic sculpture, nevertheless considered that

> Gaudier-Brzeska as a modeller was not a complete success. Modelling was not his forte, and those works that he did in clay cannot be considered in the same light as his carvings. Clay did not supply sufficient resistance and was far too soft. Gaudier was a sculptor, not a modeller, who was more in his element when he was gradually removing surplus hard stone than when patiently adding soft clay.[23]

Brodzky met Gaudier in January 1913, just as he was completing *Wrestler* (*cat.* 32) and beginning seriously to carve. It was a period of transition, not only between the impressionistic fluency of his Rodinesque portraits and figure studies and the densely modelled and structured figures carved in relief, but also between different modes of sculptural expression – intensity and formal strength expressed through ebullient character and movement or through static repose and formal subtlety.

Polychromy

PORTRAITURE represented only one aspect of Gaudier's efforts to establish himself as an artist during 1912. He continued to try to sell illustrations and decorative designs for wallpapers and posters. Ironically his quick animal and bird drawings were the only saleable items, being used in Macfall's *The Splendid Wayfaring* and in *Rhythm*. One almost accidental by-product of these vain attempts was the re-introduction into his practice of colour, which he had renounced in part because of what he considered his inability to handle paint.[24] However, necessity had forced him to use colour decoratively in his efforts to sell wallpaper and poster designs; during the previous year he had devoted considerable time and effort to poster designs for which he employed heavy curving contours, quite *art nouveau* in feeling, and gouache applied in broad slabs of somewhat sombre colour. *Macbeth* and Shaw's *Man and Superman* were both the subject of extant designs (Kettle's Yard, Cambridge) and poster designs of a bagpiper, negress and a mermaid were all presented to prospective employers only to be rejected.[25]

A spontaneous use of colour resurfaces in 1912 in pastel portrait drawings and in pigment applied to sculpture. Macfall, who was an authority on pastellists, may well have encouraged Gaudier in his use of the medium. Gaudier had also been studying neo-Impressionist colour theory with its emphasis on the use of pure colours, complementaries and the effects of optic mixing. The exhibition of work by Gauguin and Cézanne at the Stafford Gallery in November 1911 would have strengthened his awareness of Gauguin's anti-naturalistic, decorative and atmospheric use of colour and of Cézanne's constructive use of colour and brushstroke. At the Victoria and Albert Museum he saw the rhythmic linear impulse and flat colour of Japanese prints; and, on visits to Macfall and Fraser, he could take in stage designs, chap-book prints and recent prints by the Beggarstaff brothers. Cumulatively they had a liberating effect and pastel became a medium he never abandoned, even at the height of his involvement with Vorticism (pls, I, II, XVI).

At Mr Hare's suggestion he had applied gold, red and blue to one of the plasters of *The Madonna*. Though no longer visible in the present condition of the cast, the archive photograph reveals that the colour – especially the mantle which was probably the traditional blue – was laid on in loose divisionist touches.[26] A very similar application of colour can be observed in several highly characterized pastel portrait studies dating from 1912. One of these, *Japanese Head in Profile* (pl. II), employs a striking combination of extravagant line and pure colour. While the colour suggests neo-Impressionist practice, the line – possibly inspired by Japanese prints – recalls his habit of reducing his candid portrait sketches to caricature. The former owner of this pastel was Lovat Fraser for whom Gaudier also made several painted plaster sculptures, including *Cheetah* (*cat.* 26, pl. 13) and the *Ornamental Mask* (*cat.* 31, pl. 28). Since Fraser designed for the theatre and numbered the leading designer Gordon Craig among his friends, the theatrical stylization of the mask may well defer to Fraser's interests as well as being a satirical portrait. It may also owe something to the eclectic wealth of orientalizing designs visible in London as a result of the Russian ballet's season in 1912; Gaudier went to the ballet on several occasions, not only to prepare the *Firebird* (*cat.* 18), commissioned by the Lousadas, but also to make studies of Nijinsky subsequently exhibited at Dan Rider's bookshop.

Gaudier's recourse to colour and elements of abstract design to heighten movement and expressive effects may have been affected by other chance contacts with Asian art. Major Smythies owned a variety of artefacts – Tibetan dresses 'very effective both in design and colours' and a Burmese seal:

> the tiger biting the sun with very terrific movement and diabolism which qualities appeal to me much. Lately I have been digesting all the observations I made for a year or so and drawn some masks in the way I mean to sculpt them: painted so as to give the absolute characteristic complexion modified by the occasional expression but just as simple and bright as can be. I use for that the optic mixing of the colours, putting them in pure pigments side by side so as to give the resulting tone.[27]

'Diabolism' in Gaudier's satirical portrait drawings was achieved by progressively enhancing the basic linear rhythm through repetition and possibly even repeated tracing of the face and then strengthening the linear character with a thick pen or brush line of varying thickness. *Ornamental Mask* seems to have been developed from these caricatures though it is also possible to see similarities with his zoo studies from *Gorilla* (*cat.* 28, pl. 27). Unlike *The Madonna*, *Ornamental Mask* retains much of its original colouring of blue, red and purple though it has lost the gilding evident in early photographs; the leftover pigments were used to decorate Lovat Fraser's new studio.

These works with their decorative use of colour help to explain Gaudier's receptivity to the brilliance and anti-naturalistic use of larger planes of saturated colour by Gauguin, the Fauves and their English followers. Fergusson and Wolmark played their part in liberating the sense of colour allied to formal structure which resulted first in the 1913 pastel portraits of Sophie Brzeska and Horace Brodzky and later in his abstract Vorticist pastels (pls. I, XVI). He used planes of saturated colour, sometimes sculpturally as an analogue to the mass-defining planes of his sculpture and to enhance the primitivism of his effects, as in *Man and Woman* (*cat.* 38, pl. 35). At the same time Gaudier now appeared to take more of an interest in colour and design for its own sake; in November 1912 he announced to Brzeska that he was designing wallpaper friezes and tiles, in preference to illustrations.[28]

10

'Do you cut … direct … in stone?'

In the famous anecdote of Gaudier's first meeting with Epstein, direct carving is the password for sculptural modernity (see p. 59). The bold affirmative reply marked Gaudier's aspiration to be 'one of us' – the moderns. Gaudier probably did begin carving during 1912 and Epstein, then the leading avant-garde sculptor working in England, was his prime role model. Some time before they met Gaudier had modelled a small group, *Maternity* (*La mendiante*, *cat.* 16, pl. 15), based on Epstein's controversial over-lifesize carving, *Maternity*, on the facade of the British Medical Association Building in the Strand, London. However, this work of 1907–8 had been made by the traditional method of transferring a full-size clay model into stone with the assistance of pointing devices and architectural masons. During 1910–11 Epstein had abandoned it for good and begun, in close collaboration with the trained architectural and letter-carver Eric Gill, to carve into the block without preparatory models, using only a drawn design on the stone and their feeling for the material as his guide. The character of the sculpture resulted from the technique and from their emulation of archaic sculpture from India, Egypt and Assyria. When Gaudier and Epstein met in early June 1912, the older sculptor was carving the monumental, Assyrian-inspired, winged angel figure for the *Tomb of Oscar Wilde* (fig. 67). The following week Gaudier wrote describing the visit and enclosing a sketch of the Tomb to Dr Uhlemayr:

> A Russian sculptor Jacob Epstein also works here – he has just finished a tomb (sarcophagus) for Oscar Wilde in Paris. The thing will be erected at the Père Lachaise Cemetery next July. I saw it in the studio last Sunday – Oscar Wilde is flying slowly into space, his eyes shut. The whole work is treated – strongly, filled with insuperable movement and delicate feeling, in the expression and the medium – a piece of sculpture which will live for ever, only the total seems to be too small. The whole thing is massive – you know what I mean – and the sculpture seems too refined, too small. It's all carved direct in the stone without models.[1]

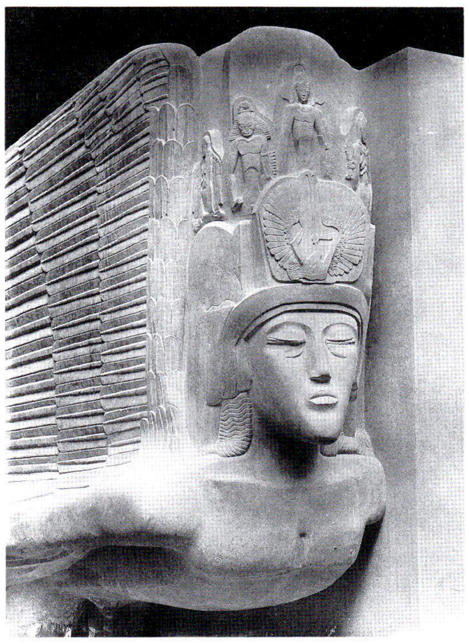

67 Jacob Epstein, *Tomb of Oscar Wilde* (detail), 1911–12. Photographed in the studio, June 1912

While the piece clearly made a great impression it would be misleading to see Gaudier's first attempts at carving solely as a result of experiencing its massive presence. Formally and stylistically it exercized no influence on any of his subsequent work. Nor was his praise untempered by criticism, since as he perceptively observed, there is a tension between the mass of the Hoptonwood stone block and the delicate relief detail of the figure, much of which was carved with a degree of technique which reflects Epstein's own debt to Eric Gill.[2] Gaudier's own relief carving in 1912–13 is characterized not by crisp edges but by a chamfered softness suggestive of weathered stone. Even in the 1913 carvings and reliefs, most of which were developed directly from life drawings, he eschewed detail to focus on the articulation of large masses through rhythmically articulated planes.

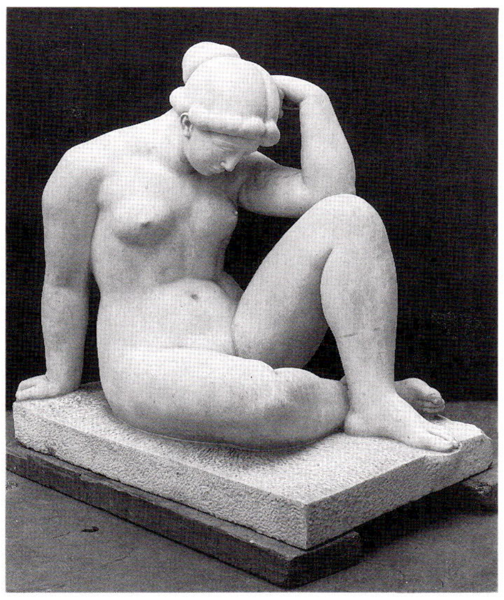

68 Aristide Maillol, *La Méditerranée*, 1905

Unlike Epstein, who yearned to work on a monumental scale – 'to carve mountains' – Gaudier applied his creed of sculpture as the relation of masses to small and, in some cases, very small pieces.[3] This was only partly a matter of necessity; with the exception of *Head of Ezra Pound* (*cat.* 79) and the garden pieces for Roger Fry and Lady Hamilton, which remained as small cut-plaster maquettes (*cat.* 71, 99, 100), he received no commissions for large carvings and could not afford to buy sizeable blocks himself. Until late 1913 his carvings were largely opportunistic unions between his life and animal drawings and the shape, density and scale of the available stone. Numerous anecdotes from Brodzky and Hamnett attest to his ingenuity in obtaining offcuts and fragments by purchase, midnight theft from masons' yards, and sometimes given freely by his amiable neighbour, Fabrucci.[4] Even a cursory examination of his sculpture underlines the truth of these stories. *Grief* (*cat.* 49, pl. 55) was carved from a wedge-shaped block which restricts the composition; the angle of the bent head and arms and legs compresses the figure inwards while the planes which define the masses are all slightly flattened, notably the very upright back. Though its immediate sources were life drawings and the pose was a traditional type of which the most recent and influential exemplar was Maillol's *La Méditerranée*, 1905 (fig. 68), the seemingly monumental volume created in the small, irregular block is nevertheless impressive.[5] *Maternity* (*cat.* 64, pl. 83) too was carved from an irregular, pyramidal block used to its limits so that one marvels at its compositional and expressive freedom. *Singer* (*cat.* 51, pls. 56–58) is a strongly columnar mass, slightly flattened front and back, indicating that little stone has been removed from the shallow block. *Samson and Delilah* (*cat.* 57) – the 'post-post embracers' as Pound called them – is a prismatic marble wedge incapable of free-standing without the plaster mound in which the narrow base of the stone is lodged. *Redstone Dancer* (*cat.* 69, pls. 97, XI), with its unusual circular plinth and marked rotational composition, may have been carved from a column rather than a rectangular block.

Other works suggest a struggle with intractable materials unsuited to three-dimensional work – the boulder-like granite *Standing Female Figure* (*cat.* 53, pls. 60–62) carved with difficulty from a stone probably primarily intended for machine-assisted, monumental masonry, and the large blocks intended for the Duchess of Hamilton's garden vases, which were left unfinished in August 1914 (*cat.* 99, 100, pls. 148, 150). Many works are essentially reliefs, not only low reliefs carved on flat slabs of stone like *Woman* (*cat.* 39) and *Love Scene* (*cat.* 73), but also *Cat* (*cat.* 70), *Mermaid* (*cat.* 55) and the stone masks which were carved from rough fragments of irregular density, the back of which was left unworked.

During 1914 Gaudier seems increasingly to have carved maquettes in plaster. The scale of the functional garden pieces envisaged would have been larger but many adventurous pieces associated with the Vorticist aesthetic, carved in green stone or metal, were palm-sized. None of his contemporaries was making tiny pieces like these; the number of extant drawings relating to these and other unrealized works as well as the care devoted to the carving of pieces such as *Torpedo Fish* (*cat.* 80), *Doorknocker* (*cat.* 81, pl. 128), *Fish* (*cat.* 93), *Duck* (*cat.* 90) and *Toy* (*cat.*

95), indicate their significance to the artist.[6] They challenged Western conventions of sculpture; they had no plinth – some, like *Toy* (*cat.* 95, pls. 136–38), could be placed in many different ways; others were functional, even fetishistic; they were designed for tactile rather than purely visual response; Hulme, for whom several were made, would carry them about in his pockets and handle them at will.[7] Gaudier's fascination with small-scale densely worked sculpture is inextricably linked with his long-standing interest in Far Eastern art forms – the hard stone carvings and applied decorative bronze figures and animals on ancient Chinese ceremonial vessels, Japanese *netsuke* and with the greenstone *tiki* (neck ornaments) of Oceania. Non-European carvings, especially African and Oceanic pieces, were being collected and studied by a number of artists – Picasso, Derain, Kirchner and Epstein among others – but larger carved wooden figures and masks were the primary focus of their interest. Epstein certainly had some small pieces; Sacheverell Sitwell recalled him carrying around 'little ivory masks of African workmanship' in his pockets, but his ambitions remained firmly fixed on sculpture of a more conventional European scale.[8] Gaudier's interests align him more closely with Gauguin who used Javanese Buddhist sculpture as well as European and Oceanic sources. His originality lay less in the overt sexuality and primitivism of pieces such as the phallic *Doorknocker* and the greenstone *Charm* (*cat.* 85, pls. 130, XIII) than in his redefinition of the scale and function of sculpture in terms of modernist geometric forms. This freedom was perhaps Gaudier's single greatest debt to non-European art.

Small and semi-abstract works such as *Toy* and *Fish*, the paperweight-like *Fawn* (*cat.* 84) and *Torpedo Fish* also enabled him to develop his ideas more quickly. Given the fertility of his powers of invention, direct carving was a slow method; he might have wished for the chance to work on a large scale just to prove he could do it but working on a smaller scale cutting plaster, stone or metal meant he could work fast without sacrificing the craftsmanship and technical pleasure of direct carving. It is tempting to wonder how his work might have developed had he chosen to try out the improvised constructional methods and cheap materials being used by Picasso, Archipenko and others in Paris; they would at least have enabled his sculpture to keep pace with the sculptural ideas he conceived on paper. He would have heard about such techniques both from French periodicals and from Lewis who, reviewing Picasso's latest work for *Blast*, spoke of 'these wayward little objects', 'small structures in cardboard, wood, zinc, glass string, etc., tacked, sewn or stuck together'.[9]

Relief Carvings

THE FIRST piece of carving Gaudier is recorded to have made was a wooden picture-frame he worked on in Paris in 1910. Relief carving offered a relatively straightforward way into the uncompromising technique of direct stone carving; the first direct carvings of both Epstein and Gill had been in relief. In March 1913, Gaudier wrote to Lovat Fraser that he was making as many reliefs as he could. It became far more than a means of self-education. His stone masks, irregular blocks and carved plaster pieces tested the limits of the technique. Relief carving was also the medium of some of his most experimental 'applied' work – the pierced forms of

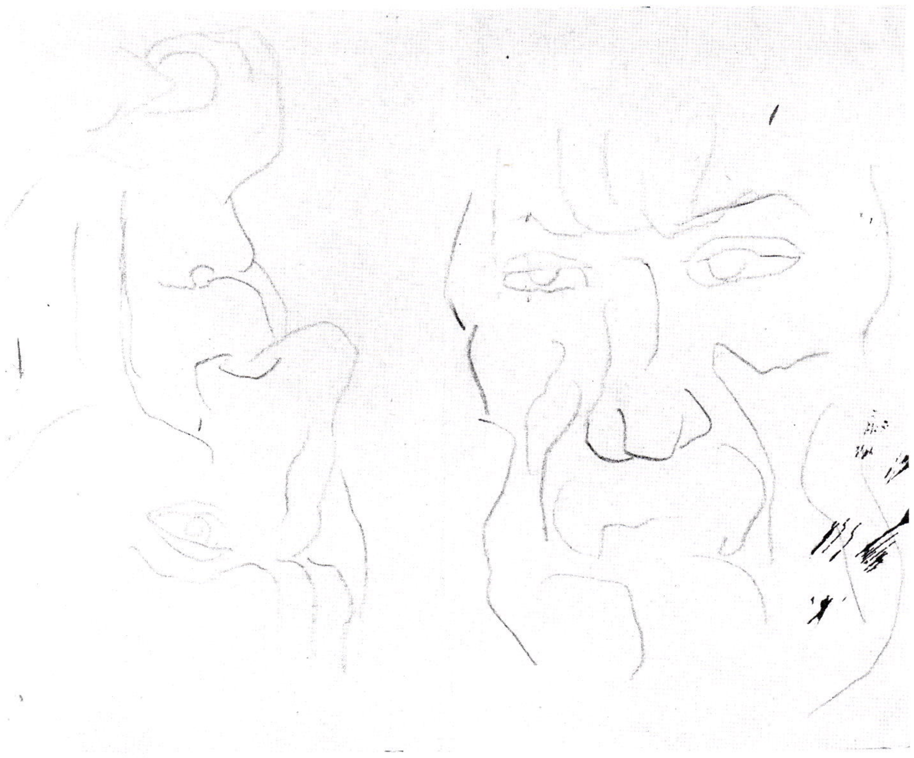

69 *Head of an Old Man*, 1912

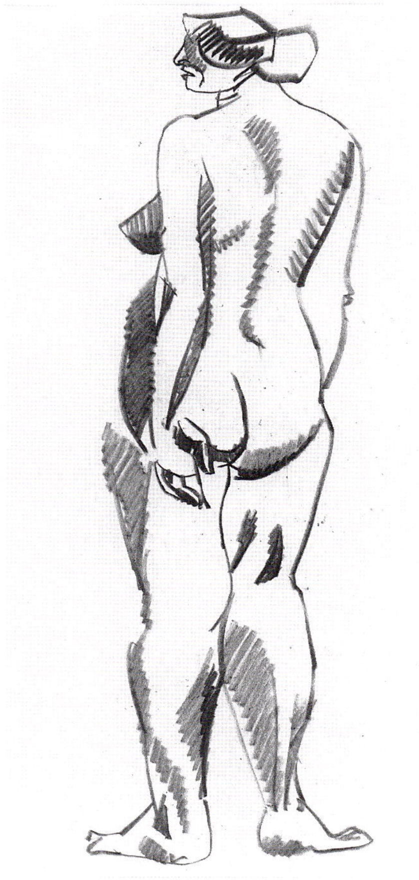

70 *Female Nude*, c. 1913

Doorknocker (*cat.* 81), *Charm* (*cat.* 85), paperweights, ornaments and medals, as well as the more smoothly decorative designs associated with the Omega Workshops – his ceramic *Cat* (*cat.* 65), furniture designs (fig. 88) and the carved plaster *Wrestlers* (*cat.* 66) are all essentially relief carvings.

Gaudier's earliest extant carvings – the tiny white marble *Head of a Man* (*cat.* 19, pl. 18) and *Religious Head* (*cat.* 20, pl. 16) transpose a type of facial study recognizable from the progressively simplified heads he sketched during 1910–12 (fig. 73). The nude life drawings begun in 1912 became the most fertile source for relief compositions. According to its first owner, John Cournos, the composition of *Weeping Woman* (*cat.* 36, pl. 33) was determined by the limitations of the stone block, but it was also directly based on nude life studies (pl. 32), probably made during the Chelsea life classes in autumn 1912.[10] The pendant *Amour* (*cat.* 35, pl. 31) also evolved from the life drawing class; at least nine pen drawings in the Orléans collection, as well as others now dispersed, show profile images of a well muscled youth with one leg advanced and either an arm across his chest in the pose of *Amour*, or with hands clasped behind his head in a pose that more closely resembles the Dartington *Boy* (*cat.* 56, pl. 75).[11] Several show the pose reversed, but two (pls. 29, 30) are directly related to the *Amour* relief.[12]

The carved figures are more compactly proportioned than those in the life drawings. The bodies are softer, fleshier, their sensuality enhanced by the serpentine curving rhythms of shoulder blades, belly and buttocks. Gaudier had told Brzeska in one of his long letters on the nature of beauty in art 'to make reliefs *tell* you must exaggerate the forms'.[13] The bulkiness of these figures may also have been informed by Maillol-like amplitude of a lifesize female nude (*cat.* 37), roughly modelled in clay, which spent some weeks in the Fulham Road studio before being destroyed. However, this pair of alabaster reliefs reflects a confluence of sources; the woman's pose of timeless grief recalls painted and sculpted figures of Eve, expelled from Paradise after the Fall, Rodin's *Eve* being the most obvious and immediate exemplar, while the youth can be read as an innocently sensual Adam-like figure. However the sensuality of the figures and his use of a coloured ground also suggests a response to the work of Eric Gill.

Gill and Epstein only began to exhibit their new directly carved sculpture in January 1911 so it is doubtful whether the newly arrived Gaudier would have seen it. His first real experience of the archaism and formal power of such work came in 1912 when a considerable amount of recent directly carved sculpture was on show in London.[14] In June 1912 the *Tomb of Oscar Wilde* was shown publicly in Epstein's Cheyne Walk studio attracting public and media interest; within weeks, his voluptuous, life-size carving *Maternity* (1910) was exhibited unfinished in the centre of the Albert Hall arena in the London Salon. During the autumn six carvings by Gill were shown alongside the works of Matisse, Picasso, Vuillard, Derain, Vlaminck, Goncharova, Larionov, Lewis, Gore, Spencer, Grant and other younger French, English and Russian painters in Fry's Second Post-Impressionist Exhibition.[15] Gaudier's sculpture has a underlying hardness and structural rigour which is the antithesis of Gill's suave, slack-muscled figures, yet their archaism and primal nudity, Gill's penchant for unusual active subjects (e.g. *Acrobats* and *The Rower*) and his obvious craftsmanship explains Gaudier's passing interest in his work. Several relief carvings of nude figures using gilt or coloured decoration, all produced during the winter and early spring of 1912–13, echo elements of Gill's style. In *Crouching Male Figure* (*cat.* 33) he employed a gold ground, possibly left over from the gilt used on the plaster *Ornamental Mask* (*cat.* 31) a couple of months before; the claw-chiselled grounds of *Weeping Woman* and *Amour* were originally red, a colour then favoured by Gill. The soft fleshiness of these figures and the pudding-bowl haircut, carved in neat parallel grooves, of the lost marble relief *Boy* (*cat.* 34) again suggest a response to Gill's style. Though there is no record of the two sculptors meeting, Gaudier continued to keep an eye on Gill's work; as late as January 1914 he made a point of going to the exhibition of work by Gill at the Chenil Gallery.[16]

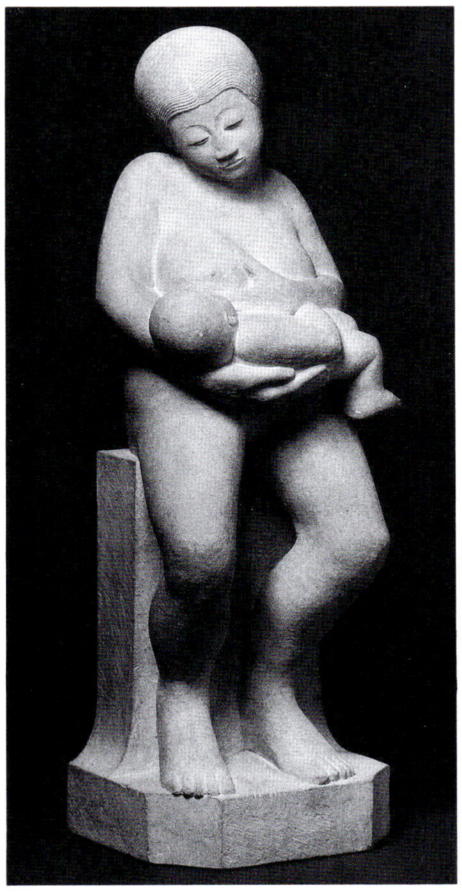

71 Eric Gill, *Mother and Child*, 1910

The lessons Gaudier had absorbed from both his mentors can be seen in two of his free-standing figures – *Singer* (*cat.* 51, pls. 56–58) and *Maternity* (*cat.* 64). *Singer*, a subject treated with a timelessness implied by the semi-nude torso draped from the hips, is a transitional work; the singer's melancholy is suggested both by her upturned head and open mouth and by the tense inward pressure of the arms twisted up behind her back, twining and grasping the long hair.[17]

Maternity is an astoundingly fresh treatment of one of the most commonly tackled of all themes. The delicate relief carving of the mother's enfolding hands is borrowed from Epstein's 1912 *Maternity*, while the elemental tenderness of the relationship between mother and child had been anticipated in both Epstein's 1908 *Maternity* and in Gill's sculptures on the same theme (fig. 71). The directness of Gill's interpretation had been much discussed by contemporary critics: for Roger Fry it expressed 'the instinct of maternity' and 'its pathetic animalism' while for C. Lewis Hind these figures represented 'the idea of maternity, reduced to the simplest form of archaic expression'.[18] Where Gill's composition is basically that of a Madonna and Child, Gaudier's *Maternity* reduces the relationship of mother and child to its animal essence. Enfolding, ovoid forms are interlocked almost as tightly as Brancusi's lovers in *The Kiss*, yet their asymmetry creates an implied rocking movement evoking the exclusive intimacy and protective warmth of the maternal role. The almost naive naturalism of this piece can also be compared with *Crouching Fawn* (*cat.* 62, pl. 80) and the new-born *Sleeping Fawn* (*cat.* 63, pl. 78), both developed directly from life drawings.

The alabaster reliefs were finished and exhibited pieces of work but the status of the three stone heads which seem to date from about the same period – *Head of Christ* (*cat.* 42, pl. 17), *Head of a Young Man* (*cat.* 44, pl. 41) and *Mask of Horace Brodzky* (*cat.* 41, pl. 43) – is equivocal. They were neither signed nor exhibited in his lifetime. Like the stone panel *Woman* (*cat.* 39, pl. 39), the carving is deepened beyond relief and the forms are broadened and stylized into facets. Both this and the careful definition of planes in rough claw-chiselled surfaces suggest that they were studies intended primarily to develop technique; the *Head of a Boy* is carved in the round though with the back of the head cursorily treated. The character and expression of the face, an overriding element in his modelled portraits, is virtually eliminated in favour of mass, structure and technique; only Brodzky's flattened ears betray the mischief characteristic of the artist's modelled portraits. Even this element of wit seems to have a secondary purpose in questioning the boundary between a relief carving and a work in the round. Studied analysis of carved form may also have been the purpose of a unique drawing of the same boy's head (pl. 42); built up with tone rather than line, the exactitude with which it parallels the sculpture's forms and the fall of light indicate that the drawing was made after, rather than in preparation for, the sculpted head. It represents a return to the method he had used to analyse Michelangelo's sculpture in the Victoria and Albert Museum and he was to return to this means of reviewing his own work at least once more in the crisp pen drawing after *Bird Swallowing a Fish*.[19]

This questioning of sculptural definition in which drawing and sculpture play complementary roles is typical of Gaudier's work; he continued to use masks as relief decoration in *Maquette for Flower Vase 1* (*cat.* 99, pl. 150) and on the projecting handles of *Maquette for Flower Vase 2* (*cat.* 100, pl. 148). Other works challenge the definition of relief; the *Mermaid* (*cat.* 55, pl. 63) growing out of her rock may be read either as a figure in the round projecting from an integral plinth or as high relief. The depth of the framing recess in *Man and Woman* (*cat.* 38, pl. 35) makes the figures appear as if on a stage or Punch-and-Judy booth, while *Samson and Delilah* (*cat.* 57, pl. 66), though actually carved in the round, is characterized by low-relief surface treatment.

The animal reliefs *Dog* (*cat.* 48, pl. 81) and *Cat* (*cat.* 70, pl. 89) play similar games with the perception and sculptural evocation of depth. Both animals are depicted curled up rather than stretched out but they are nonetheless treated in relief.[20] The design for *Dog* (fig. 78) is flattened and

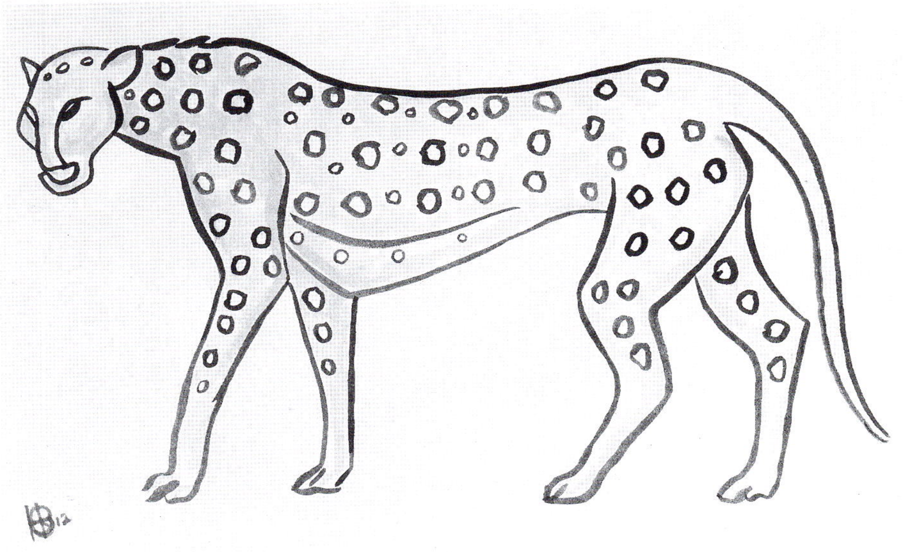

72 *Cheetah*, 1912

stylized to create a composition in which the line of the tail is echoed by the floppy ears, the curve of the dog's jaws and ruff-like upper chest. The marble *Cat*, on the other hand, uses the unevenness of the stone to evoke the soft mass of the sleeping animal. Cats were a favourite subject of Gaudier's: he attempted to capture their sinuous forms and nonchalant agility, even as a student in Bristol, and later repeatedly sketched the cat he had been given by Spencer Gore which was his companion in the Putney studio.[21] He also drew the big cats in the zoo obsessively; there are numerous profile drawings which seek to capture the soft, elastic weight of a lioness's or leopard's stride or the curious bonelessness of a sleeping cat's body set off against the more clearly articulated forms of the head and outstretched or folded legs (pl. 91). This *Cat* – definitely wild rather than domesticated – is based on these pen drawings.[22] He used a fragment of marble irregular in thickness, width and depth, emphasizing this by leaving every edge except the narrow monogrammed base rough. The subtlety of the modelling – the softened bluntness of the junction between belly and flanks, the slight dip where the ears join the skull, and seemingly casual disposition of the rangy limbs – all give the appearance of naturalism. Yet this is an artfully constructed image; the right forepaw, the angle of the head and rear limbs are adjusted to fit the stone and thrust the broad head forward. The slanting curves of muzzle, nose, eye, jaws and ears set up the compositional rhythm echoed in the angle of the bent forepaw, the curve of the shoulder, the curl of the long tail and the sharply angled rump. The unstable mass is anchored by the hard, parallel lines of the hind legs. Some areas are carved in quite high relief, with the greatest thickness where the hindquarters and paws overlap the tail, but where one might expect the highest relief at the point where muzzle and paws meet, the carving is at its most delicate, almost *rilievo schacciato*, as the muzzle seems to sink into the paws.

The psychic empathy suggested by all Gaudier's carvings and drawings of animals is noticeably absent from his reliefs of figure groups. The psychological states evoked by the lovers in Gaudier's reliefs are ambiguous; in both the primitivizing *Man and Woman* (*cat.* 38, pl. 35) and the more naturalistic *Love Scene* (*cat.* 73, pl. 93) the female appears in the dominant role as the object of desire while the male is subsidiary, a supplicant who may be rebuffed. Both female figures derive from life drawings while the head of the man in *Man and Woman* is reminiscent of *Amour*.[23] *Love Scene* is one of very few works for which a preparatory compositional drawing survives to show how the artist calculated the placing of his figures within the irregular confines of the marble panel (pl. 92) It is a rapid sketch far more cavalier in its treatment of the figures than his life drawings. The exaggerated proportions of the block in the drawing allows the creation of a psychological tension between the seemingly disinterested female and the crawling youth; in the carving the supplicant male figure is squeezed right up to the female and partly obscured by her. Compared with the naturalism of the drawing the heads of the carved figures, especially that of the male, are broadened and given a self-consciously Gauguinesque 'primitive' appearance. Indeed the enigmatic mood and style of these works are both reminiscent of Gauguin.

Gaudier was undoubtedly familiar with some of Gauguin's work from his assiduous perusal of the European art magazines and he had probably seen some of his work in Paris. His understanding may well have been deepened by the exhibition of work by Gauguin and Cézanne which took place at the Stafford Gallery in November 1911. *Manao Tupapau* (The spirit watches over her), *Vision after the Sermon* and *Christ in the Garden* were among the paintings on show. There is no documentary evidence that Gaudier saw the exhibition but there seems to be an echo of one of Gauguin's favourite motifs – a girl curled up on the ground in a foetal posture – in *Mermaid* (*cat.* 55, pl. 63). The enigmatic style of this piece is comparable to the flat linear style Gaudier seems to have developed during the autumn of 1913 and employed for decorative designs during his

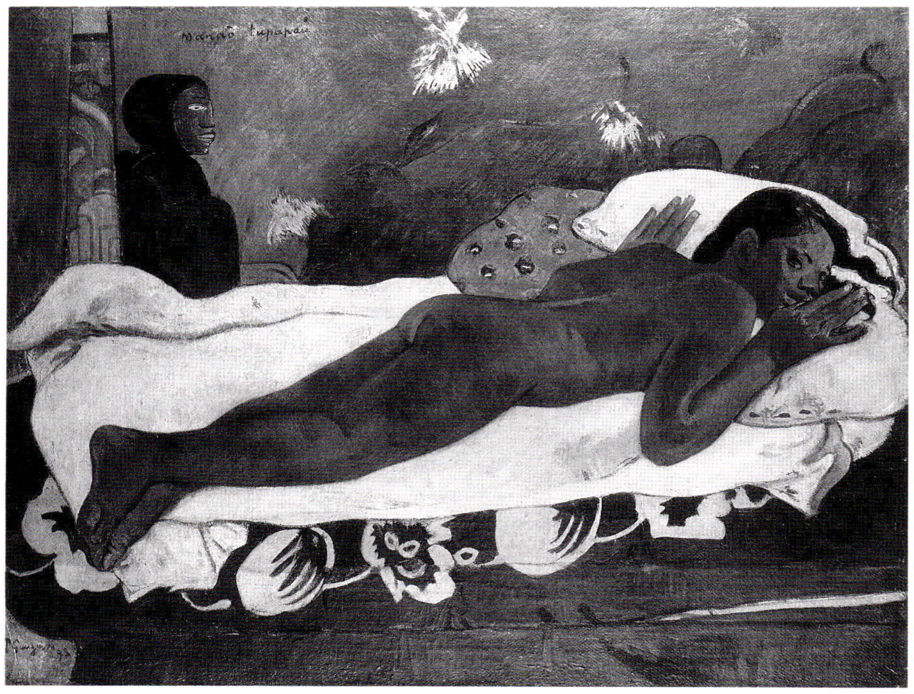

73 Paul Gauguin, *Manao Tupapau*, 1892. Exhibited at the Stafford Gallery in November 1911

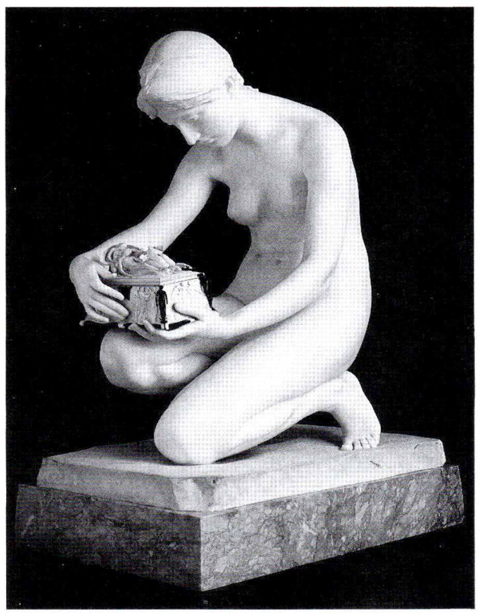

75 Harry Bates, *Pandora*, 1891

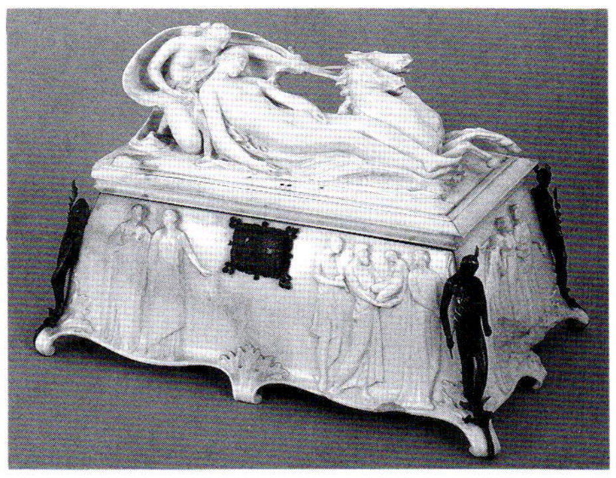

74 Harry Bates, detail showing Pandora's box from *Pandora*

association with the Omega Workshops. It seems to share the Gauguinesque and Fauve-derived simplicity of contour associated with the work of Duncan Grant and Vanessa Bell. But it also seems much closer in feeling to the fearful girl lying pressed down on her bed in Gauguin's *Manao Tupapau* (fig. 73) than it is to Rodin's supremely sensuous *Danaïde*, the work with which it has usually been compared.[24] Gauguin's dramatic use of flat saturated background colours and elements of floral and textile design are also clearly echoed in Gaudier's remarkable pastel *Portrait of Sophie Brzeska* (pl. 1).

Generally the works Gaudier studied with most attention were non-European artefacts, especially from the Far East and Polynesia, and works by leading contemporaries, Brancusi and Epstein, while he scorned the anaemic products of Academic sculptors. There is, however, one extraordinary instance in which Gaudier appropriated shamelessly from one of the senior generation of British sculptors, revealing through the rapid process of borrowing, transforming and re-using the 'amazing faculty for synthesis' recalled by Ezra Pound.[25] The carved box, to contain poems for presentation to W. S. Blunt (*cat.* 72, pl. 100), was conceived at Pound's request and carved in immense haste, under two weeks, in early January 1914. The work shows signs of Gaudier's unfamiliarity with the formal limitations imposed by the shape of the casket. The lettering, probably the first he had ever carved, is tentative in layout, lettering style and technique. On the front face of the coffer is a reclining woman, carved in relief in the marble panel. The nude female figure is most unusual in its bonelessness and complete passivity; floating on the surface of the marble like Ophelia in the brook, she projects a curiously funereal mood without any specific meaning. He may have drawn on memories of sarcophagi and tombslabs, with their recessed relief carving contained within a raised frame, but his immediate source was a work by one of the 'New Sculptors' of the Eighties and Nineties whose work he generally despised – Harry Bates' famous *Pandora* of 1891, then as now in the Tate Gallery (fig. 74). It was the exquisite, highly ornate ivory and bronze box of evils held by the kneeling Pandora that Gaudier used as his guide in this unfamiliar task (fig. 75). The dimensions, slightly sloping sides and chamfered lid resemble his own while the flaccid figure with her bent head and limply curving arms is a transcription into relief of the sleeping chariot-borne figure, carved on the lid of Pandora's box. Gaudier's resort to this surprising source may have been stimulated by extreme haste but it might conceivably also represent an effort on his part to make something suited to the taste of the elderly recipient. If that was his intention it did not succeed. Blunt did not like it, describing it as 'an absurd futurist bas-relief of a naked Egyptian woman' and promptly turning the carved side to the wall.[26]

It is ironic that Blunt should have seen this conservative placatory piece as either 'futurist' or 'Egyptian'. Early 1914 marked the height of Gaudier's engagement with the nascent London group, with Lewis, Epstein and Pound and with the Omega Workshops. This piece was altogether less challenging formally and less primitivistic than anything else he was undertaking.

11

The Fourth Dimension: Movement and Duration

GAUDIER's stylistic gymnastics should not blind us to one of the most constant elements of his art – his preoccupation with movement. His work in every medium – from zoo and studio drawings to modelled and carved sculpture – reveals his intuitive talent for suggesting organic dynamism, whether latent or active. Most striking is his ability to suggest sequential movement, to intercept an impressionistic moment while simultaneously conveying the duration of the organic continuum. He seems to have worked with a naturalist's observant eye, sensitive to the ergonomy of each species from cats and carthorses to herons and humans:

> Men do not move in one movement as with the primitives: the movement is composed, is an uninterrupted sequence of other movements themselves divisible and different parts of the body may move in opposed directions and with diverse speeds. Movement is the translation of life, and if art depicts life, movement should come into art, since we are only aware of life because it moves.

This critique, written by Gaudier in November 1912, compares 'primitive' sculpture ('the very conventional form of the primitives, which gives only an enormous sensation of serene joy or exaggerated sorrow – always with a large movement, synthetized and directed towards one end') with modern sculpture, and concludes that 'the movement of the primitive is a misconception of true movement, is a fabrication of his mind, an automatic creation that corresponds in no way with the natural movement of the living being.'[1]

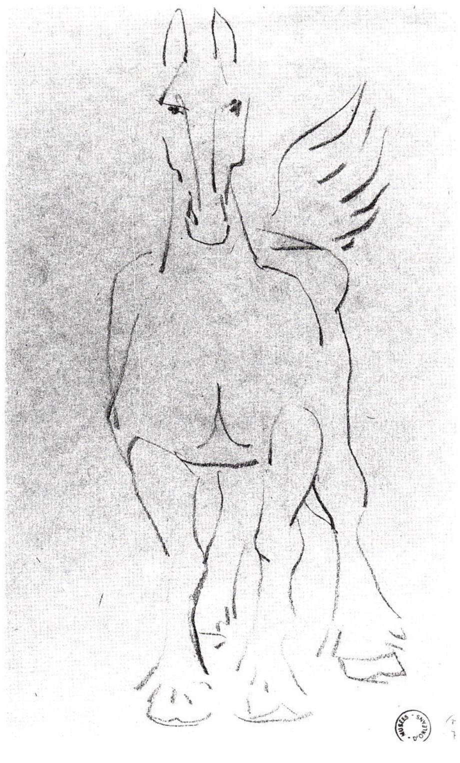

76 *Horse*, c. 1912

His interest in movement long predates this; it can be traced back through the early bird drawings, to his admiration for Rodin's *St John the Baptist* and his readings of Bergson's *Evolution créatrice*. Gaudier had made a small copy of the St John while in Paris and, as we have seen, the stance and variants of it filter into early satirical and compositional drawings (see p. 75).[2] Few of the many small naturalistic studies in wax or clay of animals and figures in movement seem to have survived; *Women Running* (*cat.* 27, fig. 30) and all the plaster animals appear to be lost or destroyed. However, in pieces such as *Women Carrying Sacks* (*cat.* 40, pl. 40) and *Workman Fallen from a Scaffold* (*cat.* 29, pl. 24), as in the street drawings, technique is subordinated to the impressionistic evocation of movement. Such works drew part of their inspiration from Rodin's modelling of figures in movement and suggest a physical and emotional abandon comparable to the tumbling, entwined figures of *The Gates of Hell*.

For all the naturalism of Rodin's figures, it is their fictive literary and symbolic context which gives them their physical and emotional freedom. Gaudier had explicitly rejected literary subject matter in favour of more down-to-earth naturalism and, in common with a number of other vanguard artists such as Matisse, Dunoyer de Segonzac, Archipenko, Duchamp-Villon, Wyndham Lewis and Duncan Grant, he used

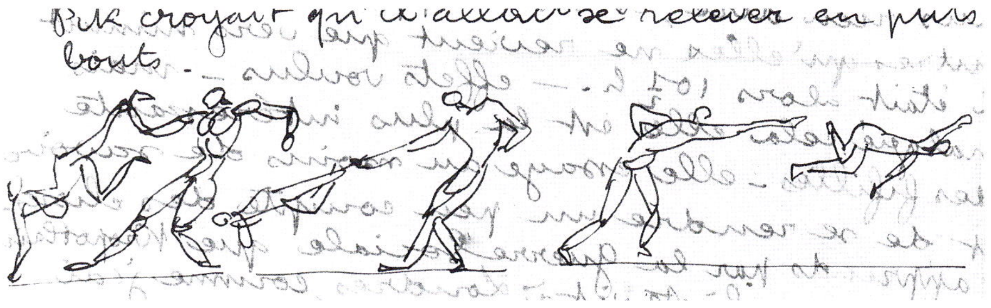

77 Wrestlers sketch in a letter from Gaudier to Brzeska, 5.12.12

wrestling, boxing and dance to explore the trained body engaged in part formalized, part spontaneous movements which nonetheless stemmed from elemental, instinctive urges. During the same month that he wrote to Sophie Brzeska with his thoughts on movement in 'primitive' and modern sculpture, he was beginning to draw at the London Wrestling Club as part of his preparation to model a statuette for Charles Wheeler. He had encountered a young wrestler modelling in his life class and admired his 'strong, taut and finely square' physique, only to discover that he worked in Wheeler's office.[3] He planned to see boxing and diving as well but became completely absorbed in the virile agility of the wrestlers.

On 5 December 1912 he wrote to Brzeska,

> Yesterday evening I went to see the wrestlers. My God I have never seen such a beautiful sight – two typical athletes – large shoulders, taut, enormous necks like bulls, small in build, firm thighs, slender ankles, feet as sensitive as hands and not tall but they fight with a fantastic vivacity and spirit, turning in the air and falling back on their hands so as to jump up on the other side; utterly incomprehensible … I stayed and drew for two hours and am going to begin the statuettes on Sunday.[4]

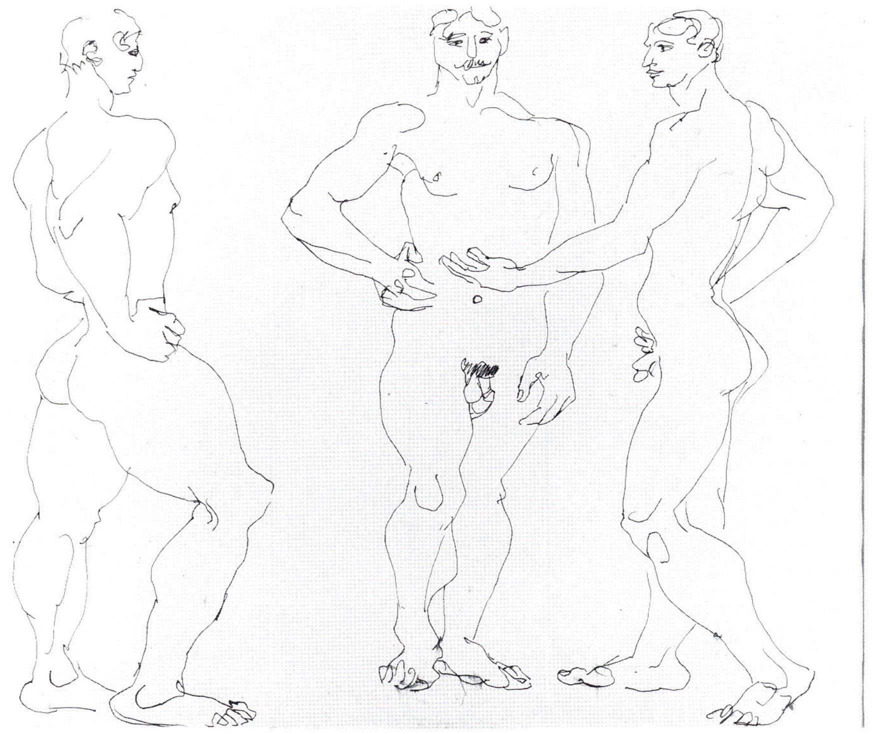

78 *Three Male Nudes Standing*, 1913

Wrestler (*cat.* 32, pls. 37, 38) marks a significant change in Gaudier's approach to modelling. In place of the impressionistic handling of clay with its overlay of Cubistic facetting, the massive figure is densely and smoothly modelled with most of the marks of process obliterated. Its emphatic masculinity and power is largely held in check but for the deceptively gentle implied pressure of the left hand and right fingers. Though still indebted to studies of the young wrestler in the life drawing class it can also been seen in relation to a series of nude studies featuring men with the athletic physique of bodybuilders (fig. 78). While dating remains uncertain, it seems to be during the winter of 1912 and spring of 1913 that his figure studies, like his modelled and carved sculpture, became markedly more massive: the shoulders broadened and musculature more marked in the men, buttocks and breasts amplified in the women so that the figures become more strongly gender-distinct. The density and restraint of these figures also suggests the passing influence of Maillol's monumental classicism. Brodzky records Gaudier working during early 1913 (*cat.* 37):

> Once at his Fulham studio he modelled a lifesize female nude...the very opposite of his usual slim Greek-like figures. It was more chubby and not unlike the thick-set figures of Maillol. Technically he had adopted a method that one might call Impressionist – built up by independent or detached small additions of clay, and with no attempt whatever at blending or graduating the touches. The surface was in no way suave. This figure remained for a long time in clay, standing on its dais ... He was not pleased with it, and I am sure it was done as an exercise or to fill in time. Certainly he never expected to find the money to have it cast in plaster, still less in bronze. He had lost interest in it. And then he suddenly decided to destroy it.[5]

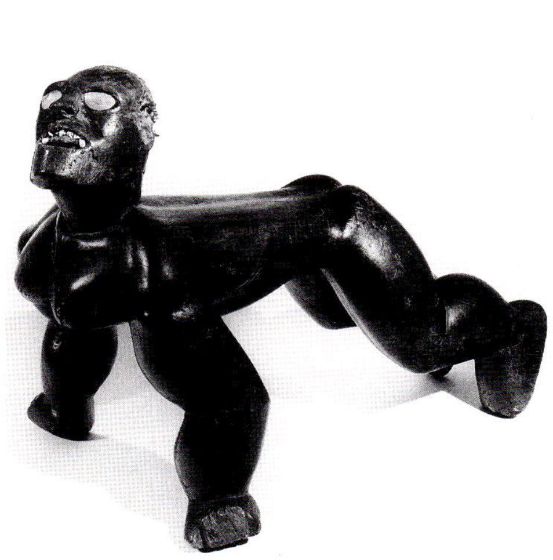

79 Hawaiian Deity

His dissatisfaction with the clay seems to have coincided with his commitment to carving. While the dating of this figure is not precise, several of Gaudier's early carvings, *Weeping Woman* (*cat.* 36, pl. 33) and the relief *Woman* (*cat.* 39, pl. 39) are similarly amply conceived. Further, Gaudier's recent visit to the British Museum was, in spite of his critical comments, prompted by an interest in the formal qualities of the 'primitive' African and Oceanic wood carvings. Among the most striking objects in the collection was the great crouching Hawaiian Deity figure (fig. 79); Henry Moore admired it from his student days and later remarked, 'It has the flat back and powerful muscles of a gorilla, combined with a tension and strain of a wrestler'.[6] While there is no proof that Gaudier saw the *Deity* figure, its proportions and style seem perceptibly to have influenced the pen and wash drawings of 1913–14 related to *Redstone Dancer* (*cat.* 69, pls. 97–99, XI) and *Caritas* (*cat.* 75, pl. 108).[7] If the figure did not have any stylistic impact on *Wrestler* the formal analogies may at least explain Gaudier's receptivity to the work during the following year.

The first of Gaudier's three surviving dance sculptures, *Firebird* (*cat.* 18, pls. 11–12), was commissioned, but references to other studies – of Nijinsky and a statuette of a dancer which belonged to Sophie Brzeska in 1912 – indicate Gaudier's own interest in the Russian ballet.[8] The *Firebird* is Gaudier's most 'posed' dance scene, literally descriptive in the same way as *The Madonna* in recording a choreographed moment of a stage

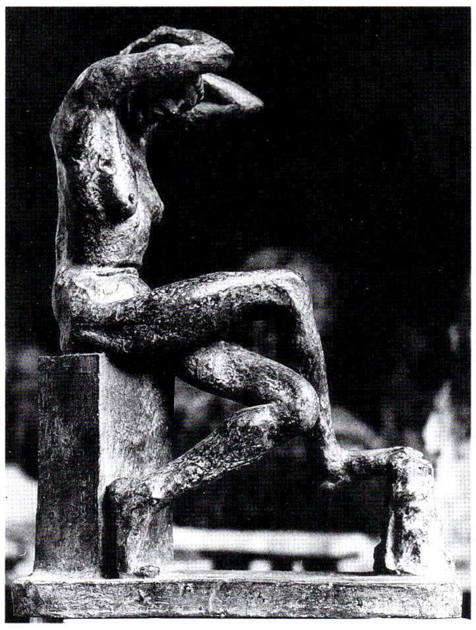

80 Jacob Epstein, *Nan Seated*, 1911

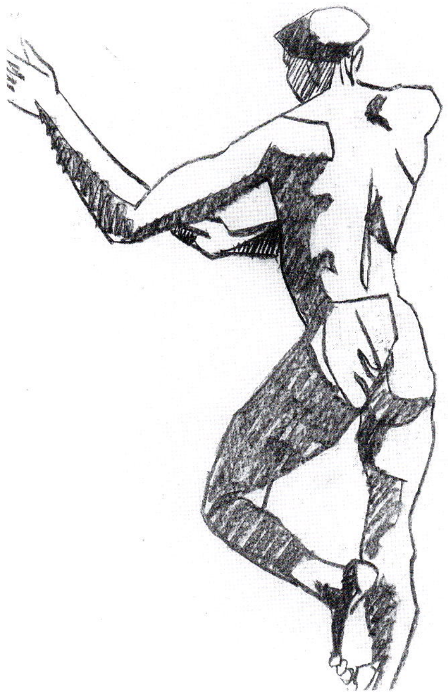

81 *Male Nude*, *c.* 1913

performance. The physical drama of the Firebird's capture is expressed through her hunched shoulders and upward gaze which suggest the impulse to flight counterbalanced by the downward pull of her captor. Its smoothly finished modelling is closely comparable to that of the portrait of *Enid Bagnold* (pl. 10) but the details of costume are stylized and softly facetted to create broader volumes and planes even within the miniature scale of the group, and may reflect the distinctive character of Bakst's costumes. The style of this work, so remote from anything else Gaudier did, is worth comparing with two other stylistically individual works – *The Madonna* (*cat.* 9) and the 1914 *Blunt Coffer* (*cat.* 72). All three were commissioned and suggest Gaudier's readiness to adopt particular styles to meet the taste of his patron.

Dancer (*cat.* 58, pls. 68–70) and *Redstone Dancer* represent completely different approaches to the sculptural suggestion of movement. The bronze *Dancer* is an astonishing piece, dionysiac in its fluidity and physical abandon, untramelled by balletic conventions of dress and implying rather than describing the precise physical postures of ballet vocabulary. On the point of stepping off her circular plinth, she seems to embody a Bergsonian world of creative energy, constant flux, interractive rhythms and blurred temporal and spatial boundaries. Stanley Casson considered it as Gaudier's masterpiece and attributed to Gaudier 'a new style in modern sculpture':

> The 'Dancer' is a figure in which movement is detected rather than seen, and detected at a moment when it is neither static nor in motion, when it is potential and not yet stopped. No sculptor, to my knowledge, has ever depicted a figure thus *descending* out of one movement into another. Rodin's definition of movement as 'transition' is here carried out more clearly than he could ever have wished and more effectively than he could ever have achieved. There is no representation of motion here, only its full and direct expression.[9]

The uninhibited quality of movement the piece evokes may have been inspired by its model, the painter Nina Hamnett; the following year, after her return from Paris where she modelled for several artists, including Zadkine and Modigliani, she described dancing naked in the studios and attracting the attention of that apostle of free dance, Isadora Duncan.[10]

Memories of several sculptures may have played a part in the evolution of the pose. Prominent among the treasures of the Orléans Museum were bronzes of animals and figures from a Gallo-Roman hoard hidden towards the end of the third century at Neuvy-en-Sullias and discovered in 1861; one of the smaller pieces is a figurine of a nude dancer, long-bodied and with legs straddled, slightly bent, and arms flung wide.[11] Another much more recent and more likely source was a bronze nude, *Nan Seated* (fig. 80) by Epstein. One Sunday in November 1912 Gaudier had seen *Nan Seated* during a visit to Epstein's Cheyne Walk studio: 'he showed me a little bronze, very beautiful, quite the nicest work of his I have seen – alive and sincere – a seated woman with her arms above her head …'[12] Gaudier's *Dancer* develops the same basic pose with the arms enfolding and framing the head; the pose can also be compared with the bent-legged stance and upraised arms of the two nude women in *Woman Carrying Sacks* (*cat.* 40, pl. 40).

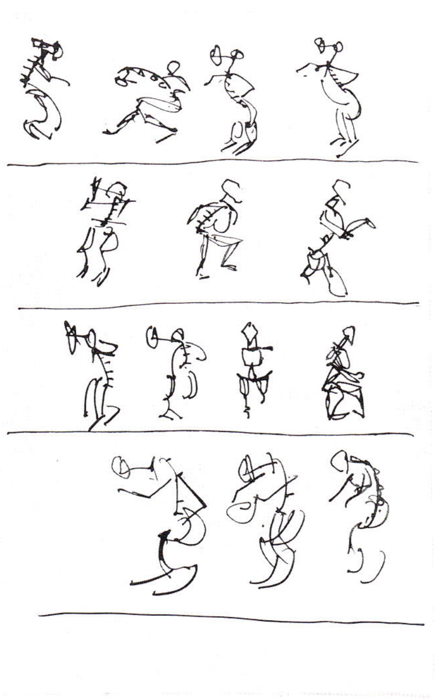

82 *Fourteen Figures in Movement*, 1913–14

Both *Dancer* and *Redstone Dancer* date from the autumn and winter of 1913–14; Gaudier was becoming friendly with Ezra Pound who had just been asked, on the strength of his expertise on Chinese and Japanese literature, to edit the papers of the great Oriental scholar, Ernest Fenollosa.[13] Gaudier's interest in Chinese culture was of long standing but it can hardly be entirely coincidental that a new graphic style of brush-drawn ideographs inspired by Chinese calligraphy made its appearance in Gaudier's work at this time. Several pen and brush drawings from a sketchbook, which apparently once belonged to Hamnett and may have been inspired by her, are rapid pictographs of sexless figures crouching, leaping and dancing (fig. 82).[14] On one level these drawings represent a return of interest in a linear graphic technique allied to a more conceptual and analytical approach to form. On another they signify a move away from 'sculptural drawings' towards a calligraphic vocabulary which asserts the two-dimensionality of the medium and the construction of the drawing as an independent entity. The figure second from the left in the top row is closely akin to a much rougher, more abandoned dancer in a brush drawing (pl. 95); this in turn is almost the reverse of a figure drawn with much greater precision and in a strongly primitivizing style (pl. 96) which anticipates *Redstone Dancer*.

Despite the brief time between the making of the two sculptures, the contrast in conception, mood, technique and attitude to material is extreme. As one recent commentator has put it, '*The Dancer* is an ember dying in the ashes of the old century, but *Red Stone Dancer* is a flame, angrily bursting into life to herald the beginning of the new order.'[15] In the *Dancer* Gaudier seems for once to have yielded to the seductive power of line almost at the expense of the figure's internal structure. In articulating his ideas on sculpture the previous year he had insisted that line is subsidiary, that it follows rather than preemptively defines the structural mass which it encloses. In *Redstone Dancer* the articulation of volumes and a far more conceptual approach to organic form dominates the composition. Both show figures in sinuous motion but the springy, supple poise of the bronze is superseded by the strenuous intensity and muscular bulk of the carving. It is an aggressive, virile piece, despite the ostensible femaleness of the breasts; the back, buttocks and upper arms are essentially masculine, their forms derived from male nude studies. A metamorphosis takes place in the transition from brush and ink drawings to the final sculpture; the figure in some of the preparatory drawings is slender and overtly female, but as Gaudier adopted a more Futurist vocabulary of re-iterated, overlapping forms the dancer's body becomes more enveloping and the movement of the limbs more geometricized and frenetic (pl. 94).[16]

In its treatment of material *Redstone Dancer* is utterly unlike the *Dancer*. In the latter the uninterrupted flow of the figure's modelling results in a wonderfully sensuous and sensual bronze, whereas *Redstone Dancer* is markedly free from sensual and erotic overtones; the smooth finish and waxing of the red Mansfield stone creates a slick, unmodulated surface. Attention is focused on the forms, their juxtaposition, rhythm and balance and not on the material qualities of the stone. The figure has been constructed by balancing masses placed in relation with one another to create a rhythmic sequence and four surprising viewpoints; the front view with its cluster of detailed elements – flipper hands, triangle features, circle and elongated circle on the breasts – contrasts sharply with the smoothly flowing convex expanse of the back.

Redstone Dancer has always been recognized as one of Gaudier's most important works; when it was exhibited at the Grafton Gallery in January 1914, T. E. Hulme praised Gaudier's sculptures and a work by William Roberts as the only things worth seeing.[17] Pound wrote in the preface for the *Memorial Exhibition* catalogue in 1918:

> [it] is almost a thesis of his ideas upon the use of pure form. We have the triangle and the circle asserted, *labled* [sic] almost, upon the face and right breast. Into these so-called 'abstractions' life flows, the circle moves and elongates into the oval, it increases and takes volume in the sphere or hemisphere of the breast. The triangle moves towards organism it becomes a spherical triangle (the central life-form common to both Brzeska and Lewis). These two developed motifs work as themes in a fugue. We have the whole series of spherical triangles, as in the arm over the head, all combining and culminating in the great sweep of the back of the shoulders, as fine as any surface in all sculpture. The 'abstract' or mathematical bareness of the triangle and circle are fully incarnate, made flesh, full of vitality and of energy. The whole form-series ends, passes into stasis with the circular base or platform.[18]

Pound has been followed by later commentators: for Levy it perfectly demonstrates 'the principle of inventive geometric simplification' and 'foreshadows … the ultimate breakdown of the cubist-abstract idiom as exemplified by the later works of Zadkine and Lipchitz'.[19] However, it is the very diversity of the echoes *Redstone Dancer* contains which makes its synthesis the more remarkable. Richard Cork, while seeing the work as 'a decisive moment' when Gaudier 'puts eclecticism on one side and embraces the new geometrical art propounded by Hulme', has identified a complex amalgam of influences from Futurist simultaneity to Indian multi-armed sculpture and Brancusi's bronze *Sleeping Muse* (1910) exhibited at London Salon.[20] Lewison cites the provocative element in this work, of measuring up to Epstein and Brancusi, a view strongly supported by an important passage in *Matka*: the account centres on Brzeska's reaction to drawings Gaudier had just brought from the studio and which showed his new, more abstract style. 'Your men have Brancusi egg-heads', Brzeska objected, while Gaudier replied that he was now only going to do sculpture like that, and had already begun 'an abstract sculpture in red stone that you've seen.' Told by Sophie that the work would be unsaleable, he retorted that Epstein and Brancusi could sell theirs. Three Brancusis had been included at the Allied Artists' show at the Albert Hall in July and Brancusi himself had been there. 'All Gaudier did was run after Epstein and Brancusi', complained Brzeska.[21]

For other commentators the dominant characteristic of *Redstone Dancer* is the 'primitive' intensity of the figure and its bent-kneed posture.[22] The features and pointed breast in the conté crayon drawing (pl. 96) do indicate 'primitive' influence but these elements are eliminated from the sculpture and a vigorous torsion replaces the crouching stance

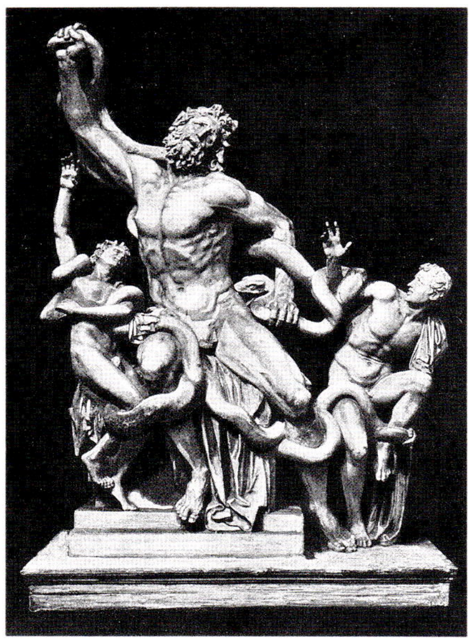

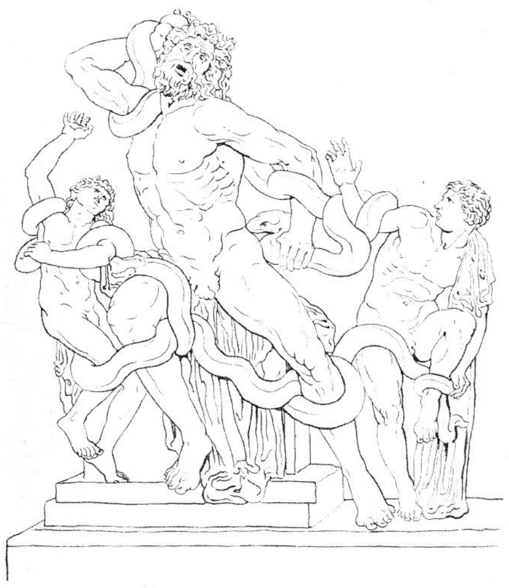

83 *Laocöon* reconstructed from *L'Illustration*, 16.6.06

84 Henri Matisse, *La Danse*, 1909

of the drawing.[23] It can be read as a riposte both to the simplification of movement in 'primitive' sculpture and to the totemic symmetry of Epstein's recent primitivistic carvings such as *Female Figure in Flenite* (fig. 90). The exaggerated twisting posture and its strenuous counter-movements recall works which Gaudier had ostensibly rejected – Michelangelo's *Dying Slave* and even the complex dynamism of late classical and Hellenistic works such as the *Laocoön* group.

A few months later, Gaudier drafted a letter attacking 'the Greeks' as part of his literary battle with Richard Aldington in the pages of *The Egoist*; in an unpublished portion of the letter he compared the *Laocöon* unfavourably with Epstein's *Female Figure in Flenite* – 'entangled bodies with no meaning save an unimportant perfection of muscles.'[24] Gaudier's familiarity with this famous Antique work probably went back to his youth in Orléans. *Laocoön* was one of the best known of all ancient sculptures but it also became news in 1906, when a sharply bent antique marble arm was excavated in Rome. It was thought to belong to the *Laocoön* and prompted renewed discussion about the sculpture's original appearance (fig. 83). Although the sculpture was not actually reconstructed with the 'new' arm until years later, a press report in the popular magazine *L'Illustration* showed the two versions side by side and provided a commentary on the implications of the altered composition:

> the position of the right arm, bent towards the head balances the lines better and gives the group more character through the pyramid composition thus achieved; further, the position is more natural, less rhetorical one might say; it expresses sorrow more intensely.[25]

L'Illustration was one of the principal illustrated magazines accessible to Gaudier through his local library in Orléans. If the work did not come to his attention then it is likely to have done so during his stay with the Uhlemayrs in Nuremberg when classical art was a subject for study and discussion with his host. Gaudier was not alone among his contemporaries in adopting the classical motif of the arm enclosing the head; one finds it in the sculpture of Matisse and Archipenko among others, but in

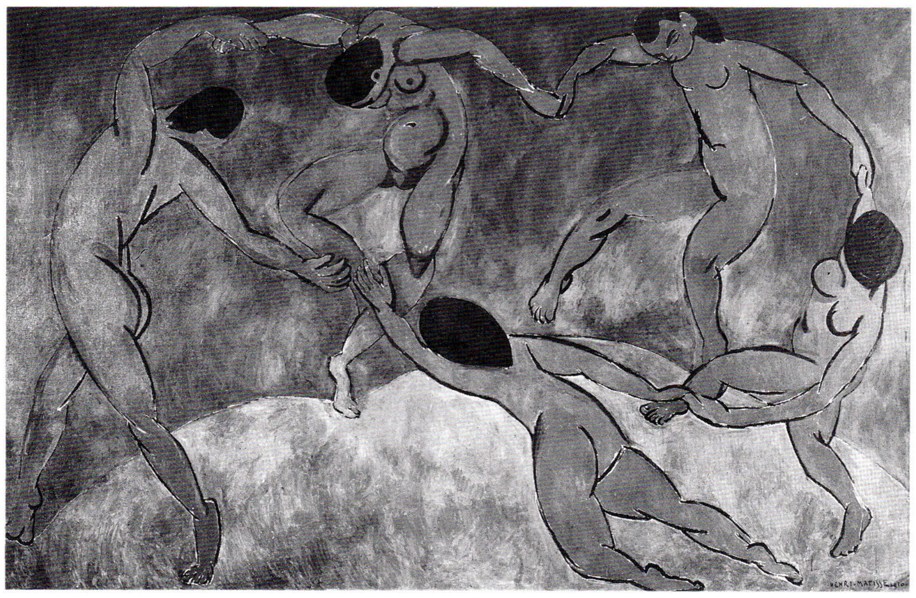

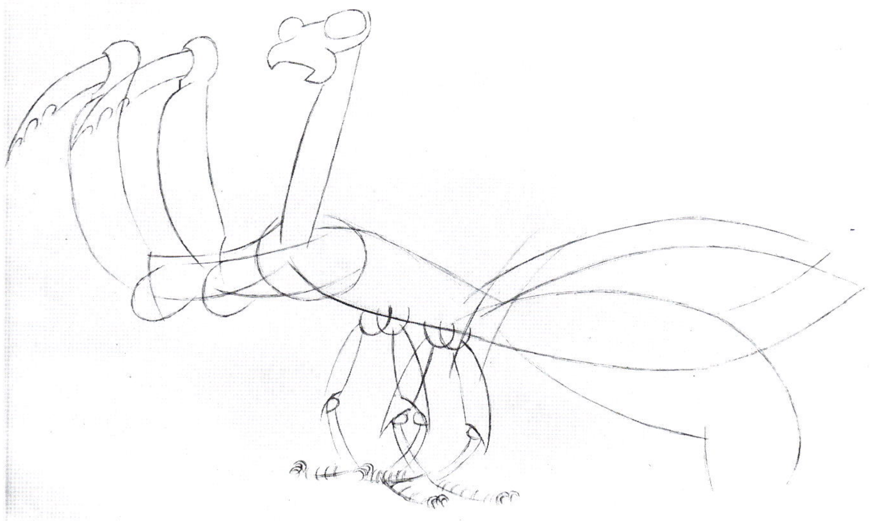

85 *Satirical Futurist Drawing*, 1913–14

Redstone Dancer this motif is combined with the expressive intensity conveyed through the figure's twisting pose and the syncopated compositional energy of the legs in a manner which is so reminiscent of *Laocoön* that a direct connection seems possible. The elaborate contrapposto of *Redstone Dancer* and the smooth shaped back can be seen as part of Gaudier's recurrent dialogue with the multi-facetted classical tradition while its formal simplification and arrogant manipulation of anatomy in the service of an abstract definition of sculptural composition seems to embody the birth pangs of modernism.

One of the best known of the preparatory drawings for *Redstone Dancer* (pl. 94) suggests the violent rhythms of the dance through a Futurist series of three superimposed variants. Work by the Futurists was well known in London by late 1913, since work by Boccioni, Carrà, Russolo, Severini and others had been included in an Exhibition of Work by Italian Futurist Painters at the Sackville Gallery in March 1912 and, with the help of Marinetti's irrepressible presence, achieved a huge amount of press coverage. Marinetti made several visits to London during 1913–14 and his showmanship and the stridently progandist typographical flourish of Russian and Italian Futurist publications greatly influenced Lewis and Pound in the evolution of the Rebel Art Centre and *Blast*. With their common interests in urban life, non-organic, geometric imagery, and the machismo of their group culture, Wyndham Lewis and the nascent Vorticists had much in common with the Futurists while needing also to assert their separate identity and thus their differences from them.[26] In June 1914, when the Futurists again had a major display of their works on show at the Doré Gallery, Gaudier played a prominent role in barracking Marinetti at one of his Futurist demonstrations.[27] His review of the London Salon the following month included a brusque dismissal of Futurism as 'impressionism using false weapons', and of their syncopated overlapping images as 'banal'.[28] A humorous drawing, dateable to 1913–14, of a curious beast, perhaps a praying mantis, satirizes this practice (fig. 85). However, Gaudier had not been above using some of the same techniques himself. The preparatory drawings for *Redstone Dancer* and several sketchbook drawings related to it deploy the Futurists' technique of syncopated, sequential images to suggest dynamic intensity.

In other works contemporary with *Redstone Dancer*, movement is not so much suggested as symbolized in a new graphic language of stiff bulbous limbs and 'flipper' hands and feet delineated with overlapping, painstakingly accurate thin pen lines which desensualize and subvert Gaudier's graphic exuberance (pl. 88). In the absence of ground line or internal modelling one is forced to an awareness of the action of the pen on an expanse of paper. It is reminiscent of the black contours of Matisse's *La Danse*, 1910 (Hermitage Museum, St Petersburg; fig. 84) and other Fauvist works included in the Second Post-Impressionist Exhibition which exerted such an influence on the work of Duncan Grant and the Omega artists. In Gaudier's work it can be seen as a counterpoint to the far more calligraphic spontaneity of the Chinese brush drawings he was producing at the same time. Both techniques encouraged extreme simplification of contour into soft gradual curves and straight lines and presage the abstract geometric arcs and angles of the Vorticist drawings.

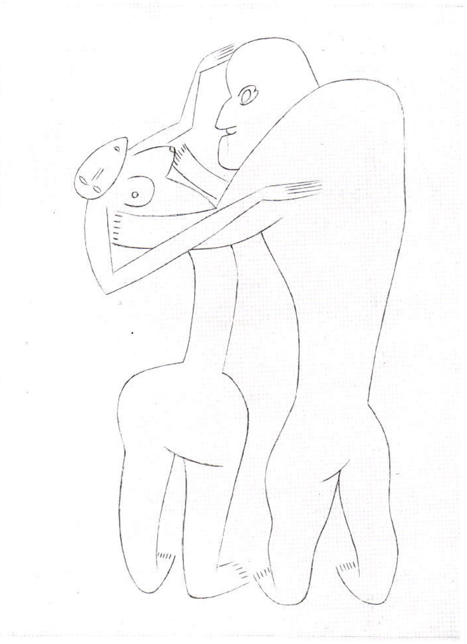

86 *Man and Woman*, 1913–14

The grappling *Wrestlers* (pl. 88), though bulky and tautly outlined, are no longer the straining, sweaty figures of the gymnasium but a flat choreography of interlaced arms and legs, more grace than grit. Even where works carry disturbing overtones of violence, as in the drawing *Man and Woman* (fig. 86), the gestures have an abstracted quality, with both action and emotion stylized and distanced. One senses a tension between the artist's impulses to observe and illustrate on the one hand and to compose autonomously on the other (fig. 87). During 1914, Gaudier's formal language, though still organically based, became increasingly geometric, formally analytical and abstracted but this did not lead to the static, somewhat lifeless forms characteristic of the figure and still-life Cubist carvings of Lipchitz and Laurens. The warmth, cruelty and dynamism of animal existence remained at the heart of his work.

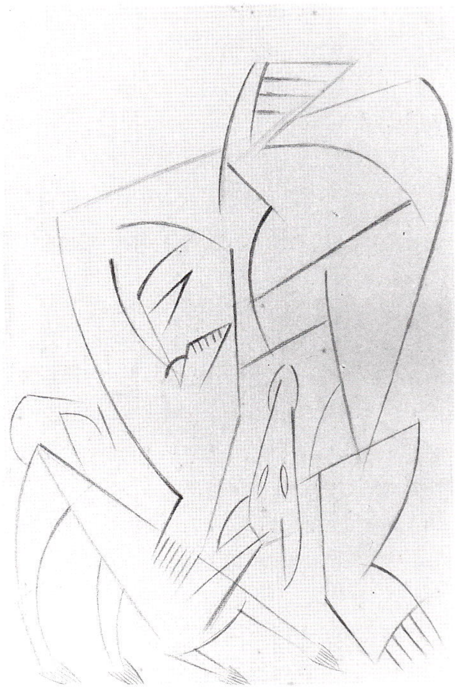

87 *Man and Dog*, *c.* 1914

12

'WE the moderns'

The summer of 1913 represented a watershed in Gaudier's activity; once he had left Wulfsberg's he had time to work as intensively as he wished. Exhibiting at the London Salon and making new contacts – with Pound, Hamnett, Fry, Gertler, Marsh and others – opened up a choice of artistic directions and signalled his emergence as a vanguard talent recognized by his peers. However, his relationship with individuals and groups was exceptionally complex; he often seems to have played one group off against the other to his own advantage, criticizing the Rebel Art Centre artists to Fry and the Omega artists to Lewis. Each friendship, each momentary allegiance acted as a whetstone to sharpen his own talent. It made him an exhilarating, infuriating and abrasive colleague. In the last resort his only allegiance was to his own work and he was still unsure of his direction. He only made a commitment to Lewis's Rebel Art Centre and the nascent Vorticist group in the late spring of 1914, remaining on friendly terms with Omega artists and with Walter Sickert's Fitzroy Street circle during the autumn and winter of 1913–14.

During that final year he devoted himself almost exclusively to drawing and carving, and a more mature artistic personality emerges for whom the autonomy of the work of art is a paramount concern. Though the impact of others – Pound, Epstein, Hulme and Brancusi – was still perceptible, he was increasingly able to subsume the lessons of their work into his own. Formally a greater unity of purpose becomes apparent – the creation of a consistent, non-naturalistic language based on organic forms. However, despite the anti-classical rhetoric of his writing, he continued to draw inspiration from the sensuous naturalism of the classical tradition to create the *Torsos* (*cat.* 59–61), *Seated Woman* (*cat.* 105) and *Mlle Borne* (*cat.* 106).

Gaudier had spent the earlier part of his career freely evoking individual character and psychological states as a satirist and portrait sculptor; carved heads such as *Head of a Young Man* (*cat.* 44), *Head of a Child* (*cat.* 22, pl. 19) and *Samson and Delilah* (*cat* 57, pls. 66–67), and reliefs such as *Man and Woman* (*cat.* 38), reveal him moving towards greater impersonality, facial expression masked in an enigmatic smile reminiscent of the heads of *kouroi* in pre-Phideian sculpture. The head and limbs become increasingly integrated as compositional elements without recognizable meaning in expression and gesture. Facial features are further reduced to a Brancusian economy of form, a triangle or emblematically abbreviated eyes, nose and mouth signposting the head.

The head itself loses its psychological and physical primacy. In *Maternity* (*cat.* 64, pl. 83) the female's bent head is absorbed into the core of the oval composition; raised arms enclose and frame the heads of the *Dancer* (*cat.* 58, pls. 68–70) and the alabaster *Boy* (*cat.* 56, pl. 75). The composition of *Boy with a Coney* (*cat.* 76, pl. 104) seems to have begun with a drawing of a standing figure with a cat upon his shoulder; in the final sculpture the ovoid form of the nestling rabbit echoes the boy's head so that their paired masses balance the feet of the kneeling figure.[1] Compositional integration is carried still further in *Redstone Dancer* where the arm is extended to anchor the head into the shoulders so that the triangular relief of the face becomes one of the grouped motifs in the larger pyramid of the figure's upper torso; at the same time the enfolding arm carries upwards and contains the energy and rotational movement of the composition. A similar transformation is apparent in the static pose but, nevertheless, remarkably dynamic composition of *Caritas* (*cat.* 75, pls. 108–9); the head, sunk into the upper torso, is completely enclosed by the abstracted form of the arms which create a powerful rotational rhythm to terminate the upward thrust supplied by the suckling children and balance the mother's lower body.[2]

Beyond the still fluctuating and evolving styles of Gaudier's work is a singleness of purpose. The flattened tubular interlace of *Wrestlers Relief* (*cat.* 66, pl. 87), the increasingly monumental volumes of *Redstone Dancer*, *Caritas* and *Seated Woman* are explorations of the figure in terms of the relation of masses. Legs are enlarged, folded, the feet integrated into the block or merely signalled by parallel striations of geometric simplicity. In *Imp* (*cat.* 78, pl. 110) they almost disappear leaving a tripartite convex column.

The shift away from the directly observed reality towards autonomous formal languages is parallelled and even anticipated in the drawings. In both media the evolution of a new and more rigorously thought through method of constructing a sculpture or drawing entailed the suppression of his natural virtuosity, his 'manual finesse' as Elsen has described it.[3] He evolved during late 1913–14 several distinct but complementary graphic styles which he used for sketches and compositional studies increasingly distanced from life drawing. These styles, though in themselves original, grew out of Gaudier's wide-ranging knowledge of ancient and non-European art forms – the paintings of the Font-de-Gaume cave in the Dordogne, the expressive brush marks of Chinese calligraphy, Oceanic carvings in the British Museum. They also connect, to a lesser extent, with the strong stylized contours characteristic of designs produced by the Omega artists, notably Duncan Grant and Vanessa Bell, and, later, with the more geometric and aggressively abstracted graphic work of Wyndham Lewis, William Roberts, Edward Wadsworth and Jacob Epstein.

IX Portrait of Ezra Pound (*cat.* 94)

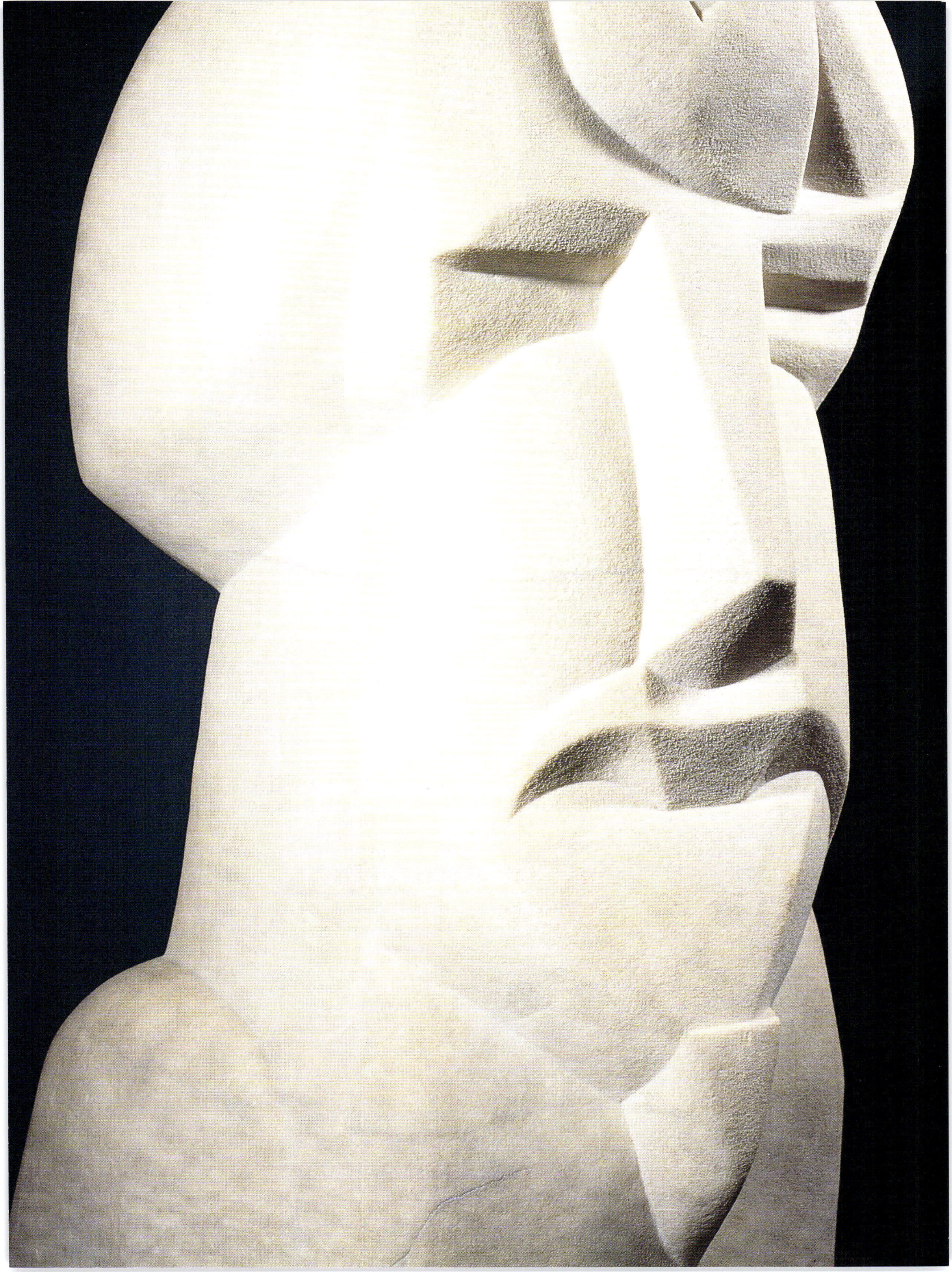

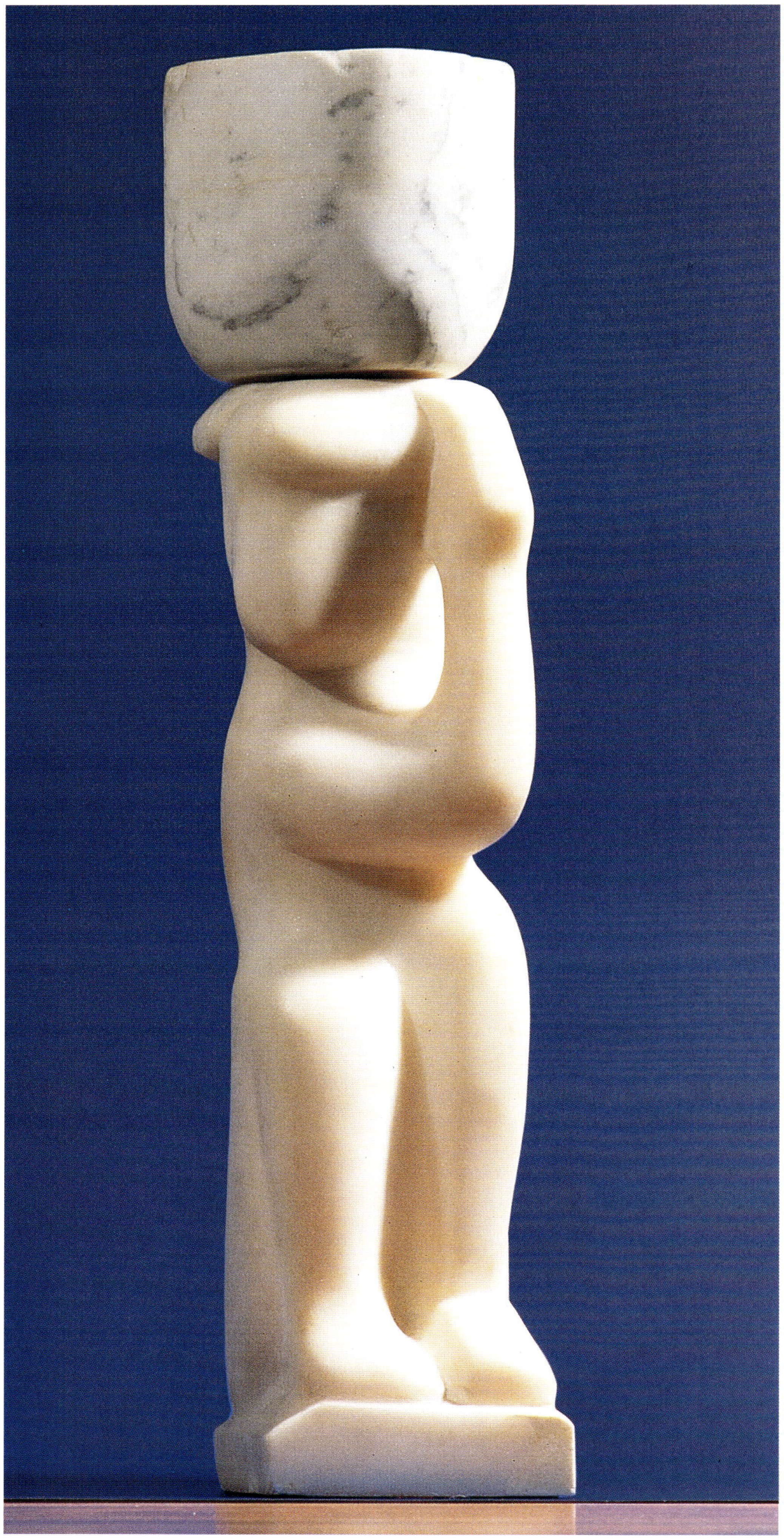

X Water Carrier (*cat.* 74)

XI Redstone Dancer (*cat.* 69)

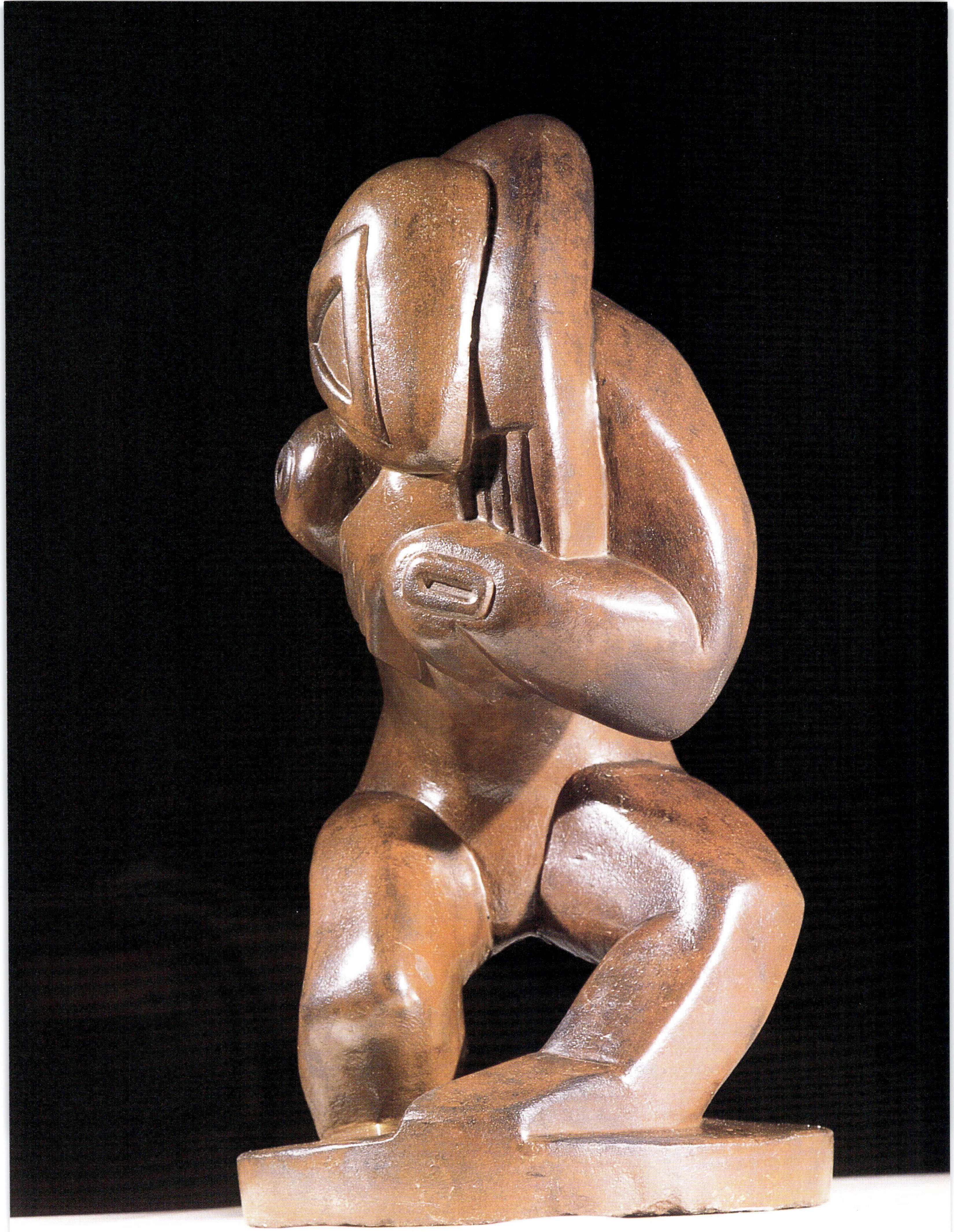

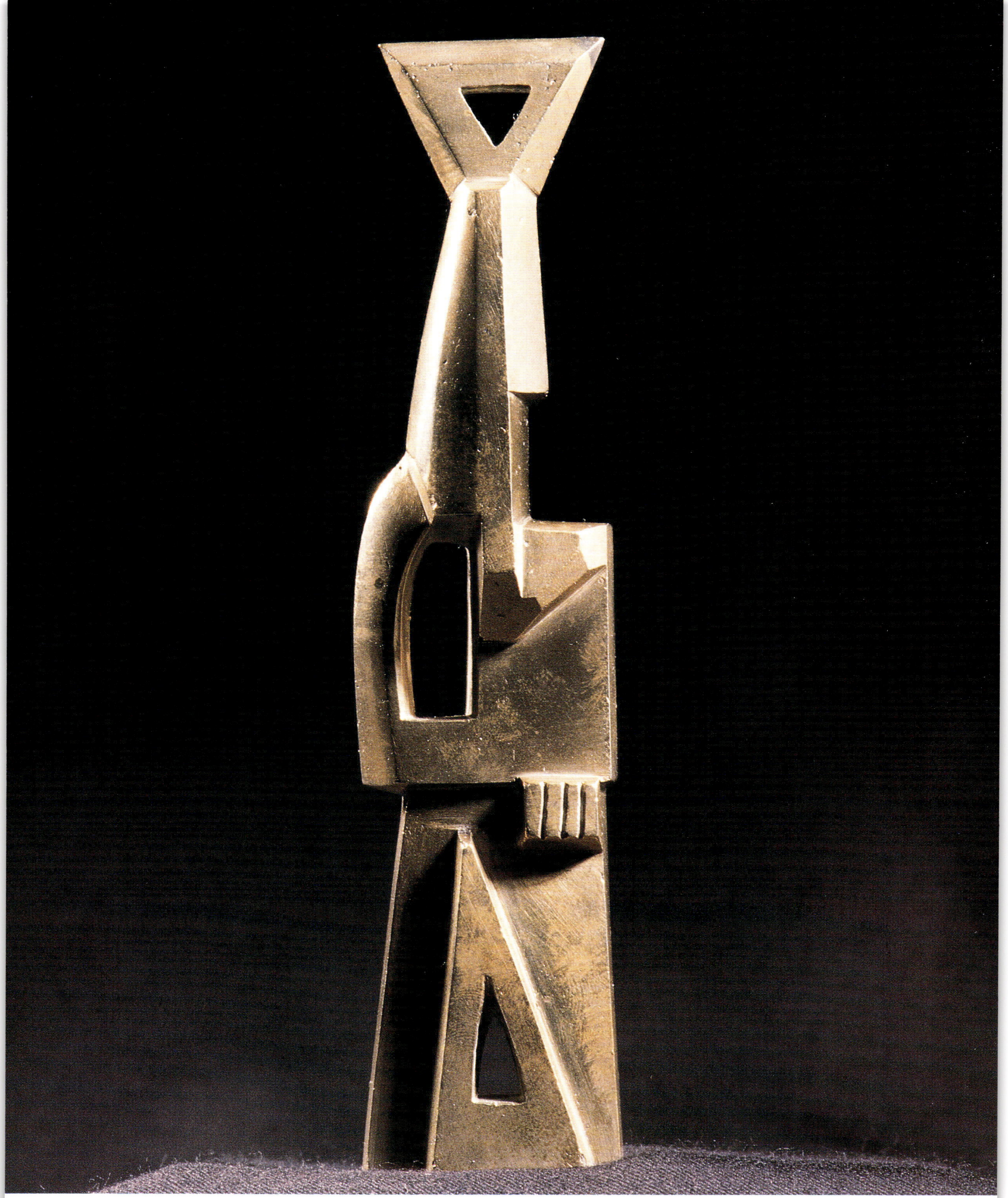

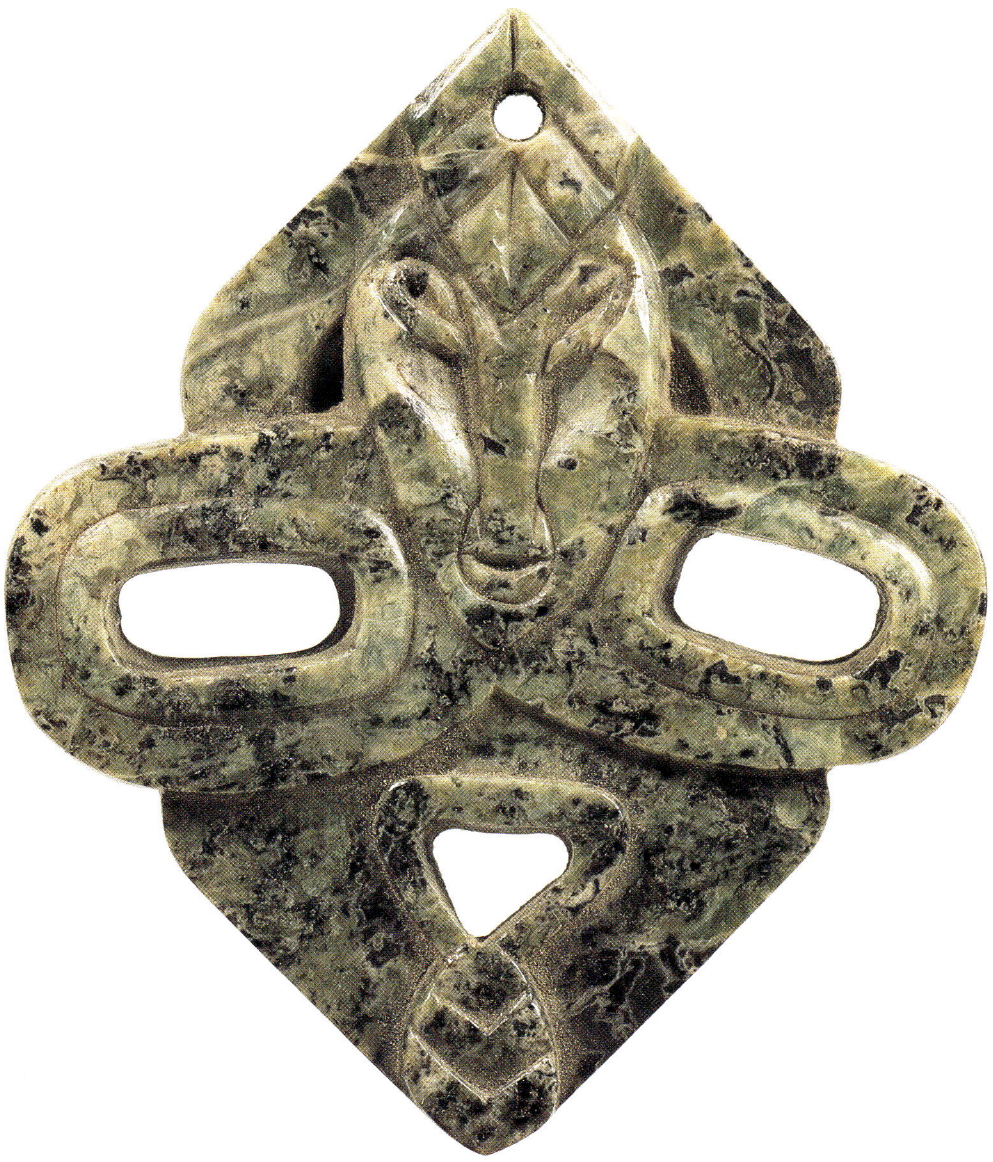

XIII Green Stone Charm (*cat.* 85)

XII Torpedo Fish (*cat.* 80)

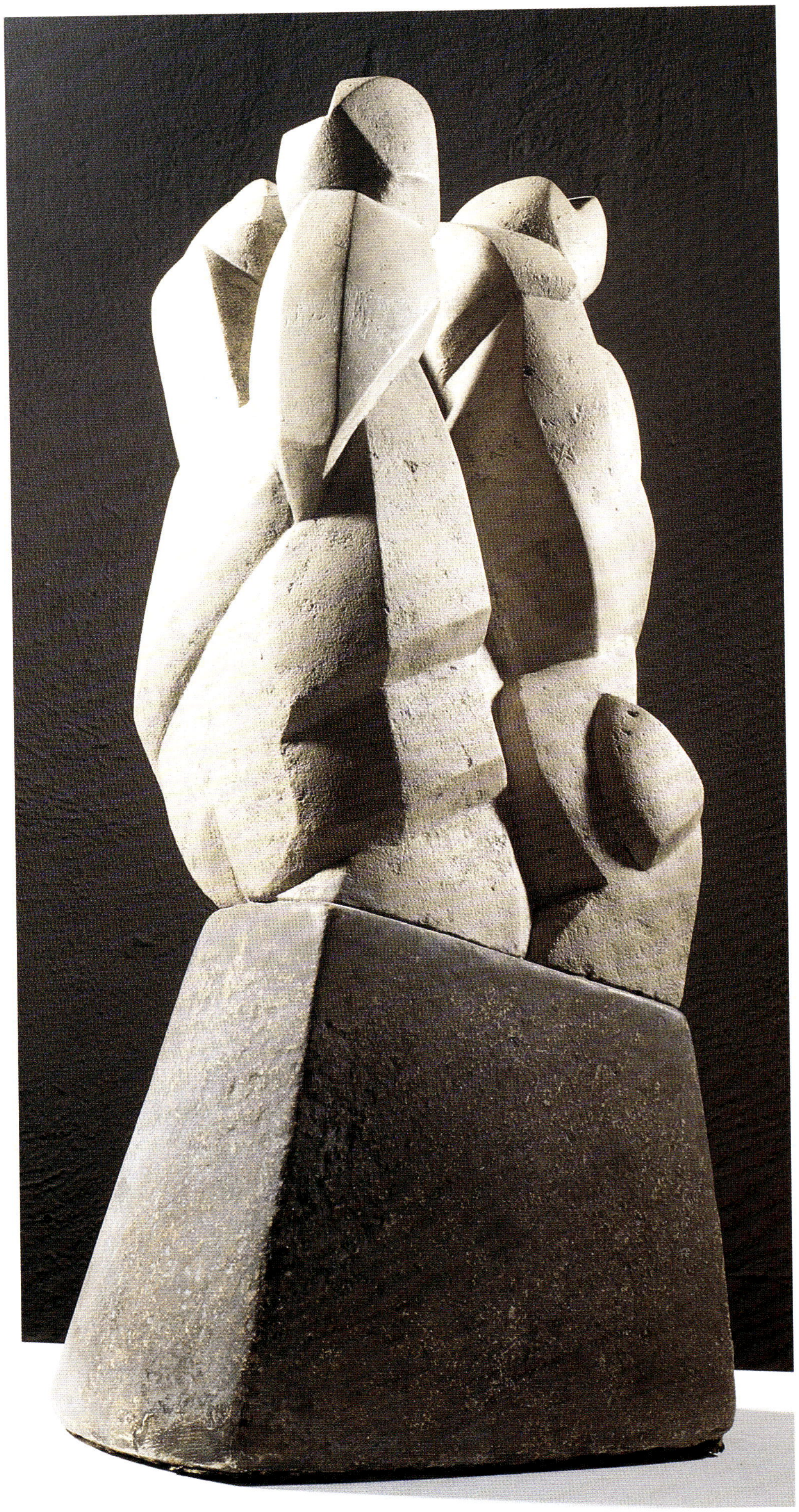

XIV Birds Erect
(*cat.* 107)

XV Seated Woman
(*cat.* 105)

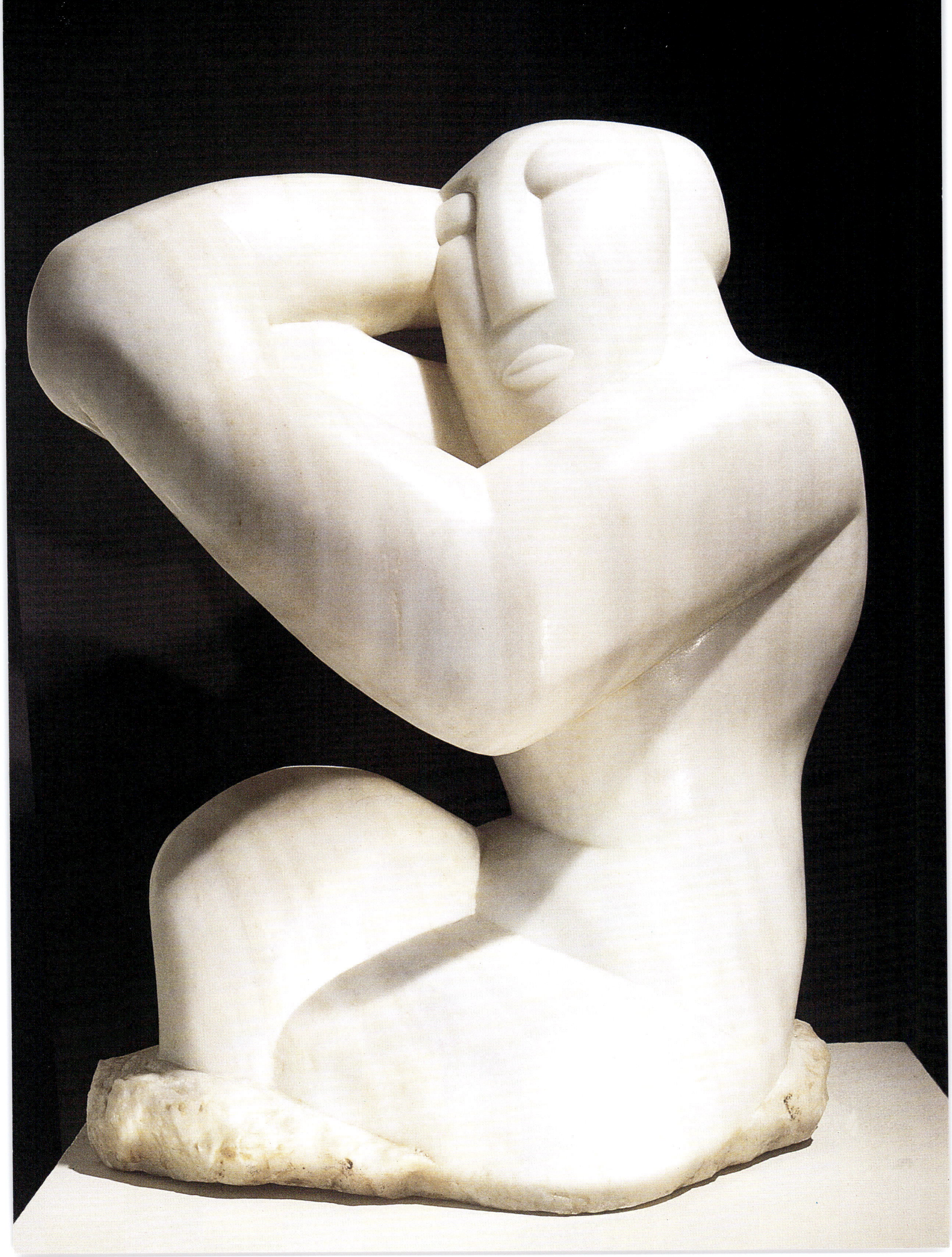

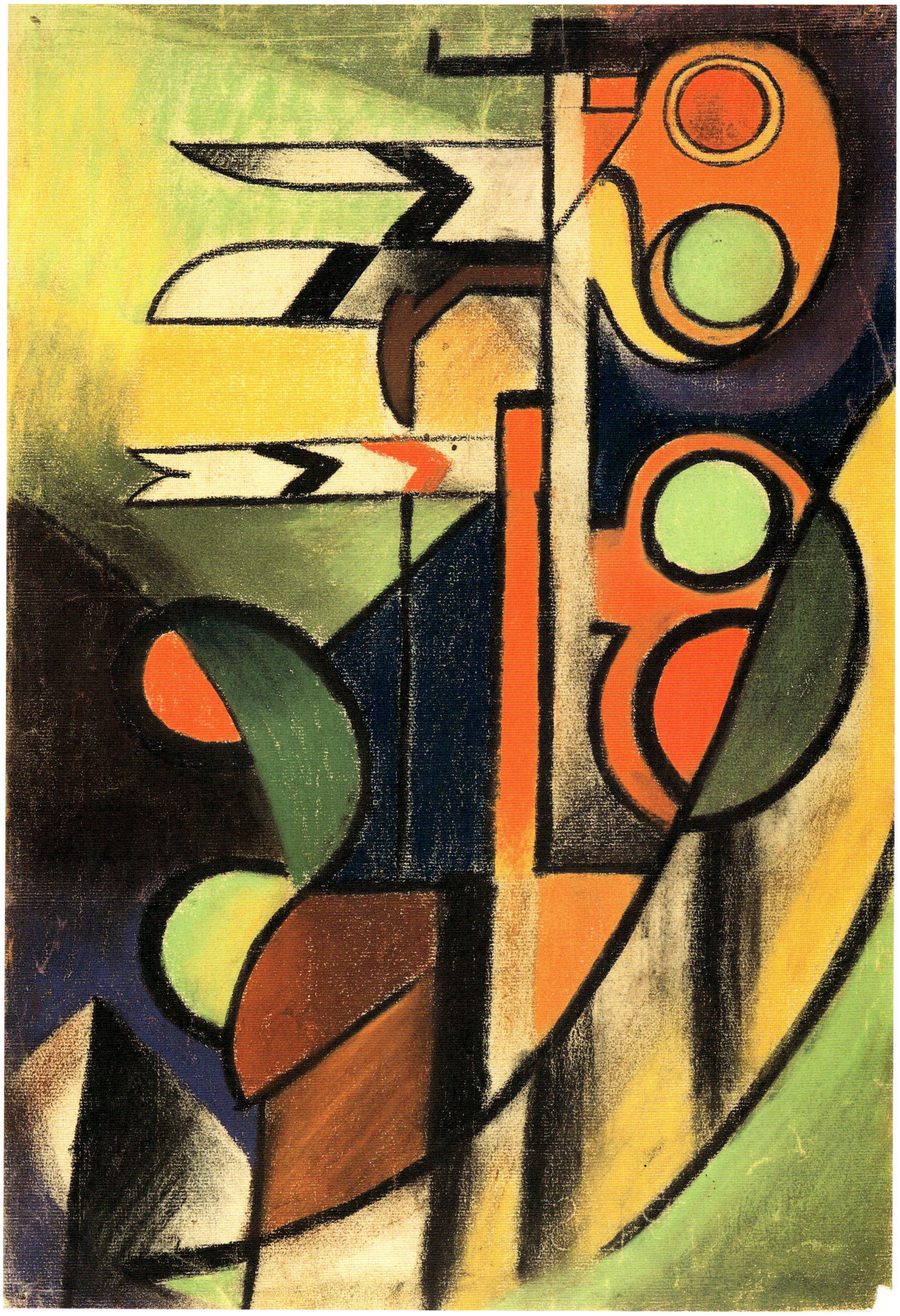

13

The Omega Workshops

THE EXACT nature of Gaudier's association with the Omega Workshops remains elusive though his amicable contact with Fry and the men and women employed at 33 Fitzroy Square lasted about nine months. Since it seems he was only an occasional visitor and did little, if any, work there the communal workshop ethos central to the enterprise was lost on him. He never appears to have been on such close terms of friendship with any of the Omega crowd as he managed to remain with Camden Town painters such as Gilman, Bevan and de Karlowska. Since the group operated relatively quietly there were no opportunities for him to make any grand gestures of support as he subsequently did for the Rebel Art Centre. When the opportunity did arise to comment on the Omega 'lounge' during his review of the Allied Artists' Salon in June 1914, his admiration for the subtlety of the carpet, inlaid tables, trays and pottery, is tempered by faint praise, as he rejected the 'prettiness' of Omega pieces in favour of the 'great strength and manliness in decoration' shown by the Rebel Art stand, and, still worse, greeted Lewis's abstractions *Night Attack* and *Signalling* as 'the start of a new evolution in painting'.[1]

His most obvious motive for joining them was financial since Fry's support, solicited by Nina Hamnett, gave him access to materials, possibly small advances and, most important, a space where his work could be seen by prospective clients, even if he did lose 25 per cent in Omega's commission on any sales. Several of his more naturalistic sculptures of 1913 – the alabaster *Boy* (*cat.* 56), *Crouching Fawn* (*cat.* 62), *Maternity* (*cat.* 64), the marble *Cat* (*cat.* 70), *Water Carrier* (*cat.* 74) and the challenging *Redstone Dancer* (*cat.* 69) – were shown for the first time at the Grafton Group exhibition in January 1914 but as Collins has remarked, 'Gaudier's talents as a sculptor and draughtsman did not fit too easily into the design activities of the Omega'.[2] His work was compared with that of other sculptors rather than being seen as part of the Workshop:

> Mr Gill's work at the Goupil Gallery, like the carving of Mr Gaudier-Brzeska and of Mr Roger Fry at the Alpine Club, will probably be classed in the public mind as of the 'Epstein' School, not because that artist is the originator of a phase of art which, indeed, is rather an archaistic reversion than an innovation, but because Mr Epstein came earlier into prominence, and gained recognition of his power of interpreting natural forms before he adopted his present extreme simplicity of design.[3]

Fawn was sold and *Redstone Dancer* taken back by Gaudier, but the remainder were deposited at Fitzroy Square for sale.[4] Fry himself was the first owner of *Boy* and also commissioned the *Maquette for a Bird Bath* (*cat.* 71) for his home, Durbins near Guildford, where there were already murals by Grant, Bell, a garden sculpture by Eric Gill and other treasures, notably *Mlle Pogany* by Brancusi. Two of Gaudier's last unfinished works – the two flower vases for which only maquettes were produced (*cat.* 99,

XVI Signals, pastel

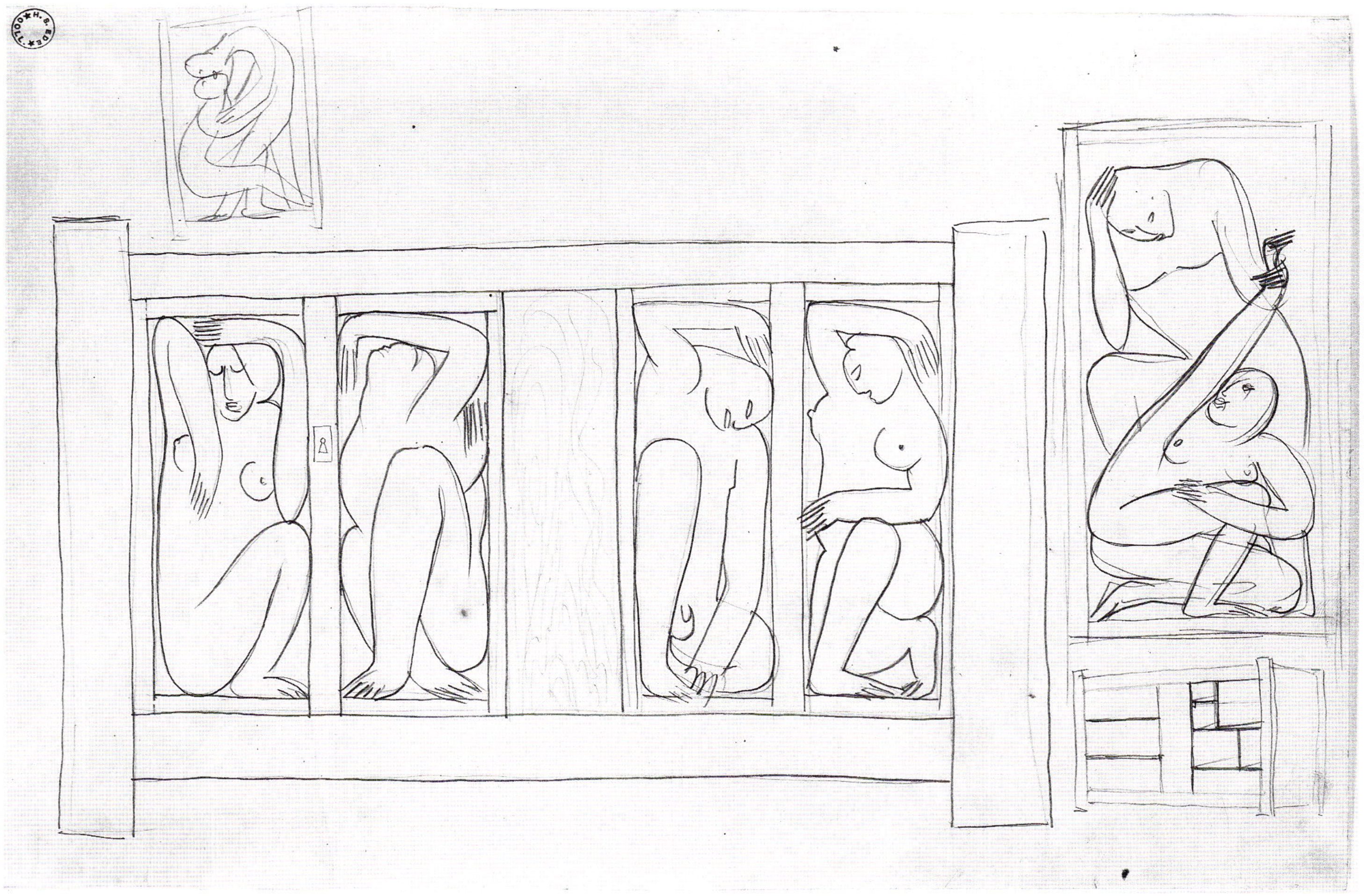

88 *Design for a Decorated Cupboard*, 1913–14

100) were intended for Lady Ian Hamilton, one of the original backers of the Omega Workshops; although Gaudier had separated from Omega by the summer of 1914 he appears to have continued to attempt to work on these vases until shortly before his return to France.

However, the wide-ranging decorative activities of the Omega and their relaxed experimental attitude to the design of furnishings rekindled Gaudier's former interest in applied design. Even before his arrival in London and during his first months in England he had prepared numerous decorative projects which had proved unacceptable to potential clients and employers. He had grasped the opportunity to decorate Lovat Fraser's studio complete with *Ornamental Mask* (*cat.* 31) and *Cheetah* (*cat.* 26). He had made tile designs. He had also witnessed the wild efflorescence of primitivizing design and colour with which Gore, Ginner, Lewis, Gill and Epstein had responded to the decoration of Madame Strindberg's Cabaret Theatre Club during the summer of 1912.[5] He had probably seen or heard about some of the other decorative interiors with nude, animal and still life themes already produced by Grant and Bell. Pastels using an intense palette of blues, green, yellows, oranges and strong black contours, like *Study of Cauliflower on a Table*, seem to reflect his response to Grant's work.[6] Even if Gaudier remained diffident about his ability as a painter, he can have been in little doubt of his capacity to undertake large-scale drawings of figures of nudes, animals and plants such as adorned the screens, chimney pieces and furniture already produced by Grant and Bell.[7]

The sketchbooks and other drawings dateable to 1913–14 contain designs for two- or three-dimensional decoration (fig. 80). One of the graphic styles developed during the autumn of 1913, with convex, fine pen contours, lent itself particularly well either to painting or to low-relief carving in wood or plaster as revealed by the kinship between drawings related to the *Wrestlers* relief, (*cat.* 66, pl. 88, fig. 89), his drawings for the *Marquetry Tray* (*cat.* 67) and a design for a painted or carved cupboard (fig. 88).[8] The increasingly autonomous character of Gaudier's designs did not in these instances lead him towards abstraction but rather to primitivism infused with the memories of classical poses. The gracefully crouching nudes, posed like caryatids, in the Omega cupboard design converted with equal ease to a design for a wooden *Newel Post* (*cat.* 68, pl. 85) and foreshadow one of the preparatory drawings for one of his last and most classical works, *Seated Woman* (*cat.* 105, pls. 154–56). The architectural strength and oppositional character of the *Wrestlers* relief has been transmuted in the preparatory drawings for the *Marquetry Tray* into a more ambiguous pairing, the rhythmically undulating figures suggesting harmony rather than conflict.

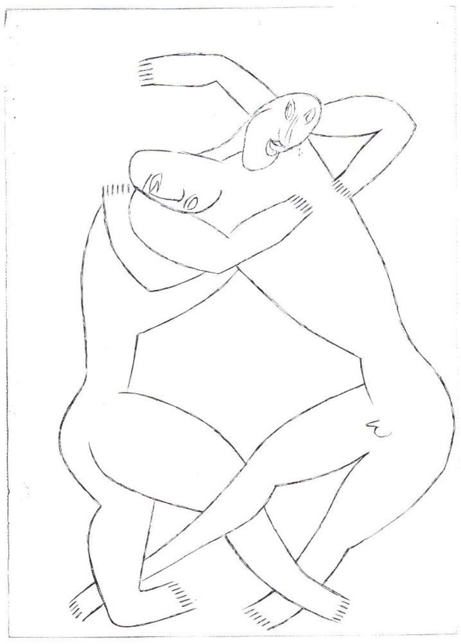

89 *Wrestlers*, 1913–14

The uncluttered decorative balance of these works and their formal ingenuity makes one regret that so few of Gaudier's ideas for applied decoration came to fruition. In addition to the charming ceramic *Cat* (*cat.* 65, pl. 103), there are also witty (if not altogether practical) designs for a 'singing woman' jug and for a number of Chinese and African-inspired ceramics with animal and wrestler designs[9]. Still more lightheartedly he seems to have painted animals in gouache on an Omega box.[10] There was to be an equally playful element in the 'toys' and 'ornaments' he carved for Hulme, Lewis and other friends associated with the Rebel Art centre.

However, Hulme and Pound's preoccupation with intensity of expression and the aggressively heterosexual exuberance of the Rebel Art Centre presented an increasingly sharp contrast with the Omega. Primitivistic themes were common to artists in both groups but Epstein's primitivism was wide-ranging and direct, embracing the formal volumes, radically transformed proportions and themes of procreation and birth. The slightly haphazard amateurism and technical shortcomings of Omega productions may have jarred on Gaudier's rigorous sense of craftsmanship. It probably went against the grain of his beliefs about direct carving to have to make maquettes in plaster for translation into another medium. Socially, too, Gaudier had far more in common with the intellectual, cosmopolitan, déclassé men of the Rebel Art Centre than with the more decorously English, Bloomsbury atmosphere of Fry's circle. A further important factor in Gaudier's relative detachment was that he was a sculptor rather than a painter. However responsive he was to the graphic influence of Cézanne and Matisse filtered through the work of Bell and Fry, it was other sculptors, above all Epstein and Brancusi, and Hulme, who was speaking and writing about sculpture as a vanguard medium for modern art, with whom he had a stronger kinship.

14

Gaudier, Epstein and Brancusi

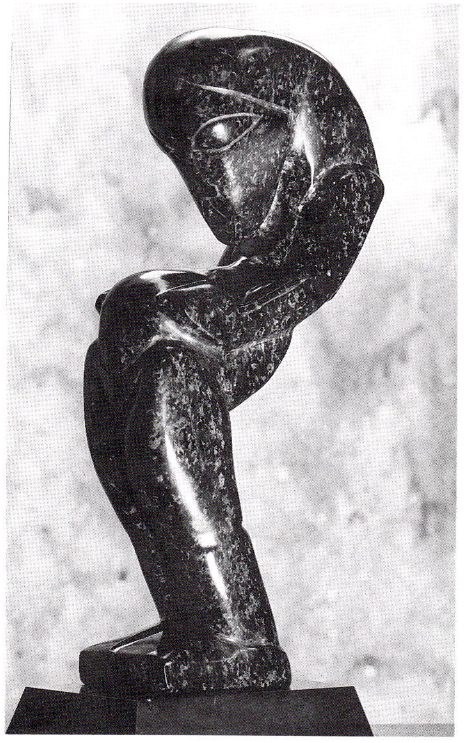

90 Jacob Epstein, *Female Figure in Flenite*, 1913. Exhibited at the London Salon, July 1913

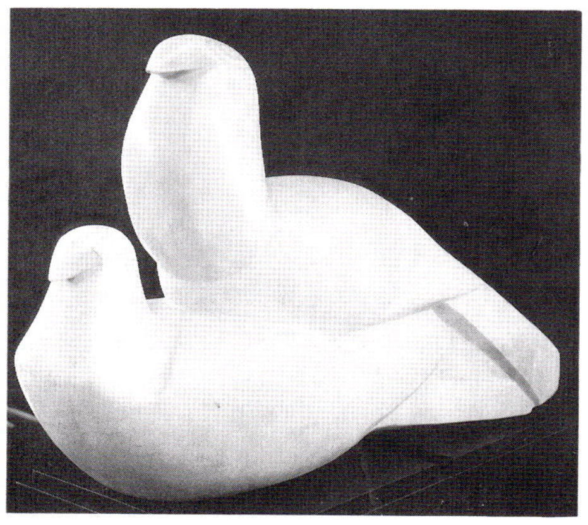

91 Jacob Epstein, *Doves 2*, 1913

Epstein remained and Brancusi became central figures for Gaudier as a modernist sculptor. Brancusi's work was known to him primarily through Epstein who had become friendly with him during his visits to Paris in 1912–13 to install the *Tomb of Oscar Wilde*. Brancusi's habit of working in series, progressively refining the lucidity of his forms, exercized a profound influence on Epstein's practice during 1913–14. He abandoned the detailed surface treatment of the stone which Gaudier had criticized in the Tomb, producing during 1913–15 series of carved pieces – three versions of his copulating marble *Doves*, two versions of *Venus* in marble, a relief and two pregnant female figures in serpentine called *Figures in Flenite*. All were characterized by simplified forms and sexually explicit themes carved direct in smoothly finished hard stone.[1]

Gaudier encountered the full impact of the latest direct carving at the Allied Artists' Salon in the Albert Hall in June 1913. Not only was Epstein showing the s-shaped *Female Figure in Flenite* (fig. 90), but Brancusi was exhibiting three pieces – *Sleeping Muse* in bronze (fig. 93), a stone sculpture and a bronze head. These were hailed by Fry as the most important pieces in the exhibition.[2] Both the bronzes were sold and the stone piece was retained and included in the Post-Impressionist Exhibition at the Doré Galleries. Though Gaudier had been carving for the previous six months all the pieces he was showing were bronze portraits and figures. Some, like the cubistic *Alfred Wolmark* and the powerful *Wrestler*, were daring when compared with most contemporary modelling (as is reflected in the dismissive press reports), but they were comparatively tame beside the formal radicalism of Epstein's and Brancusi's carvings. His excitement at seeing the work and at meeting Brancusi, who came over to London for the show, is reflected by Brzeska who complained that Gaudier had spent all his time 'running after Epstein and Brancusi'.[3]

Only a couple of months later, after visiting Epstein's London studio at a garage in Lamb's Conduit Street on 7 October, Gaudier wrote to Brzeska, 'he's doing the most extraordinary statues, absolute copies of Polynesian work with Brancusi-like noses'.[4] Epstein's *Doves 2* (fig. 91), together with the Brancusi stone carving and three Zadkines, were included in the Post-Impressionist and Futurist Exhibition at the Doré Gallery in October. It was perhaps as a result of this exhibition that Pound was moved to declare, in a letter to his mother, 'Epstein is a great sculptor.'[5] Gaudier responded, as Epstein had, to the craftsmanship and the formal lucidity of Brancusi's work; pure oval 'eggheads' and reductive geometric features became part of his graphic and sculptural vocabulary, in *Redstone Dancer*, in drawings for sculpture, in *Caritas* and in the little sketch group, *Monkeys* (*cat.* 103).

The stimulus he received from Epstein was more profound; much more obviously than Brancusi, who rejected suggestions that African art influenced his sculpture, Epstein showed how the formal and expressive lessons of 'primitive' carving could be absorbed into his own work. He was already knowledgeable about the art of ancient and non-European cultures which he collected, studied in the British Museum and which resonated in the novel forms, the monumentality and the confrontational sexuality of his work. A distinctive group of Gaudier's sculptures, *Redstone Dancer*, *Caritas*, *Head of Ezra Pound* and the *Men with Bowl* (*cat.* 98) and large wash drawings such as *Man and Horse* (fig. 92), are characterized by massive, clumsy figures, chunky as if hewn from wood. The solid bulbous forms, similarly long-bodied proportions and stylized heads render the drawings related to *Redstone Dancer* (*cat.* 69, pls. 97, XI) and *Caritas* (*cat.* 75, pls. 106–7) immensely sculptural. So distinctive is their style that a specific source can be suggested – the great Hawaiian Deity figure (fig. 79), already cited as a possible source for *Wrestler*.

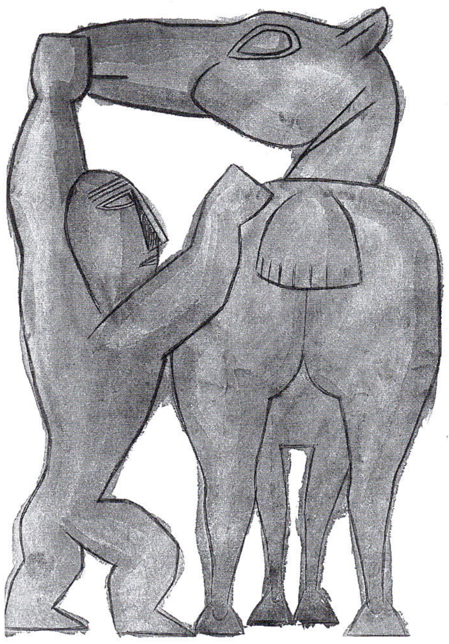

92 *Man and Horse*, 1913–14

Several carefully finished compositional drawings on maternity themes show Gaudier exploring the sculptural possibilities of a pair of children suckling from their standing mother, grappling with the awkwardness of stance and the disparity in scale between infants and mother. In the pencil drawing (pl. 106) two wriggling infants suckle, clasped in their mother's arms. Despite the simplification of forms, this is a crowded, busy composition and the whole thing is too top-heavy for transposition to sculpture. The handling of the legs and triangular indication of the face reveal a link with *Redstone Dancer*. In the Paris study (pl. 107) a single enormous child, clasped in his mother's arms, prepares to suckle while another child clings to her leg; the forms are massive to the point of clumsiness and the features far more Polynesian but the group remains unbalanced. A final preparatory drawing in black ink and brush is very close to the final composition with a strong tripod, pyramidal composition; it is faintly reminiscent of an African anthromorphic stool and the self-conscious primitivism of the composition is emphasized by the mother's pendulous breasts.[6] In the sculpture itself, the formal simplification of the children suggested in this drawing is sustained but their relationship to the nursing mother is essentially animal, its primitivism intensified, as they reach up to suckle as Romulus and Remus are depicted suckling from the she-wolf in classical tradition. The mother's pose – breast thrust forward and rump thrust back – is reminiscent of the stance of some of the large apes, though the extravagant curve of the mother's body seen in profile almost exactly mirrors that of Epstein's *Female Figure in Flenite* (fig. 90). It may also be relevant that Epstein had exhibited a drawing entitled *Feeding Young Runts* (pigeons) in his first solo exhibition at the Twenty-One Gallery in December 1913.

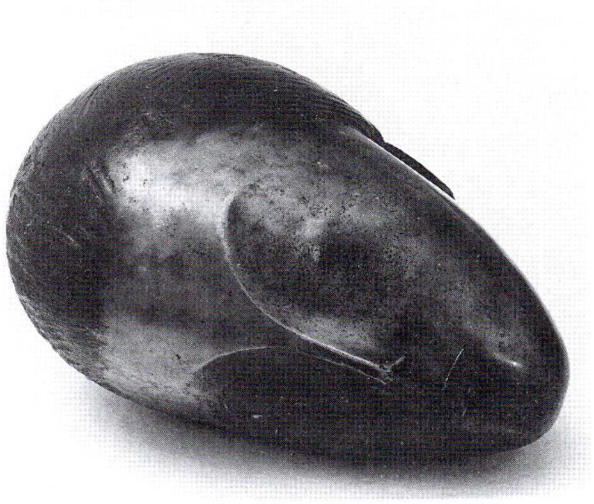

93 Constantin Brancusi, *Sleeping Muse*, 1910

Caritas is a flamboyantly provocative piece; the relationship of mother and child in *Maternity* (*cat.* 64) had been emotional, intimate, the mother's embrace private, enclosed. In *Caritas* the act of nurturing is flaunted. Sexually allusive and explicit themes, often in the guise of evocations of primitive societies, were taken up by a number of artists during the pre-war years; they are an underlying motif in the decoration of the Cabaret Theatre Club (the Cave of the Golden Calf) in Gill's priapic *Golden Calf* and, more in a coded way, in Lewis's *Design for the Drop-Curtain*.[7] However it was in Epstein's *Doves* and flenite pieces that some of the most challenging imagery could be seen. The themes of these sculptures and drawings by Gaudier – a mother suckling her young, a

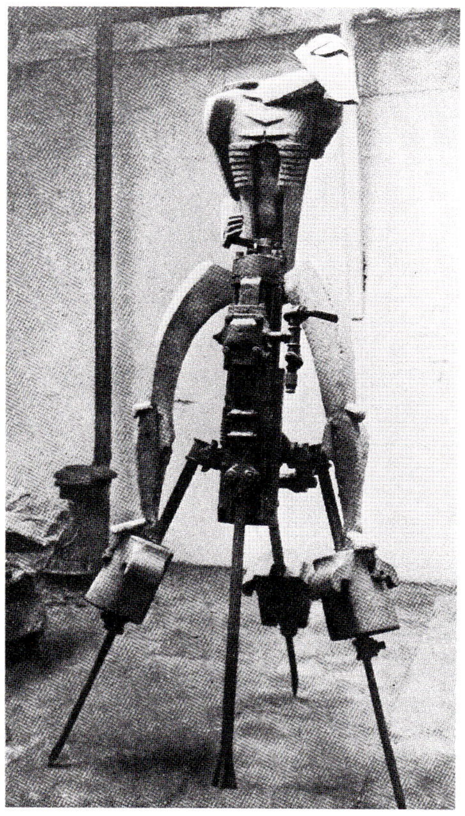

94 Jacob Epstein, *Rock Drill*, 1913. Photographed in the studio

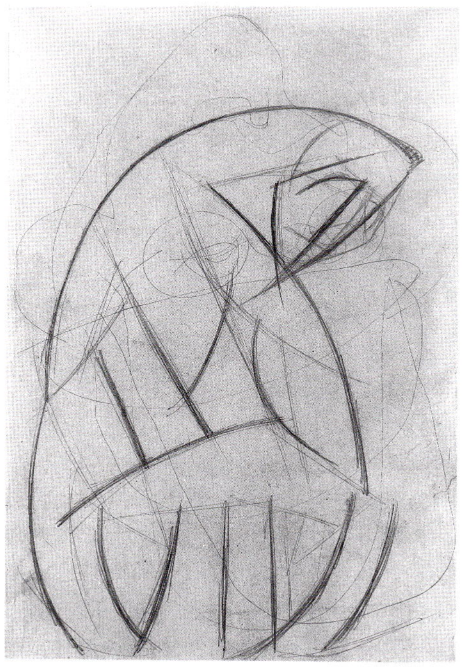

95 Drawing after Epstein, *Bird Pluming Itself*, 1914

nude mother with a child, a man with a horse – evoke an archaic indefinite past. More rarely, as in the cut plaster *Men with a Bowl* (*cat.* 98) and the greenstone *Charm* (*cat.* 85, pl. 130, XIII) the form, treatment of material and theme are directly inspired by a 'primitive' source – in the one case an African or Oceanic carving, in the other a Maori *tiki* (neck ornament).[8]

During the winter of 1913 Pound accompanied Gaudier to Epstein's studio where they saw *Rock Drill* (fig. 94), the mechanistic white plaster figure perched on a real industrial rock drill, its drill arm projecting like a giant phallus. It was by far his most revolutionary piece to date and was not exhibited until 1915. Epstein later recalled Gaudier's enthusiasm for it: 'Pound started expatiating on the work. Gaudier turned on him and snapped, "Shut up, you understand nothing!"'[9] Both Gaudier and Brzeska attended Epstein's first one-man show at the Twenty-One Gallery in the Adelphi in December; it included a selection of portraits, carvings and drawings including studies for *Rock Drill*.[10] When Pound and Brzeska met at the opening of the first London Group show in March 1914, they agreed that Epstein was the dominant presence.[11] Pound praised all three of his exhibits, *Female Figure in Flenite*, *Birds 2* and a smaller carving (now lost), *Bird Pluming Itself*, which he described as 'like a cloud bent back upon itself – not a woolly cloud, but one of those clouds that are blown smooth by the wind. It is gracious and aerial.'[12]

The profound impression made by *Doves* and *Rock Drill* is evident in the clear-cut, slightly convex masses and large pointed snout of *Dog* (*cat.* 96, pl. 140). Neither completed nor included in the *List of Works*, Gaudier probably considered this piece a private study, so close was it to Epstein's work. Nevertheless the weighty stillness of the older artist's figures has been replaced by lightness, mobility and a subtle element of humour. Like *Sleeping Fawn* (*cat.* 63, pl. 78) the carving has no integral plinth, encouraging informal presentation.

The relationship between Epstein's *Doves 2* and the masterly *Bird Swallowing a Fish* (*cat.* 97, pl. 142), one of Gaudier's most accomplished works, has been widely recognized.[13] The convulsive action is intensified rather than diminished by the geometricized forms. The composition pivots around the engorged beak. The moment of violence in the natural world is rendered more menacing by the engulfing of the mechanistic, phallic fish, which lends the piece a distinctively Vorticist aggressive tension. Gaudier also seems to have examined closely the other Epstein bird carving praised by Pound: a drawing of a *Bird Pluming Itself* (fig. 95) is surely a study inspired by the Epstein sculpture. This drawing bears an obvious relationship with the preparatory drawings for *Bird Swallowing a Fish* (pl. 144) which reveal the dynamism between predator and prey who clash in a cat's cradle of intersecting lines of force. There is an exhilarating sense of the design's momentum as the drawings switch between the relatively naturalistic, in which webbed feet still support the bird, the gestural energy of the brush drawing (pl. 143) and the abstracted elegance of the Cambridge drawing (pl. 144).

The symmetry and sexual overtones of the piece can also be seen as in part a response to Epstein. Their sense of composition was, in fact, very different; Gaudier's figures are fluid, organic, often twisting and turning, whether in repose or in movement, while Epstein, impressed by the frontality of Egyptian, Assyrian, African and Oceanic carving, tended throughout his career to create totemic symmetrical compositions which have the energy and compressed power of architectural rather than organic structures. However, during 1913–14 Gaudier produced a significant group of symmetrical pieces, all related in material, style and content to watercolours, drawings and sculptures by the older man; some of the preparatory drawings for *Doorknocker* (*cat.* 81, pl. 128) indicate, like *Charm* (*cat.* 85, pls. 130, XIII) its inspiration in Maori *tiki* (neck ornaments) or, conceivably, carvings from the northwestern peoples of North America. Others signal the sexuality of the same type of African carvings that stimulated Epstein's watercolour *Totem*.[14] A preoccupation with themes of procreation and birth had been apparent in Epstein's work since 1908 and dominated the content of his drawings and carvings from 1910–14, with recurrent motifs of potency, coition, pregnancy and birth – all hitherto taboo subjects but themes which resonated with contemporaries including Gill, Lewis, Hulme and Pound. Gaudier was highly receptive to the punning *épatisme* implicit in using an erect phallus as a doorknocker or in equating creative and sexual potency, as Epstein had done with *Rock Drill*. Many of the small 'toys' and 'ornaments' in which he developed these sexually explicit designs were for the private use of Hulme, Lewis and others within the Rebel Art Centre. The assertive heterosexuality of the group was part of their *esprit de corps*. They employed 'virile' as a term of critical praise to be contrasted both with the effete aestheticism of an earlier generation and with the covert sexuality and prudery of the English establishment.

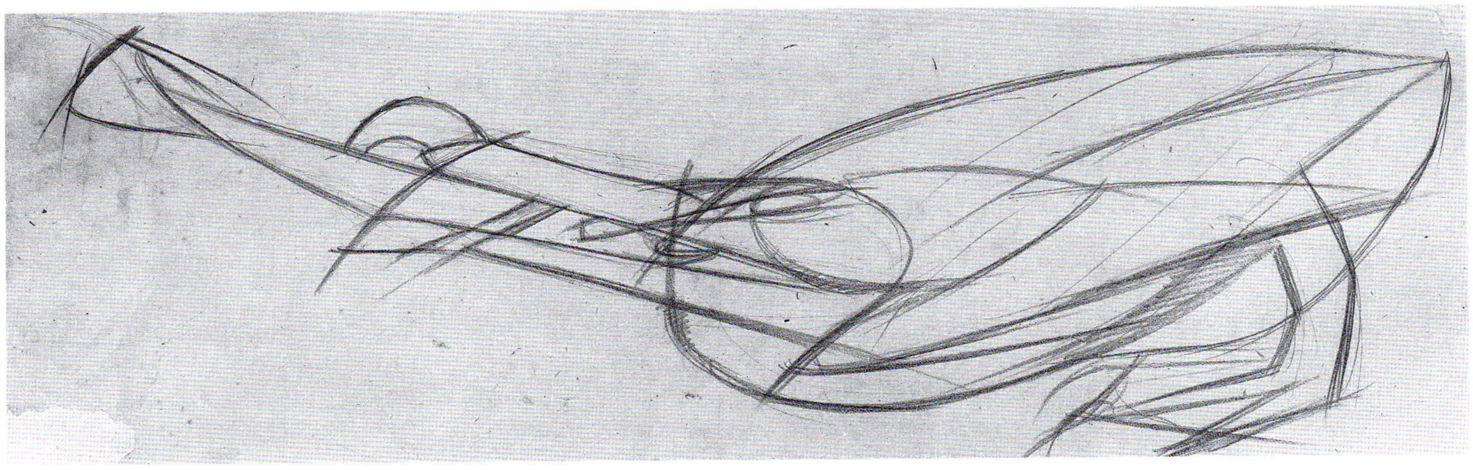

96 Study for *Bird Swallowing a Fish*, 1914

15

Gaudier's Vorticism

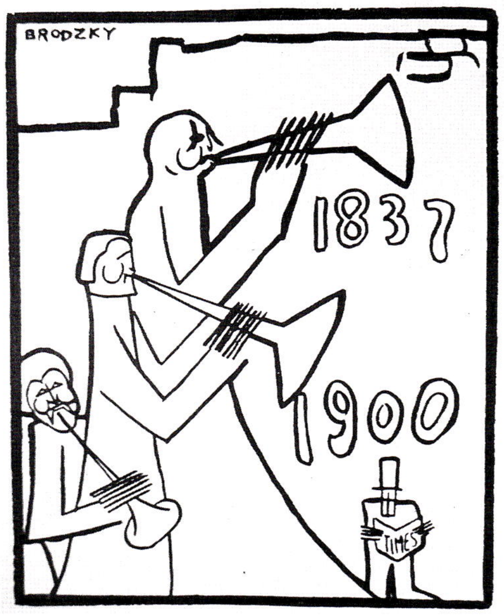

97 Horace Brodzky, *The Lewis-Brzeska Pound Troupe*, from the *Egoist*, 15.7.14

IN July 1914 Brodzky's cartoon, *The Lewis-Brzeska-Pound Troupe* (fig. 97), in the first issue of *Blast*, identified Gaudier as one of the triumvirate trumpeting the Vorticist cause. However, his had been a belated 'conversion' to the Rebel cause and his work, if not his writing, suggests a fundamental ambivalence towards its tenets. His friendship with Pound, developed in the wake of the Allied Artists' Salon in July 1913, did not lead to an immediate alliance. Gaudier became involved with the Omega Workshops during the autumn of 1913, at just the period when Wyndham Lewis, Frederick Etchells, Cuthbert Hamilton and Edward Wadsworth had left at Lewis's instigation in the aftermath of his row with Fry over the Omega's showing at the Ideal Home Exhibition.[1] Lewis in particular was unremittingly hostile to the Omega thereafter, sentiments which Gaudier did not share; he was not involved in the preliminary planning for Lewis's new magazine, *Blast*, in December 1913, and appears to have maintained a reserved attitude to Lewis, who later admitted that he had never known Gaudier well.[2] Fry wrote to friends: 'The Lewis gang do nothing else even now but abuse me. Brzeska, who sees them, says he's never seen such a display of vindictive jealousy among artists.'[3] Nor did he exhibit alongside Lewis, Epstein, Nevinson, Wadsworth and Hamilton in 'the Cubist Room' in the Brighton exhibition, *The Camden Town Group and Others*, in December 1913. On the contrary, he was exhibiting with Fry and the Omega artists in the Grafton Group exhibition at the Alpine Gallery, and was friendly enough with the Fitzroy Street group to have been proposed for election to the London Group by Harold Gilman.

The evolution of Gaudier's work during the latter part of 1913 and the early months of 1914 should therefore be understood less as part of the still inchoate Vorticist movement than in terms of Gaudier's emulation of Brancusi and Epstein, and of his relationships with Pound, Hulme and, more distantly, other members of the Pound-Lewis circle. It was only after Lewis set up his Rebel Art Centre in Great Ormond Street during March 1914 that Gaudier emerges as more strongly affiliated with that group than with any other.[4] Though his changing allegiance was signalled by the *Head of Ezra Pound*, exhibited at the Whitechapel Art Gallery in May, it was as late as June that he ended his long neutrality; in early June he became a signatory of Rebel Art Centre artists' letters to the *Observer* and the *Egoist*, dissociating themselves from Futurism; he played a prominent role in barracking the Futurists Marinetti and Nevinson at the Doré Gallery; he signed the Vorticist manifesto and wrote 'Vortex Gaudier-Brzeska' for *Blast* (see pp. 279–82).

His personal links with Pound, first established during the summer of 1913, were strengthened in December by the decision of Pound and Dorothy Shakespear to purchase two sculptures – *Torso 3* (*cat.* 60) and *Samson and Delilah* (*cat.* 57) – using poetry prize money given by Yeats. By the beginning of January Gaudier was hastily producing the *Blunt Casket* (*cat.* 72) in support of Pound's planned presentation and dinner for the poet.[5] Shortly after they had both visited Epstein and seen the great machine-mounted plaster figure, *Rock Drill*, Gaudier embarked at Pound's request upon a monumental portrait of the poet on which he worked throughout February and March. Throughout the period he was seeing a good deal of Pound, hearing readings of his poetry and discussing common interests, the most significant of which was their enthusiasm for Far Eastern art.

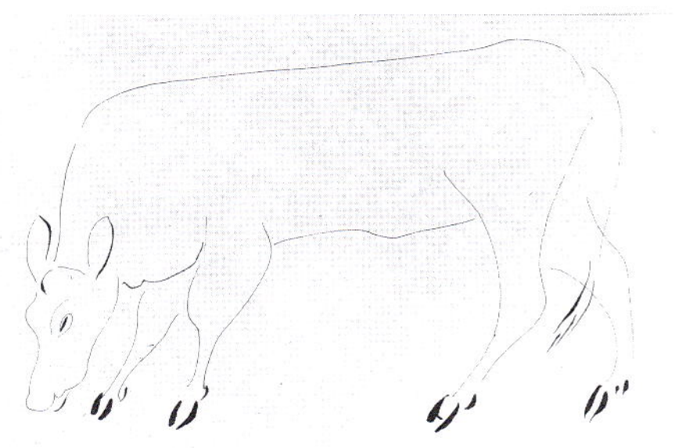

98 *Study of a Cow*, *c.* 1913

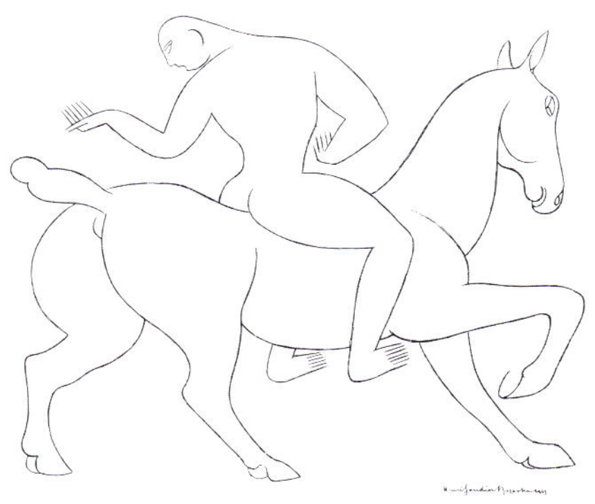

99 *Man on Horseback*, 1913

Chinese and Japanese art exercized a fascination which went back to Gaudier's childhood and the watercolour of a *Tiger's Head* copied from a print after a late nineteenth-century Chinese model and visible in his sketch of his bedroom in Orléans (fig. 7).[6] In 1910, after seeing an exhibition of Japanese prints and sword hilts (*tsuba*) in Paris, he had written to Dr Uhlemayr, 'I have not stopped proclaiming in the teeth of opposition, that the yellow civilization is better than our own.'[7] His conviction was strengthened by the prints and other works he saw in the Victoria and Albert Museum and the British Museum collections and then given new focus through his friendship with Pound. The poet's own interest in the Far East was similarly enduring and profound, being reflected in *The Cantos*, in his 'translations' from Chinese and Japanese, and in other works. An influential friend was the poet and British Museum curator Lawrence Binyon, whom he had first met in 1909. Binyon had already published a good deal on the art of the Far East as well as European art.[8] In 1913 he was put in charge of the newly created oriental prints and drawings section within the museum. During the same year Pound himself was entrusted with the executorship of the papers of the scholar Ernest Fenollosa. It was almost certainly Pound who introduced Gaudier to Fenollosa's *Epochs of Chinese and Japanese Art* which was a specific source for a passage in 'Vortex Gaudier-Brzeska'.[9]

Pound recalled Gaudier's attentive study of Chinese calligraphy: 'he was so accustomed to observe the dominant line in objects that, after he had spent what could not have been more than a few days studying the subject at the museum, he could understand the primitive Chinese ideographs (not the later more sophisticated forms)'.[10] He employed black and coloured china inks and brushes not only to create his own cryptic signs, such as his own monogram, dancing figures and his strong gestural study for *Bird Swallowing a Fish* (pl. 143), but also for the discipline the technique imposed in simplifying the forms of his studies of Ezra Pound (pls. 119, 120) and preparatory drawings for *Redstone Dancer* and *Caritas*.[11] Using a far finer brush and an exquisite delicacy of touch he also produced animal studies which fuse Chinese brush technique with the free-flowing contours of the Font-de-Gaume animals in *Stags* (fig. 34) and *Study of a Cow* (fig. 98). The spontaneity and variation of density and weight of the brush line suggested the idiosyncrasies of organic form and movement.

No less important were Chinese sculpted objects such as the small densely carved animals in jade and other hard stones, and early bronze figures and animals which were both free-standing and small applied decorations on ceremonial vessels. The elegant springy drawing, *Man on Horseback* (fig. 99) with its distinctive long-backed, short-legged form and insistent convexity seems inescapably related to early Chinese bronzes such as the small bronze *Tapir* of the 5th or 6th century BC (Zhou Dynasty), now in the British Museum.[12] Pound, reviewing Gaudier's sculpture at the London Group exhibition in March 1914, referred to the '"snuggly" comfortable feeling' of Gaudier's animals and compared *Boy with a Coney* (*cat.* 76, pl. 104) with Zhou bronze animals.[13] Possibly Gaudier knew this type of piece through Pound since there was as yet virtually no sculpture of this early period in London's public collections and there had been relatively little study of early Chinese bronzes.[14] However, during the autumn of 1913 he and Sophie visited an exhibition of Chinese art at the Whitechapel Art Gallery; among the textiles and bronzes on show were two Zhou bronze vessels lent by George Eumorfopoulos, a selection of Han and Tang ceramics including a white Tang horse and a number of small carved figures and animals.[15] Many Chinese animal figures in hard stone are depicted seated or crouching with their legs tightly tucked or folded beneath them in a manner reminiscent of Gaudier's *Crouching Fawn* (*cat.* 62, pl. 80) which, however, was opportunistically based on a pen drawing – one of a large number carried out on the same day.[16] The Oriental tradition of small but exquisitely carved functional and decorative objects probably had more impact on the small 1914 pieces such as *Small Fawn* (*cat.* 84), *Duck* (*cat.* 90) and *Brass Toy* (*cat.* 95) which redefine sculpture as something to be carried, handled and used.

Head of Ezra Pound (*cat.* 79, pl. 121) was, on the other hand, the largest sculpture Gaudier carved. It brings together the preoccupation with the strong, virile and anti-sentimental, which characterized the Futurist and Pound-Lewis circle, with the concentrated, semi-abstract qualities of an ideogram. According to Epstein, Pound had asked Gaudier to make it 'virile'; Brodzky, who regarded the bust and all Gaudier's more abstract work as 'unrepresentative', recalled that, 'its purpose and beginnings were entirely pornographic. Both the sculptor and the sitter had decided upon that. Brzeska [i.e. Gaudier] informed me … that it was to be a phallus.'[17] Mimetic likeness was to be all but abandoned; Pound recalled Gaudier muttering repeatedly, 'You understand it will not look like you, it *will* … *not* … *look* …like you. It will be the expression of various emotions which I get from your character.'[18]

Paradoxically this is the one portrait for which Gaudier definitely made preparatory studies; 'he made first a number of drawings', Pound recalled, and at least some of the carving was carried out from life with the poet 'on a shilling wooden chair in a not over-heated studio with railroad trains rushing overhead.'[19] Brodzky was still more emphatic that the drawings 'in charcoal reinforced with Indian ink … were made direct from Pound before and while the carving was in progress.'[20] All the drawings are executed in brush and ink with the cursive clarity, gestural energy and formal balance of Chinese calligraphy, but also with an expansiveness which spills over the edges of the paper. Pound's rather narrow eyes and level brows metamorphose into a sign reminiscent of a Chinese ideogram, the nose is narrowed and lengthened, the mass of bushy auburn hair and moustache acquire a geometric clarity and his neat goatee beard takes on a life of its own (pls. 119–20).

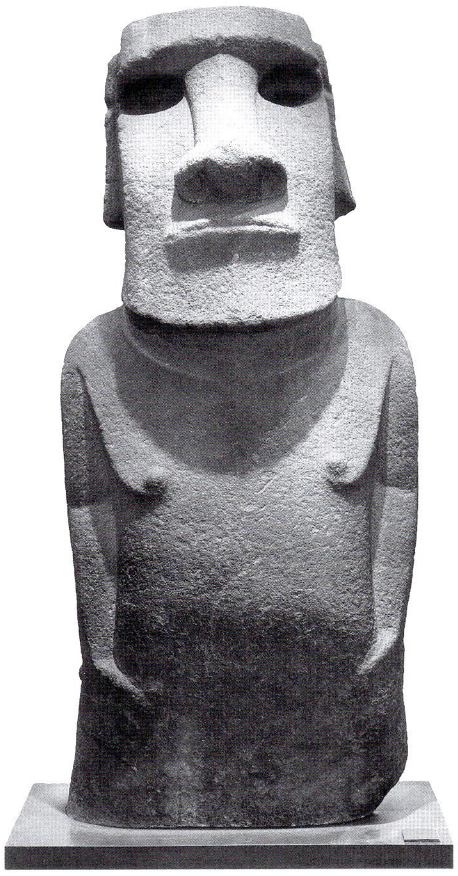

100 *Hoa Hakanani'a*, Orongo, Easter Island

The sculpture changed considerably in the course of carving, as Pound's letters indicate. In early March he wrote, 'Bx's bust of me begins to look like Father Tiber. It will be less outrageous than I thought, and eternally calm – which I ain't.'[21] On 10 March, 'Brzx's column gets more gravely beautiful and more phallic each week. I think it will have a deal of energy as a composition of masses.'[22] The Benington photographs of Gaudier working on it in his studio (fig. 45) show the partly roughed out head with black-outlined features very different from the completed work – larger, angled eyes, a higher hairline, a furrowed brow and comically upturned moustache, which was probably a joke. However, in retrospect Pound admitted to preferring the unfinished stone:

> The bust of me was most striking perhaps two weeks before it was finished … it was perhaps a *kinesis*, whereas it is now a *stasis*; but before the back was cut out, and before the middle lock was cut down, there was in the marble a titanic energy, it was like a great stubby catapult, the two masses bent for a blow.[23]

The *Head of Ezra Pound* could function as an anti-classical colossus symbolic of the struggle being conducted between the traditionalists, such as the poet Richard Aldington, and the protagonists of the new art led by Hulme and Pound. Its prototype was no fragment of Greek statuary but the great stone Easter Island figure *Hoa Hakanani'a* which then stood outside in the portico of the British Museum (fig. 100). If the monumentality of the piece conferred on Pound the status of presiding guru at the centre of the vortex of modernism, its phallic imagery, like that of *Rock Drill* with its driller figure penetrating the virgin rock, equated creative and sexual potency.[24] Pound went further than Gaudier in underlining this meaning; during the artist's lifetime it was exhibited and reproduced as *Head* or *Bust of Mr Ezra Pound* but Pound himself implied a priestly, almost mystical role by naming it *Hieratic Head of Ezra Pound* in his 1916 *Memoir*.[25]

Both Pound and Gaudier were active participants in the debates about the new art being conducted in the pages of *The Egoist*. Responding to Aldington's defence of the Hellenistic tradition, Gaudier contrasted the rationality of later Greek and Hellenistic sculpture with the intuitive works produced by so-called barbaric people of archaic Crete; he asserted that 'the sculptors of to-day differ from these later Greeks not in tendency but in *kind*.'

> The modern sculptor is a man who works with instinct as his inspiring force. His work is emotional. The shape of a leg, or the curve of an eyebrow, etc., etc., have to him no significance whatsoever; light voluptuous modelling is to him insipid – what he feels he does so intensely and his work is nothing more nor less than the abstraction of this intense feeling … This sculpture … is continuing the tradition of the barbaric peoples of the earth (for whom we have sympathy and admiration).[26]

Gaudier's rejection of later Hellenistic art, including some of the most admired masterpieces, had already taken shape in 1911 but the language of intensity and abstracted feeling which he now employed reflected the

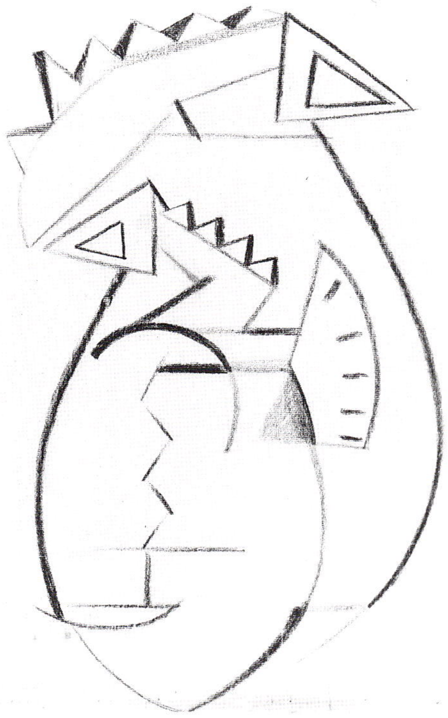

101 *Design for Vorticist Ornament*, 1914

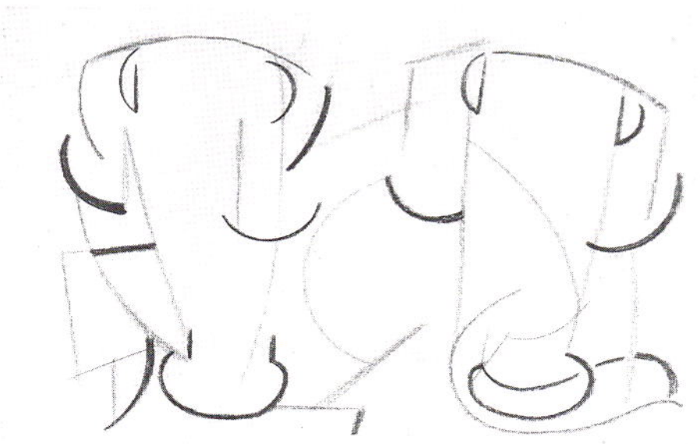

102 *Two Cows' Heads*, 1914

influence of T. E. Hulme. In February Pound placed Gaudier alongside Epstein and Gill as the new generation of distinctively modern sculptors in his report of Hulme's lecture 'Modern Art and its Philosophy' at the Quest Society.[27]

Hulme's lectures and writings, published during 1913–14 in the *New Age*, were complemented by the personal influence of the convivial, if exclusively male, salons he hosted at the home of his companion Mrs Ethel Kibblewhite in Soho Square and at which Gaudier, Pound and Aldington were frequent guests.[28] For Hulme, the break-up of the Humanist post-Renaissance intellectual and artistic world had resulted in 'a state of slush' which was being superseded by the emergence of 'a new geometric art ... different in kind from the art which preceded it'.[29] In Egyptian, Indian and Byzantine art he saw an alternative to the sensuous, naturalistic Greek norm: 'everything tends to be angular, curves tend to be hard and geometrical' and 'the representation of the human body, for example, is often entirely non-vital, and distorted to fit into stiff lines and cubical shapes of various kinds.'[30] Artists, such as Epstein, as he saw it, were looking back to these archaic styles as a stepping-stone to the new abstract, geometrical art which represented the way ahead. Hulme's writings, drawing on the writings of Bergson and Wörringer, stressed the purely formal and philosophical bases for this recourse to artforms which could be seen as antithetical to classical norms; Epstein's current work seemed to illustrate the validity of his theories. Hulme's emphasis was primarily on form but Gaudier, like Epstein, was also interested in meaning and emotion. For the practitioner, as opposed to the philosopher, archaic and non-European art offered stirring examples of direct carving, and primal emotional intensity in expressing movement, transcendental power or sexual union, which were the polar opposite of the anaemic gentility, covert carnality, hackneyed themes and overworked surfaces of academic contemporary art.[31]

A mechanistic, impersonal abstraction using geometric forms does not really exist in Gaudier's work since even the metallic crispness of *Torpedo Fish*, *Fish* and drawings for small scale sculptures (figs. 104, 105) remain essentially humanistic, alluding to the relationship of parent and child or animal or even of a new born creature breaking out of the egg (fig. 101). The intersecting arcs and networks of energy in the drawings relating to *Bird Swallowing a Fish* and *Stags* never relinquish contact with the blind instinctive violence of nature which gave rise to them.

The primal emotion which fuelled some of Rebel artists' best work gave rise to a tension between the abstraction and meaning which some were quick to point out. Lewis, Epstein and Gaudier were the targets of a broadside from Walter Sickert who, despite the provocative realism of his own Camden Town bedroom scenes, was revolted by the 'Pornometric gospel' he identified as central to the Rebel Art Centre creed:

> We hear a good deal about non-representational art. But while the faces of the persons suggested are frequently nil, non-representation is forgotten when it comes to the sexual organs. Witness Mr Wyndham Lewis's 'Creation' exhibited at Brighton, Mr Gaudier-Brzeska's drawing in last week's *New Age* [pl. 94] and several of Mr Epstein's later drawings.[32]

Vorticism was never a movement unified round a single coherent philosophy. Each one of the artists affiliated with the Rebel Art Centre tended to have a different relationship with the mosaic of fiercely held opinions trumpeted in *Blast*. Initially they asserted no independent creed and were united primarily in a hostility to Futurism sharpened by their underlying kinship in seeking an 'Art that is strong, virile and anti-sentimental'. Gaudier's sympathies with the manifesto in *Blast* were limited; he might agree that 'The artist of the modern movement is a savage' but he was far from wishing either to reject the past or to espouse the industrialized machine aesthetic: 'this enormous, jangling, journalistic, fairy desert of modern life serves him as Nature did more technically primitive man'.[33] Nor was he responsive to the mystical tendency of Kandinsky's *On the Spiritual in Art* of which an excerpt was published in *Blast*, in Wadsworth's translation. Gaudier's seminal essay 'Vortex Gaudier-Brzeska' (see pp. 279–82) develops Pound's definition of the Vortex, which itself derives in part from his definition of Imagism in poetry as 'that which presents an intellectual and emotional complex in an instant of time.' The Vortex was not just as 'the point of maximum energy' but also the carrying forward of the past into the future: 'All the past that is vital, all the past that is capable of living into the future, is pregnant in the vortex NOW.'[34]

However widespread the interest in atavistic themes of tribal ritual, dance and the hunt, or in the techniques and formal inspiration offered by culturally remote artefacts, nobody apart from Hulme had attempted to sum up the shifting balance of cultural values before Gaudier's 'Vortex Gaudier-Brzeska' essay. This tour-de-force history of world sculpture in three pages exalts modern sculptors as urban heirs to 'the barbaric peoples of the earth', seeking inspiration from the formal strength of prehistoric, archaic and worldwide artistic traditions.[35] Its highly compressed and allusive language owes much to the character of Pound's Imagist poetry and early Cantos but it also contains Gaudier's own inimitable mixture of bombast and deadly seriousness in its incantatory rhythms and extravagant language. He pursues 'the fruitful sphere' of each epoch from the Palaeolithic period through Egyptian, Greek, Indian, Assyrian, European, Chinese, Mexican, African and Oceanic art. The Western classical tradition is soundly blasted; the Greeks accused of narcissism ('he petrified his own semblance') and of a merely secondary feeling for form; 'solid excrements in the quattro e cinquecento, liquid until the seventeenth century, gases whistle till now'.

'Vortex Gaudier-Brzeska' drew together several disparate elements – the underlying search for new forms of expression, a golden age-tinted vision of primeval cultures different from the enervated and worn out classical tradition they sought to reject. It captured the romantic primitivism shared by the Fauves, Expressionists and many in the English avant-garde of harking back to a vaguely evoked primitive, semi-nomadic life close to and dependent upon nature. It celebrated the primal drives of man's survival ('his manhood was strained to the highest potential – his energy brutal – his opulent maturity was convex'). Bypassing the partisan infighting of *Blast*'s manifesto and its hit-lists of the blasted and blessed, it takes a global historical view.

Gaudier had once complained to Uhlemayr that through inexperience his 'line lacked snap and vigour'. The roots of 'Vortex Gaudier-Brzeska' lay back in Gaudier's solitary studies in Paris and London when he had worked out his idea on sculptural volumes and planes by studying Michelangelo. Now, armed with the epigrammatic edge of Imagism, he was able to elevate sculpture to a central role in modernism:

> Sculptural energy is the mountain.
> Sculptural feeling is the appreciation of masses in relation.
> Sculptural ability is the defining of these masses by planes.

Form is discussed and evoked in three-dimensional terms of spheres, pointed cones, of phallic convexities. There are echoes of the notes Gaudier had begun to make in Paris about the styles of different eras and cultures and to his recent museum discoveries, references to the cave paintings of the Font-de-Gaume and to the Assyrian sculptures in the British Museum collections. There are echoes, too, of his theoretical readings of Nietzsche and Bergson. His friendship with Pound is evident in the section on Chinese art, only 200 words long, but the most specific in this masterpiece of polemical synthesis: it traces Chinese art from the Palaeolithic to the 'artistic ruin and sterility' of the Ming. It has been convincingly argued that the single most enigmatic but precise reference derives both from a bronze drum acquired by the British Museum in 1903 and from Fenollosa: 'The features of Tao-t'ie were inscribed inside the square with the rounded corners – the centuple spherical frog presided over the inverted truncated cone that is the bronze war drum.'[36]

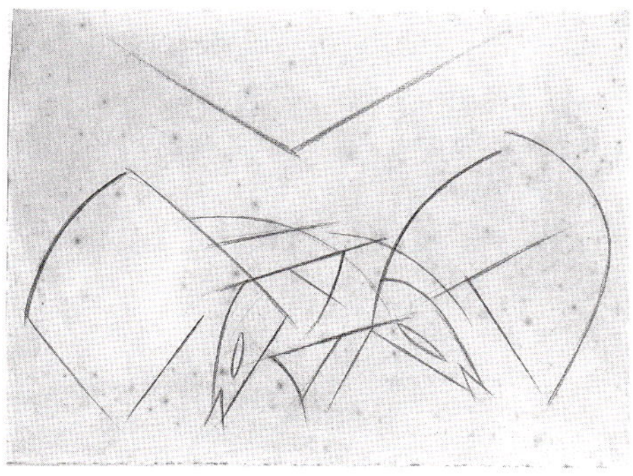

103 Study for *The Stags*, 1914

The praise which greeted this essay stands in contrast to the mixed reception which the few examples of his more abstract work received. After *Redstone Dancer*, *Boy with Coney*, *Alabaster Group (Stags)*, a marble *Torso* and *Maternity* had been exhibited in the first London Group show in March, Konody remarked, 'of Mr Gaudier-Brzeska's affectations in carved stone it is difficult to speak with patience.'[37] Another critic admitted 'we found Mr Brzeska's *Alabaster Group*, 112, quite unintelligible till a chance inspiration revealed a pair of antlered deer as the suggestion of the design' (fig. 103).[38] But the 'Vortex' essay was greeted as 'extremely good reading' even by an ardent defender of classical art, the poet Richard Aldington, who connected Gaudier's rejection of classical tradition with his espousal of the key modernist tenets – admiration for the art of 'primitive' cultures, 'virile' and geometric art:

> Mr Gaudier-Brzeska is really a wild, unkempt barbarian, with a love of form and a very clear knowledge of the comparative history of sculpture. He is the sort of person who would dye his statues in the gore of goats if he thought it would give them a more virile appearance; if he were a Naturalist he would chain slaves to rocks in order that he might reproduce their contortions. Fortunately he is not a Naturalist, and his worst crimes consist in a somewhat terrifying abuse of all Greek sculpture whatsoever, and of everything which is not, tremendously virile and cannibalistic and geometric.[39]

For Ford Madox Hueffer it was 'the most pleasurable piece of writing of the lot'.[40] Even Pound was amazed and impressed:

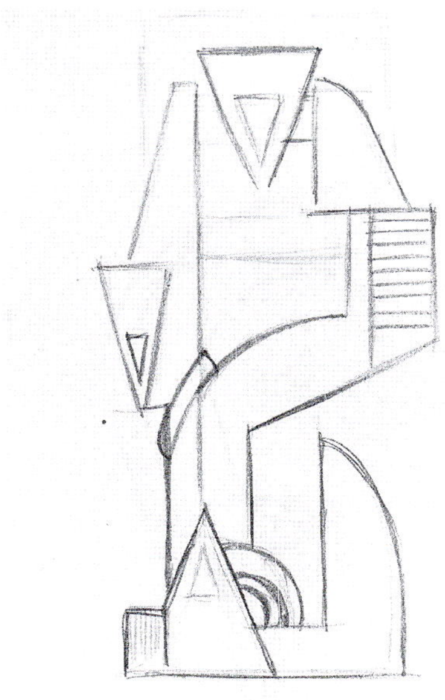

104 *Vorticist Figure*, 1914

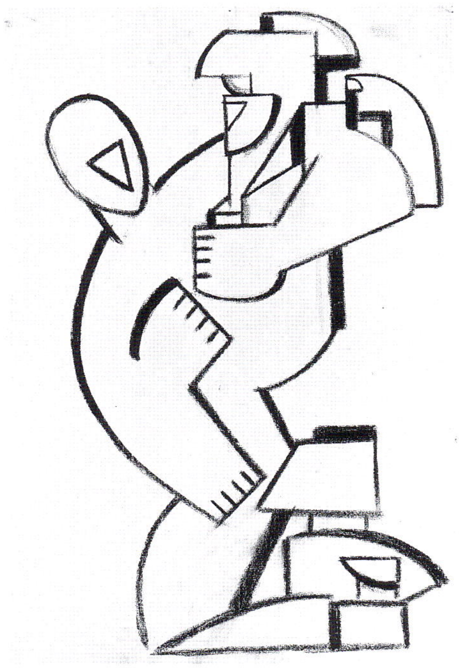

105 *Design for Sculpture (Mother and Child)*, 1914

> It is not merely a remarkable document from a man whom most people remember a twelve-month before as speaking English with difficulty, it is a remarkable arrangement of thought. I confess that I read it two or three times with nothing but a gaiety and exhilaration arising from the author's vigour of speech ... [it] will become the text-book in all academies of sculpture before our generation has passed from the earth.[41]

Vorticism was still in the process of evolution. The sculptural focus and brilliance of Gaudier's essay marked his new role as one of the key shapers of and spokesmen for the group. Epstein might have been expected to take the more dominant role, but he was holding aloof, never signed the Vorticist manifesto in spite of his closeness to Hulme and only exhibited *Rock Drill* a year later. Privately Pound still rated Epstein's work more highly than Gaudier's, though he thought the latter more promising.[42] In his 1916 *Memoir* Pound uses Gaudier's writings, even more than his work, to annexe Gaudier for Vorticism. In an interview as late as the Fifties, he continued to assert Gaudier's central role.[43]

Gaudier's work continued to follow two, if not more, separate directions; there was the growing abstraction of some of his drawings and pastels, the direct dependence upon primitive models apparent in *Men with Bowl* and the classicism of *Mlle Borne* and *Seated Woman*.[44] The crisply facetted and increasingly abstracted character of Gaudier's carving was apparent in his small carved stone and metal pieces; some, like *Duck* (*cat.* 90), retain an identifiable integrated form, however simplified. But in others forms assume an independent life; in drawings arcs, zig-zags and strictly patterned mechanistic shapes drift in overlapping planes and segments where depth and surface are further confused by a studied variation in the weight of conté crayon lines. A drawing from a sketchbook which also contains preparatory drawings for *Torpedo Fish* (*cat.* 80, pl. 123) is clearly based on the *Rock Drill* but now with head, hands and feet all geometricized into the triangles which, once merely incised or carved to indicate the face, now dominate the composition (fig. 104). *Torpedo Fish* has the look and feel of an implement for which one has yet to divine the purpose; its pierced triangular head is strongly reminiscent of Lewis's mannekin *Enemy of the Stars* (1912), and its analogy to the human form sufficiently ambiguous that Pound reproduced it inverted. He planned other pieces of this kind of which several seem to have been lost. At least three drawings show a stylized mother and child (fig. 105); the repeated hands faintly echo the flipper hands of the *Wrestler* relief and its associated drawings and the repeated arm recalls *Redstone Dancer* but from the solidity and abstracted intricacy of these figures and the overlapping spatial ambiguity of some of the drawings one can infer the growing influence of Cubism on the Vorticist artists. Gaudier was aware of Archipenko's recent work, since his *Dancer* (1912) had been reproduced in *The Sketch* a few months before Gaudier's *Stags* were reproduced there.[45] But the spatial and temporal ambiguities of Analytical Cubist painting may also have been becoming more familiar. Another likely link, given rhythm and change of pace conveyed by curvature and strength of line alone in these drawings, was Edward Wadsworth, some of whose prints, like *Yorkshire Village* (1914), have a powerful Cubist structure combined with a purely abstract patterning and syncopation of three tones.[46]

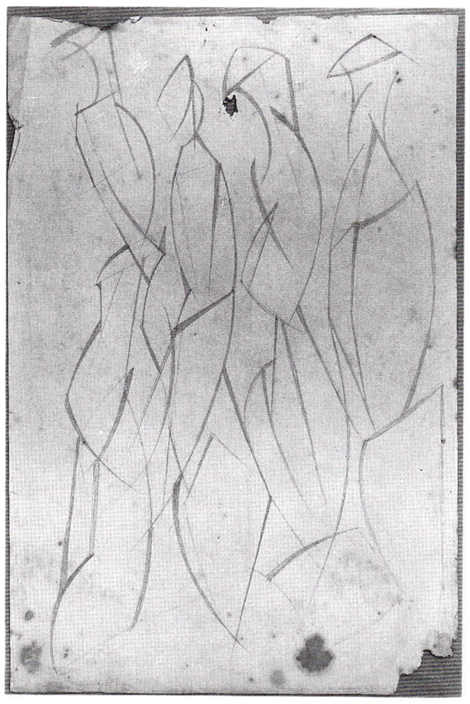

106 *Four Figures* (study for *Birds Erect*), 1914

Birds Erect (*cat.* 107, pls. 161–63) is the apogee of these experiments in abstraction, yet its shifting convex planes and slanting, syncopated composition are removed from the mechanistic geometry of Vorticism. Had it been carved in France at this period it would probably now be regarded as one of the early masterpieces of Cubist sculpture – analytically subtle, yet intuitive in the ever fluctuating perspectives it offers; the forms rising from their integral but mountain-like base seem analogous to the hillside villages painted by Derain, Braque and Picasso in 1909–10. Brodzky claimed the piece originated from cacti growing on the studio windowsill but the only surviving preparatory drawing (fig. 106) suggests Gaudier's street drawings of only one or two years before; the people walking in the park talking and showing off their clothes has been reduced to a prismatically stylized group, not unlike clustered but psychologically isolated city dwellers in Kirchner's contemporary *Five Women on a Street*.[47]

Alongside the densely clustered grouping of *Birds Erect* the unitary repose of *Seated Woman* (*cat.* 105, pls. 151–52) may seem an astonishing *volte-face*, a reversion to the classical nostalgia perhaps betrayed by *Grief*. Yet the underlying sculptural concerns are identical in the delicate syncopation of masses and their defining planes and in the artists's responsiveness to the character of his materials.

Gaudier's apparent ambivalence towards abstraction and modernism have always been the subject of speculation, especially since remarks made to Aldington just before his departure for France, and in correspondance to friends during the war hinted at his desire to turn back to a sensuous naturalistic style. Epstein and Lewis were among many artists who turned their backs, at least temporarily, as apects of their pre-war abstraction in the aftermath of the First World War. But in Gaudier's case even his most outspoken pieces of rhetoric had asserted a formal approach always based on observation of nature, and had allowed all his admired contemporaries the freedom, once unshackled from the restraints of the classical norm, to choose their own models. His conclusion for the direction of modern sculpture was not prescriptive:

> WE the moderns: Epstein, Brancusi, Archipenko, Dunikowski, Modigliani, and myself ... have been influenced by what we liked most, each according to his own individuality, we have crystallized the sphere into the cube, we have made a combination of all possible shaped masses – concentrating them to express our abstract thoughts of conscious superiority.[48]

CONCLUSIONS

Gaudier was in many ways a paradoxical figure – an eclectic pioneer, an untutored artist better read and more versatile in his craftsmanship than most of his peers, a Frenchman who wrote one of the most succinct and witty histories of sculpture in English, an incisive critic of classical art who produced some of the most beautiful classical sculptures of the twentieth century, a prodigious inventor of forms who chose to work in a slow, intractable medium, an outsider who yearned for acceptance but who demonstratively flouted conventions. His work embraced caricature, naturalism and geometric abstraction; a few sculptures are a triumphant synthesis of all three. Even in his most formally experimental phase, during 1914, few pastels and drawings and no surviving sculptures explore abstraction without recognizable figurative references.

In his letters from the trenches Gaudier continued to define sculpture in terms of plane, mass, line and surface, and to identify his starting point as living form; he planned an essay for *Blast* on 'the Need for Organic Forms'.[1] He told Pound 'I believe I shall develop a style of my own which, like the Chinese, will embody both a grotesque and a non-grotesque side.'[2] This suggests a line of development consistent with the expressive and formal versatility of his pre-war work. A few months later, he told Pound 'it is not much use going farther in the research of planes, forms etc. If I ever come back I shall do more "Mlles G" [*Torso*] ...'[3]

Fry, among others, saw his Vorticist experiments as merely a temporary diversion from his essential naturalism. In the post-war period many of his erstwhile allies in the Rebel Art Centre, including Epstein, Lewis and Wadsworth, were to return to more traditional figurative work and in France, too, there was a tendency to accomodate rather than to reject the past. In the context of British and European early Modernism he exhibited a characteristic need to learn from a multitude of sources outside the canon. He shared an ambivalence towards abstraction with Brancusi, Archipenko, Duchamp-Villon and Boccioni. More than any of these, with the possible exception of Archipenko, Gaudier continued to hold a recurrent and creative dialogue with the Greek tradition. At a superficial level this was clothing classical poses in modernist formal garb; at a deeper level it was a re-engagement with the sensuous subtlety of contrapposto and with the immediacy and vigour of the human presence which, at its best, was represented in classical sculpture from ancient Greece to the Renaissance.

Despite his apparent rejection of his family roots, Gaudier remained profoundly bound by them, not least in his quixotic return to fight for France. He never abandoned the respect for nature and craftsmanship instilled by his father. His acute observations of nature, its casual violence, resilience, beauty and unselfconscious being, were his patrimony and a lifelong pleasure, perhaps especially amidst the mud and devastation of the Western Front. His insistence on the integrity of materials and craftsmanship can be traced back to the craft traditions of his family; it fused readily with the ethos of direct carving and truth to materials, itself derived in part from the British Arts and Crafts tradition, pioneered during 1910–11 by Gill and Epstein, and passed on to Moore, Hepworth, Skeaping and Underwood during the Twenties.

Gaudier's continuing sympathy with Bergsonism also allied him with a wider European avant-garde – the Cubists, Simultanists, Expressionists and Futurists. In 1910 Franz Marc, the other great *animalier* among the pre-war avant-garde, explained his choice of subject by reference to 'my feeling for the organic *rhythm* of all things, to encompass a pantheistic empathy with the vibrating and pulsating flow of blood in nature, in trees, in animals and in the air ... I can see no better way to this "animalizing" of art, as I should like to call it, than the animal picture.'[4] Gaudier's view was less mystical yet his work, especially the animal drawings and sculptures, convey intense empathy for the animal pulse in nature. In this he stood somewhat apart from his fellow Vorticists; Bergson was 'blasted' in *Blast* and Hulme, an erstwhile Bergsonian, perceived the new austere geometric art as moving 'away from the messiness and confusion of nature and natural things.'[5] Gaudier's own emphasis on emotion rather than reason, and on carrying forward all that was valuable in the art of the past into the new art as 'heirs of the barbaric peoples of the earth', is essentially Bergsonian. The intense vitality of so much of Gaudier's work implies an underlying kinship between human and animal which is atavistic rather than sentimental or anthropomorphic. It seems to render tangible the idea that all – sleeping fawn or cat, suckling mother, seabird and prey or wary lovers – dance to the same cosmic rhythm.

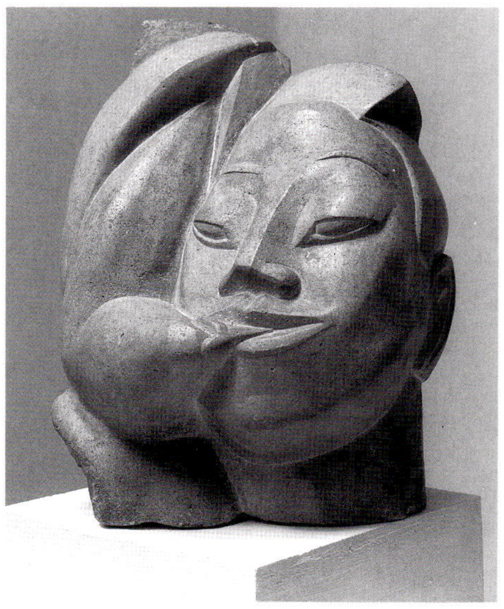

107 Frank Dobson, *Pigeon Boy*, 1920

To Gaudier's contemporaries, his gadfly personality, his passionate engagement in his art and his talents as a polemicist impressed them as much as his work. Pound, who was probably closest to him, and whose *Memoir* reflects what he had learnt from Gaudier, esteemed his promise more than his actual achievement, giving pride of place to Epstein. Although Pound kept and treasured examples of Gaudier's work throughout his life, he rated him more as a symbol of sacrificed and wasted talent. Frank Dobson, six years Gaudier's senior, was the sole contemporary sculptor to respond more or less immediately to Gaudier's work when he carved the *Kneeling Female Figure*, in about 1915, and later *Pigeon Boy* (1920, fig. 107). Dobson almost certainly knew Gaudier's work before the War since he had exhibited at the Allied Artists in 1913 and 1914 and knew, amongst others, Edward Marsh and Mark Gertler; he may have seen the Memorial Exhibition in 1918.[6] Another contemporary, Leon Underwood, who was a year older than Gaudier, only caught up with his work during the Twenties when he began to work in stone.

The aesthetic of direct carving in stone and of truth to materials assumed growing importance during the Twenties. At first Gaudier was little remembered other than by sculptors who had encountered Pound's *Memoir*, discovering there not only a selection of his sculpture and drawings dominated by his later, more experimental pieces, but also his *Blast* essays and reviews. Few of his sculptures, and none of his more Cubist or Vorticist pieces, were then in public collections. The most vitriolic rejection of Pound and Gaudier came from the American Lorado Taft who, in his 1917 lectures at the Art Institute of Chicago, dismissed the 'caricatures' of Matisse, Brancusi and Archipenko, and used Gaudier as a leading exemplar of the 'deluded youths' who 'for mischief or through sheer imbecility' had 'turned to this form of prostitution'.[7] Frank Rutter, whose role in setting up the Allied Artists' Association would certainly have made him familiar with Gaudier's work, omitted him from his 1926 *Evolution in Modern Art* but, by the late Twenties, one or two critics, their awareness heightened by the work of the newly emergent British sculptors, began to acknowledge Gaudier's posthumous influence. 'It should not be forgotten that the work of a Frenchman, Henri Gaudier-Brzeska (1891–1915), who lived for a time in England, and had a deep intuition of sculpture's origins and development, has influenced the younger school of British sculptors.'[8] In 1927 Wilenski, reversing his private dismissal of Gaudier, only two years earlier, as an artist who would never be important, called him 'the most original architectural sculptor so far produced by the modern movement'.[9] In 1928 Stanley Casson, while dismissing Vorticism and accusing Gaudier of 'frittering away his abounding energy in futile manifestoes that were manifest to no one and that no one read', acknowledged that 'he had the makings of a very great sculptor': he detected in *Dancer* 'in his interpretation of movement ... a new style in modern sculpture'.[10]

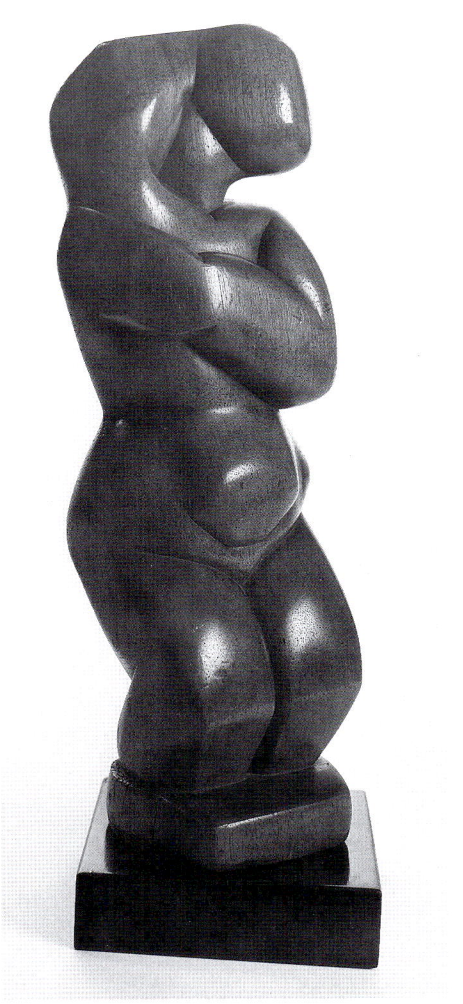

108 Henry Moore, *Standing Woman*, 1923

Henry Moore came across a second-hand copy of Pound's *Memoir* in about 1922 and was deeply affected by both the work and Gaudier's thoughts on the definition of sculpture. A notebook list he made of possible subjects includes 'Stone carrier, Woman kneeling, Horse with turned head, Speed – deer – legs doubled beneath it.'[11] One sees echoes of Gaudier in several early pieces, such as the marble *Dog*, 1922 (Henry Moore Foundation), *Standing Woman*, 1923 (fig. 108), and one or two of his early tightly interwoven *Mother and Child* groups.[12] Writing in 1930, Moore expressed views which reflect his discussions with Epstein as well as the impression made by Gaudier:

> The sculpture which moves me most is full-blooded and self-supporting, fully in the round, that is, its component forms are completely realized and work as masses in opposition, not being merely indicated by surface cutting in relief; it is not perfectly symmetrical, it is static and it is strong and vital, giving out something of the energy and power of great mountains.[13]

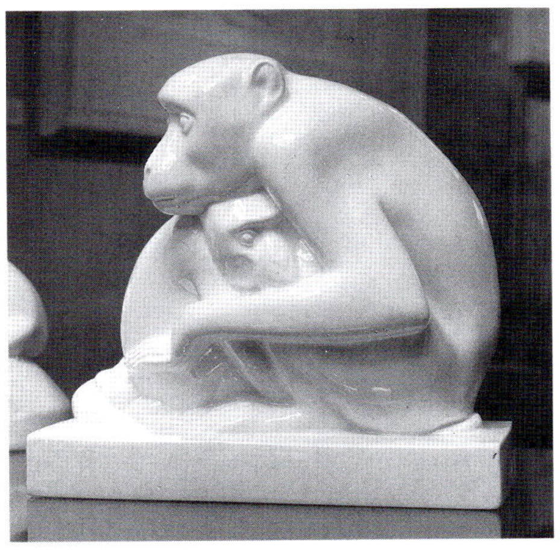

109 John Skeaping, *Monkeys*, 1927

During the Thirties, Moore's and Epstein's paths diverged sharply but Gaudier's influence endured; in 1934 when he set out his aims as a sculptor in *Unit One*, Moore identified the key points as truth to material, the fully three-dimensional realization of form, observation of nature, the fusion of abstract and human qualities to achieve intensity of expression, and innate vitality.[14] The terms in which these principles are set out are Moore's own but Gaudier's writing echoes through them. During the Sixties, at the request of Jim Ede, Moore patinated several casts of *Bird Swallowing a Fish* (retaining one himself) and *Maquette for Flower Vase 2* (*cat.* 100).

Gaudier's example relayed through Pound was also a vital inspiration for Leon Underwood's 1922–23 *Brains Below the Belt* and 1923 *Mountain God*.[15] During the later Twenties both Barbara Hepworth and John Skeaping made small *animalier* carvings in hard stone; Richard Bedford,

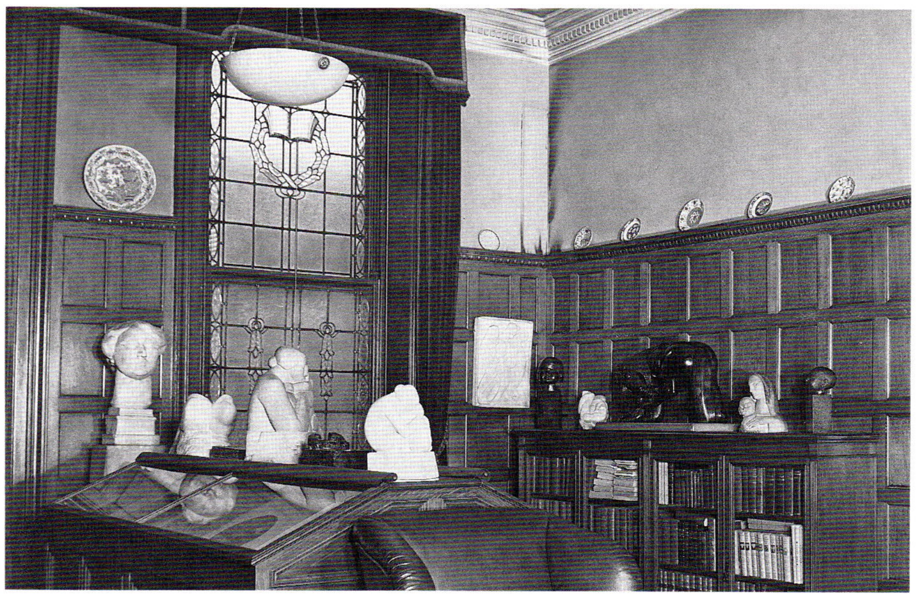

110 *Mlle Borne* and *Maternity* with Barbara Hepworth's *Doves* (1929) and *Mother and Child* (1927), Frank Dobson's *Pigeon Boy* (1920) and John Skeaping's terracotta *Madonna and Child* (*c.* 1926) in the home of George Eumorfopoulos, 1935

of the Victoria and Albert Museum's sculpture department, and Alan Durst, were also making animal pieces. It is likely that they were drawing inspiration, as Gaudier had, from Chinese and Japanese carving but they may also have known about Gaudier's animal carvings. As has recently been pointed out, several important collectors of Oriental art, such as George Eumorfopoulos, began to collect modernist carvings during this period, responding to their characteristic density, abstracted forms and rhythmic fluency (fig. 110).[16] Skeaping was perhaps Gaudier's real successor as an *animalier* but in the longer term he seems more closely allied to the dramatic *animalier* tradition of Barye (fig. 109).[17]

The publication of Ede's and Brodzky's books was timely, coinciding with this undercurrent of appreciation by artists and critics. In 1932, Wilenski reasserted the prime importance of Pound's *Memoir* in assessing Gaudier's work and likened him to Brancusi in his search for permanent universal forms: 'he experimented with the geometricization of his visual experience and also with geometrical combinations based on natural structure'.[18] He identified *Brass Toy (Torpedo Fish)*, *Bird Swallowing a Fish* and some of the animal and bird brush drawings reproduced by Pound, as works studied by modern sculptors to help them 'arrive at the development of their own creed.' The following year E. G. Underwood judged that Gaudier 'had a profound influence on the development of modern English sculpture … an artist of undoubted genius'.[19]

Since then there has been a degree of consensus in recognizing Gaudier's role as a direct carver, formal innovator and thinker in a pioneering period of modernism but also in acknowledging, often regretfully, that although there are individual works of importance – *Redstone Dancer*, *Bird Swallowing a Fish*, *Head of Ezra Pound* and some of the geometrically abstracted drawings and sculptures, notably *Birds Erect* – there was no single dominant style. For Levy, Gaudier's oeuvre is 'a microcosm of the *avant-garde* at a time when there was a genuine, evolving *avant-garde* in action.'[20] For Cole, on the other hand, he produced a number of 'highly individual sculptures' but 'it cannot be said that Gaudier ever achieved a recognizable style.'[21]

Gaudier's importance has continued to be assessed through his writing, quite apart from the evidence of his work. Thus Zilczer could claim in 1981,

> Two sculptors active in the first decades of this century, Eric Gill and Henri Gaudier-Brzeska, represented the dual origins of the direct carving aesthetic in Britain. Gill's advocacy of direct carving derived directly from the Arts and Crafts tradition. Gaudier-Brzeska's use of the technique on the other hand was more closely tied to the advent of modernism.[22]

Gaudier's clear identification with the English avant-garde, itself marginalized in treatments of European modernism, has contributed to his invisibility as a French artist. After Gaudier was killed, Pound's friend the writer and critic Rémy de Gourmont published almost the only tribute to appear in France. He went entirely on Pound's word since he had never heard of Gaudier; he was distinctly foggy about Vorticism, identifying Epstein as its leader and the *Tomb of Oscar Wilde* as a Vorticist work.

> He was 23 or 24 and seemed destined for fame. Like Epstein, like the painter Lewis, Brzeska (he exhibited only under this name) was a great admirer of the art of the ancient Orient, of the sculptural forms of the Egyptians, Assyrians and Chinese. But, writes, Pound, he was no imitator but a seeker. He had studied deeply and the remained his own man. Like all real sculptors, and they are a rare breed, he liked to attack the stone direct. He had, as the English say, 'the sense of the material'.[23]

So far as the writers engaged in Cubism and other modern movements were concerned, Gaudier did not exist. In 1919 André Salmon, passing over the claims not only of Gaudier but also of Rembrandt Bugatti and François Pompon, lamented the dearth of innovative animaliers.[24] Once again in 1945 Gaudier was passed over in discussions of direct carving and *animalier* sculpture in an important book on sculpture in France.[25] Subsequent studies have similarly served to underestimate the significance of French political, social and intellectual life in his formation and, in the understandable eagerness to lament his loss to English twentieth-century art, to overlook the likelihood that Gaudier's career after the war might well have taken place in France. From the European, later twentieth-century perspective of constructive sculptural techniques, improvised materials and readymades – in short from the perspectives of later Cubist, Futurist and Dada sculpture – Gaudier could also be seen not as a pioneer but as part of an anti-industrial rearguard of artists, wedded to traditional materials and seeking in the archaic and primitive a formal language through which to express their dissidence.[26] The attractions of 'primitive' sculpture, like those of direct carving, were less a matter of structure or form than of spiritual affinities and mystic union between sculptor and material, a reading framed more by German Expressionism than by the English avant-garde.

Until the 1950s only a few of Gaudier's earliest works could be seen in any French public collection; these were given to Orléans by his parents.

Alerted to the importance of their son's work by Pound's *Memoir*, Gaudier's parents were frustrated in their attempts to track it down by a combination of Gaudier's adoption of Brzeska's name, her inheritance of his Estate and her subsequent intestacy.[27] Ede was reticent about his acquisition of the Brzeska Estate; it was only after further correspondence with the Gaudier family during the Fifties that he began to give and sell substantial quantities of drawings and some sculptures to the Orléans museum and to the French national collections.[28] In 1956, introducing the first exhibition of Gaudier's work to take place in France, at Orléans, the curator, Jacqueline Auzas-Pruvost, acknowledged that the exhibition would introduce the work of an unknown artist and make its audience aware of the loss his death represented to French art. In 1965 the Salle Gaudier-Brzeska opened at the Musée National d'Art Moderne in its former home in the Palais de Tokyo.[29] Roger Sécretain's *Un sculpteur "maudit". Gaudier-Brzeska*, published in 1979, was the artist's first biography in French. As Sécretain pointed out other factors militated against recognition – Gaudier's pseudo-Polish identity and residual local rancour at his refusal to undertake national service.[30] It was only in 1992 that Pound's text was published in French and in 1993 that the exhibition, held in Orléans and Toulouse in belated celebration of the artist's centenary, attracted a measure of national attention.

Stories of the desperation and tragedies of Gaudier's and Brzeska's lives will, no doubt, continue to move and inspire those who hear them. The immediacy, vitality and apparent spontaneity of Gaudier's work will continue to delight; and there are life and animal drawings of supreme quality. Perhaps that is enough to justify a reputation and a following. Gaudier's stature as a pioneer of modernism, however, rests upon more than this. There are more than a dozen sculptures of which each is a quite outstanding example of its kind. Their variety as he tried out one idea and then another, responded to this or that commission or opportunity to prove himself, reveals both his youth and an astounding versatility. His work can be seen as a fascinating paradigm of this exploratory, transitional period when the very definition of sculpture was being challenged all over Europe. Playfully experimental works can be seen naturally enough as evidence of the artist's immaturity; but they often reveal the wide range of visual sources he was assimilating and the aesthetic positions he was trying out; they complement the violent swings of mood and opinion, of hero-worship, artistic brotherhood and rejection which signal the tension between the outsider's desire for approval and the artist's need to assert an individual voice. The sculptures suggest a deeper seated ambivalence towards the classical tradition and the redefinition of the sculpture while the letters and writings provide a fascinating and articulate counterpoint. It was because of these uncertainties, not despite them, that Gaudier exercized a catalytic influence on British sculptors during the Twenties.

The exhilaration which much of his work still stimulates and the affection it often inspires surely also stems from his arrogant self-confidence. Untrammelled by the customary restraints and systematic exercizes of art school training, he experimented in competing styles with apparently nonchalant ease and intelligence, responding directly with verve and individuality. There is very little of caution, prudence or dogged perseverance about him, except in the consistent determination with which he pursued his calling. More perhaps than any of his contemporaries he can be seen as a role model of an artist who ignored boundaries. For the majority of them the realization of artistic talent and ambition was fostered by attendance at art schools during which their practice and understanding of art were guided by the conventional hierarchies of the *beaux arts* – drawing after the Antique, the Old Masters and from life, to painting and sculpture and, to a lesser extent, to the graphic arts – rather than by the less highly esteemed decorative arts. If the methods and goals of training sculptors were slightly less rigidly prescribed – taking in architectural decoration and ornamental masonry – they were nevertheless just as strongly tied to assumptions about the pre-eminence of classical, allegorical and historical genres and of large-scale public work. From the Realists and Impressionists onwards many had of course rebelled, abandoning academies or rejecting their teachings and hallowed models. Nevertheless most still attended art schools and imbibed some of the values. Among Gaudier's friends and contemporaries in Britain few lacked art training altogether. For Gaudier, lacking access to conventional training and driven to seize any opportunity, his relationship with this tradition was ambivalent. In many respects, he trained himself as a draughtsman using some of the same models as did his contemporaries at the Slade or the Ecole des Beaux-Arts. But he studied cheap popular art-forms such as magazine illustration and satirical prints with the same critical deference as Michelangelo. Hence, his exceptional freedom of technique. His selectivity among the cultures of both the classical and the modern worlds, from both East and West, from large sculpture and very small, displays an almost postmodern fluency and lack of inhibition.

Gaudier overcame his extreme outsider status – as untrained artist, poor, radical, foreign without the benefit of contacts – to become one of the leaders of the British avant-garde within three years of his arrival. He was a sign of the opportunities for radical intervention that the exhaustion of the classical tradition had opened up. To look at his work today is to feel the energy and sense of purpose that characterizes the dissolution of an old order and the bursting into chaotic but vigorous life of the new.

PHOTOGRAPHER'S NOTE

by David Finn

SHORTLY after the idea for this book was born, I started on a photographic adventure that for a variety of reasons took almost fifteen years to complete. During this time I visited Kettle's Yard in Cambridge to photograph Gaudier-Brzeska's sculptures; the Tate Gallery in London; the Museum in Orléans; the Pompidou Centre in Paris; Tirolo in Italy where Mary Rachewiltz, Ezra Pound's daughter, lives; Hamilton College, NY, where two sculptures are on extended loan from Omar Pound, Ezra Pound's son; the Hirshhorn Museum in Washington, D.C.; and the Museum of Modern Art in New York.

In her text Evelyn Silber has pointed to the influence of Rodin, Epstein, Gill, Archipenko, and Brancusi on Gaudier-Brzeska's sculpture, but my photographs of their works, which I have taken for other projects, involved a different experience from that of photographing Gaudier-Brzeska's. For the most part I found that they make statements in their sculpture which can be captured in a few photographs taken from different angles. Gaudier-Brzeska's sculptures, on the other hand, invite a virtually endless number of photographs. Details shot from almost every possible angle reveal compositions that are often breathtaking.

The only other artist I know who created work of such diversity is Henry Moore, and it is fascinating to speculate about the relationship between the two. Moore, only seven years younger, was sixteen years old when Gaudier-Brzeska was killed. He was in secondary school in Castleford, and had begun only recently to show a talent for drawing and an interest in sculpture. He was still in the army when the *Memorial Exhibition* of Gaudier-Brzeska's works opened in June 1918, and so would not have had an opportunity to see his works. He did see photographs published in Ezra Pound's 1916 biography, and in 1922 he read Gaudier-Brzeska's powerful essay on sculpture in *Blast*, when Moore was a student at the Royal College of Art.

I am sure that the female torso carved by Moore in 1929 (no. 29 in his catalogue raisonné) was not in any sense a copy of the female torso carved by Gaudier-Brzeska in 1913; both seem to be original conceptions. Yet they share the same spirit. The bulging forms of many of Gaudier-Brzeska's works like *Wrestler* are distinctly Moore-like, as are the intertwining abstractions in *Caritas* and *Birds Erect*. Despite the variety of his output, I have rarely photographed a work of Moore's that did not lend itself to being photographed from as many different angles as I found in Gaudier-Brzeska's work. Moore's works are visual feasts for the searching photographer's eye and I had the same experience when photographing Gaudier-Brzeska's sculptures.

I find it hard to imagine how a young man of twenty-three could produce such a remarkable body of work. I keep reminding myself that Keats was only twenty-five when he died and yet he is acknowledged by all to be one of our greatest poets. It is not the legend that surrounds these towering figures that inflames my imagination, but the quality of their work, and it challenges credulity that they could have been produced at such an early age.

As I photographed one work by Gaudier-Brzeska after another, I asked myself, 'Is this truly a great work, or am I reading something into it?' My camera always gave me the same answer. Discovery is the key word to describe the experience. I couldn't believe all the wonderful forms I was finding through my camera lens. Even looking at the back of a sculpture like *Dog*, or at some of the tiny ornaments, or at some of the carved plaster vases, there was always some surprise, some remarkable composition, even sometimes a hidden face in what appeared to be an abstract form. Although he worked as a sculptor for only four or five years at most, this was no amateur, no halting student finding his way. He was a genius – a genius like Moore – out of whose mind and hand extraordinary forms miraculously emerged.

It is a source of great personal satisfaction that my photographs of Gaudier-Brzeska's work have now been published together with Evelyn Silber's brilliant text, written after what I know was exhaustive and patient research over many years.

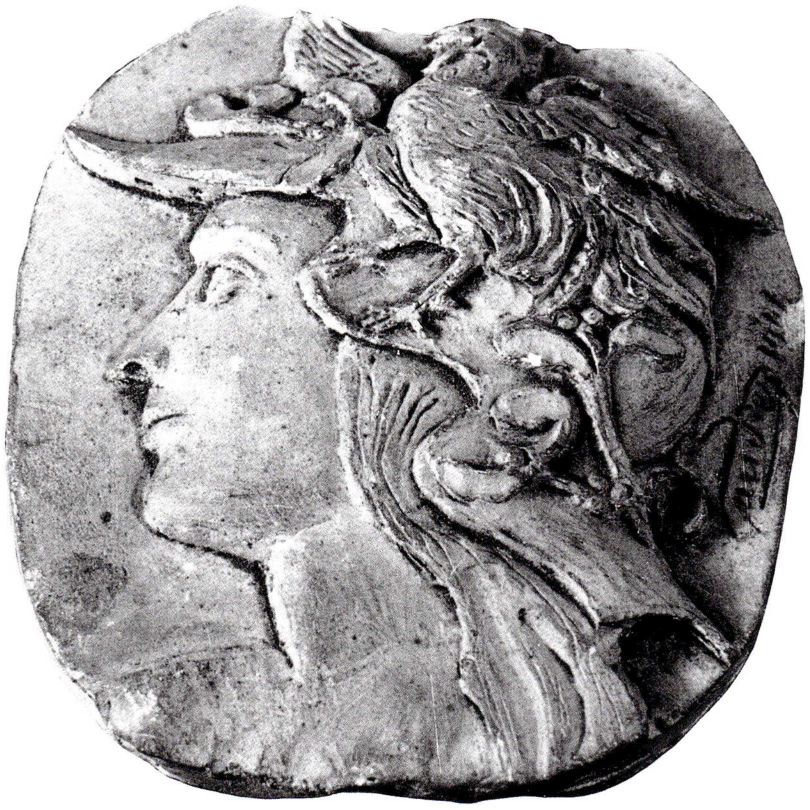

1 Medallion of Minerva (*cat.* 1)

2 So-called Portrait of Mme Gaudier (*cat.* 3)

3 Terracotta Mask (*cat.* 8)

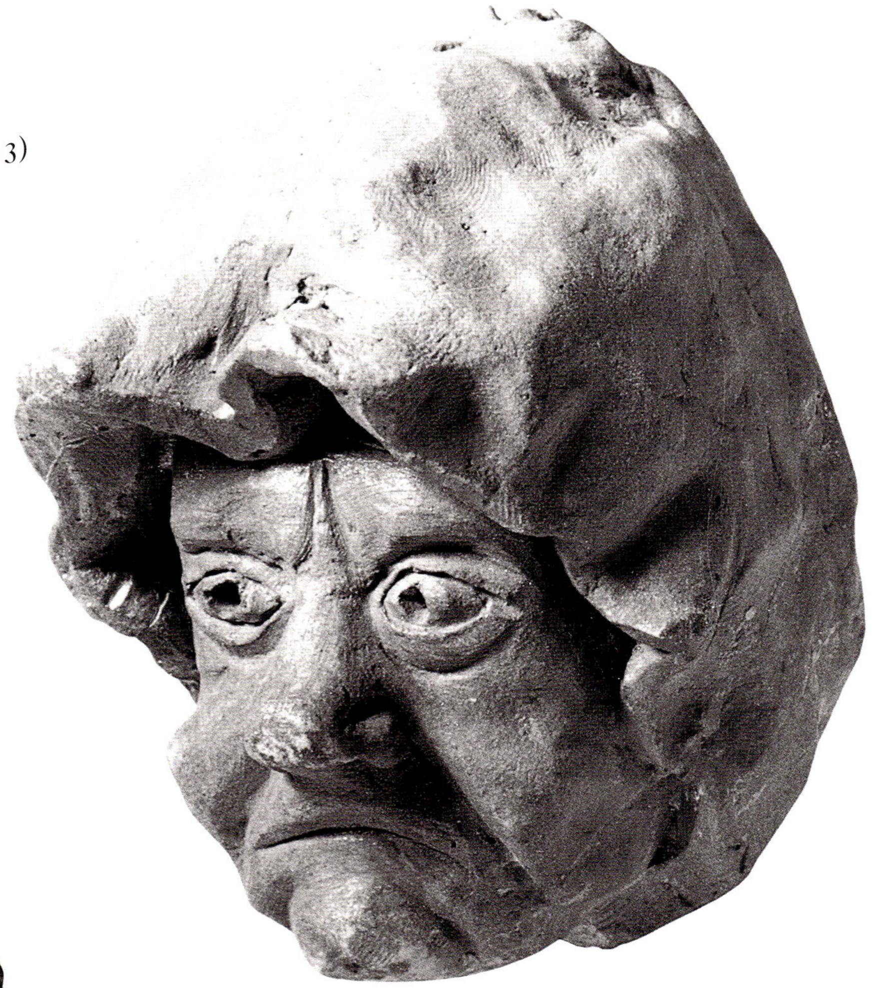

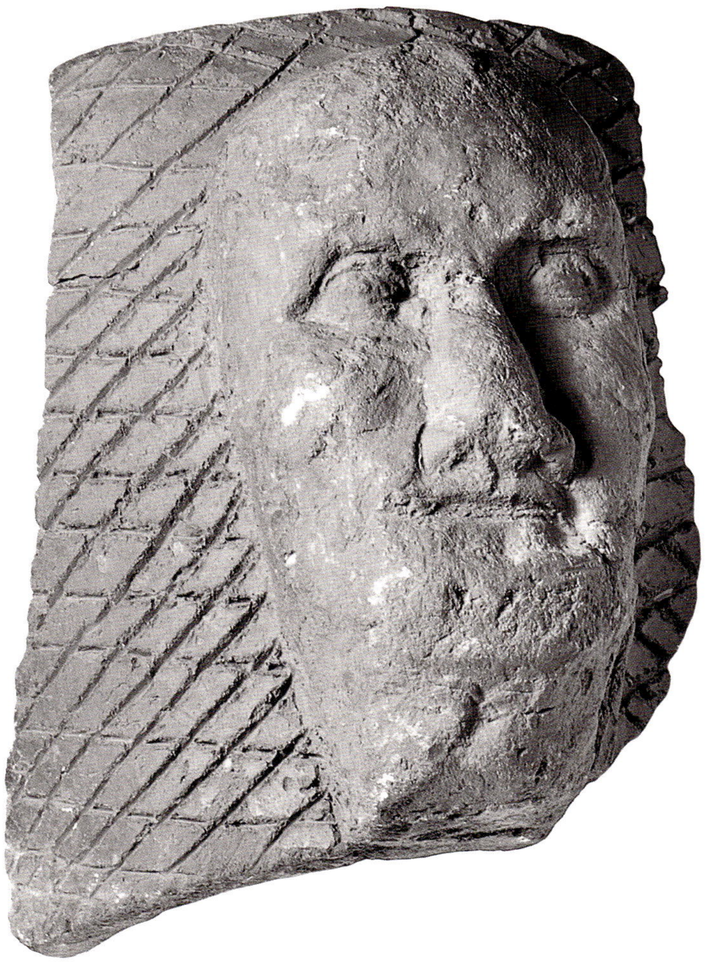

4 Portrait of M. Gaudier (*cat.* 2)

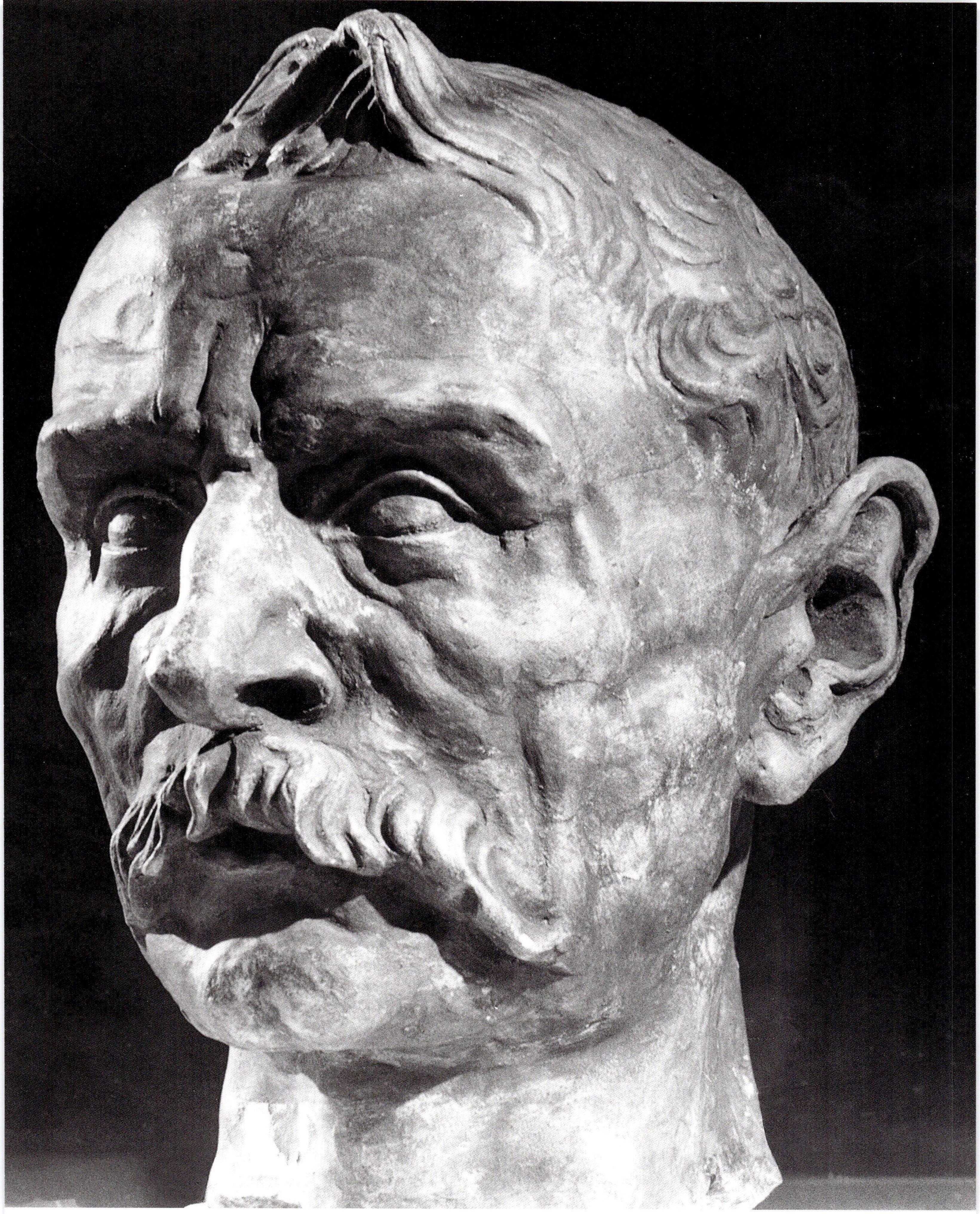

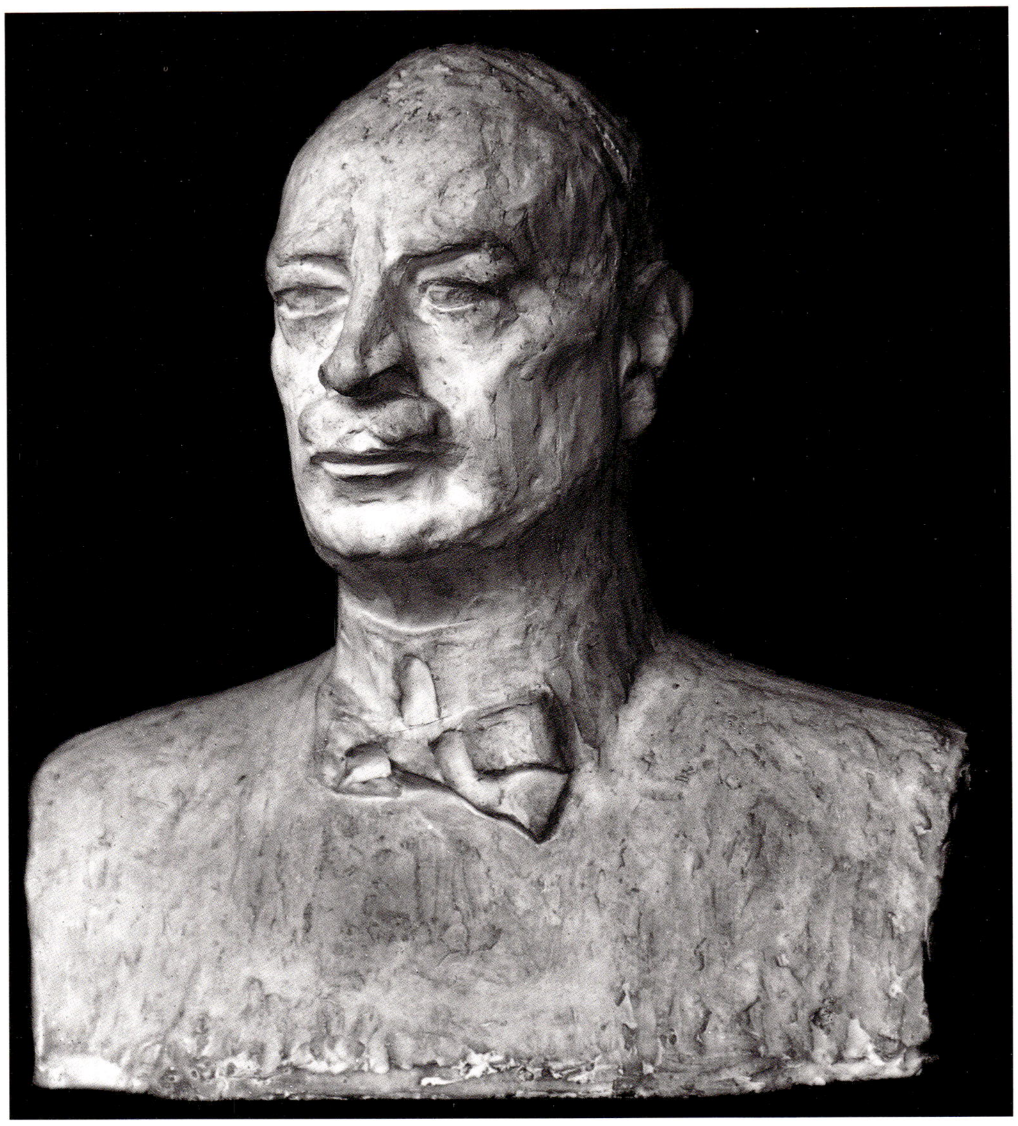

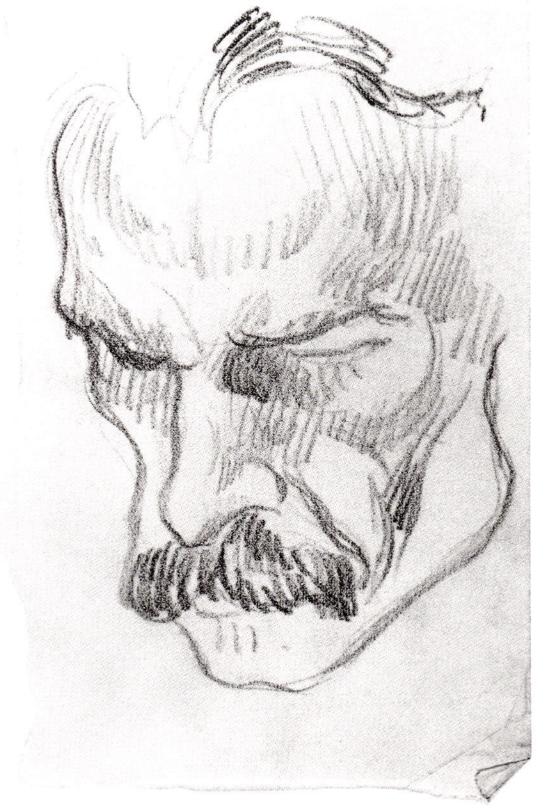

5 Haldane Macfall (*cat.* 11)

6 Sketch of Haldane Macfall, pencil

7 Major Smythies (*cat.* 12)

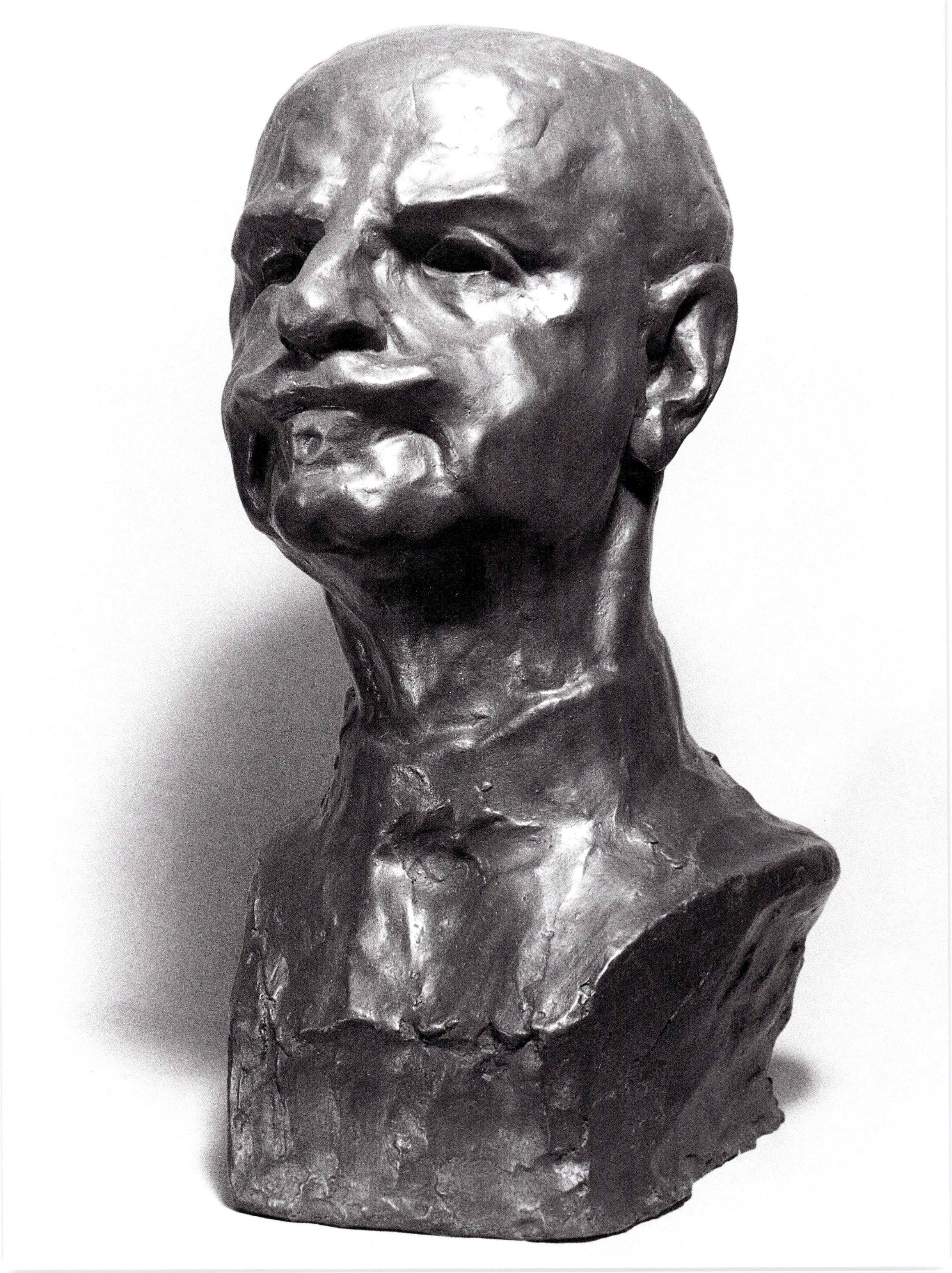

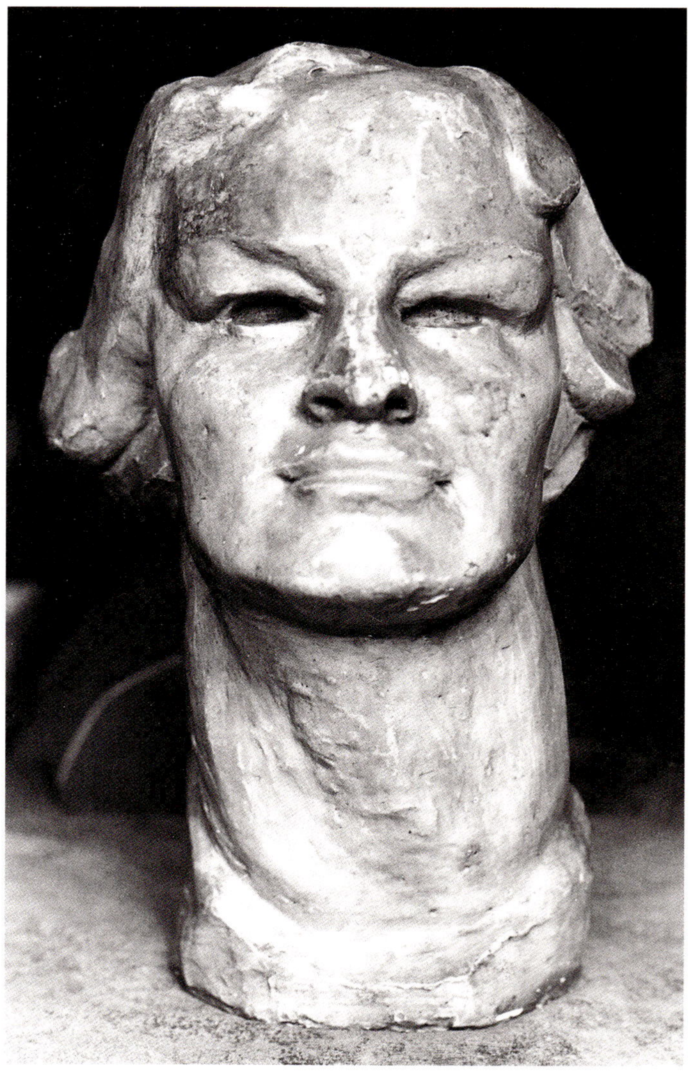

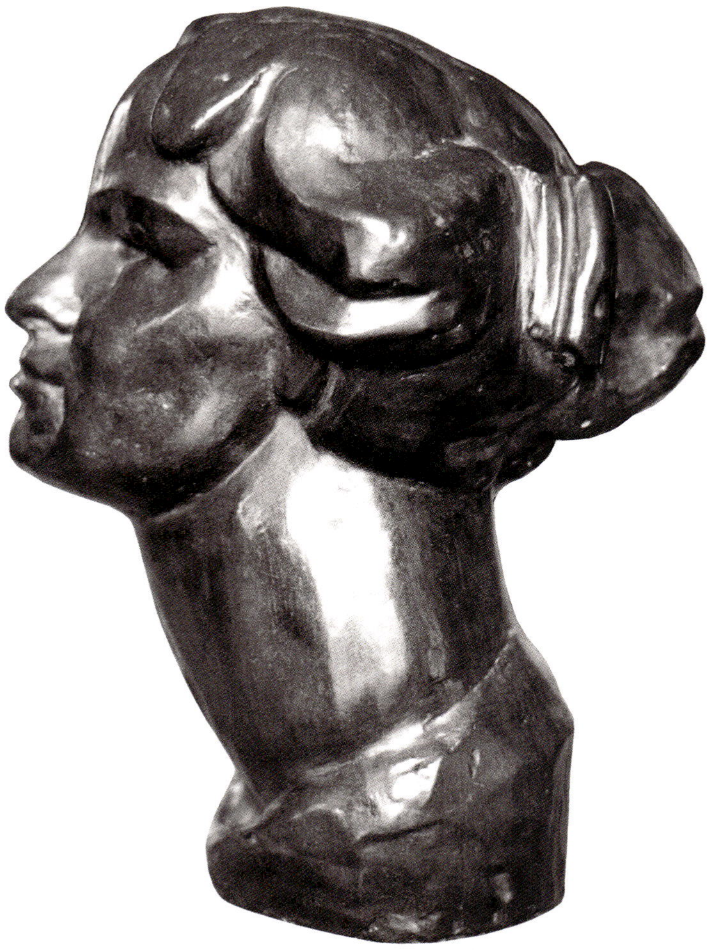

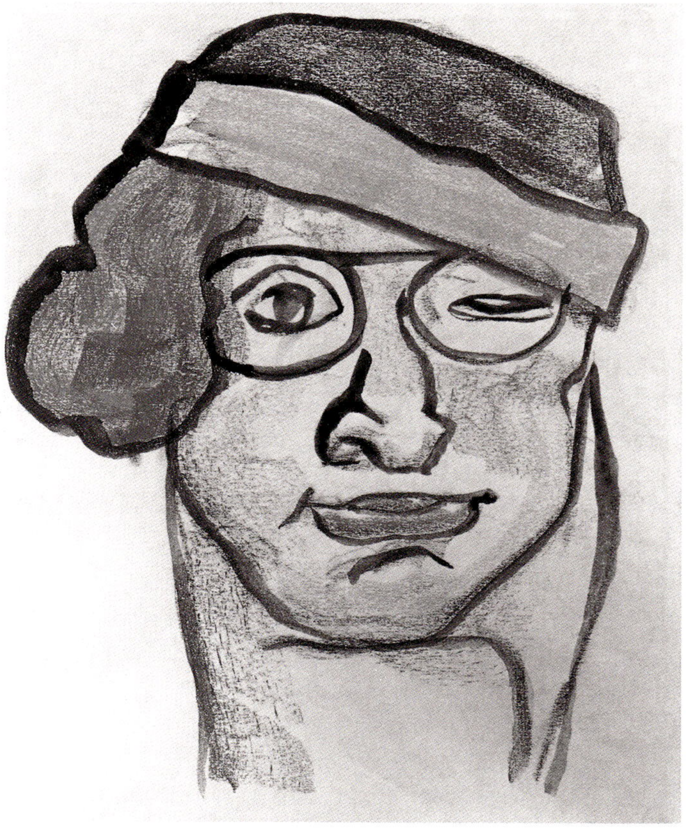

8 Enid Bagnold (*cat.* 17)

9 Sketch of Enid Bagnold, ink and pastel

10 Enid Bagnold (*cat.* 17)

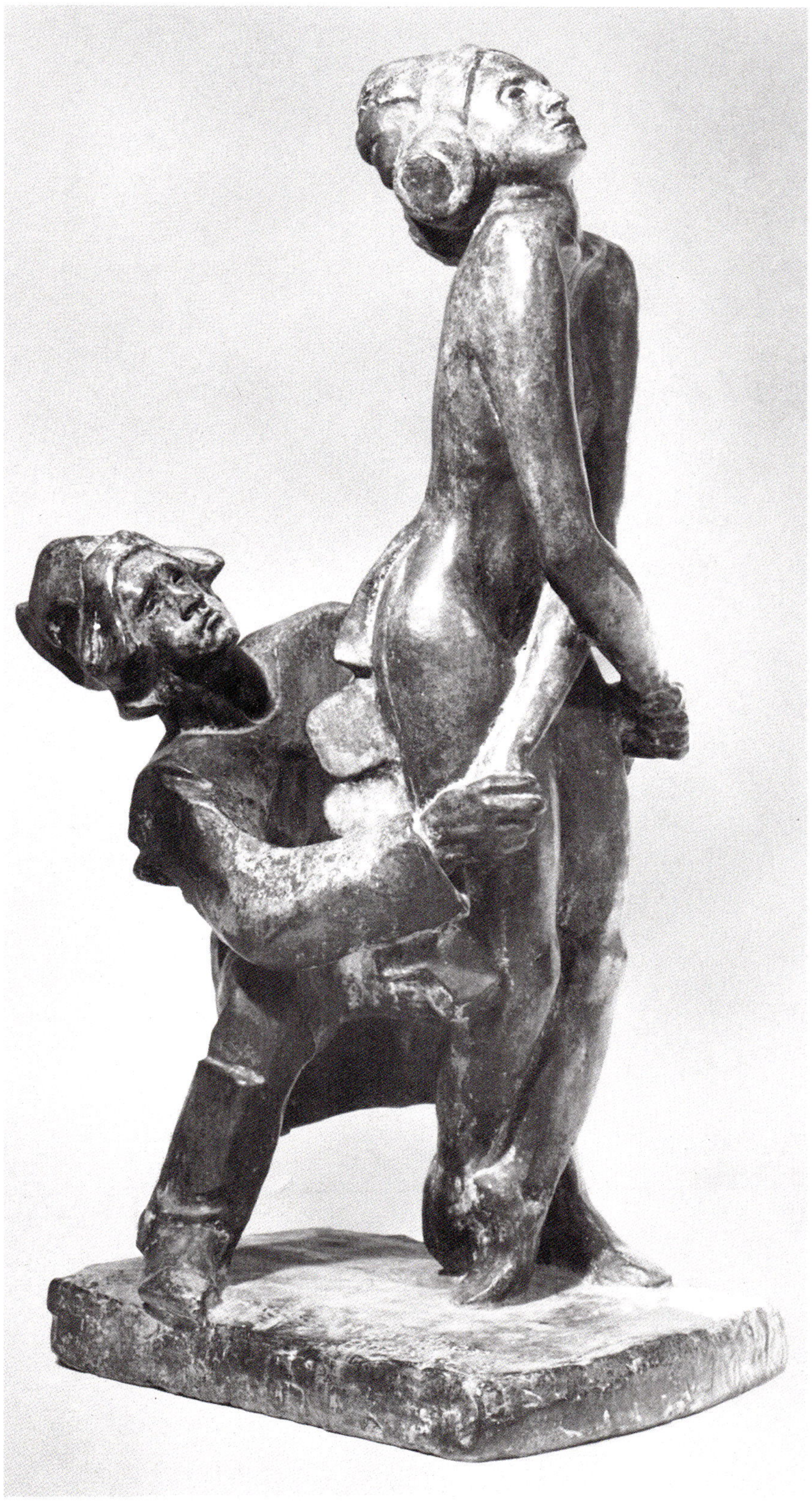

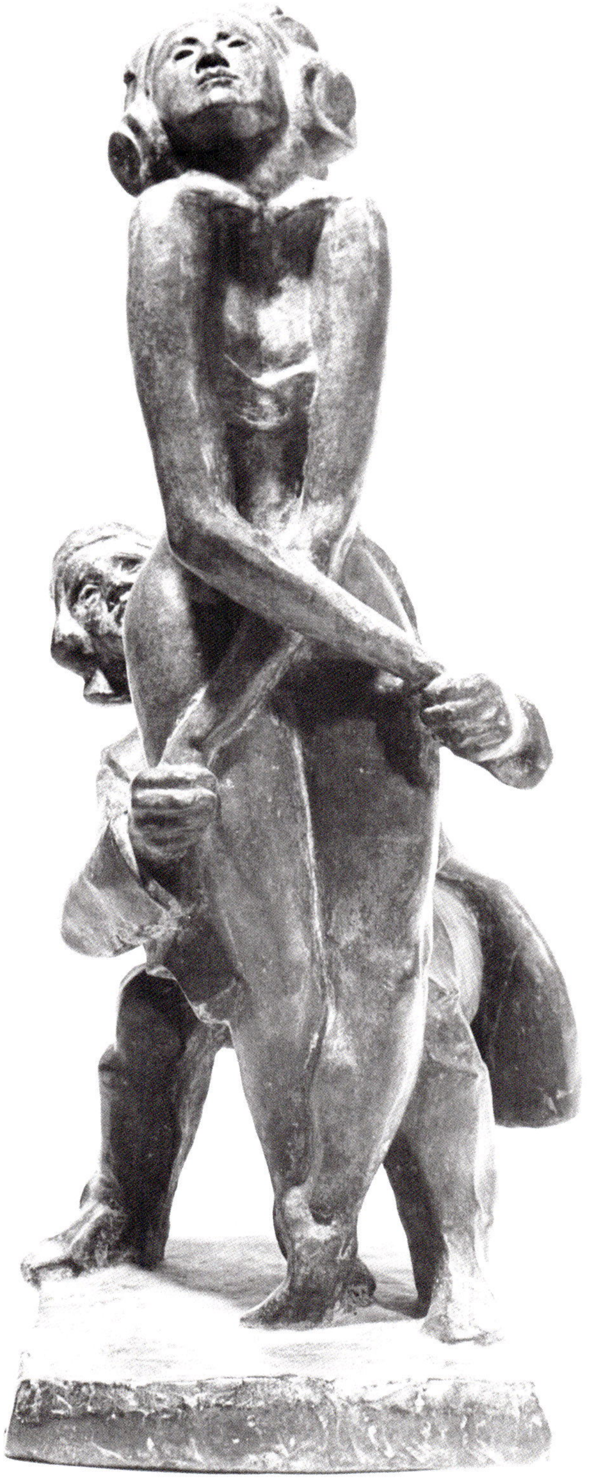

11, 12 Firebird (*cat.* 18)

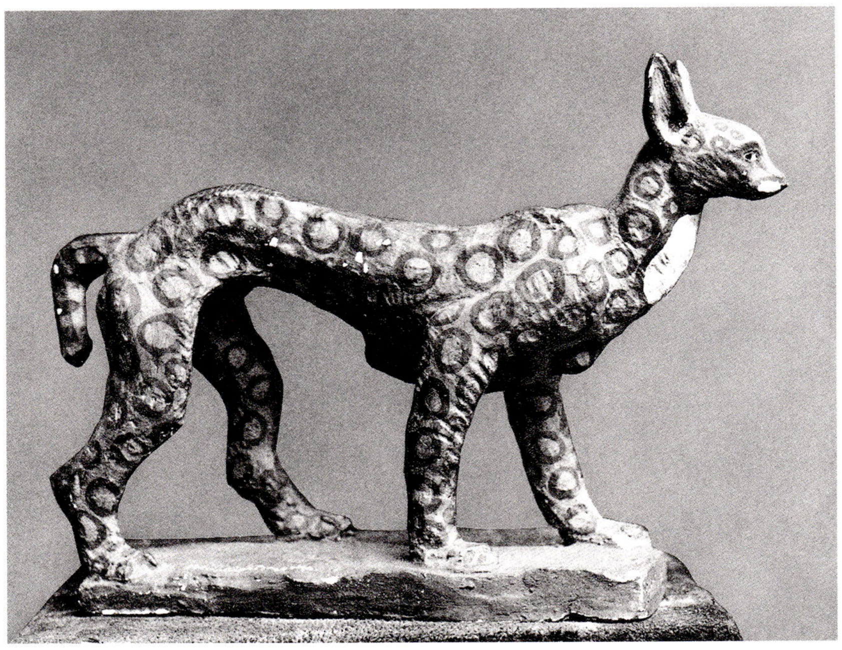

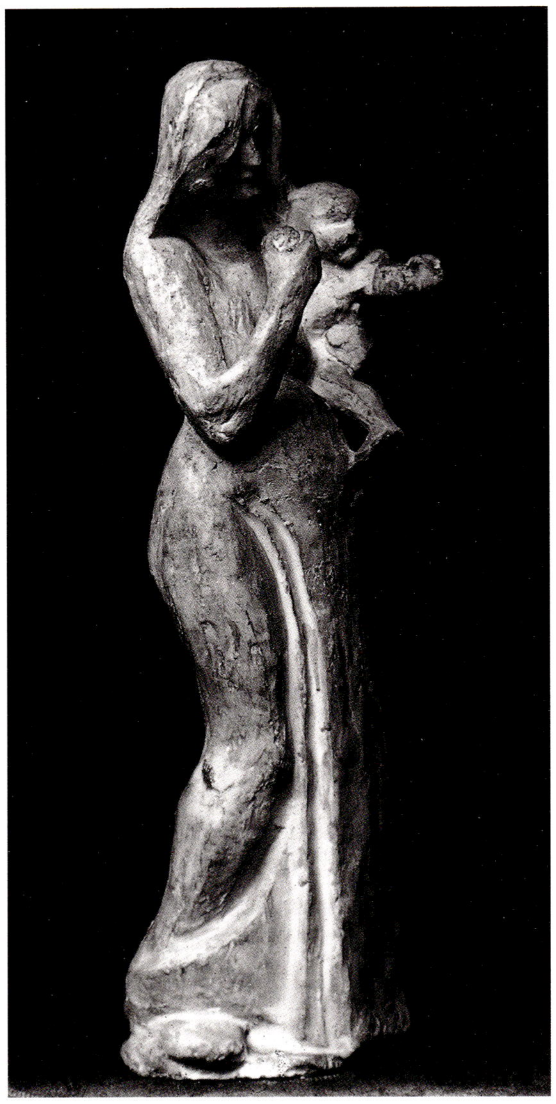

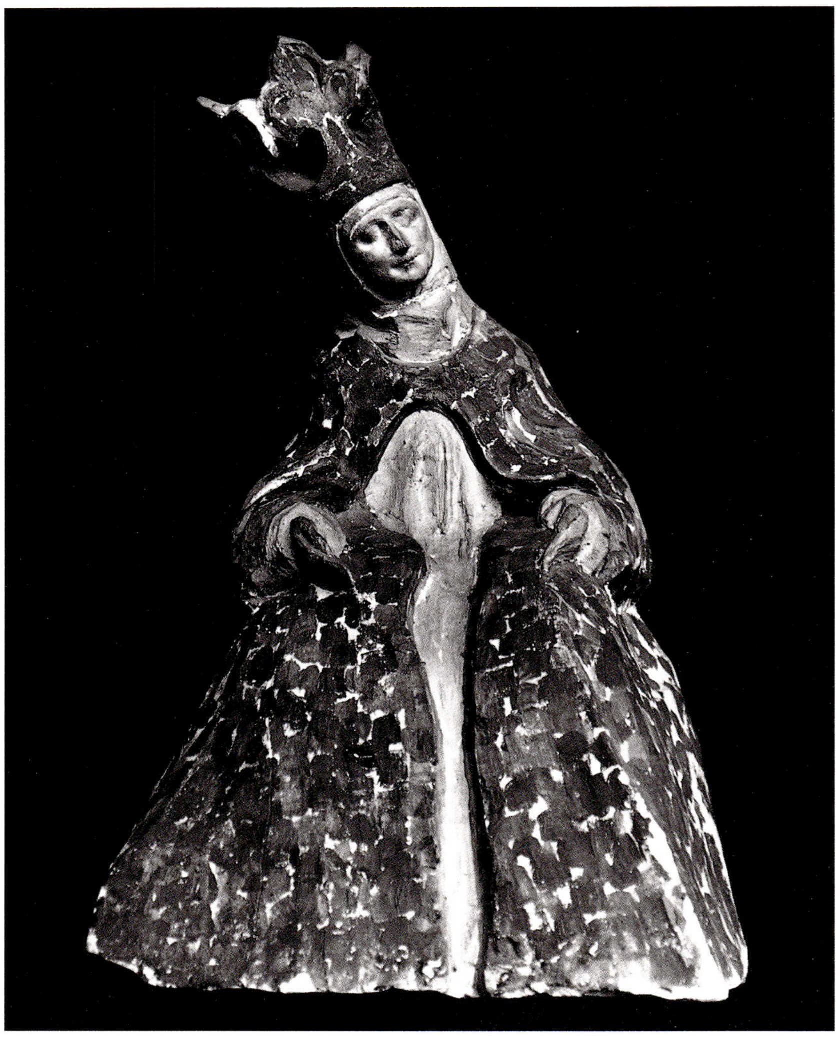

13 Cheetah or Jungle Cat (*cat.* 26)

14 The Madonna of 'The Miracle' (*cat.* 9)

15 Maternity (*cat.* 16)

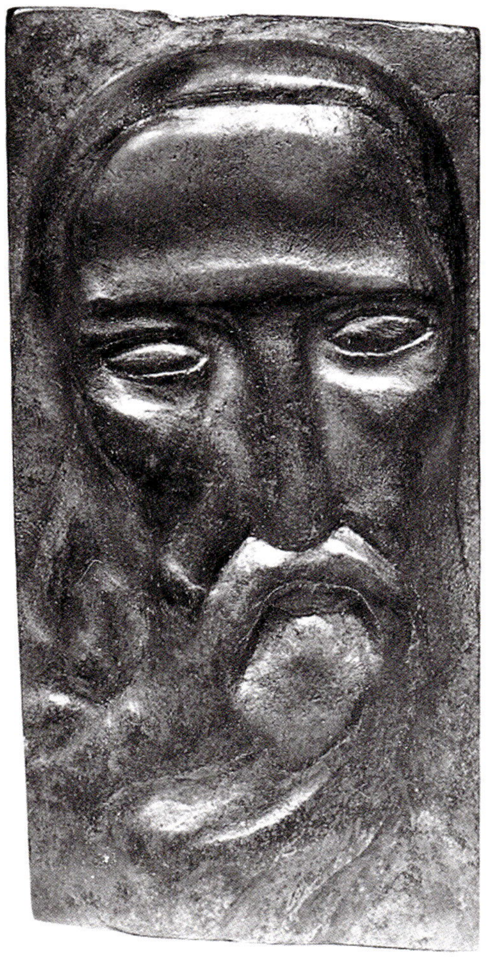

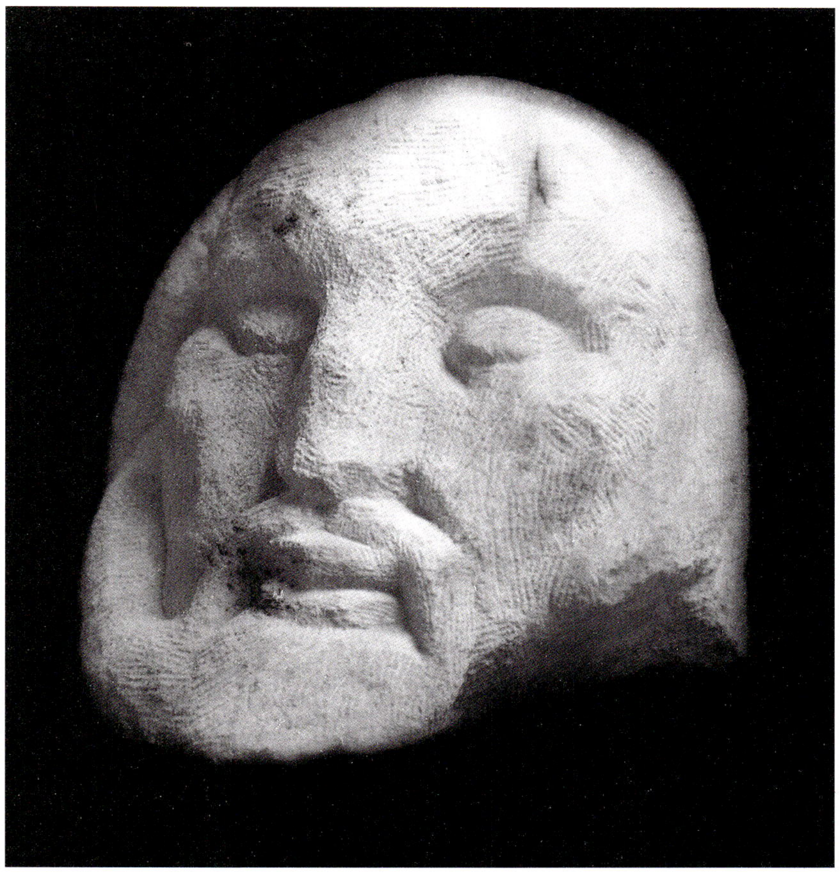

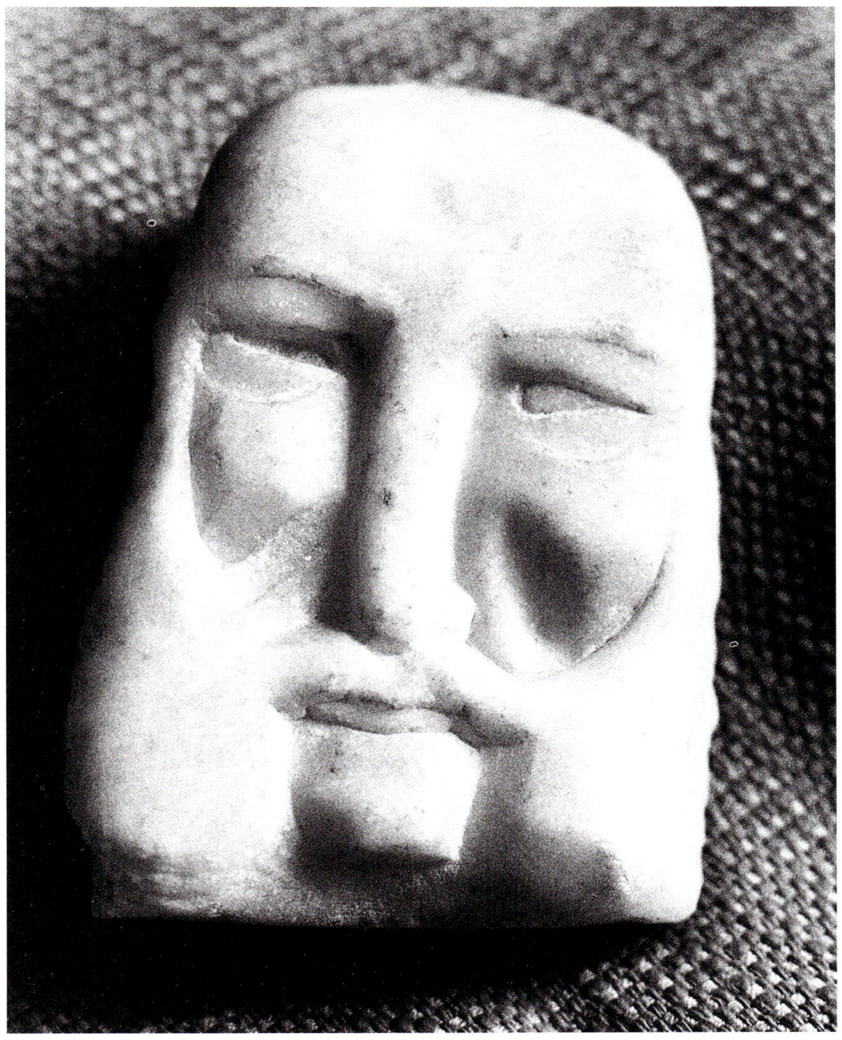

16 Religious Head (*cat.* 20)

17 Head of Christ (*cat.* 42)

18 Head of a Man, relief (*cat.* 19)

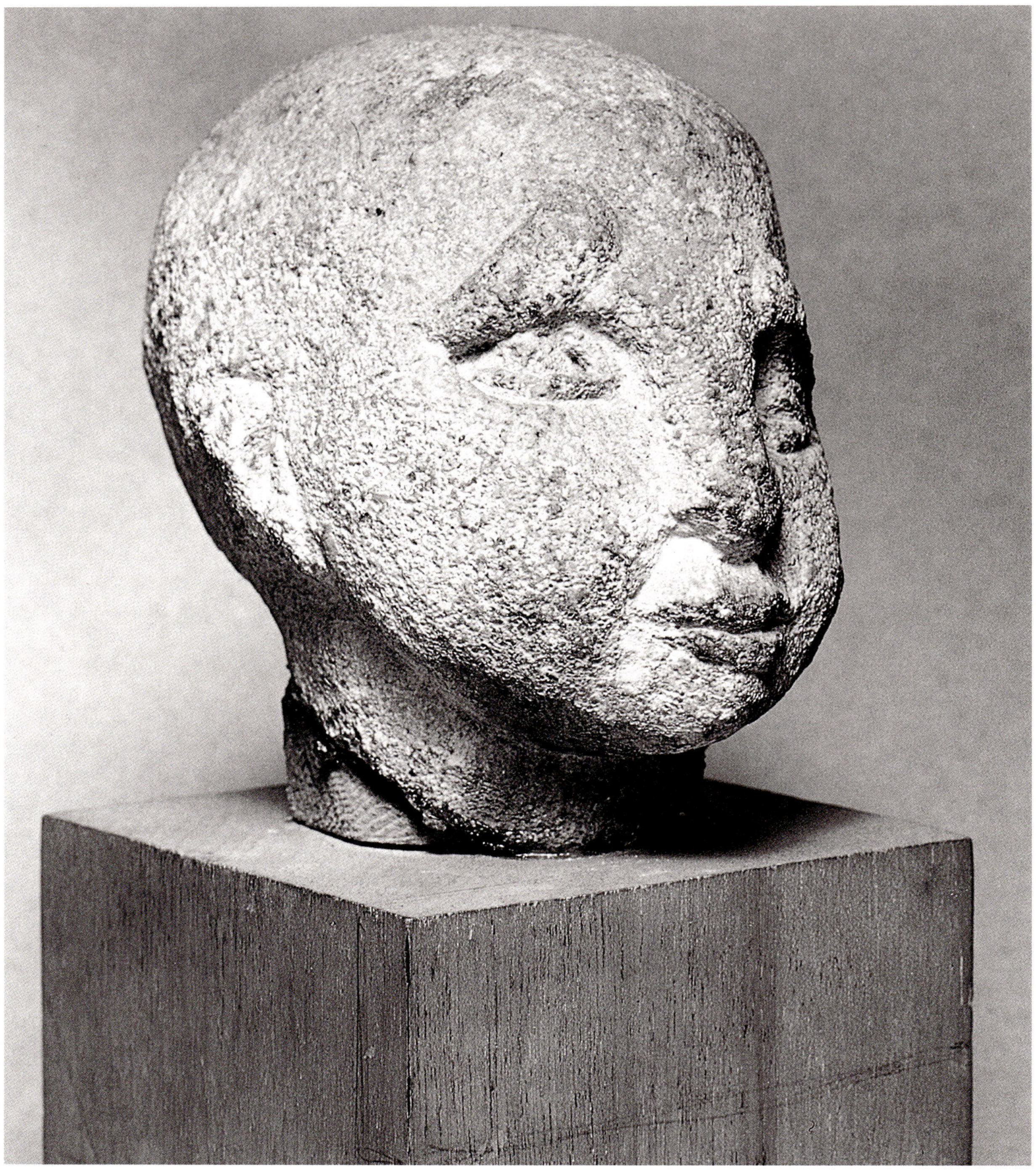

19 Head of a Child (*cat.* 22)

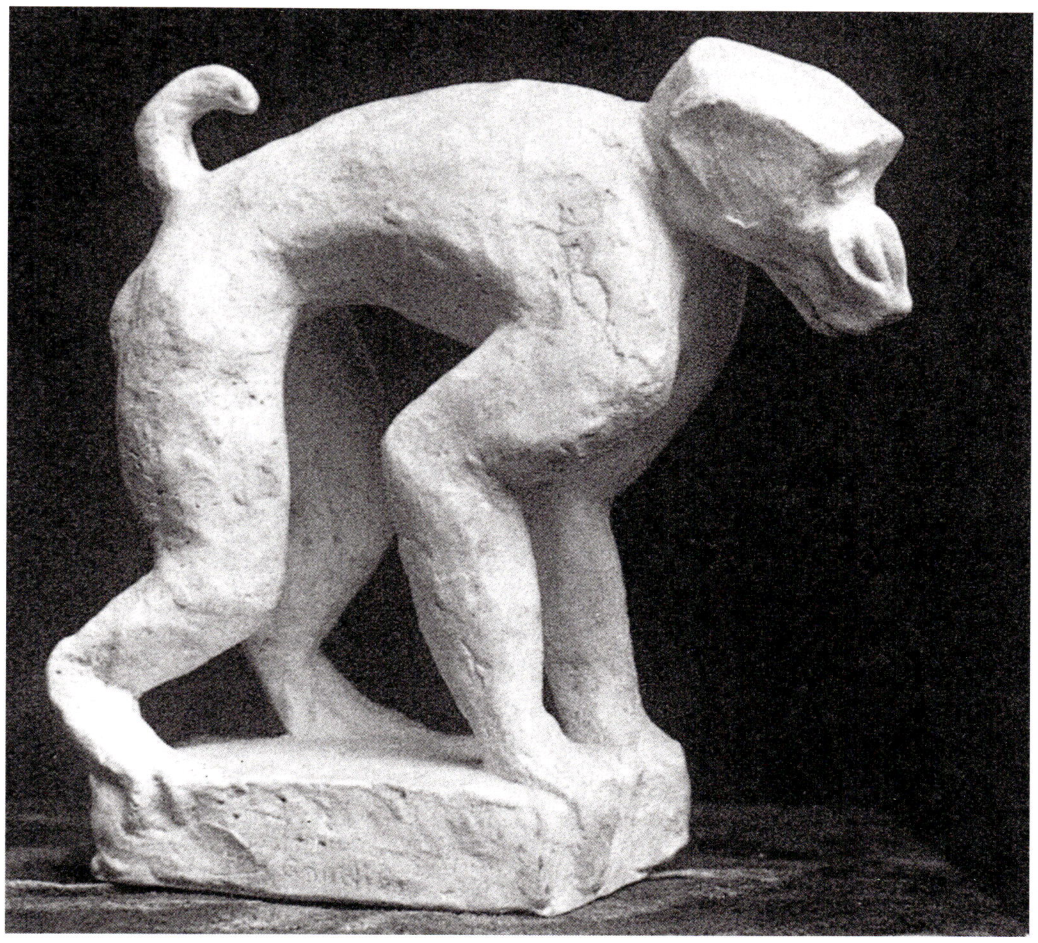

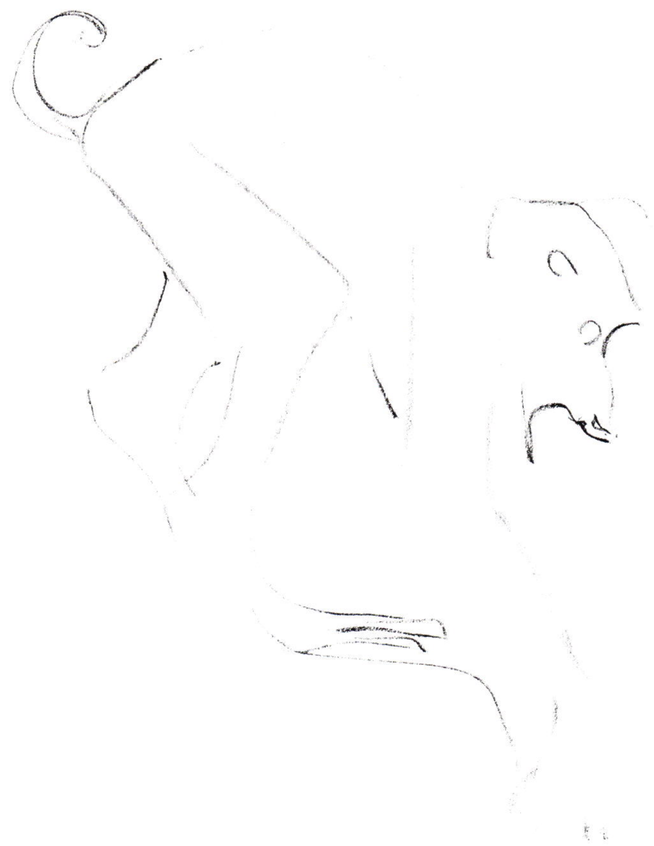

20 Monkey (*cat.* 23)

21 Sketch of Monkey, conté crayon

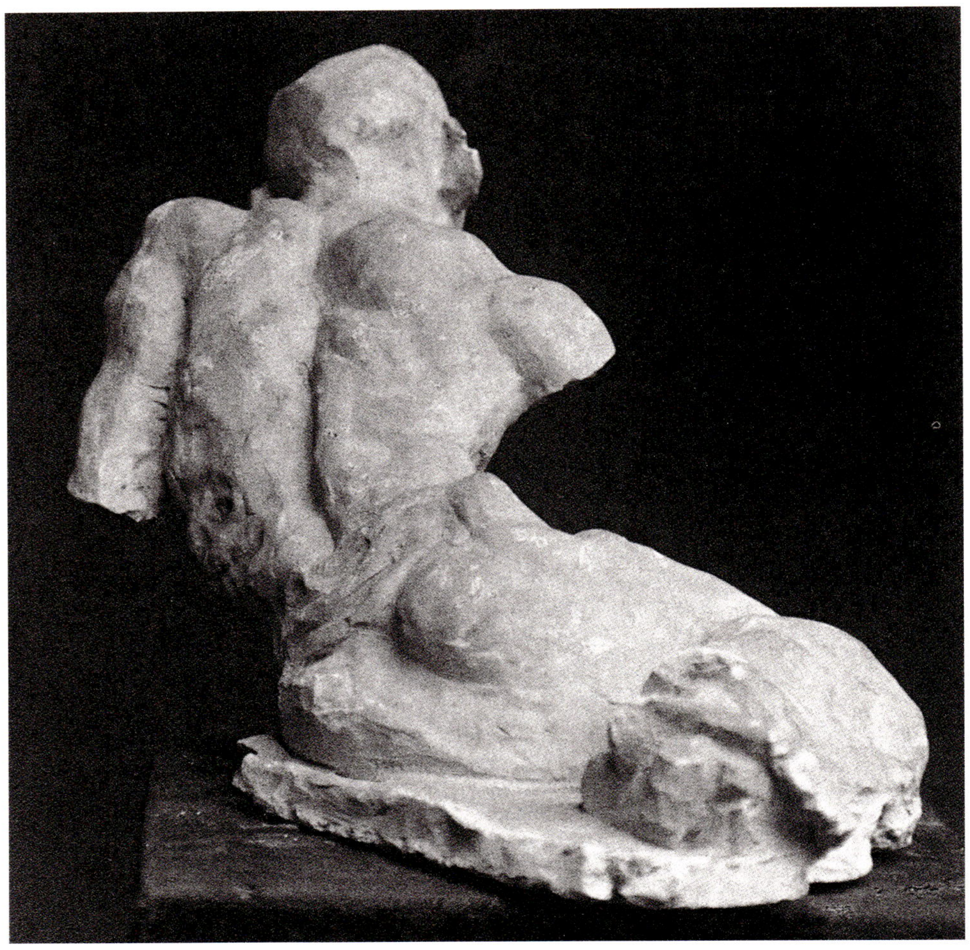

22, 23
Workman Fallen from
a Scaffold (*cat.* 29)

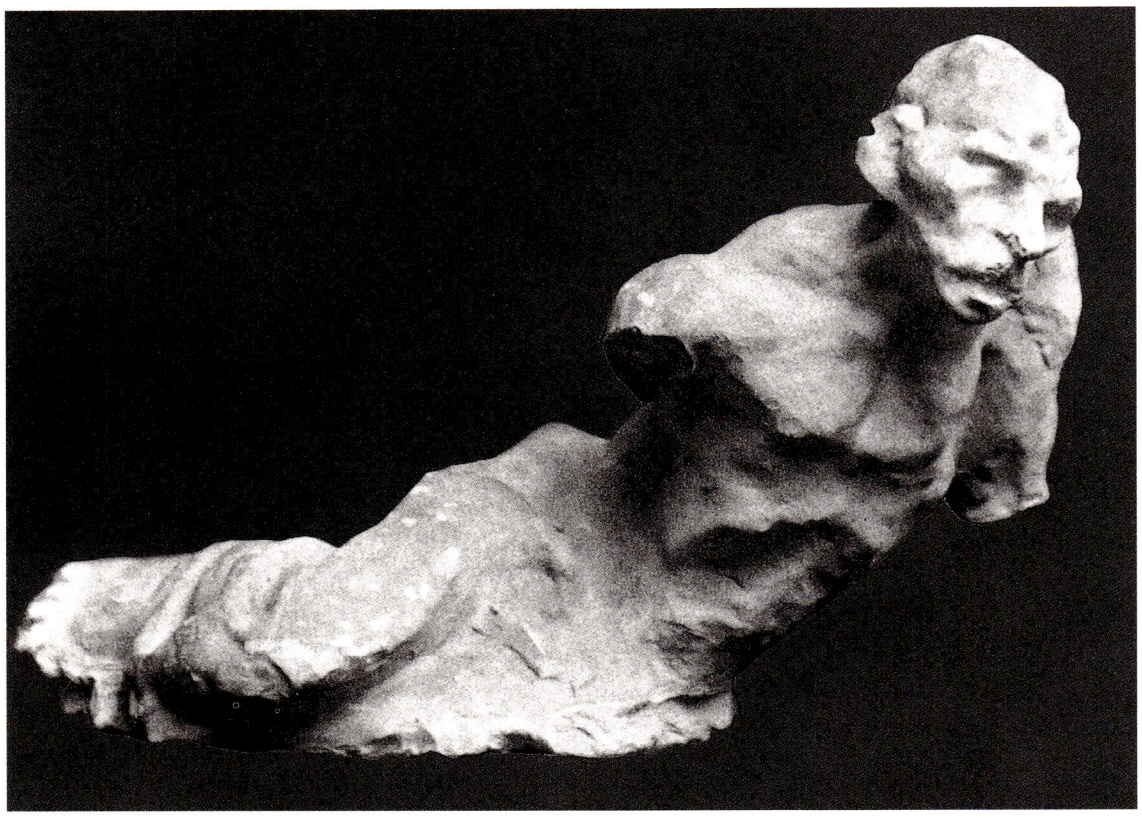

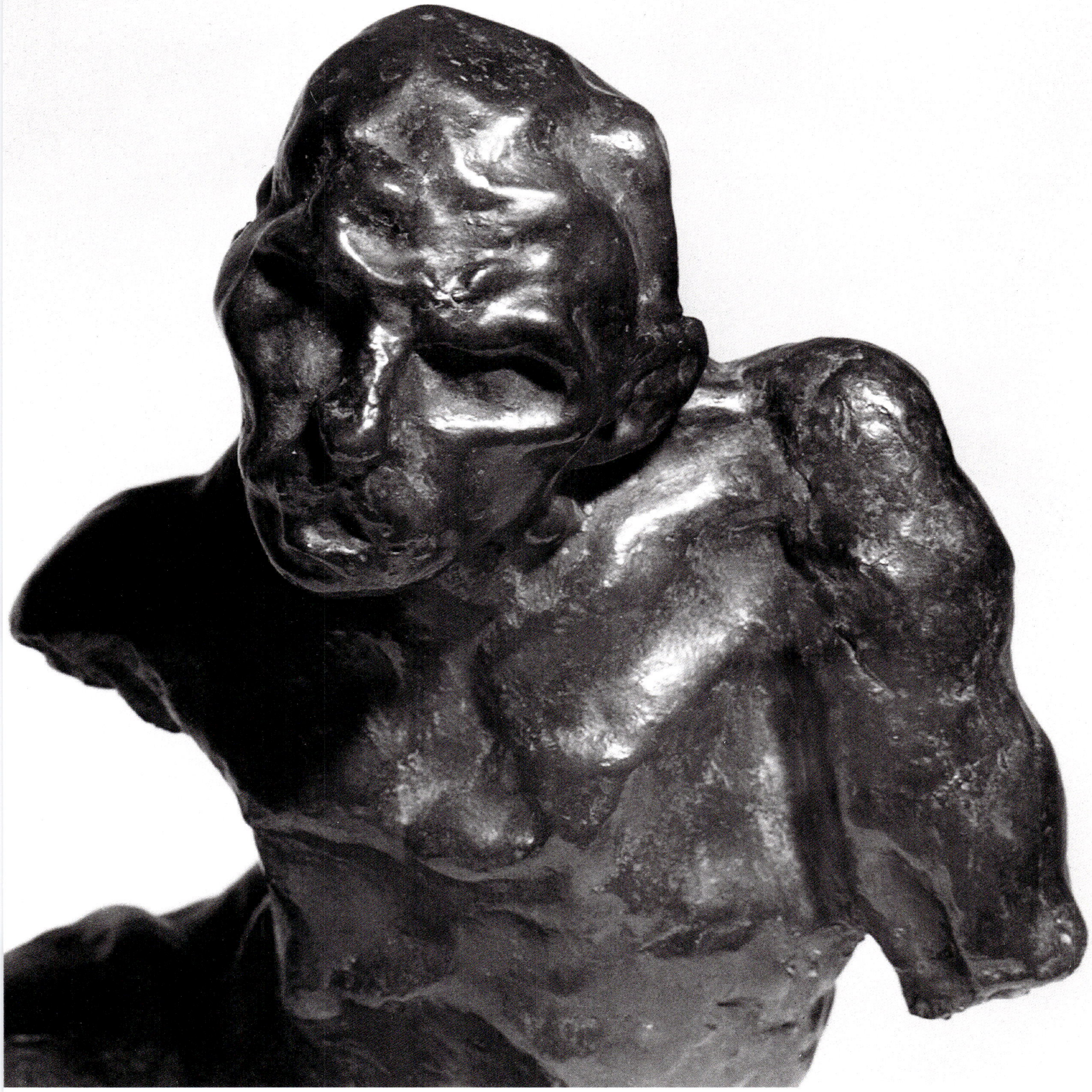

24 Workman Fallen from a Scaffold (*cat.* 29)

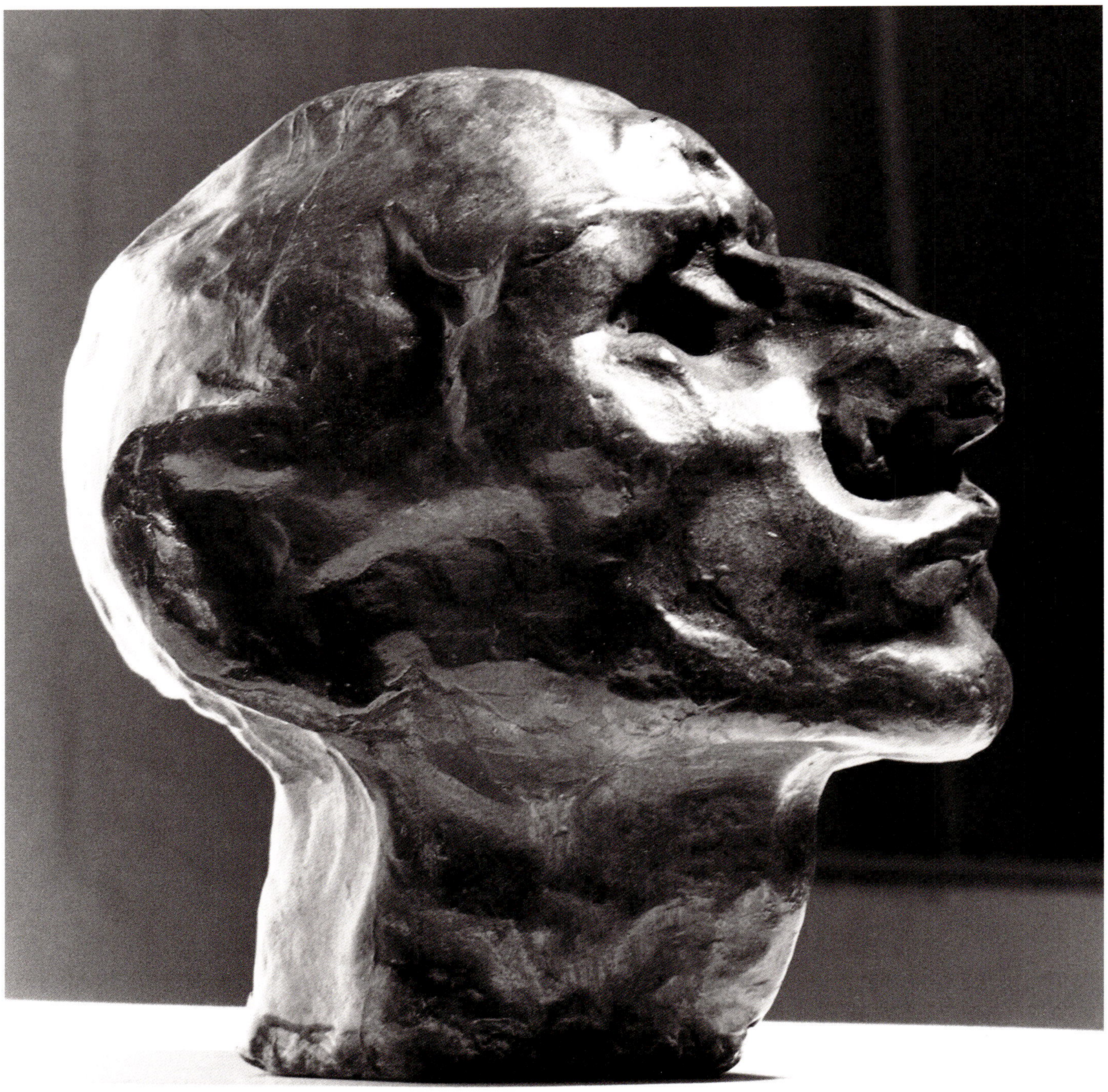

25, 26 Head of an Idiot (*cat.* 30)

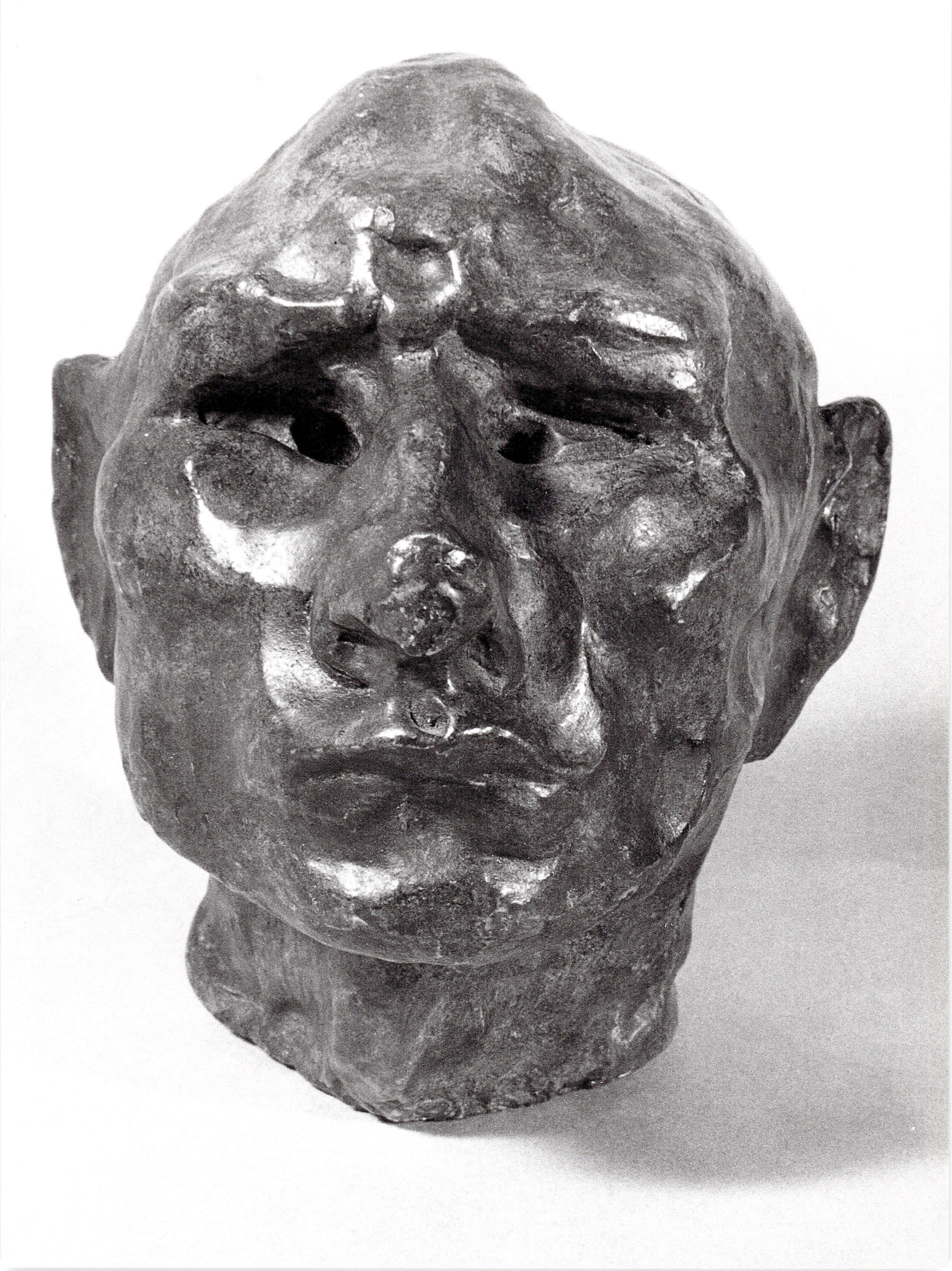

27 Gorilla (*cat.* 28)

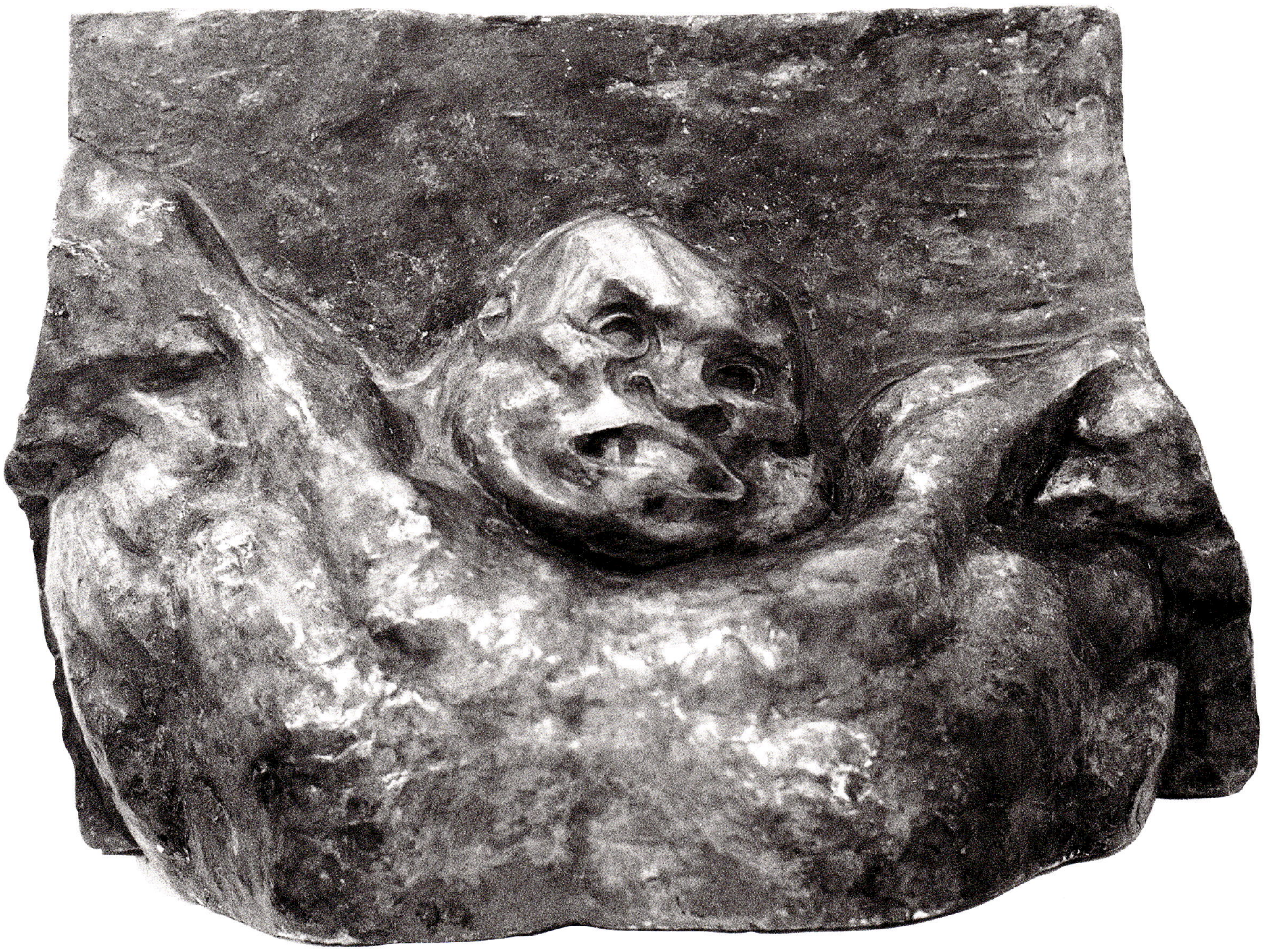

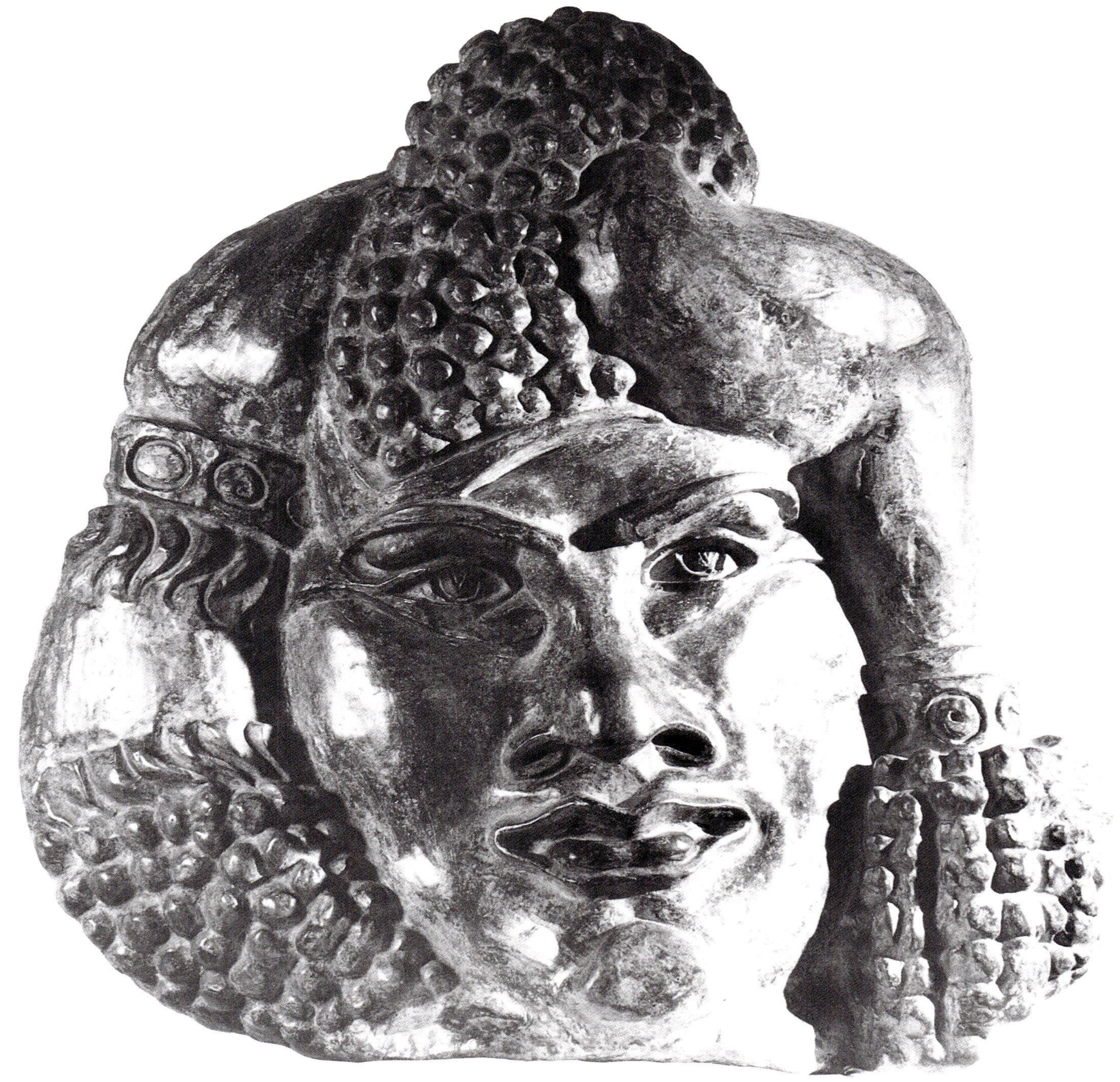

28 Ornamental Mask (*cat.* 31)

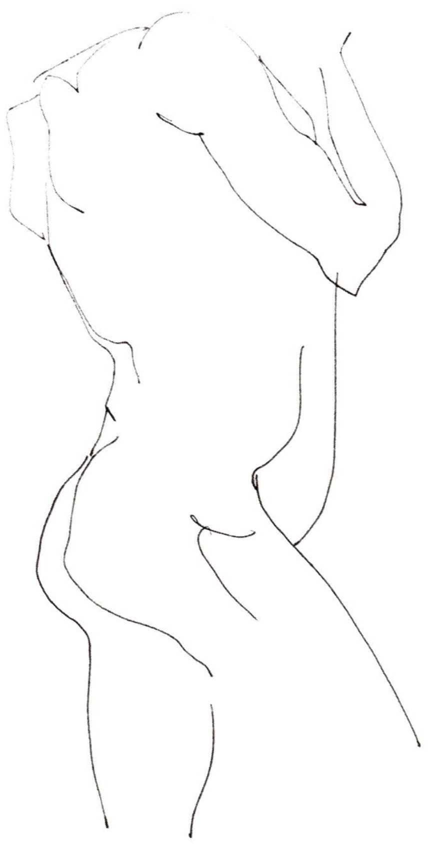

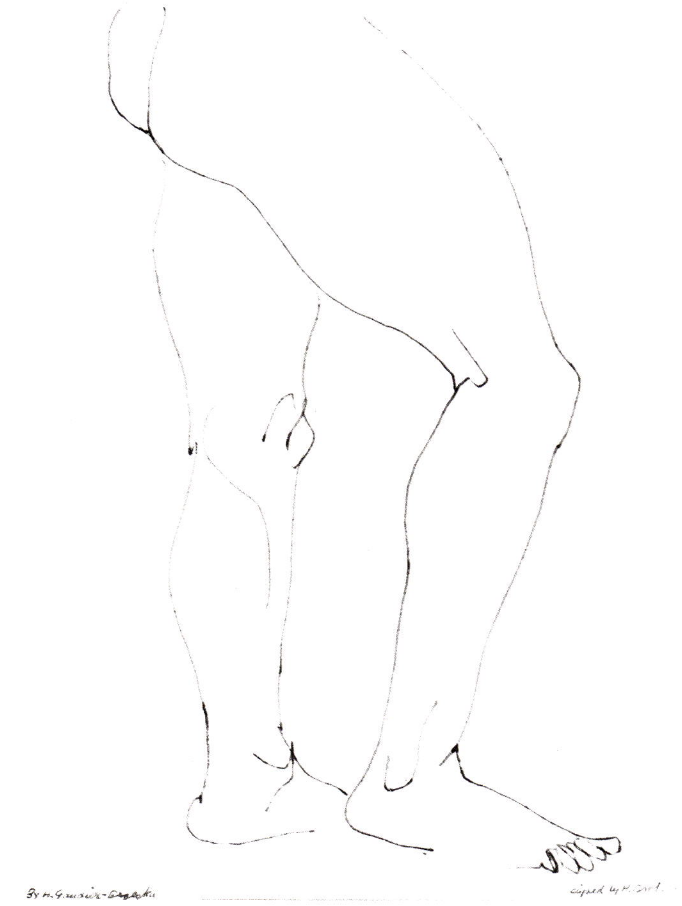

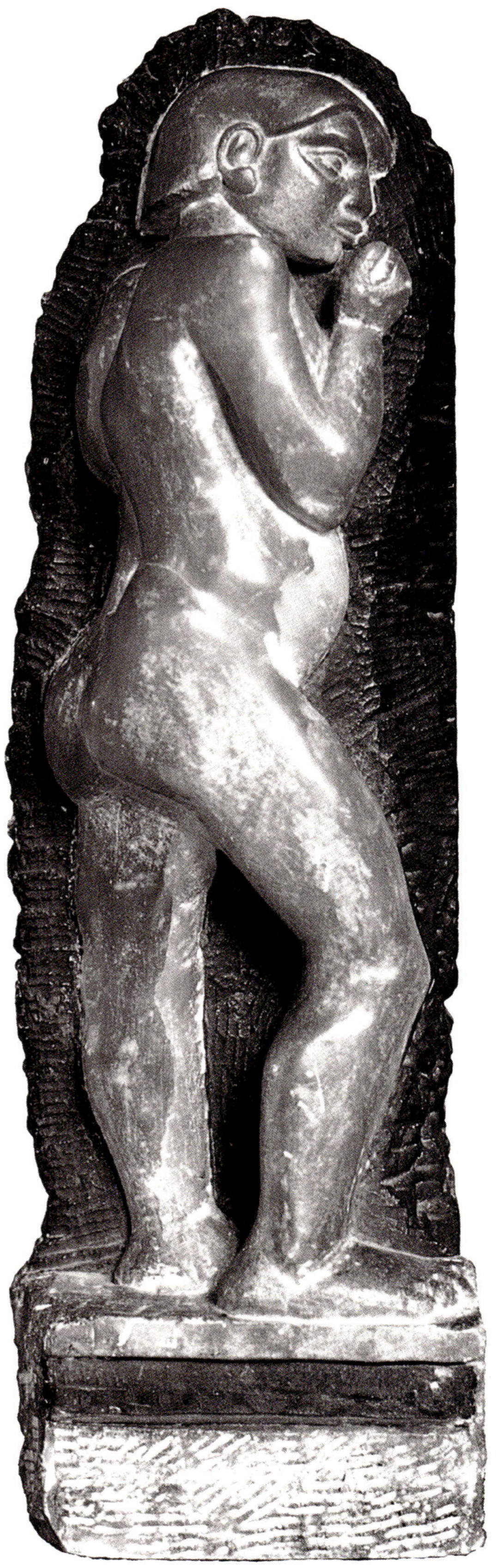

29 Boy, profile nude study, ink

30 Study of legs

31 Amour (*cat.* 35)

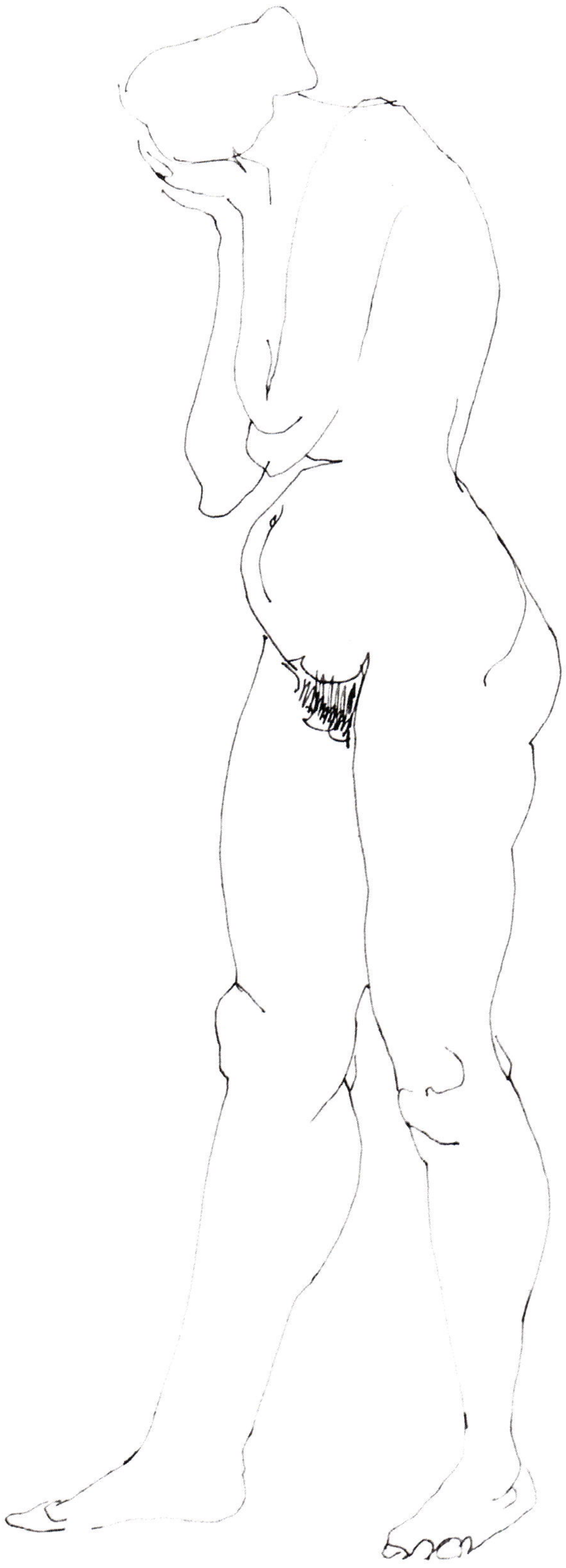

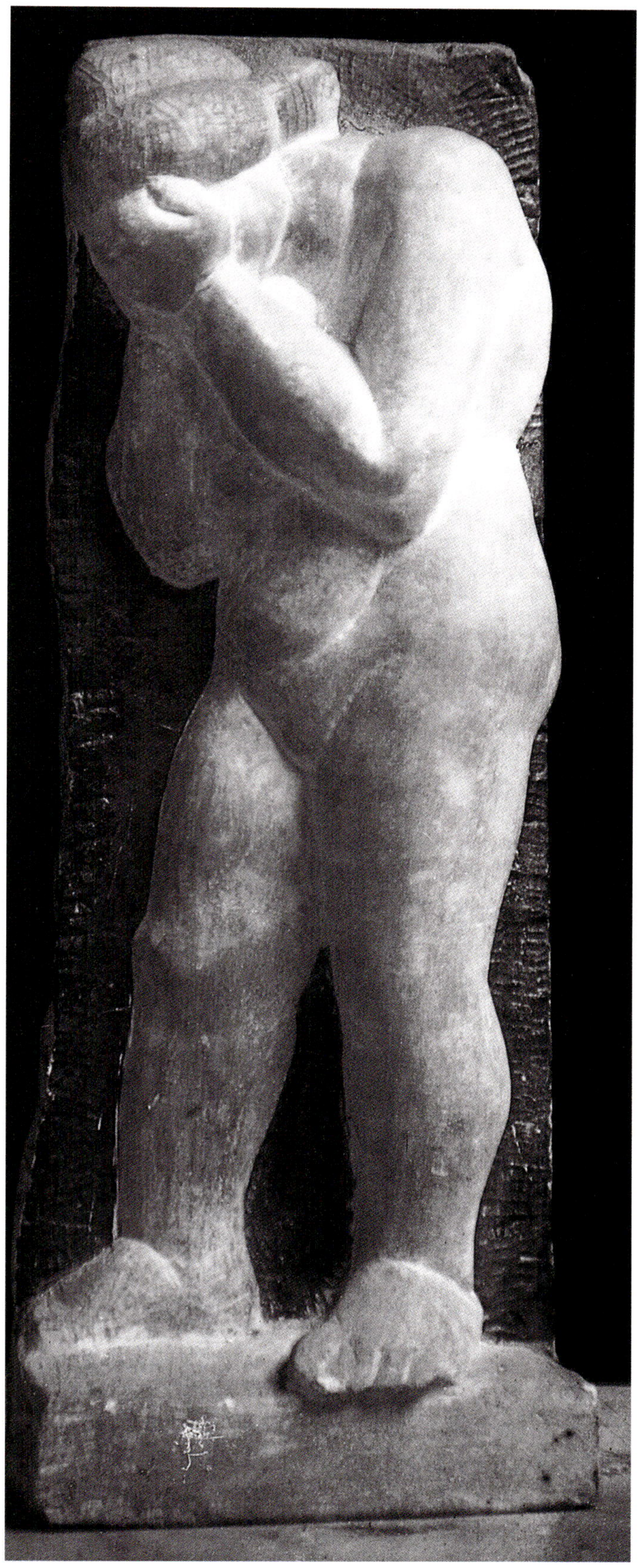

32 Weeping woman, life study

33 Weeping Woman (*cat.* 36)

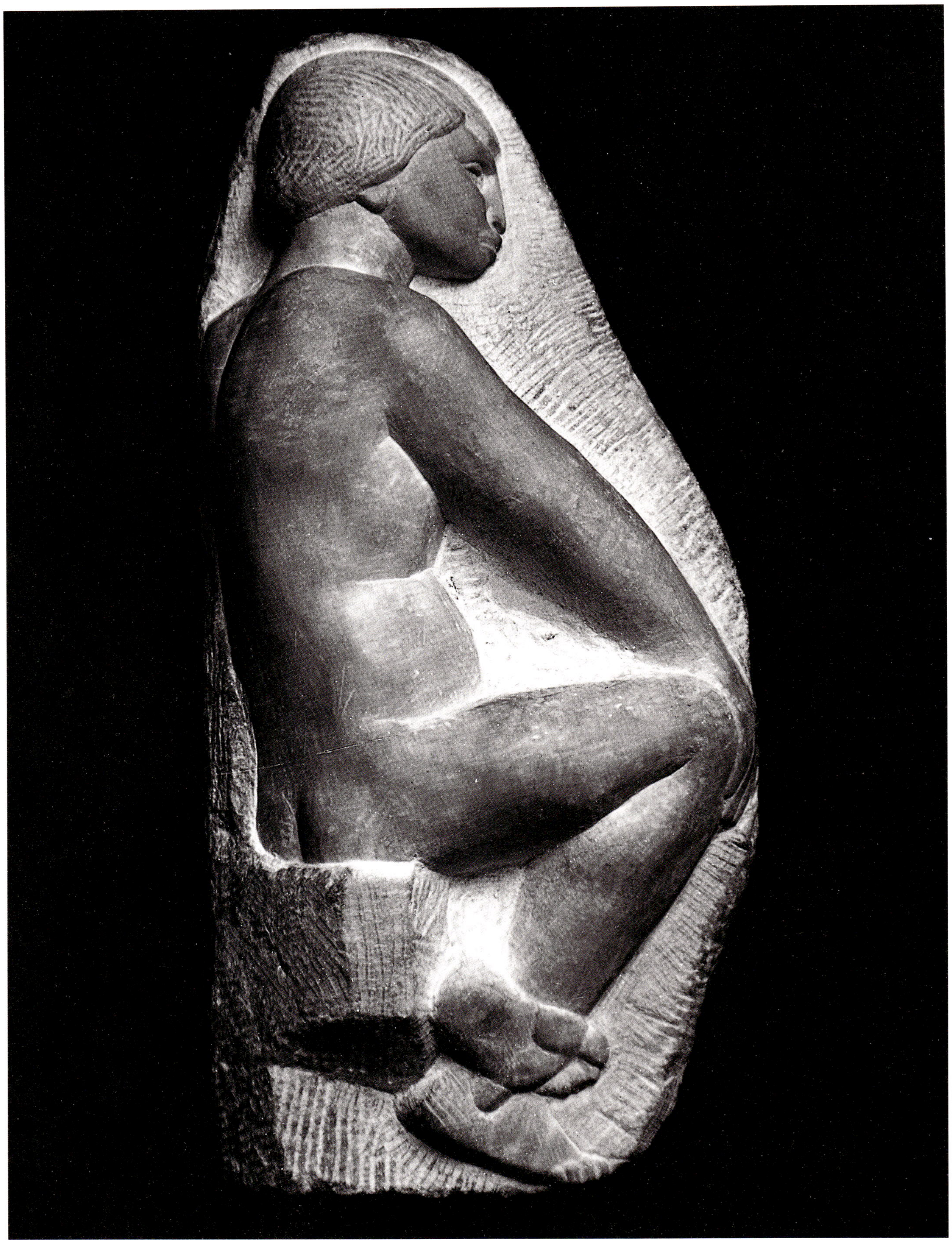

34 Boy, relief (*cat.* 34)

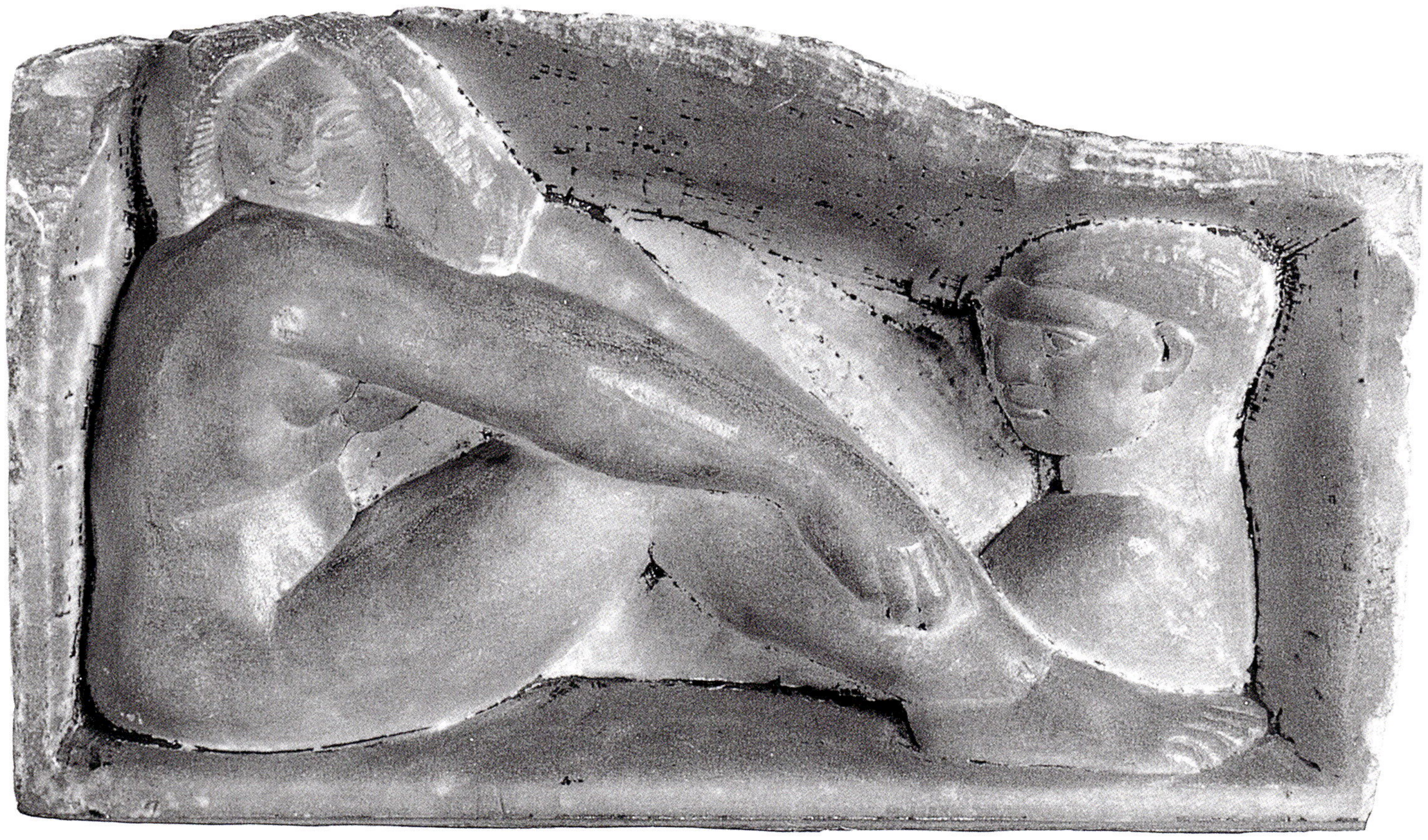

35 Man and Woman (*cat.* 38)

36 Seated female nude, life study

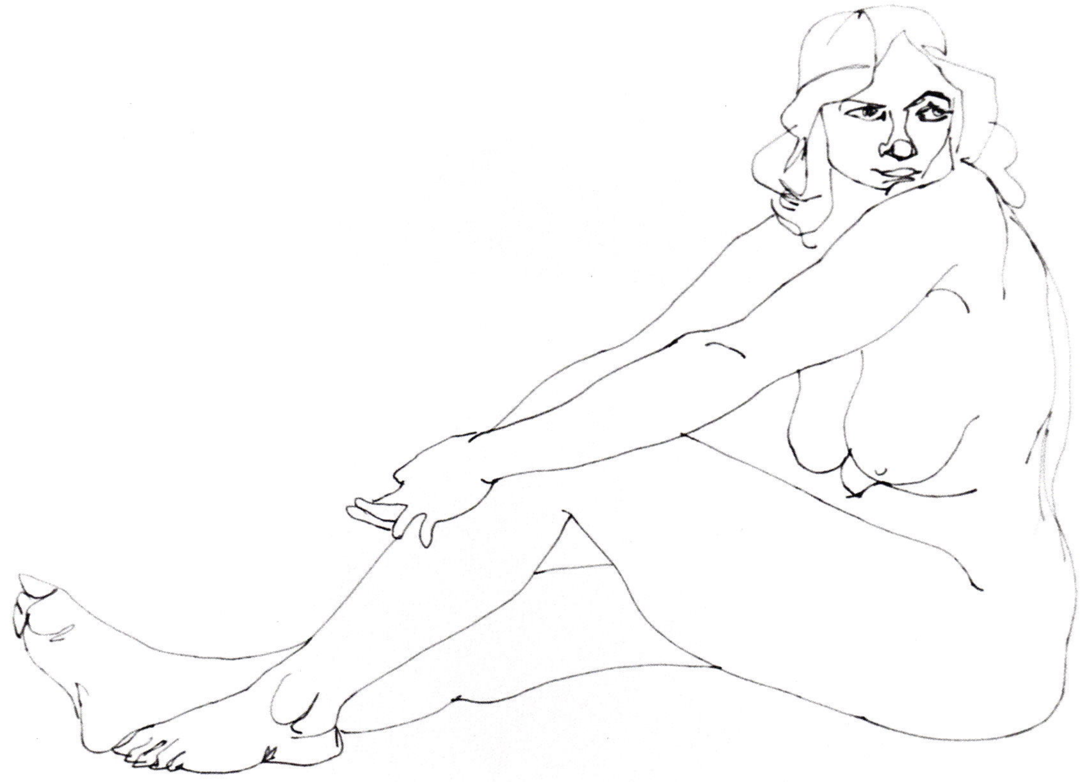

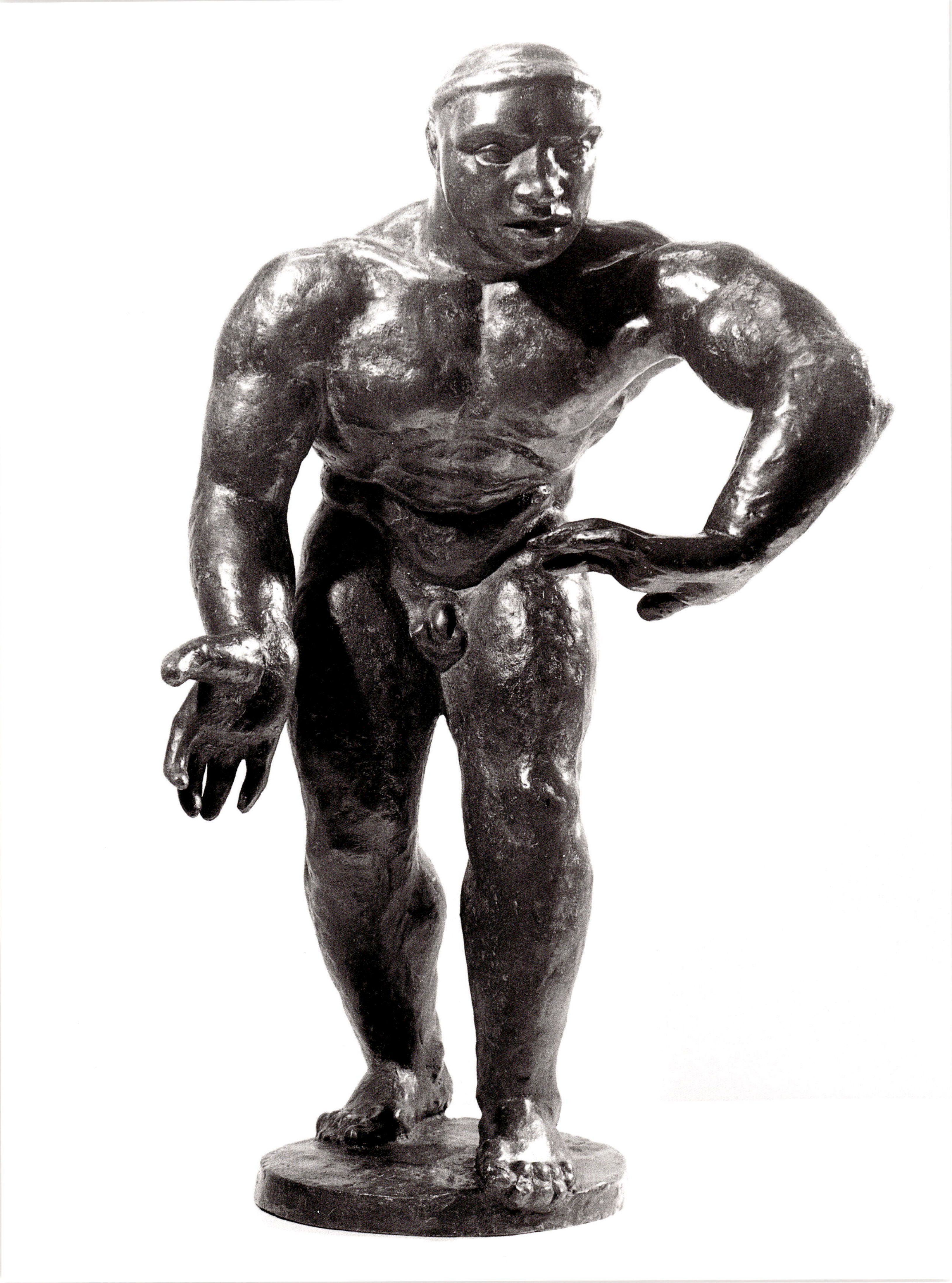

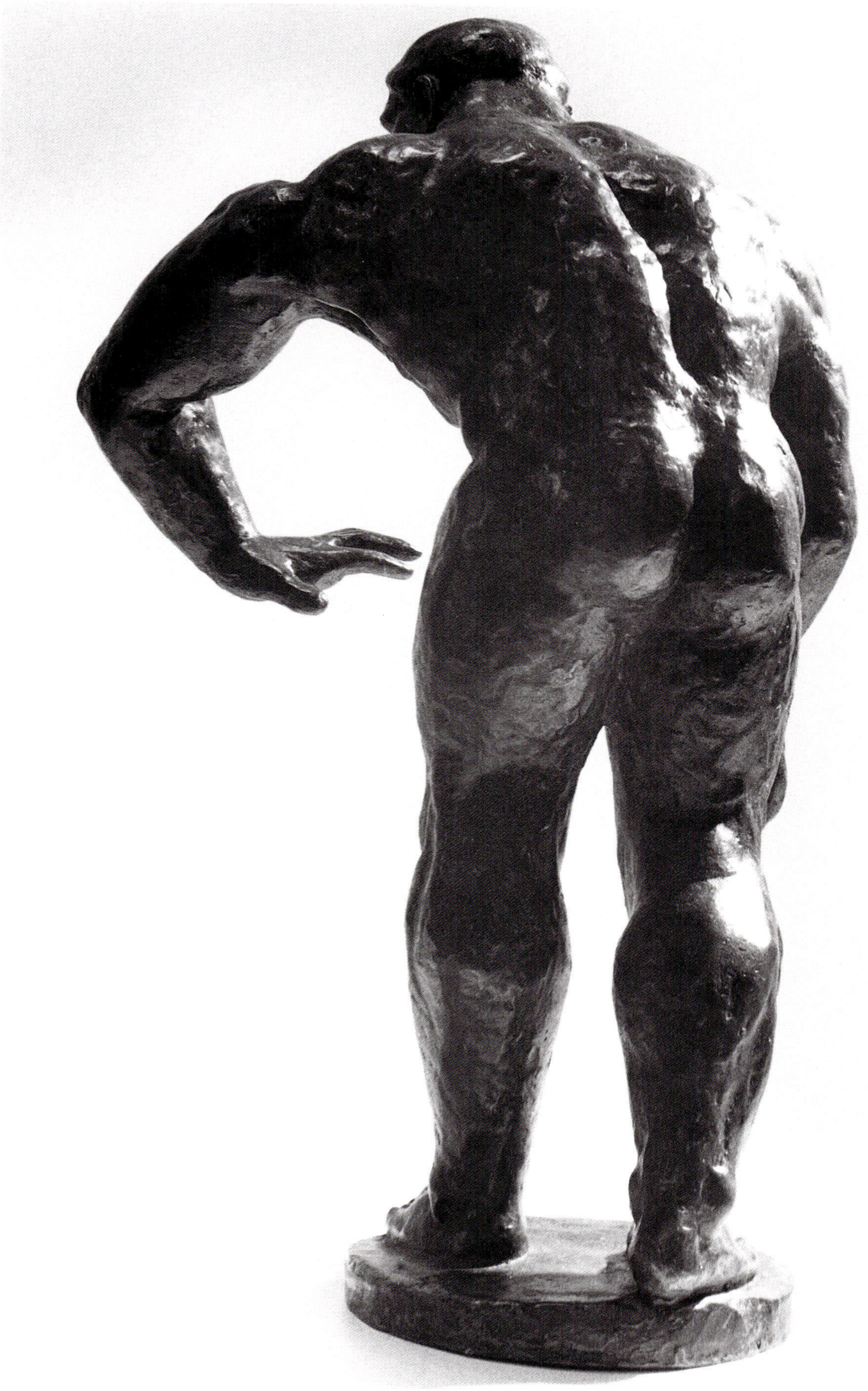

37, 38 Wrestler (*cat.* 32)

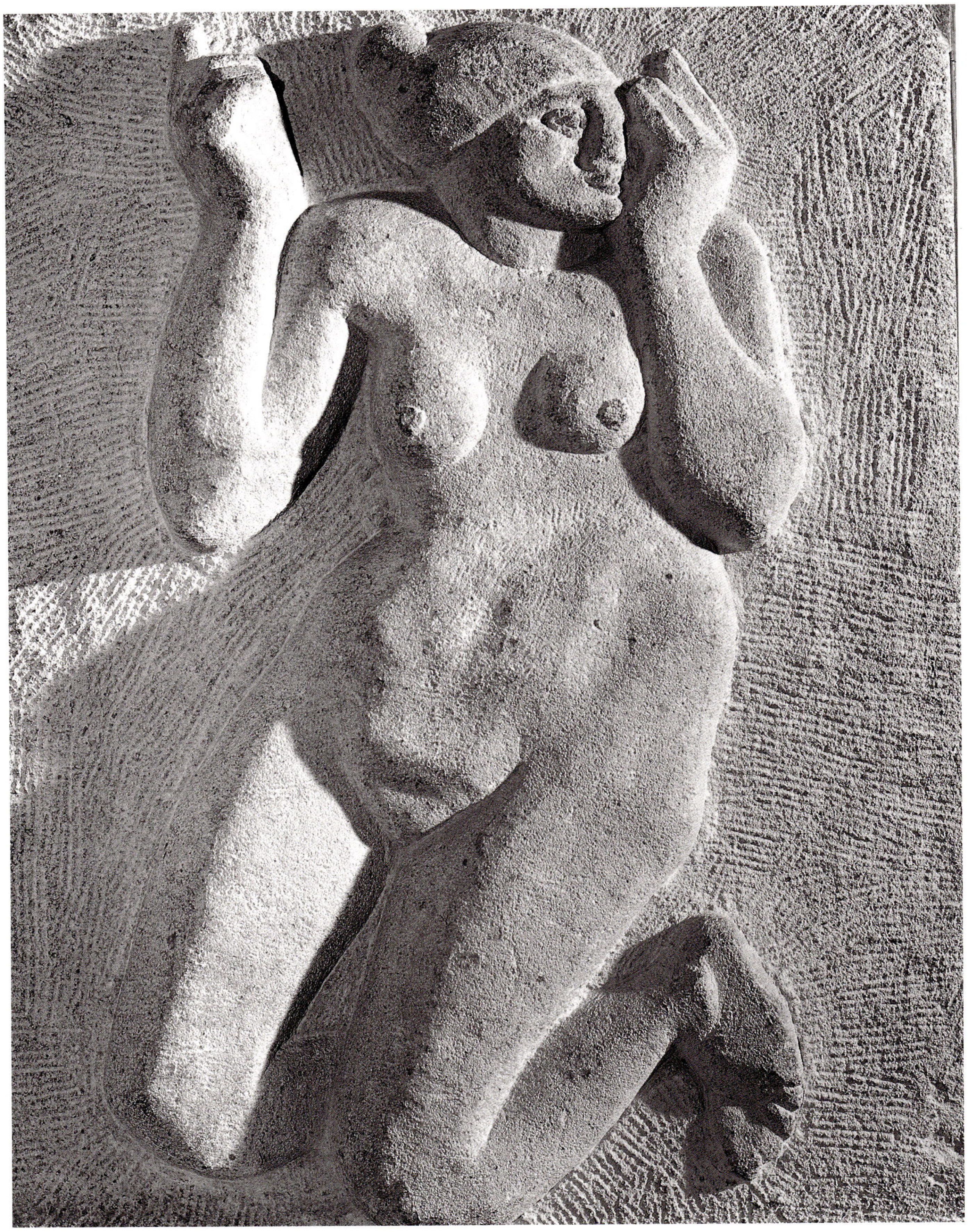

39 Woman (*cat.* 39)

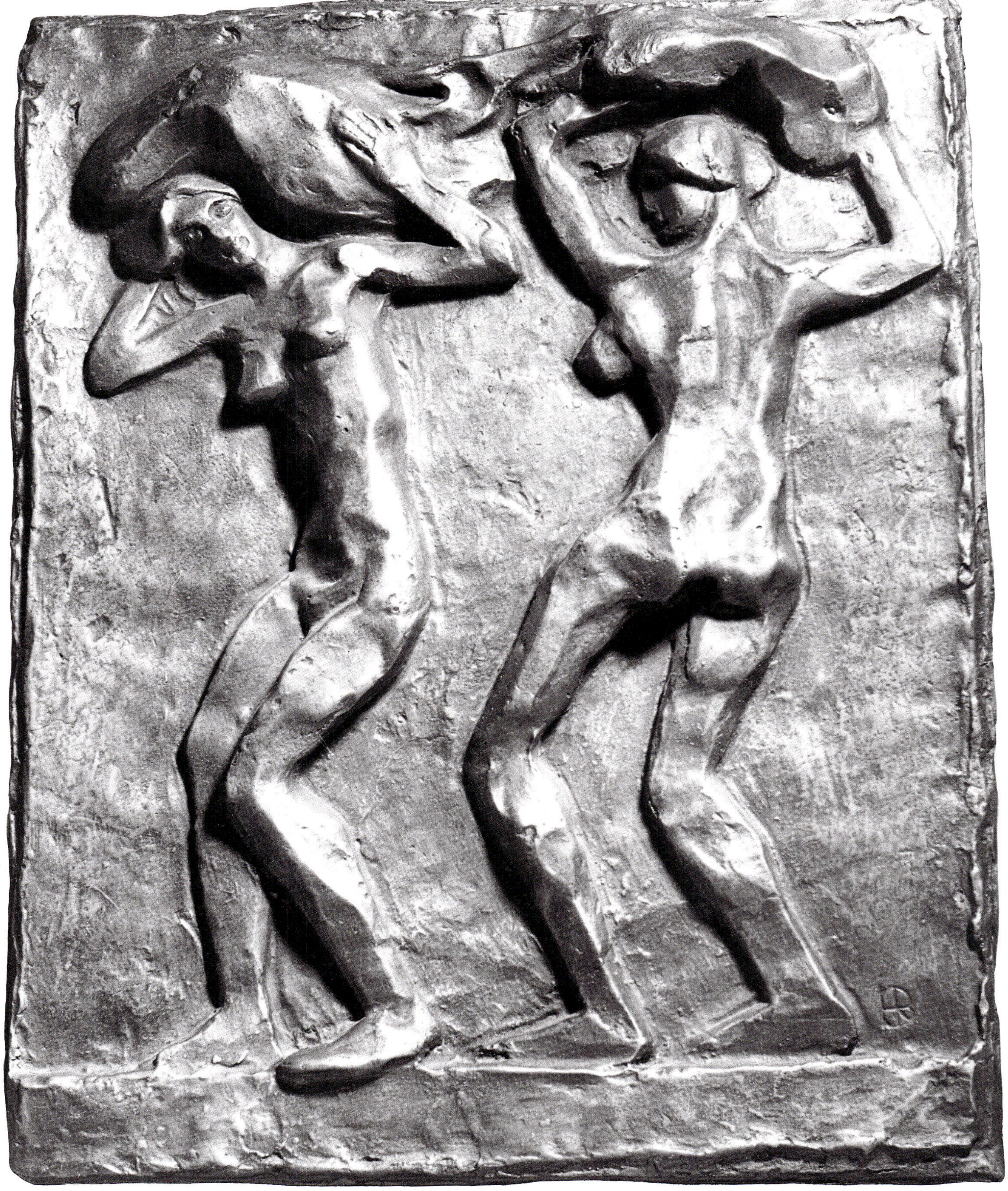

40 Women Carrying Sacks (*cat*. 40)

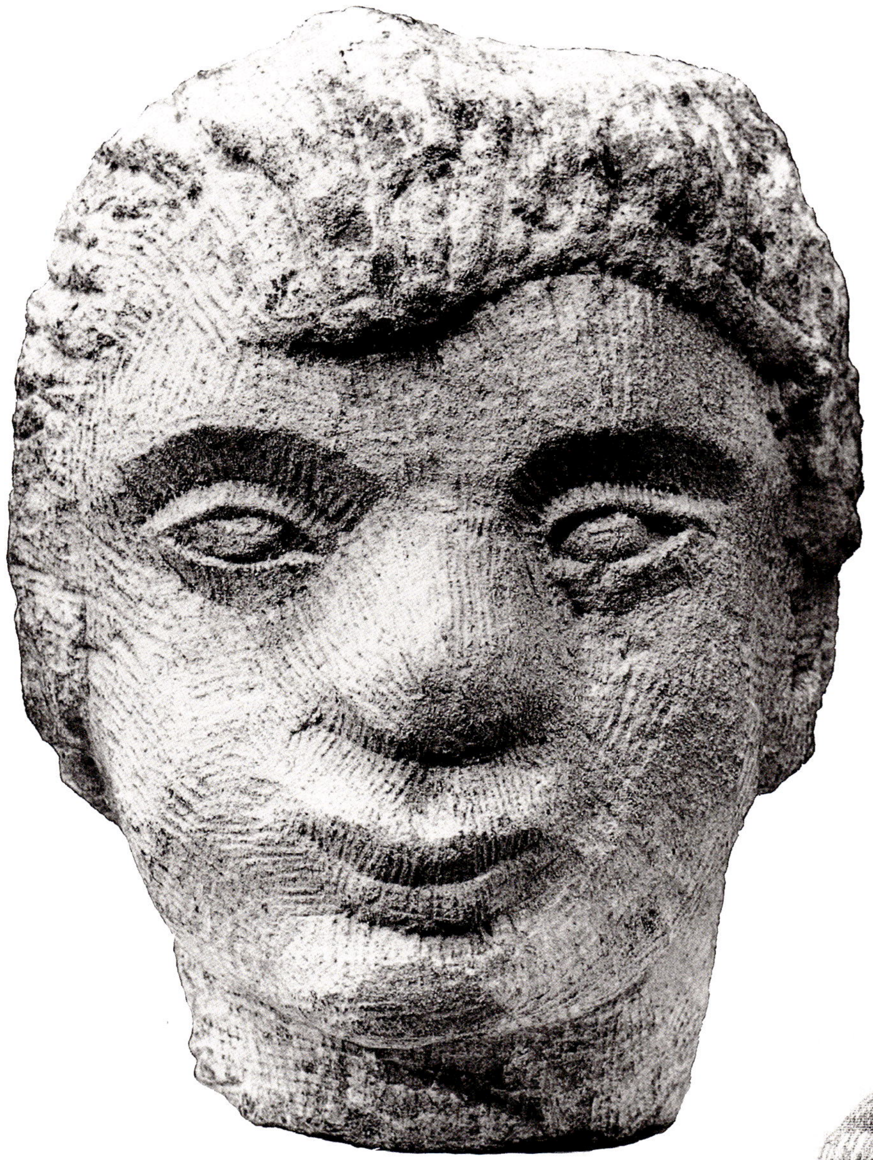

41 Head of a Young Man (*cat.* 44)

42 Head of a Boy, pencil

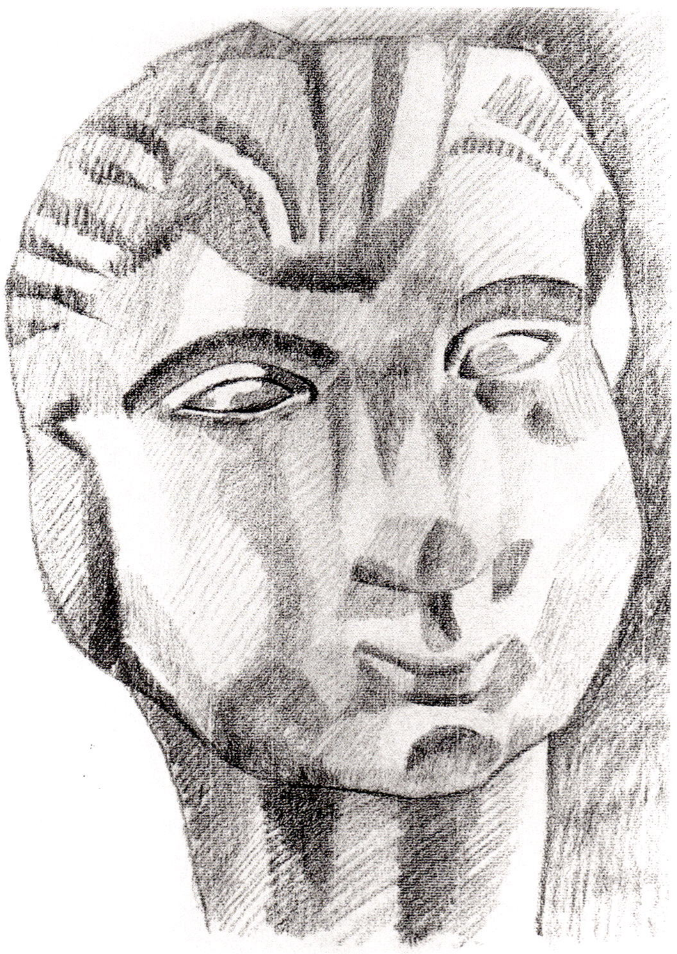

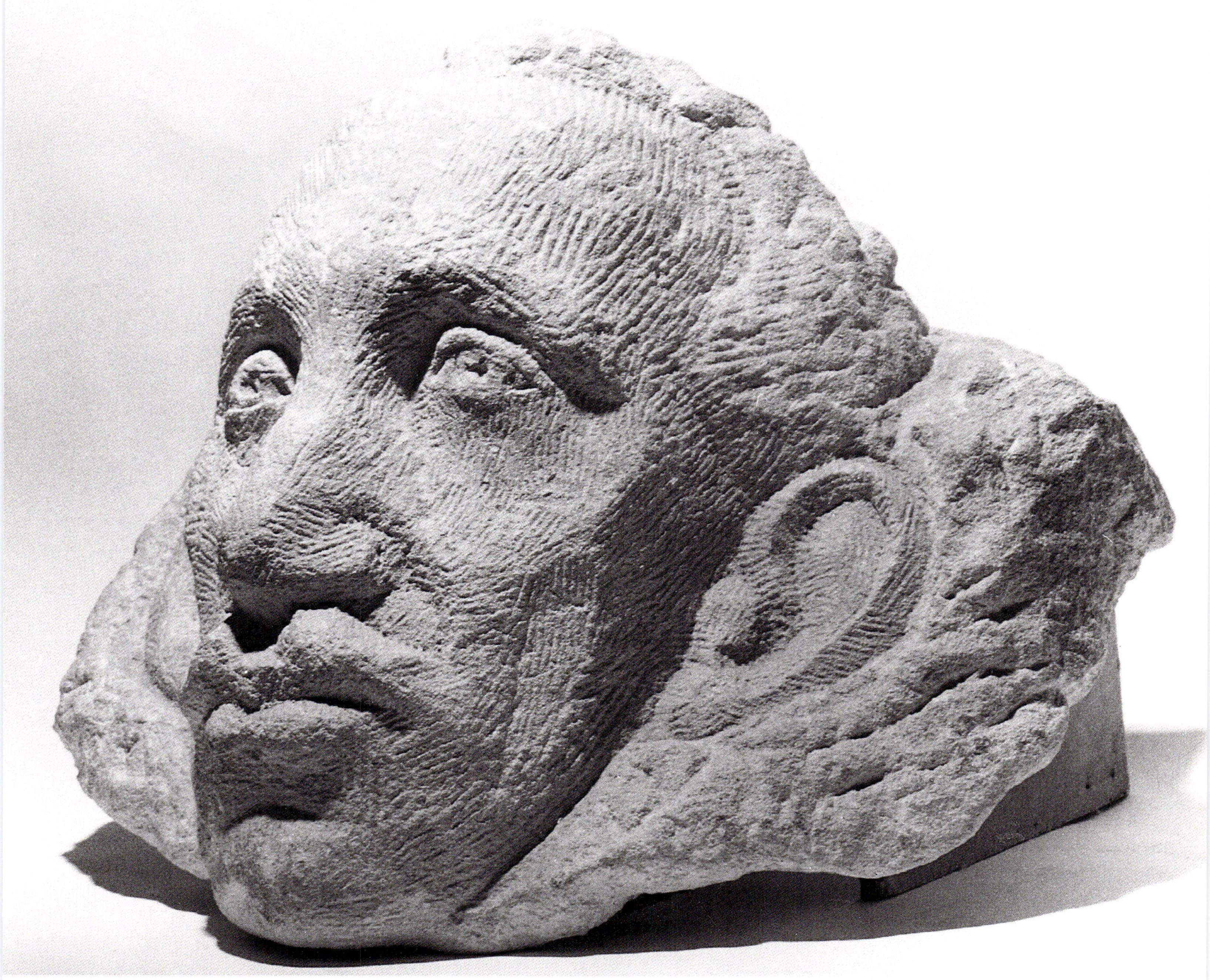

43 Horace Brodzky, Mask (*cat.* 41)

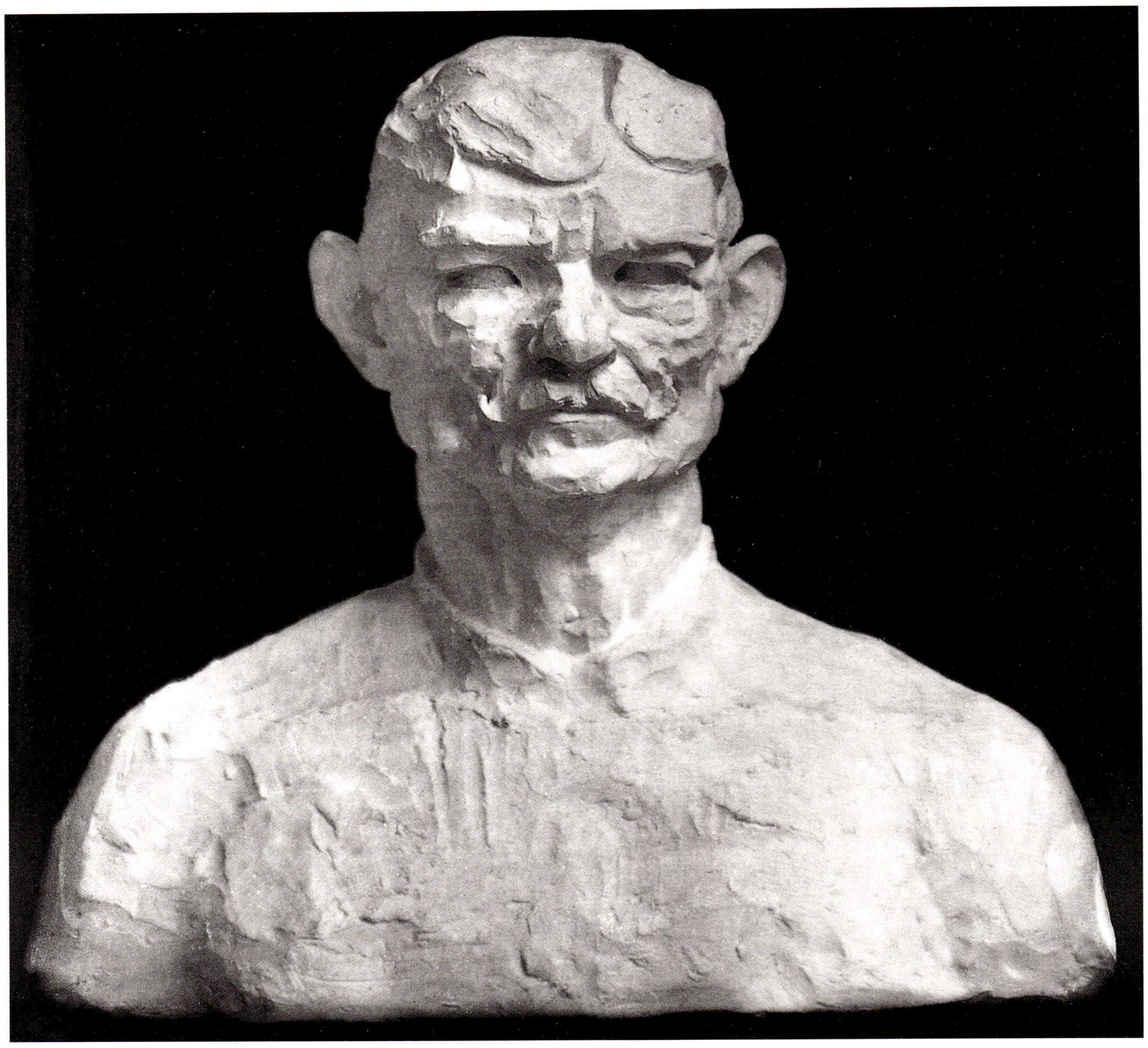

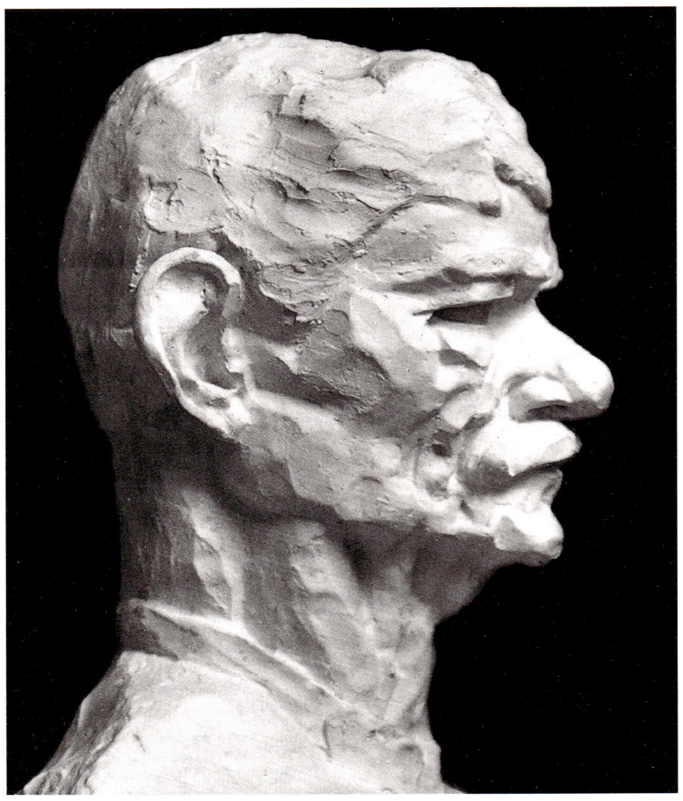

44, 45 Frank Harris
(*cat.* 45)

46, 47 Alfred Wolmark (*cat.* 46)

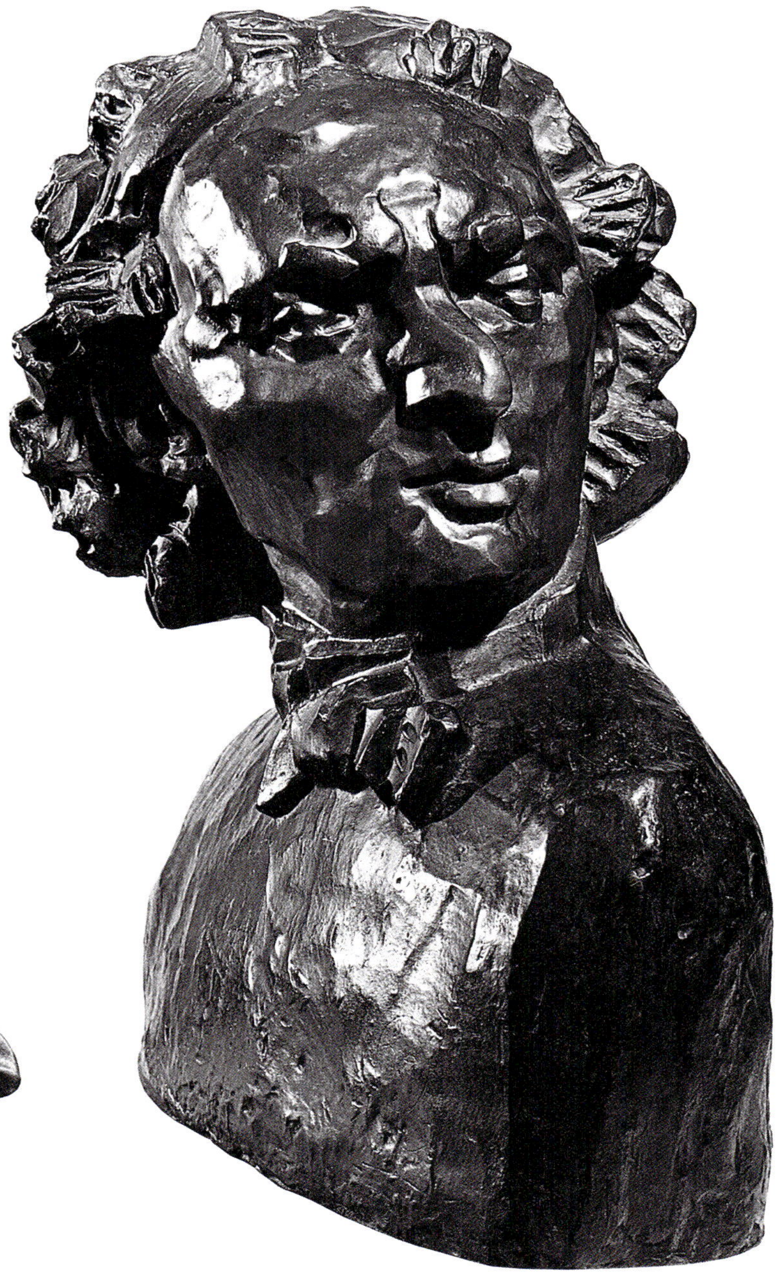

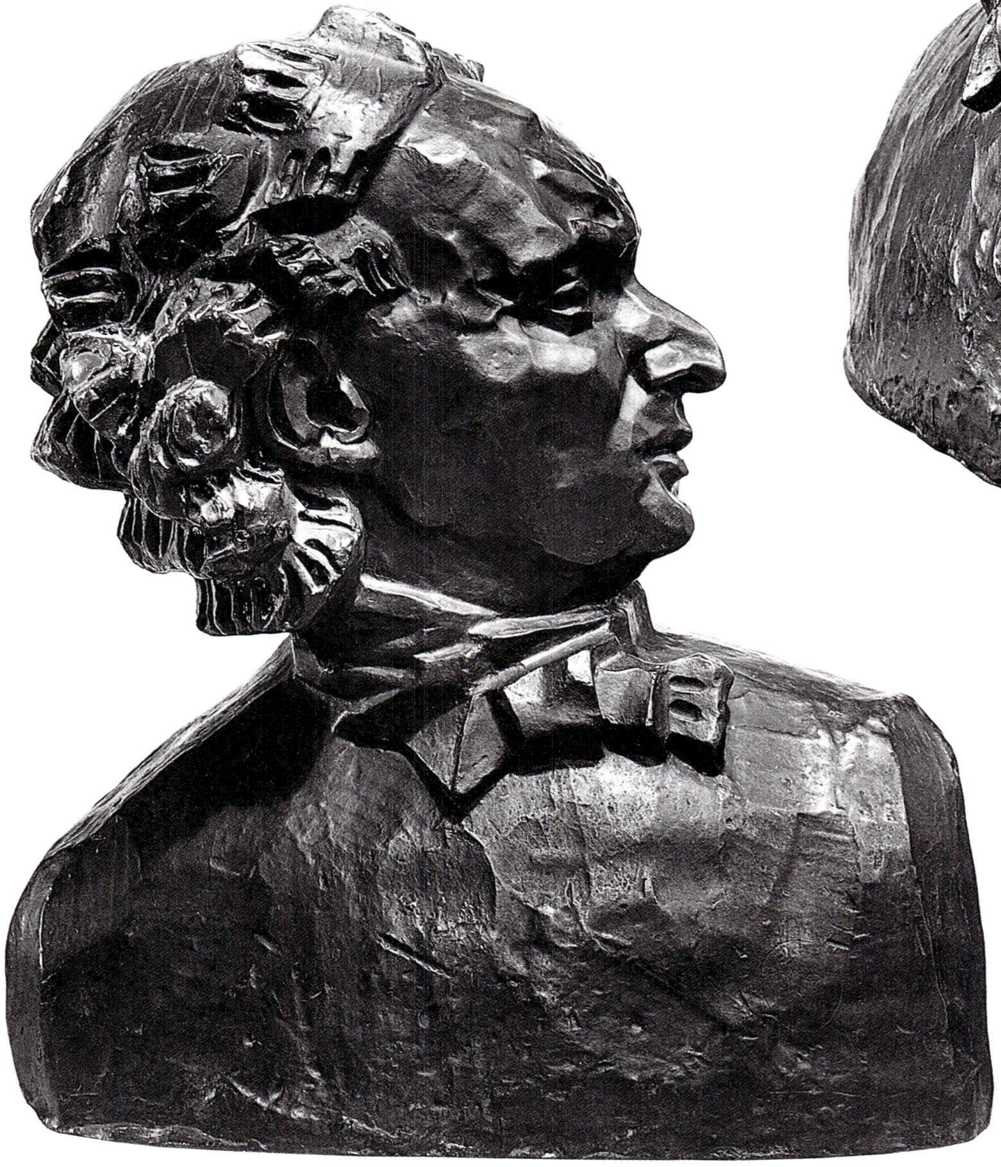

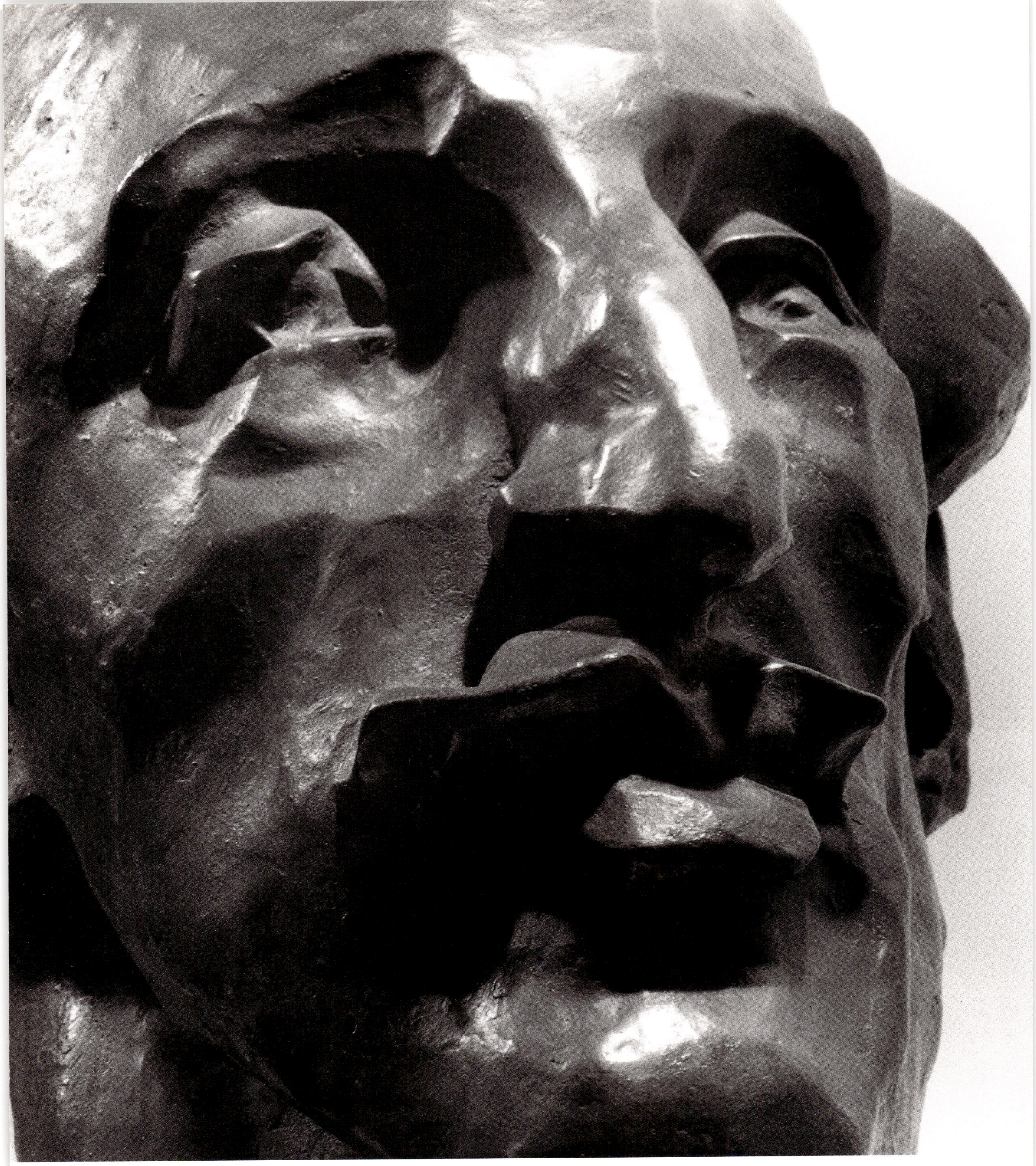

48 Horace Brodzky (*cat.* 47)

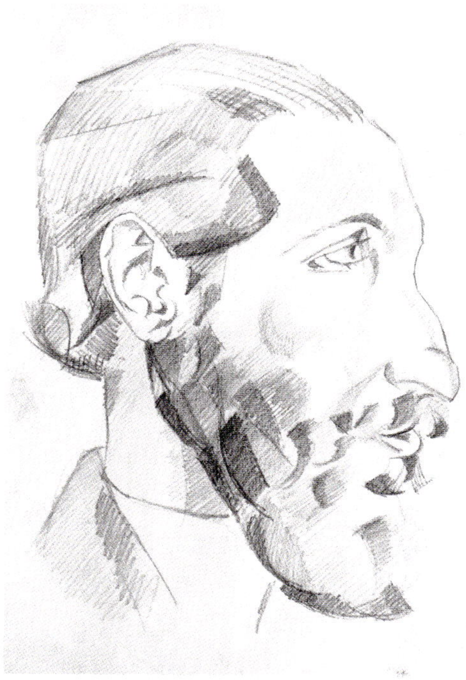

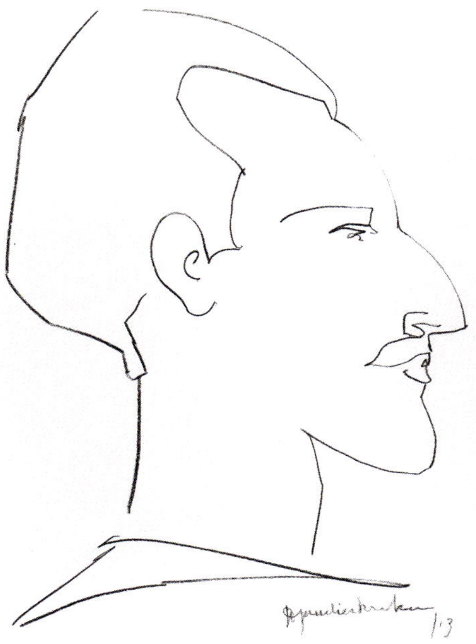

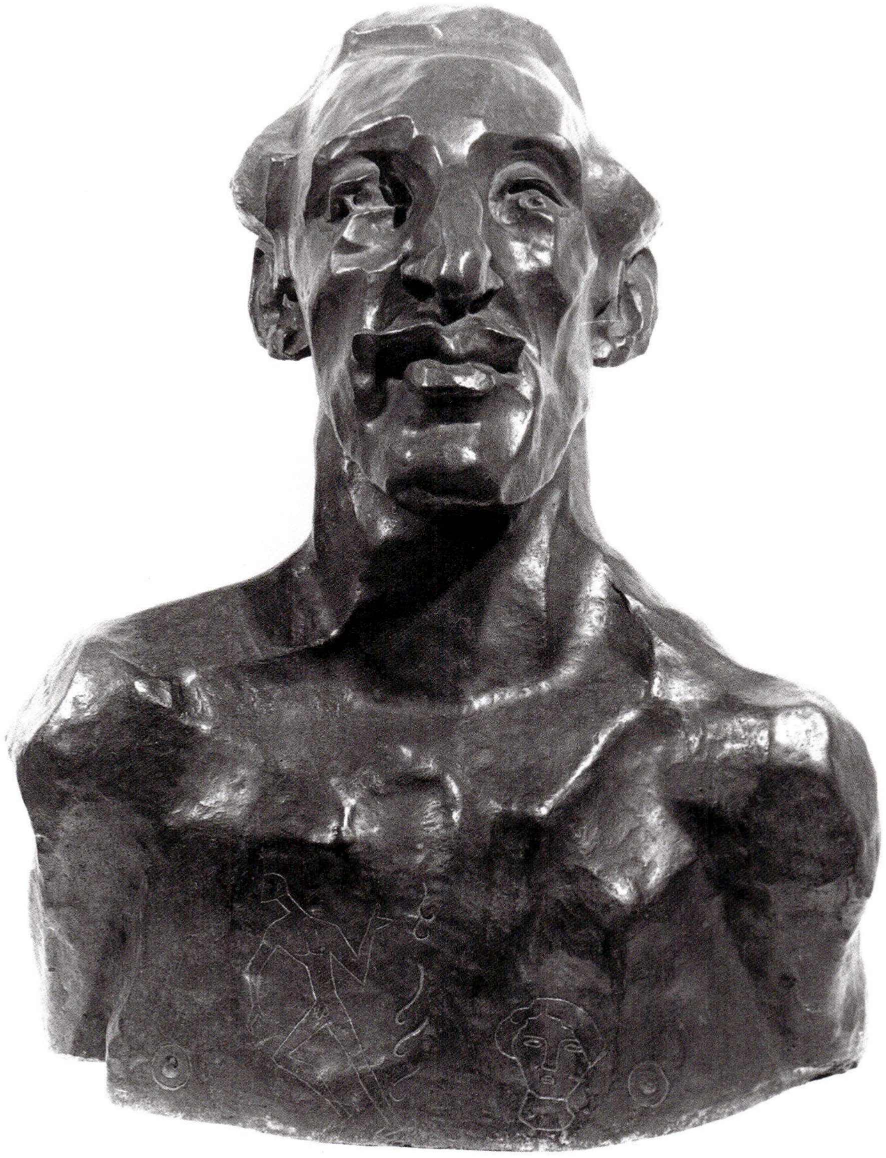

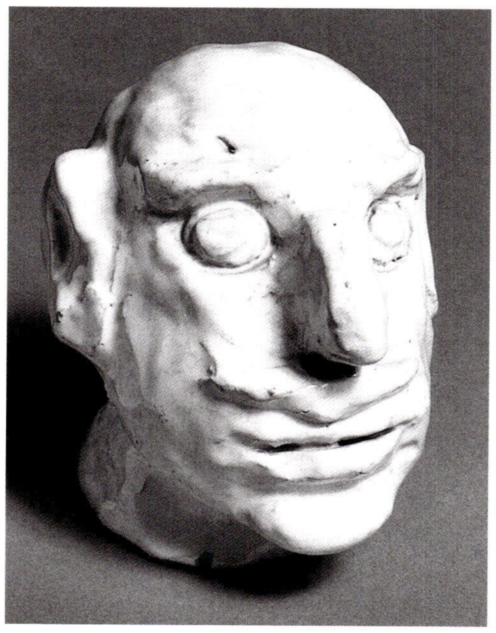

49 Profile head of Horace Brodzky, pencil

50 Portrait of Horace Brodzky, crayon

51 Pottery Head (*cat.* 111)

52 Horace Brodzky (*cat.* 47)

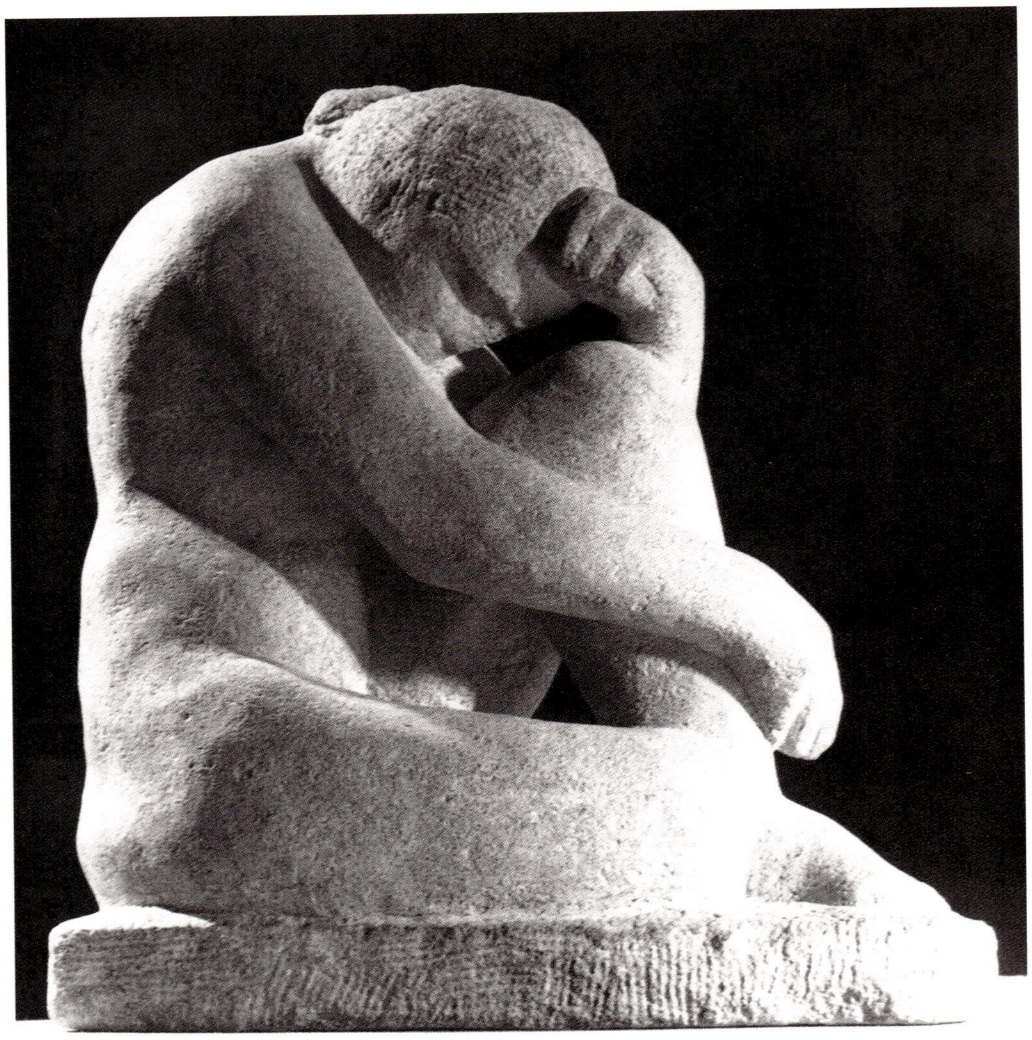

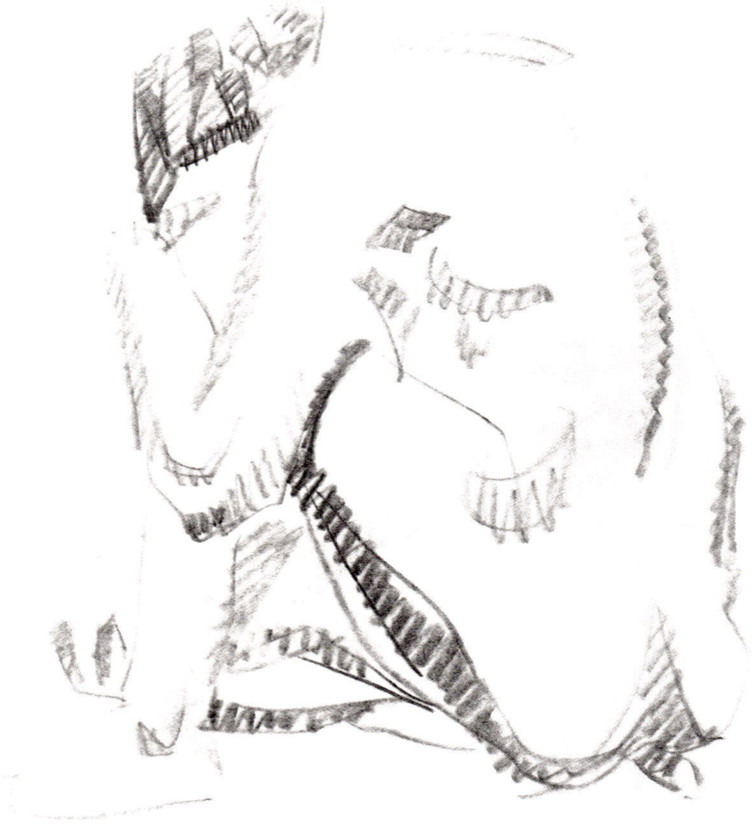

53 Grief (*cat.* 49)

54 Seated Woman (Study for Grief)

55 Grief (*cat.* 49)

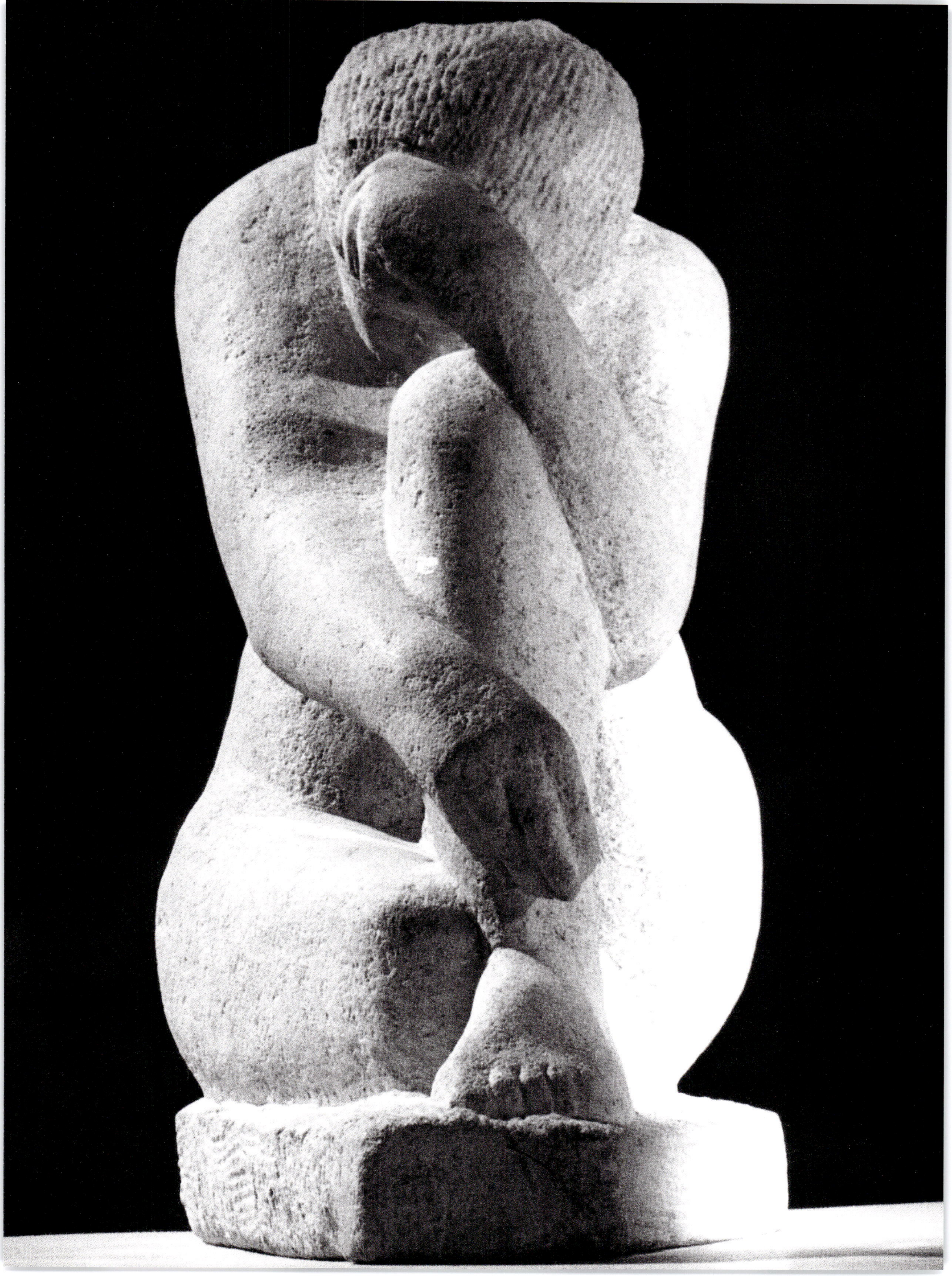

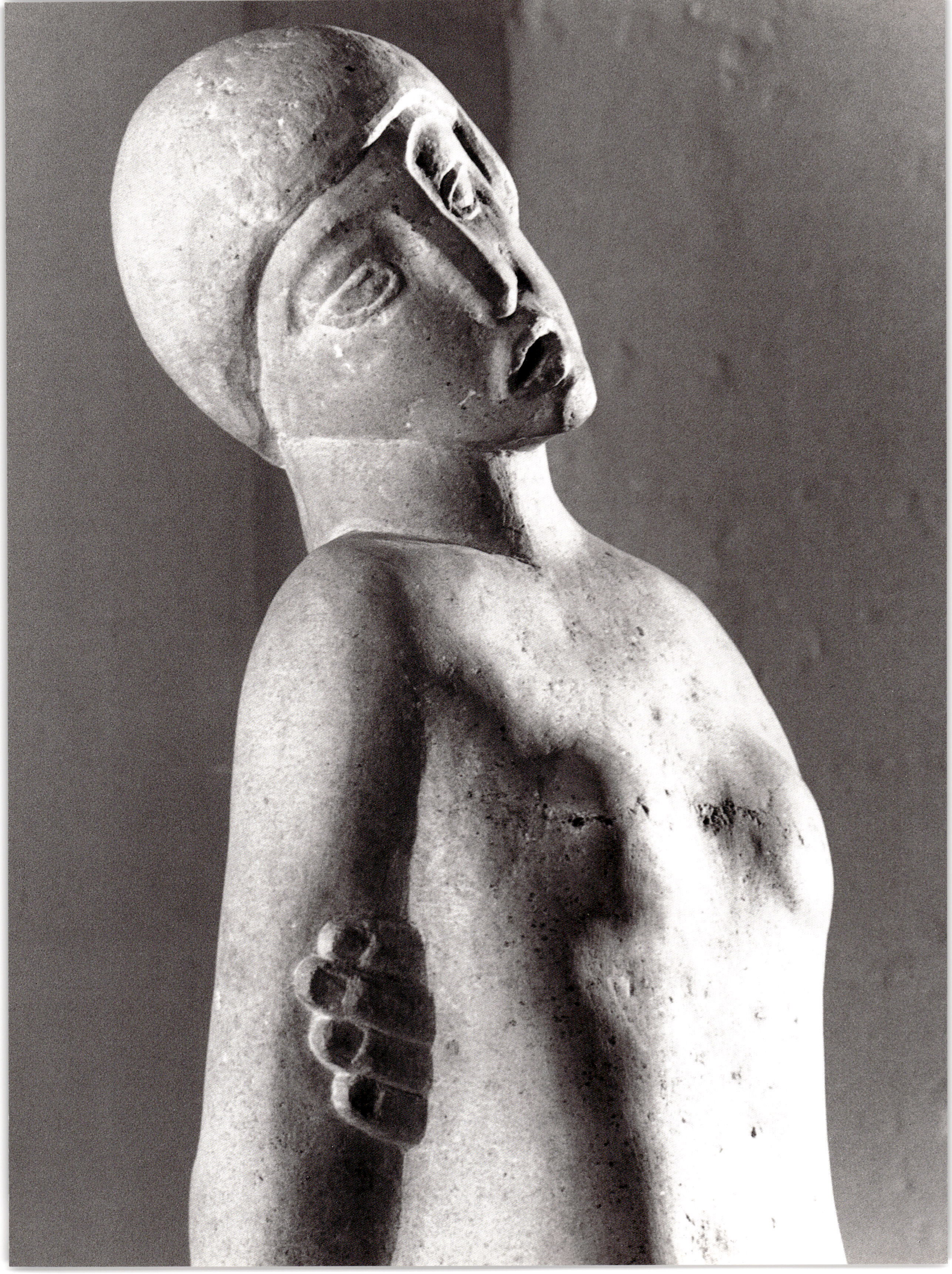

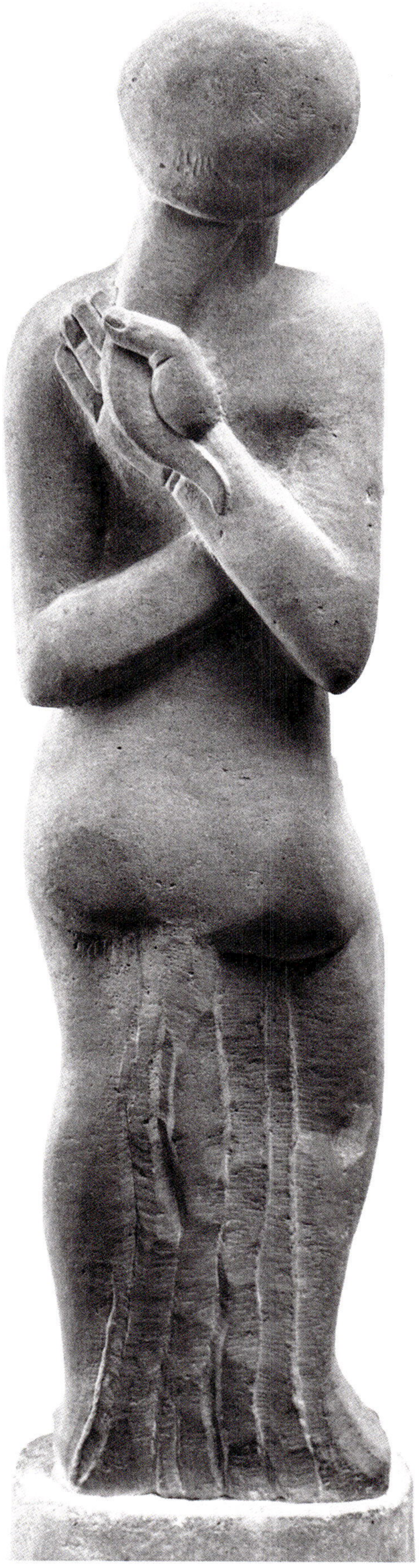
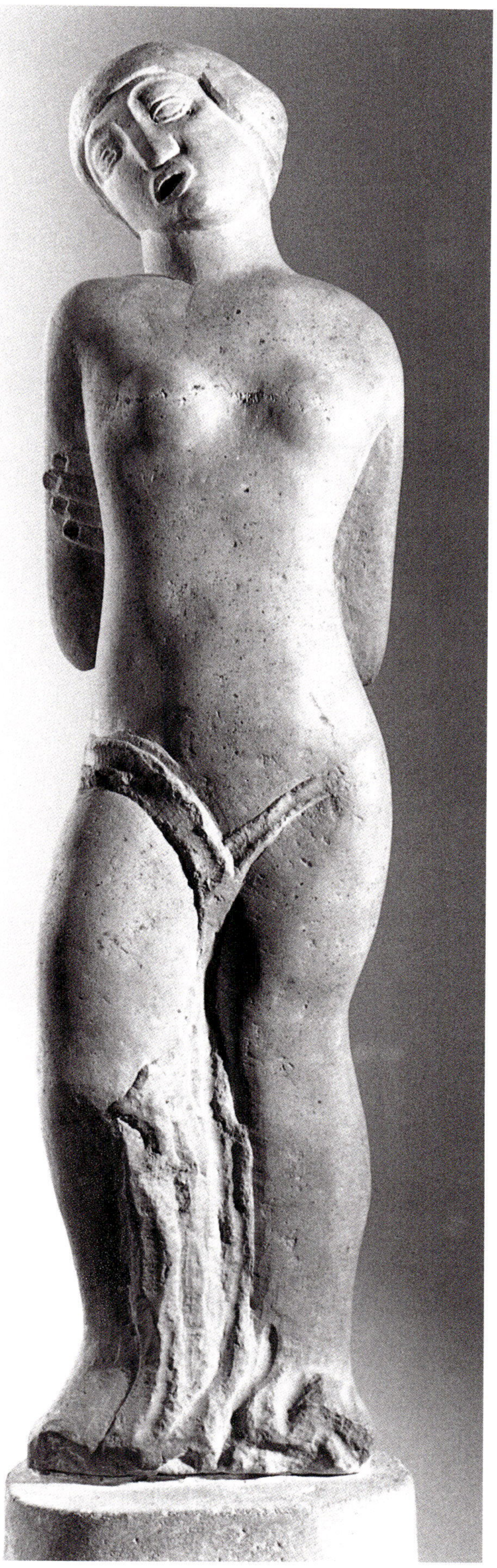

56–58 Singer (*cat.* 51)

59 Sketch for Standing Figure (*cat.* 54)

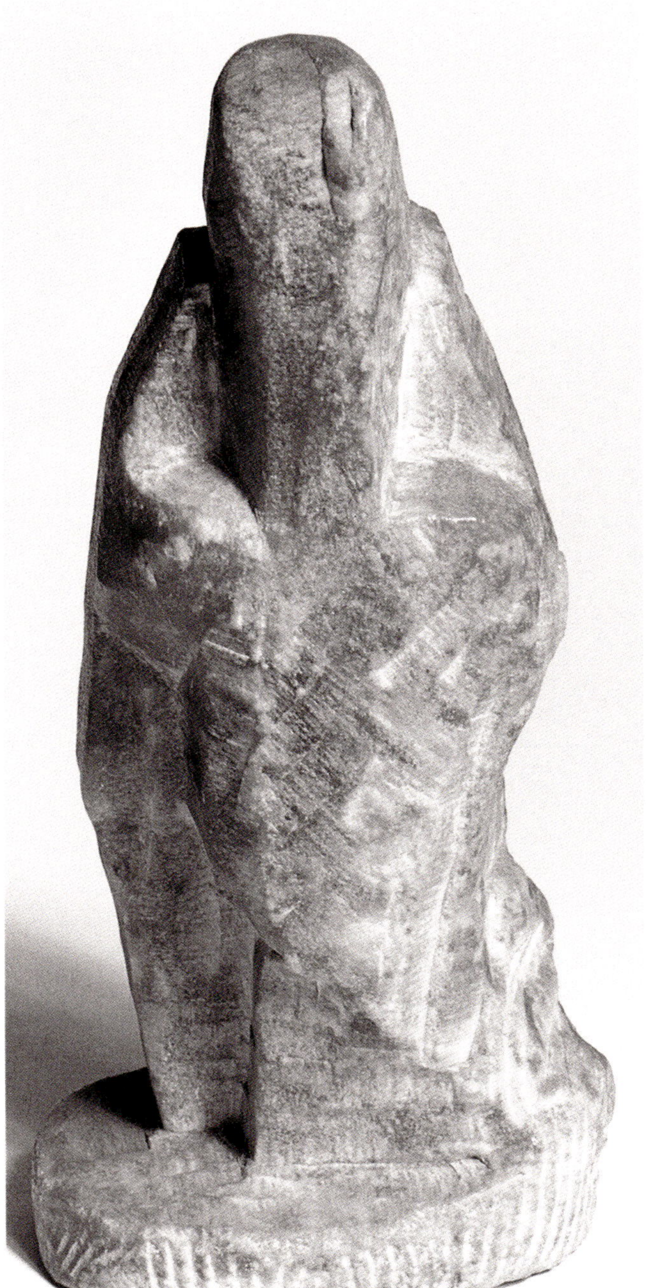

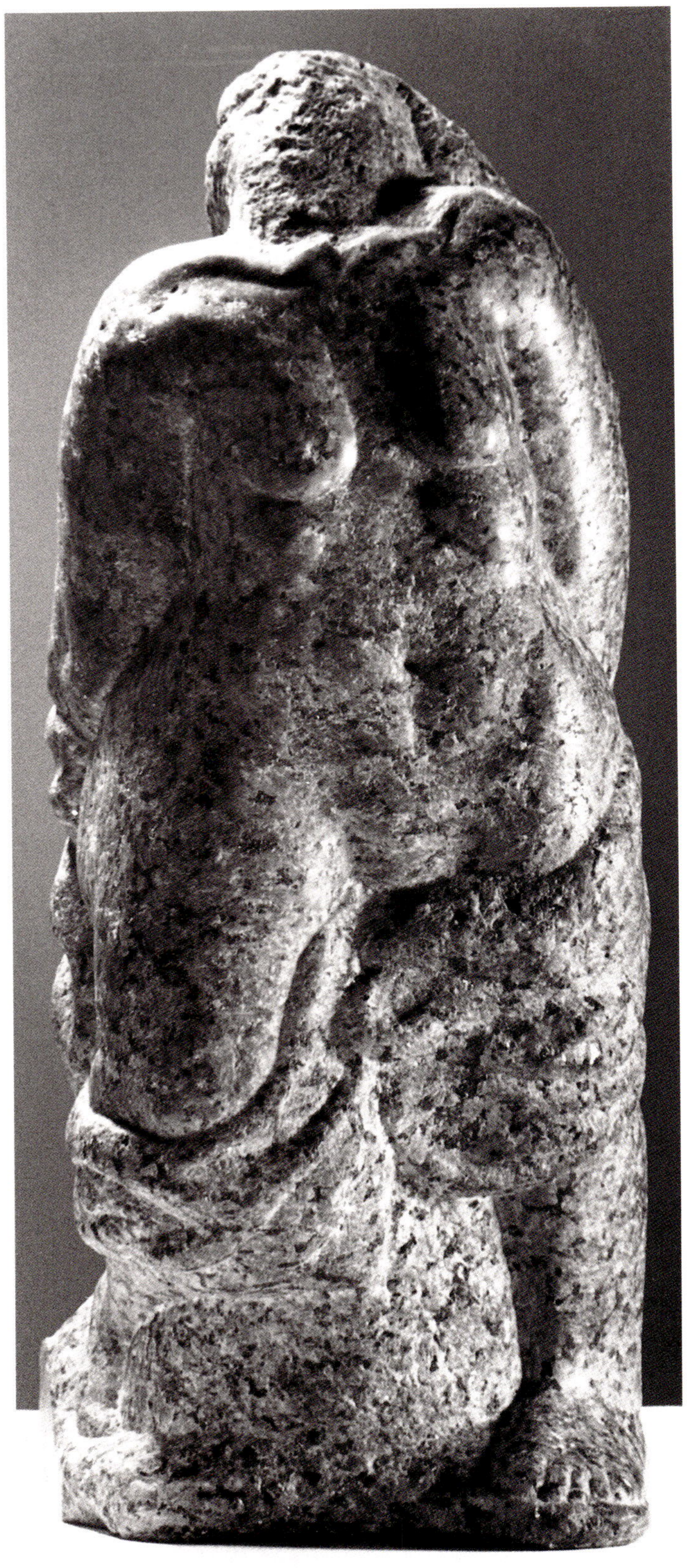

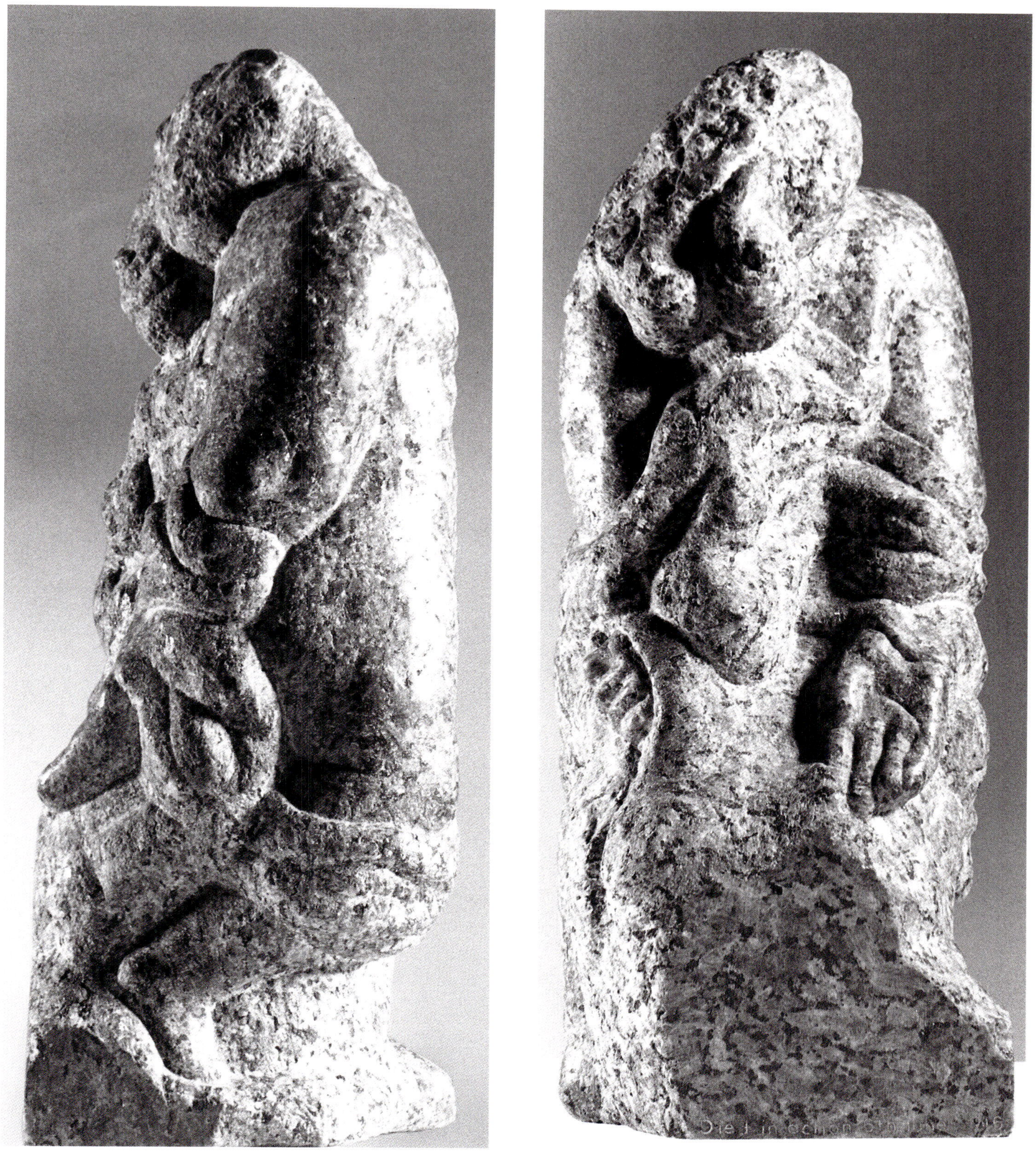

60–62 Standing Female Figure (*cat.* 53)

63, 64 Mermaid (*cat.* 55)

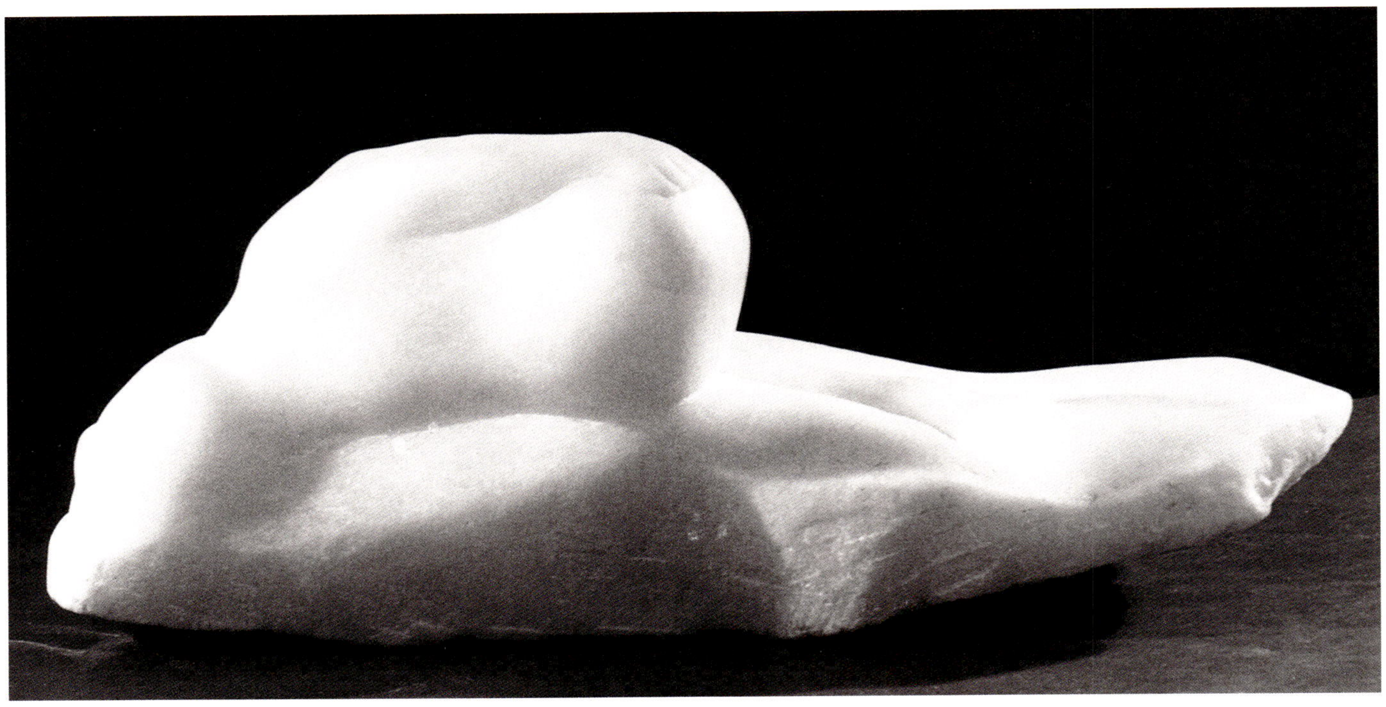

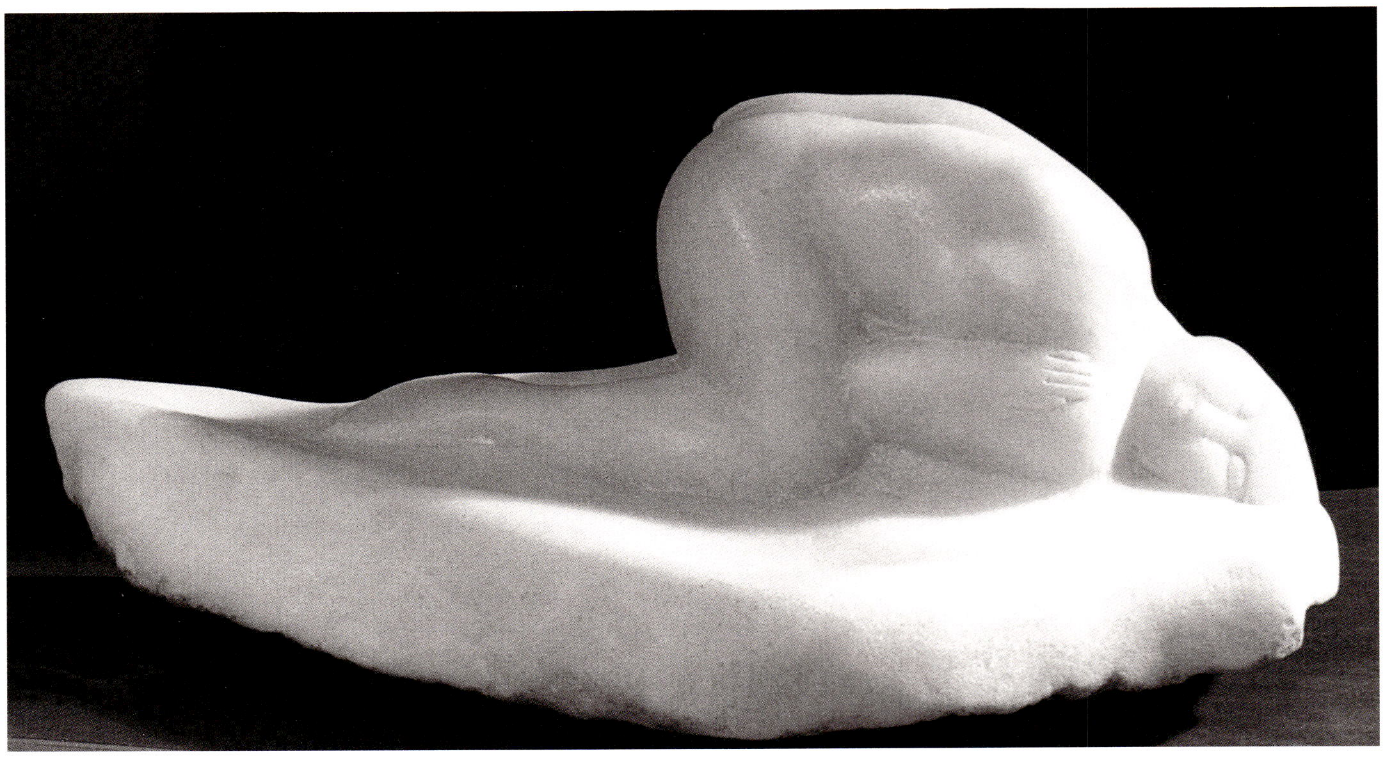

65 Female Figure (*cat.* 50)

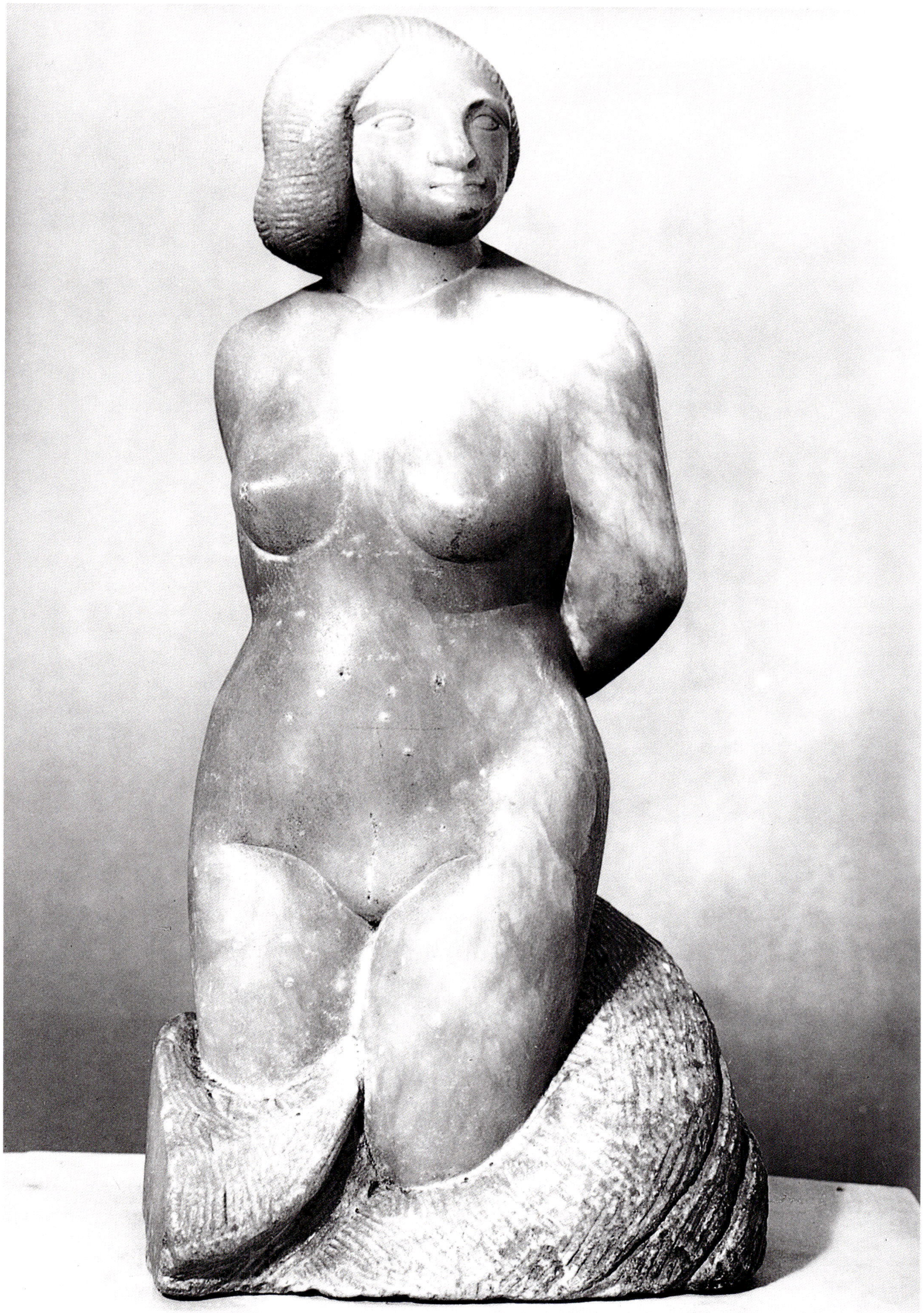

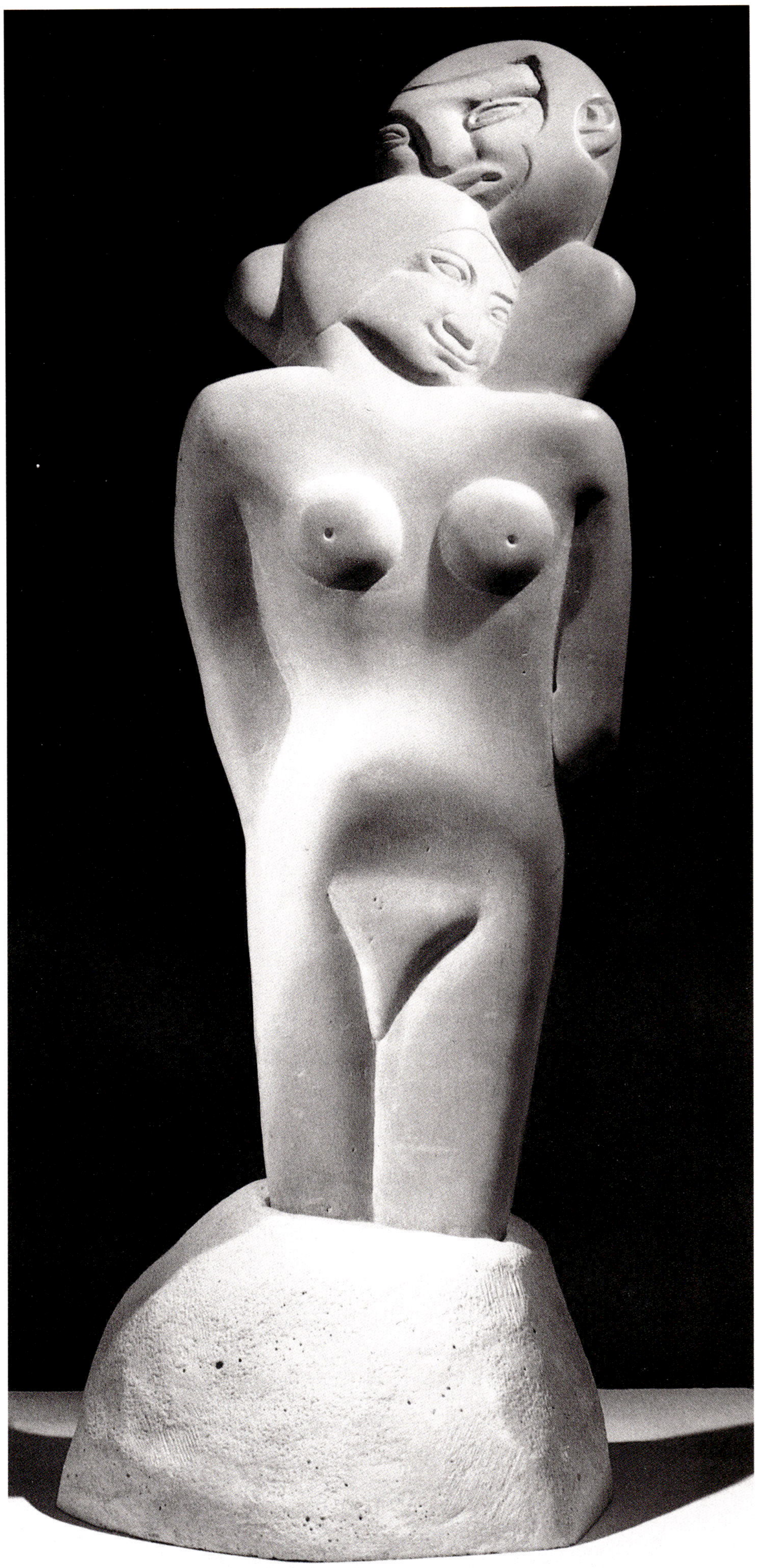

66, 67 Samson and Delilah (*cat.* 57)

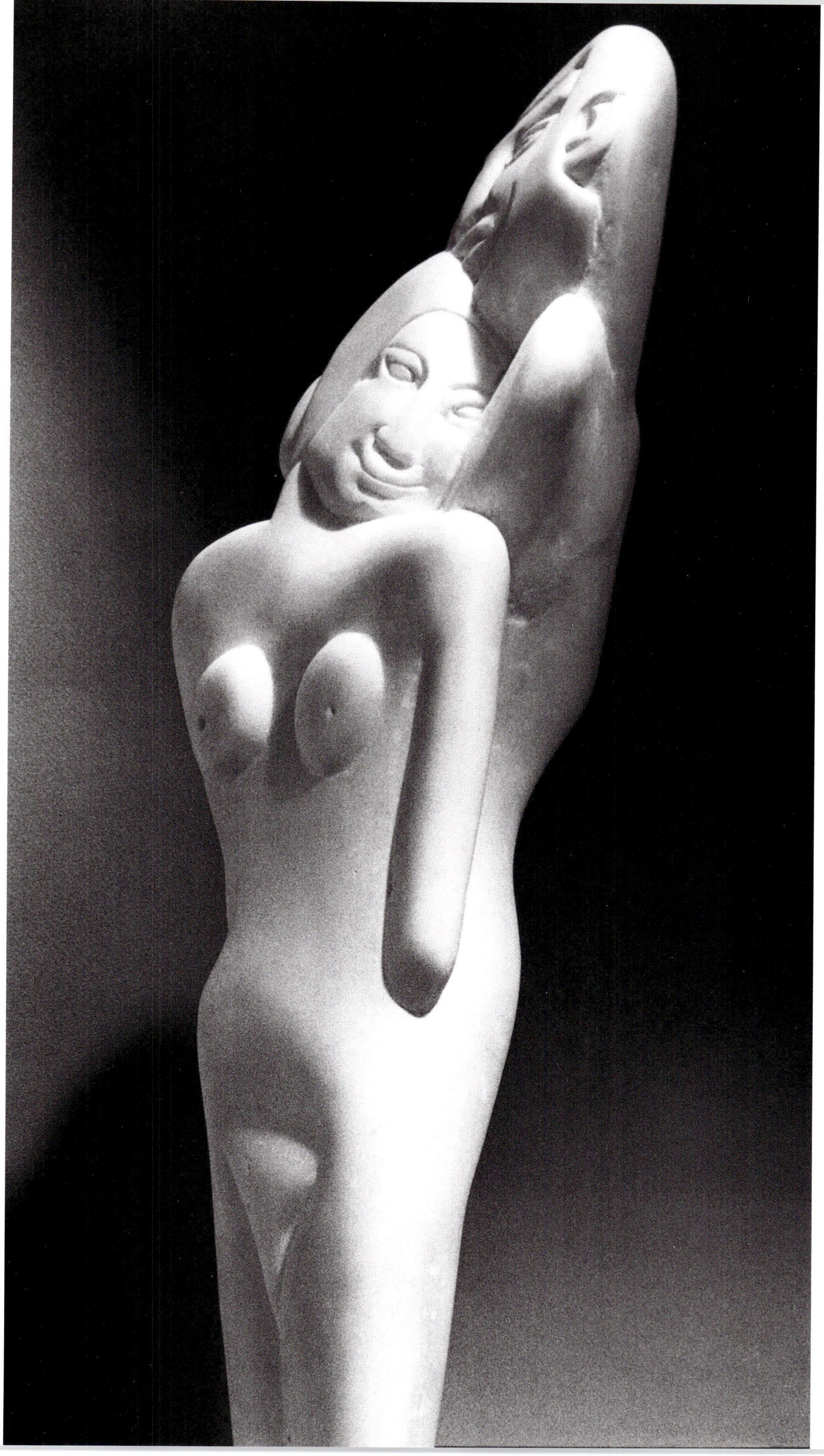

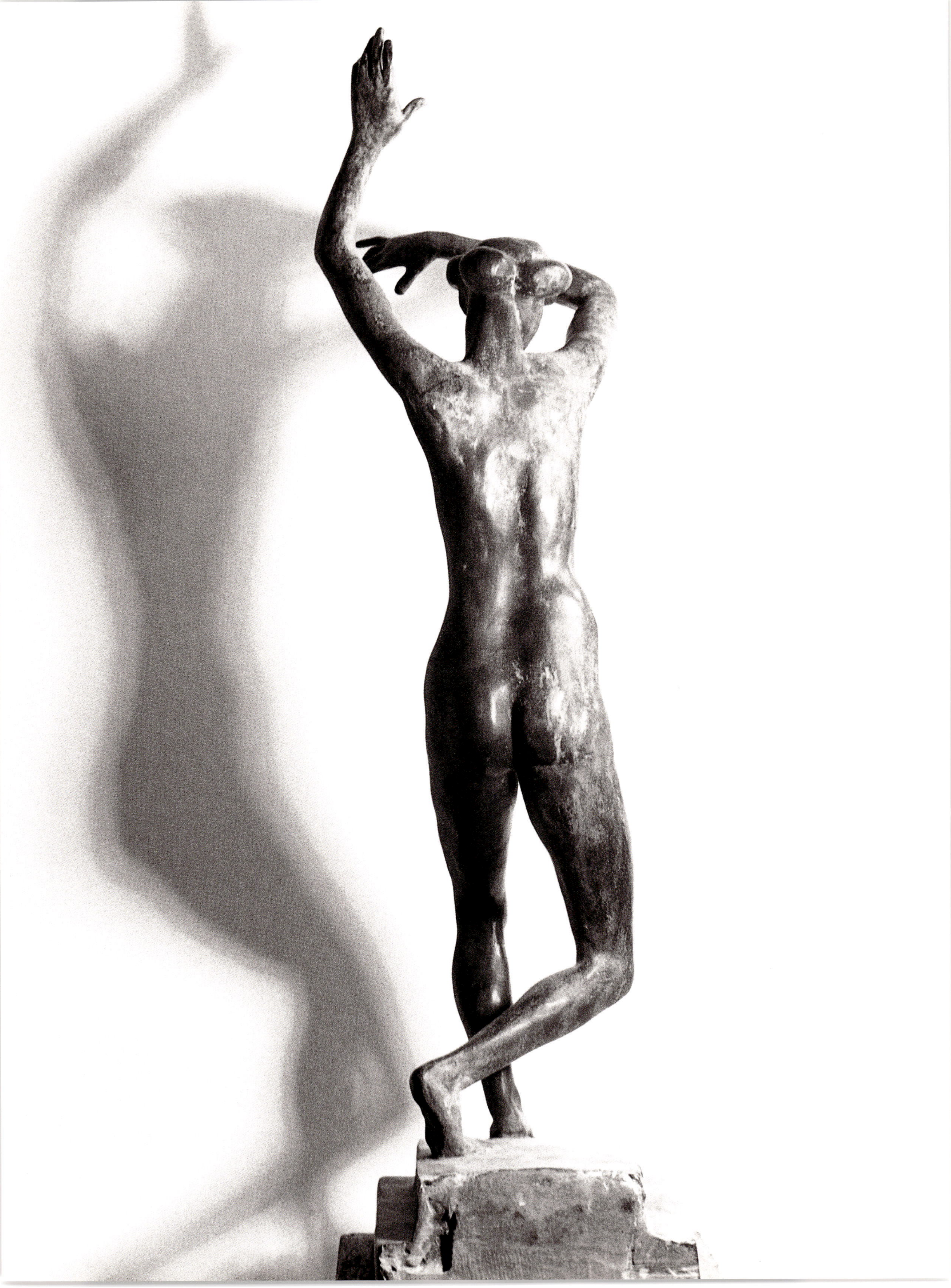

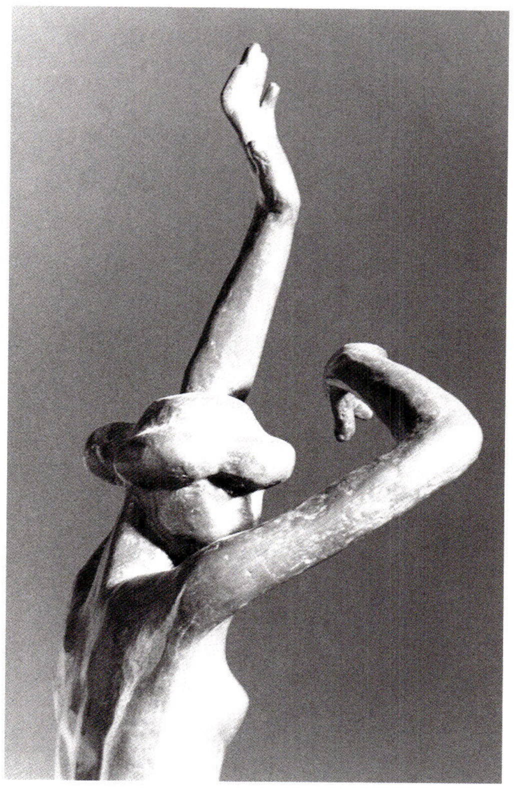

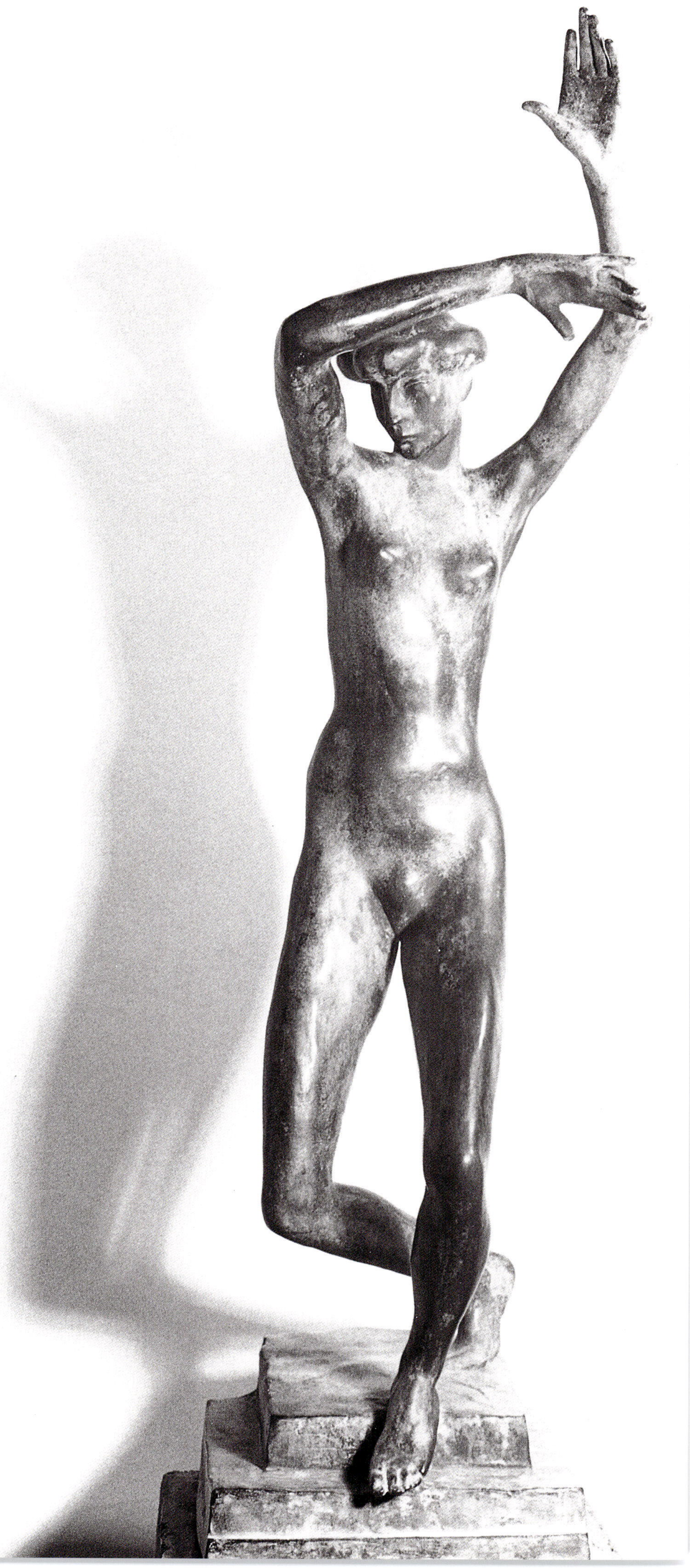

68–70 Dancer (*cat.* 58)

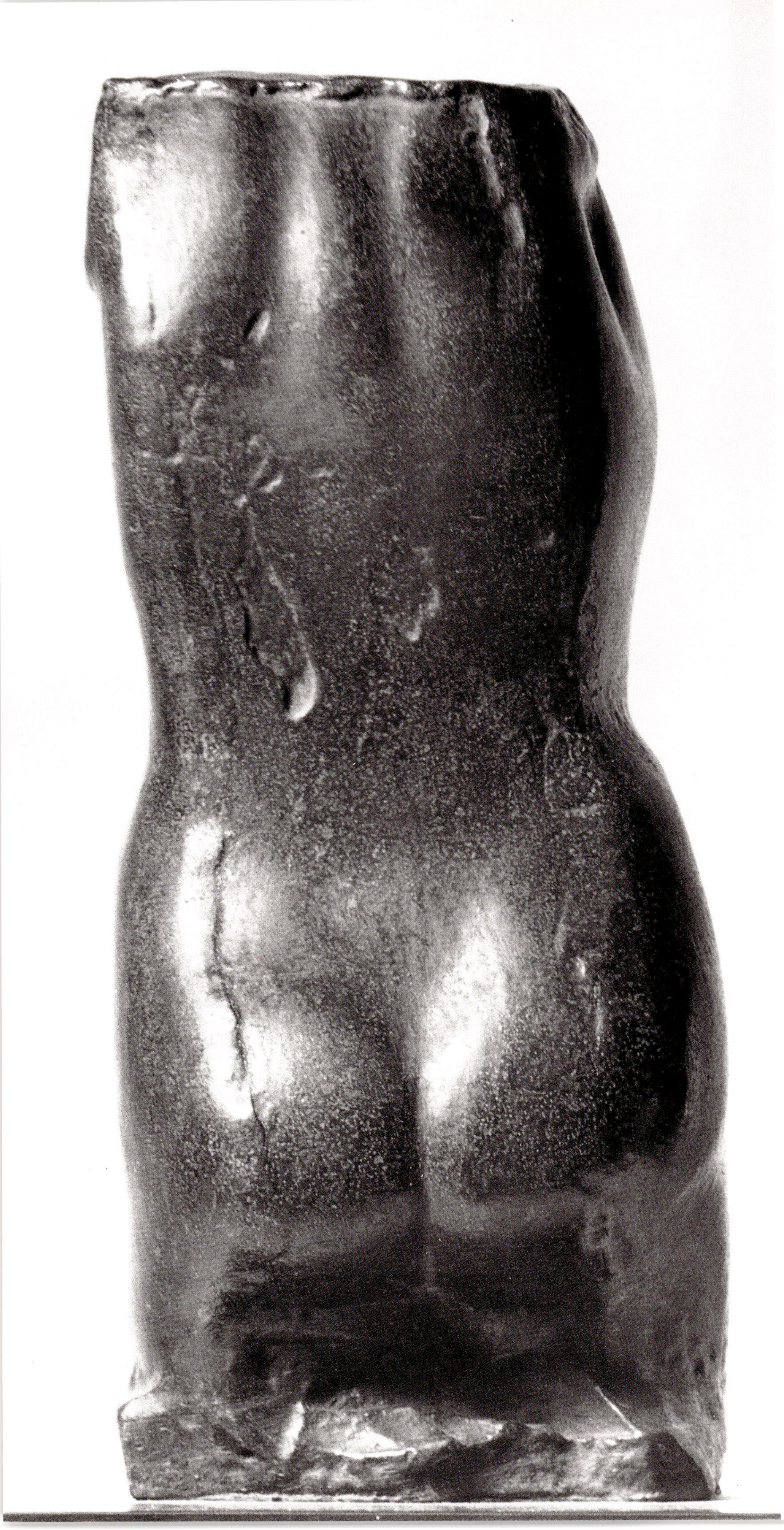

71, 72 Torso 2 (*cat.* 59)

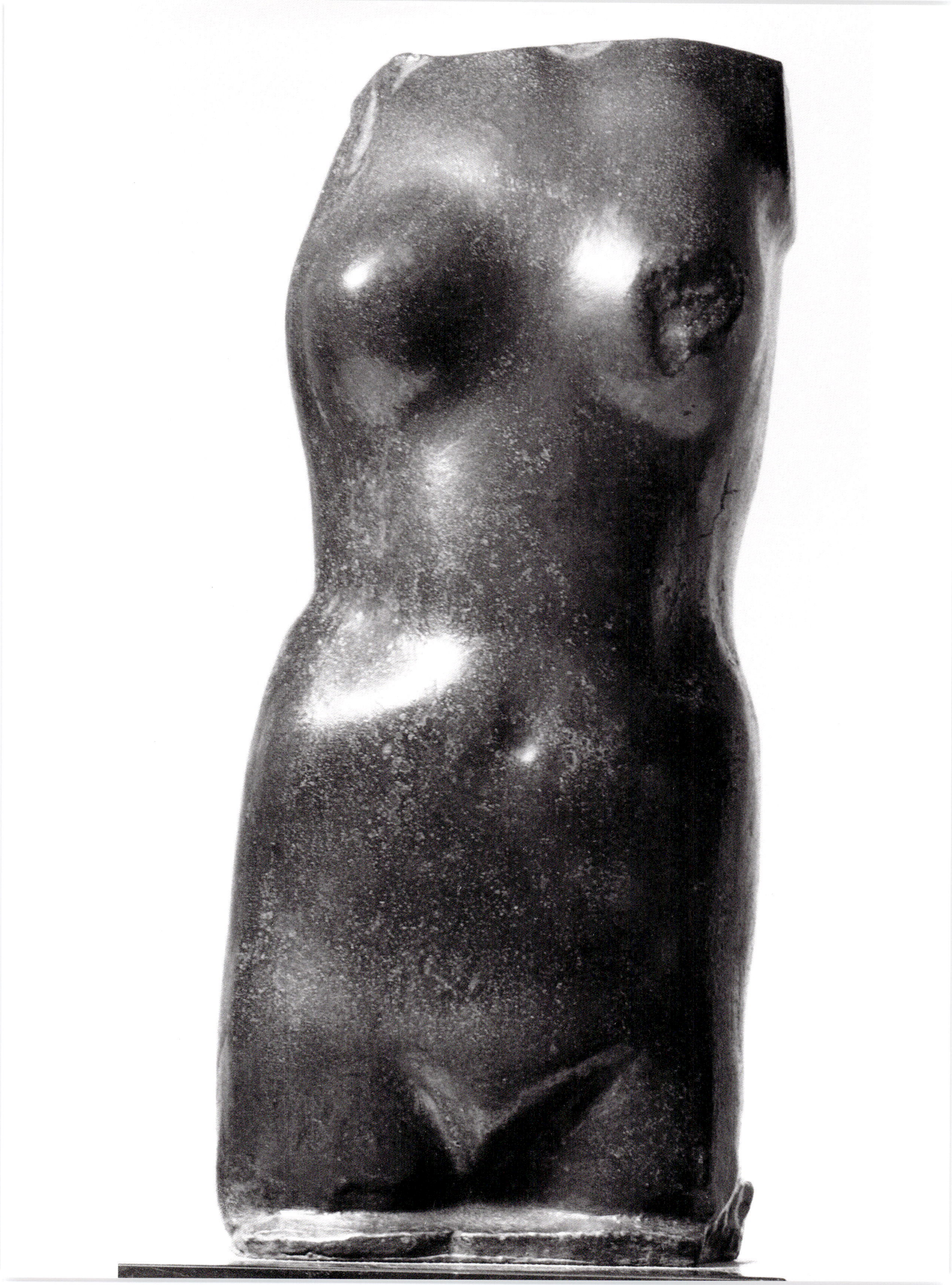

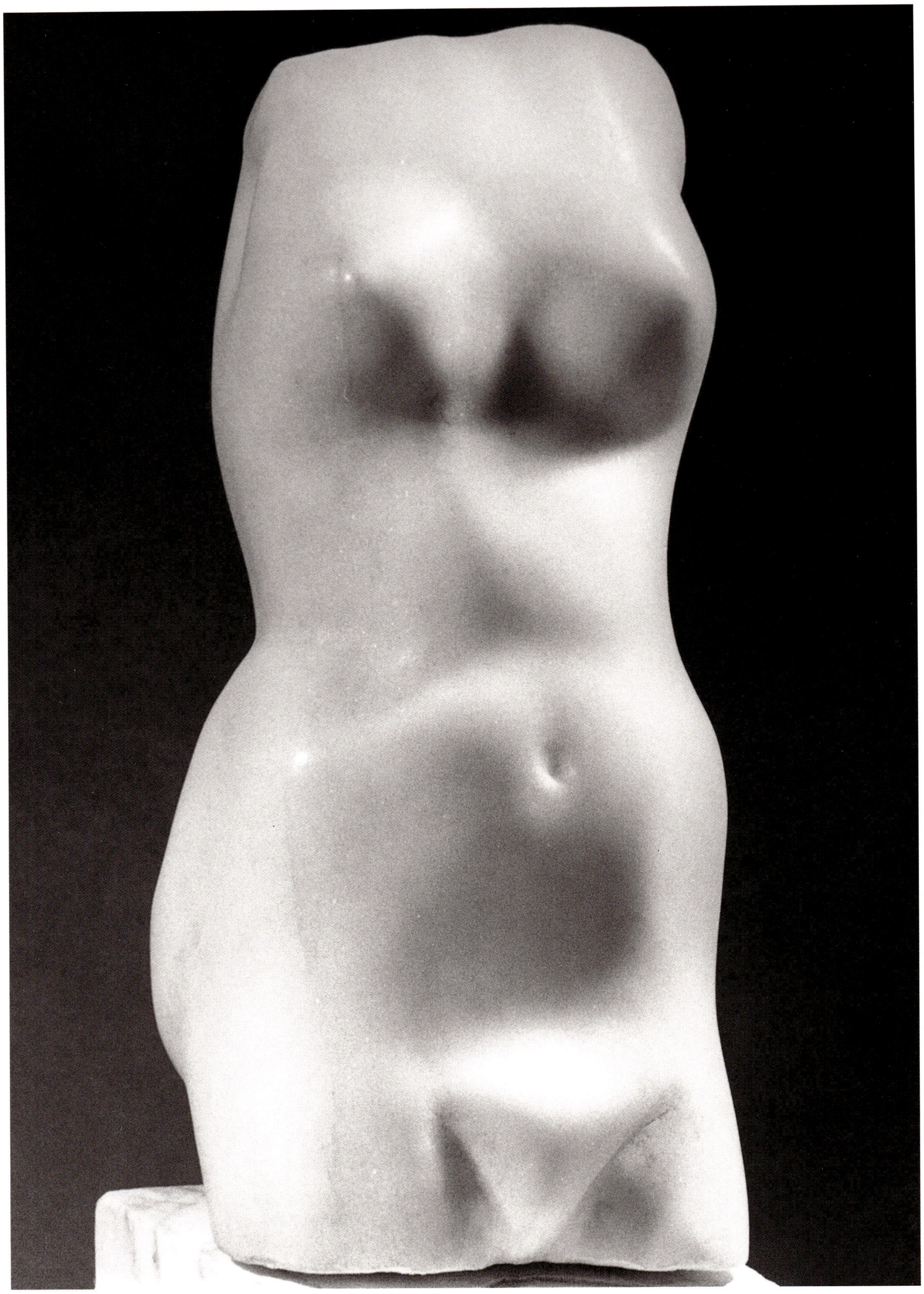

73, 74 Torso 3 (*cat.* 60)

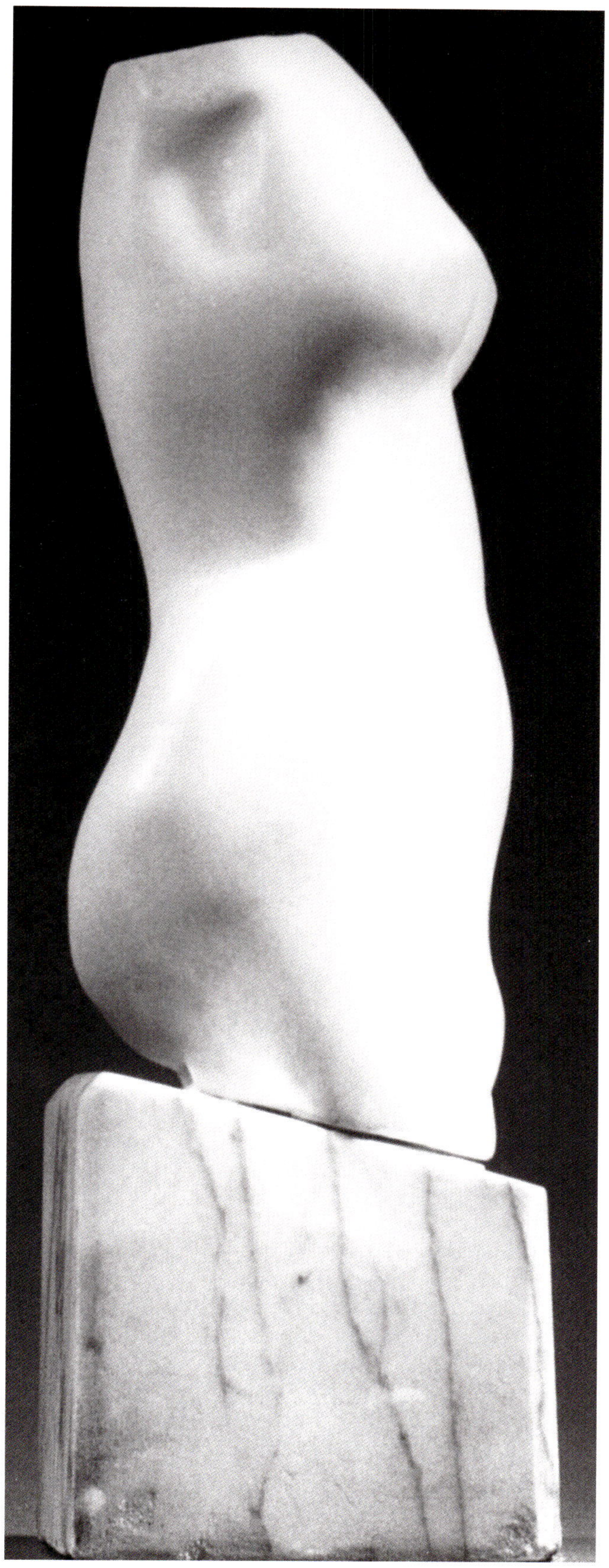

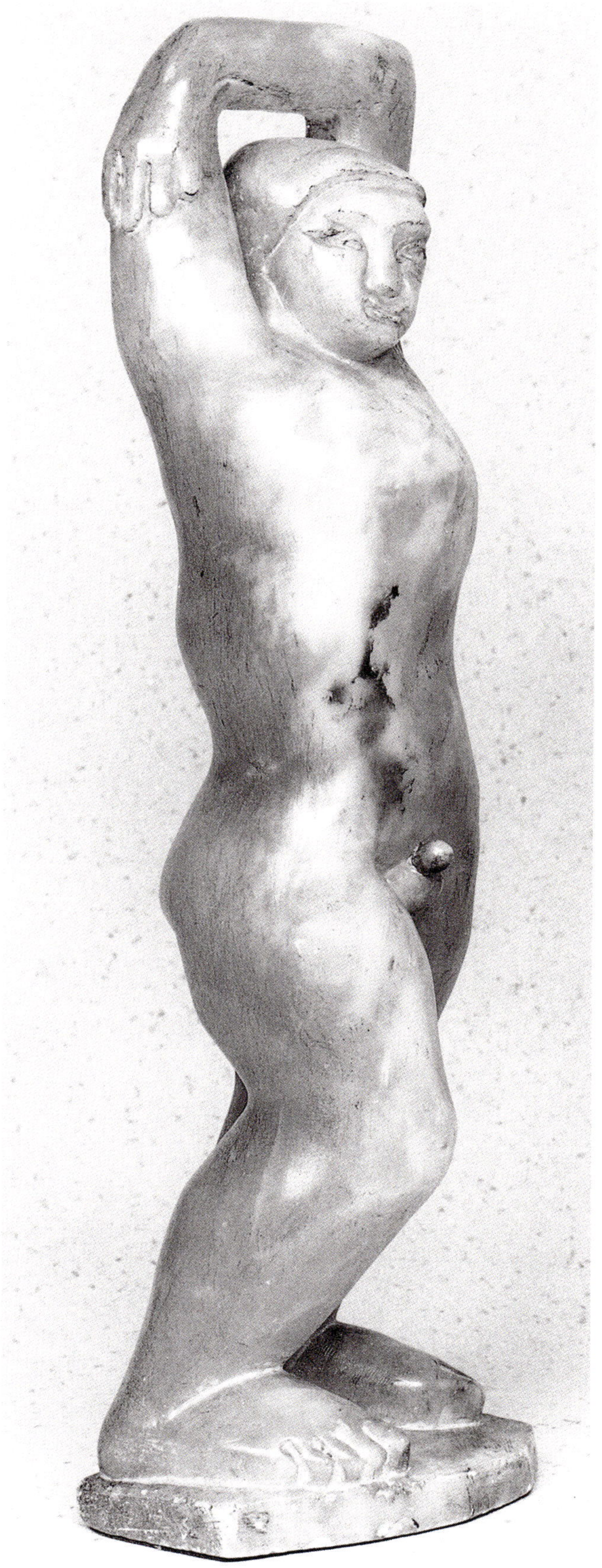

75 Boy (*cat.* 56)

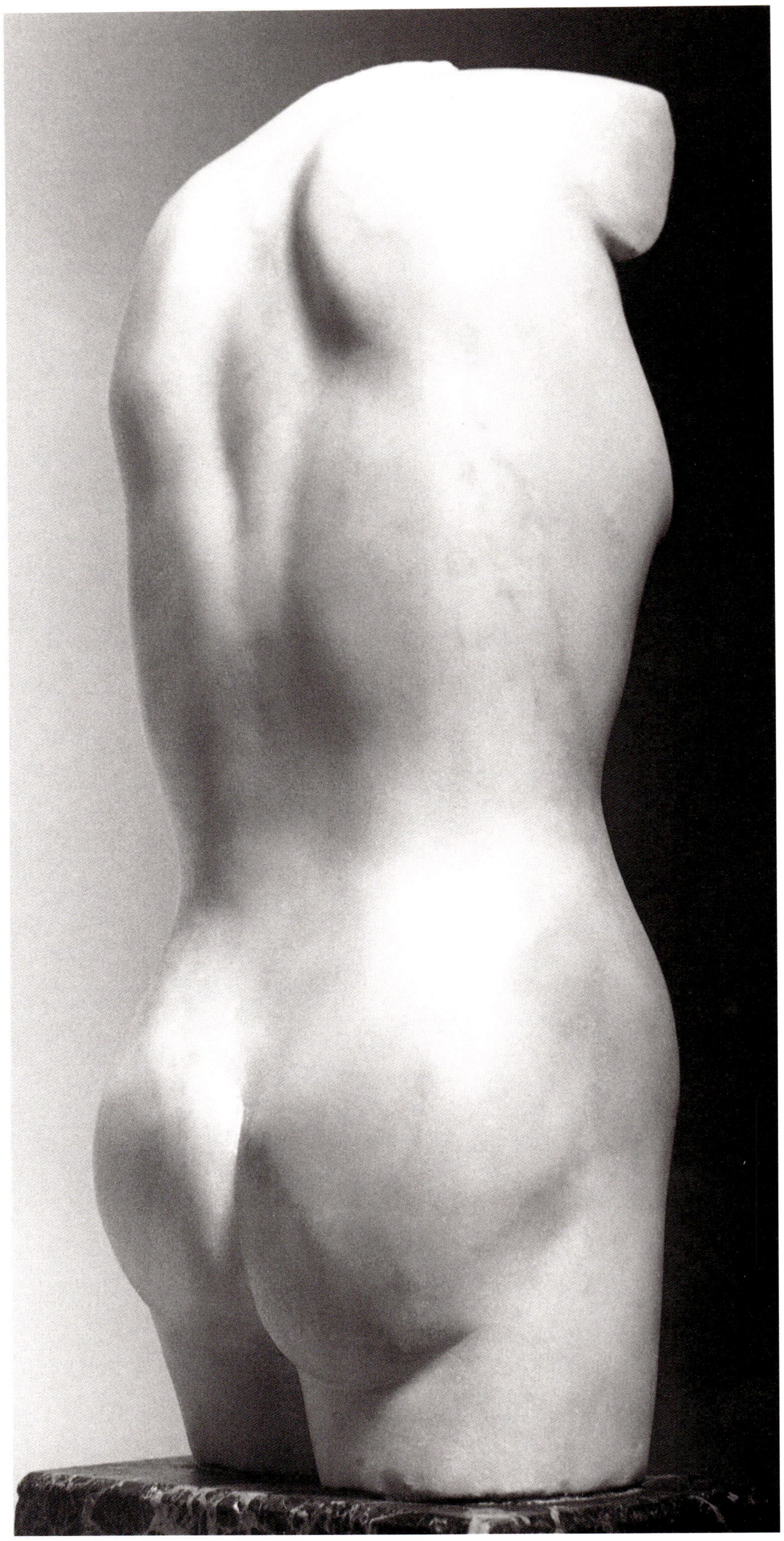

76, 77 Torso I
(*cat.* 61)

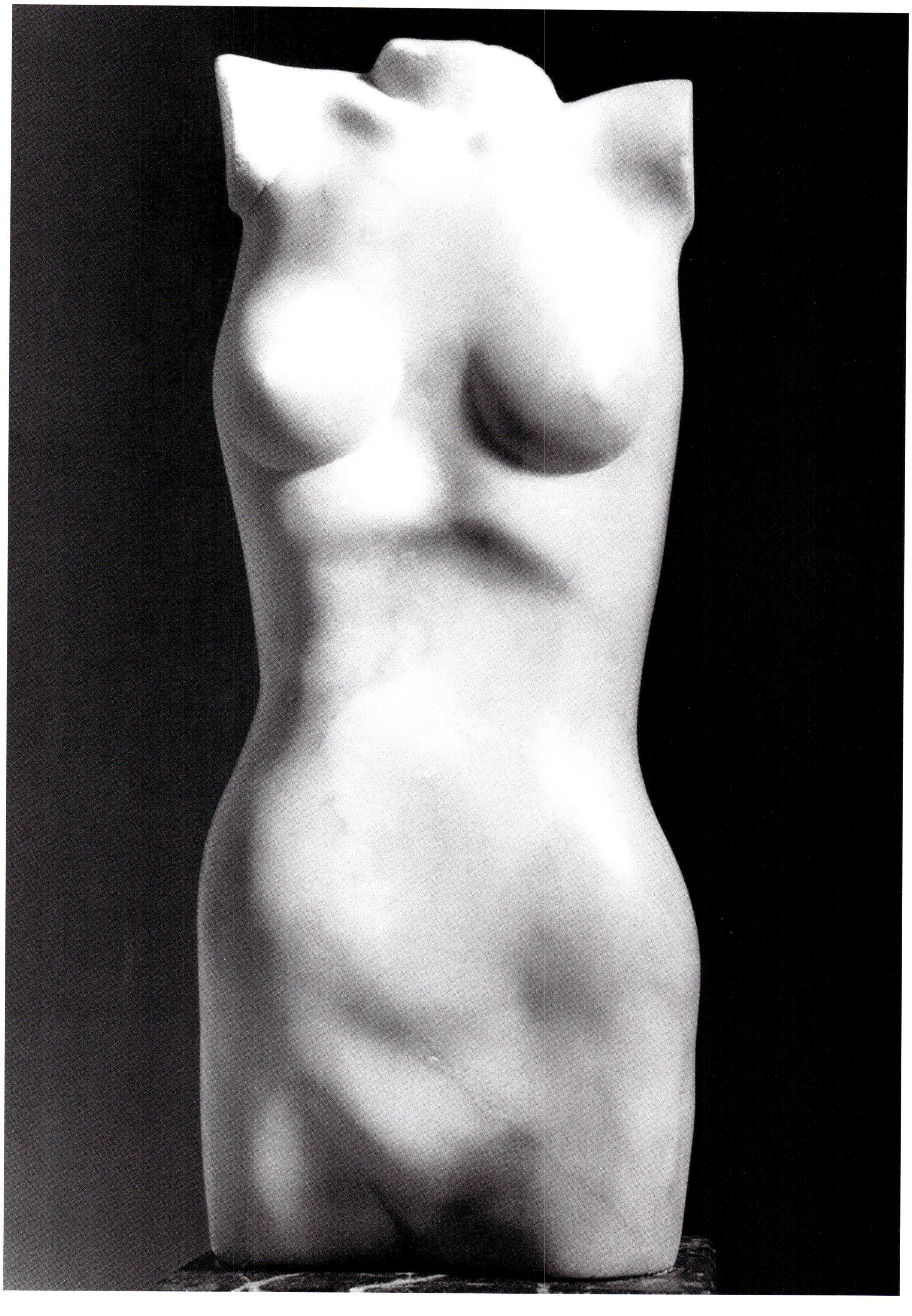

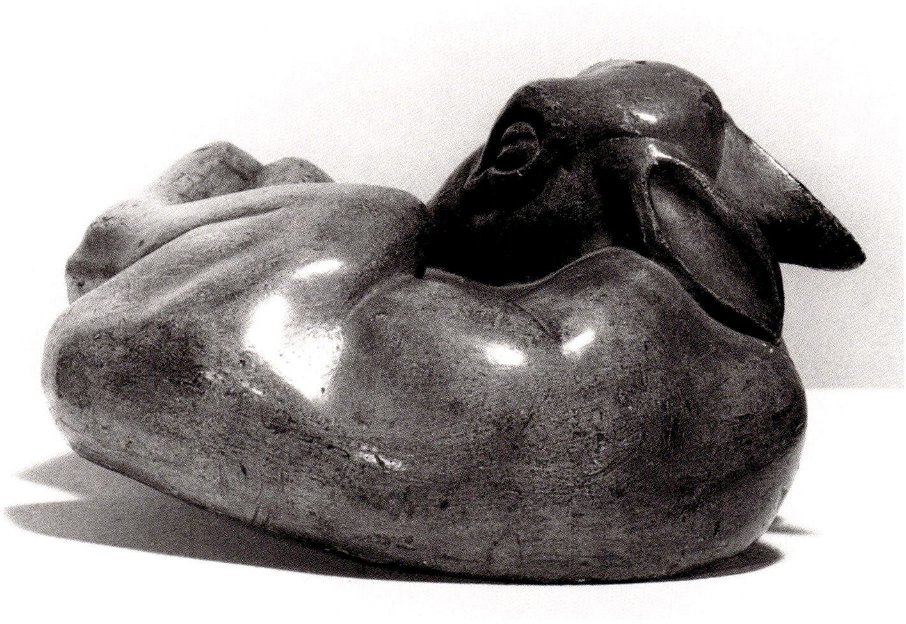

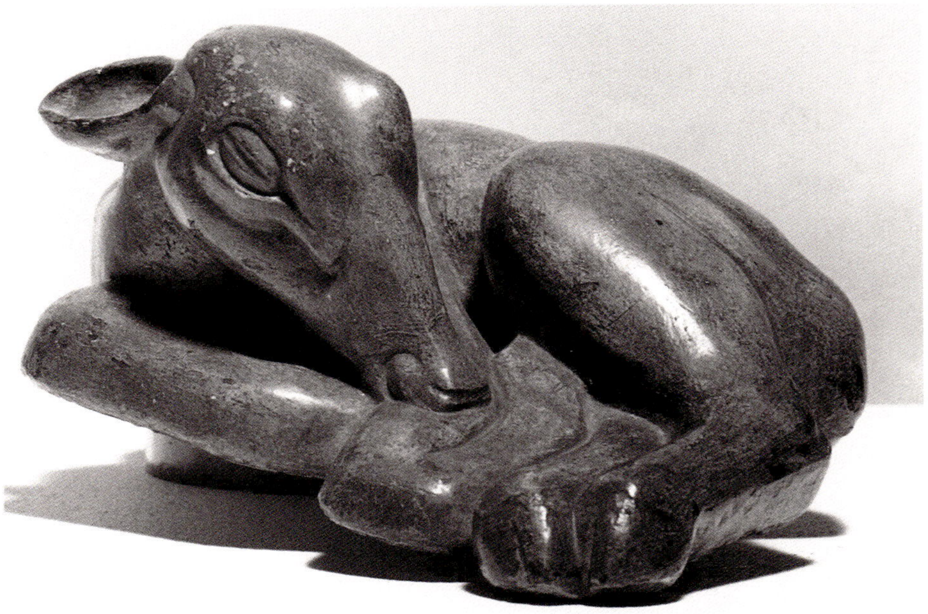

78, 79 Sleeping Fawn
(*cat.* 63)

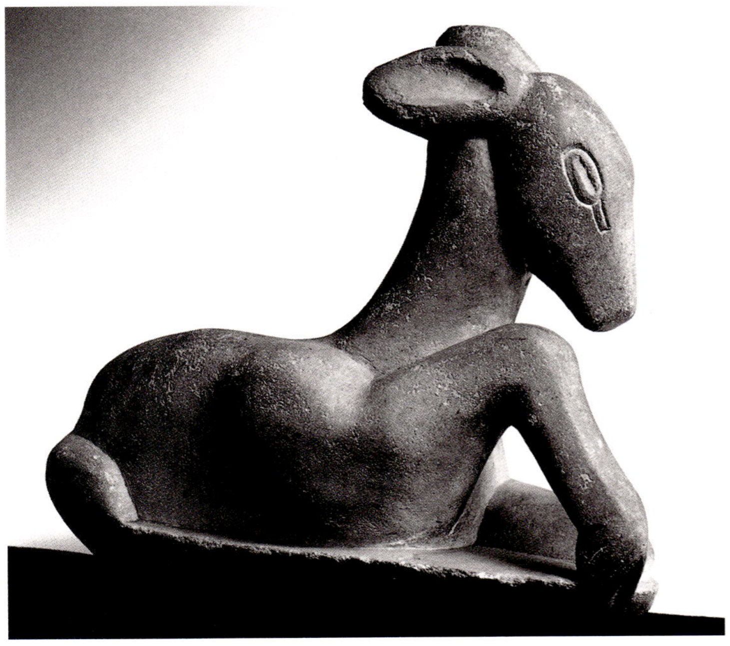

80 Crouching Fawn (*cat.* 62)

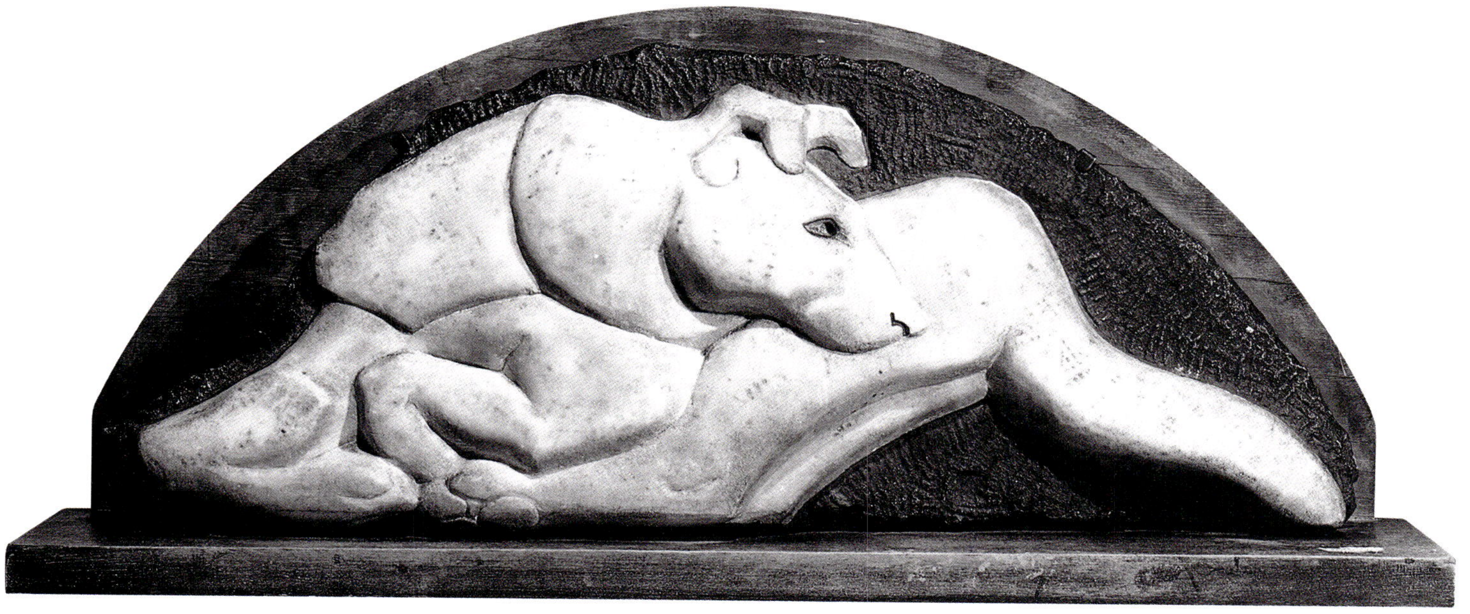

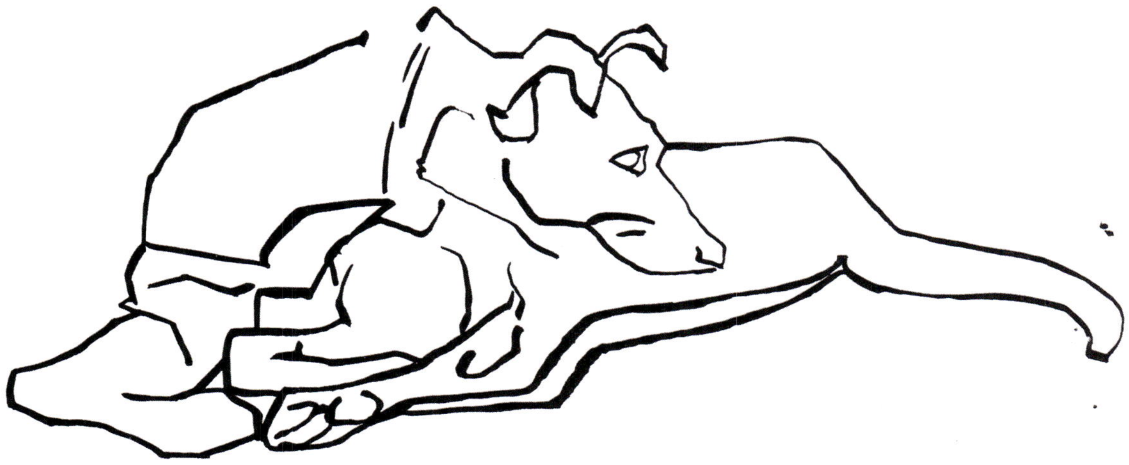

81 Dog (*cat.* 48)

82 Study for Dog

83, 84 Maternity (*cat.* 64)

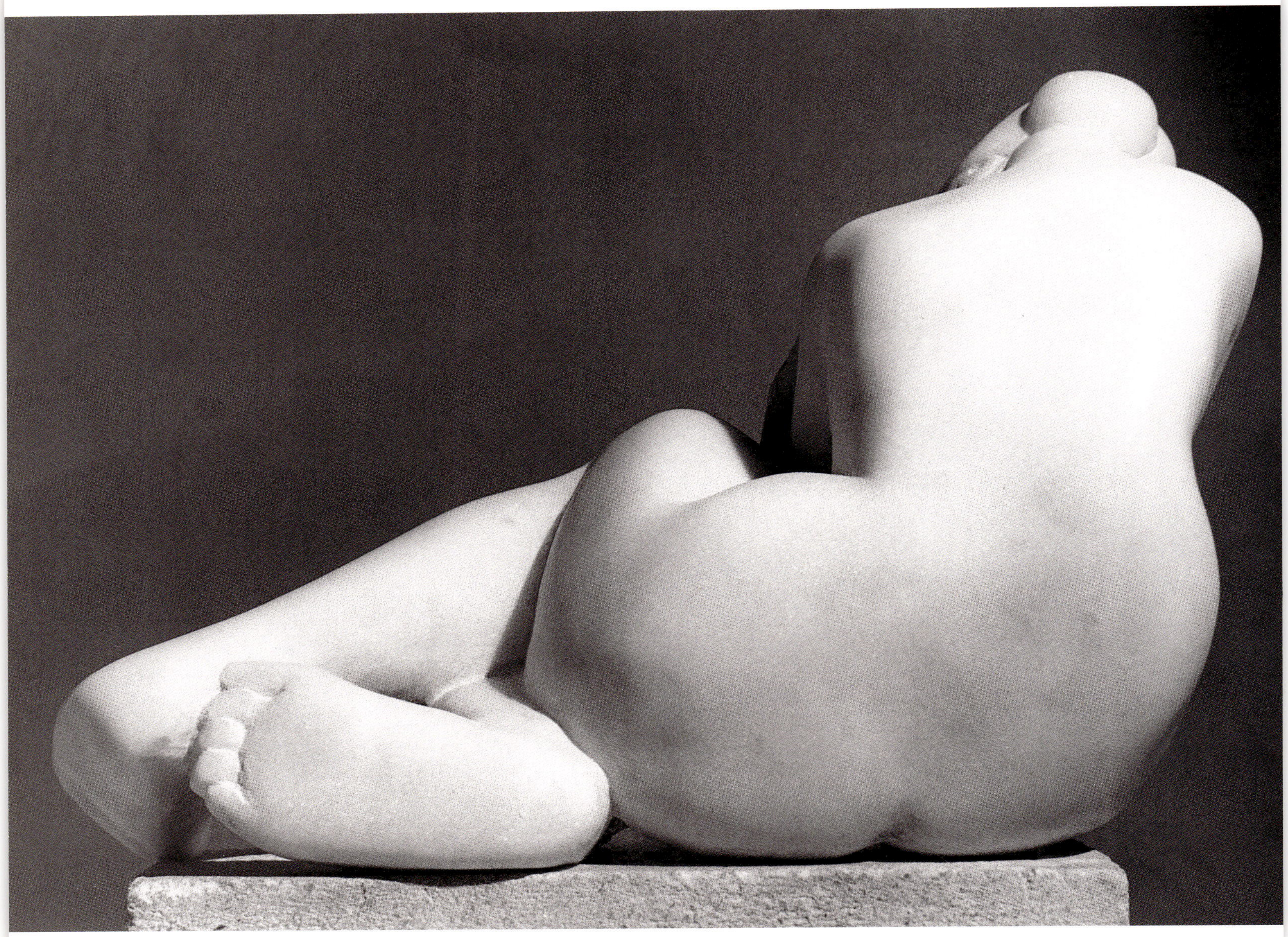

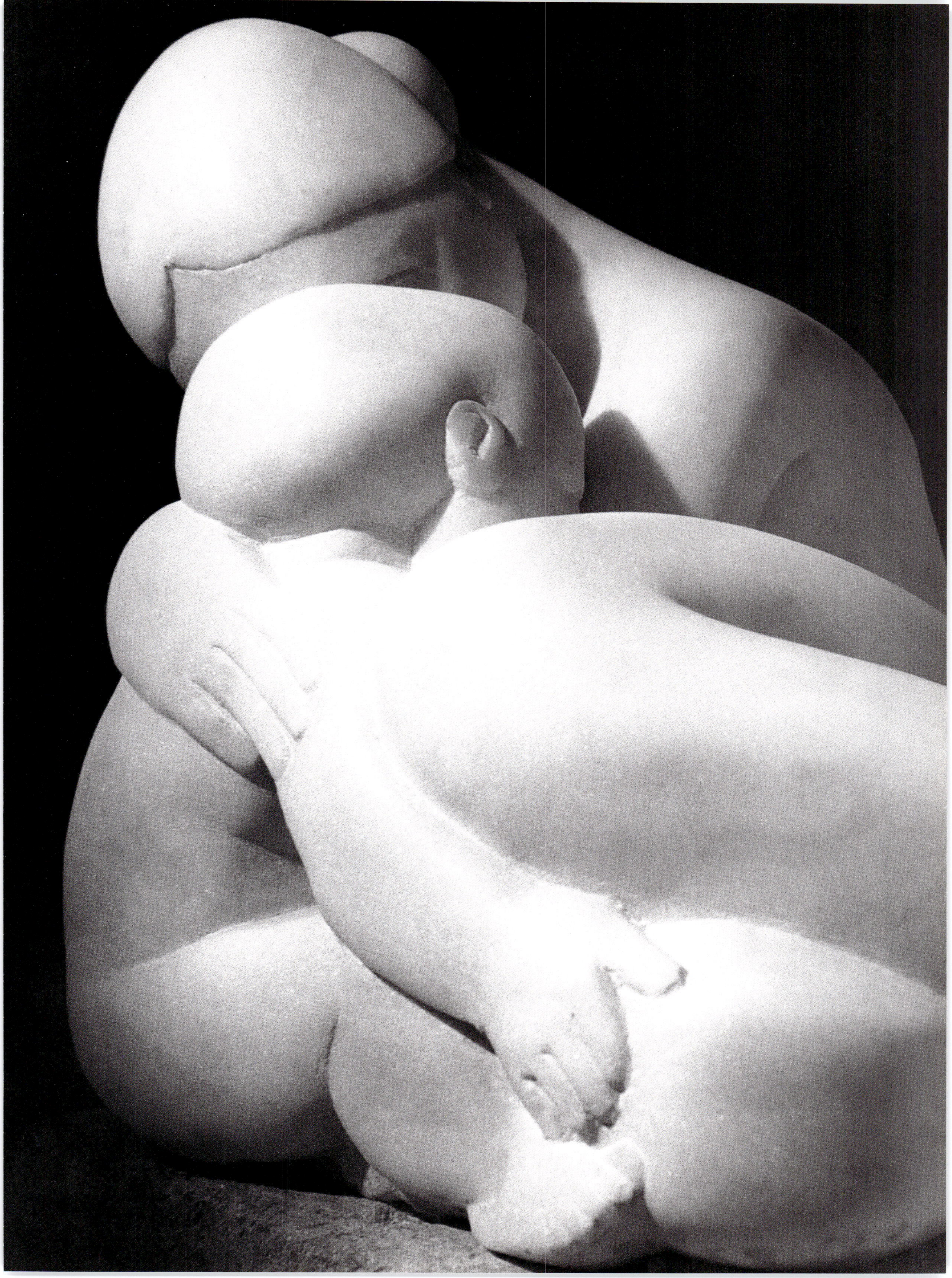

85 Crouching Boy (*cat.* 68)

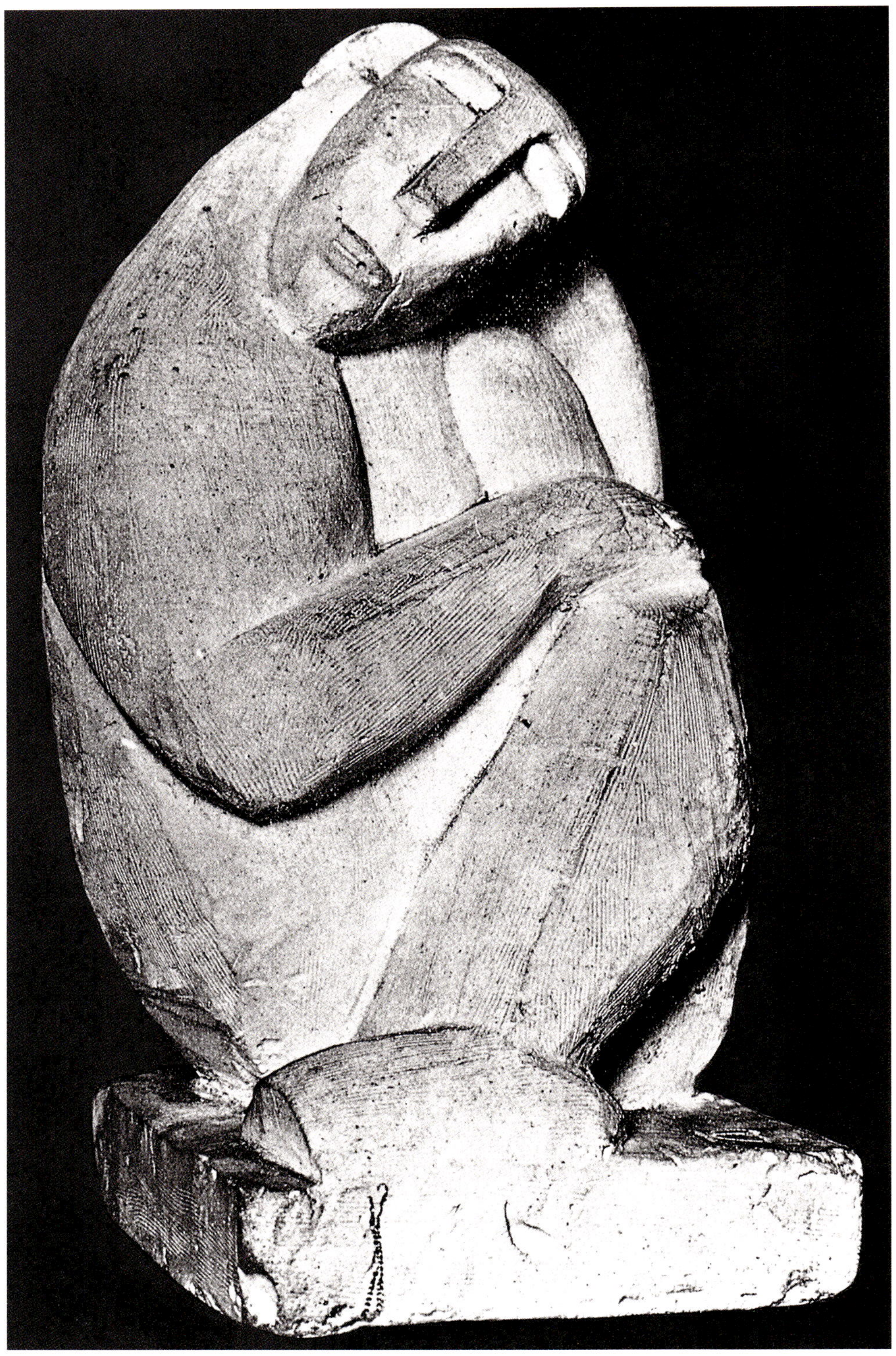

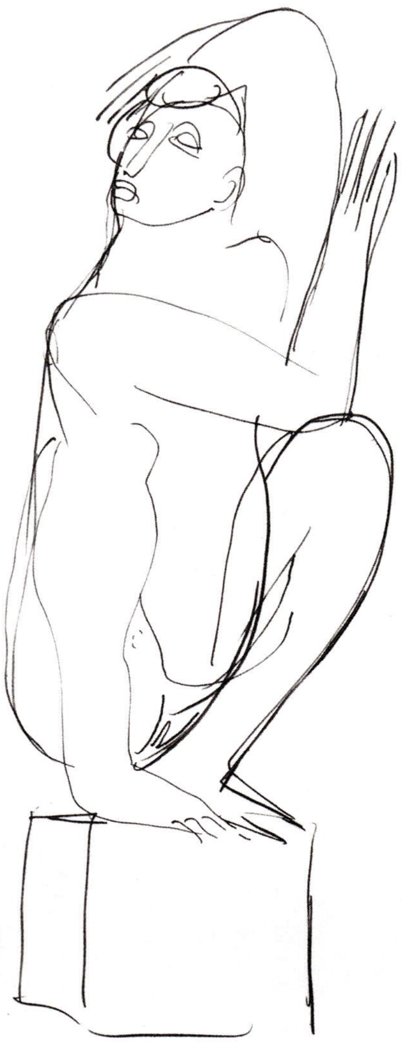

86 Crouching Figure, ink

87 Wrestlers (*cat.* 66)

88 Study for Wrestlers, pencil

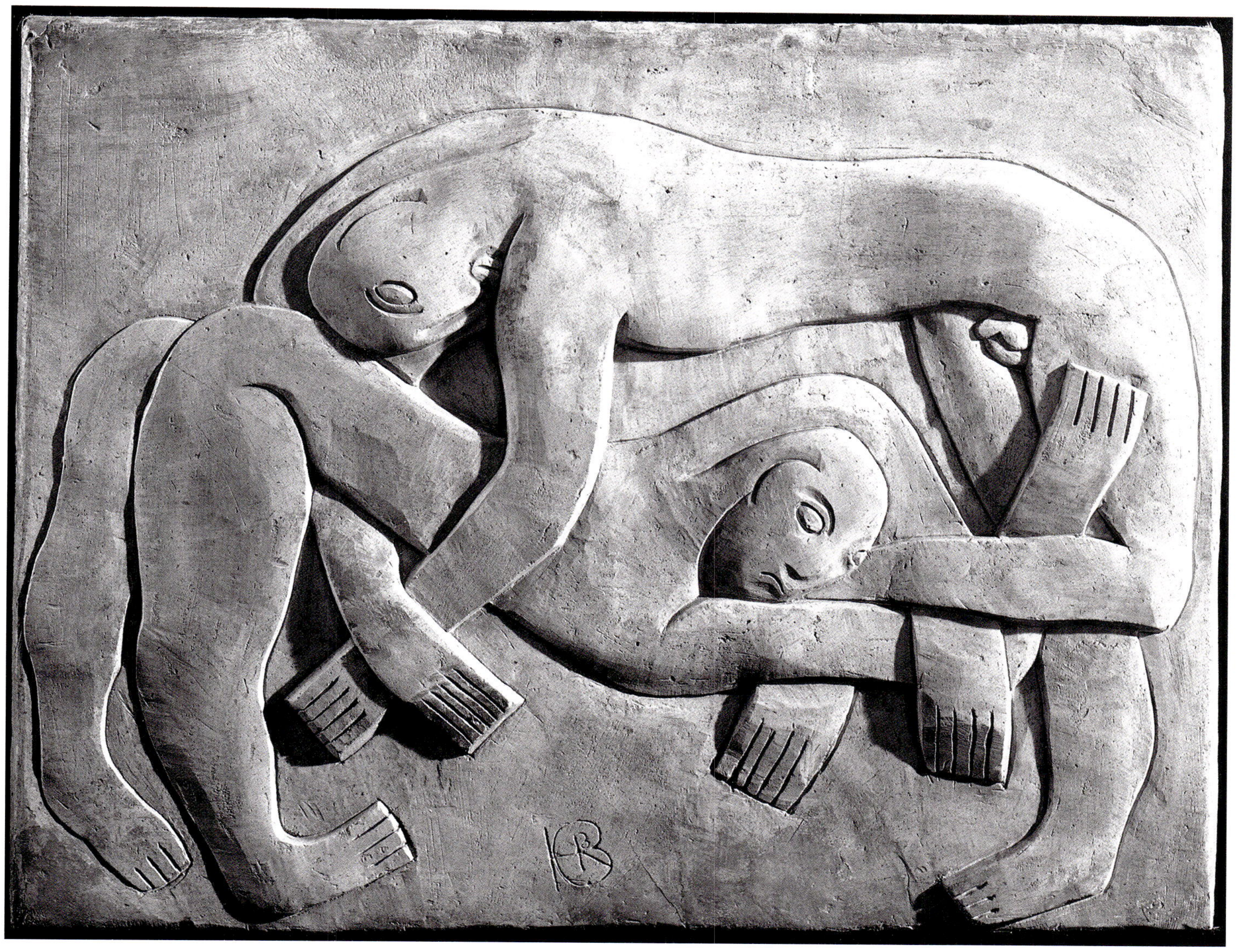

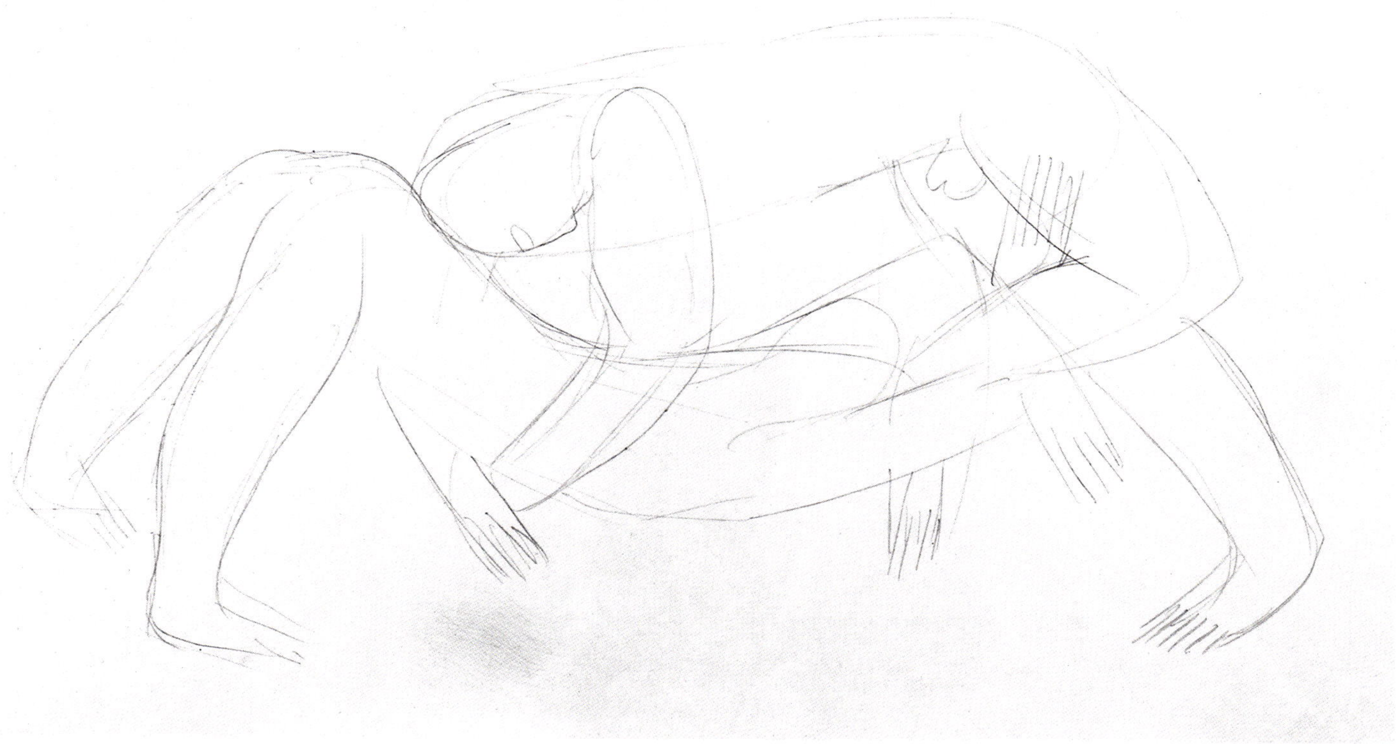

89, 90 Cat (*cat.* 70)

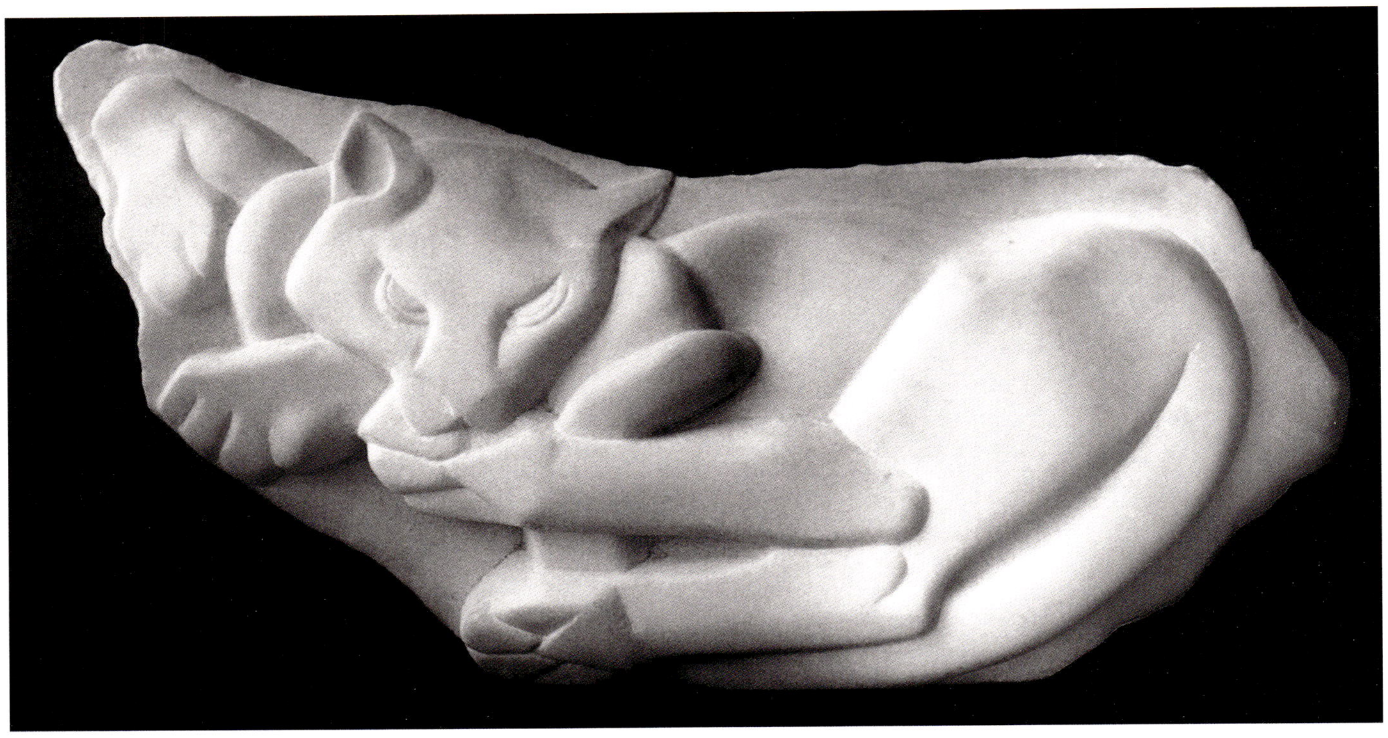

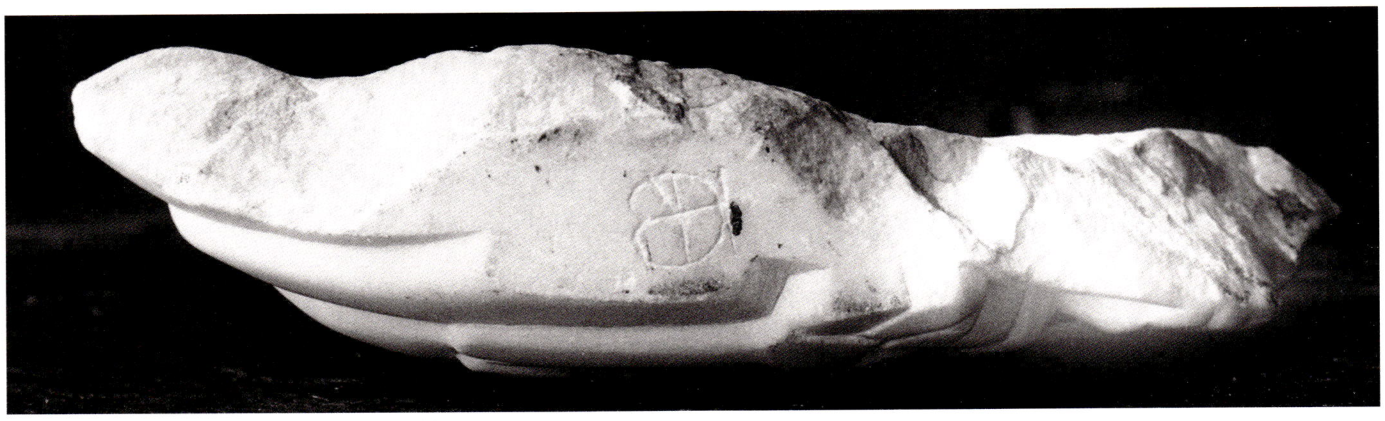

91 Lioness, ink

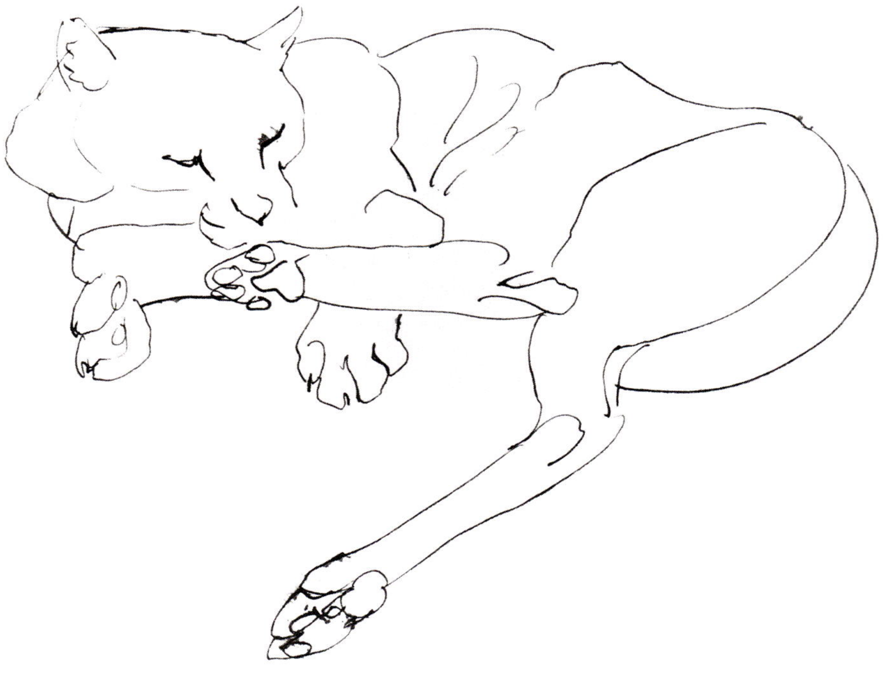

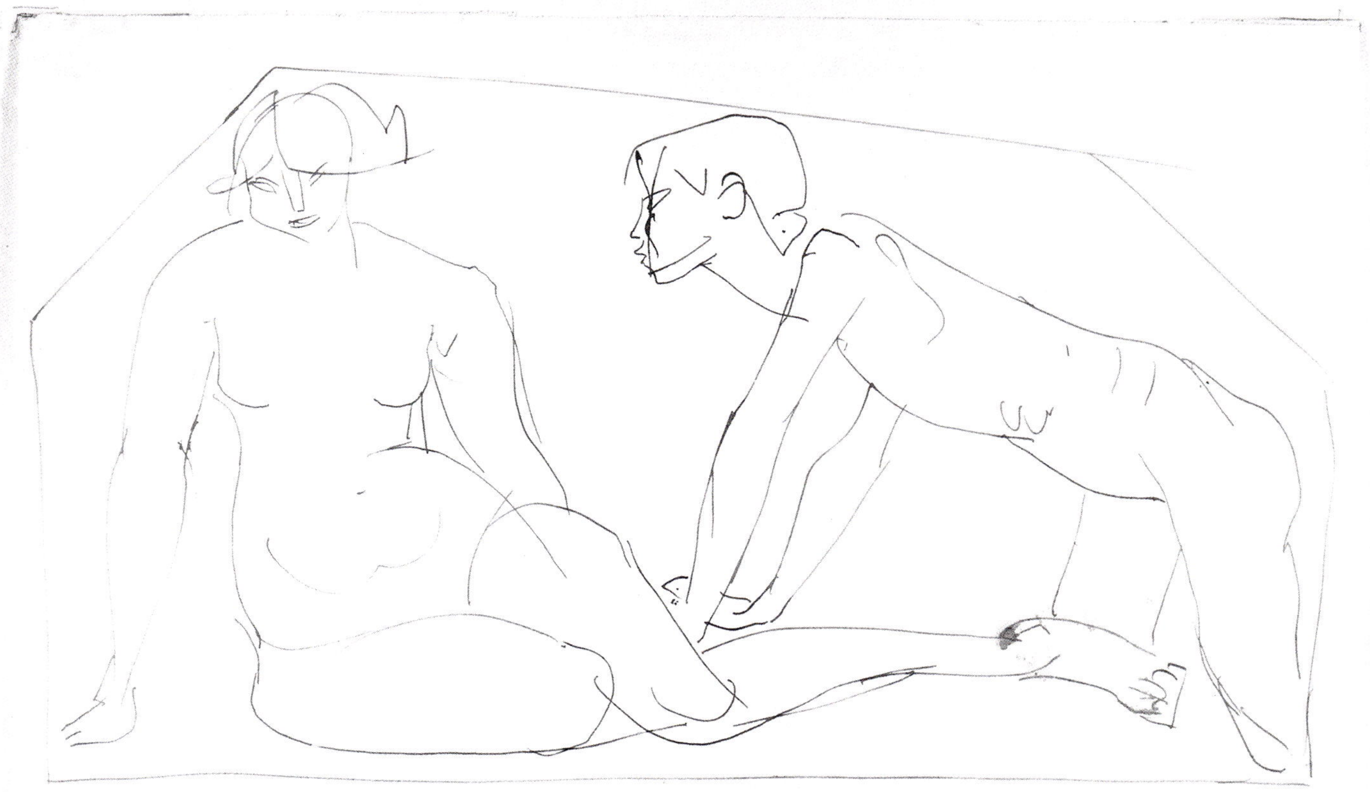

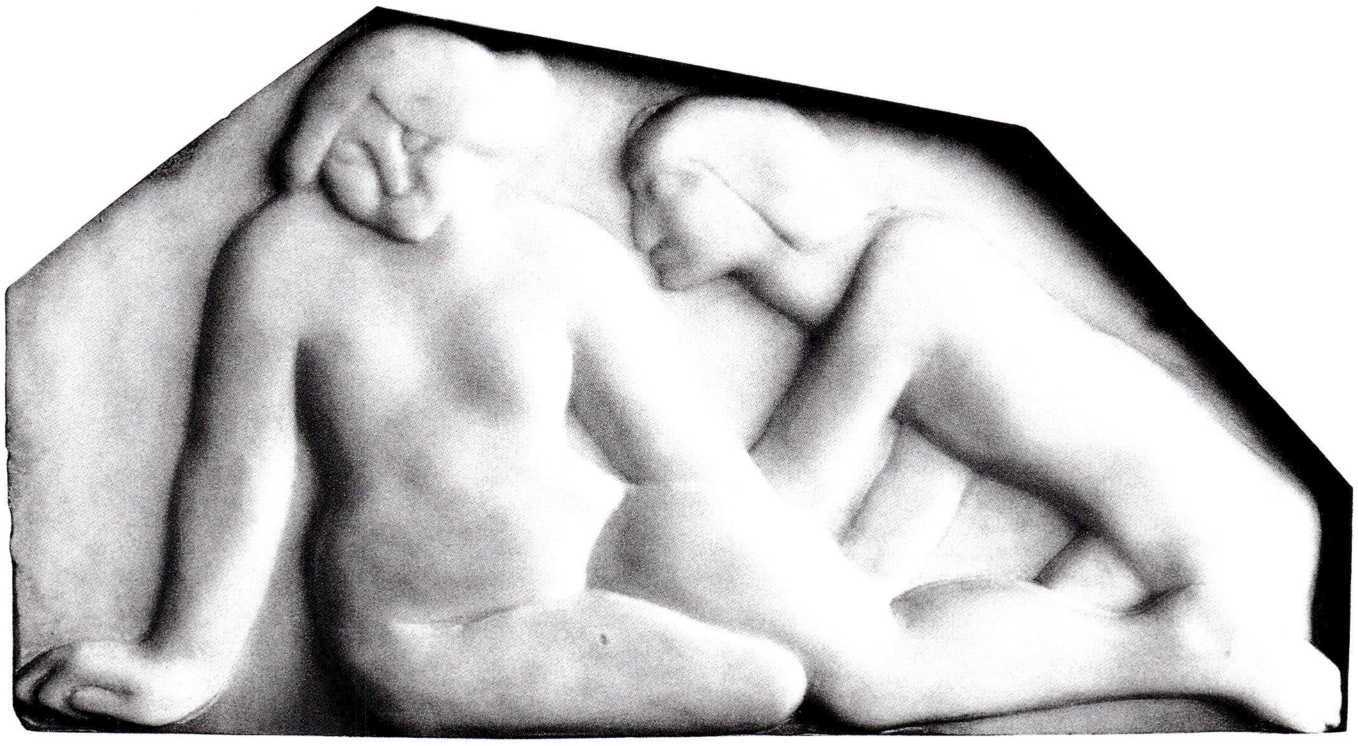

92 Study for Love Scene

93 Love Scene (*cat.* 73)

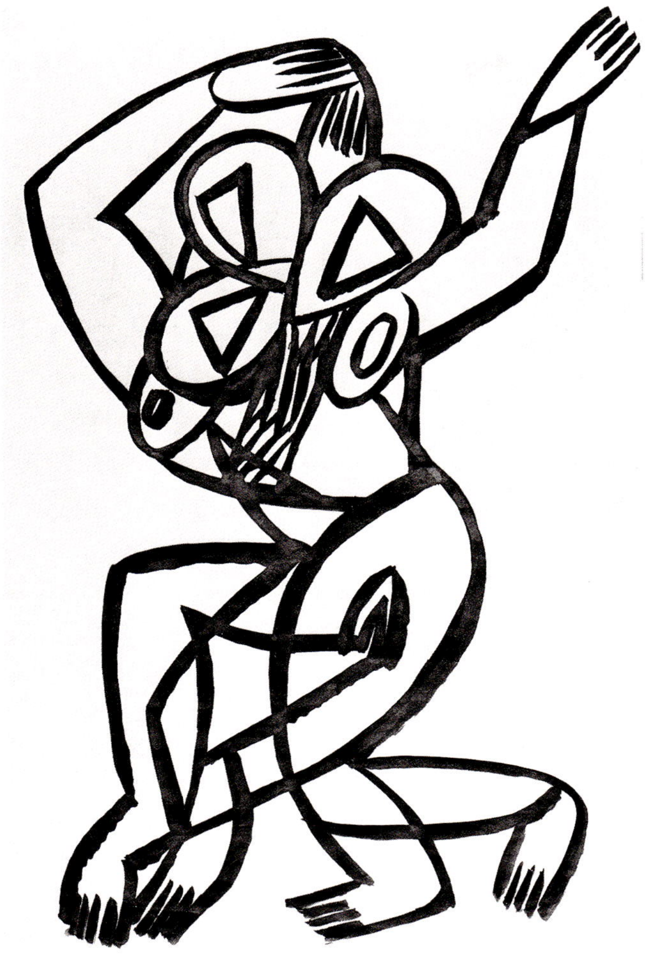

94 Study for Redstone Dancer

95 Dancing Woman, ink and brush

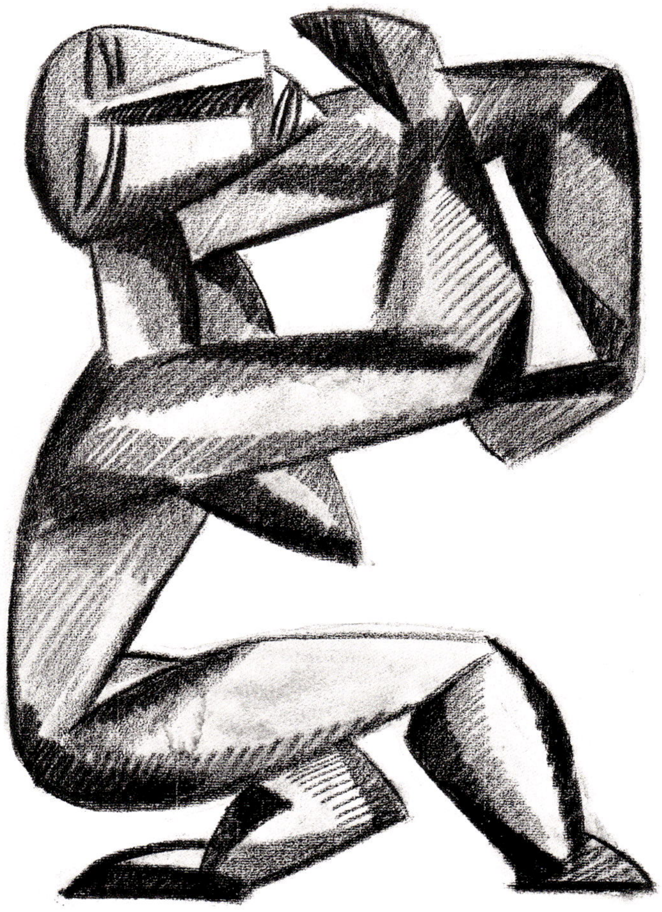

96 Dancing Woman, watercolour and conté crayon

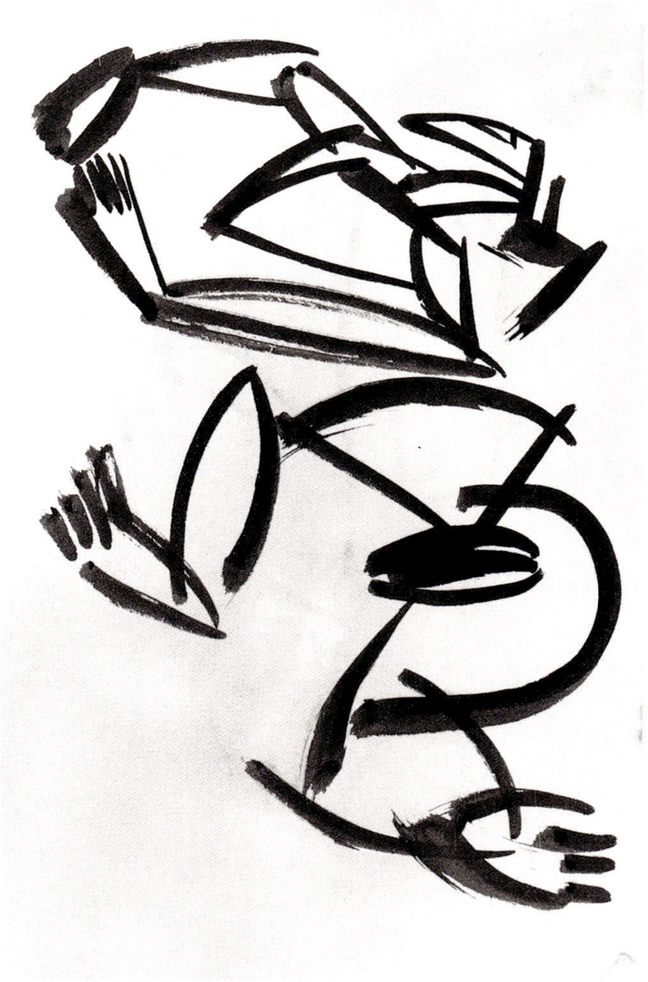

97–99 Redstone Dancer (*cat.* 69)

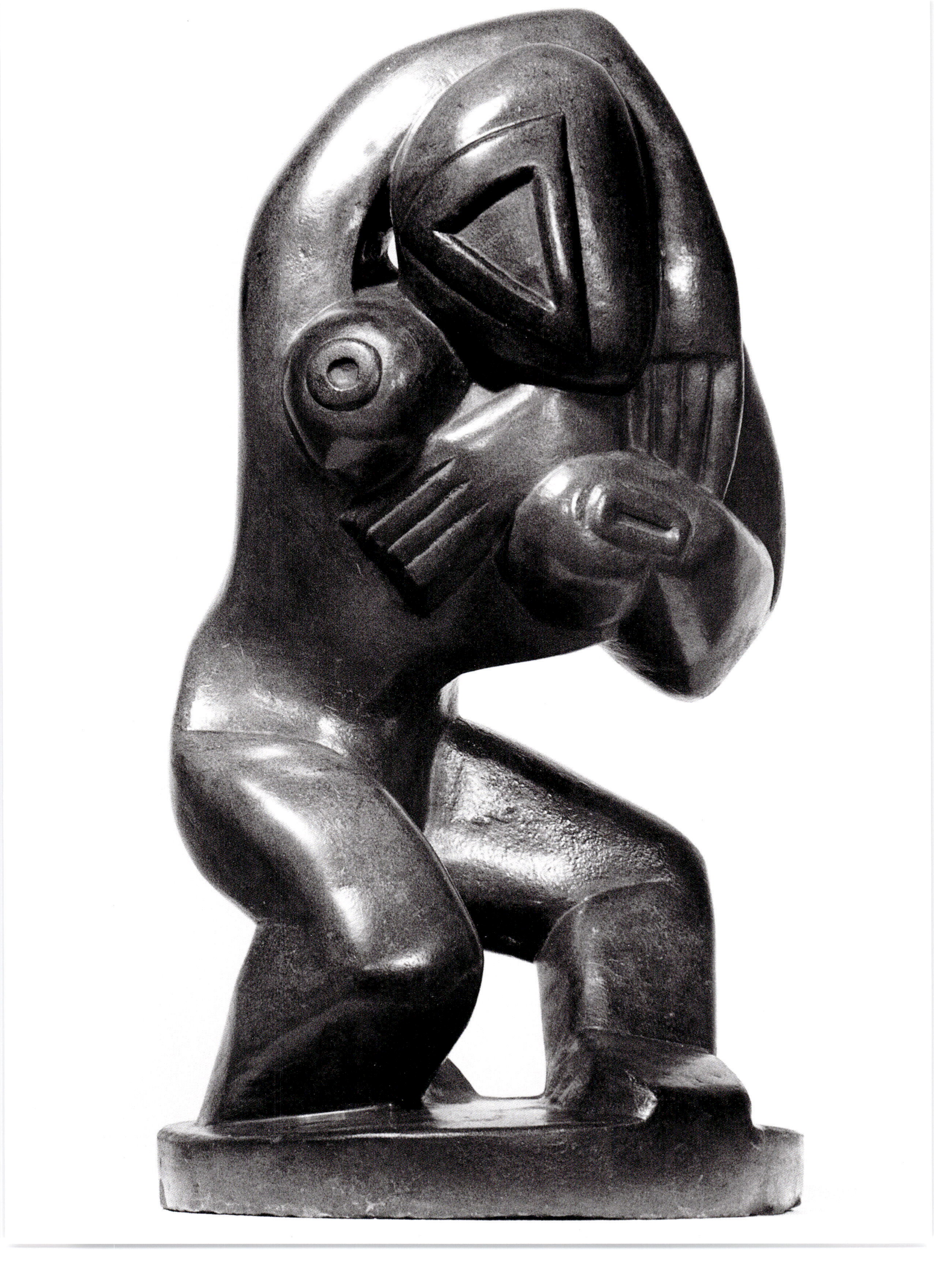

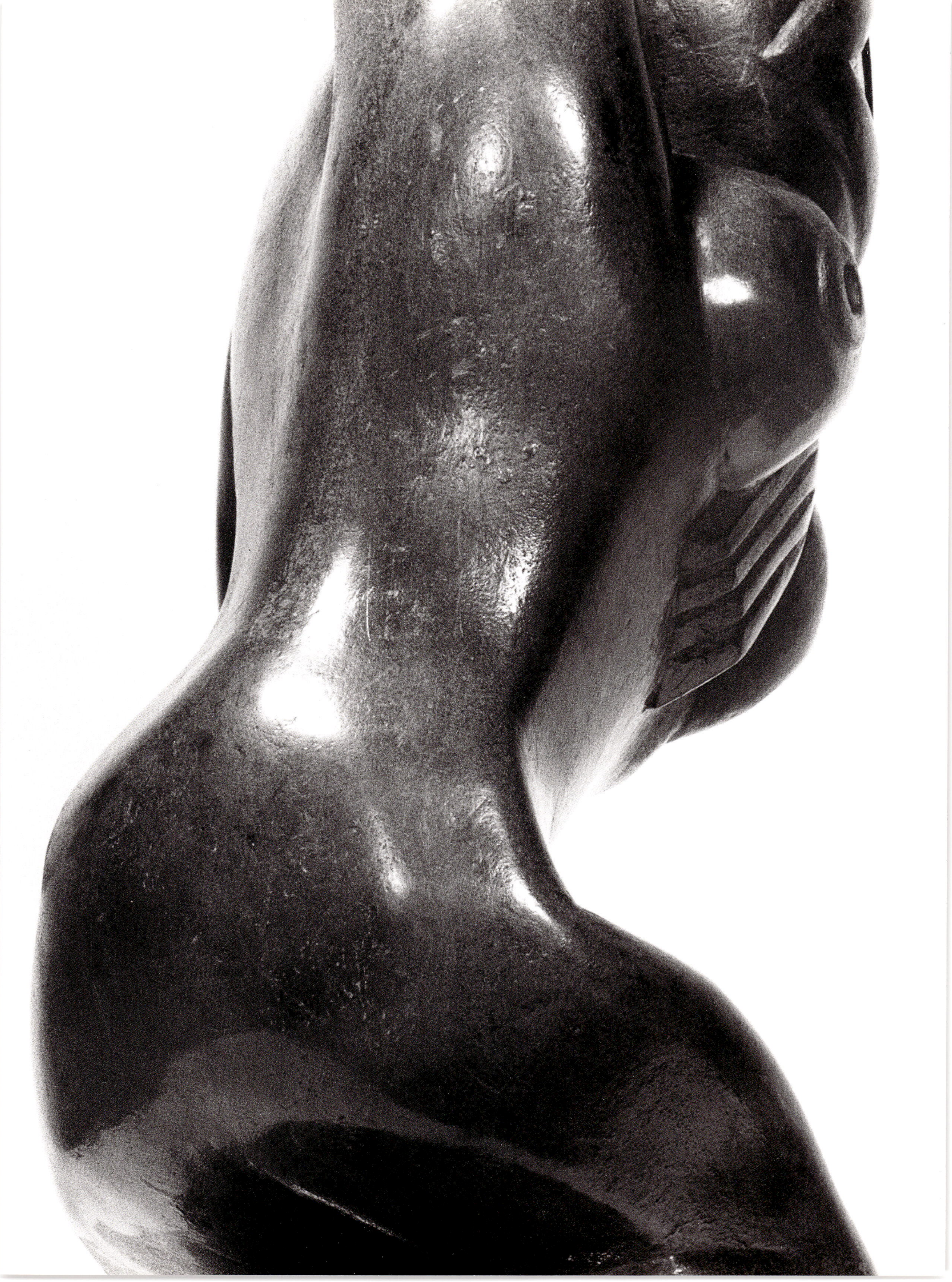

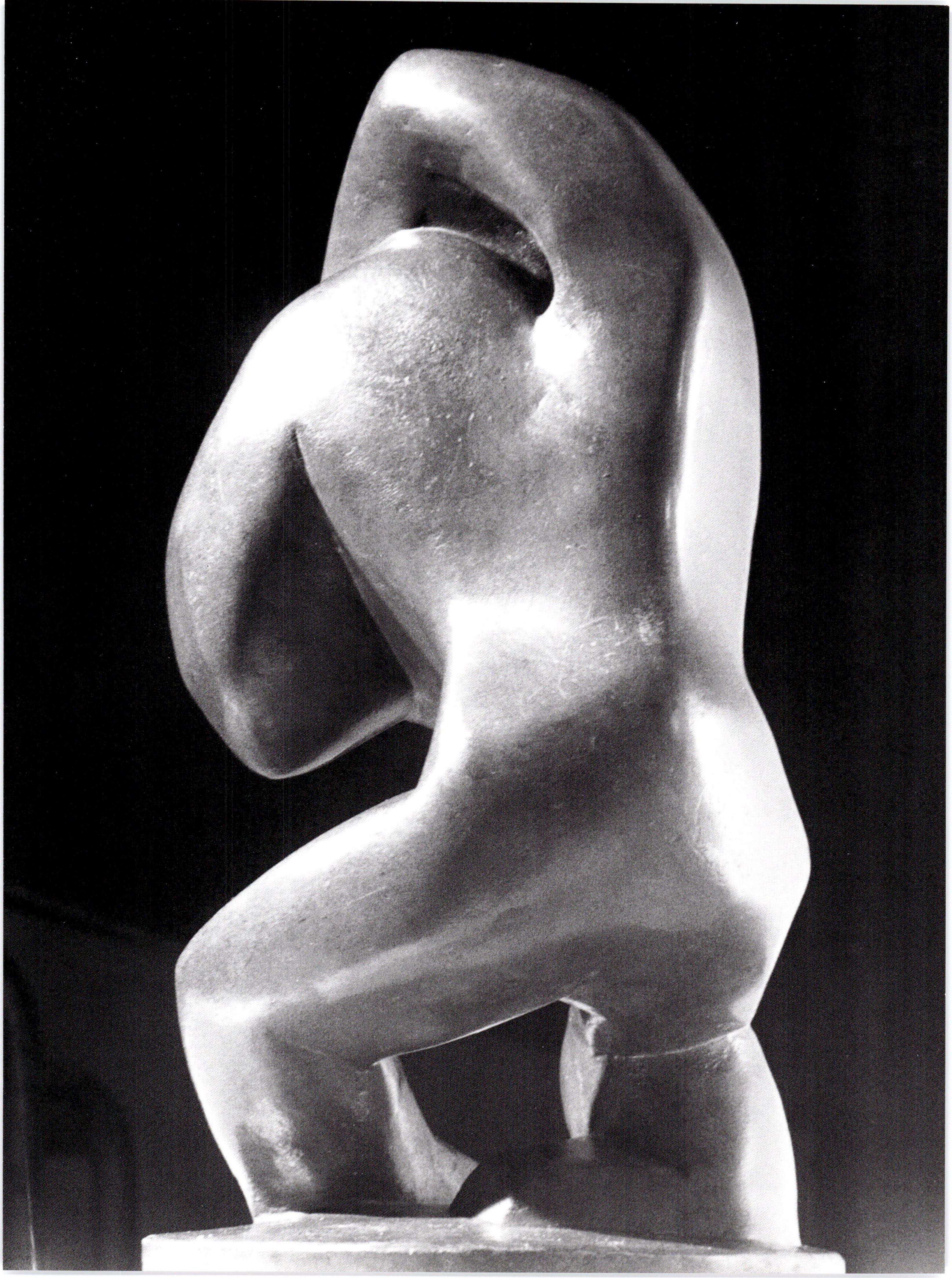

100, 101 Coffer for Wilfred Scawen Blunt (*cat.* 72)

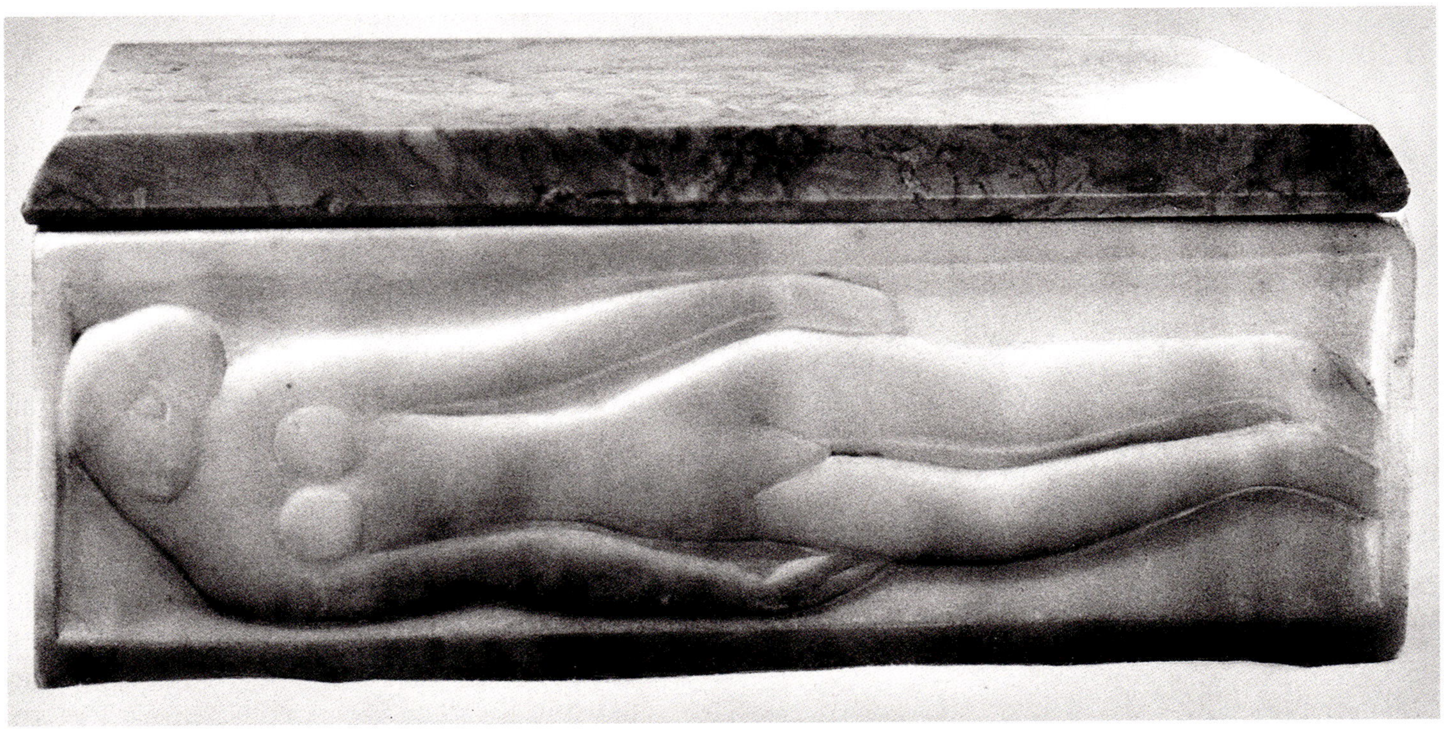

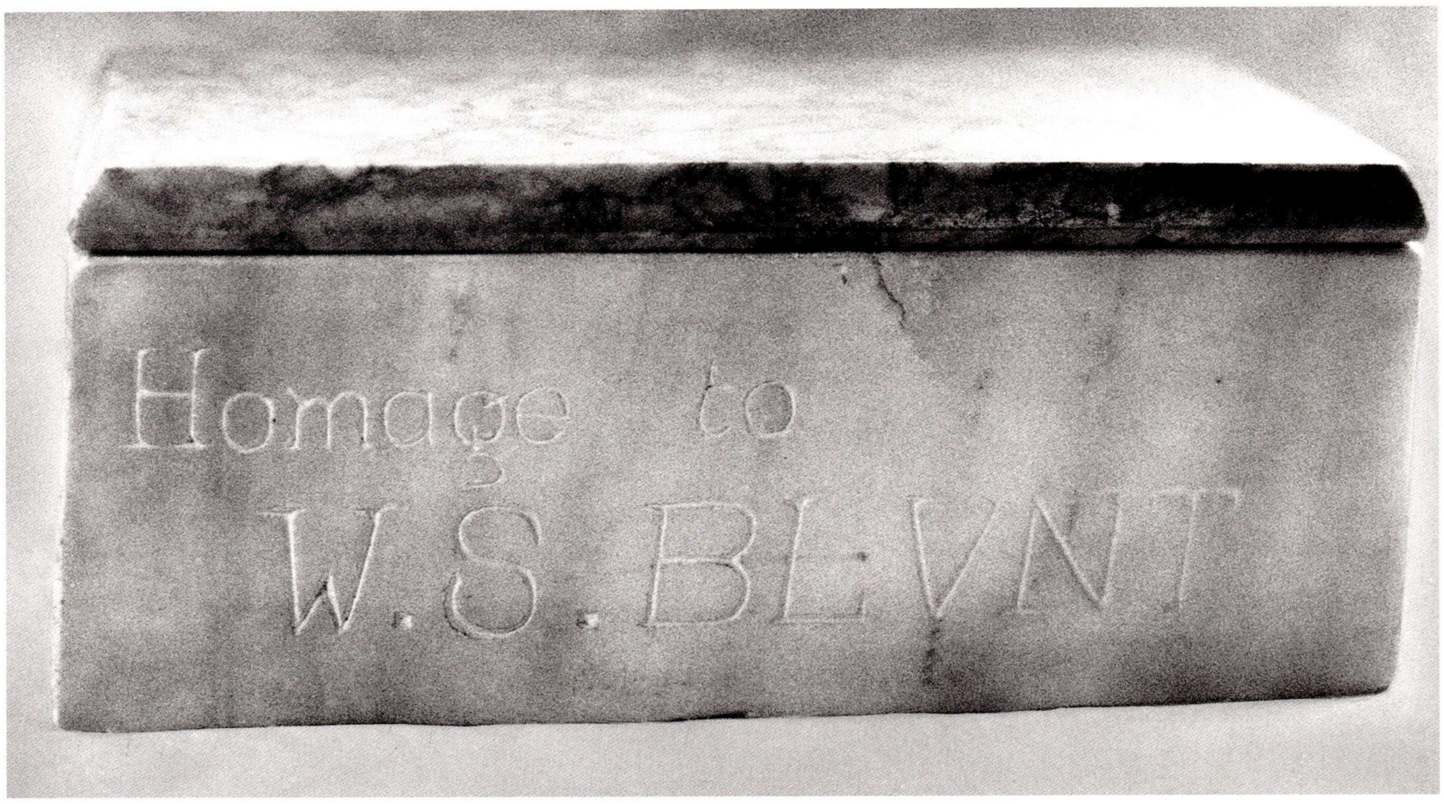

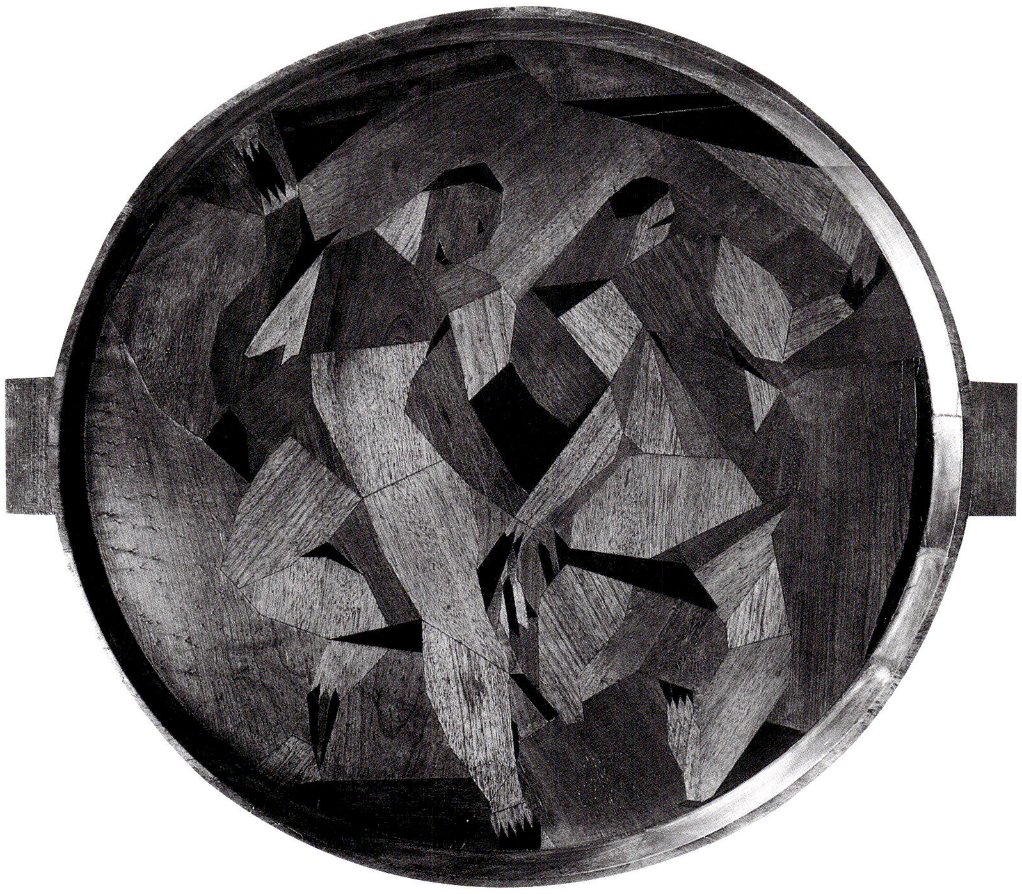

102 Round Tray (*cat.* 67)

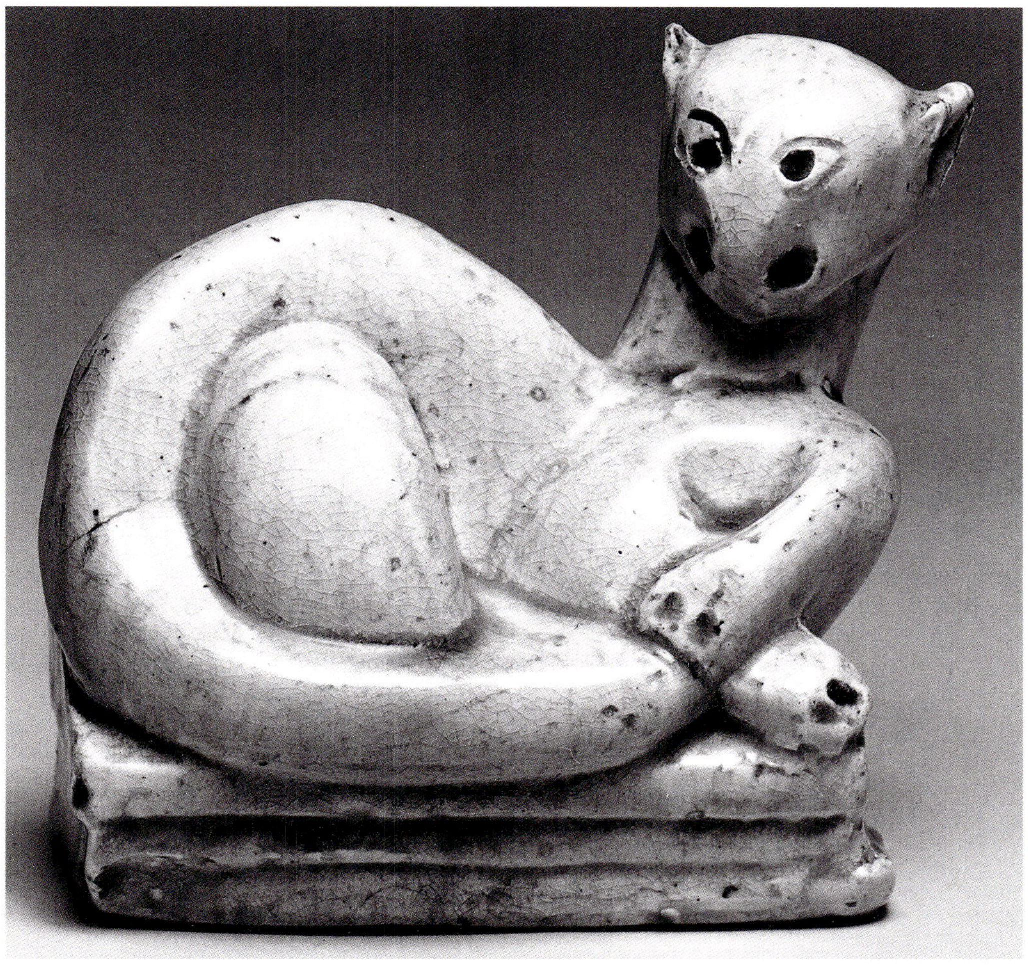

103 Cat (*cat.* 65)

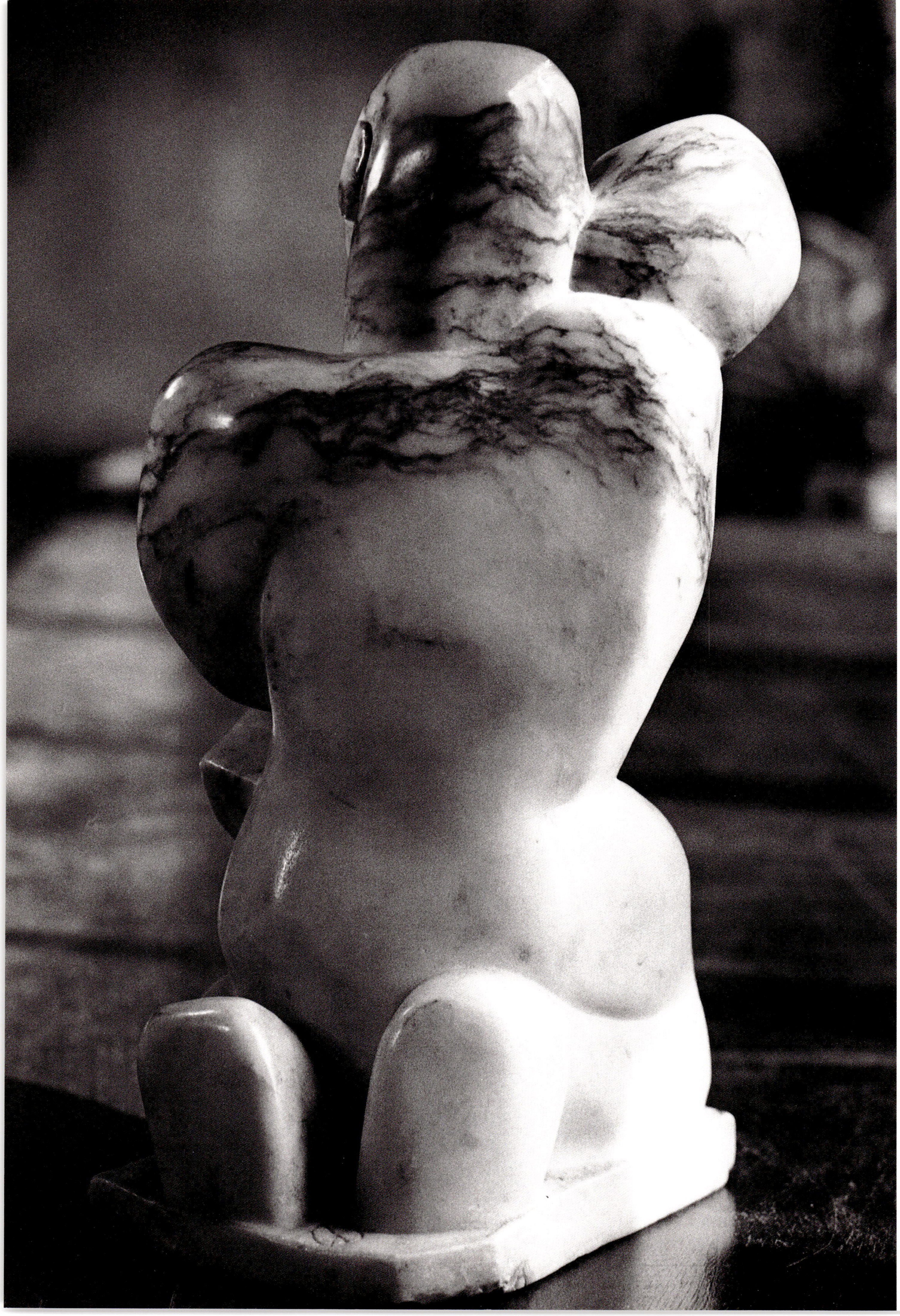

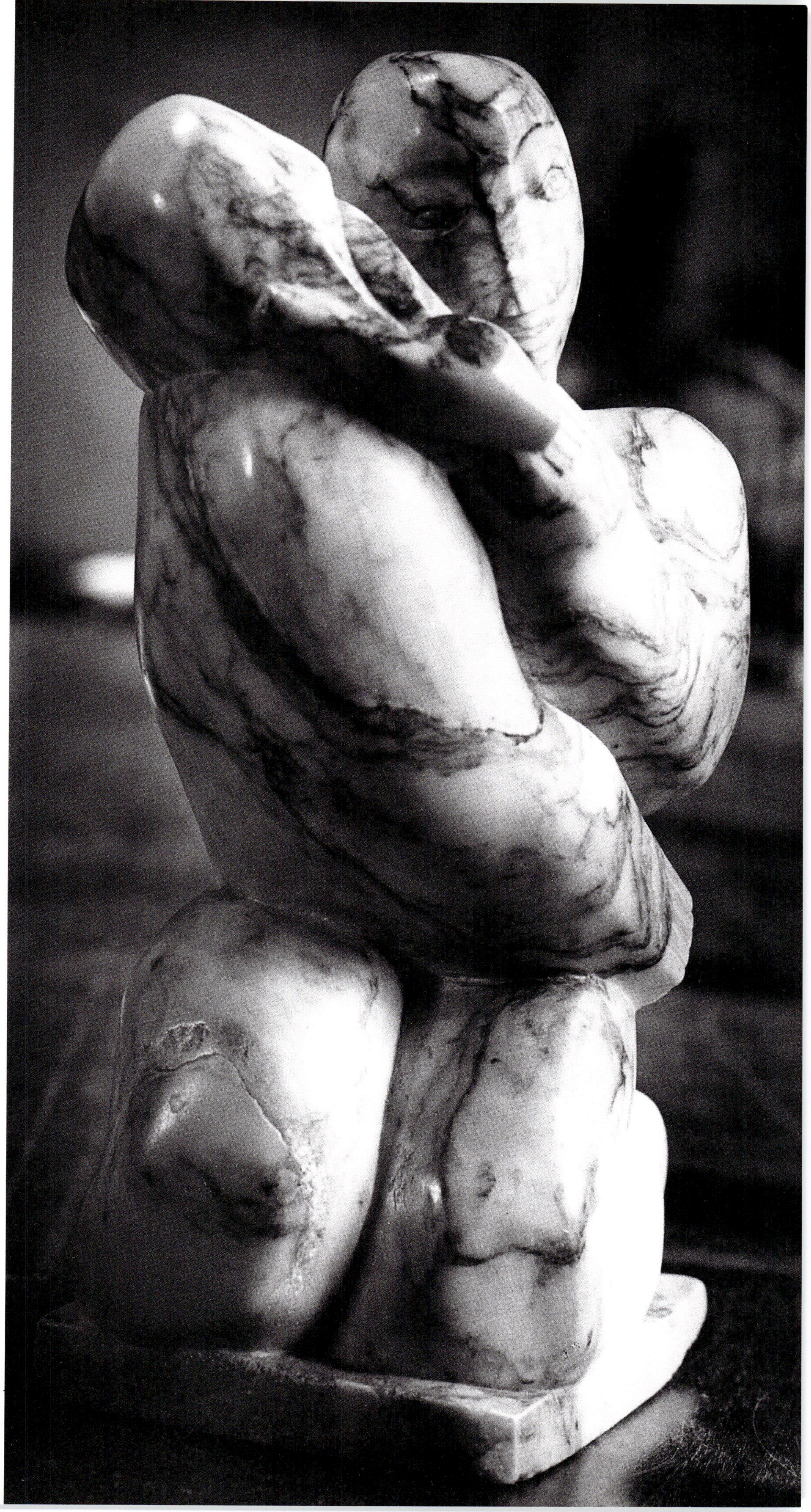

104, 105
Boy with a Coney
(*cat.* 76)

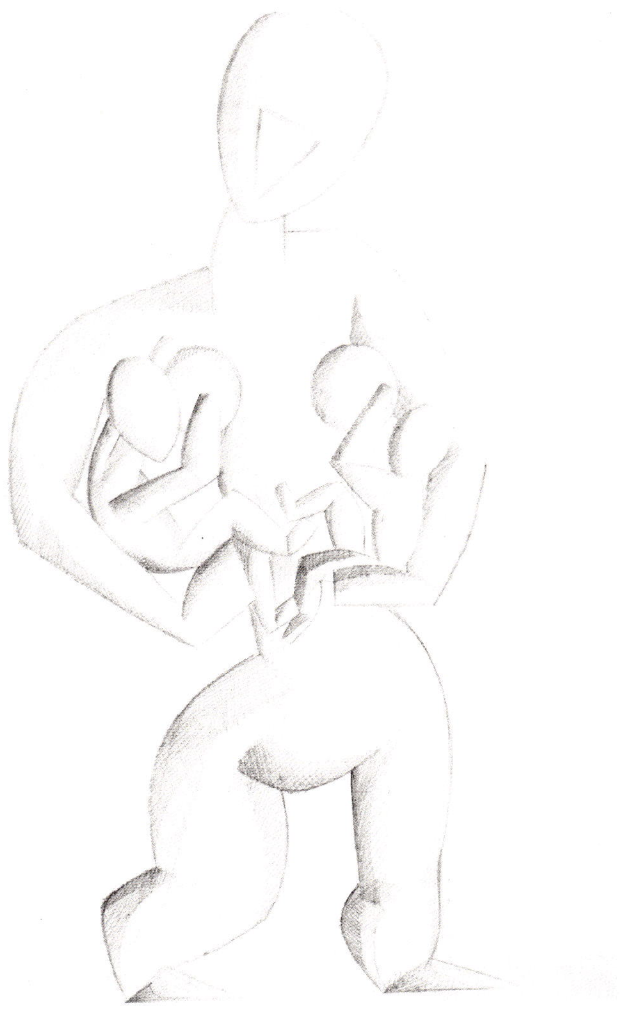

106 Study for Caritas, pencil

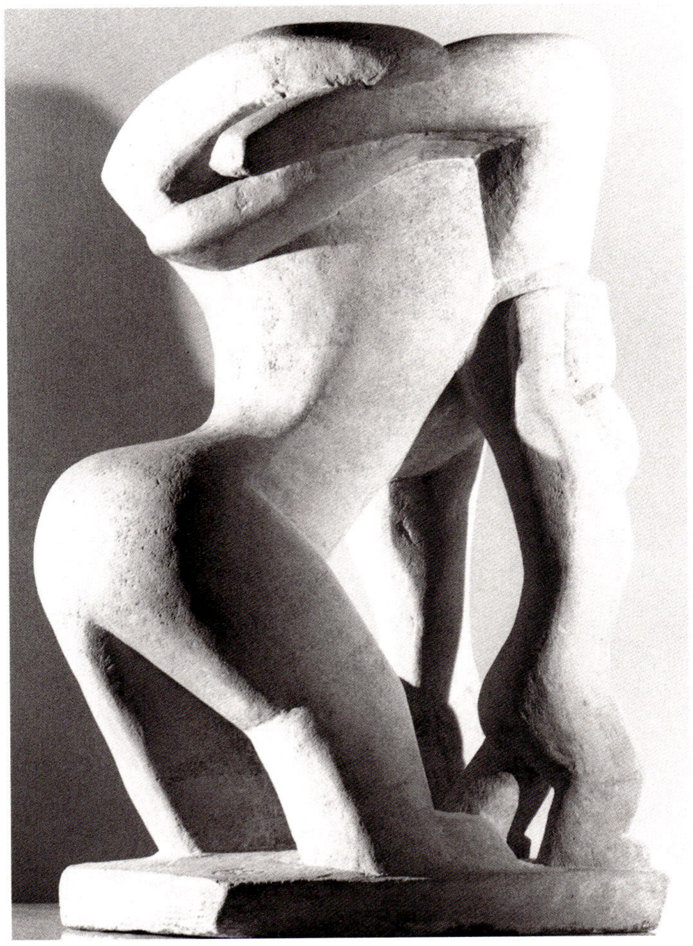

108, 109 Caritas (*cat.* 75)

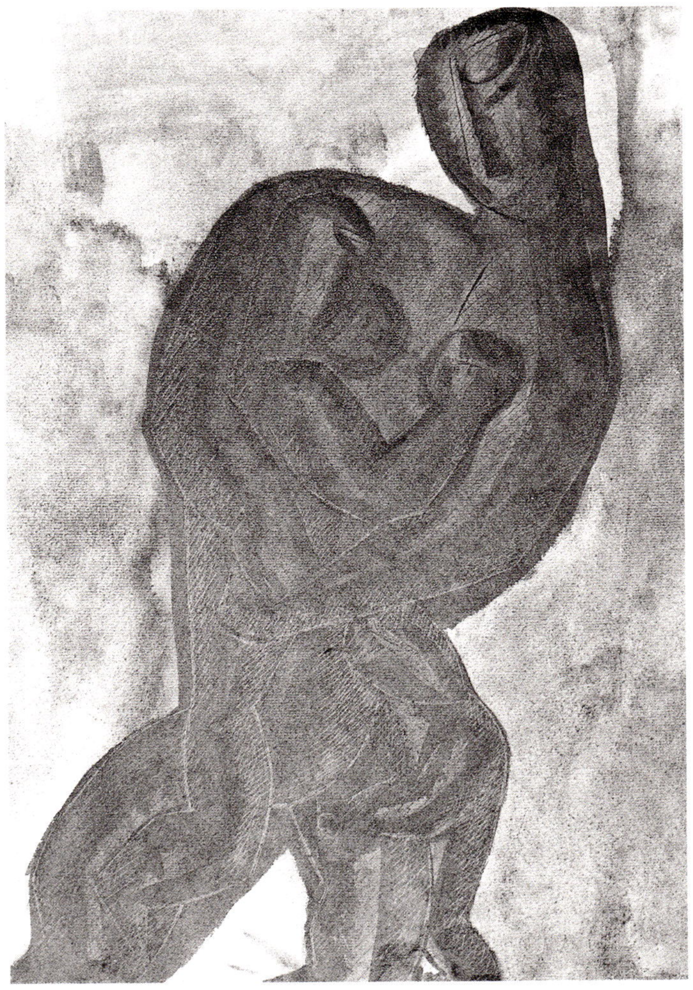

107 Study for Caritas, ink and wash

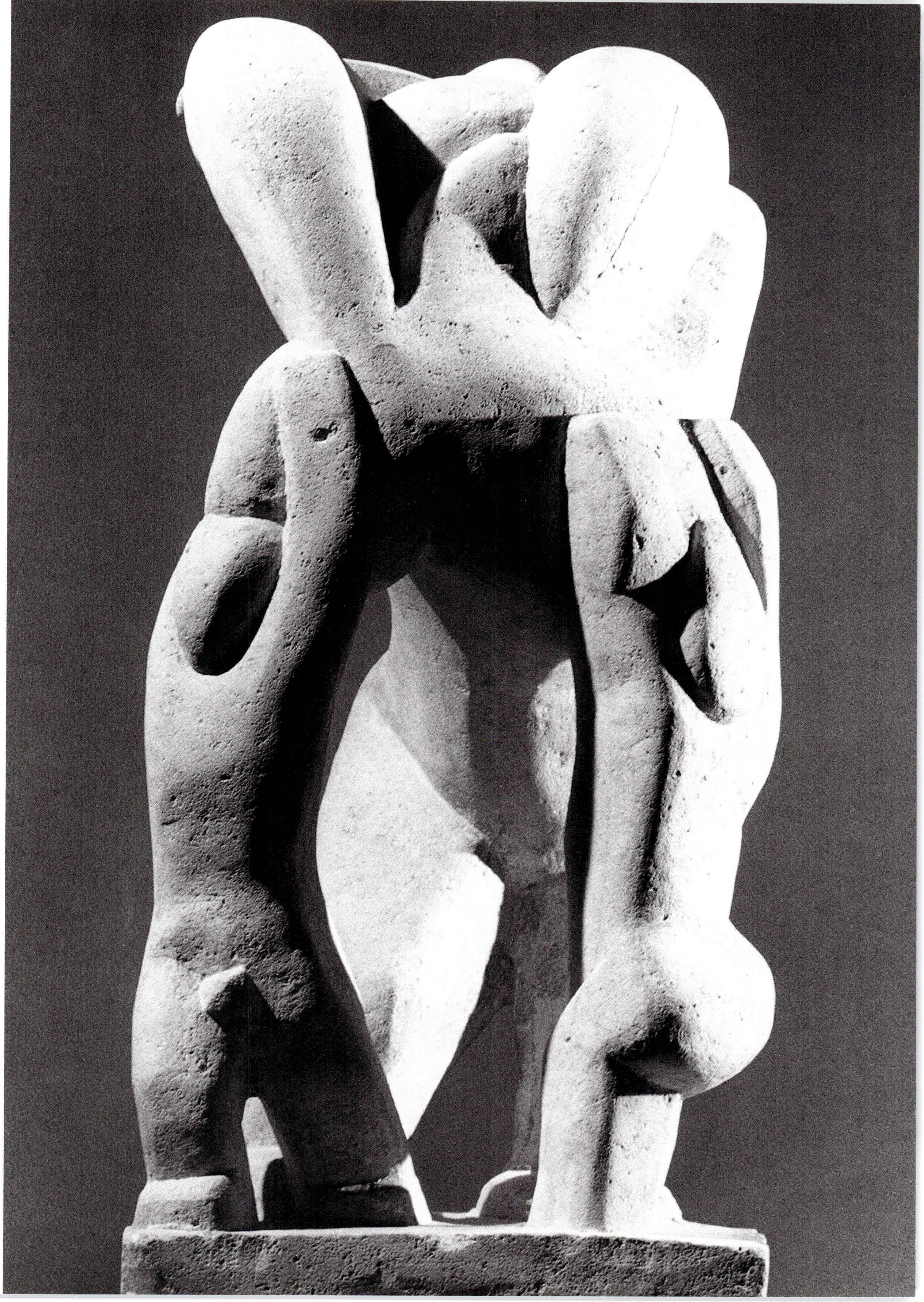

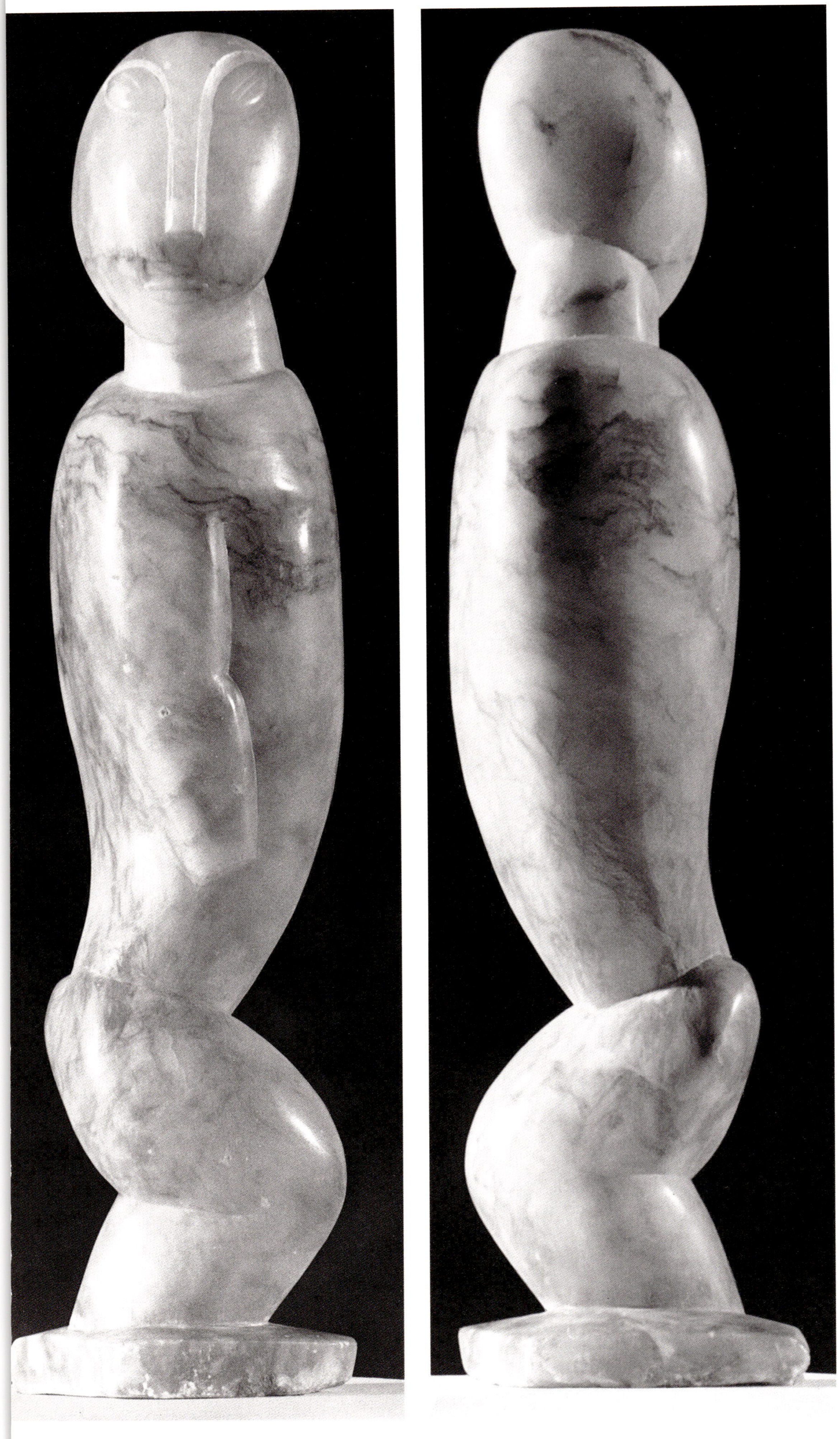

110–112
Imp (*cat.* 78)

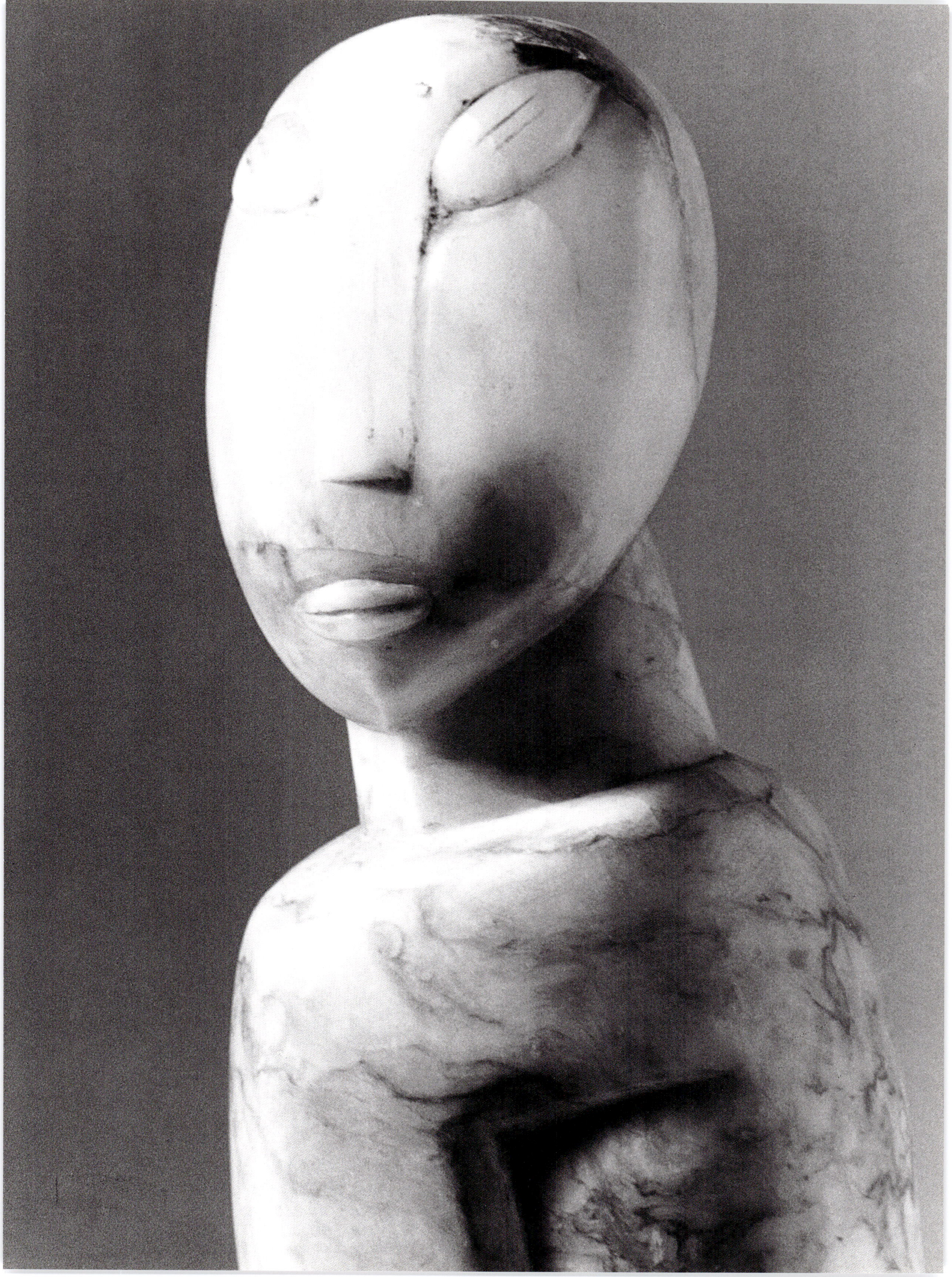

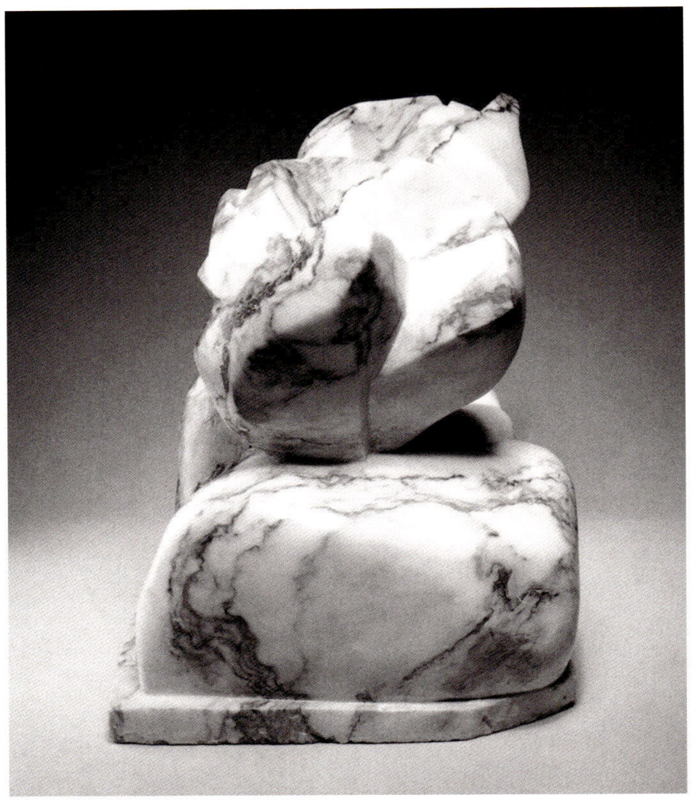
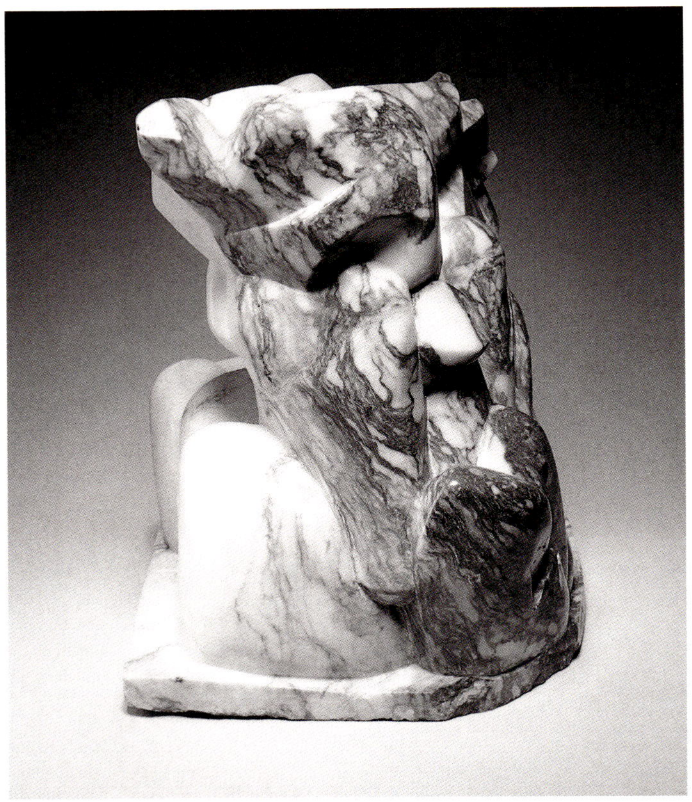
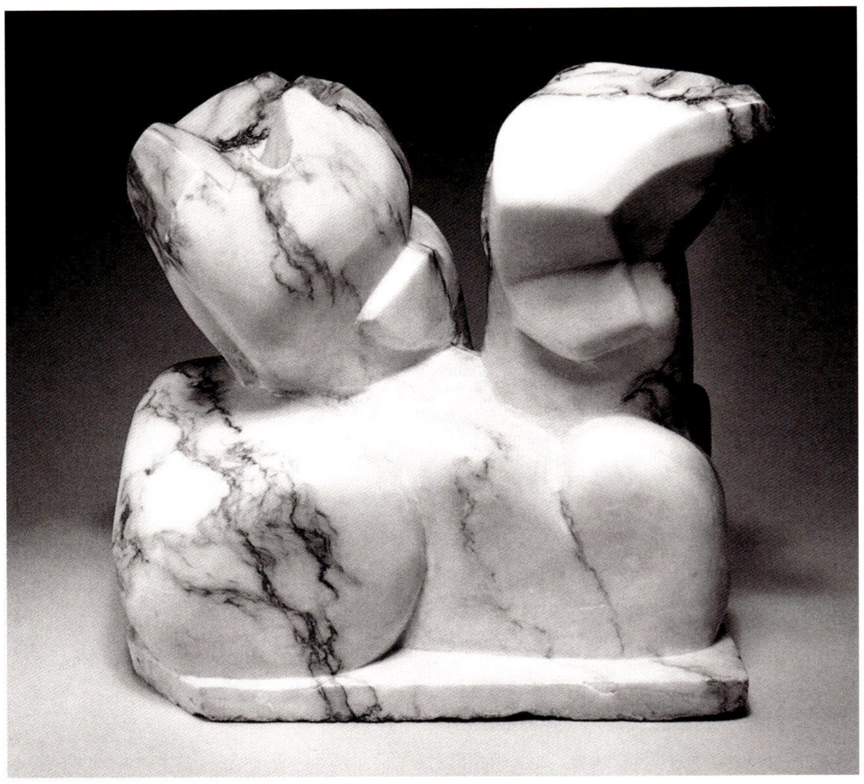

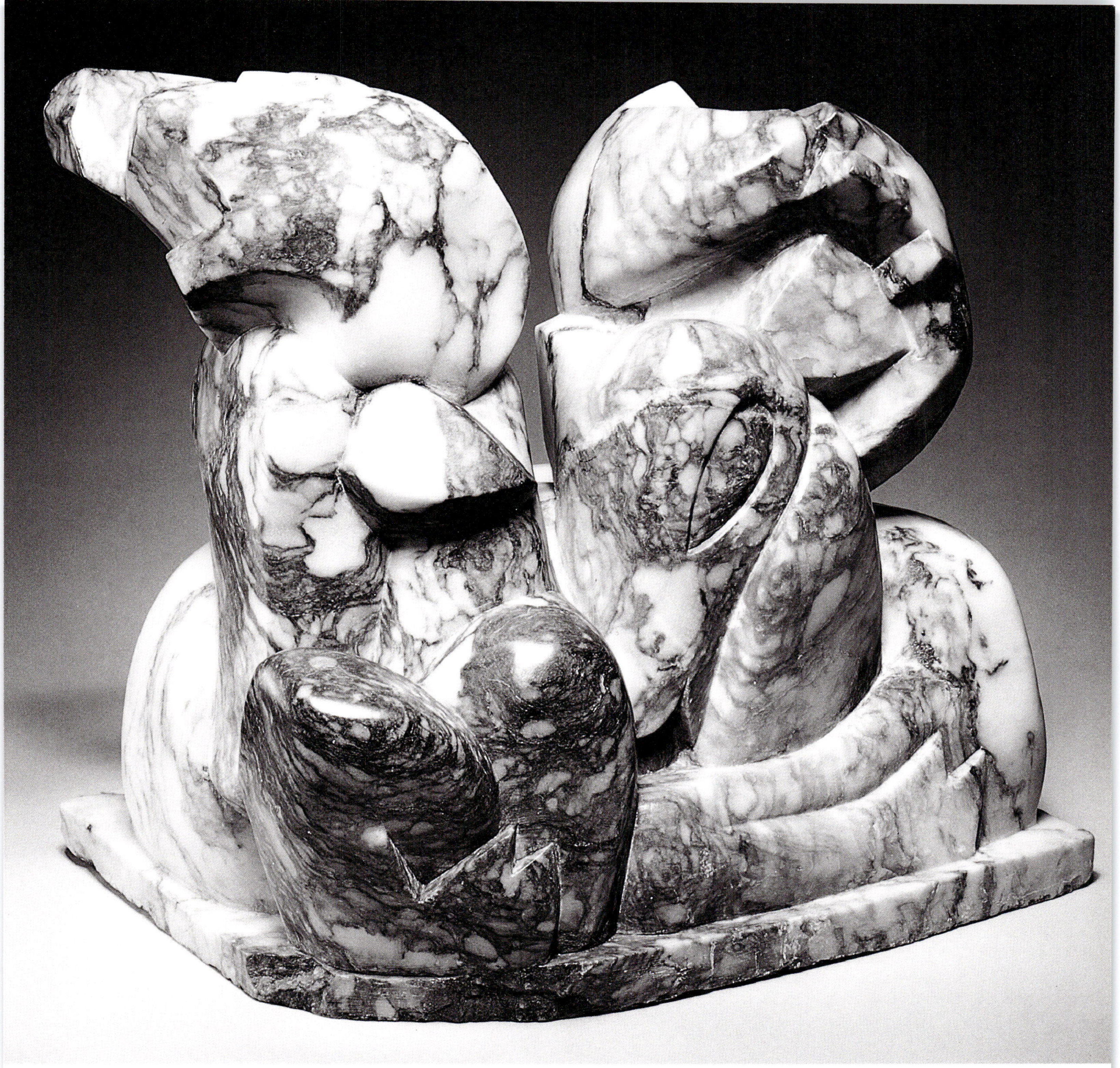

113–116 Stags (*cat.* 77)

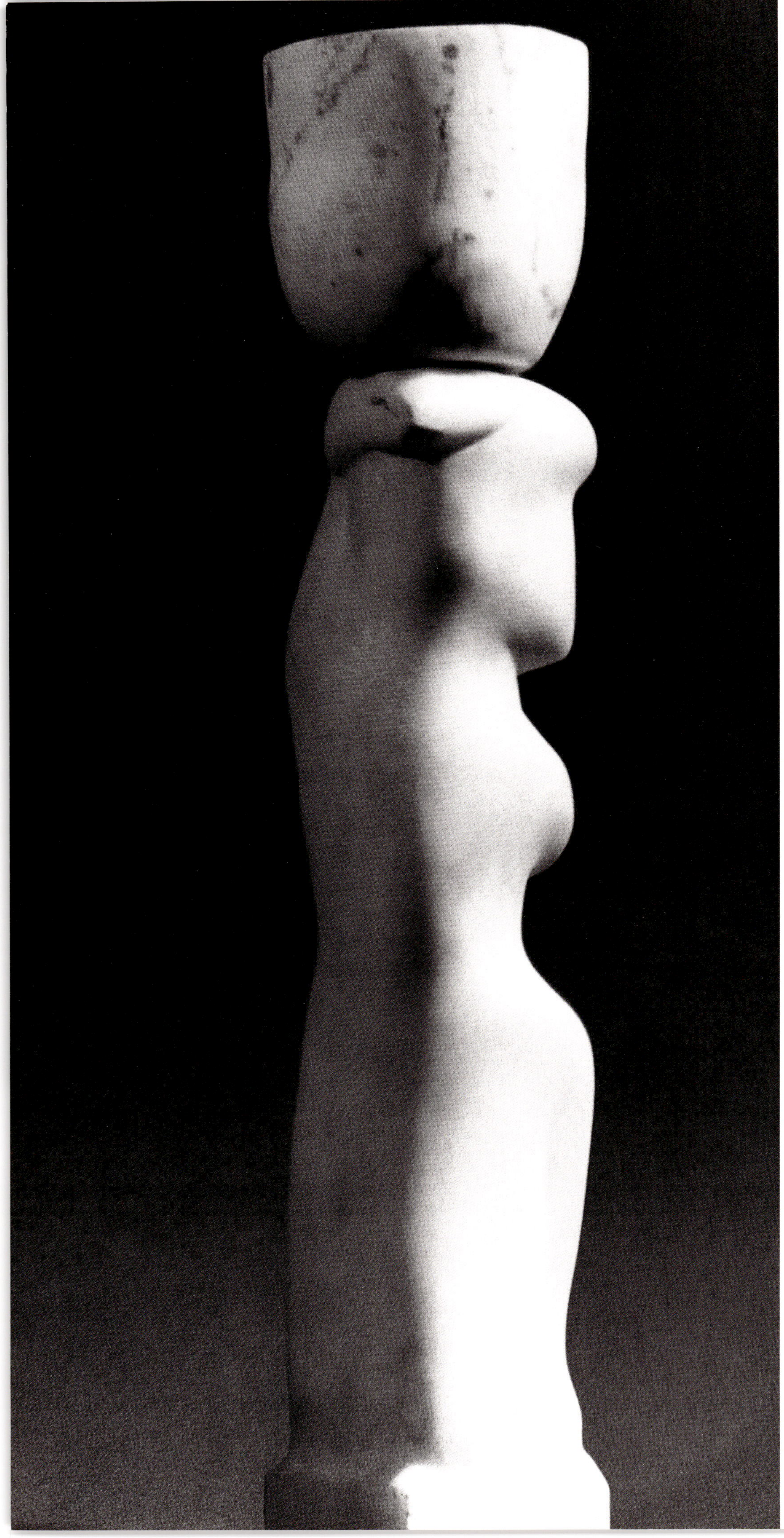

117, 118
Water Carrier
(*cat.* 74)

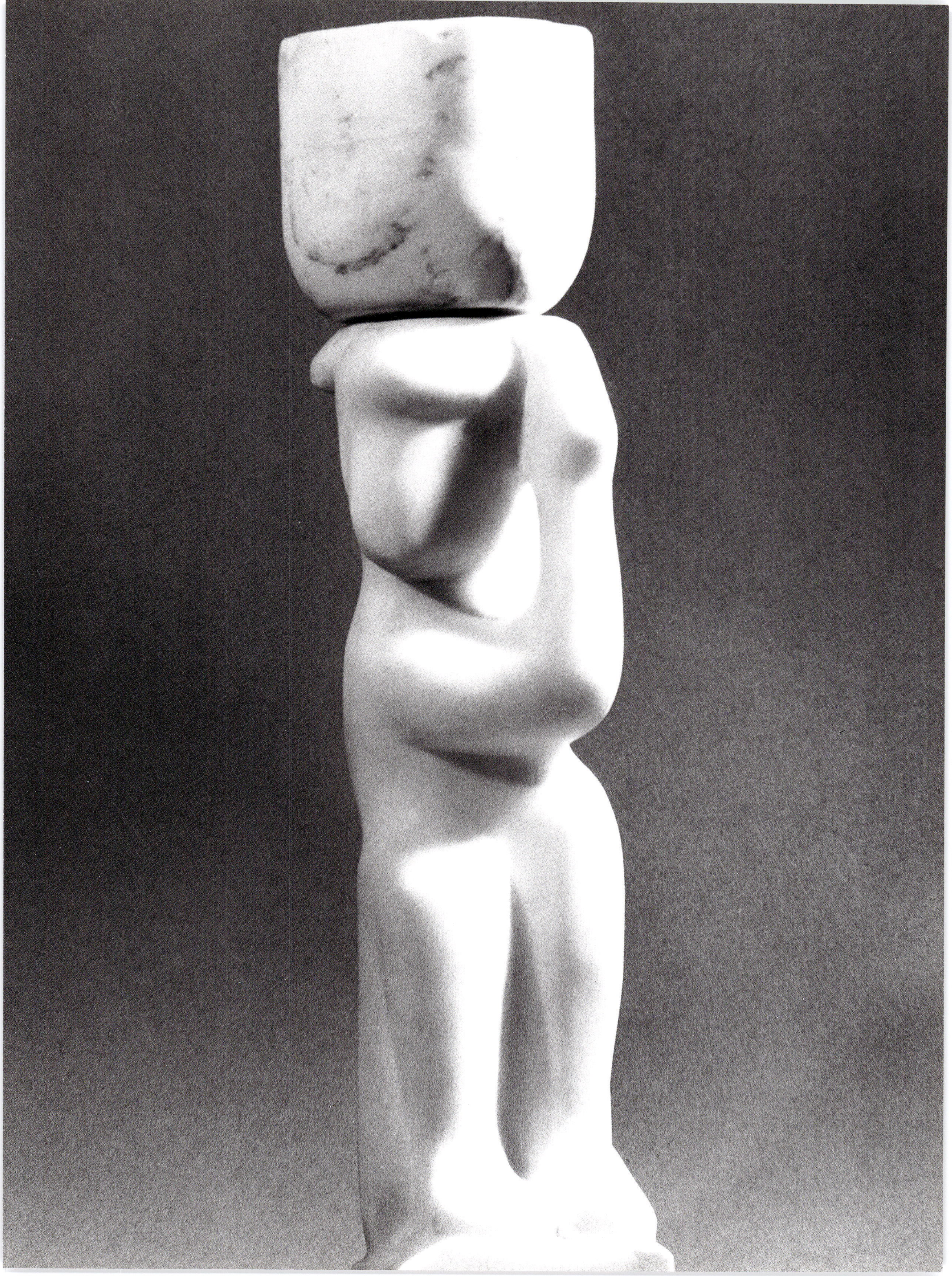

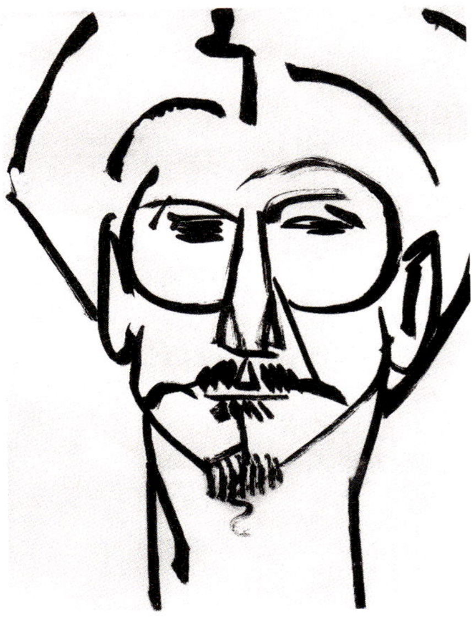

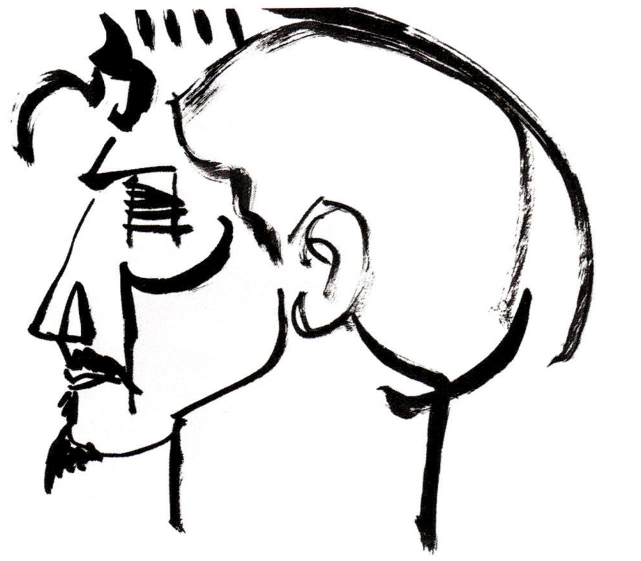

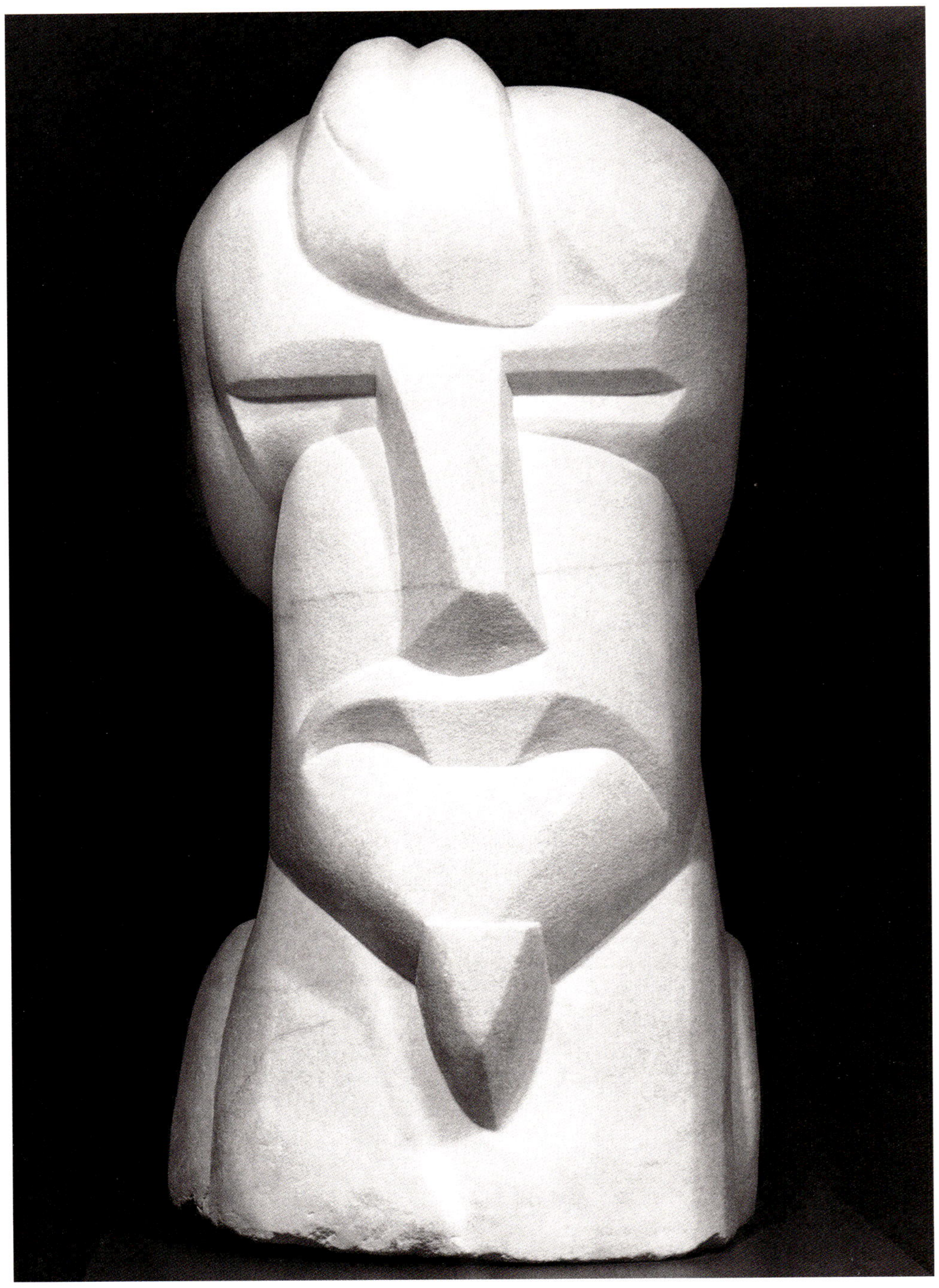

119 Study for Head of Ezra Pound

120 Study for Head of Ezra Pound, profile

121, 122
Head of Ezra Pound
(*cat.* 79)

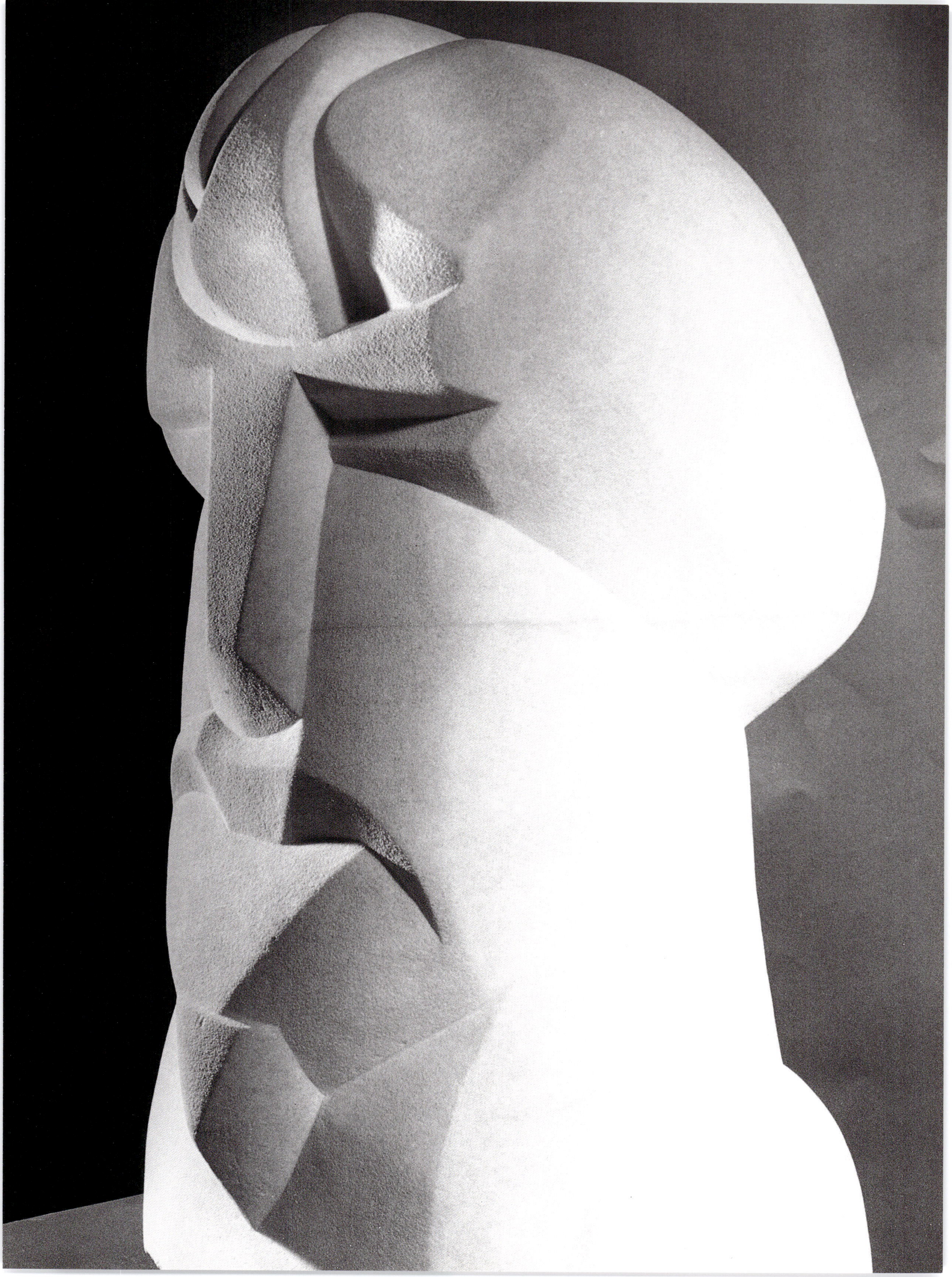

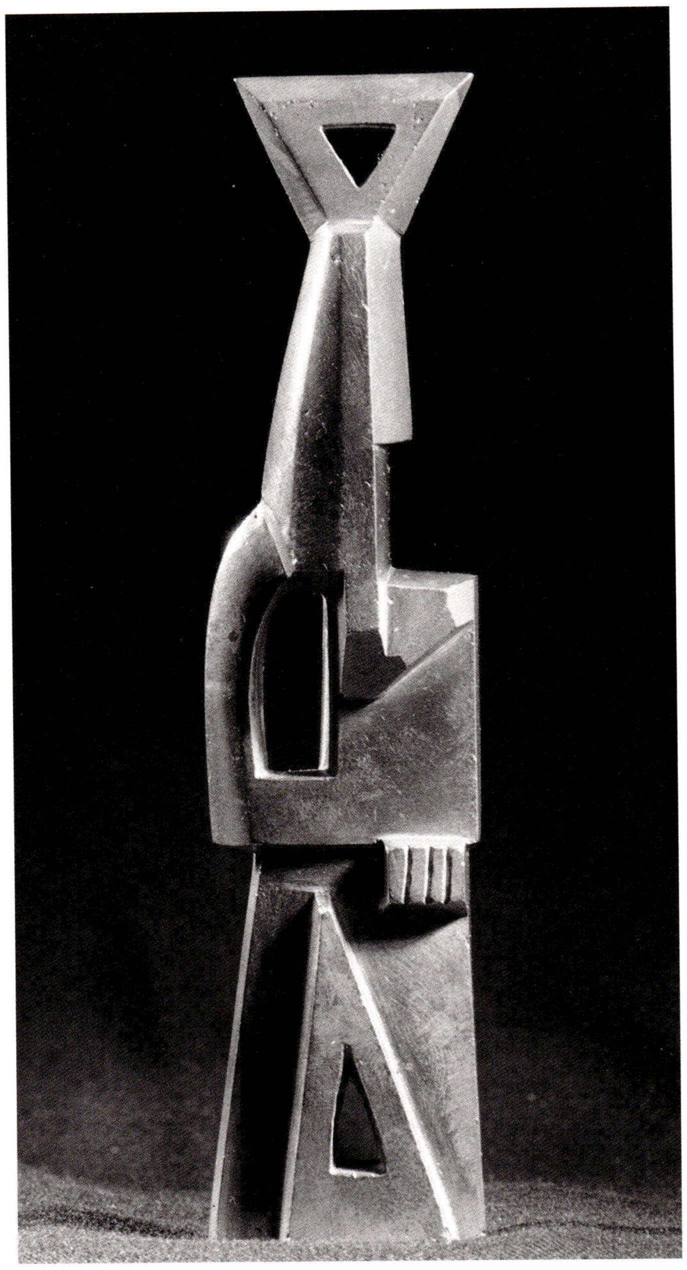

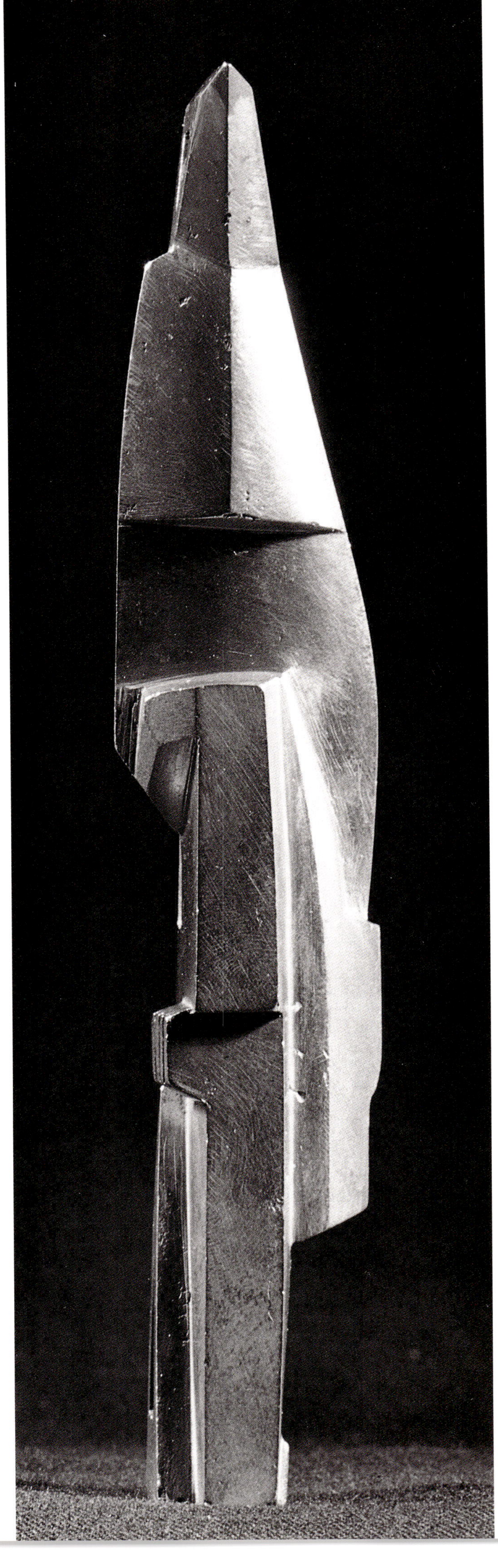

123 Torpedo Fish, actual size (*cat.* 80)

124–126 Torpedo Fish (*cat.* 80)

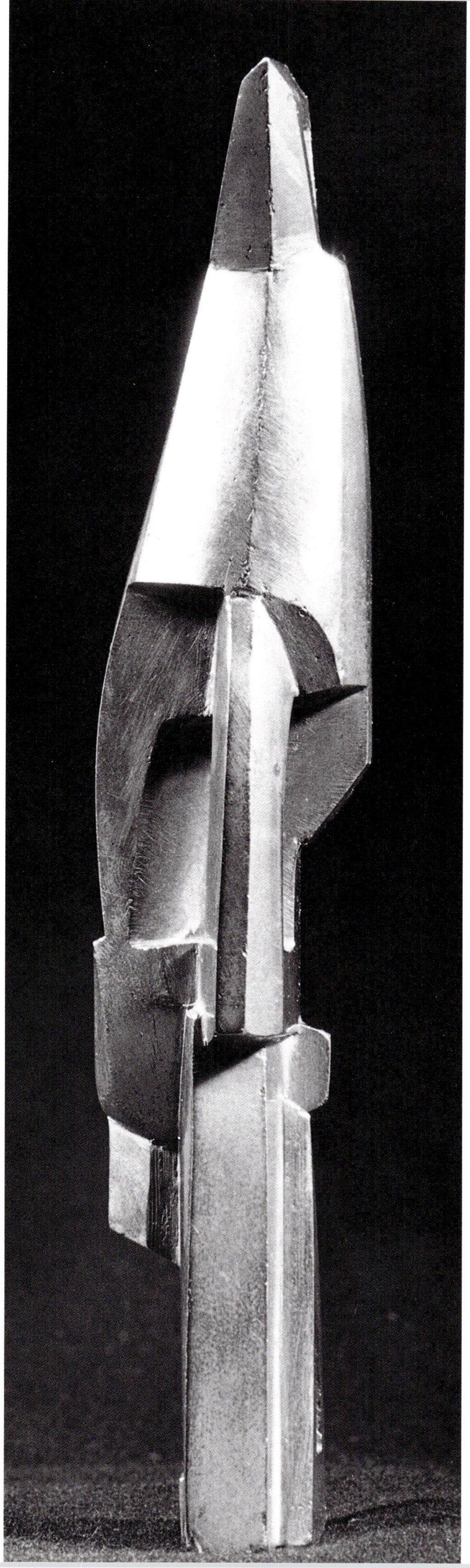

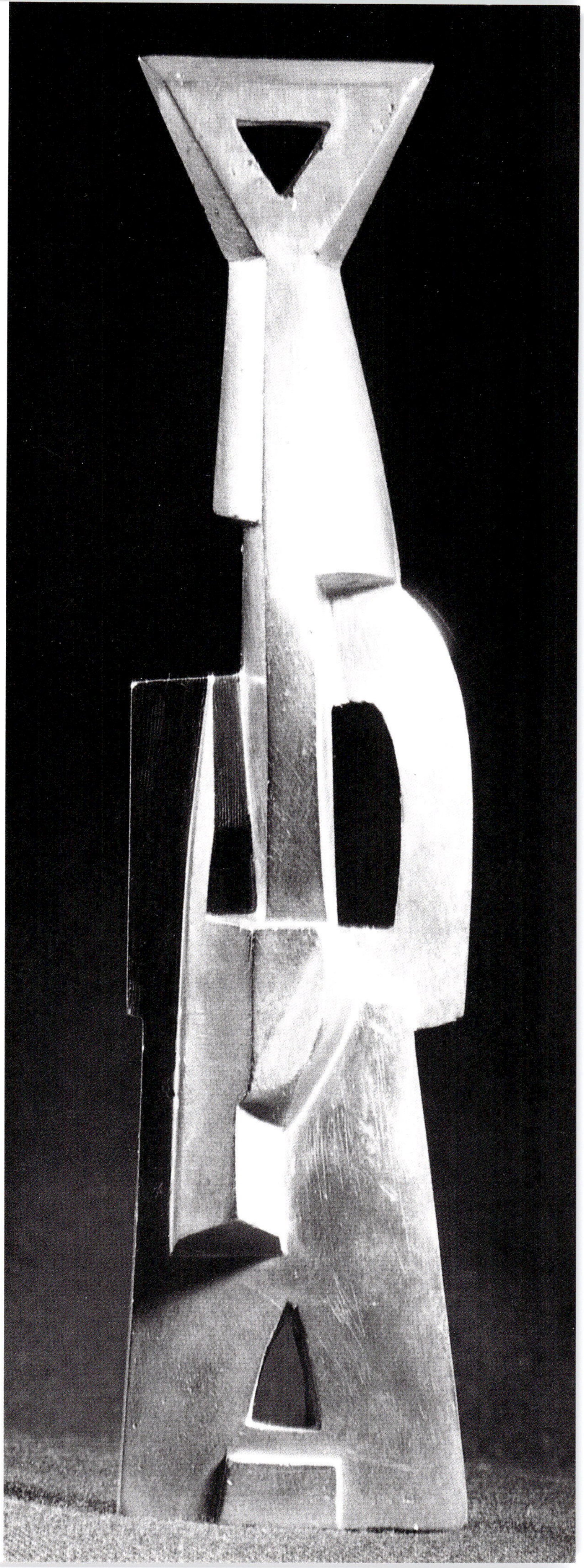

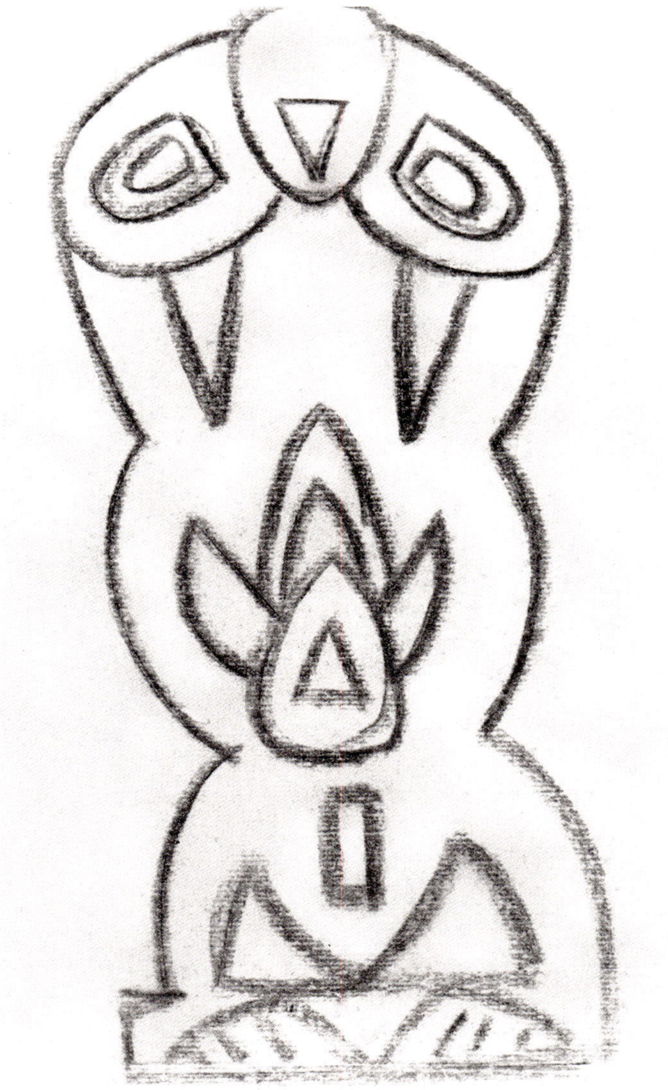

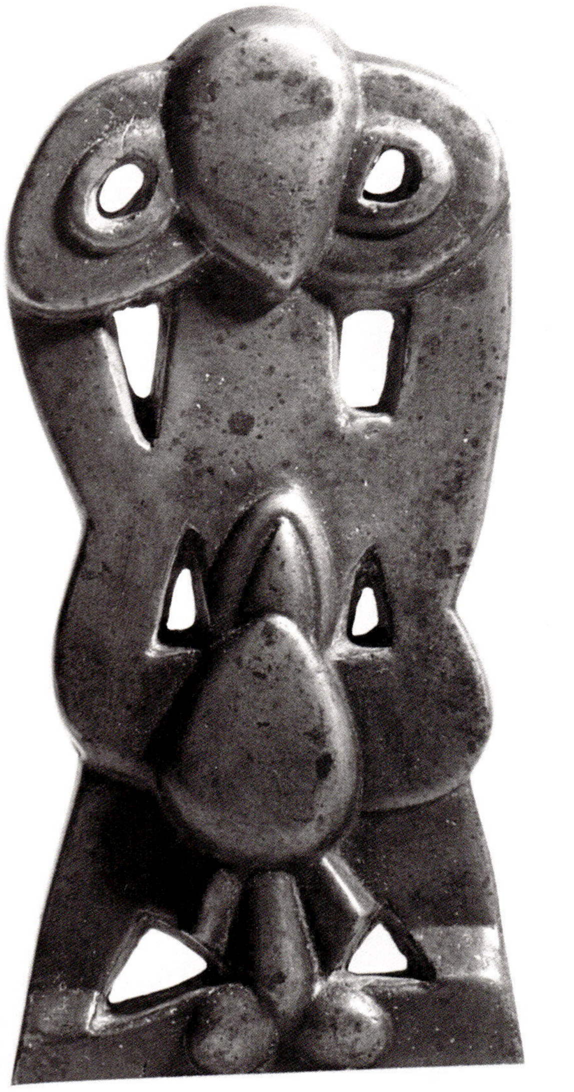

127
Drawing for
Doorknocker,
conté crayon

128 Doorknocker
(*cat.* 81)

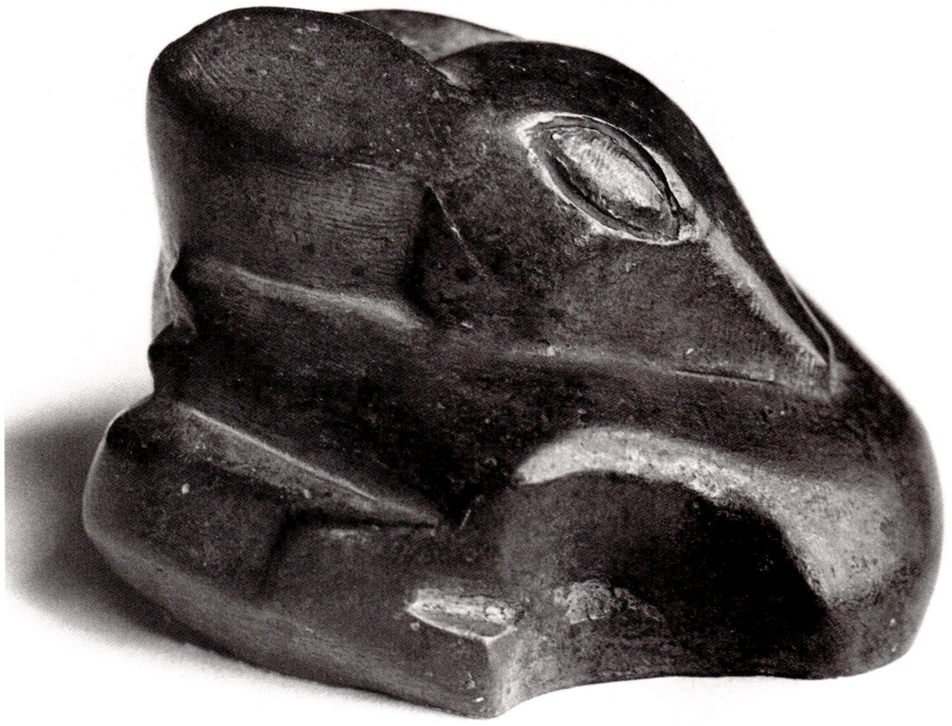

129 Small Fawn
(*cat.* 84)

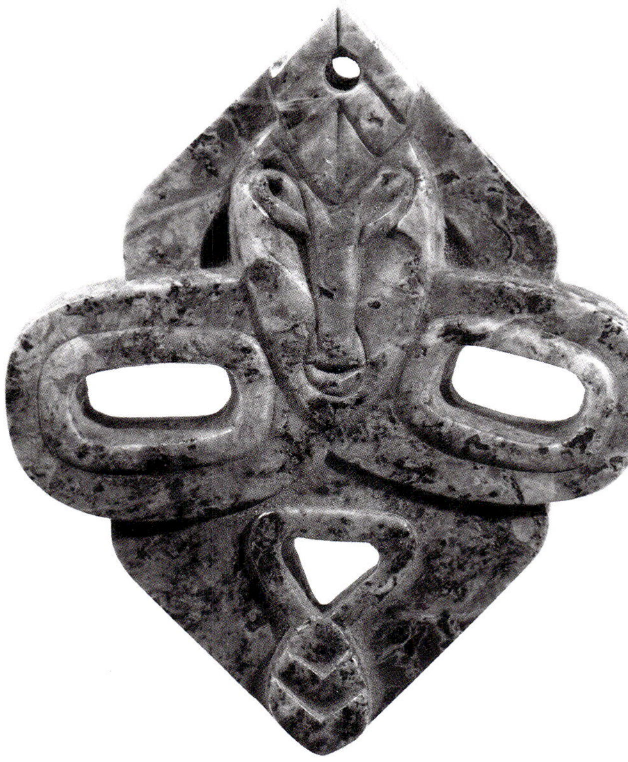

130 Green Stone Charm (*cat.* 85)

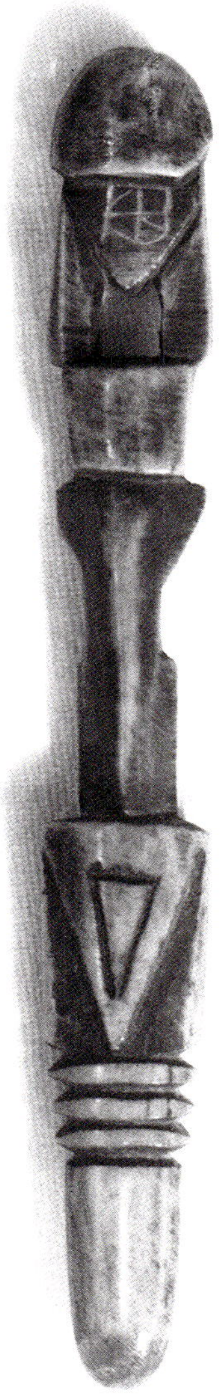

131 Ornament (*cat.* 101)

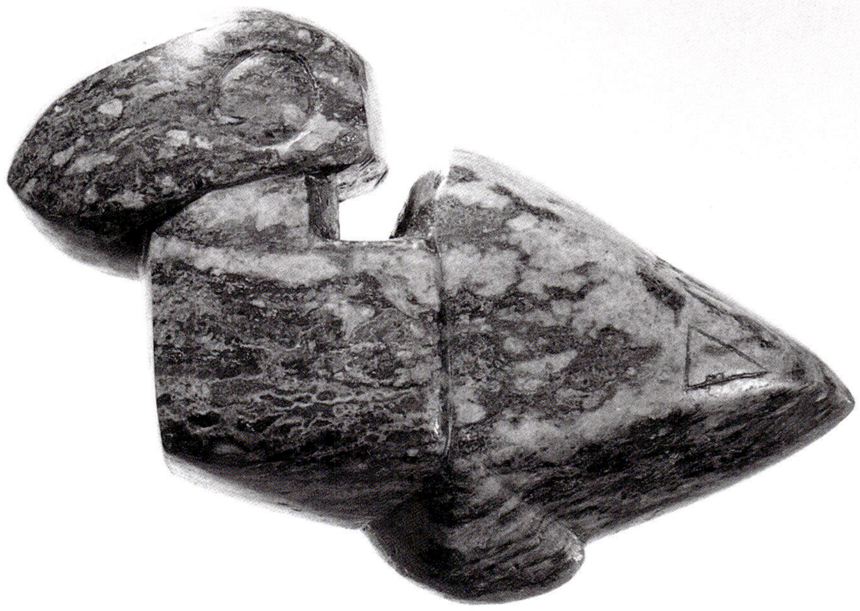

132 Duck (*cat.* 90)

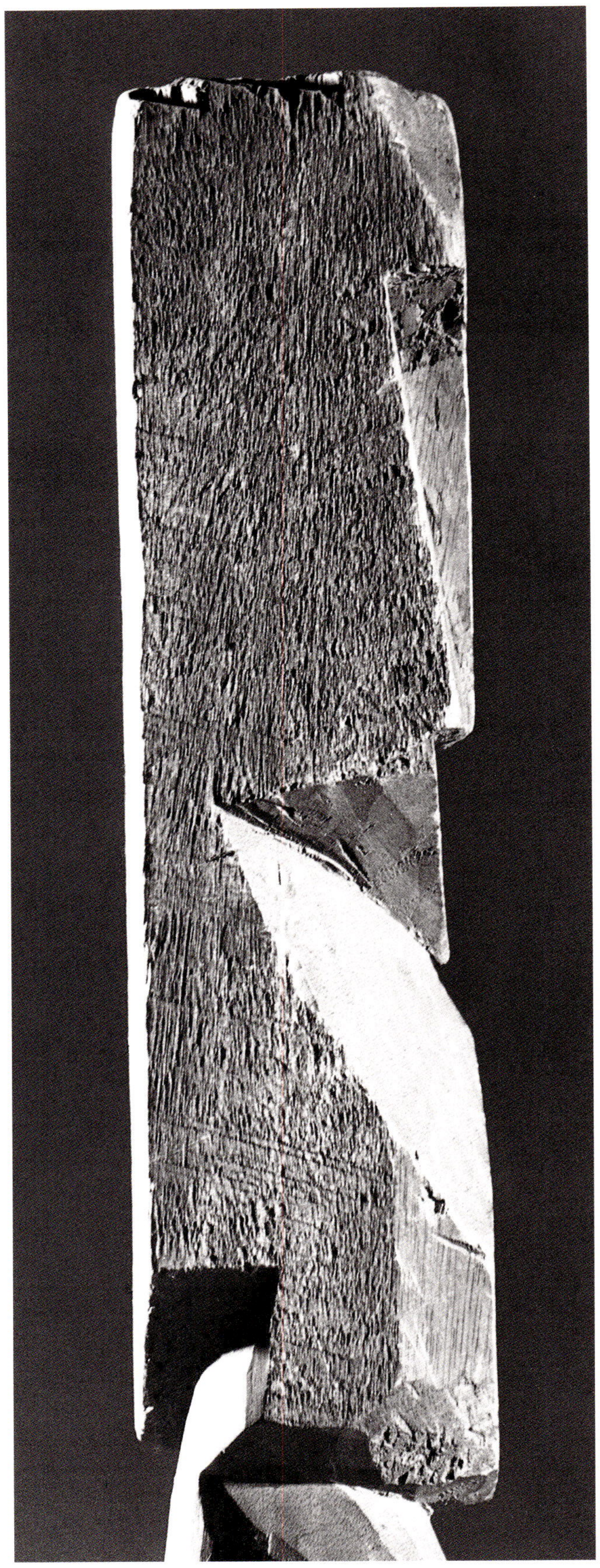

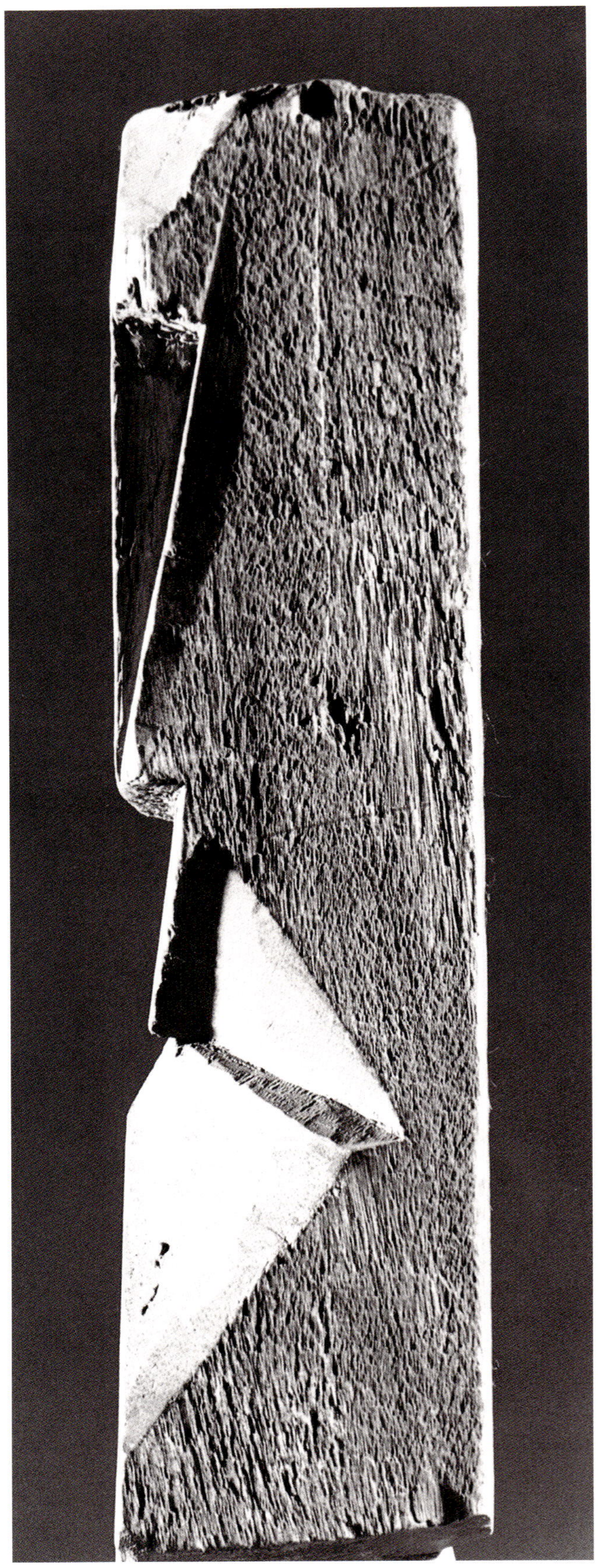

133, 134 Portrait of Ezra Pound, details (*cat.* 94)

135 Portrait of Ezra Pound (*cat.* 94)

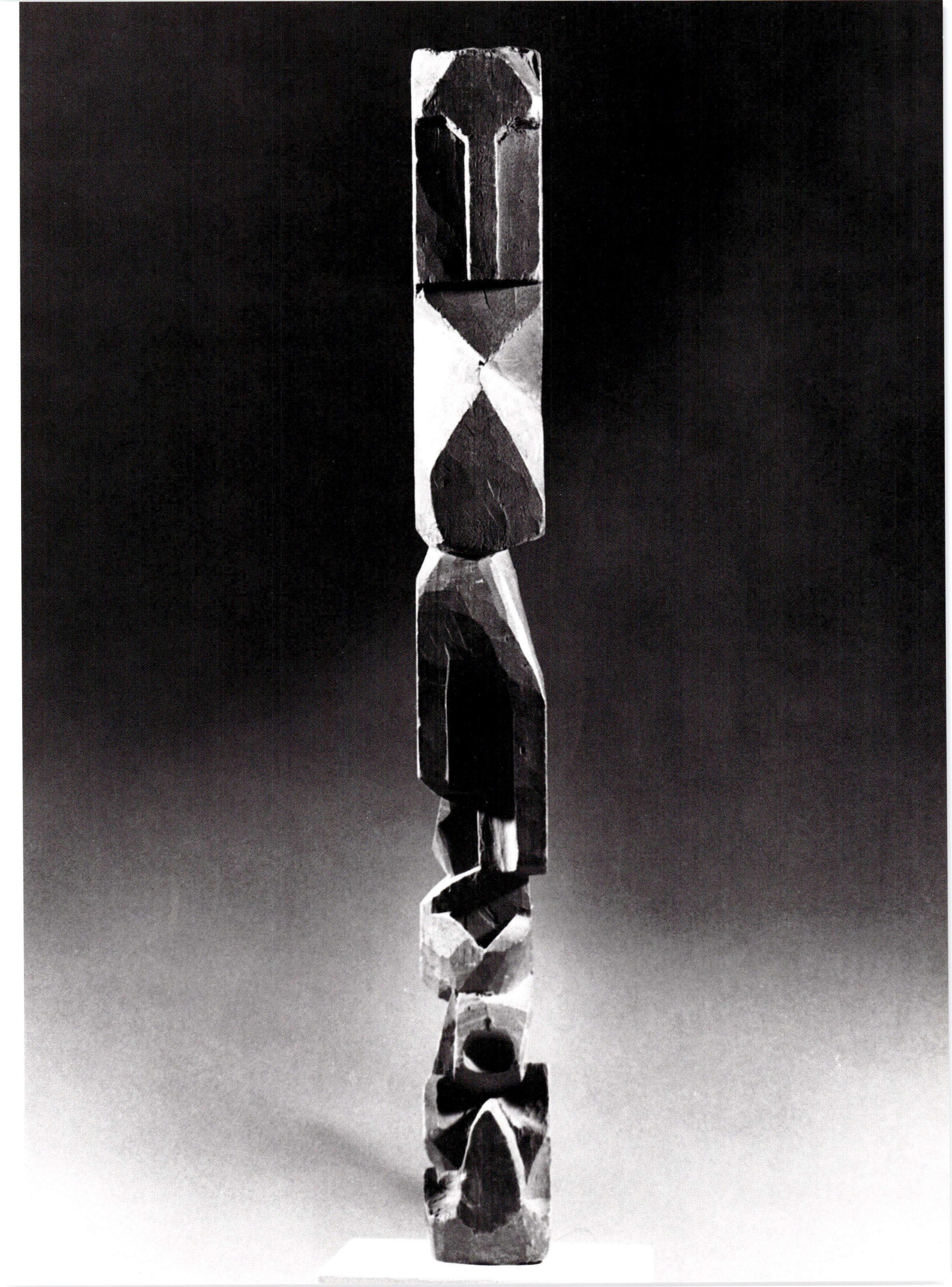

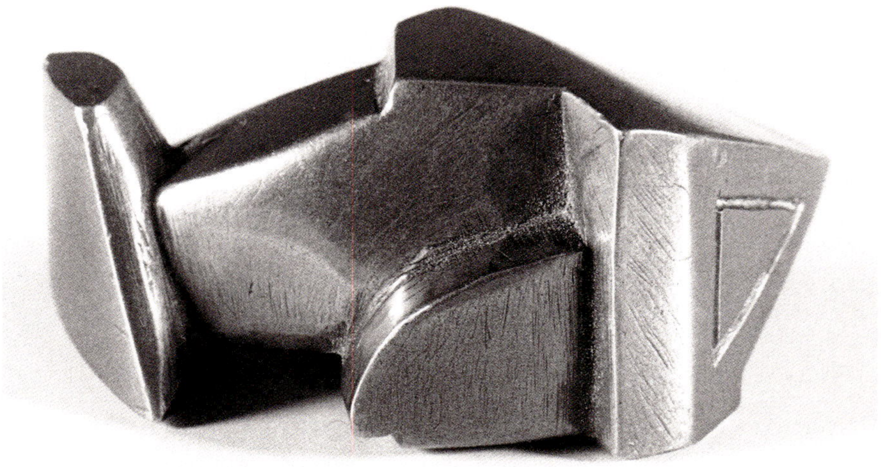

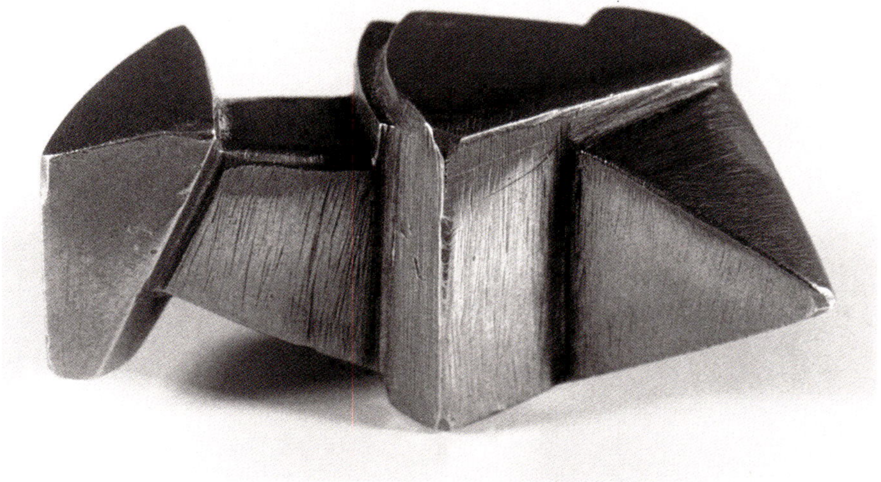

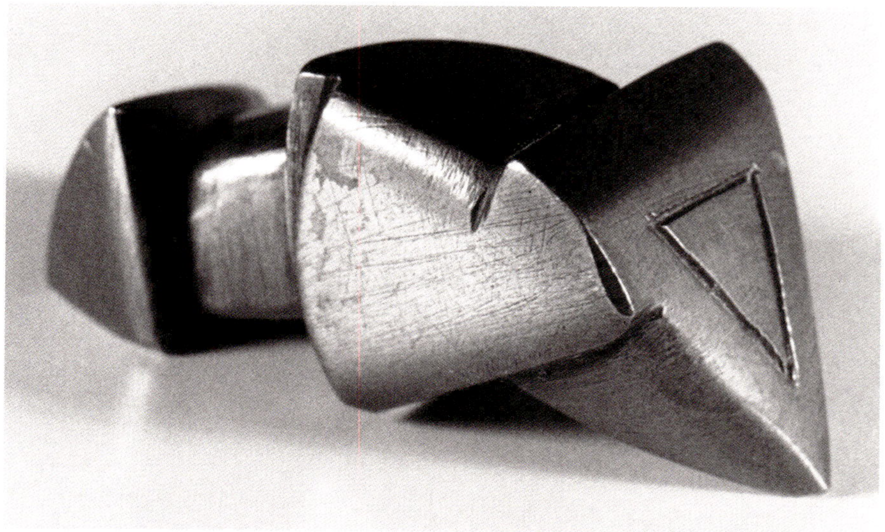

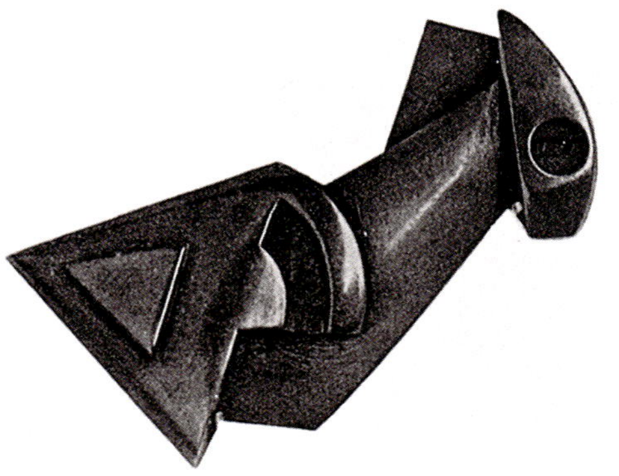

139 Fish (*cat.* 93)

136–138 Toy (*cat.* 95)

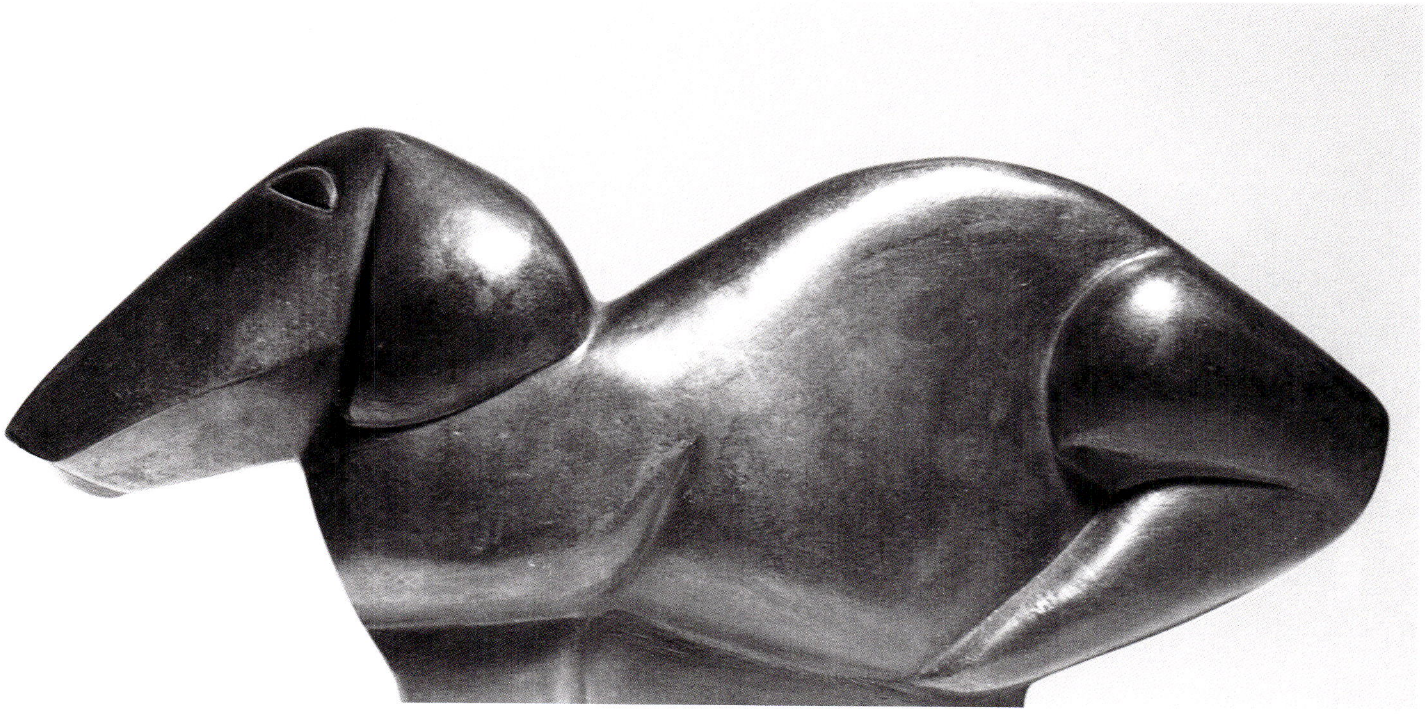

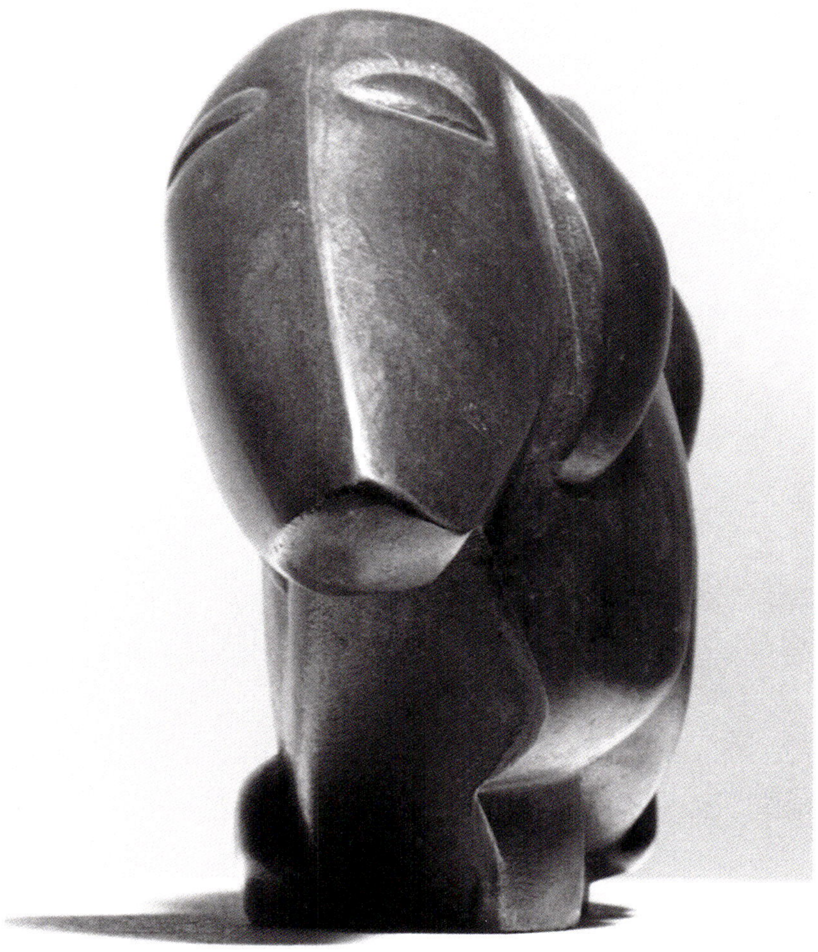

140, 141 Dog (*cat.* 96)

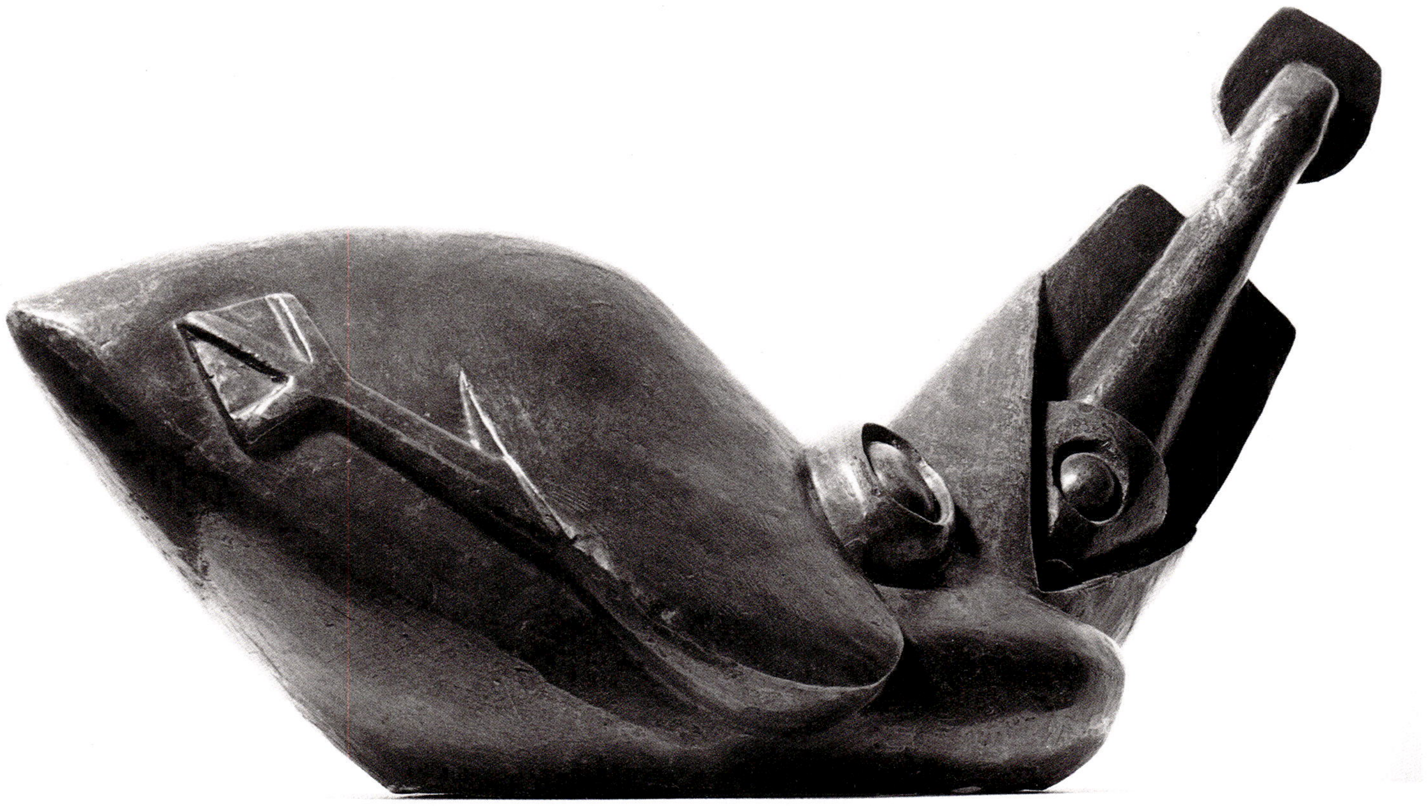

142 Bird Swallowing a Fish (*cat.* 97)

143 Study for Bird Swallowing a Fish, ink and brush

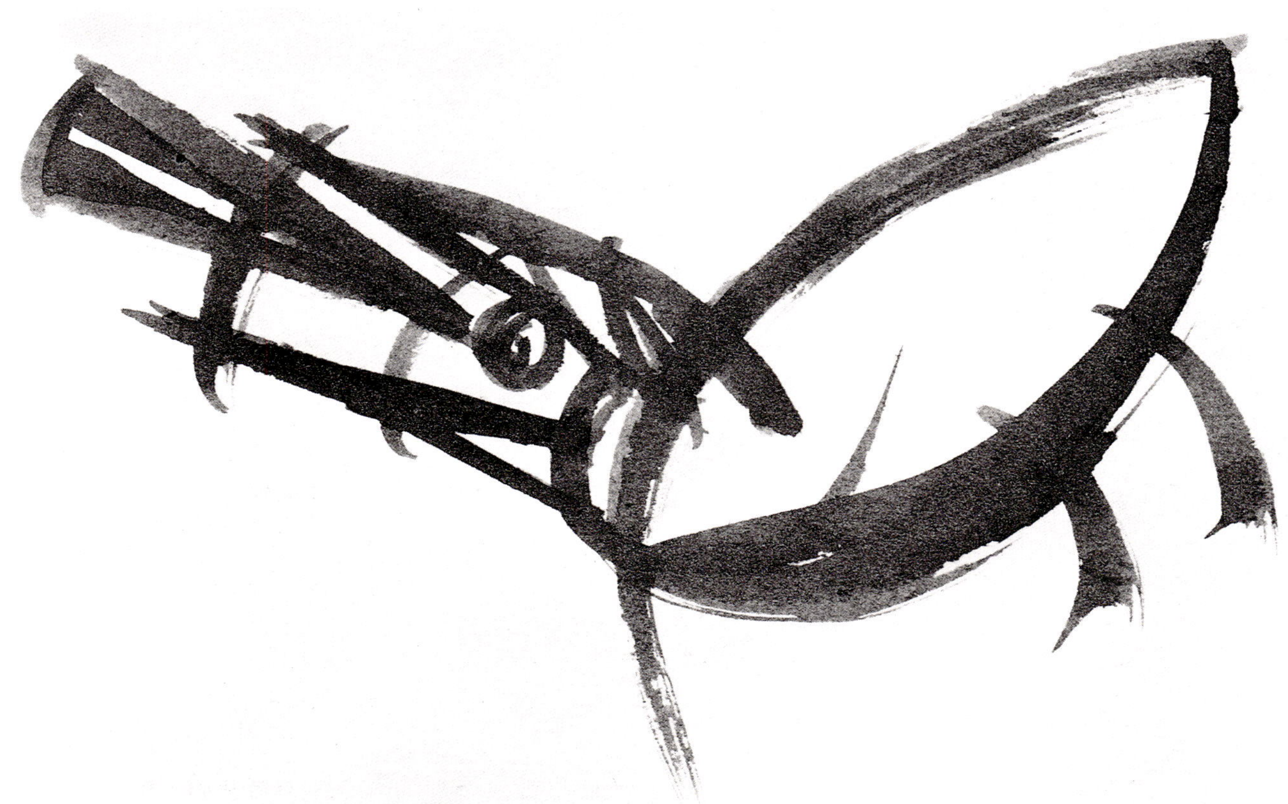

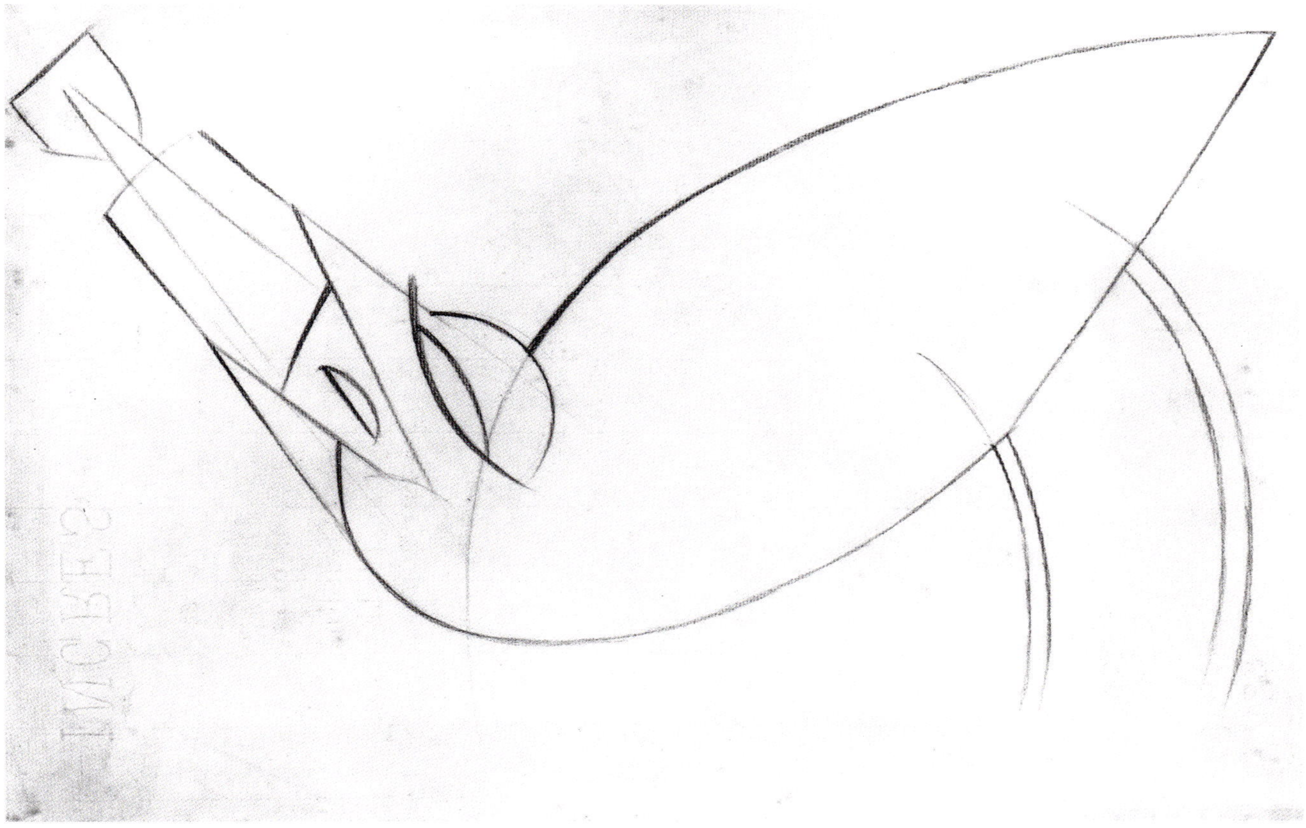

144 Study for Bird Swallowing a Fish, pencil

145 Bird Swallowing a Fish (*cat.* 97)

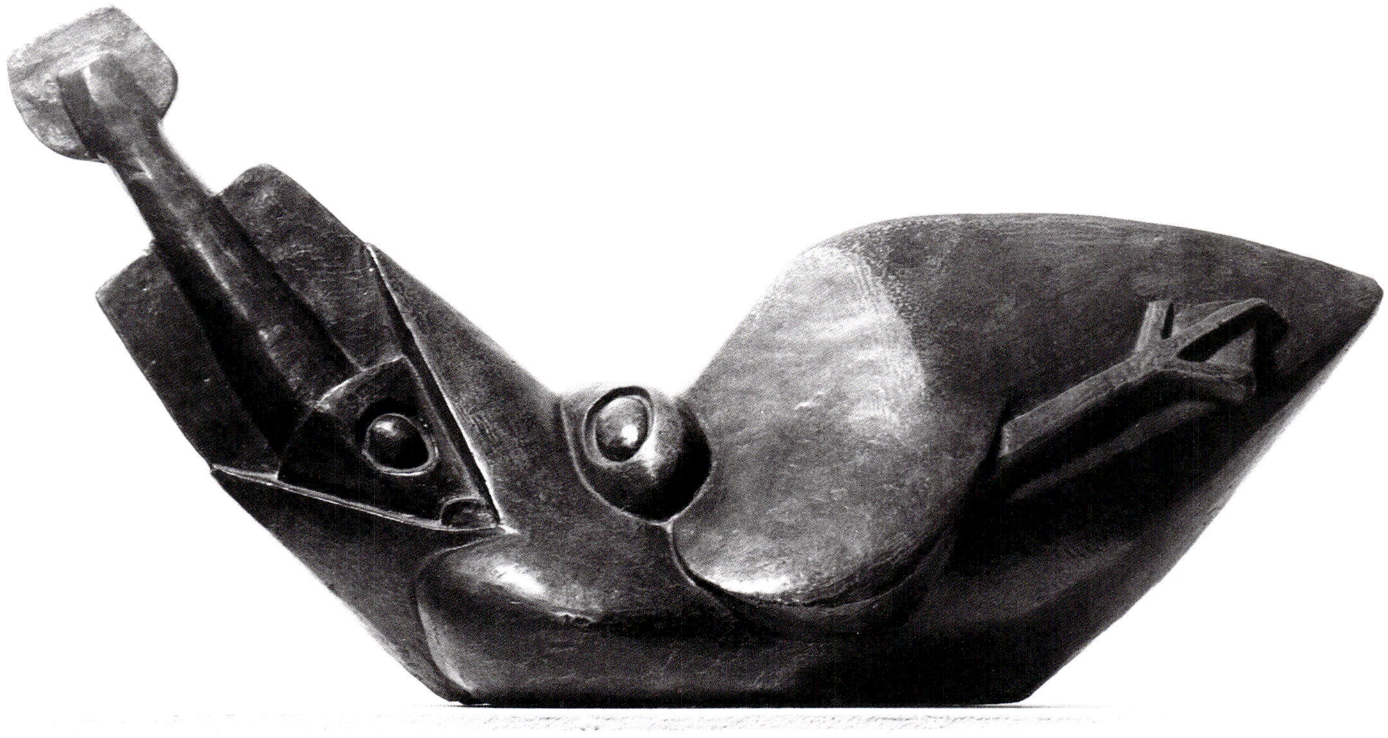

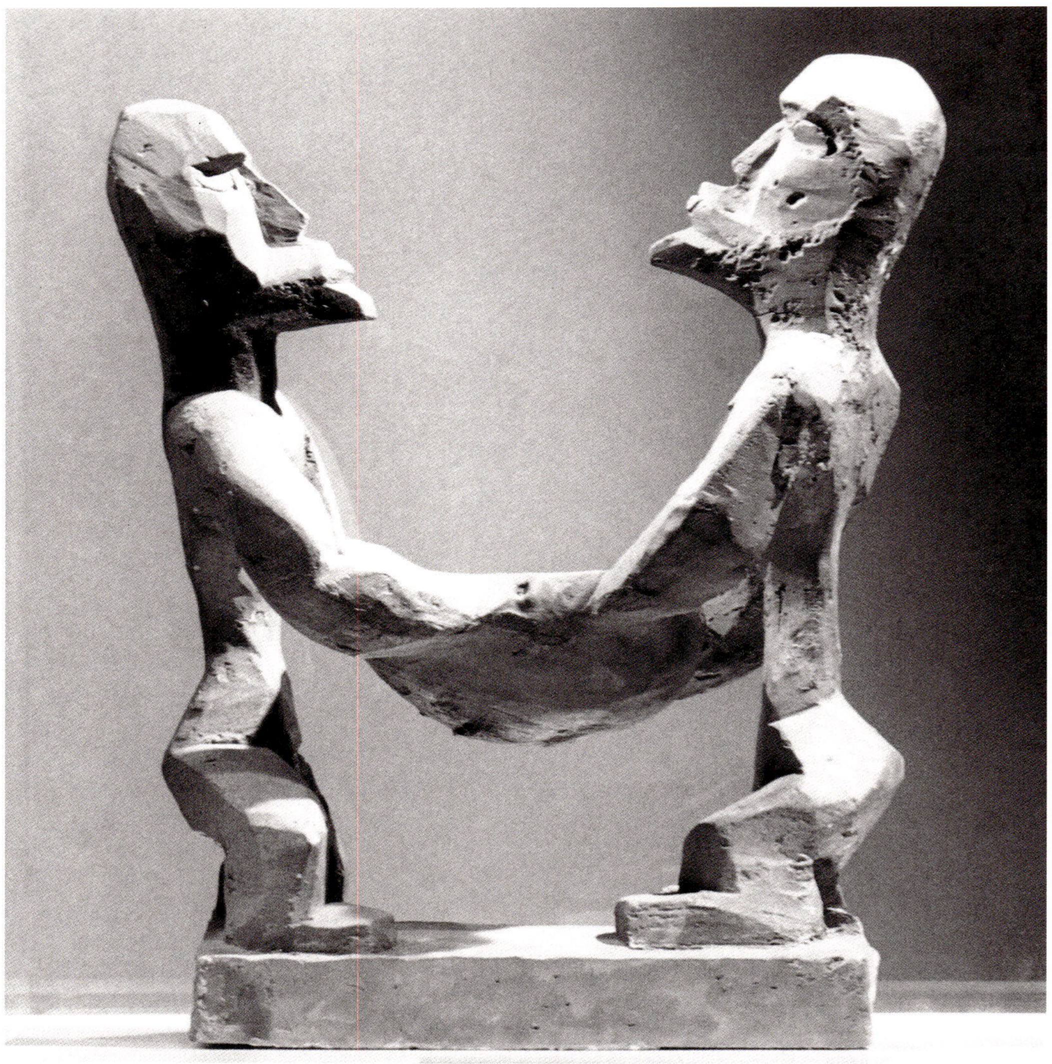

146 Men with Bowl (*cat.* 98)

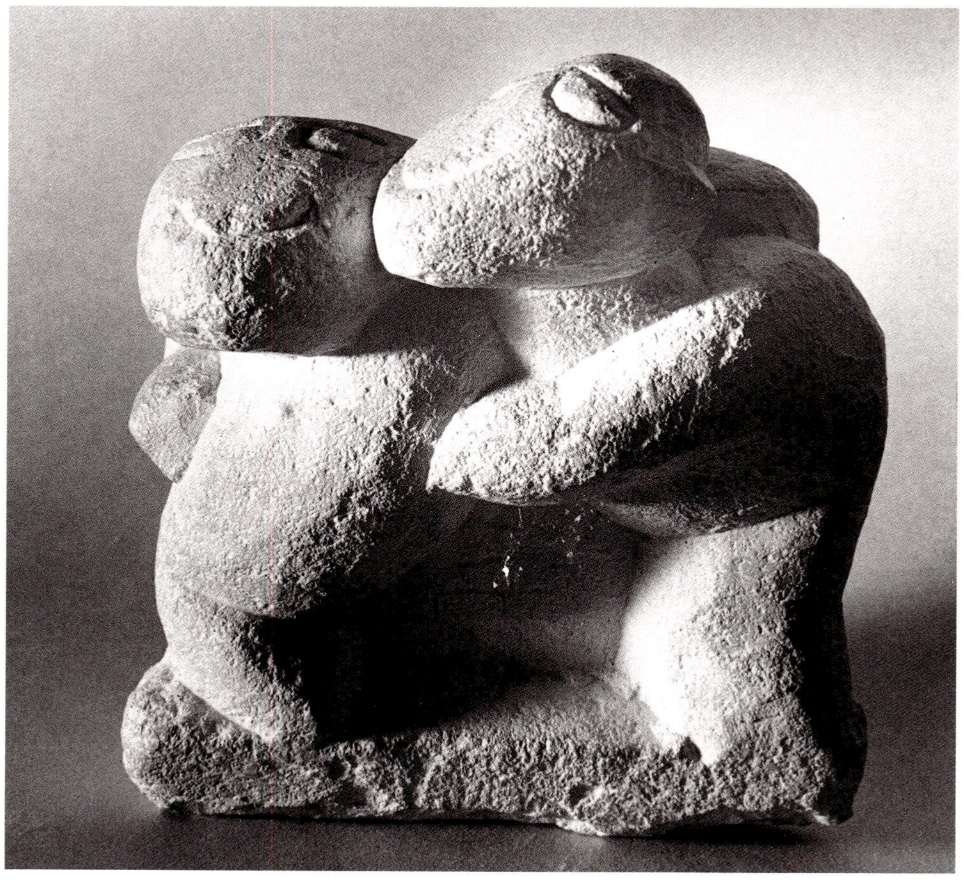

147 Monkeys (*cat.* 103)

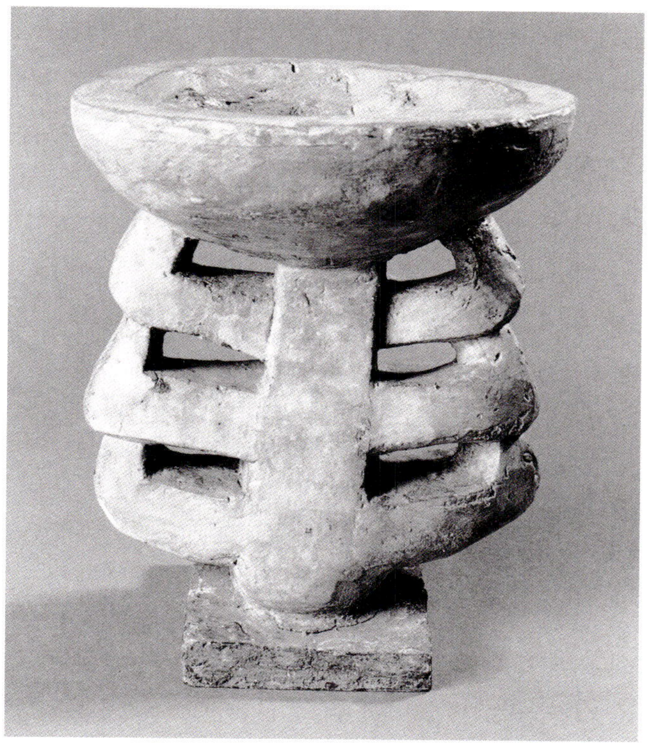

148 Maquette for Flower Vase 2 (*cat.* 100)

149 Maquette for a Bird Bath (*cat.* 71)

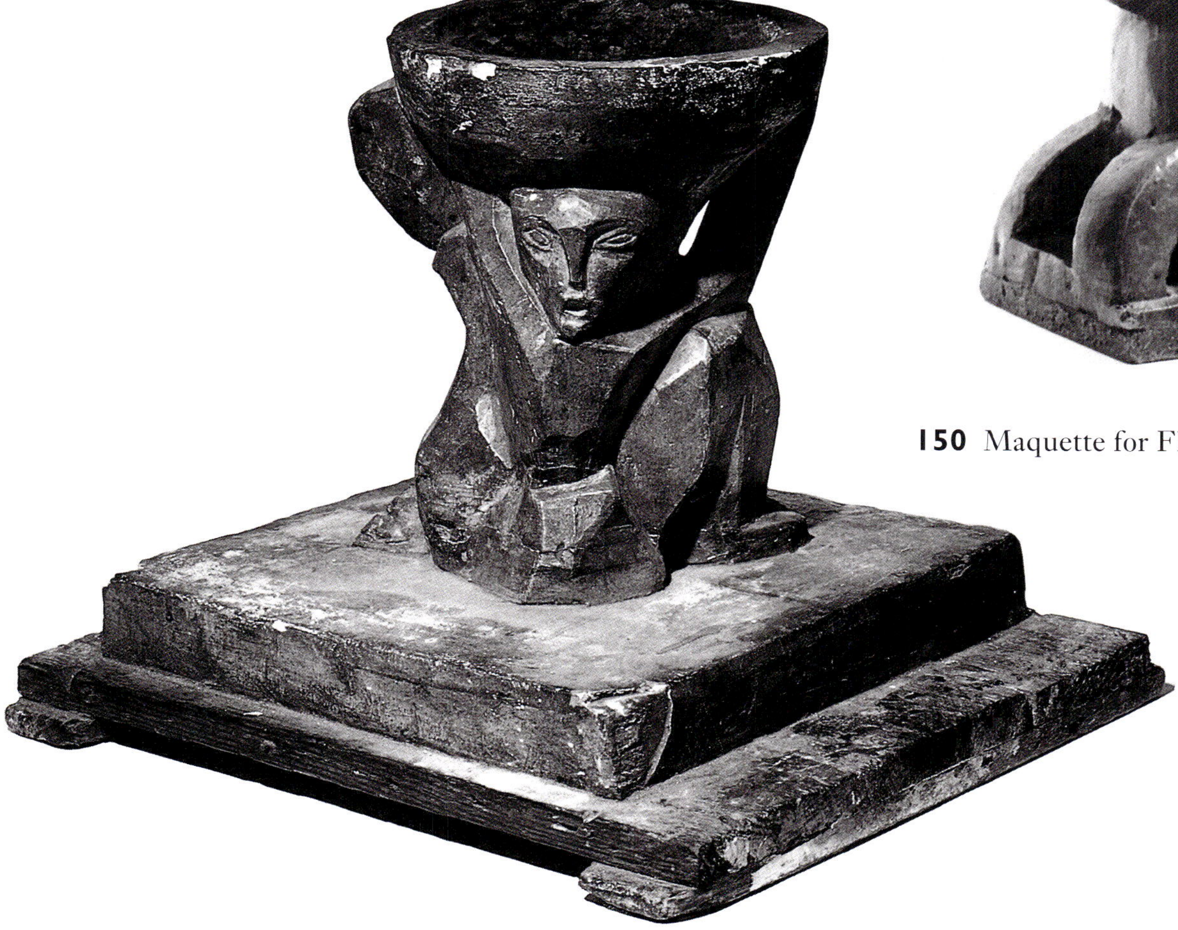

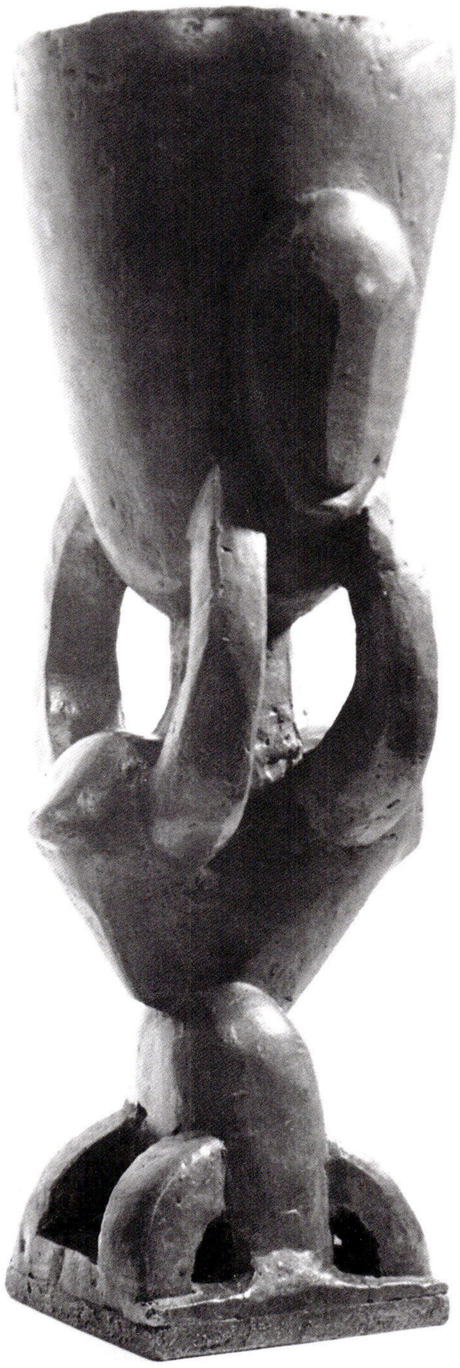

150 Maquette for Flower Vase 1 (*cat.* 99)

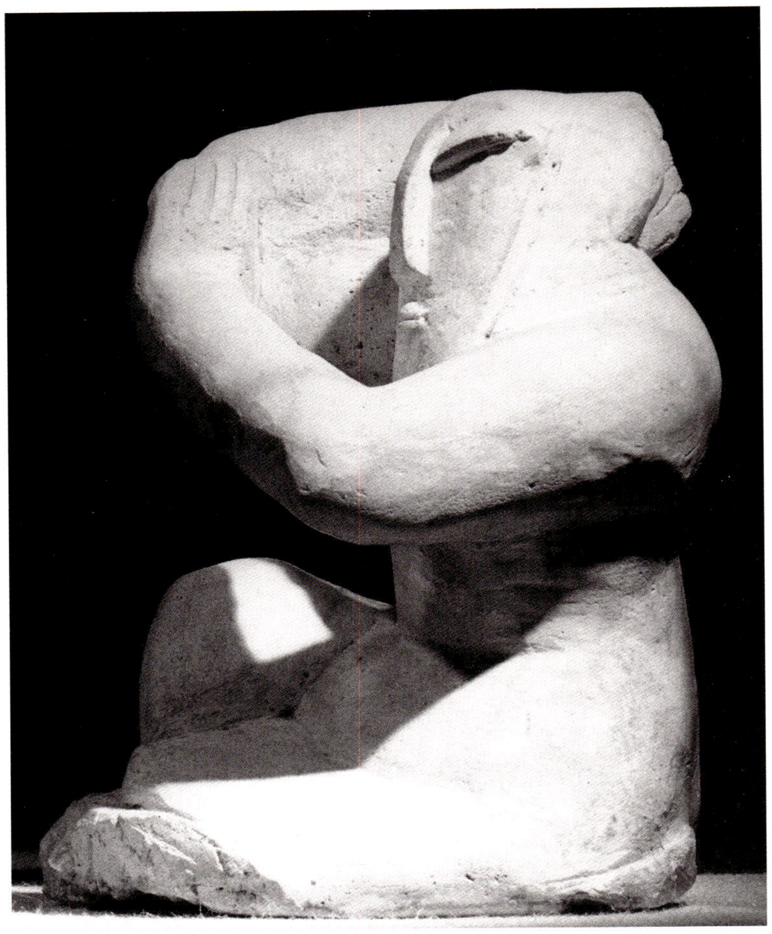

151, 152 Study for Seated Woman (*cat.* 104)

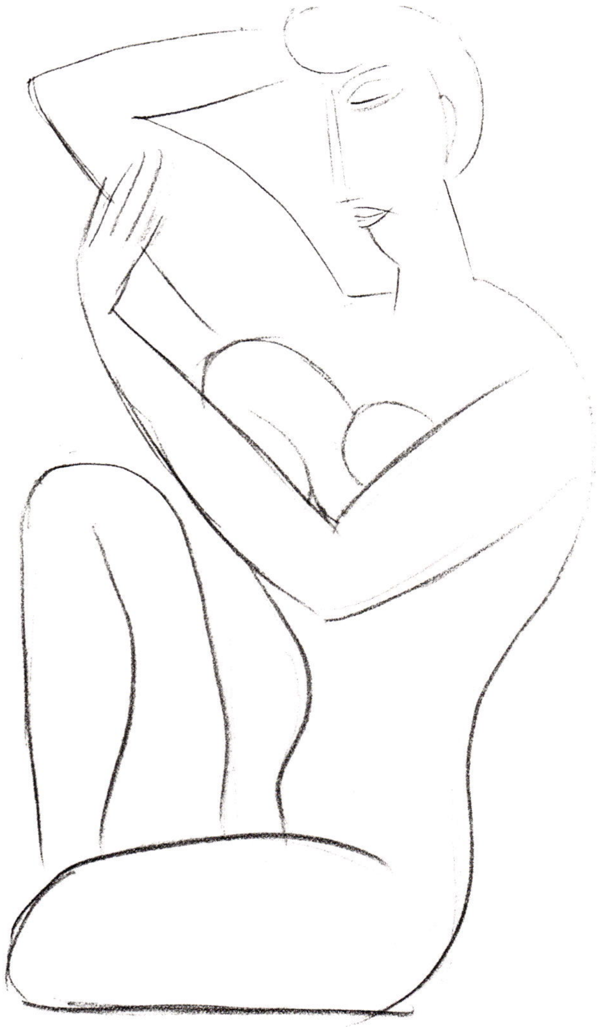

153 Study for Seated Woman, pencil

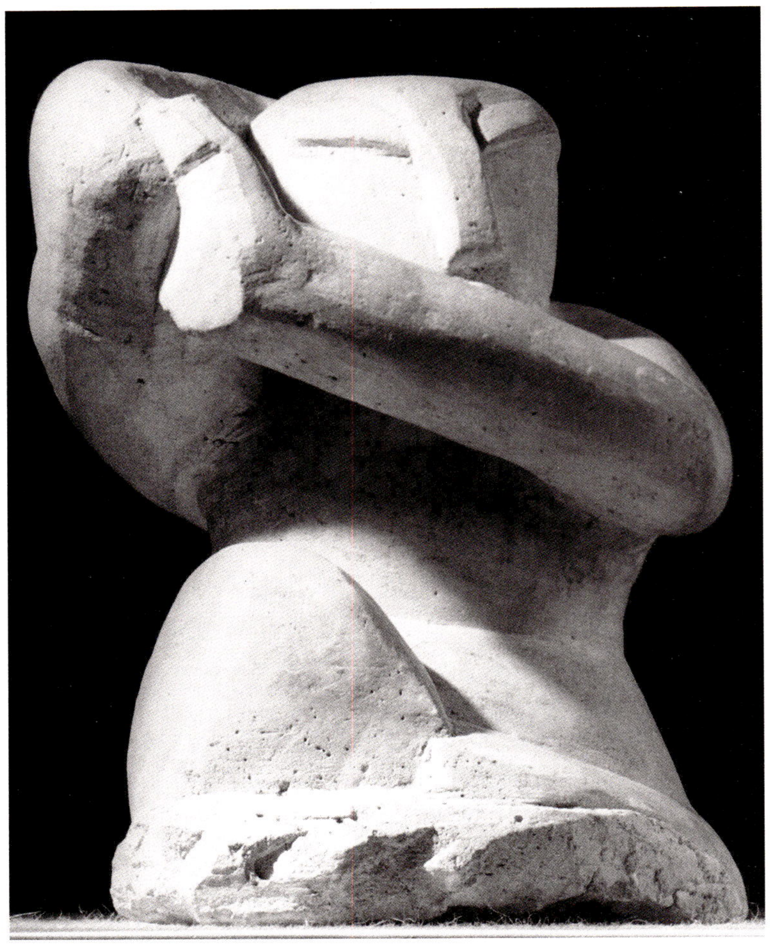

154 Seated Woman (*cat.* 105)

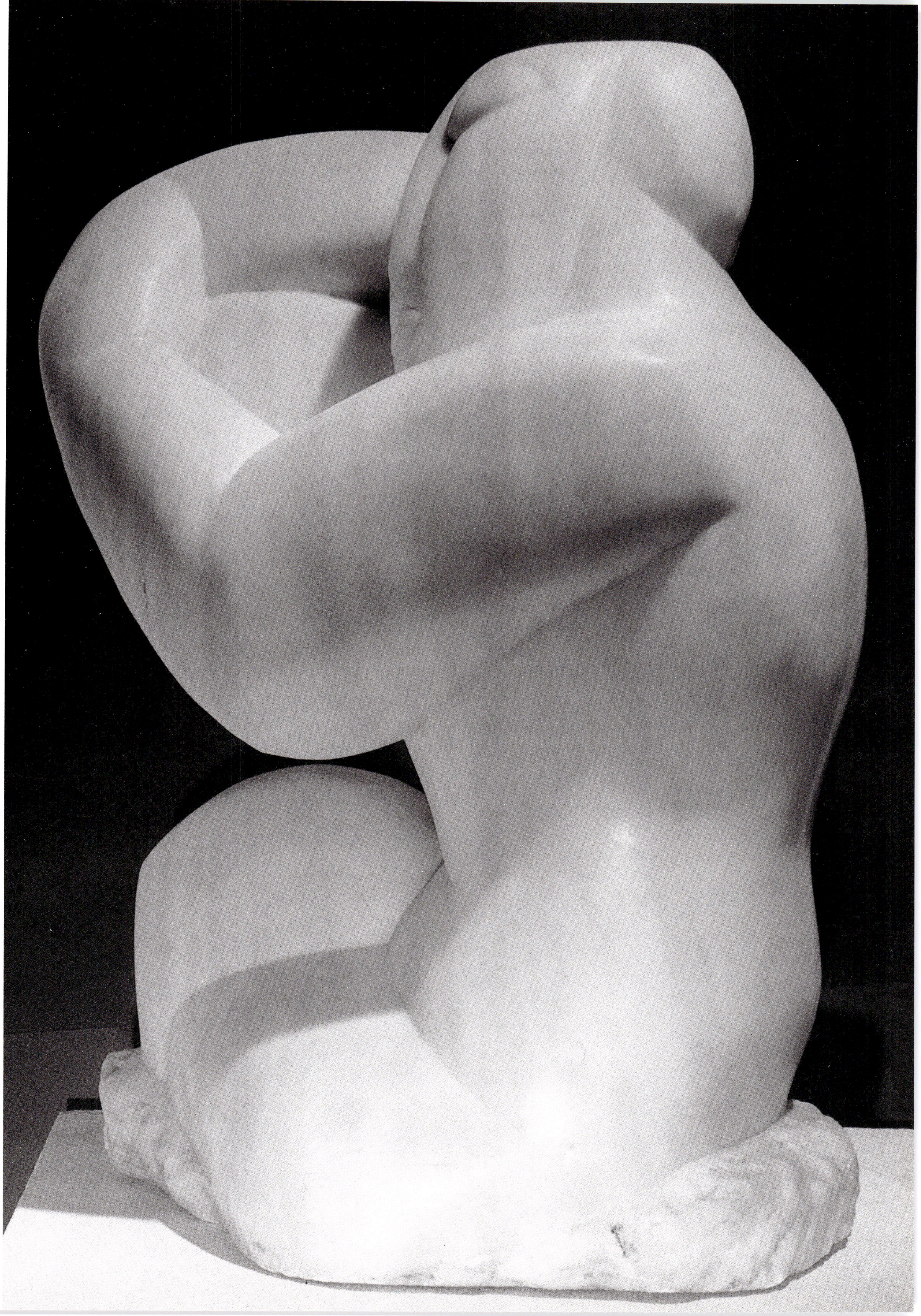

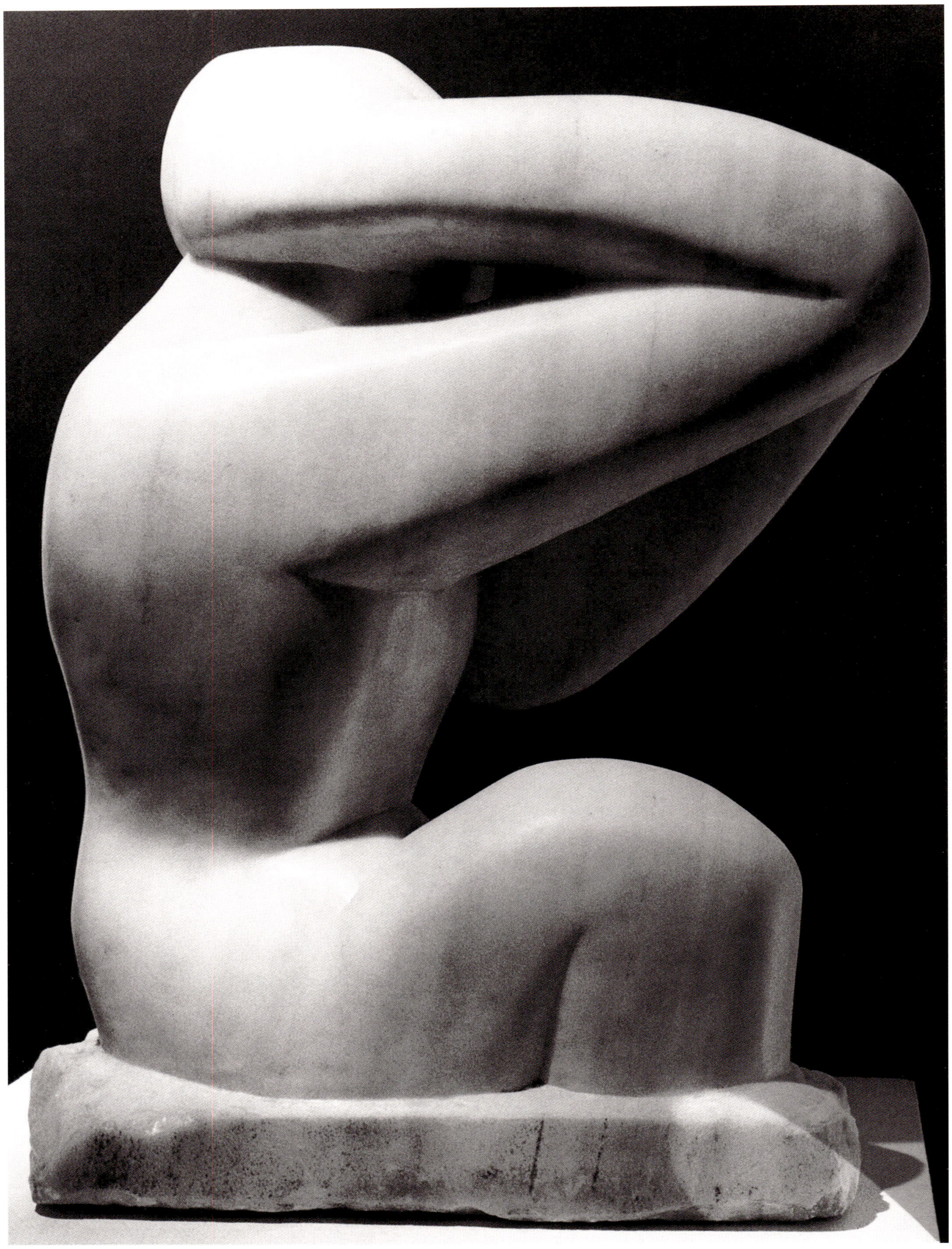

155, 156 Seated Woman (*cat.* 105)

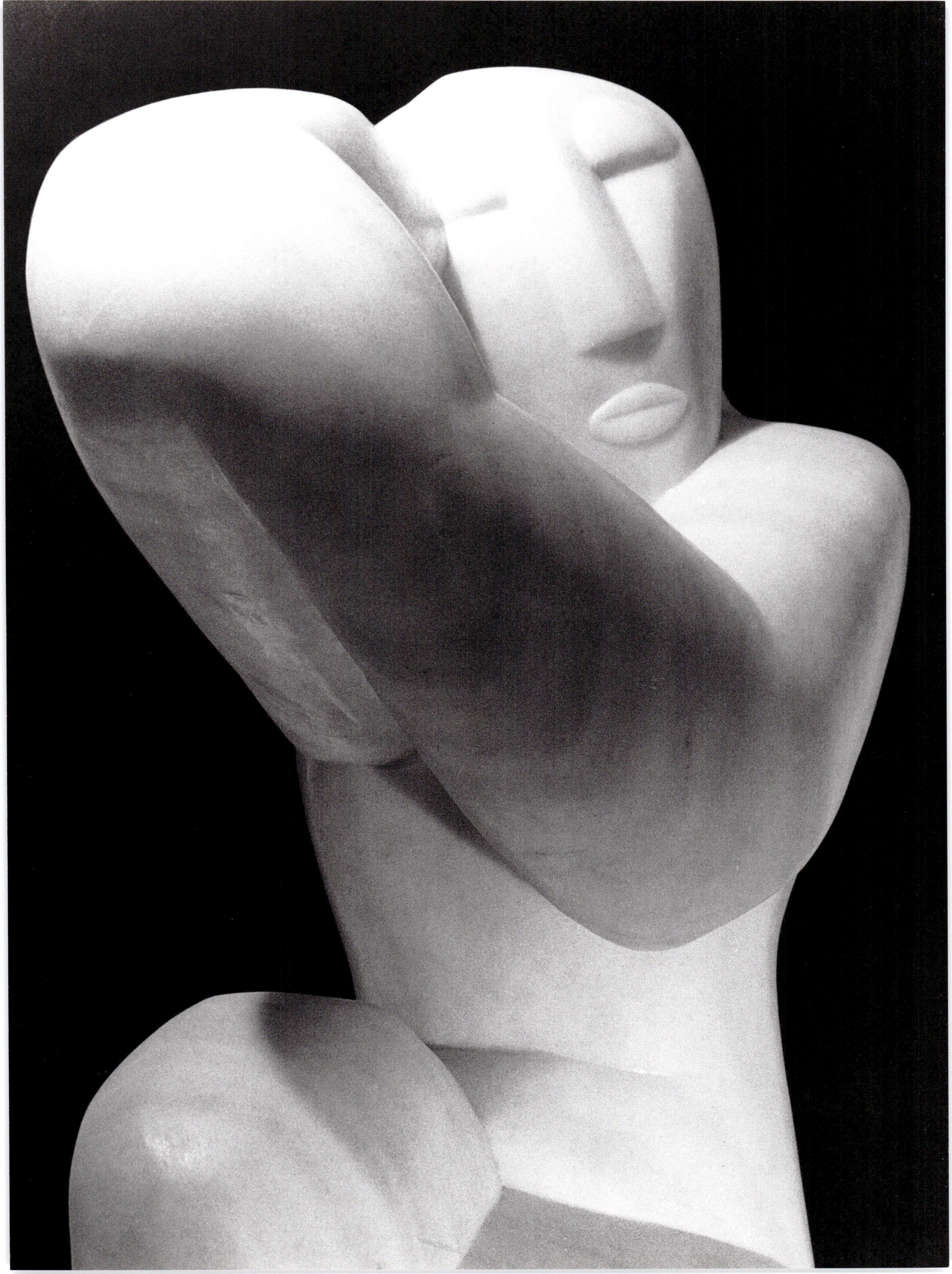

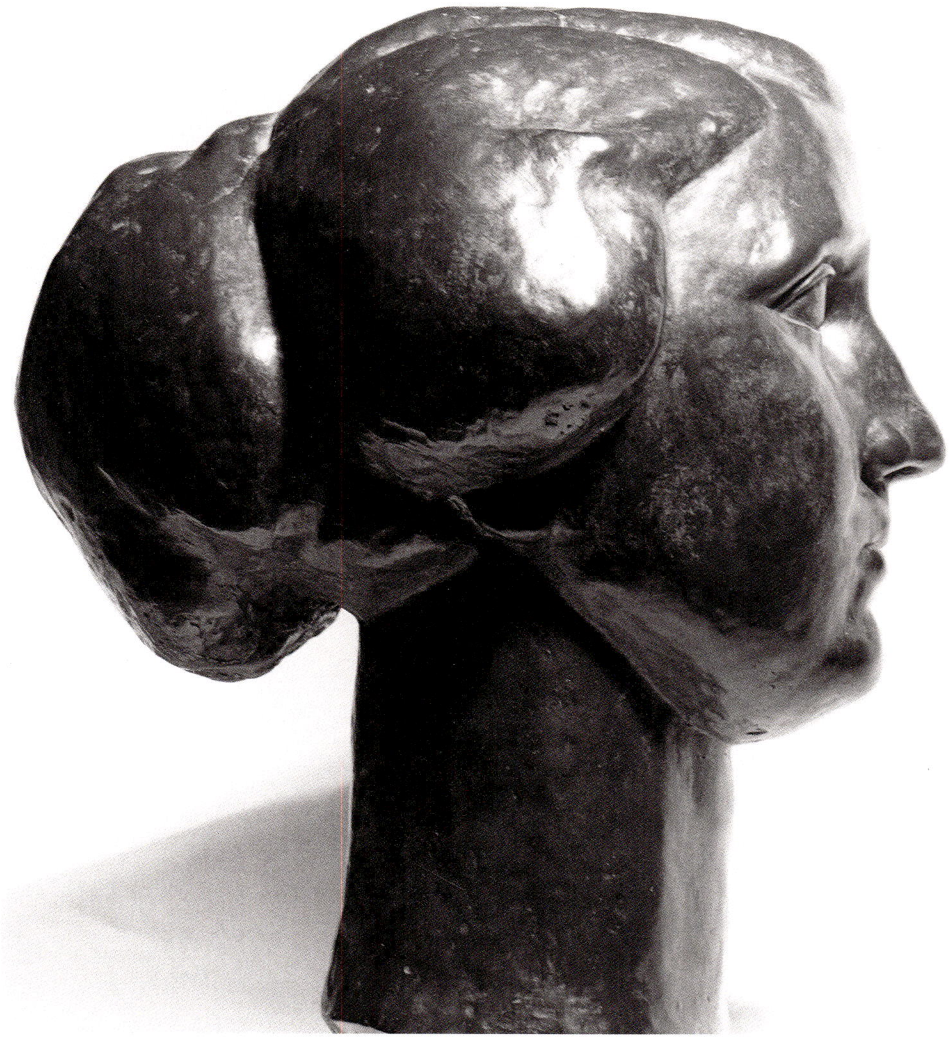

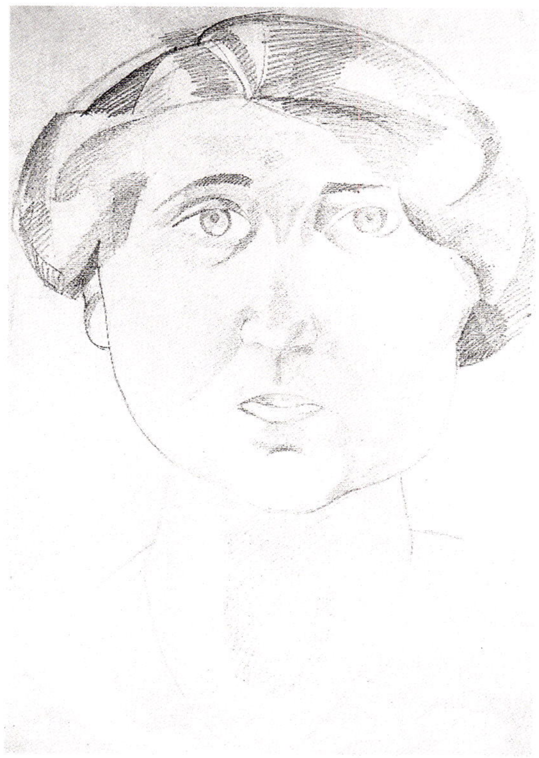

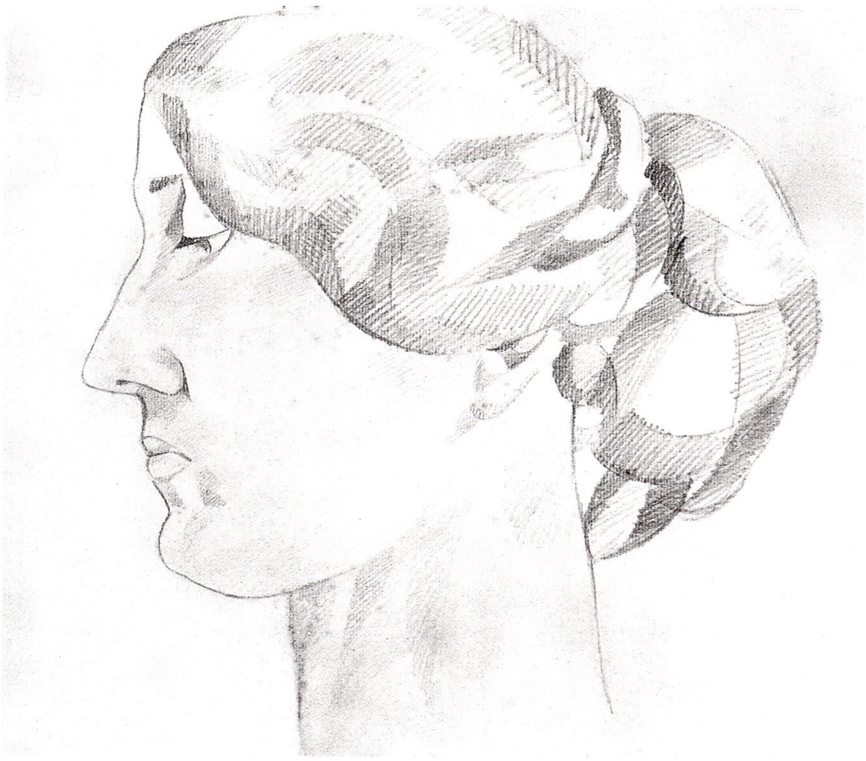

157, 160 Mlle Borne (*cat.* 106)

158 Study for portrait of Mlle Borne

159 Study for portrait of Mlle Borne, profile

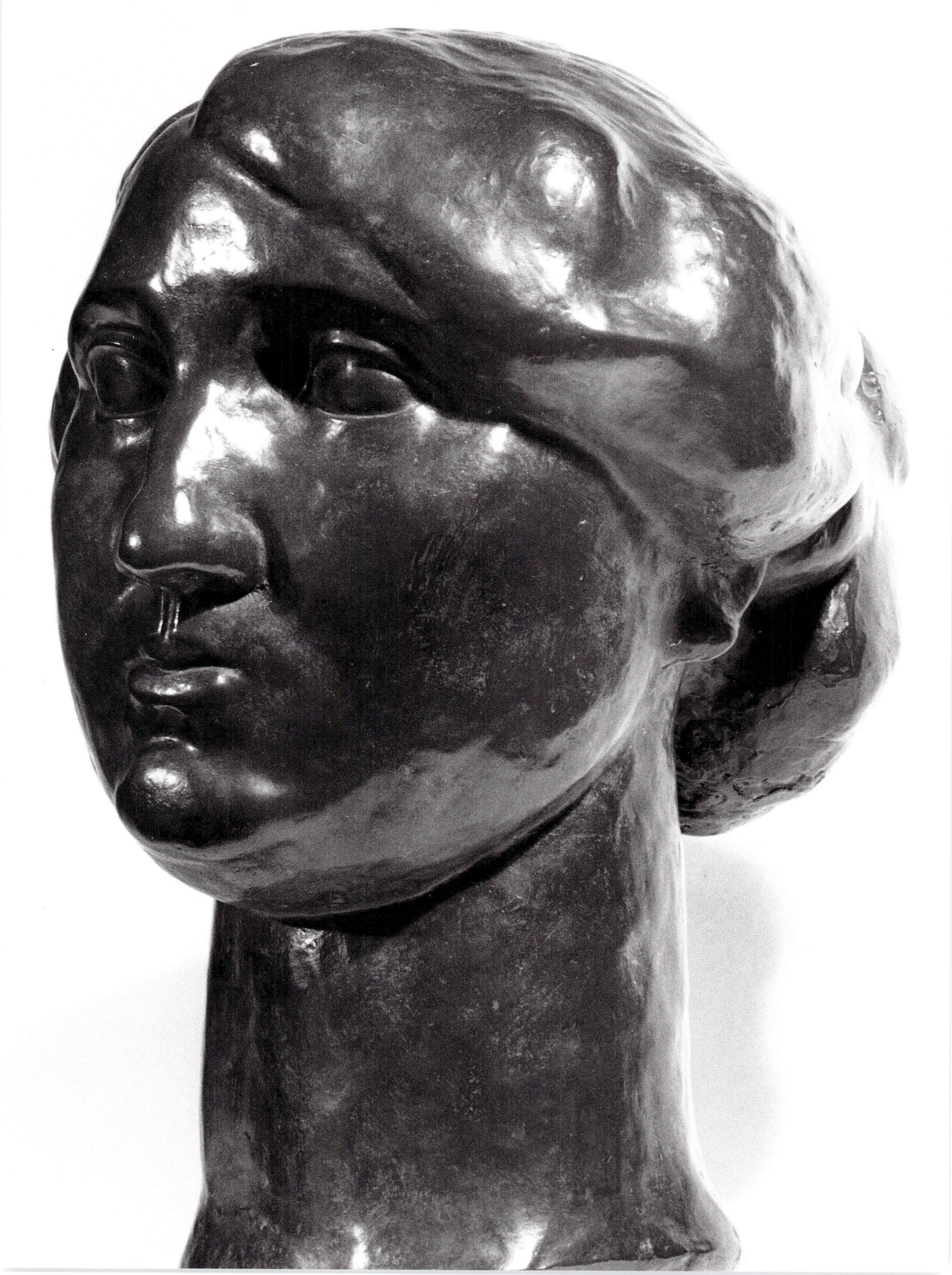

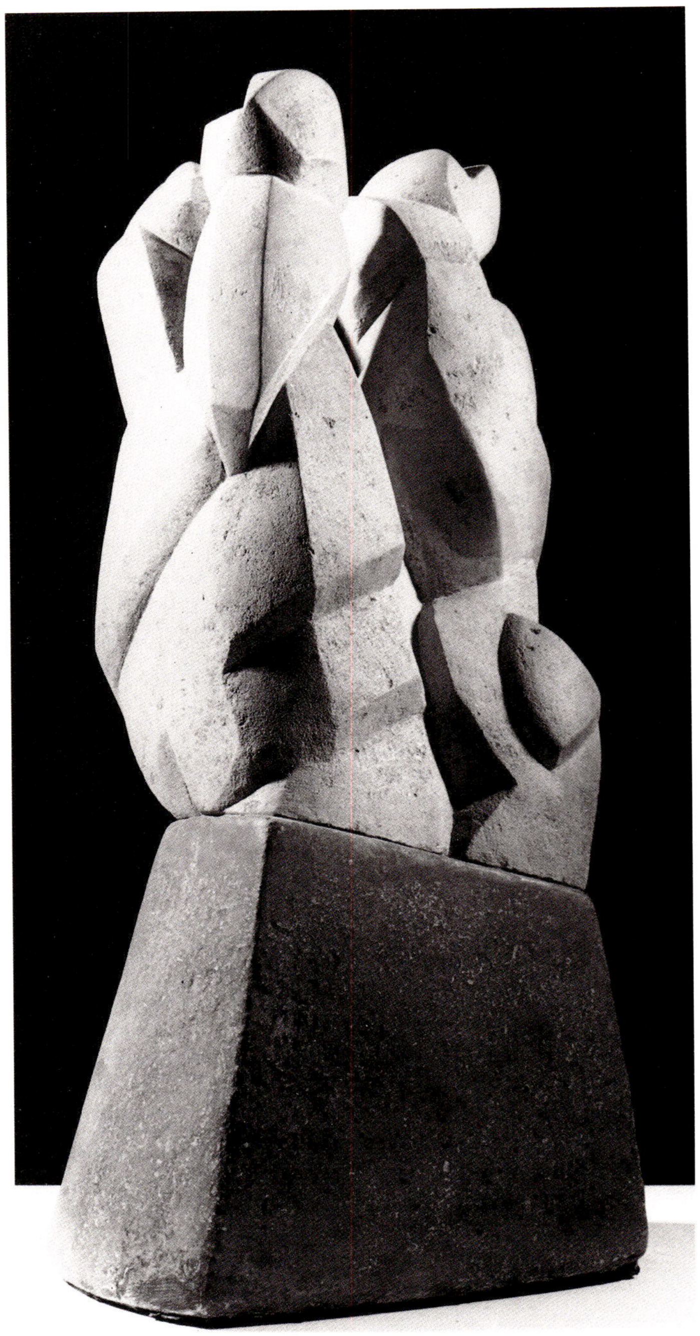

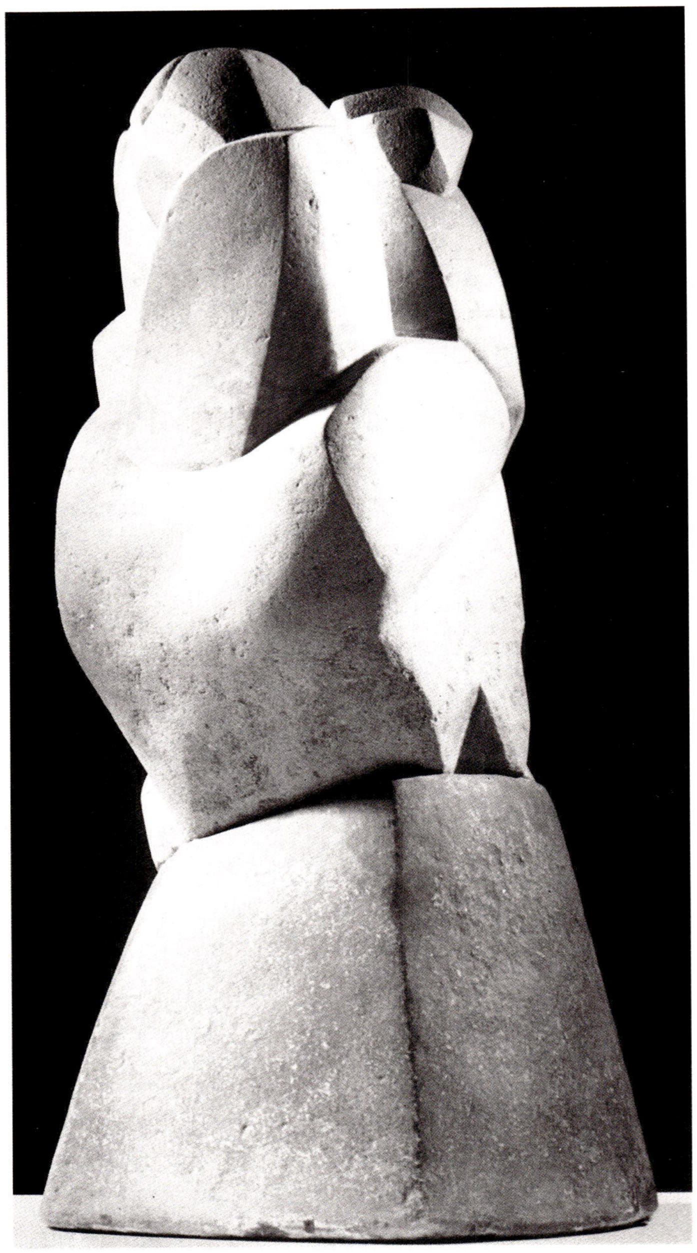

161–163 Birds Erect (*cat.* 107)

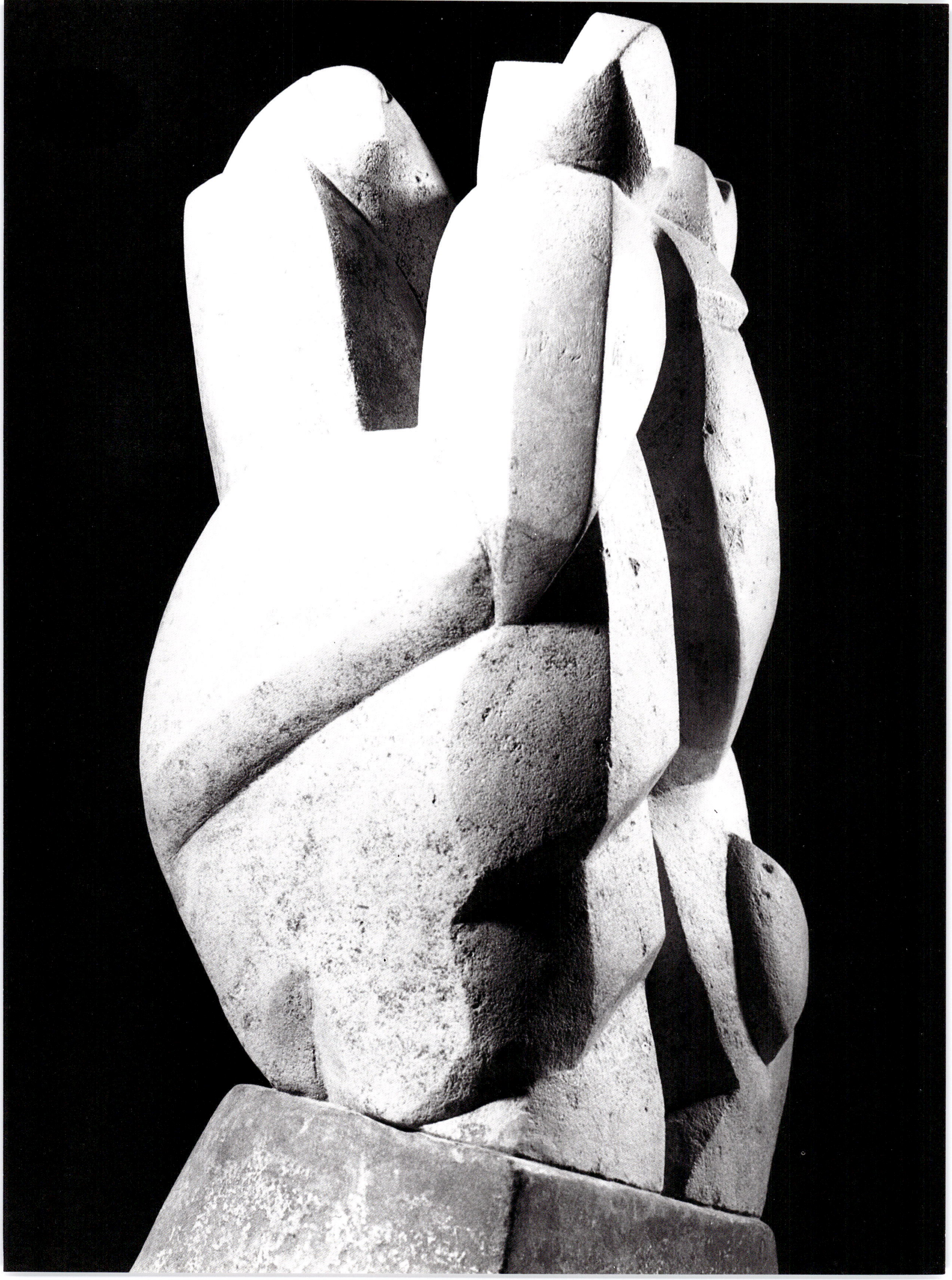

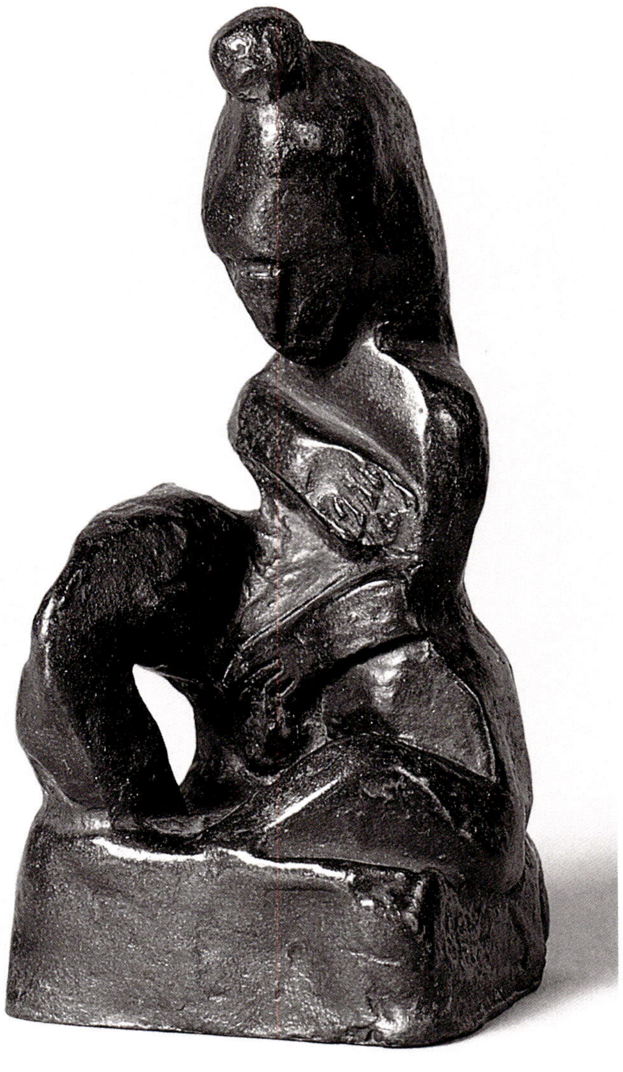

164 Erotic Sketch (*cat.* 115)

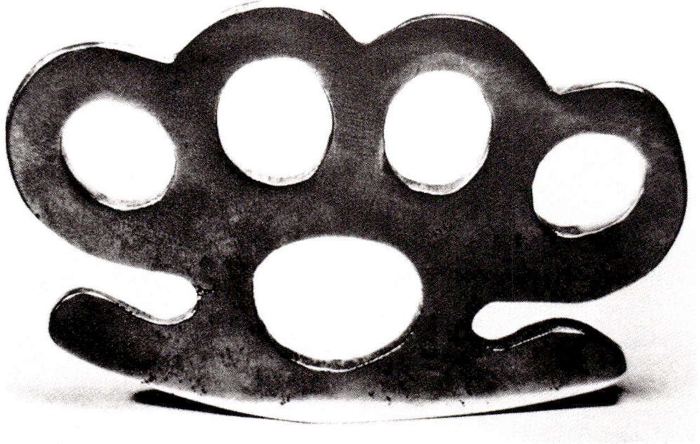

165 Knuckle-Duster (*cat.* 88)

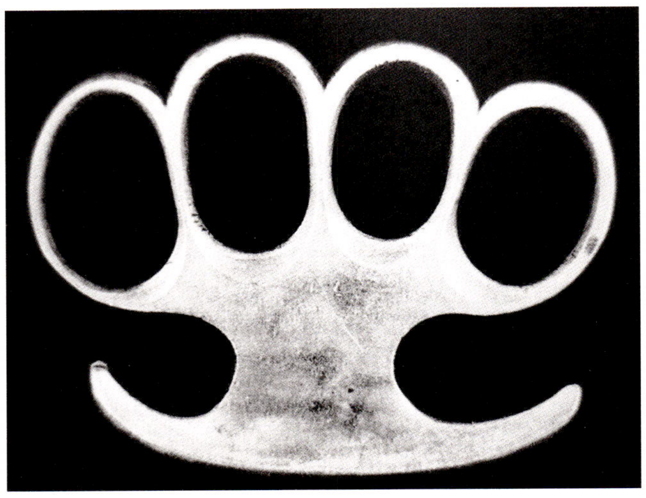

166 Knuckle-Duster (*cat.* 89)

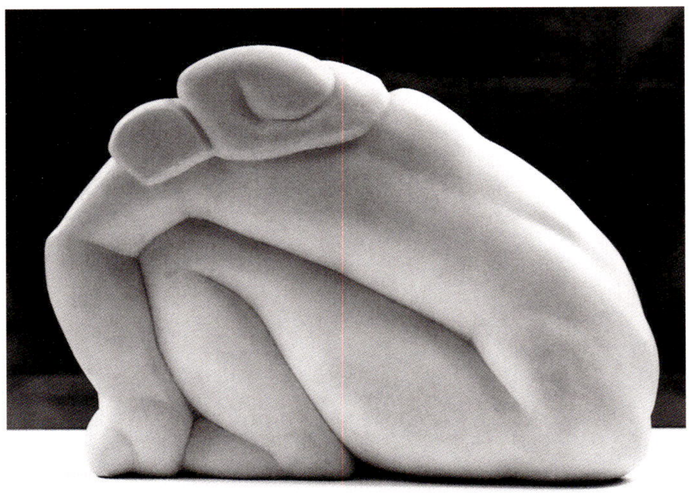

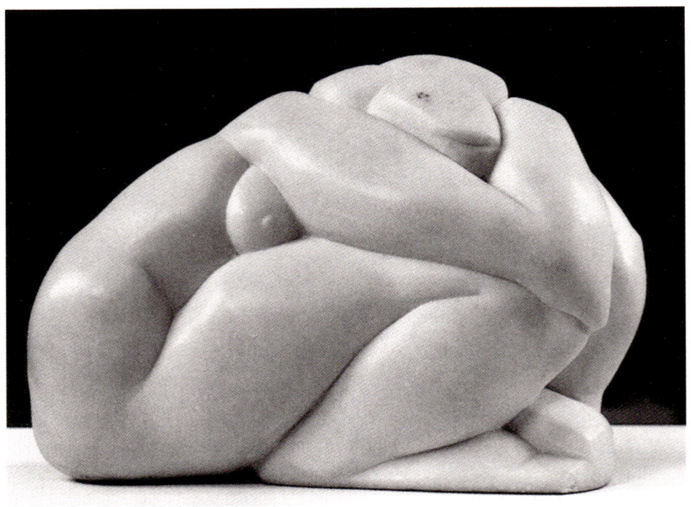

167, 168 Crouching Figure (wrongly attributed)

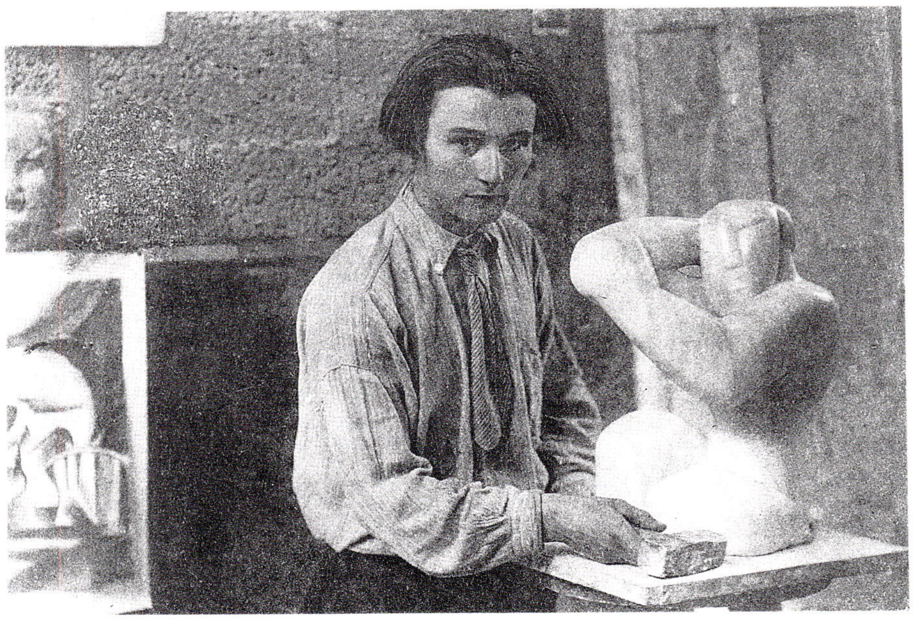

111 Gaudier in his studio, mid-1914. Visible are *Seated Woman* (*cat.* 104), *Terracotta Mask* (*cat.* 8) and a pastel still life. Photograph by Walter Benington

The Oeuvre: sources

CONSTRUCTING a convincing chronology of Gaudier's sculpture and estimating the extent of his oeuvre are both remarkably complicated tasks, considering the brevity of his career. Though he sold comparatively few works and the bulk of his oeuvre was inherited intact by Sophie Brzeska in 1915, many works have vanished and those which survive are stylistically and technically heterogeneous. Most of it is neither signed nor dated. His sculpture was constantly at risk – from the fragility of its materials, from his temper and self-critical tendency to destroy or abandon work that did not satisfy him. A number of works, now lost, were photographed by Walter Benington during visits to the studio in mid-1912 and again in early and mid-1914, as well as at the *Memorial Exhibition* in 1918.[1] Others are known only through letters or other written sources and these do not necessarily provide either unequivocal evidence for dating or much information about appearance. Finally, Brzeska's intestacy, and the subsequent history of the Estate, accounts for both the survival of much material which might otherwise have been lost, and the proliferation of posthumous casts.

Gaudier's List of Works

The primary source for Gaudier's sculptural oeuvre and its chronology is the artist's own *List of Works* drawn up on 9 July 1914, shortly before his return to France.[2] It is reproduced in full by Ede in his 1930 *Life of Gaudier-Brzeska* and comprises sixty-one sculptures and objects plus pastels, drawings, oils and prints.[3] It is systematically arranged – by year, title, medium, size, owner and price. There are also brief comments; where works were subsequently lost or broken, these may be virtually all that is known about them. Under 1912 we find, for example, the *Pot à fleurs* (*cat.* 13) 'flanqué de 4 têtes bas relief'; made of terracotta and measuring '3′ × 2¾′ × 2′ à peu près', it was sold for five guineas to 'R. M. Cocks or Cox', who lived 'near Chichester, Sussex'. Apparently never photographed and soon broken in a house move, almost its only existence is in the *List*.

Gaudier's indications of medium and technique are specific and seemingly reliable, but the *List* is neither complete nor chronologically accurate save in the broadest terms. Among the omissions are minor works, maquettes and incomplete sketches which might have been destroyed by the artist at a later date but survived to become part of the Estate, e.g. *Erotic Sketch* (*cat.* 115) and *Sketch for Standing Figure* (*cat.* 55). Major sculptures, such as *Dancer* (*cat.* 57, sold in his lifetime to Sidney Schiff) and *Birds Erect* (*cat.* 107), are also omitted. Since some works had been presented or sold, many of the sizes must have been estimated and some dates are demonstrably inaccurate, reinforcing the impression that he was jotting work down as he remembered it; there is documentary evidence for the dating of two of the *Torsos* (*cat.* 59, 60) and *The Embracers* (*cat.* 56) before the end of 1913, but in Gaudier's *List* they appear in 1914 after the *Head of Ezra Pound* (*cat.* 79) which was carved in March–April 1914. As he began to show his work more frequently, exhibition dates provide a *terminus ante quem*; these, too, highlight many inconsistencies in the *List of Works*. The Grafton Group exhibition took place in January 1914, yet Gaudier lists three of the five works exhibited – *Vase* (*cat.* 74), *Fawn* (*cat.* 62) and *Redstone Dancer* (*cat.* 69) – as works of 1914. The London Group exhibition took place in March so that the works exhibited there and listed in the published catalogue, including *Boy with Coney* (*cat.* 76) and *Stags* (*cat.* 77), must have been completed by early March though both works appear well on in the 1914 listing. Dependence on the *List of Works* for the chronology and size of works must therefore be cautious.

The *List of Works* is more revealing about the very variable pattern of work Gaudier looked back on in 1914; only one work, the terracotta *Mask of Sophie Brzeska* (*cat.* 7), is listed for 1911, reflecting his poverty and lack of access to materials; no carvings are listed before 1913 but the first eight entries for 1913 are carvings, which thereafter dominate his output. Many works remained in plaster and only eight bronze casts – *Major Smythies* (*cat.* 12), *Firebird* (*cat.* 18) and six casts from a pierced alabaster *Ornement* (*cat.* 87) – are included, apart from the late, small works in chiselled as opposed to cast bronze.

Ezra Pound not only owned sculptures and drawings but also, for a while during the War, looked after a large part of the studio contents.[4] He included a list of thirty-five works – nearly all carvings in stone, brass or plaster – in his 1916 *Memoir*.[5] There are occasional descriptive details but he made no pretence of completeness or chronological accuracy.

Ede, in possession of most of the Estate, including all the letters and writings, and with first-hand information from owners of Gaudier's work and others who had known him, annotated Gaudier's original *List of Works* and added a *Supplement* of thirty-three works, thus yielding a corpus of ninety-four sculptures. Ede's list includes a number of works which he had never seen, such as the painted alabaster *Angel* (*cat.* 110), described by Pound as 'a scandalous satire', and three works made in the trenches, which were already lost and probably destroyed. He also included the *Bust of Middleton Murry* (*cat.* 21) which was destroyed while still in the clay. However, he did not incorporate other works referred to in correspondence or in Sophie Brzeska's writings.

Gaudier's own record, the work of Pound and Brodzky and Ede's researches appear to leave little scope for otherwise unknown works by Gaudier to come to light, but the complete disappearance of some works mentioned in these sources, the youthful heterogeneity of his oeuvre and the extent of his subsequent influence on later sculptors has led to a number of 'new' sculptures being attributed to him. Only a handful of these have won general acceptance. In most cases stylistic and technical compatibility has been further supported by reliable provenance from people closely associated with Gaudier (e.g., the wooden *Portrait of Ezra Pound*, *cat.* 94, and the recently discovered *Standing Female Figure*, *cat.* 53). Certain other works (e.g., *Crouching Figure*, the variant *Doorknocker cat.* 81, 82, and the *Reclining Woman cat.* 102, appear to match items described in Gaudier's *List of Works* but were either 'lost' or not photographed. The attribution of some works remains open to question and one, *Crouching Figure*, is here rejected as Gaudier's work.

Gaudier's Estate

Sophie Brzeska inherited the mass of sculptures, plasters, fragments, drawings and sketchbooks scattered all over the floor and on every surface of the studio. Ezra Pound, Renée Finch and the Victoria and Albert Museum all temporarily stored some works during the War. Fifty sculptures and a similar number of drawings from the Estate and private collections were shown in the *Memorial Exhibition* at the Leicester Galleries in June 1918; these included some works omitted from the *List of Works*, such as *Dancer* (*cat.* 57), *Birds Erect* (*cat.* 107) and *Mlle Borne* (*cat.* 106).[6] It is also certain that some plasters were cast in bronze for sale during the show.[7] However, several important pieces were not included; the American collector, John Quinn had, with Pound's encouragement, been negotiating to purchase works even before Gaudier's death; he bought *Dog* (*cat.* 48) from Frank Harris, *Cat* (*cat.* 70) and *Watercarrier* (*cat.* 74) from the Omega Workshops and bought *Stags* (*cat.* 77), *Birds Erect* (*cat.* 107) and *Seated Woman* (*cat.* 105) from the *Memorial Exhibition*.[8] After the exhibition several of the pieces still belonging to Brzeska were sent back to the Victoria and Albert Museum where they had been deposited for safety in 1916, and the original plaster of *Dancer* (*cat.* 57) was presented to the Museum.

Following Brzeska's committal to Gloucester Mental Hospital in November 1922 a receiver was appointed to her Estate and an attempt was made to sell the work to raise funds for her hospital costs notwithstanding her healthy bank account. Despite the discreet opposition of the museum staff, the works deposited at the Victoria and Albert Museum were sent to Stevens's Auction Rooms in Covent Garden but no sale seems to have taken place. The Treasury Solicitor became the next holder of the Estate, in March 1925, on account of Brzeska's intestacy. Efforts to trace her next-of-kin through advertisements in London and Gloucester papers failed, not surprisingly, and on 12 January 1926 the Treasury was granted probate on an Estate of which Gaudier's work formed almost the entirety.[9] Wilenski's valuation for the Official Solicitor valued the collection at £545, based on past prices, but at only about £250 'for practical purposes', given the quantity to be dispersed. He considered many of the drawings valueless and that the artist 'was never popular and never will be'. Sculpture, drawings, notebooks and writings were forwarded in April 1926 to the Tate Gallery where H. S. Ede was the curator responsible for them. The Leicester Galleries were at this stage willing to offer £220.[10] However, *Redstone Dancer* (*cat.* 69), *Singer* (*cat.* 51) and *Imp* (*cat.* 78) were acquired for the Tate collection together with seventeen drawings in late 1926, all through Frank Stoop who purchased and presented them through the Contemporary Art Society. The CAS also acquired *Love Scene* (*cat.* 73) and *Woman* (*cat.* 39) from Stoop, though they were not to find homes in public galleries for many years.

The remainder of the collection, now mostly comprising drawings and plasters but still holding carvings including *Head of a Young Man* (*cat.* 44), *Mermaid* (*cat.* 55), *Caritas* (*cat.* 75), *Imp* (*cat.* 78), *Doorknocker* (*cat.* 81) and *Dog* (*cat.* 96), was then offered to London dealers. During the autumn of 1927, Ede himself made an offer of £60 for the rest of the Estate, which the Treasury Solicitor was willing to accept. However, on

13 October Ede withdrew, saying that he expected a friend, the artist Edward McKnight Kauffer, to make an offer in his stead. On the same day the Director of the Tate, Charles Aitken wrote to the Treasury Solicitor:

> As far as I can judge £60 is a fair price for what is left of the Gaudier Brzeska Collection, as most of the drawings are slight, and placing any number on the market would entail trouble . . . Messrs. Brown & Phillips [Leicester Galleries], I believe, offered £210 for the whole collection before all the best things were taken for this gallery and the Contemporary Art Society, so I think £60 for what is left seems fair.
>
> I understand that Mr McKnight Kauffer is prepared to offer £60 for the collection with Mr Ede's approval and, as Mr Kauffer is an outsider, I think it would be better for him to purchase the collection, rather than Mr Ede, who is an official here.[11]

The offer was accepted. Between 1927 and 1929 McKnight Kauffer also negotiated the purchase of the copyright on all the writings which enabled Ede to quote extensively from Gaudier's correspondence and Brzeska's writings in his *Life of Gaudier-Brzeska*, subsequently republished as *Savage Messiah*.[12]

However beneficial to the long-term survival of Gaudier's oeuvre and reputation, the purchase of the Estate by McKnight Kauffer and Ede's immediate acquisition of that material from him were questionable decisions. The next Director of the Tate, J. B. Manson, instituted a discreet enquiry into the circumstances of Ede's acquisition of the Estate in 1931 shortly after the publication of *Savage Messiah*. Ede defended himself in a letter, supported by other correspondence, to C. H. Collins Baker, who was charged with the enquiry:

> The following correspondence will show that I first suggested buying the Gaudiers after they had been lying around at the gallery for over a year, inspected by the Gallery trustees, the CAS, members of the Executive Committee, the Leicester Galleries and V. Stocks of the Treasury and after these people had taken what they wanted and pronounced the rest more or less worthless. As Dr Brown told me this morning, had it not been for my offer the drawings and papers would probably have been burnt since they had been lying around for so long and no one would give anything for them.
>
> The sale to E. McKnight Kauffer was finally made with the full concurrence of the Treasury who themselves were prepared to sell to me. The Tate, the CAS, the Leicester Galleries and the Goupil all refused to take them and several individuals I spoke to did not even bother to come and see them.[13]

Baker was able to exonerate Ede, after interviewing him and inspecting the dossier of correspondence:

> Before you came I had taken the impression that you had been injudicious qua privileged civil servant in securing the papers etc., to which you had 'privileged access'. From the dossier you showed me I gathered that my impression was quite wrong: I see that you, Dr Aitken and Dr Brown were all alive to this obvious objection to a civil servant buying in that way. So far as I can tell you were most correct; and I shall make it my affair to correct the 'die' from which my false impression came.[14]

Chronology

The *List of Works* can be used only with caution as a guide to the chronology of Gaudier's sculpture. Other primary sources, such as drawings, letters and other documents, are of variable assistance. Gaudier filled sketchbooks and notebooks but there are few extant drawings which relate to specific sculptures. Thus they do not generally help to date sculpture other than quite broadly. Letters – both Gaudier's and others' – and Brzeska's draft autobiographical novel, *Matka*, do contain passing references to work seen, bought or completed and these are incorporated into this catalogue, although dating is often a matter of deduction given the debatable degree of fictionalization in Brzeska's writing and the periods of months which often separated her writing from some of the events described.

Pound's partial catalogue, Ede's *Supplementary List* and Brodzky's book drafted in 1919 all allocate dates, though few have gone unchallenged. Levy simply followed Gaudier's and Ede's datings, but both Cole and Lewison have been concerned to establish a chronology for Gaudier's sculpture. Cole's suffers from a lack of supporting evidence and explanation; he backdates several works apparently on stylistic grounds. *Mlle B* (which he was able to identify from documentary sources as *Mlle Borne*, *cat.* 106) and *Love Scene* (*cat.* 73) are both redated from 1914 in Gaudier's *List of Works* to 1912. *Man and Woman* (*cat.* 38), dated 1914 in Ede's *Supplementary List*, is also dated to 1912 by Cole. As Lewison has pointed out, the redating of the stone carvings relates to a debate about when Gaudier first began to carve stone, the medium upon which his reputation as a vanguard sculptor largely depends and the virtues of which he famously trumpeted in his brief writings.[15]

Gaudier himself did not lay claim to a single carving before 1913; Ede, in his *Supplementary List*, placed just one carving, *Monkeys* (*cat.* 103), in 1912. Brodzky dated *Man and Woman* (*cat.* 38) and *Woman* (*cat.* 39) in 1912, and *Amour* (*cat.* 35) in 1912–13, but neither produced any arguments in support of these dates. Cole argued that Gaudier began carving soon after he met Epstein in early summer 1912 when the latter was completing his first major direct carving, the *Tomb of Oscar Wilde*, but that he thought so little of his early efforts that he omitted them from his *List of Works*.[16] While dismissing the famous Harris-Brodzky-Pound story of Gaudier beginning to carve in order to live up to his boast to Epstein that he did indeed carve direct (see above p. 59) as an 'elaborate but delightful fantasy', Cole appears nevertheless to accept its essential veracity. As Lewison points out, however, there seems to have been a sharp divide in Gaudier's mind – at least in July 1914 – for, having listed no carvings at all for 1912, the first eight entries for 1913 are all carvings with the information repeated more than once that they are all works in 'taille directe'.[17] Indeed, of the 1913 sculptures in the *List*, only four – the busts of Harris, Wolmark and Brodzky (*cat.* 45–47) and the *Wrestler* (*cat.* 32) – were modelled. Lewison concedes that Gaudier might previously have made carvings by the more traditional method of transferring a design first worked out in clay and cast in plaster into stone, but elsewhere leans to the view that Gaudier always carved direct and began to carve only in 1913. He also regards Brodzky's datings as particularly unreliable.

It seems hardly credible that someone as adventurous, manually adept and as aware of the history of sculpture as Gaudier would have necessarily have waited meekly until Epstein was at hand in order to try out carving himself. He had spoken of his intention to learn the technique of carving wood for cabinet-making and of having taken up the chisel and boaster to Dr Uhlemayr as early as March and May 1910; in August 1910 he had told Kitty Smith he was carving a wooden picture frame. He also notes in the *List of Works* that he had given a terracotta *Self-Portrait* (*cat.* 6) to an Italian wood sculptor, possibly as payment in kind for lessons in wood-carving technique or the loan of tools. In April 1911 he portrayed himself to Kitty Smith as 'a very stern boy always thinking of clay, stones, chisels and bodies to sculpt'. Clearly if he was not actually carving, the ambition to do so was already there. No explicit references to carved work have so far been discovered either in Brzeska's *Matka* or in Gaudier's letters before early 1913, but he may well have made experimental pieces which have not survived or were never included in the *List* because they were regarded as studies.

The discussion has overlooked the existence of one small carving, *Religious Head* (*cat.* 20), which can convincingly be dated in June–September 1912, since the initials incised on the back allude cryptically to the brief friendship between Gaudier, Brzeska, Mansfield and Murry. Closely related to it in material, scale and style is the so-called *Portrait of 'Ezra Pound'* (*cat.* 19). The humorous character of this piece – a portrait of a man with mutton-chop whiskers – can be plausibly compared with the satirical edge of Gaudier's street drawings, pastels and modelled portraits in 1912. Meeting Epstein may have stimulated further efforts, such as the rather Egyptian *Head of a Child* (*cat.* 22).

There seem much stronger grounds for dating Gaudier's commitment to carving as his primary technique to the beginning of 1913. This would be consistent not only with the *List of Works* but also with the availability of tools, stone and space in which to make the extra noise and mess that carving entailed. In February 1913, on Sophie's return from Dodsford to the new studio at 454a Fulham Road, they argued about the impossibility of her living in the studio not only because of the terms of the lease but also because, with her intense dislike of noise and mess, it was impossible for her to be there 'especially if he is cutting stone'.[18] It has been overlooked that previously they had perforce lived and worked in the same rooms whereas from January 1913 Gaudier had a separate studio, acquired at least in part because he hoped to do a substantial carving. As he wrote to Uhlemayr on 6 January:

> I have taken this studio in the hopes that it will bring me more work. Anyhow, I can work better here than in ordinary rooms – though what I really want to do is to sculpt a large statue in hard stone, and for that I must get a commission. All this year I have been reduced to doing little statues in plaster and bronze, and portraits, which haven't in the least satisfied my desires or my ability.[19]

While it would have been possible for him to have done a little carving before, especially after Sophie had left town in September, his freedom to work on a larger scale was greatly increased once he had a studio, first at

454a Fulham Road and, from September 1913, under railway arch 25 in Putney (figs. 36–37).

Nevertheless the chronology of many works in 1913 and 1914 is uncertain. However one looks at it, this was a period of tremendous technical and stylistic change and both Cole and Lewison have been tempted to group some works according to preconceived notions of stylistic development, from naturalism and Rodinesque bravura towards a more simplified, abstracted geometric style. In March 1913 Gaudier wrote to Lovat Fraser, 'I carve as many reliefs as I can and it is a long job enough but I shall manage to drop in one evening coming back from town'.[20] This would suggest that some at least of the carved reliefs (*cat.* 33–36) are more or less contemporary with the modelled portraits of *Brodzky* (*cat.* 47) and *Wolmark* (*cat.* 46). A superficial and then more profound knowledge of Cubism becomes apparent during 1913; after July 1913 Brancusi's influence became tangible, though Gaudier's own artistic personality becomes increasingly distinct with works such as *Redstone Dancer* (*cat.* 69), *Stags* (*cat.* 77), *Torpedo Fish* (*cat.* 80) and *Birds Erect* (*cat.* 107).

This trajectory towards modernist semi-abstraction, firmly placed within the discourses of Cubism, Vorticism and Primitivism, throws up special problems for the 1914 carvings: at least two works listed in early sources for that year – *Love Scene* (*cat.* 73) and *Mlle Borne* (*cat.* 106) – with their naturalistic, almost classical, approach to form, do not fit into this preconceived pattern. Nor does *Seated Woman* (*cat.* 105), well documented as one of Gaudier's last works. Both Cole and Lewison place *Mlle Borne* in 1912 and Lewison is particularly critical of Brodzky's 1914 dating. Cole also dates *Love Scene* in 1912 though Lewison, dating it 1913–14 and noting the accomplishment of the carving and the stylistic similarity to *Mlle Borne*, appears to waver in his conviction of Brodzky's inaccuracy.[21] The evidence of Brzeska's writings (*cat.* 106 and above p. 44) indicates that *Mlle Borne* dates from summer 1914 and must be seen alongside *Birds Erect* (*cat.* 107) and *Seated Woman* (*cat.* 105) as one of the last completed works. This demonstrates that *Love Scene*, *Seated Woman* and *Mlle Borne* can be seen with the three *Torso* studies of Nina Hamnett as part of Gaudier's recurrent dialogue with the classical tradition. Similarly, the genesis of the *Blunt Coffer* (*cat.* 72) underlines the continuing eclecticism of his sources, his willingness, despite his outward show of arrogance, to adjust his approach according to medium, mood and client and to work in several styles simultaneously.

Casts

Only *Major Smythies* (*cat.* 12), *Firebird* (*cat.* 18), *Bird Swallowing a Fish* (*cat.* 97) and the now lost *Ornement* (*cat.* 87) were definitely cast during Gaudier's lifetime so that nearly all bronzes are posthumous casts. Several works appear to have been cast – with Brzeska's reluctant consent – for the *Memorial Exhibition*, where *Monkey* (*cat.* 23), *Football Player* (*cat.* 32), *Letterweight* (*cat.* 87) and a *Fawn* (*cat.* 63) are listed as bronzes. *Dancer* (*cat.* 57) was probably also cast at this time. Between 1918 and 1935 a few bronzes were cast from plasters at the instigation of the collectors or dealers into whose possession they came – the Leicester Galleries and Zwemmer's. Major Smythies was incensed at the proliferation of posthumous casts or 'trade bronzes': 'the very idea of an edition of a bronze untouched by the artist, would have revolted the craftsman in him.'[22]

The major proliferation of casts from carvings as well as plasters took place during the 1960s, partly through Mervyn Levy, the Mercury Gallery, Anthony d'Offay Gallery and private owners, but largely at the instigation of H. S. Ede. Though Ede's records were very casually kept, so that ultimate edition sizes are sometimes in doubt, nine or twelve was the usual maximum. The sale of some of these casts, in addition to disseminating Gaudier's work into public and private collections by sale, enabled Ede to present sculptures and drawings to a variety of collections; he made major gifts to the Musée National d'Art Moderne in Paris and to the Musée des Beaux-Arts in Orléans, which for the first time established Gaudier as a French sculptor whose work could be seen in the context of European rather than British modernism. Any doubts about the desirability of all these casts, especially those taken from carved works and from plasters of which earlier bronzes already existed, must be balanced against the fact that Ede's trading played an extremely important part in fostering Gaudier's reputation. They also helped ensure the survival of the unique ambience of Ede's home and collection at Kettle's Yard, Cambridge, which he presented to the University in 1967.[23]

This Catalogue

This catalogue aims to include all Gaudier's recorded work with evidence of dates wherever possible. Where a year but no specific month is indicated, the sequence in which works appear is not intended to suggest an exact order. Works for which only literary references are available and for which no date can be advanced are listed at the end of the catalogue, as is work previously attributed to Gaudier but here rejected.

The titles of Gaudier's works are a frequent cause of confusion since there are several works with similar of identical titles, such as *Torso*, *Ornament*, *Toy*, and many with no single established title in the artist's lifetime. Wherever possible works are titled as in Gaudier's lifetime and *List of Works* with alternatives and variants also given. Where there are several very similar titles and no clear early source I have adopted the same nomenclature as Cole to avoid adding to the confusion.

Notes on individual pieces provide supporting evidence for their dating and the circumstances of their making. It has not proved possible to locate or follow the provenance of all the bronze casts through the sale rooms; those listed are in public collections or well documented in private collections. Isolated auction references are not included.

Gaudier's drawings are so numerous and widely dispersed that it has not proved possible to include lists of related drawings; some related drawings are discussed and illustrated in the text but a catalogue raisonné of Gaudier's drawings remains to be compiled.[24]

THE CATALOGUE

All measurements are given in centimetres, with inches in brackets.

1908

1 **Medallion of Minerva (pl. 1)**

Plaster, oval, 10 × 8 (4 × 3¼), signed and dated 'Gaudier 1908', Gaudier family; Orléans, Musée des Beaux-Arts, 1956
Exhibited: Orléans, 1993, 1
Literature: Cole (1978), p. 48, illustrated

1910

Heads

Brzeska's *Journal* (Orléans, Musée des Beaux-Arts) describes her first visit to Gaudier's rooms in May–June; there she saw modelled heads and had her own portrait modelled.

October–November

2 **Portrait of Monsieur Gaudier (pl. 4)**

Painted clay, 27.3 × 21.9 × 24.1 (10¾ × 8½ × 9½)
G. Gaudier; Orléans, Musée des Beaux-Arts, 1922
Exhibited: Orléans, 1956, 1, there dated 1908
Literature: Cole (1978), no. 1, p. 48

Mentioned in Gaudier's *List of Works* and almost certainly modelled, as Cole suggests, during his stay at St Jean de Braye during autumn 1910.

3 **So-called Portrait of Madame Gaudier (pl. 2)**

Clay mask, 80 × 60 × 60 (31½ × 23½ × 23½), Mme Baillet; M. Petit, 1960; private collection
Literature: S. Fauchereau, 'Gaudier-Brzeska, la caricature, les futurismes', *alfabeta*, 84, 1986, pp. 56–57

This recently discovered terracotta head, which originally belonged to Gaudier's sister and has remained in St Jean de Braye, has been identified as a portrait of the artist's mother largely on the oral testimony of an aged local inhabitant to the present owner, describing her as 'a small, wrinkled, shrewish woman who always wore a sort of bonnet' (author's translation of letter from present owner, 19.3.93). Sophie Brzeska's still less flattering description of her on the only occasion when she and one of Gaudier's sisters visited her cottage at Combleux, is similar: 'La mère, mince, rouge de figure dans un affreux bonnet gris comme celui des novices dans les couvents qui donne l'air d'un chauve-souris à la femme' ('The mother, thin, with a red face and a dreadful grey bonnet like the ones worn by novices in convents, which makes the woman look like a bat').

However, the same passage in *Matka* (Orléans) also describes the modelling of a portrait of a local woman whose description matches this piece: 'une femme âgée d'un type fort en bonnet blanc – assise devant Ailé [i.e. Gaudier] qui la modèle en terre' ('an old woman of the strong type in a white bonnet – sitting in front of Ailé who is modelling her in clay', Orléans, MBA 93–2–1, section 136). No name is given to this sitter who could conceivably have been *Mère Rouzeau* (*cat.* 5) whose portrait is included in the *List of Works* while no portrait of Madame Gaudier is mentioned.

4 **Portrait 'Chican' mask**

Plaster, 1½ lifesize, given to Chican, Combleux (Loiret); location unknown.
Literature: Cole (1978), no. 018, p. 127

Chican – literally the quibbler or 'artful dodger', for the word relates to our chicanery – was presumably a caricature as the description in Gaudier's *List of Works* implies: 'moulage sur glaise modellée d'après nature, style naturel, caractère très exagéré' ('cast of work in clay modelled from life, natural style, very exaggerated character').

5 **Portrait Mère Rouzeau, mask**

Plaster, lifesize, given to M. Rouzeau, Combleux (Loiret), 1910
Literature: Cole (1978), no. 019, p. 127, mistakenly dates it to 1914.

Mentioned in Gaudier's *List of Works*. See also *cat.* 3.

6 **Self-Portrait**

Clay, lifesize, probably destroyed
Literature: Ede, *Life*, pp. 192–93; Cole (1978), no. 01, p. 125

Described in the *List of Works* as having been given to an Italian woodcarver in Paris. It was in August 1910 that Gaudier wrote to Kitty Smith that he was carving a picture frame to train himself in carving technique; the gift could well have been in exchange for advice or equipment.

1911

7 **Portrait Mask of Sophie Brzeska**

Terracotta, lifesize, probably destroyed (see *cat.* 8 below)
Literature: Ede, *Life*, p. 192; Cole (1978), no. 2, p. 49

This piece was described as, 'terre sèche, grandeur nature, proprietaise Gaudier-Brzeska conservé souvenir' in Gaudier's *List of Works*. In *Matka* (CUL), fol. 14a, Brzeska describes Lovat Fraser's admiration for this mask, made a year earlier, on his first visit to the studio in spring 1912. On 17 November 1912, Gaudier wrote to Brzeska 'I have hung my beloved's mask above my bed, and the shadow it makes on the wall is so utterly like my Sisik's that I am constantly startled, thinking it is she. Kisses, sweet dear, I hold you to me in love and tenderness.' (Ede, *SM*, p. 199)

Cole's identification of the *Terracotta Mask* (*cat.* 8) as Sophie Brzeska is open to question. Even allowing for its heavily abraded state it is so remarkably unlike the pastels and drawings of the sharp-featured Brzeska and the technique is so crude that it seems an unlikely candidate for Fraser's admiration. Gaudier made several modelled portraits of Sophie, most of which do not seem to have got beyond the clay; there are references to a head modelled in his room in Paris soon after they met and several efforts at her portrait made during the autumn of 1912.

8 **Terracotta Mask (pl. 3)**

Terracotta, 25.4 × 20.3 (10 × 8), Cambridge, Kettle's Yard
Literature: Ede, *Life*, pl. LXII; Cole (1978), no. 2, p. 49

This mask was discovered and identified as a portrait of Sophie Brzeska by Cole on the basis of a 1914 photograph of Gaudier in his studio where it can be seen, hanging on the wall behind him (fig. 111). The identity of the portrait is doubtful. Its simplified, archaizing features relate most closely to the masks on the two *Garden Ornaments* (*cat.* 99, 100), begun but never completed in August 1914. It is also worth noting that the *Pot à fleurs* (*cat.* 13) modelled for Macfarlane Cocks the following year was in terracotta with four heads on the sides. The present condition of the work makes a definitive judgment impossible.

1912

February

9 **The Madonna of 'The Miracle' (pl. 14)**

Painted plaster 53.3 × 34.3 × 40.5 (21 × 13½ × 16), T. Leman Hare; H. S. Ede; Cambridge, Kettle's Yard
Unpainted plaster, *Memorial Exhibition*, 1918; location unknown, probably destroyed
9 bronzes cast 1960s from painted plaster, 54 × 34 × 40 (21¼ × 13¼ × 15¾)
3 casts remain at Kettle's Yard
Paris, Musée des Beaux-Arts, 1992
Exhibited: London, *AAA*, July 1913, 1214; Bristol, Royal West of England Academy, October 1913 to January 1914, 786 as *The Miracle*; *Memorial Exhibition*, 1918, 25 as *The Madonna of 'The Miracle'* (painted plaster, lent by L. Hare)
Literature: Pound claims Gaudier was promised £100 for the piece (*Memoir*, p. 43); Ede, *Life*, p. 194, as *Madonne*; Brodzky, illustrated opposite p. 50; Cole (1978), no. 3, p. 50

A statuette of Maria Carmi as the Madonna in Max Rheinhardt's production, 'The Miracle' was commissioned by Leman Hare on 10 February 1912. He bought the plaster for £5. Brzeska's *Matka* (CUL), fol. 15d, records Mrs Leman Hare arriving at the studio to offer the commission and to urge Gaudier and Brzeska to accompany them to the last performance which was to take place that very night: 'There is a large number of people who admire Maria Carmi as much as we do. So my husband had the idea to ask Lord Northcliffe and a few other gentlemen whether they might not like to contribute to having a bust made of this divine *Madonna*. Lord Northcliffe was enchanted with the idea . . . We are going to have a copy cast in bronze to offer to Madame Carmi and then fifty or so in plaster which will sell easily'. Gaudier's account to Haldane Macfall (12.2.12, National Art Library) was cooler and less fantastical: 'Mrs Hare came down to Paulton Square [sic] while we were packing things up and all dusty, telling us that Mr Hare wanted me to make a statuette of Maria Carmi as the Madonna at Olympia – off we went as tired as could be, made about sixty sketches of the subject, came back home, having had a discussion at Pembroke Road, at 1 o'clock yesterday, and spent the whole morning putting up the clay for the thing.' He intended to complete it the following evening. He goes on, 'Mr Hare gave me a very good idea: he suggested that I should indicate on the plaster cast the different colours: gold, red and blue – and this I will do.' On 26 February Gaudier told Macfall that the mould was complete and he was about to cast it. The scheme for an edition in bronze went no further though Lord Northcliffe gave Gaudier £5 as a gift.

In 1916 both casts seem to have been with the Hares though their ownership was unclear; Brzeska claimed the Hares had paid only £2 or £4 for the casting of the second plaster by Parlanti and that both casts were hers though she proposed to give the painted plaster to the Hares and to share the proceeds of the sale of the 'white Madonna' with them; Mr Hare stated that Gaudier had given the painted Madonna to Mrs Hare and that he had paid £11 for the second in three instalments (correspondence from Sophie Brzeska to Mr and Mrs Hare, 20.6.16, 5.7.16 and 23.7.16 and Mr Hare to Sophie Brzeska, 3.7.16, Q. Keynes).

The work is reproduced from an archive photograph by Walter Benington (pl. 14). In its present condition, colour and brushstroke are indistinguishable.

10 Small Mask of Maria Carmi

Painted plaster, Mrs G. Lovat Fraser (1930)
Literature: Cole (1978), no. 05, (p. 125)

Not mentioned in the *List of Works* but in Ede's *Supplement*. According to Cole, it is mentioned in 1912 correspondence as having been given to Lovat Fraser.

March–April 1912

11 Haldane Macfall (pl. 5)

Plaster, 109 × 18 × 51 (43 × 7 × 20), H. Macfall; probably destroyed
Exhibited: London, *AAA*, 1913, 1215; *Memorial Exhibition*, 1918, 64
Literature: *Matka* (CUL), fols. 21, 22, 25; Brodzky, pp. 37–38, illustrated opposite p. 96; Cole (1978), no. 6, p. 53

Mentioned in the *List of Works* and sold to Macfall for £2 10s, the price of casting in plaster.

March–April 1912

12 Major Smythies (pl. 7)

Plaster, 44.4 × 22.8 × 23.4 (17½ × 9 × 9¼), inscribed 'H Gaudier Brzeska' S. Brzeska Estate; F. Stoop, 1930; Contemporary Art Society; London, Tate Gallery
1 bronze cast commissioned by Smythies from Gaudier for £12, 1912. 5 numbered bronzes cast by Morris Singer Foundry on behalf of CAS, 1971. brown patination, 44.5 × 23 × 23.5 (17½ × 9 × 9¼), stamped 1971 MORRIS/SINGER FOUNDERS/LONDON
1. Major Raymond-Smythies; Manchester City Art Gallery, 1922
2. London, Tate Gallery
3. Southampton City Art Gallery, 1972
4. Birmingham Museums and Art Gallery, 1973
unnumbered, Cambridge, Kettle's Yard
Exhibited: *Memorial Exhibition*, 1918, 97 (plaster) as *Head of a Military Officer*
Literature: *Matka* (CUL), fols. 14d, 26a, Brodzky, pp. 76–78, illustrated opposite p. 62; Levy, p. 29, pl. 71; Cole (1978), no. 5, p. 52; Cole (1995), 95, p. 28

Major R. H. Raymond Smythies was fifty-two years old and had been retired from the Army (Prince of Wales Volunteers) for ten years when he sat for his portrait at Gaudier's suggestion. Smythies was sufficiently pleased with it to pay for its casting in bronze ('Sold to Major Smythies for the cost of casting: bronze £12.0.0. plaster £1.10.0', *List of Works*). On 24.4.12 Gaudier wrote to tell him, 'I have retouched the head so that the little that had been spoilt by the wet cloth has come back again . . . I have asked [the foundry] for a light green and blue patina of old Pompejan bronze, which, I believe, is what you prefer' (Manchester City Art Gallery). The patina has aged to a dark green close to black. During the Memorial Exhibition it was exhibited as *Head of a Military Officer* at Major Smythies' request.

13 Pot à fleurs

Terracotta, flanked by four heads in bas-relief, *c.* 91.4 × 83.8 × 61 (36 × 33 × 24), sold for five guineas to R. Macfarlane Cocks; broken 1919.
See *cat.* 15.

14 Two demi-statuettes

Terracotta, 25.4 × 10.2 × 7.6 (10 × 4 × 3), sold for one guinea to R. M. Cocks.
See *cat.* 15.

15 Platter

Terracotta 'tête bas relief au fond', 91 × 68.6 (36 × 27), sold for one guinea to R. M. Cocks.
Literature: Ede, *Life*, pp. 192–93; Brodzky, pp. 169–74; Cole (1978), nos. 031–033, p. 129

Macfall, writing to Brodzky (2.10.19, National Art Library), recalled that Macfarlane Cocks gave Gaudier a cheque for £30 for several small things in case he could not find a market elsewhere. 'Poor Henri in a sad moment sent him two or three things which it is too sad to think had ever come from his hands.' Two had been smashed and 'Cocks now only has the one he likes – the flower bowl which Macfall recalls as 'three females surrounding a bowl-shaped hollow'. On 21.10.19 (National Art Library) he reported that the *Flower Bowl* had been broken in a house move. In *Matka* (CUL), fol. 32c, there is a reference to a vase with masks made for Mr Fox (i.e., Cocks).

April–May 1912

16 Maternity (La mendiante, pl. 15)

Plaster, *c.* 46 (18), T. Leman Hare, 1912; location unknown
Exhibited: *Memorial Exhibition*, 1918, 1 as *La mendiante*
Literature: Cole (1978), no. 02, p. 125 *Maternity*, dated to 1913

Described in Gaudier's *List of Works* as 'Maternité statuette plâtre 1½' Lant à peu près £3 T Leman Hare. 35 Pembroke Road Kensington' and identified as a work of 1912. This piece and its purchase in 1912 are described in the Brzeska's *Matka* (CUL, fol. 6 numeration following fol. 16). The Hares examined the piece in clay during a visit to the studio but asked why the figure did not have eyes; Gaudier, playing up to them, took a ball of clay and pretended to make eyes both for the mother and for the child she holds in her arms, while actually leaving the work unaltered; the Hares purchased the work for £2, Gaudier commenting after their departure that casting in plaster would cost a little more than £1, leaving 15 shillings for him to buy more clay.

May 1912

17 Enid Bagnold (pl. 10)

Plaster, incised 'Henri Gaudier Brzeska 1912' on back of collar, 47 × 27 × 32 (18½ × 10½ × 12½), E. Bagnold (Lady Jones); Viscountess Astor
1 bronze cast (April 1930), 46 (18), Lady Jones; Viscountess Astor
Exhibited: *Memorial Exhibition*, 1918, 76 (plaster); London, J. and E. Bumpus, *Henri Gaudier-Brzeska*, 1931, 37 (bronze)
Literature: Cole (1978), p. 21, illustrated but not included in catalogue. E. Bagnold *Enid Bagnold's Autobiography*, 1969, pp. 65–70; A. Sebba, *Enid Bagnold, A Biography*, 1986, pp. 32–35

In March 1912 Gaudier wrote to Bagnold 'to know whether you could sit now for the portrait head I promised to give you' (Sebba, p. 33). In a letter to Macfall (10.5.12, National Art Library) Gaudier wrote, 'I have just finished a vase and am portraying Miss Bagnold next Sunday 12th inst.' At the end of May Bagnold wrote to her mother, 'Gaudier has done a *wonderful* head. Very big, rather over life size in clay, with hair and combs and neck and a bit of collar. It's simply extraordinary, exactly like' (Sebba, p. 33). Ewart Wheeler helped Gaudier take the clay head on a handcart to Lovat Fraser's studio on 23 November 1912. On 30 November Gaudier related to Sophie, 'Yesterday evening I met Enid Bagnold in the King's Road; she asked me to do a plaster cast of her head, and I told her it would cost £3, so I shall make 35s. on her, which will do for casting a statue, which I will begin tomorrow – I have sent Parlanti to get the model from Fraser.' (Ede, *SM*, p. 21)

In 1930 Enid Bagnold, by then Lady Jones, was living in Hyde Park Gate where Jacob Epstein was a neighbour. In April, 1930, he arranged for the bust to be cast for her, probably by Parlanti, at a cost of £17.

June–July

18 Firebird (The Russian Ballet, pls. 11, 12)

2 plaster casts from original clay (1 extant), signed 'Gaudier Brzeska' on base
1. T. Leman Hare; location unknown
2. O. R. Drey; location unknown
1 bronze cast by Parlanti, 1912: J. Lousada 1912; destroyed by bombing. 10 bronze casts subsequently cast, 61 × 33 × 27 (24 × 13 × 10½)
1. Washington, Hirshhorn Museum; purchased by J. Hirshhorn by 1977
2. Lord Harewood
Exhibited: London, *AAA*, 1913, 1212; London, Whitechapel Art Gallery, *Twentieth Century Art*, 1914, 179; *Memorial Exhibition*, 1918, 2 as *The Russian Ballet*
Literature: Ede, *SM*, pp. 156–57; Brodzky, illustrated opposite p. 36; Levy, p. 17, 29, pl. 73; Cole (1978), no. 14, p. 61

Julian Lousada commissioned this group showing Adolph Bolm and Tamara Karsavina in the Ballet Russe production of Stravinsky's *The Firebird*, which was performed in London for the first time during the Ballet Russe season from 12 June–1 August, 1912. The sculpture depicts the moment when Ivan Tsarevitch captures the Firebird. Lousada received a plaster and paid £20 for one bronze cast, the highest price paid for any of his works in his lifetime. Gaudier wrote to Sophie, 'I saw the bronze group at Parlanti's on Saturday, and I agree it's a scandal that such a beautiful little group should be flung away for a profit of £7 – still it is better than nothing' (14.10.12). On 14 November he wrote again to Sophie, 'The Lousadas want to change the colour of the group to light green. It has now the marvellous patine of old bronze. I have written to Parlanti to make it green like the leaves of a cabbage.' Another plaster was painted and exhibited, together with Nijinsky drawings, in Dan Rider's Bookshop in November 1912, and was later sold to Leman Hare for £6. Gaudier's *List of Works* states that another plaster went to O. R. Drey.

19 Head of a Man (Portrait of Ezra Pound, so-called, pl. 18)

Marble, 12.7 × 9.5 (5 × 3¾)
H. S. Ede; private collection
Literature: Cole (1978), no. 24, p. 73

Not mentioned by Ede, *Life*, or in *List of Works*. The head bears no resemblance to Pound though there are similarities with some of the heads sketched in his library and street drawings. Comparison of the modelling and style of the eyes, together with the limited technique, suggests an early date.

June–August

20 Religious Head (pl. 16)

Marble, 12.7 × 5.7 (5 × 2¼), inscribed on reverse
Z M
v
P K
S. Brzeska Estate; H. S. Ede; Cambridge, Kettle's Yard; stolen 1977
12 numbered bronze casts by John Mills 1965 (correspondence, Kettle's Yard) but correspondence with Sydney and Hirshhorn Museum, Washington, from Ede, states edition of 9 taken in 1965. Casts have Roman numeral on reverse.
1. Cambridge, Kettle's Yard; stolen 1988
2. Tate Gallery
6. Sydney, Art Gallery of New South Wales, 1968
Unnumbered, Paris, Musée National d'Art Moderne, 1966
Literature: Ede, *Life*, p. 205; Cole (1978), no. 23, p. 72

Not included in the *List of Works* but in Ede's *Supplement* as *Deity*, alabaster, and dated to 1914.

The inscription on the reverse refers to the short-lived but intense friendship of Gaudier (P[ik]) and Sophie (Z[osienka]) with Middleton Murry (M) and Katherine Mansfield (K) which began in June–July and was over in early September 1912 when Gaudier's drawings were published in the September issue of *Rhythm*.

June–August

21 Middleton Murry

Clay (destroyed)
Literature: Ede, *Life*, p. 204 as *Bust of Middleton Murry*; Brodzky, pp. 42, 45–49; J. M. Murry, *Between Two Worlds*, 1935, pp. 224–25; Cole (1978), p. 22

A head of the writer and editor of *Rhythm* was modelled during the brief but intense friendship of Gaudier and Brzeska with Murry and Katherine Mansfield during the summer of 1912. Murry recalled the head as 'something strongly like and strangely unlike me – strangely unlike in the sense that it became massive, heroic, hieratic, the head of a sort of brooding demiurge', a description strangely evocative of the later *Head of Ezra Pound* (*cat.* 79). It was left in the studio and pelted to destruction with bricks by the artist, Sophie Brzeska and Horace Brodzky in 1913.

22 Head of a Child (pl. 19)

Limestone with traces of pigment, 9.8 × 7.9 × 9.8 (3¾ × 3 × 3¾)
H. S. Ede; the Cardiff Gallery; Cardiff, National Museum of Wales
Exhibited: *Memorial Exhibition*, 1918, 15 Carving of a head in stone; Cambridge, 1983, 16
Literature: Cole (1978), no. 7, p. 54

There is no documentary evidence to help date this carving; it appears to reflect the study of ancient Near or Far Eastern sculpture. Cole and Lewison both date it to 1912 after Gaudier met Epstein.

October

23 Monkey (pl. 20)

Plaster, 21.5 (8½), apparently signed 'H. Gaudier', probably destroyed.
2 bronze casts were made before 1930.
1. H. Macfall (1918)
2. F. C. Johnson (1943)
Exhibited: London, Zwemmer Gallery, *Drawings and Sculpture by Some Contemporary Sculptors*, 1930, 45

Monkey (no medium given); Leeds, 1943, 60 *Baboon* (bronze, lent by F. C. Johnson)
Literature: Ede, *Life*, p. 204, listing plaster and 2 bronzes; Ede, *SM*, p. 173; Brodzky, illustrated opposite p. 67; Cole (1978), no. 025, p. 128

In a letter to Sophie Brzeska, Gaudier writes, 'Since you left [early October] I have done . . . a little statue of a monkey, one of a lynx, one of a puma . . .' (28.10.12) There may be a reference to one of these animals in a letter to Lovat Fraser in March 1913: 'I have had one of those animals cast in plaster when you come you see whether you like it' (7.3.13, private collection).

24 Lynx

Clay, destroyed
See *Monkey* (*cat.* 23)
Related drawing: Lynx, pencil, 19.2 × 25.7 ($7\frac{1}{2}$ × 10), inscribed 'C'est ce lynx que je viens de faire en terre' ('This is the lynx which I have just made in clay')
Exhibited: Orléans, 1957, 21

25 Puma

Clay, destroyed
See *Monkey* (*cat.* 23) and *Cheetah* (*cat.* 26).

26 Cheetah (Jungle Cat, pl. 13)

Painted plaster, C. L. Fraser; Leicester Galleries; location unknown.
Mentioned in Gaudier's *List of Works* as 'Animal (cheetah) plâtre peint, 18″ long, 6″ haut, 2″ epais £2'.
Exhibited: *Memorial Exhibition*, 1918, 19 (A. Serval)
Literature: Ede, *Life*, p. 114, pl. XXI; Brodzky, illustrated opposite p. 78; Cole (1978), no. 07, p. 126, illustrated

In a letter to Brzeska on 16 October 1912, Gaudier writes, 'I've done a little jungle cat that I like, and I am going to do another at once'. There are two related watercolours (fig. 72). See also *Monkey* (*cat.* 23).

October

27 Two Women Running.

Clay, destroyed
Literature: Ede, *Life*, pp. 120–21, pl. XXIII

In a letter to Sophie Brzeska 28.10.12, Gaudier described how on the previous Sunday afternoon 'I half-finished the plaster group: two women running. Now that it is finished it seems to me like an allegory – the Spirit of Liberty drawing women towards a nobler life.' A small group with two clothed, running figures appears on the modelling stand in a humorous drawing of the studio which accompanied the letter. He mentions it again the following week: 'I stuck at the little group which I told you about, and finished it this morning, after having changed it for the better by broadening the planes.' (3.11.12)

28 Gorilla (pl. 27)

Plaster, 38.1 × 50.8 (15 × 20), H. Macfall, 1918; Zwemmer Gallery (before 1930); M. Levy and A. d'Offay; Anthony d'Offay
A single bronze cast was taken by Anton Zwemmer in 1938 from a plaster thought to have then been destroyed but subsequently found broken at Zwemmer's. A numbered edition of 7 was taken before 1973 by Morris Singer Foundry. Cole states that there are 11 bronze casts in all.
1939 cast, private collection, USA. (Levy, 1965)
1. Lord Harewood
Exhibited: London, *Memorial Exhibition*, 1918, 33; London, Zwemmer Gallery, *Drawings and Sculpture by Some Contemporary Sculptors*, 1930, 47 *Chimpanzee* (plaster cast); London, Zwemmer Gallery, *Christmas Exhibition*, 1938–39, 1 *Gorilla* (bronze); Leeds, Temple Newsam, *Roy de Maistre, Henri Gaudier-Brzeska*, 1943, 58 (bronze), where it is stated that this was the unique cast.
Literature: Brodzky, plaster illustrated opposite p. 117; Levy, no. 69, p. 29; Cole (1978), no. 16, p. 63

Not included in the *List of Works* but in Ede's Supplement as a work of 1912. The formal daring of the cut-off, semi-relief format, the monumentality of the work and its exaggerated expression all suggest a date after *Monkey* (*cat.* 23) and *Lynx* (*cat.* 24).

29 Workman Fallen from a Scaffold (pls. 22–24)

Clay, 29.2 × 38.1 ($11\frac{1}{2}$ × 15), H. S. Ede; Orléans, Musée des Beaux-Arts, 1956
Plaster, E. Wheeler; Leicester Galleries, location unknown.
1 or 2 bronze casts *c.* 1918, 29.5 × 38.8 × 35.9 ($11\frac{1}{2}$ × $15\frac{1}{4}$ × $14\frac{1}{4}$)
1. A. E. Anderson; London, Victoria and Albert Museum, 1921; transferred to Tate Gallery T03727
2. ?E. Wheeler; location unknown
Exhibited: *Memorial Exhibition*, 1918, 16 (lent by Flt Sgt Wheeler, no medium given); Leeds, 1943, 57 (clay); Cardiff, 1953, 3 (plaster); Orléans, 1956, 7 (plaster); Orléans, 1993, 4 (clay)
Literature: Ede, *Life*, pp. 141, 204; Brodzky, pp.

123–24, illustrated opposite p. 79; Cole (1978), no. 17, p. 64

Brodzky states that the subject was inspired by an incident Gaudier had seen in Paris and that originally 'this figure had both arms complete, and depicted the man in the act of rising from the ground in agony.' This appears to be supported by a very slight sketch in Orléans (MO 453 verso). The records for this piece are confused and contradictory; Ede's Supplement to the *List of Works* records three versions, the original clay broken and in Ede's own possession, a plaster owned by Wheeler, and the bronze given to the Victoria and Albert Museum. However, according to Brodzky the original clay was given to Wheeler and the arms were broken off while it was in his possession and before 1918. A reference by Gaudier to Wheeler buying 'a tiny statue for himself for £2' (Gaudier to Brzeska, 24.11.12) may refer to this piece.

The archive photographs taken by Benington (pls. 22, 23) indicate that a plaster was exhibited at the *Memorial Exhibition*. The clay original was in Ede's possession in 1943 when he lent it to the Leeds exhibition and annotated Philip Hendy's draft exhibition catalogue, stating that a bronze had been given to Wheeler. This might indicate that Wheeler had had a bronze cast from his plaster or might indicate a confusion with the bronze owned by Anderson and given to the Victoria and Albert Museum in 1921. Ede lent a 'plaster' to both Cardiff and Orléans but this almost certainly refers to the clay which Ede then presented to Orléans; there it was assumed to be a plaster until conservation was undertaken in 1984. At that time the material was found to be unfired clay, its surface obscured by a thick layer of paint which also concealed numerous old breaks and damage, some of which had been made good with plaster.

A date in the latter part of 1912 appears plausible given the freedom and Rodinesque vigour of the modelling.

30 Head of an Idiot/Head of a Jew (Self-Portrait, pls. 25, 26, III)

Plaster, 18.1 × 14 × 16.5 (7 × 5½ × 6½)
L. Fraser; A. Fraser; Zwemmer Gallery; A. Zwemmer; London, Victoria and Albert Museum, 1951; transferred to Tate Gallery
Edition of 7 bronzes cast for Anton Zwemmer in 1939.
1. Zwemmer Gallery; A. Conger Goodyear; Albright-Knox Art Gallery, Buffalo, NY
2. Mercury Gallery; Scottish National Gallery of Modern Art, 1977
3. Lady Tredegar; A. Thompson; Leicestershire Museums, Arts and Records, 1953
4. Art Gallery of Auckland, New Zealand
Exhibited: *Memorial Exhibition*, 1918, 21 (plaster, lent by A. Fraser); London, Zwemmer Gallery, *Drawings and Sculpture by Some Contemporary Sculptors*, 1930, 44 no medium; Leeds, 1943, 59 (bronze)
Literature: Ede, *Life*, p. 205; Brodzky, illustrated opposite p. 66; J. Cournos, *Autobiography*, New York, 1935, p. 257; Levy, p. 29, pl. 75; Cole (1978), no. 18, p. 65

Exhibited under the title *Head of a Jew* at Dan Rider's Bookshop and in Lovat Fraser's studio, where it was admired by John Cournos who asked whose work it was. He describes it as 'a tiny sculptured head of an idiot boy'. Levy affirms that Brodzky identified it as a satirical self-portrait.

December 1912

31 Ornamental Mask (pl. 28)

Painted and gilded plaster, 76.2 × 68.6 (30 × 27), C. L. Fraser; Baroness d'Erlanger; H. S. Ede; D. Hughes; Dr O. Ghez; Geneva, Musée du Petit Palais
7 bronze casts (6 numbered and 1 *hors du commerce*) by Fiorini, 1969–70. 70 × 68 × 21 (27½ × 26¾ × 8¼), green patination
4. Belfast, Ulster Museum
5. D. Hughes; Orléans, Musée des Beaux-Arts, 1971
Unnumbered Cambridge, Kettle's Yard
Exhibited: *Memorial Exhibition*, 1918, 45
Literature: H. Macfall, *The Book of Lovat*, 1923, p. 53; Ede, *Life*, pp. 90, 194–95; Brodzky, p. 40, illustrated opposite p. 124; Cole (1978), no. 4, p. 51; Belfast, Ulster Museum, *Catalogue of Twentieth-Century Sculpture*, 1988, pp. 31–33; Mercury Gallery, *Henri Gaudier-Brzeska*, 1995, 12

Commissioned by artist and theatre designer Claud Lovat Fraser (1890–1921) who paid £5 for its casting in plaster by Parlanti. Two letters from Gaudier to Lovat Fraser (16.12.12 and 7.1.13 enclosing Parlanti's invoice of 6.1.13, private collection) confirm that the plaster was collected by Parlanti on 17 December. Gaudier proposed to go to Fraser's studio the Saturday after it was delivered to paint it. It hung in Lovat's studio until his death. Brodzky relates that Gaudier used the paint which remained after the completion of the *Ornamental Mask* 'to decorate Fraser's studio, painting the staircase and other woodwork in primitive colours.' The gilding has gone but some of the original pigment – blue, red and brown – survives.

December 1912–February 1913

32 **Wrestler (Football Player, pls. 37, 38, VIII)**

Plaster, signed on top of base 'Gaudier-Brzeska 1912'
S. Brzeska Estate: H. S. Ede; Mrs Burra; destroyed 1959, except for damaged head, 11.8 ($4^5/_8$),
Cambridge, Kettle's Yard, 1971
One bronze cast was made in 1918; location unknown.
Two lead casts commissioned by Ede predate 1930.
3 bronzes cast *c.* 1945 for Mrs Burra, stamped on base 'Nicholas, Ben, Toke' Lead, 60 × 35.1 × 35.7 ($23^1/_2$ × $13^3/_4$ × 14)
1. H. S. Ede; Leeds City Art Gallery, 1943
2. H. S. Ede; W. Staite Murray; F. L. S. Murray; H. Diamond; J. H. Hirshhorn; Hirshhorn Museum of Art
Bronzes:
1. N. Burra; Cardiff, National Museum of Wales, 1972
2. Mrs R. Burra; B. Burra; Bristol City Art Gallery, 1984
3. T. Burra
Exhibited: London, *AAA*, 1913, 1213; *Memorial Exhibition*, 1918, 61 *Football Player* bronze
Literature: Ede, *Life*, pp. 141, 144–46, 196; Brodzky, illustrated opposite p. 32; Cole (1978), no. 18 and 09, pp. 66–67, 126; Cole (1995), pp. 63, 165

In November 1912 Gaudier met Charles Wheeler (brother of the actor Ewart Wheeler), an engineer with manufacturing contacts in Birmingham, who proposed to recommend Gaudier to design motor mascots and electric radiator ornaments. 'On top of this he is very much interested in sport, and has commissioned me to make two little statues in plaster – one of a wrestler and the other of a bather – which he will have cast in bronze by one of his firms. In his office he has the very wrestler I liked so much – a wonderful boy, strong, taut and finely square. I am going to see wrestling in the evenings two or three times, which will give me good sketches' (Gaudier to Brzeska, 28.11.12). On 2 December he saw the wrestling for the first time. Meeting Sophie off the train from the Midlands in mid-February 1913, Gaudier announced that *Le Lutteur* was just finished and ready for casting in plaster (*Matka* [CUL], fol. 67). Only the wrestler seems to have been made.

Included in Gaudier's *List of Works* as '*Lutteur*, plâtre, 2¼' haut'. However, when deposited by Brzeska at the Victoria and Albert Museum it appears to have been called *Football Player* (V & A record 2.6.16), under which title it was exhibited in 1918. This seems to have led Cole to assume the existence of a separate sculpture of a football player (no. 09, p. 126). However, a receipt from the Museum (19.4.23) includes the description '*Football player or wrestler*' and it was as *Wrestler* that the plaster was listed in Wilenski's appraisal of the Brzeska Estate.

1913

33 **Crouching Male Figure**

Stone, gilded, probably relief, location unknown
Exhibited: London, Grosvenor Gallery, *International Society of Sculptors, Painters and Engravers*, 1913, 8 *The Golden Figure* (gilded plaster)
Literature: Brodzky, p. 41

Not included in the *List of Works* or in Ede's Supplementary List. According to Brodzky, it was a carving of a 'crouching male figure' which he did not reclaim after the exhibition both because he had not paid his hanging fee and because 'the work had never pleased him, and he had gilded it to conceal an important break.' It may conceivably be identical with 40 but Brodzky, who compiled most of his book in 1919, only shortly after the *Memorial Exhibition*, did not identify it as 40 which was shown there. Brodzky was unaware of its whereabouts, though he knew it had been rescued and eventually sold to a woman and that a squabble about payment with the sculptor had ensued.

The dating of this and the following works in Spring 1913 is based not only on their technical and stylistic similarities, but also on Gaudier's letter to Lovat Fraser in March that year when he described carving 'as many reliefs as I can'.

34 **Boy, relief (pl. 34)**

Seravezza marble, location unknown
Exhibited: London, *Memorial Exhibition*, 1918, 9 (lent by Miss/Mrs Kinnear)
Literature: Ede, *Life,* pp. 194–95; Cole (1978), no. 06, illustrated

Described in Gaudier's *List of Works* as 'Garçon bas-relief Marbre Seravezza circa 1½' haut ⅞" large £5.5.0 M. Kinnear old cow Regents Park'. Gaudier appears to have sent a 'white marble relief' which could be this work or *Love Scene* (*cat.* 73) with *Singer* (*cat.* 51) on consignment to the Chenil Gallery, probably in early 1914 (*Matka* [CUL], fol. 148b).

35 **Amour (pl. 31)**

Alabaster, gilded ground now much darkened, plinth originally incised 'AMOUR' but inscription obliterated

before 1985, 46.3 × 13 × 9 (18¼ × 5 × 3½).
A. Kohnstamm; family descent; Christie's 7/8.11.85 (183) illustrated; Tate Gallery
Exhibited: *Memorial Exhibition*, 1918, 34 *High-relief* (lent by A. Kohnstamm); ACGB, *Henri Gaudier-Brzeska*, 1956, 14 (lent by Mrs E. Kohnstamm)
Literature: Pound, p. 130, no. 34 'Boy in alabaster, high relief against gilt background, early'; Ede, *Life*, p. 194; Brodzky, illustrated showing original inscription, opposite p. 97; Cole (1978), no. 029, p. 128

Described in the *List of Works* as 'Amour bas relief garçon alabâtre taille directe circa 1′ haut 3″ ou 4″ large £6. Al Kohnstamm, Hampstead. demi poli, fond doré'. The Kohnstamm brothers, leather manufacturers, were important early patrons of Alfred Wolmark and Jacob Epstein. A passage in *Matka* (CUL), fol. 82b, written in January 1914 but referring to events dated (fol. 86b) June 1913, describes the artist George Banks's admiration for 'mon gars en alabâtre' which may be this piece or the Dartington *Boy* (*cat.* 61).

Both this piece and *cat.* 36 were developed from life drawings made at evening class in late 1912 (pls. 29, 30, 32).

36 Weeping Woman (pl. 33)

Alabaster, *c.* 30.5 × 8–10 (12 × 3–4), J. Cournos; Mrs H. Payne Whitney; location unknown
Exhibited: *Memorial Exhibition*, 1918, ? 99 *Bas-relief: Nude* (stone) 1912
Literature: Pound, p. 130, no. 31 (Chubby figure with bowed head, alabaster, early, unimportant); C. W. Beaumont and M. T. H. Sadler (eds), *New Paths. Verse. Prose. Pictures. 1917–18*, 1918, illustrated; Ede, *Life*, pp. 194–95; J. Cournos, *An Autobiography*, London, 1935, p. 258; Cole (1978), no. 03, pp. 30, 125; J. Lewison, 'Gaudier-Brzeska's "Weeping Woman"', *Burlington Magazine*, CXXIX, 1987, pp. 243–44

Included in *List of Works* as 'Femme pleurante, bas-relief'. Cournos recalled that Gaudier had told him, 'The size and shape of the alabaster were responsible for making her a sentimental woman weeping.' A reference in *Matka* (CUL), fol. 88a, datable to about June–July 1913, refers to Cournos choosing this piece as a gift instead of another 'statuette' offered to him by Gaudier.

37 Standing Woman

Clay, lifesize, destroyed by sculptor
Literature: Brodzky, pp. 79–80

'Once at his Fulham studio he modelled a lifesize female nude . . . the very opposite of his usual slim Greek-like figures. It was more chubby and not unlike the thick-set figures of Maillol. Technically he had adopted a method that one might call Impressionist – built up by independent or detached small additions of clay, and with no attempt whatever at blending or graduating the touches. The surface was in no way suave. This figure remained for a long time in clay, standing on its dais . . . He was not pleased with it, and I am sure it was done as an exercise or to fill in time. Certainly he never expected to find the money to have it cast in plaster, still less in bronze. He had lost interest in it. And then he suddenly decided to destroy it.'

38 Man and Woman (pl. 35)

Alabaster relief, remnants of bronze pigment on bevelled edge, red on background and yellow on figures, 20 × 32.5 (7¾ × 12¾), depth 5.6 (2¼). Signed with monogram on left return side. B. Marchesi; Leicester Gallery; Leeds City Art Gallery, 1935 as *Odalisque*
Exhibited: *Memorial Exhibition*, 1918, ? 38 *Bas-relief*, alabaster, 1912
Literature: Ede, *Life*, p. 206; Brodzky, illustrated opposite p. 99 as *Bas-relief* – stone (1912); Brodzky, *Drawings*, pl. 92; Cole (1978), no. 12, p. 59

Not included in Gaudier's *List of Works* but in Ede's Supplementary List as *Seated Woman and Slave*, a stone or alabaster relief of 1914, owned by Madame Blanche Marchesi. Cole follows Brodzky in dating it to 1912 while Lewison suggests 1912–13 on the basis of comparison with *Mermaid* (*cat.* 55) and the use of the monogram signature. The male head is closely related to that of several late 1912 nude studies and is technically close to *Woman* (*cat.* 39) while the woman's pose reverses that in a stylo-pen life drawing (pl. 36), both suggestive of an early 1913 date.

39 Woman, relief (pl. 39)

Bath stone, 56.5 × 40.6 (22¼ × 16)
S. Brzeska Estate: F. Stoop, 1930; Contemporary Art Society; Hull University Art Gallery
Exhibited: *Memorial Exhibition*, 1918, 99 *Bas-relief: Nude*, stone, 1912
Literature: Brodzky illustrated opposite p. 110 as *Bas-relief* (stone) 1912; Cole (1978), no. 11, p. 59

Cole places this in 1912 but Lewison (Cambridge, 1983, 25) associates its primitivism and self-conscious use of chisel marks with a slightly later date, comparing it with *Female Figure* (*cat.* 50) and *Sepulchral Figure* (*cat.* 49). I would compare the composition, theme, broadening and flattening of the planes with *Women Carrying Sacks* (*cat.* 40) while the detail of the carving of the eye, nose and brow is identical to that of *Amour* (*cat.* 35).

40 Women Carrying Sacks (pl. 40)

Plaster, 34.9 × 28 (13¾ × 11), incised with 'HGB' monogram
H. Brodzky; Lady Epstein; Walsall, Garman-Ryan Collection
2 bronze casts with black patina taken by Brodzky, 1930s
Four casts taken by Lady Epstein, 1964, 35.9 × 28.3 × 4.6 (14 × 11 × 1¾)
1. Private collection, by 1934
2. Location unknown
3. Cambridge, Kettle's Yard
4. Piccadilly Gallery, 1965; M. Oliphant; Sotheby's 26.11.69 (324) illustrated; J. Hirschhorn; Washington, Hirshhorn Museum of Art
5. M. Levy (1965)
Exhibited: *Paintings, Drawings and Sculpture by Contemporary Artists*, 36 Bridge Street, Cambridge, 1933, 4 *Bronze plaque* (exhibited for the first time)
Literature: Brodzky, illustrated opposite p. 44; Levy, p. 29, pl. 74; Cole (1978), no. 15, p. 62, dates 1912

Not included in Gaudier's *List of Works* or Ede's *Supplementary List*. The use of the 'HGB' monogram is found in at least one dated work of 1912, *Cheetah* (fig. 72) but the flattening and facetting of the planes in the arms and legs point to a date in early 1913, when the artist was preoccupied with relief carving. The composition bears an obvious relationship with that of *Woman* (*cat.* 39).

41 Horace Brodzky, Mask (pl. 43)

Portland stone relief, 35.6 × 38.1 × 16 (14 × 15 × 6¼), S. Brzeska Estate; H. S. Ede; Cambridge, Kettle's Yard
9 casts in artificial stone cast by R. A. Rowe, 1965
2 casts, Cambridge, Kettle's Yard
Exhibited: *Memorial Exhibition*, 1918, 43 *Head of a Man* stone) 1912; Leeds, 1943, 71
Literature: Ede, *Life*, p. 196; Cole (1978), no. 20, p. 68

Mentioned in Gaudier's *List of Works* as 'Brodzky masque pierre Portland gran[d]eur nature'. The head was at the Leicester Galleries in 1918 (Cole cites a letter from the Leicester Galleries to Sophie Brzeska, 25.10.18 'There are certainly a few of the remaining sculptures we should be glad to see housed elsewhere . . . the stone head of Brodzky') so it was presumably included in the *Memorial Exhibition* though not identified as Brodzky.

42 Head of Christ (pl. 17)

Bath stone, twice lifesize, destroyed.
Literature: Pound, 1916, pl. XIV; Ede, *Life*, p. 196, pl. XXX; Cole (1978), no. 04, p. 125

Gaudier's *List of Works* includes a *Head of Christ*, twice lifesize in Bath stone, as a work of 1913, grouped with the *Head of a Boy* (*cat.* 44) and *Mask of Horace Brodzky* (*cat.* 41). Pound illustrates this piece as *Head of Christ* (very early work, destroyed by sculptor). This same head was illustrated by Ede and called *Head of a Man*.

43 Head

Stone, 30.5 (12), S. Brzeska Estate; H. S. Ede; location unknown
Exhibited: Leeds, 1943, 70

This appears neither in the *List of Works* nor in Ede's Supplement. Confusingly, Ede, when annotating the Leeds catalogue, dated it to 1913 and compared it with the *Head of Christ* (*cat.* 42); at the same time he suggested it was a work Gaudier had made overnight in order to impress Epstein (see p. 59).

44 Head of a Young Man (pl. 41)

Sandstone, 31 (12¼), S. Brzeska Estate: H. S. Ede; Kunsthalle Bielefeld
12 numbered, artificial stone casts by Fiorini, 32 × 24.5 × 20 (12½ × 9½ × 7¾)
1. Cambridge, Kettle's Yard; Paris, Musée National d'Art Moderne, 1964
2. and 3. Private collections
6. and 7. Cambridge, Kettle's Yard
8. London, Tate Gallery
? Sydney, Art Gallery of New South Wales (1985)
Exhibited: *Memorial Exhibition*, 1918, 43 (stone 1912)
Literature: Ede, *Life*, p. 206; Brodzky, p. 179; M. Ménier, *La Revue du Louvre*, 1965, p. 2; Cole (1978), no. 9, p. 56; Kunsthalle Bielefeld, Katalog, pp. 65–66

Gaudier's *List of Works* mentions 'Tête d'enfant masque' twice lifesize in Portland stone, as a 1913 work. Ede includes a separate entry for it as *Head of a Boy* in his supplementary list as a 1914 work but accepted in a letter to R. Morphet (Tate Gallery, 1967) that this dating was too late, and suggests 1912 or even 1911. Cole, following Ménier, identifies it with the early months of Gaudier's friendship with

Epstein, i.e., the latter part of 1912. Lewison suggests early 1913 on the basis of its kinship with the *Mask of Brodzky* (*cat.* 41), and suggests that Gaudier might have made a mistake in material when making out his list.

March 1913

45 Bust of Frank Harris (pls. 44, 45)

Plaster, probably destroyed
Literature: Ede, *Life*, p. 196; Cole (1978), no. 030, p. 129, illustrated

Recorded in Gaudier's *List of Works* as 'Frank Harris, buste, plâtre, grandeur nature'. Harris commissioned the portrait in November 1912. On 14 November 1912, Gaudier told Sophie, 'This morning I had a letter from Frank Harris. He says he will come on Sunday, and I have laid in two cwts. of clay.' Because of Harris's departure for USA the modelling of the bust was delayed until the following spring. In a letter to Lovat Fraser (7.3.13) in which he also mentions current work on carvings in relief, Gaudier wrote, 'I am doing Frank Harris portrait it is half done and promising.' It is also referred to in a letter from Gaudier to Dr Uhlemayr, 12.3.13 (Cole). It must have been complete by late April as Gaudier wrote asking for another front view photograph of the bust (29.4.13).

46 Portrait of Alfred Wolmark (pls. 46, 47)

Painted plaster, 67.3 (26½), signed with monogram, dated '13', Liverpool, National Museums on Merseyside (Walker Art Gallery)
6 bronzes, 65 × 55 × 40 (25½ × 21½ × 15¾), cast 1954–60 by Art Bronze Foundry (London), Ltd.
1. Leicester Galleries; private collection (on loan to Scottish National Gallery of Modern Art, Edinburgh)
2. P. Granville; Southampton City Art Gallery, 1955
3. Walker Art Gallery, National Museums on Merseyside.
4. P. Granville; York City Art Gallery
5. J. Shaw; Christie's 3.11.67 (76); Fine Art Society; C. and L. Handley-Read; Birmingham Museum and Art Gallery, 1973
6. P. Granville; Paris, Musée National d'Art Moderne (1960)
Exhibited: London, *AAA*, 1913, 1217; London, *AAA*, March 1916, 39
Literature: Ede *Life*, pp. 196–97; Cork, *Vorticism*, 1, p. 169; Liverpool, Walker Art Gallery, *Foreign Catalogue*, 1977, pp. 311–12; Cole (1978), no. 22, pp. 70–71

Described as 'Cubique' in *List of Works*.

47 Portrait of Horace Brodzky (pls. 48, 52)

Plaster painted pale green, nude male figure and girl's head incised on front. Signed and dated on back 'H Gaudier Brzeska 1913' with a dedication in shorthand, 60.4 × 53.3 (23¾ × 21)
H. Brodzky; Cambridge MA, Fogg Art Museum, 1964
6 bronze casts, 70 (24), of which 3 were cast in 1931–32 and a further 3 in 1956.
1. M. V. Hill; Bristol Museum and Art Gallery, 1951
2. H. S. Ede; Leeds City Art Gallery
3. H. Brodzky; private collection
4. H. Brodzky; Cambridge MA, Fogg Art Museum, 1964
5. London, Tate Gallery, 1957
6. Ottawa, National Gallery of Canada, 1958
Exhibited: London, *AAA*, 1913, 1216; London, J. and E. Bumpus, *Henri Gaudier-Brzeska*, 1931, 38 (bronze, lent by Captain V. Hill)
Literature: Ede, *Life*, p. 196; Brodzky, pp. 18, 67–69, illustrated opposite p. 51; Levy, p. 29, pl. 76; Cole (1978), no. 21, p. 69

Described as 'Cubique' in *List of Works*. The signature on the back was identified by Brodzky as Gaudier's personal shorthand. Incised on the chest are the nude figure of a running man and a woman's head.

48 Dog (pl. 81)

Marble, background painted red, on grey wooden base, 24.1 × 48.2 (9½ × 19), inscribed with HGB monogram on reverse
F. Harris by 1916; J. Quinn, April 1916; Quinn Estate 1924–27; American Art Association Inc, *The John Quinn Collection*, Feb. 9–11, 1927, no. 687, illustrated; S. Lustgarten; Chicago, Art Institute, 1953
Literature: Ede, *Life*, p. 204; Brodzky, p. 30, 166, illustrated opposite p. 80; Cole (1978), no. 26, p. 75; J. Zilczer, *"The Noble Buyer": John Quinn Patron of the Avant-Garde*, Washington, 1978, p. 159

Brodzky describes this as one of several small pieces exhibited at Bedib's Bookshop in St Martin's Lane where numerous drawings were also deposited for sale.

49 Grief (Sepulchral Figure, pls. 53, 55).

Bath stone, 41 × 37 × 20 (16¼ × 14½ × 7¾) inc. base.
A. Wolmark; Leicester Galleries, 1954; Earl of Sandwich; London, Tate Gallery, 1962

3 casts made for Leicester Galleries, 1918
1. G. Eumorfopoulos, 1918; Leicester Galleries, *c.* 1943
2. Leicester Galleries; *c.* 1930 M. Oliver; Christie's 12.6.81 (74); Mercury Gallery, stolen 1985
3. Lady Tredegar; Sotheby's 28.3.62 (148); A. Thompson; Leicestershire Museums, Arts and Records Service, 1963
Exhibited: London, *AAA*, March 1916, 40 *Grief* lent by A. Wolmark; *Memorial Exhibition*, 1918, 89; London, Beaux-Arts Gallery, 1952, 11; Leicester Galleries, *Artists of Fame and Promise*, 1954, 152; Leeds, 1943, 65 (lent by Leicester Galleries)
Literature: *The Egoist*, 16.2.14, p. 80, illustrated; Ede, *Life*, p. 196; Brodzky, illustrated opposite p. 33; Cole (1978), no. 25, p. 74

Exchanged with Alfred Wolmark in return for his *Portrait of Gaudier-Brzeska* (Orléans, Musée des Beaux-Arts). Described in *List of Works* as 'statuette funéraire fini ciseau'.

50 Female Figure (Venus, pl. 65)

Alabaster, 37.8 × 18.3 × 8.8 (14¾ × 7¼ × 3½), incised on back 'H Gaudier-Brzeska 1913'
Roland, Browse & Delbanco; Manchester City Art Gallery, 1946
Exhibited: Edinburgh, 1972, 22
Literature: Ede, *SM*, p. 247; Cole (1978), nos. 27 and 010, pp. 31, 76, 126; Cole (1995), p. 72

This figure is here tentatively identified as 'my little alabaster Venus' sold for £3 to a visiting Jewish collector from Kraków to whom Wolmark had introduced him (Gaudier to Brzeska, 8.10.13 and *List of Works*). While the robustly modelled nude is more Gauguinesque than idealized, the wave-like curves of stone around the thighs, a feature probably suggested by the limited height of the alabaster offcut from which it is carved, may have prompted the title. The unusual full signature and date could have been done for the purchaser's benefit. Cole lists this figure and *Venus* separately and dates this figure to both early 1913 and August 1913. Lewison dates it to early 1913, relating it to *Woman* (*cat.* 39) in their common dependence on a Gauguinesque model, and also to Archipenko's *Mother and Child*, 1910.

51 Singer (Chanteuse Triste, pls. 56–58, IV)

Derby stone, 85 × 22 × 16 (33½ × 8¾ × 6¼)
S. Brzeska Estate; F. Stoop; Contemporary Art Society; Tate Gallery, 1930
Exhibited: London, Goupil Gallery, *London Group*, 1915, 45 *Singer*; London, Doré Gallery, *Vorticist Exhibition*, 1915, item e *Singer*; *Memorial Exhibition*, 1918, 100 *The Singer*, 1913
Literature: *The Egoist*, 16.2.14, p. 80, illustrated; Pound, 1916, pp. 89–90, pls. XXIII, XXIV (*Chanteuse Triste*); L. Taft, *Modern Tendencies in Sculpture*, 1921, pl. 56; Ede, *Life*, p. 196; Cole (1978), no. 28, p. 77; Lewison (1983), no. 42; Cole (1995), p. 90

Gaudier's *List of Works* for 1913 describes this as '*Chanteuse*, statuette in hard Derby stone', which may explain, as Lewison suggests, why so many point marks are visible in the otherwise smooth surface. A reference in *Matka* (CUL) fol. 132c, dateable to late 1913, indicates that both Kohnstamm, the purchaser of *Amour* (*cat.* 35), and a woman considered purchasing this piece. Shortly before the opening of the 1914 London Group exhibition Gaudier consigned it with 'the white marble relief' to the Chenil Gallery (*Matka*, fol. 148b). Pound describes it as 'earlier period' which may well mean before he became friendly with Gaudier in July–August 1913. A year later Gaudier listed the piece in his 'will' as being with Alfred Wolmark.

52 Infant Hercules

Grey stone, broken during move to Putney studio, destroyed
Literature: Ede, *Life*, p. 204; Pound, pp. 49, 128; Cole (1978), no. 08, p. 126

Pound suggests that it dated from the same period as *Chanteuse Triste* (*cat.* 51), i.e. mid-1913, and that it was broken during the move to the Putney studio leaving the head, 'about half the size of a fist', as the kitten's plaything.

53 Standing Female Figure (pls. 60–62)

Granite, 41 × 12.1 × 16.5 (16¼ × 4¾ × 6½). Family descent; Mercury Gallery 1989
Edition of 7 numbered bronzes with founder's mark, *Paris*, inscribed on back 'Henri Gaudier Brzeska Figure 1913', cast pre-1989
Exhibited: London, Whitechapel Art Gallery, *Twentieth Century British Art*, 1914, 155 *Figure*; Mercury Gallery, *Henri Gaudier-Brzeska 1891–1915*, 1991, 1, illustrated
Literature: R. Cole, 'A Gaudier-Brzeska sculpture rediscovered', *Burlington Magazine*, CXXXII, 1990, p. 874

The sculpture exhibited at the Whitechapel Art Gallery alongside *Head of Ezra Pound* (*cat.* 79),

Maternity (*cat.* 64), *Firebird* (*cat.* 18), *cat* (*cat.* 70) and *Fawn* (*cat.* 63) was not photographed by Benington and was not included in the 1918 *Memorial Exhibition*. It does not appear in either the *List of Works* or Ede's Supplement. In addition to the provenance via family descent and the style of the carving, the attribution is based on an old photograph showing the piece on a base with 'HGB', and on a label 'no. 155 "Figure" BASALT, GAUDIER BRZESKA' and a brass plate 'HGB 1913'. The subject, despite its ostensible femininity, appears to relate to Gaudier's 1910 Prometheus drawings (fig. 53).

54 Sketch for Standing Figure (pl. 59)

Alabaster, 20 × 10 × 6 (7¾ × 4 × 2½), S. Brzeska Estate; H. S. Ede; Cambridge, Kettle's Yard
Literature: Cole (1978), no. 012, p. 127

55 Mermaid (pls. 63, 64)

Marble, 11.4 × 27.5 × 17.5 (4½ × 10¾ × 6¾), S. Brzeska Estate; H. S. Ede; Cambridge, Kettle's Yard
9 unnumbered bronze casts by Fiorini on behalf of H. S. Ede in 1964–66, 11.5 × 28 × 18 (4½ × 11 × 7)
1. Cambridge, Kettle's Yard, Paris, Musée National d'Art Moderne, 1964
2. Cambridge, Kettle's Yard
3. London, Tate Gallery
4. H. S. Ede; Bielefeld, Kunsthalle, 1967
Exhibited: London, J. and E. Bumpus, *Henri Gaudier-Brzeska*, 1931, 34 (marble); London, Zwemmer Gallery, *Gaudier-Brzeska: pen and ink drawings*, 1936, 3 (marble)
Literature: Ede, *Life*, p. 206; Levy, p. 29, pl. 77; Cole (1978), no. 33, pp. 82–83; Lewison (1983), no. 26, p. 40

First mentioned in Ede's supplementary *List of Works* dated 1914. Cole dates to 1913 while Lewison suggests a date after October 1913 on the basis of its 'Polynesian look' which he relates to Gaudier's letter to Brzeska (8.10.13); '[Epstein] is making some extraordinary statues like the Polynesians, absolute copies, with Brancusi-like noses'. He also suggests, by analogy, a late 1913 dating for *Woman* (*cat.* 39), *Man and Woman* (*cat.* 38) and *Love scene* (*cat.* 73). The seal-like metamorphosis of the body and its fusion with the block, as well as stylistic details of the hands and eyes, suggest a date later than this group of reliefs and closer to *Wrestler Relief* (*cat.* 66) and Gaudier's association with the Omega Workshop.

56 Boy (pl. 75)

Alabaster, 46.9 (18½)
Omega Workshops; R. Fry; London, Delbanco Gallery; Mr and Mrs L. Elmhirst; Devon, the Dartington Hall Trust
Ede arranged the casting of 3 bronzes in 1968 on behalf of the Elmhirsts, 45 × 11.5 × 10 (17¾ × 4½ × 4), unnumbered
1. Mr and Mrs Elmhirst; Cambridge, Kettle's Yard
2. Mr and Mrs Elmhirst; Paris, Musée National d'Art Moderne, 1971
Exhibited: London, Alpine Gallery, *Grafton Group*, 1914, 46 *Boy*; ACGB, *Henri Gaudier-Brzeska*, 1957, 11, as *Male Nude*; Edinburgh, Leeds, Cardiff, *Henri Gaudier-Brzeska Sculpture*, 1972, 29 as *Boy*; Cambridge, 1983, 43
Literature: Pound, p. 129, no. 30 'Boy, in plaster. Omega shops, unimportant'; Ede, *Life*, p. 196; Cole (1978), no. 38, pp. 88–89; Lewison (1983), no. 43

Included in *List of Works* as 'Garçon, statuette, alabâtre, circa 1¼' haut, 3″ × 4″' and handled by Omega Workshops.

Cole states that this work was completed at the Omega Workshops, Gaudier having taken advantage of the availability of a decent piece of stone. However, there is a reference in *Matka* (CUL), fol. 86b, to George Banks's admiration for 'mon gars en alabâtre', and on fol. 130b to Fry's admiration for it and his request that Gaudier let him have it to sell at Omega for £20. This would suggest an early to mid-1913 dating rather than autumn. Lewison points to its similarity to the School of Michelangelo, *Nude Slave*, exhibited at the Burlington Fine Arts Club as part of an exhibition of Italian sculpture in 1912; the piece was reproduced in the *Burlington Magazine*, August 1912.

57 Samson and Delilah (The Embracers, pls. 66, 67)

Marble, 55 × 19 × 14 (21½ × 7½ × 5½), E. Pound, 1913; Paris, Musée National d'Art Moderne, 1967
3 plaster casts, 2 bronze casts, 1 cast by Nasini, Rome *c.* 1933/4
Plaster:
1. E. Pound; Cambridge, Kettle's Yard
2. London, Tate Gallery
Bronzes:
1. E. Pound; Anthony d'Offay; private collection
2. Washington, Hirshhorn Museum
Exhibited: *Memorial Exhibition*, 1918, 39
Literature: Ede, *Life*, p. 200; Cole (1978), no. 41, p. 92; O. Pound and A. W. Litz, *Ezra Pound and Dorothy Shakespear Their Letters 1909–1914*, 1984, p. 287

Described in the *List of Works* as 'Samson et Dalilah

groupe erotique. Seravezza marble 1¾′ haut circa. £5. Ezra Pound 5 Holland Place Kensington' and dated to 1914. It must, however, have been complete by December 1913 when Ezra Pound wrote to Dorothy Shakespear about the purchase of *Torso 3* (*cat.* 59), adding, 'I don't think we've either of us space for the post-post embracers.'

Autumn

58 Dancer (pls. 68–70)

Plaster with traces of red and green pigment, on wooden base supported by armature, 79 × 18.5 × 18.5 (31 × 7¼ × 7¼), signed 'H Gaudier Brzeska 1913' on side of base
S. Brzeska; London, Victoria and Albert Museum, 1918; transferred to Tate Gallery
2 casts before 1918
1. S. Schiff; Mrs V. Schiff; Sir E. Beddington-Behrens; S. Beddington-Behrens; location unknown
2. G. Eumorfopoulos; the Hon. E. Knollys; private collection.

Sir E. Beddington-Behrens, with the cooperation of the Tate Gallery, arranged for 4 further casts to be made from the original plaster by Fiorini under the supervision of the sculptor David Wynne, 1965; these are unnumbered but dated '1965'.
1. Sir E. Beddington-Behrens; Oxford, Christ Church Picture Gallery, 1965
2. Sir E. Beddington-Behrens; Paris, Musée National d'Art Moderne, 1965
3. London, Tate Gallery
4. Mr and Mrs D. Wynne
A further cast from the original plaster was taken by Fiorini in 1966/67
5. H. S. Ede; Cambridge, Kettle's Yard – incised 'No. 4' on side of base.
Exhibited: *Memorial Exhibition*, 1918, 11
Literature: Ede, *Life*, p. 204; Levy, p. 29, pl. 70; Cole (1978), no. 32, pp. 33, 81

Cole, following Brodzky, suggests that Sophie Brzeska was the model, but Brzeska's writings and other evidence indicate that the model was the painter Nina Hamnett, whom Gaudier had met at the Allied Artists. Curiously, the piece is omitted from the *List of Works*. Sidney Schiff purchased *Dancer* and a round pedestal for £10 paid in two instalments on 14.11 and 1.12.13.

59 Torso 2 (pls. 71, 72)

Clay (probably destroyed) from which 2 plaster casts taken, 1 with a chipped left breast given to Brodzky, the other to Wolmark, according to Cole
Patinated unchipped plaster, 19.5 (7⅝), Orléans, Musée des Beaux-Arts
Chipped plaster, H. Brodzky; Earl of Sandwich
3 bronze casts made from Brodzky's plaster in 1930; 5 bronze casts from Wolmark plaster
Bronzes:
1. Sir Brinsley Ford (chipped)
2. Tate Gallery (chipped)
3. Mr and Mrs Elmhirst; Paris, Musée National d'Art Moderne, 1964 (unchipped)
4. Sir Colin and Lady Anderson (unchipped; Edinburgh, 1972, 24)
5. Sotheby's 8.10.85 (45) illustrated; Mercury Gallery
6. A. E. Allport; location unknown (unchipped)
7. Cambridge, Kettle's Yard (unchipped)
Exhibited: London, *AAA*, March 1916, 41 *Torso* lent by A. Wolmark; *Memorial Exhibition*, 1918, 8 (identified as plaster cast of Torso in Victoria and Albert Museum)
Literature: Ede, *Life*, p. 205; Brodzky reproduces the chipped plaster cast opposite p. 16; Levy, p. 29, pl. 68; T. Materer, 'Henri Gaudier's "Three Ninas"', *Paideuma*, 4, 2–3, 1975, pp. 323–24; Cole (1978), no. 30, p. 79

Unlike the two marble *Torsos* (*cat.* 59, 60, 61), this one was omitted from Gaudier's *List of Works*. Gaudier described *Torso* to Major Smythies as 'a marble statue of a girl in the natural way, in order to show my accomplishment as a sculptor' (Smythies quoting Gaudier in a letter to Ede, 1929; private collection, repr. Ede, p. 255). The close resemblance to *Torso 3* would suggest that this may have been a study for it.

60 Torso 3 (pls. 73, 74, V)

Marble, 20.7 × 8.5 × 8.5 (8¼ × 3½ × 3½); including plinth 27.5 × 8.6 × 8.5 (10¾ × 3½ × 3½), E. Pound; private collection, on loan to Hamilton College, Clinton, New York
Exhibited: *Memorial Exhibition*, 1918, 18
Literature: Ede, *Life*, p. 200; T. Materer, 'Henri Gaudier's "Three Ninas"', *Paideuma*, 4, 2–3, 1975, pp. 323–24; Cole (1978), no. 31, p. 80, dating 1913–14; O. Pound and A. W. Litz, *Ezra Pound and Dorothy Shakespear Their Letters 1909–1914*, 1984, pp. 286–87

Described in *List of Works* as 'Torse de femme, marbre Seravezza 7″ haut £10 Mrs O. Shakespeare Portrait de Nina Hamnett peintre', and placed among the works of 1914.

According to Pound this torso preceded *Torso 1*:

'He had, if I remember rightly, just finished one torse and was working on the one now at the "South Kensington".' They were complete by December 1913 when Dorothy Shakespear wrote to Ezra Pound warning him that her uncle, Henry Tudor Tucker, 'is wanting to know the price of Brzeska's torse, of which he has heard so much from us – so you had better keep your eye on it if you really mean to get it.' On December 16 Pound replied that he had written to Cournos about buying the torso and that he thought it was as good as theirs 'provided he [Gaudier] don't want argosies in return.' He went on to suggest that Dorothy's uncle could buy 'the flat-bellied torse if he needs it.' By 30 December the sculpture was in Dorothy's possession: 'Brzeska's torse doesn't seem to feel the cold particularly.'

This torso is far more compact and fleshy, especially around the hips and belly than *Torso 1* (*cat.* 61).

61 Torso 1 (pls. 76, 77)

Sicilian marble, 25.2 × 98 × 77 (10 × 38½ × 30¼) excluding base
S. Brzeska; London, Victoria and Albert Museum, 1915; transferred to London, Tate Gallery T03731
Polyester resin casts with white aggregate taken 1976,
1. Bielefeld Kunsthalle
2. Cambridge, Kettle's Yard
3. Southampton Art Gallery
4. H. S. Ede; Paris, Musée National d'Art Moderne, 1977
Exhibited: London, Goupil Gallery, *London Group*, 1914, 115 (£38)
Literature: Pound, p. 128, no. 7; Ede, *Life*, p. 200; Brodzky pp. 177–78; T. Materer, 'Henri Gaudier's "Three Ninas"', *Paideuma*, 4, 2–3, 1975, pp. 323–24; Cole (1978), no. 29, p. 78, dated 1913; Lewison (1983) no. 54, dated 1914; O. Pound and A. W. Litz, *Ezra Pound and Dorothy Shakespear Their Letters 1909–1914*, 1984, pp. 286–87.

Described in *List of Works* as 'Torse de femme (Nina Hamnett)'. Gaudier lists *cat.* 60 and 67 as works of 1914 but the correspondence between Dorothy Shakespear and Ezra Pound in December 1913 indicates that at least two of the torsos were complete by December 1913 while Pound recalled that this was the second carved torso to be completed.

62 Crouching Fawn (pl. 80)

Bath stone, 30.4 × 25.3 (12 × 10)
Mrs B. Mayor; Lady Rothschild; private collection (on loan to Birmingham Museums and Art Gallery)
5 casts made on behalf of owner in 1920s but Cole claims 12 casts in all
Exhibited: London, Alpine Club Gallery, *Grafton Group*, 1914, 47; *Memorial Exhibition*, 1918, 94; London, J. and E. Bumpus, *Henri Gaudier-Brzeska*, 1931, 39 (lent by Mrs B. Mayor)
Literature: Pound, p. 129, no. 23; Ede, *Life*, p. 198; Brodzky, pp. 176, 182; Cole (1978), no. 48, p. 100

Described in Gaudier's *List of Works* as 'Faun statuette, Bath stone, 1′ × 10″ × 5″, sold £15 – 25 per cent commission for Omega to Mrs Mayor, Campden Hill'. One ear was damaged by being attacked by a woman with an umbrella at the Leicester Galleries during the *Memorial Exhibition* but after Mrs Mayor had purchased it.

63 Sleeping Fawn (pls. 78, 79)

Seravezza marble, R. Drey; Mrs W. Crocker, San Francisco; private collection
Painted plaster, R. Drey (after 1914); Leicester Galleries, 1918; London, Victoria and Albert Museum, 1939; transferred to Tate Gallery (T03728)
1918–39 12 casts made for Leicester Galleries as required (letter O. Brown to Tate Gallery 30.8.1960)
11.5 × 23.5 × 25.5 (4½ × 9¼ × 10)
1. Leicester Galleries, *c.* 1930; C. Rutherston; Mrs Rutherston-Powell; Sotheby's 22.7.77 (70) illustrated; Christie's 9.3.90 (216) illustrated
2. Cambridge, Kettle's Yard
3. Eastbourne, Towner Art Gallery, 1977
4. Private collection
Exhibited: London, Whitechapel Gallery, *Twentieth Century Art*, May 1914, no. 208; *Memorial Exhibition*, 1918, 98; Leeds, 1943, 66 (bronze, lent by E. le Bas)
Literature: Ede, *Life*, p. 196, pl. XXXVI (marble); Ede, *SM*, marble illustrated opposite p. 84; Cole (1978), no. 39, pp. 33, 90

Described in the *List of Works* as 'Faon statuette marbre Seravezza' 6″ × 4″ × 5″ sold for five guineas to Raymond Drey. Lewison (Cambridge, 1983, no. 50) queries whether the Tate plaster can be identified with the marble described in Gaudier's *List* and lent by Drey to the *Memorial Exhibition*, since the latter included 4 different fawns. Lewison would identify the Tate plaster *Fawn* with no. 96 *Fawn* bronze (1913) and dates 1913–14. Cole states that Drey commissioned the carving in November 1913, after a clay model he had seen in the studio.

64 Maternity (pls. 83, 84, VII)

Seravezza marble, 21.5 (8½); including limestone base, 29.5 × 30 × 22.5 (11½ × 11¾ × 8¾)

Omega Workshops; Mrs O. Strachey; R. Fry; G. Eumorfopoulos; Mrs W. Sedgwick; H. S. Ede; Paris, Musée National d'Art Moderne, 1964
8 unnumbered bronze casts by Fiorini on behalf of H. S. Ede, 1960s, 27.5 (9½)
2 casts, Cambridge, Kettle's Yard
3. Kettle's Yard; V. Waddington: private collection, 1966;
4. Melbourne, National Gallery of Victoria
5. London, Tate Gallery
6. Bielefeld Kunsthalle, 1967
Exhibited: London, Whitechapel Art Gallery, *Twentieth Century Art*, 1914, 156 *Maternity*; Birmingham, Royal Birmingham Society of Artists and London, Heal's Mansard Gallery, *The Modern Movement in Art*, 1917, lent by R. Fry; *Memorial Exhibition*, 1918, 35
Literature: R. Fry, *Burlington Magazine*, XXIX, 1916, pp. 209–10, illustrated, owned by Mrs O. Strachey; Ede, *Life*, p. 196; Ede, *SM*, pp. 132, 240, 259, illustrated; Brodzky, pp. 176, 177, 180, illustrated opposite p. 17; Cole (1978), no. 34, pp. 84–85; J. Collins, *The Omega Workshops*, 1972, p. 71

Gaudier's *List of Works* places the piece in 1913, a date supported by a passage in *Matka* (CUL), fol. 117, in which Alfred Kohnstamm is described spending a long time at the studio looking at *Maternity* before deciding that at £40 it was too expensive. The same page contains references to Paul Morand and the Ranee of Sarawak who visited the studio in September 1913. It was deposited at the Omega Workshops for sale, whence it was sold to George Eumorfopoulos for £20, 25 per cent of which was commission. Collins suggests a date in early 1914 because it was not included in the January Grafton Group show but was included in the March London Group show, and suggests Omega took possession after the end of the Whitechapel Show (June) and before Gaudier's 9 July *List of Works* was drawn up. However '*Maternity* (stone)', the description in the London Group catalogue seems to refer to *Caritas* (*cat.* 75). The naturalism of the treatment can be compared with the Gill's three direct carvings of nude *Mother and Child* of 1910 (Leeds Museums and Galleries, Cardiff, National Museum of Wales, fig. 71) which one critic described as 'animal and pathetic'.

65 Cat (pl. 103)

Moulded earthenware with ceramic glaze, 11.8 (4⅝), 'Ω' inscribed beneath base. 6 versions of this piece glazed in different colours were made for the Omega Workshops. Four are known to survive.
1. Contemporary Art Society; Bristol Museum and Art Gallery (brown glaze)
2. Contemporary Art Society; Bristol Museum and Art Gallery (brown glaze)
3. R. Bevan; Anthony d'Offay (pale green glaze)
4. Location unknown
Literature: R. Fry, 'Gaudier-Brzeska', *Burlington Magazine*, XXIX, 1916, illustrated. Pound, p. 129, 'no. 26 Model of cat for porcelain (Omega shops)'; Ede, *Life*, p. 204; Levy, pl. 65; Cole, no. 37, p. 88; Lewison (1983), no. 45; J. Collins, *The Omega Workshops*, 1983, pp. 71–72; Crafts Council, *The Omega Workshops 1913–17. Decorative Arts of Bloomsbury*, 1984, C14

The piece was press-moulded in two sections with details of eyes and claws added by hand. At this time Omega ceramics were made by George Schenk of Mitcham. According to Cole *Cat* was glazed in cream, black, dark blue and brown. Collins suggests a date as late as May–June 1914 because sketches of a cat in a similar position appear on the other side of the paper on which Gaudier's review of the London Salon (*The Egoist*, 15.6.14) was drafted but Gaudier often reused paper and had more or less parted from Omega by then. Stylistically it seems much closer to *cat.* 66.

66 Wrestlers relief (pl. 87)

Carved plaster relief 72.4 × 92.1 (28½ × 36¼), signed in monogram; S. Brzeska Estate; H. S. Ede; Boston, Museum of Fine Arts, 1965
9 herculite casts on behalf of Ede by John W. Mills, June 1965, 71 × 92.5 × 7.5 (30 × 36½ × 3)
1. H. S. Ede; Paris, Musée National d'Art Moderne
2. Private collection
3. and 7. H. S. Ede; Cambridge, Kettle's Yard
6. Private collection; Tate Gallery
(number unknown); Mercury Gallery; Middlesborough Art Gallery, 1977
Exhibited: London, *Memorial Exhibition*, 1918, 69
Literature: Pound, p. 130, no. 32 Ede, *Life*, p. 200; Brodzky, pp. 31–32, illustrated opposite p. 98; Levy, p. 30, pl. 82; Cole (1978), no. 42, p. 93; F. Koslow, 'The Evolution of Henri Gaudier-Brzeska's Boston *Wrestlers* Relief', *Bulletin of Boston Museum of Fine Arts*, 1981, pp. 38–49

Brodzky relates that the canvas upon which the plaster rests was used in 1912, first for a thickly impasted oil painting of a Whitechapel Jewish fruit-seller to which Gaudier refers in a letter to Brzeska

28.10.12 (University of Essex), and then for a Gauguinesque tropical landscape 'hot in colour, with a dull red sky and exotic palm-like trees'. The painting, *The Jewish Fruitseller*, detached in 1966 from the relief, is also in Boston, Museum of Fine Arts. Koslow dates the carved plaster to 1913–14 though it appears as a work of 1914 in Gaudier's *List of Works*, a date accepted by Lewison. Its robust simplicity, primitivism, careful placing within the panel and carved technique, analogous to low relief wood carving, suggest a relationship with the Omega Workshops period.

67 Round Tray (pl. 102)

Mahogany carcase, inlaid with Andaman pedouk, oak, walnut and ebonized wood. Diameter *c.* 64 (25¼).
Made by John Joseph Kallenborn.
C. R. W. Nevinson, 1914; Sir Charles Strong; Sotheby's 8.3.78 (39) illustrated; London, Victoria and Albert Museum
Exhibited: London, *Memorial Exhibition*, 1918, 102
Literature: R. Fry, *Burlington Magazine*, XXIX, 1916, illustrated (wrestlers); N. Hamnett, *Laughing Torso*, 1932, p. 43; Cole (1978), no. 36, p. 87; J. Collins, *The Omega Workshops*, 1983, p. 73, pl. 26; Anthony d'Offay, *The Omega Workshops*, 1984, no. 36

Designed for the Omega Workshops. Collins proposes a date during winter 1913 at the same period when Grant and Bell were producing designs for marquetry trays. Hamnett recalled, 'I brought Henri round one day and he did a design for a tray which was eventually carried out in inlaid woods.' Gaudier drew several versions with wrestlers grappling in different positions, but the composition chosen also evokes a dance.

Another wooden tray, oval with inlaid and painted decoration is attributed to Gaudier by Cole, no. 36, p. 87. The design bears no resemblance to Gaudier's style and, in the absence of supporting evidence associating it with Gaudier, the attribution is not accepted here.

68 Crouching Boy (Newel Post, pl. 85)

Carved plaster, signed in monogram, lost
Literature: R. Fry, *Burlington Magazine*, XXIX, 1916, pp. 209–10, illustrated; Pound, p. 129 as 'Boy, in plaster. Omega shops, unimportant'; Cole (1978), no. 035, pp. 135–36, illustrated; J. Collins, *The Omega Workshops*, 1983, pp. 72–73, pl. 27
Related drawings: Cole (1978), p. 130, illustrated

69 Redstone Dancer (pls. 97–99, XI)

Mansfield stone, polished and waxed, signed in monogram on base, 43 (17), S. Brzeska Estate; London, Tate Gallery
1 bronze cast by M. Gillespie, 1969
Cambridge, Kettle's Yard
Exhibited: London, Alpine Club Gallery, *Grafton Group*, 1914, 50; London, Goupil Gallery, *London Group*, May 1914, 113 (£100); *Memorial Exhibition*, 1918, 72
Literature: Pound, dating 1913, pp. 129, 137–38, no. 27, pls. XXI, XXII; Ede, *Life*, p. 198; Levy, p. 30, pl. 83; Cole (1978), no. 43, pp. 94–96.; Lewison (1983), p. 39, no. 56

Described in *List of Works* as 'Danseuse statuette grès rouge Mansfield, 1½' poli à la cire'. Gaudier's date of 1914 has rightly been challenged by Lewison since the work was included at the Alpine Club Exhibition in January. A suggestive passage in *Matka* (CUL), fol. 129a, immediately preceeding Brzeska's account of her first meeting with Nina Hamnett which took place in autumn 1913, contains Brzeska's criticisms of Gaudier's new style of 'Brancusi eggheads' and Gaudier's mention of 'an abstract sculpture in red stone that you've seen'.

70 Cat (pls. 89, 90)

Seravezza marble, 18 × 41 (7 × 16), varying depth, incised signature in monogram on base
Omega Workshop; J. Quinn; E. Pound;
M. de Rachewiltz; Collection Brunnenburg
Exhibited: London, Alpine Gallery, *Grafton Group*, 1914, 49; London, Whitechapel Art Gallery, *Twentieth Century Art*, 1914, 188.
Literature: Pound, p. 128, pl. XVIII; Ede, *Life*, p. 194; Cole (1978), no. 46, p. 99

Included in *List of Works* for 1913. Pound paid a deposit on Quinn's behalf, 7.9.15 and completed the transaction 7.2.16.

71 Maquette for a Bird Bath (pl. 149)

Plaster, inscribed 'scale ⅛ in.', 22 (7½; without base), base 6.3 × 26.7 × 26.7 (2½ × 10½ × 10½), R. Fry; A. Fry; London, Mercury Gallery; McMaster Art Gallery, University of Hamilton, Ontario
2 casts in 2 pieces cast by Fry, 4 casts in one piece *c.* 1960, sold by Beaux Arts Gallery (Cole)
Maquette scaled up by Jane Truzzi-Franconi, 1992, and an edition of 3 cast by Morris Singer on behalf of G. Raffles.
1. G. Raffles

2. Private collection
3. McMaster Art Gallery, University of Hamilton Ontario
Exhibited: *Memorial Exhibition*, 1918, 103 (vase plaster)
Literature: Cole (1978), no. 54, p. 107; Lewison (1983), no. 115; J. Collins, *The Omega Workshops*, 1983, pp. 73–74

Not listed by Ede. Commissioned by Roger Fry for the garden of his home, Durbins, where it would have been a companion to Eric Gill's nude female figure, exhibited as *Garden Statue* in the Second Post-Impressionist and Futurist Exhibition at the Grafton Gallery in October–December 1912. Collins proposes a date in winter 1913.

1914

72 **Coffer for Wilfred Scawen Blunt (pls. 100, 101)**

Pentelic marble body with lid in grey, pink-veined Sienese marble. Incised on opposite side from nude relief, 'Homage to W. S. BLUNT', incised signature in monogram on base, 11.4 × 26.3 × 12.2 (4½ × 10¼ × 4⅞), private collection
Literature: E. Pound, *Poetry*, March 1914; Pound, p. 129, no. 11; Ede, *Life*, p. 198; Cole (1978), no. 49, pp. 36, 101; E. Longford, *Pilgrimage of Passion*, 1979, pp. 393–96, presentation illustrated; O. Pound and A. W. Litz, *Ezra Pound and Dorothy Shakespear Their Letters 1909–1914*, 1984, pp. 300, 303

Carved in less than two weeks during January 1914, the casket was commissioned by Ezra Pound for £6 on behalf of W. B. Yeats, T. Sturge Moore, John Masefield, Victor Plarr, Frederic Manning, Richard Aldington, F. S. Flint and Pound himself, to contain scrolls of dedicatory verse by each poet. It was presented to Blunt at 'the Peacock Dinner' held at Blunt's home, Newbuildings Place, near Horsham, on Sunday 18 January 1914.

The proposal of a dinner and the form of presentation was only agreed between Pound's emissary, Lady Gregory, and Blunt on 28 December 1913. Gaudier was approached to make the casket during the following week; on 4 January Pound wrote to Lady Gregory, 'Gaudier-Brzeska is making a marble pen-box or reliquary or whatever it may be. I hope his decoration won't be too ultra-modern.' Its completion was a close-run thing; on 13 January Pound's future wife, Dorothy Shakespear, was asking him nervously, 'Has Blunt's trough been accomplished?' Pound replied the following day, 'Brzx *says* the sarcophagus will be done in time.'

Though this must have been one of the first works produced in 1914, 'Coffret, marbre pentélique et de Sienne, 1′ × 4″ × 6″' is the seventh work noted by Gaudier for 1914 in his *List of Works*. Pound described it as a 'very fine bas relief of a woman, on a small marble pyx presented to Wilfred Scawen Blunt.'

73 **Love Scene (pl. 93)**

Seravezza marble, 23.5 × 40.6 × 6 (9¼ × 16 × 2¼), unsigned
S. Brzeska Estate; F. Stoop; Contemporary Art Society, 1930; Doncaster Museum
Exhibited: *Memorial Exhibition*, 1918, probably 60 *Nude Man and Woman*
Literature: Pound, 1916, p. 160; Brodzky, illustrated opposite p. 81; Ede, p. 198; Cole (1978), no. 10, p. 57

Cole dates this work 1912 but also identifies it with '*Scène d'Amour*' in Gaudier's *List of Works* where it appears as a work of 1914. Lewison points out that since the *List* was compiled in July 1914 it is unlikely that Gaudier got the date of the work so far wrong. A dating in early 1914 is accepted here on the grounds of the similarity of the relief carving with that on the *Blunt Coffer* (*cat.* 72). In *Matka* (CUL), fol. 148b, Brzeska mentions in the course of a discussion about the imminent March 1914 London Group opening that Gaudier has consigned 'a white marble relief' and *Chanteuse Triste* (*cat.* 51) to the Chenil Gallery where he has hopes of selling them. A marble relief, priced at £20, is mentioned again as being in the care of the Chenil Gallery in Gaudier's 'will' 5.8.14 (reproduced in part by Cole, 95, p. 90). Wilenski's valuation of Brzeska's Estate includes '*Adam and Eve* marble relief, length 15 in.' (Cole, 95, p. 191)

This is one of very few sculptures for which a preparatory drawing is extant (pl. 92). Ede identified himself as the donor of this panel to the CAS but his dedication on the verso of the drawing ('To Frank Stoop from Ede an allusion to a most generous gift. June 1930') probably acknowledges Stoop's purchase and donation from the Brzeska Estate.

74 **Water Carrier (Vase statuette, pls. 117, 118, X).**

Seravezza marble figure and grey-veined, Sicilian marble cup, 41.3 × 12.4 × 9.7 (16¼ × 4⅞ × 3⅞)
Omega Workshops; J. Quinn; E. Pound; private collection on loan to Emerson Gallery, Hamilton College, Clinton, New York
Exhibited: London, Alpine Gallery, *Grafton Group*, 1914, 45 Vase, marble
Literature: Pound, p. 128, no. 9; Ede, *Life*, p. 198; Cole (1978), no. 45, p. 98, dating 1913–14

Described in *List of Works* as 'Vase, statuette, 1½′ × 3″ × 2″, with the note 'poli – pot en Sicilien – statue en Seravezza.' Purchased together with *Cat* (*cat.* 70) from Omega Workshops by Ezra Pound for John Quinn in 1916.

75 Caritas (Maternity, pls, 108, 109)

Portland stone, 47 (18½), S. Brzeska Estate; H. S. Ede; Orléans, Musée des Beaux-Arts
2 casts in artificial stone, both Cambridge, Kettle's Yard
Exhibited: London, Goupil Gallery, *London Group*, 1914, 111 (*Maternity* stone); London, *Vorticist Exhibition*, 1915, d as *Caritas*
Literature: Pound, p. 129, no. 29, pl. XVII; Ede, *Life*, p. 198; L. Taft, *Modern Tendencies in Sculpture*, 1921, pl. 57; Cole (1978), no. 44, p. 97; B. Cassat, *La Caritas: Une Oeuvre de Gaudier-Brzeska*, 1992; Cole (1995), p. 77

Described in the *List of Works* for 1914 as 'Maternité, group, 3 figures'. This work, together with *Stags* (*cat.* 77) and *Boy with Coney* (*cat.* 76), were exhibited in March at the Goupil Gallery. Cole states that Gaudier worked on this piece at the same time as on *Redstone Dancer* but Brzeska who was taken to see the latter in the studio and describes it in detail (fols. 129 and 133), only refers to *Caritas* explicitly much later and together with *Head of Ezra Pound* and being 'stone champagne corks' – 'trois tire-bouchons en pierre' (*Matka* [CUL], fol. 155b).

76 Boy with a Coney (pls. 104, 105, VI)

Red-veined alabaster, 34 × 16.8 × 13 (13⅜ × 6⅝ × 5⅛), incised signature in monogram on base
E. Pound; M. de Rachewiltz; Collection Brunnenburg
Exhibited: London, Goupil Gallery, *London Group*, 1914, 114 (£55); London, *AAA*, 1914, 1347; Doré Galleries, *Vorticist Exhibition*, 1915, a; *Memorial Exhibition*, 1918, 68
Literature: *The Egoist*, 16.2.14, p. 80 (related drawings); Pound, 'Exhibition at the Goupil Gallery', *The Egoist*, 16.3.14, p. 109; Gaudier-Brzeska, 'Allied Artists' Association', *The Egoist*, 15.6.14, p. 227; Pound, p. 129, no. 15; Ede, *Life*, p. 200; Cole (1978), no. 53, p. 106

Described in the *List of Works* as 'Enfant au lapin, statuette, alabâtre veiné rouge, 11″ haut'. Datable to early spring 1914.

77 Stags (pls. 113–116)

Red-veined alabaster, 34.9 × 34.3 (13¾ × 13½), J. Quinn; S. Lustgarten; Chicago, Art Institute
Exhibited: London, Goupil Gallery, *London Group*, 1914, 112 *Alabaster group*; *Memorial Exhibition*, 1918, 44
Literature: *Sketch*, 25.3.14 illustrated; *Blast* 1, 1914, xvii illustrated; Pound, pp. 45, 129, no. 14, pl. XXV; Ede, *Life*, p. 200; Brodzky illustrated opposite p. 44; B. L. Reid, *The Man from New York*, 1968, p. 374; Cole (1978), no. 52, pp. 104–5

Considering the importance of the piece remarkably little is known about it. Pound, who was a frequent visitor in early 1914 as he sat for his portrait, placed 'the works in veined alabaster, the *Stags* and *The Boy with a Coney*' together after the *Torsos* (*cat.* 59–61). From a reference in *Matka* (CUL), fol. 148b, datable to about March 1914, Brzeska and Gaudier entertained hopes that Pound would purchase this and 'the brass thing' (possibly *Doorknocker*, *cat.* 81, 82). Gaudier corresponded with Pound from the trenches about the sale of the work to John Quinn; at the time the sculpture was in the keeping of Renée Finch (Gaudier to Pound, 20 and 26.3.15). It was eventually sold to Quinn from the *Memorial Exhibition* for £260.

78 Imp (pls. 110–112)

Red-veined alabaster, 40.6 (16)
S. Brzeska Estate; H. S. Ede; London, Tate Gallery
Exhibited: London, Goupil Gallery, *London Group*, 1915, 96 (*Statuette in alabaster*); *Memorial Exhibition*, 1918, 28
Literature: Pound, p. 129, no. 28, pl. XXVII; Ede, *Life*, p. 205; Levy, p. 30, pl. 81; Cole (1978), no. 57, p. 110

Not included in *List of Works* but included in Ede's Supplement. The lowest segment had been broken off and misaligned during restoration. The alignment was corrected during restoration at the Tate Gallery in 1992.

79 (Hieratic) Head of Ezra Pound (pls. 121, 122, IX)

Pentelic marble, 91.4 × 61 (36 × 24), F. Madox Hueffer; E. Pound; R. Nasher
Synthetic stone cast on base by Isamo Noguchi, Collection Brunnenburg on loan to Fondazione Cini, Venice.
Exhibited: London, Whitechapel Gallery, *Twentieth Century Art*, 1914, 154 as *Bust of Mr Ezra Pound*; Milan, Undecesimo Triennale, 1957; London, Royal Academy, *British Art in the 20th Century*, 1987, 58

Literature: *Blast 2*, July 1915, illustrated p. 84 as *Head of Ezra Pound*; Pound, pp. 48–50, 129, no. 13; L. Taft, *Modern Tendencies in Sculpture*, 1921, pl. 58; Brodzky, pp. 58–62; Levy, p. 30, pl. 78; Cork, *Vorticism*, I, pp. 179–83; Cole (1978), no. 50, p. 102, F. A. Koslow, 'Gaudier-Brzeska and Ezra Pound', *The Print Collector's Newsletter*, XVI, 1985, pp. 153–69; L. Tickner, 'Now and Then: the *Hieratic Head of Ezra Pound*', *Oxford Art Journal*, 16, 1993, pp. 55–61; Cole (1978), p. 79

It is not clear whether the idea for a portrait originated with Gaudier or Pound but it soon evolved into a commission from Pound who purchased the marble block because he objected to Gaudier's intention to do it in plaster. Work began in January or early February, soon after Pound's return from Colemans Hatch, Sussex, where he had been assisting W. B. Yeats. Preceded and possibly accompanied by a series of 'Chinese' ink and brush drawings (pls. 119–20), the carving took 'two solid months of sheer cutting' including 'spare days for reforging the wornout chisels'. Photographs by Walter Benington show the carving in progress (fig. 45) and there are references to the evolution of the carving in Pound's letters to Dorothy Shakespear throughout March. It was only with the publication of Pound's Memoir that this piece acquired its familiar title, *Hieratic Head of Ezra Pound*, though Cole claims the title was jointly chosen.

It is included in *List of Works* as 'Ezra Pound, buste', sold for £2 10 shillings to Ford Madox Hueffer, 'vendu prix du marbre' and for many years it stood in the front garden of South Lodge, Campden Hill Road, where Hueffer lived with Violet Hunt. Subsequently in Pound's possession, it was sited at Brunnenberg.

80 Torpedo Fish or Toy (Ornement torpille, pls. 123–126, XII)

Cut bronze with incised signature in monogram on base, 15.9 × 3.8 × 3.2 (6¼ × 1½ × 1¼)
Original cut bronze T. E. Hulme; G. Freyer; D. Freyer; Anthony d'Offay; Toronto, Art Gallery of Ontario, 1985
9 numbered bronze casts by M. Gillespie, 1968, from the original cut brass. Inscribed on bottom edge 'HGB */9'
1. Paris, Musée National d'Art Moderne, 1968
2. London, Tate Gallery
3. Sotheby's 1.11.87 (70) illustrated; Mercury Gallery
4. and 6. Cambridge, Kettle's Yard
7. Bielefeld Kunsthalle
Exhibited: *Memorial Exhibition*, 1918, 23 *A Toy* carved in brass, lent by Mrs Kibblewhite
Literature: Pound, pp. 25, 129 as *Toy*, pl. XVI (reproduced upside down); R. H. Wilenski, *The Meaning of Modern Sculpture*, 200; Cole (1978), no. 63B, p. 117

The *List of Works* describes 'Ornement torpille bronze ciselé', sold for £2 to T. E. Hulme as well as a plaster model of the same piece which remained with the artist's possession. Pound groups this *Toy* with the two *Doorknockers*, describing this as 'the first experiment and the best of the three, but Gaudier made about a dozen small carvings during 1914. Epstein recorded that 'From Gaudier-Brzeska [Hulme] commissioned some small works which Gaudier thought it great fun to do. These were small brass carvings in a somewhat abstract style, and Hulme would carry them about in his pocket, and handle them while talking' (*Let There Be Sculpture*, 1940, p. 75). Few were exhibited and there is no clear chronological sequence.

81 Doorknocker (pl. 128)

Cut brass, 17.7 (7)
S. Brzeska Estate; H. S. Ede; Cambridge, Kettle's Yard 12 cast by Fiorini on behalf of Ede. Not apparently numbered but all have a small tongue at the back where Ede added a tongue to the original in order to use it as a doorknocker on his house in London.
1. Paris, Musée National d'Art Moderne, 1964
2. Private collection
3. Cambridge, Kettle's Yard
4. London, Tate Gallery
7. Sydney, Art Gallery of New South Wales
variant – London, Gimpel Fils, 1964; Washington, Hirshhorn Museum of Art – 17.7 × 18.8 (7 × 7½)
Exhibited: London, *AAA*, 1914, 1288 or 1349
Literature: *The Egoist*, 15.6.1914; Pound, p. 129; Brodzky, p. 90; Cole (1978), no. 62, p. 116; Lewison (1983), no. 97

Two doorknockers are included in Gaudier's *List of Works*, one 7 inches and one 8 inches long, 'taillé à même le bloc de bronze pas de coulage, poli'. The 7-inch one sold to Mrs Raphaël, 34 Hans Place. In 1930 Ede had mislaid the one which belonged to him, but the measurements of the Kettle's Yard piece are closer to 7 inches than 8 inches. The Hirshhorn piece is incised rear centre with artist's monogram and 'H Gaudier-Brzeska' and is slightly different in size from the Cambridge one, as well as being characterized by some small pits not present in the other casts.

82 Doorknocker 2

Cut and polished bronze, *c.* 17 (6¾), Mrs Raphael; location unknown
Exhibited: London, *AAA*, 1914, 1288 or 1349
Literature: Ede, *Life*, p. 198

This piece has not been identified with any certainty; it has been suggested that the Hirshhorn cast of *Doorknocker 1* (*cat.* 81) is the second piece but Ede, rightly in my view, was sceptical of the notion that Gaudier cut two virtually identical pieces by hand.

83 Insect Statuette

Portland and Bath stone, *c.* 76 (29⅞), location unknown
Exhibited: London, *AAA*, 1914, 1344
Literature: Ede, *Life*, p. 198; Cole (1978), no. 021, p. 127

Described in the *List of Works* as 'Insecte, statuette, pierres Portland and Bath, 2½′ haut', this sizable piece seems to have vanished without trace.

84 Small Fawn in Brown Stone (pl. 129)

Bath stone, 8.5 × 7 × 6.5 (3⅜ × 2¾ × 2½), D. Shakespear; E. Pound; O. Pound
5 bronze casts with varying patina by Nasini, Rome, unnumbered
3 casts – Collection Brunnenburg
Exhibited: London, Doré Gallery, *Vorticist Exhition* 1915, small object b; *Memorial Exhibition* 1918, 17 (dated 1913)
Literature: Pound, no. 23 or 24, pl. XVIII; Ede, *Life*, p. 198; Brodzky, p. 178; Cole (1978), no. 47, p. 100

Described in Gaudier's *List of Works* as 1914, 'Faun statuette, Bath stone coated with resin ['enduite de résine'], 3″ × 2″ × 2″ sold for £1 10s to Mrs E. Pound.' When attending the *Blast* dinner on 15 July 1914 Gaudier placed a small *Fawn* sculpture on Pound's plate in lieu of the 10 shilling price of the dinner which he could not afford; this might well have been this piece, given its scale, style and subsequent ownership. Conceivably the Pounds also paid him an additional sum for it. Pound contributes to the confusion surrounding the various *Fawn* pieces by reproducing this piece but identifying it with the *Crouching Fawn* (*cat.* 62), sold from the Alpine Gallery. This palm-sized piece functions well as a paperweight and may have been intended for this purpose. A *Paperweight* (*cat.* 87) owned by G. Hyde-Lees was exhibited in the Vorticist Exhibition in 1915.

85 Green Stone Charm (pls. 130, XIII)

Polished green Irish marble, 10.1 × 8.9 (4 × 3½), E. Pound; Anthony d'Offay; Los Angeles, private collection
Single bronze cast, late 1970s
1. Anthony d'Offay
Exhibited: Doré Galleries, *Vorticist Exhibition*, 1915, small object c; *Memorial Exhibition*, 1918, 22; Cambridge, 1983, no. 94
Literature: Pound, p. 129, no. 22; Ede, *Life*, p. 198; Brodzky, p. 56; Cole (1978), no. 58, p. 111

Gaudier describes several small ornamental pieces in his *List of Works*, two of which were in green stone, e.g. *Ornement, relief ajouré* in green Irish marble, and *Fish*, of which this seems to be the first, though the measurements given 7.6 × 7.6 (3 × 3) are approximate. Brodzky connected it with Gaudier's fascination with 'primitive' body and facial decoration; he wore the charm round his neck. It was used for the design impressed on the cover of the first edition of Pound's book.

86 Fish

Polished, green Irish marble, 5 × 2 (1¾ × ¾)
Literature: Ede, *Life*, p. 198

The only reference is in Gaudier's *List of Works* where this piece, *Charm* and *Relief Ornament* are grouped together as the first items listed in 1914. Drawings of fishes handled naturalistically and in a radically simplified, geometric manner can be found in one of Gaudier's small sketchbooks (Chenil Blue Book, sheet size to perforated edge *c.* 20.5 × 12.4 (8 × 5), private collection, detached leaves Orléans MO 638–59). It contains drawings related to a project for a medal or tray, *Torpedo Fish* (*cat.* 80), the cut brass *Fish* (*cat.* 93) and *Toy* (*cat.* 95) but nothing to indicate a more precise dating.

87 Ornament, relief (Paperweight)

Polished alabaster, 17.7 × 6.4 (7 × 2½), T. E. Hulme; G. Hyde Lees (1918); location unknown
6 bronze casts, including one half-thickness.
Exhibited: *Memorial Exhibition*, 1918, 27 *Letter-weight* bronze
Literature: Pound, p. 133; Ede, *Life*, pp. 198, 205

Grouped with the green marble *Fish* (*cat.* 86) and *Charm* (*cat.* 85) at the beginning of the 1914 entries in the *List of Works* where it is described as 'Ornement, relief ajouré, alabâtre, 7″ × 2½″' and 6 bronze replicas are mentioned. Ede adds the information that one half-thickness replica was owned by R. Fry and another by Mr Holley. Ede also adds in his Supplement, an alabaster *Paperweight*, owned in 1918 by G. Hyde-Lees and of which several brass reproductions existed. This information converges with Pound's reference to Gaudier's method of reducing life drawings to their relative masses 'working down to the simple design of his alabaster paperweight from a series of red "incomprehensible" skeletons of the human figure.' It seems feasible to suggest that they refer to the same object.

88 Knuckle-Duster (pl. 165)

Cut brass 7.6 × 11.4 (3 × 4½), G. Raffles; private collection
Exhibited: Cambridge, 1983, 96
Literature: Cole (1978), no. 65B; Cork, *Vorticism*, 1, p. 160; Lewison (1983), no. 96

This knuckle-duster was made for T. E. Hulme who described its meaning to Kate Lechmere: 'The two pieces curving out sideways at the bottom are the woman's parted legs. The central hole is her vagina, and the four holes at the top are the woman's head tossing and turning as she achieves orgasm.' (K. Lechmere interviewed by R. Cork)

89 Knuckle-Duster (pl. 166)

Cut brass, *c.* 7.6 × 11.4 (3 × 4½), private collection, Los Angeles
Literature: Cole (1978), no. 65A, p. 117
Cole alludes to references in Brzeska's *Journal* (Essex University Library) to knuckle-dusters cut in brass for Hulme and Lewis.

90 Duck (pl. 132)

Marble, 8.3 (3¼), S. Brzeska Estate; H. S. Ede; Cambridge, Kettle's Yard
12 bronze casts by Fiorini from the marble, 1964–68 and 1 separate casting in lead on behalf of H. S. Ede, 6.5 × 12 × 4 (2½ × 4¾ × 1⅝)
1. Paris, Musée National d'Art Moderne
2. Private collection
3. Cambridge, Kettle's Yard
4. London, Tate Gallery
5. H. S. Ede; private collection
Exhibited: Orléans, 1956, 5
Literature: Cole (1978), no. 55, p. 108

91 Medal

Perforated and chiselled iron, polished, *c.* 10 (3⅞) diameter, location unknown
Literature: Ede, *Life*, p. 200

Grouped with *Torpedo Fish* (*cat.* 80), *Fish* (*cat.* 93) and *Relief Ornament* (*cat.* 87) by Gaudier in his *List of Works* for 1914. Purchased by T. E. Hulme for 10 shillings. This and *cat.* 92 may be connected to the circular abstract design in red wash reproduced on the title page of Ede's *Life*.

92 Medal

Perforated and chiselled bronze, polished, *c.* 10 (3⅞) diameter, sold for £1 5s to an unknown buyer from Cheshire; location unknown
Literature: Ede, *Life*, p. 200
Mentioned in the *List of Works*.

93 Fish (pl. 139)

Chiselled bronze, approx 12.7 × 5.1 (5 × 2; *List of Works*) Mrs E. Kibblewhite; location unknown
Exhibited: *Memorial Exhibition*, 1918, 24
Literature: Pound, p. 25, pl. XVI (describes as cut brass); Ede, *Life*, p. 200; Cole (1978), no. 64, p. 117

A small blue sketchbook, datable to 1914 (Chenil Blue Book, sheet size to perforated edge *c.* 20.5 × 12.4 [8 × 4⅞] private collection, detached leaves Orléans MO 638–59) contain many drawings of fish, both naturalistic and stylized.

94 Portrait of Ezra Pound (pls. 133–35, IX)

Wood, 73 × 17.2 × 17.2 (28¾ × 6¾ × 6¾)
J. Rodker; London, Hanover Gallery; New Haven, Yale University Art Gallery
Exhibited: Cambridge, 1983, 70
Literature: Pound, p. 49; Cole (1978), no. 51, p. 103

The piece appears to have been hewn from a square-sectioned length of cut timber. It is not mentioned in Gaudier's *List of Works*, nor in any other early publication on Gaudier. Pound claimed enigmatically that the sculptor 'preferred a small sketch made later, to the actual statue', i.e. *cat.* 94. Its first documented owner was John Rodker, whose Ovid Press published a portfolio of 20 Gaudier drawings, mostly belonging to Pound, in 1919. It has generally been accepted as Gaudier's work.

95 Brass Toy (pls. 136–38)

Cut brass, 0.6 (¼)
Made by artist for father of vendor; Sotheby's 26.11.69 (63) illustrated; G. Raffles

Literature: Cole (1978), no. 63A, p. 117; Lewison, Kettle's Yard, no. 95
Not mentioned in *List of Works*.

96 **Dog (Dachshund, pls. 140, 141)**

Marble (damaged), 15.2 × 35.3 (6 × 14), H. S. Ede; Sir Dyer Simpson; J. D. Simpson (Edinburgh, 1972)
1 aluminium cast, patinated brown, Cardiff, National Museum of Wales, 1966
12 bronzes cast by Fiorini on behalf of H. S. Ede, 1964, 15.5 × 35.5 × 8 (6⅛ × 14 × 3⅛), no inscription or cast number. A further 3 numbered casts were taken by Bernard Meadows at the Royal College of Art, *c.* 1965–70, from a plaster owned by J. Wood Palmer.
1. Kettle's Yard; Paris, Musée National d'Art Moderne, 1964
2. and 10. Cambridge, Kettle's Yard
3–6. Private collections
7. Washington, Phillips Collection
8. Sydney, Art Gallery of New South Wales
11. London, Tate Gallery
(Meadows 1/3) Sotheby's 12.5.83 (102); Mercury Gallery
Exhibited: London, J. and E. Bumpus, *Henri Gaudier-Brzeska*, 1931, 40
Literature: Ede, *Life*, p. 205, pl. XXVII; Ede, *SM*, 'Marble sketch' or unfinished marble opposite p. 84; Cole (1978), no. 56, p. 109

Cole refers to Sophie calling it 'Dachshound'. The marble was broken while in Ede's possession and subsequently repaired and entered the collection of Sir Dyer Simpson, chairman of the insurance company, following settlement of the claim (Ede to R. Morphet, Tate Gallery, 1961). It was presumably as a result of this that the cast(s) in plaster were taken to facilitate the making of the aluminium and later bronze casts.

A somewhat unresolved study, its close relationship to aspects of Epstein's *Rock Drill* and *Doves* (both 1913) may account for its omission from the *List of Works*. It was not exhibited in Gaudier's lifetime.

97 **Bird Swallowing a Fish (Sea Bird, pls. 142, 145)**

Carved plaster, painted green, 31.7 (12½)
S. Brzeska Estate; H. S. Ede; Cambridge, Kettle's Yard
Bronze, 31 × 60 × 29 (12¼ × 23⅝ × 11⅜), not apparently numbered.
1. Artist's Estate; New York, private collection (destroyed)
1964 casts:
1. H. Moore Estate
2. Cambridge, Kettle's Yard
3. London Tate Gallery
4. Paris, Musée National d'Art Moderne, 1964
5. Bielefeld Kunsthalle
6. Private collection
7. Anthony d'Offay; Edinburgh, Scottish National Gallery of Modern Art, 1980
8. H. S. Ede; Otterloo, Kröller-Müller Museum, 1968
Exhibited: London, *AAA*, 1914, 1345 *Bird*, £50, gunmetal; *Memorial Exhibition*, 1918, 95 (*Sea Bird*)
Literature: Ede, *Life*, p. 205; Levy, p. 30, pl. 80; B. L. Reid, *The Man from New York*, 1968, p. 250; Cole (1978), no. 66, pp. 118–19

Gaudier's *List of Works* mentions only a plaster of this piece but a bronze cast had also been made and was exhibited in the London Salon. Correspondence between John Quinn and Ezra Pound in 1915–16, and between Pound and the Leicester Galleries in 1918, alludes to the existence of a single bronze cast as well as a plaster. Quinn's offer to have a second cast made for Pound was refused. Ede (letter to Tate 17.6.64) stated that one or two casts had been made in Brzeska's lifetime, of which one was destroyed by fire in New York, though in 1975 he stated that only one cast had been made in Brzeska's lifetime. Cole stated that notes left by Sophie suggest she arranged for 3 casts (letter to Scottish National Gallery of Modern Art 22.11.82).

Ede had 6 bronzes cast from the original plaster by Fiorini and patinated by Henry Moore in 1964. Ede had a further 4 cast by John W. Mills (Mills to R. Cole, 13.12.77).

98 **Men with Bowl (pl. 146)**

Plaster, painted brown, 31 × 26.5 × 14.5 (12¼ × 10⅜ × 5¾), M. Levy; Orléans, Musée des Beaux-Arts
4 bronze casts by Gaskin's Foundry, London, *c.* 1965, 30.5 (12)
The Cardiff Gallery; Mrs Bowen; Cardiff, National Museum of Wales, 1992
London, Mercury Gallery
Cambridge, Kettle's Yard
Exhibited: Cardiff Gallery, 1953, no. 7
Literature: Cole (1978), no. 59, p. 112

Not included in the *List of Works* or Ede's Supplement but the attribution has never been questioned. Possibly intended as a garden ornament or bird bath. The clay or plaster has been cut into jagged facets in a manner that fuses Cubism with African wood carving.

99 Maquette for Flower Vase 1 (Garden Ornament 2, pl. 150)

Clay (destroyed), plaster, 63.5 × 21.5 × 22 (25 × 8½ × 8⅝) cast for Ede 1935; London, Hanover Gallery, 1957; London, Tate Gallery (T365)
3 bronze casts by Susse Frères for Hanover Gallery
1. Hanover Gallery; Mrs D. Ogden Stewart; H. Diamond; J. H. Hirshhorn; Washington, Hirshhorn Museum
2. Cambridge, Kettle's Yard
1 bronze cast by order of the Trustees, 1961, London, Tate Gallery (T403)
Exhibited: *Memorial Exhibition*, 1918, 60; Leeds, 1943, 81; Orléans, 1956, 72
Literature: Brodzky, pp. 134–37; Cole (1978), no. 60, p. 114; J. Collins, *The Omega Workshops*, 1983, pp. 74–75, pl. 28

This and *cat.* 100 were maquettes for two stone flower-vases, commissioned in Spring 1914 through the Omega Workshops as part of Omega's redecoration of the entrance hall of 1 Hyde Park Gardens for Lady Ian Hamilton. The two maquettes differ radically, this one having a very deep bowl while *cat.* 100 has a very shallow one. Neither was particularly functional. Their dissimilarity may indicate that they represent alternative solutions to the design, only one of which would have been chosen for carving. At any event they were never completed. Two large blocks of greyish stone were delivered to the studio but proved, according to Brodzky's account, impossible to carve. After several days' work during which he broke several points on the stone, Gaudier had only carved a shallow groove in the top of one block. In October 1914 when Brodzky visited the abandoned studio, 'The stones lay there in the yard, the grass sprouting between them, now firmly embedded by their weight in the ground.'

100 Maquette for Flower Vase 2 (Garden Ornament 3, pl. 148)

Carved plaster, 35 × 28 × 26 (13¾ × 11 × 10¼), Cambridge, Kettle's Yard on loan to Leeds City Art Gallery
1 early cast in lead made on Ede's instructions, pre-1943. 37 (12¾)
6 bronzes cast by Fiorini and patinated by Henry Moore, 1964 and 2 cast by R. Rowe, *c.* 1965, 36 × 28 × 27.5 (14⅛ × 11 × 10⅞), unnumbered, London, Tate Gallery
2 casts Cambridge, Kettle's Yard.
Paris, Musée National d'Art Moderne, 1964
Exhibited: Leeds, 1943, 82
Literature: Brodzky, pp. 134–37; Cole (1978), no. 61. p. 115

With *cat.* 99, commissioned by Lady Ian Hamilton in Spring 1914 and left unfinished in September on Gaudier's final departure for France.

101 Ornament (carved toothbrush, pl. 131)

Bone, 17.1 (6¾), signed in monogram, R. Bevan; Anthony d'Offay
Exhibited: *Memorial Exhibition*, 1918, 28A
Literature: Ede, *Life*, p. 200; Levy, p. 30, pl. 84; Cole (1978), no. 69, p. 124; Cole (1995), 95, p. 99

A 1914 work described as 'Ornement, os, 3″ × ¼, taillé dans manche de brosse à dent et enfumé' in the *List of Works*. Purchased by Mme Karlowska (Mrs Robert Bevan) for 10 shillings. Levy claims this as the only survivor of Gaudier's wartime carving but this cannot be correct.

102 Reclining Woman

Seravezza marble relief, 25.4 × 10.2 (10 × 4), Renée Finch; location unknown

This is one of the last items in Gaudier's *List of Works*, described as 'Femme couchée, relief' in Seravezza marble. It was sold to Renée Finch at the auction in aid of the Spencer Gore exhibition, after the artist's death in March 1914. Renée Finch, a French artist long resident in London, was a fellow member of the London Group, serving on the hanging committee for its first exhibition in March 1914, together with Epstein, Spencer Gore, Edward Wadsworth and J. B. Manson. She became especially friendly with Sophie Brzeska and, with Stanislawa de Karlowska, helped to console Sophie after Gaudier's departure for France. Several of Gaudier's works including *Stags* (*cat.* 77) and *Seated Woman* (*cat.* 105) were stored at her home in the King's Road. *Crouching Figure* has been identified with this 'lost' work but Gaudier clearly indicates that this was a relief, which *Crouching Woman* is not. The work was considered lost but has recently been identified on the grounds of scale, style and technique with a small alabaster piece carved on both sides (Christie's 23.11.93 [114] illustrated).

103 Monkeys (pl. 147)

Sandstone 17.7 × 16 × 10.5 (7 × 6¼ × 4⅛), S. Brzeska Estate; H. S. Ede; Cambridge, Kettle's Yard
12 unnumbered casts in composite stone by Fiorini on behalf of Ede, 1964–68, 18 × 15 × 9.5 (7⅛ × 5⅞ × 3¾).

Cambridge, Kettle's Yard (2 casts)
London, Tate Gallery
Paris, Musée National d'Art Moderne, 1966
Sydney, Art Gallery of New South Wales, 1968
Literature: Ede, *Life*, p. 204; Cole (1978), no. 13, p. 60

Not mentioned in *List of Works*. Cole proposes that the piece was begun in 1912 and changed in 1914 by cutting triangular designs on heads, but there seems no reason to suppose such a long drawn out process for what is essentially an informal sketch. The grouping of several figures and the balance of simple masses are recurrent themes in 1914; compare *Caritas* (*cat.* 75) and *Birds Erect* (*cat.* 107).

104 Study for Seated Woman (pls. 151, 152)

Plaster, 30.5 × 27.5 × 23.6 (12 × 10⅞ × 9¼), Espace Cardin, Paris, 6.12.85; Orléans, Musée des Beaux-Arts

The source of this maquette for one of Gaudier's last sculptures remains obscure.

105 Seated Woman (pls. 154–156, XV)

Marble, 47 × 34.5 × 28 (18½ × 13½ × 11)
J. Quinn, 1918; H. Wesson-Bull and P. Loomis; Cambridge, Kettle's Yard; Paris, Musée National d'Art Moderne, 1964
7 casts by Michael Gillespie on behalf of Ede, of which 1 unnumbered, 47 × 34.5 × 21.5 (18½ × 13½ × 8½)
O. Bielefeld Kunsthalle
1. and 4. Private collections
2. and 5. Cambridge, Kettle's Yard (0/6 and 5/6)
3. London, Tate Gallery
5. Australia, Private collection
6. Bradford Art Galleries and Museums
Exhibited: London, *AAA*, March 1916, 1; *Memorial Exhibition*, 1918, 80; New York, Sculptors' Gallery, *Seven English Modernists*, 1922
Literature: Pound, 1916, pp. 68, 160, pl. 19; L. Taft, *Modern Tendencies in Sculpture*, 1921, p. 28, pl. 55; S. Cheney, *A Primer of Modern Art*, 1924, illustrated; Ede, *Life*, p. 200, pl. XLIV; Cole (1978), no. 67, pp. 120–21

Described in *List of Works* where it is the last sculpture entry as '"Femme assise" marbre pentélique strié poli à la cire'. Pound identifies this as 'his last or almost his last work.' In a letter from the trenches Gaudier refers to 'a big marble, a sleeping woman, which you have never seen' (Gaudier to Pound, 20.3.15).

106 Mlle (Marie) Borne (pls. 157, 160)

Bronze, 40 × 29.8 × 34.2 (15¾ × 11¾ × 13½)
Original plaster: G. Eumorfopoulos; location unknown
Ede, 1930, lists 3 bronze casts
1. G. Eumorfopoulos (by 1930); Sotheby's 1940; D. Angus; Leicester Gallery, *c.* 1947
2. H. S. Ede (by 1930)
3. Viscount Tredegar (by 1943)
Cole estimates the total number of bronze casts at 12.
1. Mercury Gallery, London
2. E. Estorick; Cambridge, Kettle's Yard
3. Grosvenor Gallery; Cardiff, National Museum of Wales, 1978
4. Kettle's Yard; Paris, Musée National d'Art Moderne, 1964
Exhibited: *Memorial Exhibition*, 1918, 101 *Bust of Mlle B*, plaster, 1914
Literature: Ede, *Life*, p. 205; Brodzky, plaster illustrated opposite p. 111 (dated 1914); Levy, p. 29, pl. 72; Levy, p. 29, pl. 72; Cole (1978), no. 8, p. 55 (dated 1912); Cole (1995), p. 88, dates 1914

Not included in Gaudier's *List of Works*, but a plaster and three bronzes are listed in Ede's Supplement for 1914. Brodzky follows this dating but Cole and Lewison are agreed in placing it in 1912 on the basis of its style. A *Bust; Mlle Borne* was among the plasters deposited for custody at the Victoria and Albert Museum by Sophie Brzeska at the end of May 1916 and returned to her two years later just before the opening of the Leicester Galleries *Memorial Exhibition* where it was shown as *Mlle B*. This identification has a radical effect on the dating of the portrait since Marie Borne was a young Frenchwoman, teaching in England, whom Sophie and Henri met while on holiday at Littlehampton in late September 1913. She kept in touch with Sophie and was sufficiently friendly with her in 1914 not only to suggest her own parents at Chamy as possible hosts for Sophie, who was hoping to return to France for part of the summer, but also to rent lodgings with Sophie in London from June to September 1914. There she was escorted assiduously by Gaudier, somewhat to Sophie's alarm, as she observed the attraction between them. The outbreak of war lead to Mlle Borne's departure. The whole episode is recounted by Brzeska in *Matka* (CUL), fols. 161–64. The context of the story suggests that on their first meeting, Brzeska rather than Gaudier had taken notice of her. In the light of this evidence both drawings and sculpture must be dated in the summer of 1914.

107 **Birds Erect (pls. 161–63, XIV)**

Limestone, 68.3 (27), New York, Museum of Modern Art
One cast in artificial stone, Cambridge, Kettle's Yard
Exhibited: *Memorial Exhibition*, 1918, 56 *Birds erect*; London, Royal Academy, *British Art in the 20th Century*, 1987, 60
Literature: Pound, 1916, p. 161, pl. xx; Brodzky, p. 92; Levy, p. 30, pl. 79; Cole (1978), no. 68, p. 123; Lewison (1983), no. 111

Not included in *List of Works* and thus, judging from its style and accomplishment, one of his last works. Pound stresses that 'the representative element is very slight' and relates the piece to the formal experiments begun with the *Toy* (*Torpedo Fish*, *cat.* 80) and its preparatory drawings. Brodzky states this work was inspired by cacti on the studio window-sill.

While in the trenches Gaudier produced several small sculptures from the materials to hand, all of which appear to have been lost. Ede lists these as two *Groups* in wood and soft stone; 'Monsieur Ménager [Gaudier's C.O.] tells me that Gaudier did three or four small bits of sculpture in the trenches, either from the butts of rifles or in soft stone, using only his penknife. These works were preserved for a little while, and then thrown away to make room for clothing.' (Ede, *Life* pp. 187, 206)

108 **Maternity**

Walnut wood; lost
Literature: Ede, pp. 187, 206

'I am doing some little pieces of sculpture. A few days ago I did a small Maternity statue out of the butt end of a German rifle; it's magnificent walnut wood and I managed to cut it quite successfully with an ordinary knife. The Captain has asked me to do it to give as a present to someone.' (Gaudier to G. Gaudier, 12.11.14)

UNDATABLE WORKS

109 **'Little Dancer'**

Medium unknown, *c.* 50–60 (19⅝–23⅝), destroyed
Literature: Ede, *Life*, p. 145

In a letter to Brzeska (28.11.12) Gaudier planned to make his projected wrestler and bather statuettes (*cat.* 32) 'the size of your little dancer'. This suggests a single figure rather than the *Firebird* group, though the inspiration may also have been the Ballets Russes. *Dancer* (*cat.* 58) is dated 1913 in the plaster so cannot be the work referred to here.

110 **Angel**

Painted alabaster, destroyed
Literature: Pound, 1916, pp. 49, 128

Described by Pound as having 'enormous breasts, in alabaster with its robe painted scarlet and with the face of an ignominious Dante' and 'a scandalous satire', though whether of religious art or of a particular personality such as Amy Lowell, whose ample form Gaudier had admired at the Dieudonné dinner in July 1914, is unknown. Pound refers to other lightheartedly satirical pieces including a 'tiny clay model' of his cat trying to see something under the shelf upon which it was placed which was 'a parody of all religion, a kneeling posture, a derision of all self-humiliating religiosity', and parodies of himself and Sophie Brzeska in wax 'which parodies she threw at him or at the stove'. See also *cat.* 111 below.

111 **Pottery Head (pl. 51)**

Earthenware, glazed white, *c.* 10.2 (4), Cambridge, Kettle's Yard
Literature: Cole (1978), no. 011, p. 127

Cole identifies this as a likely Omega piece although its resemblance to *Head of an Idiot* and the *Head of Brodzky* is striking.

112 **Serpents Entwined**

Wax (damaged on top by melting in sun); probably destroyed
Literature: Ede, *Life*, p. 205

113 **Mask of Man's Head**

Wax

Mentioned as a work in his possession by H. S. Ede in correspondence with Philip Hendy, Leeds City Art Gallery, in 1942 during preparations for the 1943 Leeds exhibition.

114 Woman, Statuette

Plaster or bronze, *c.* 10 (3⅞)
S. Brzeska; T. E. Hulme; location unknown

An undated letter, datable to August–September 1914, from T. E. Hulme to Edward Marsh, 'I have a very little clay statuette by H. Gaudier which Mlle Brzeska gave me, about 4 inches high, of a woman [illegible] and have had it cast. I could give you another cast if you liked it' (photostats of Hulme correspondence, University of Hull).

115 Erotic Sketch (pl. 164)

Bronze, 12.1 (4¾), Dr J. A. Jellicoe; Leicester Galleries; Dr N. Goodman 1933; Victoria and Albert Museum, 1971; transferred to Tate Gallery (T03732)
Literature: Cole (1978), no. 024, p. 128 as *Figure Study*

This slight sketch of a masturbating female figure is not recorded in any early literature but the possibility should be considered that it is *cat.* 114.

Rejected work

Crouching Figure (pls. 167, 168)

White marble, 22.2 × 30.5 × 10.2 (8¾ × 12 × 4), Sotheby's, 1955; Leicester Galleries, 1957; Minneapolis, Walker Art Center
Exhibited: Orléans, 1956, 12; London, Arts Council, 1956, 10; Edinburgh, SNGMA, 1972, 28; Arts Council, *Vorticism and Its Allies*, 1974, 106; Whitechapel Art Gallery, *British Sculpture of the Twentieth Century*, 1981, 44; London, Royal Academy, *British Art in the 20th Century*, 1987, 62
Literature: Cole (1978), no. 35, p. 86; C. Harrison, *English Art and Modernism 1900–1939*, 1981, p. 107, pl. 46; R. Cork, 'The Vorticist Circle, Bomberg and the First World War', in *British Art in the 20th Century*, 1987, pp. 139–40

Little is known about this work before its appearance at auction in 1955; a provenance in John Quinn's collection suggested by the sale catalogue is not supported by the extensive correspondence and documentation on Quinn's collecting activity and the dispersal of the Estate 1924–27. Notwithstanding the weakness of the provenance and its stylistic oddities it has been widely accepted and exhibited as Gaudier's work. Cole suggests it was begun in 1913 and completed in 1914; he identifies it with the 1914 relief, 'Femme couchée relief, marbre Seravezza 10″ × 4″ sold to Renée Finch, 247 Kings Road, for 18/- vendu à l'enchère pour l'exposition Spencer Gore' in Gaudier's *List of Works* (*cat.* 102). However, it is not a relief carving. Harrison identifies this and *Maternity* (*cat.* 64) as 'among his most successful works'. Cork accepts it as evidence of the plurality of Gaudier's stylistic experiments and as 'a *tour de force* of direct carving'. Lewison, however, has queried the attribution to Gaudier and suggested a follower, such as the young Leon Underwood. I share his scepticism. While the piece has the compactness and improvisational composition so often found in Gaudier's carving from stone fragments, certain aspects of the figure, notably the elongated and mannered handling of the limbs, are completely uncharacteristic. Though accomplished, it seems considerably later than 1913–14.

VORTEX GAUDIER-BRZESKA

THROUGH ITS PUBLICATION in the first issue of *Blast* in June 1914 and its inclusion in Ezra Pound's 1916 *Memoir*, 'Vortex Gaudier-Brzeska' became the best known of Gaudier's few writings. Pound, Aldington and Hueffer acknowledged it as one of the finest literary efforts stimulated by the Rebel Art Centre and Vorticism. I have suggested elsewhere in this text that Gaudier's writings were as well if not better known than his sculpture for some years after his death.

The cryptic intensity of the essay, with its echoes of Imagism and Pound's own obliquely evocative cross-references, justifies its publication in full. The typographic flourishes were not entirely those of Lewis; the autograph manuscript* reveals that the typography was in part a translation of Gaudier's own idiosyncratic layout, underlinings and calligraphic changes of scale. The autograph text contains very few alterations though Zadkine's name was included and then deleted from the roll call of 'moderns'.

* Princeton University Library; reproduced in E. Pound, R. de Gourmont, M. Ménier and F. Koslow Miller, *Henri Gaudier-Brzeska par Ezra Pound*, Toulouse, 1992, pp. 284–88).

VORTEX.

GAUDIER BRZESKA.

Sculptural energy is the mountain.

Sculptural feeling is the appreciation of masses in relation.

Sculptural ability is the defining of these masses by planes.

The PALEOLITHIC VORTEX resulted in the decoration of the Dordogne caverns.

Early stone-age man disputed the earth with animals.

His livelihood depended on the hazards of the hunt—his greatest victory the domestication of a few species.

Out of the minds primordially preoccupied with animals Fonts-de-Gaume gained its procession of horses carved in the rock. The driving power was life in the absolute—the plastic expression the fruitful sphere.

The sphere is thrown through space, it is the soul and object of the vortex—

The intensity of existence had revealed to man a truth of form—his manhood was strained to the highest potential—his energy brutal—HIS OPULENT MATURITY WAS CONVEX.

The acute fight subsided at the birth of the three primary civilizations. It always retained more intensity East.

The HAMITE VORTEX of Egypt, the land of plenty—

Man succeeded in his far reaching speculations—Honour to the divinity !

Religion pushed him to the use of the VERTICAL which inspires awe. His gods were self made, he built them in his image, and RETAINED AS MUCH OF THE SPHERE AS COULD ROUND THE SHARPNESS OF THE PARALLELOGRAM.

He prfeerred the pyramid to the mastaba.

The fair Greek felt this influence across the middle sea.

The fair Greek saw himself only. HE petrified his own semblance.

HIS SCULPTURE WAS DERIVATIVE his feeling for form secondary. The absence of direct energy lasted for a thousand years.

The Indians felt the hamitic influence through Greek spectacles. Their extreme temperament inclined towards asceticism, admiration of non-desire as a balance against abuse produced a kind of sculpture without new form perception—and which is the result of the peculiar

VORTEX OF BLACKNESS AND SILENCE.

PLASTIC SOUL IS INTENSITY OF LIFE BURSTING THE PLANE.

The Germanic barbarians were verily whirled by the mysterious need of acquiring new arable lands. They moved restlessly, like strong oxen stampeding.

The SEMITIC VORTEX was the lust of war. The men of Elam, of Assur, of Bebel and the Kheta, the men Armenia and those of Canaan had to slay each other crully for the possession of fertile valleys. Their gods sent them the vertical direction, the earth, the SPHERE.

They elevated the sphere in a splendid squatness and created the HORIZONTAL.

From Sargon to Amir-nasir-pal men built man-headed bulls in horizontal flight-walk. Men flayed their their captives alive and erected howling lions : THE ELONGATED HORIZONTAL SPHERE BUTTRESSED ON FOUR COLUMNS, and their kingdoms disappeared.

Christ flourished and perished in Yudah.

Christianity gained Africa, and from the seaports of the Mediterranean it won the Roman Empire.

The stampeding Franks came into violent contact with it as well as with the Groeco-Roman tradition.

They were swamped by the remote reflections of the two vortices of the West.

Gothic sculpture was but a faint echo of the HAMITO-SEMITIC energies through Roman traditions, and it lasted half a thousand years, and it wilfully divagated again into the Greek derivation from the land of Amen-Ra.

VORTEX OF A VORTEX ! !

VORTEX IS THE POINT ONE AND INDIVISIBLE !

VORTEX IS ENERGY ! and it gave forth SOLID EXCREMENTS in the quattro é cinquo cento, LIQUID until the seventeenth century, GASES whistle till now. THIS is the history of form value in the West until the FALL OF IMPRESSIONISM.

The black-haired men who wandered through the pass of Khotan into the valley of the YELLOW RIVER lived peacefully tilling their lands, and they grew prosperous.

Their paleolithic feeling was intensified. As gods they had themselves in the persons of their human ancestors—and of the spirits of the horse and of the land and the grain.

THE SPHERE SWAYED.

THE VORTEX WAS ABSOLUTE.

The Shang and Chow dynasties produced the convex bronze vases.

The features of Tao-t'ie were inscribed inside of the square with the rounded corners—the centuple spherical frog presided over the inverted truncated cone that is the bronze war drum.

THE VORTEX WAS INTENSE MATURITY. Maturity is fecunditty—they grew numerous and it lasted for six thousand years.

The force relapsed and they accumlated wealth, forsook their work, and after losing their form-understanding through the Han and T'ang dynasties, they founded the Ming and found artistic ruin and sterility.

THE SPHERE LOST SIGNIFICANCE AND THEY ADMIRED THEMSELVES.

During their great period off-shoots from their race had landed on another continent.—After many wanderings some tribes settled on the highlands of Yukatan and Mexico.

When the Ming were losing their conception, these nel-Mongols had a flourishing state. Through the strain of warfare they submitted the Chinese sphere to horizontal treatment much as the Semites had done. Their cruel nature and temperament supplied them with a stimulant: THE VORTEX OF DESTRUCTION.

Besides these highly developed peoples there lived on the world other races inhabiting Africa and the Ocean islands.

When we first knew them they were very near the paleolithic stage. Though they were not so much dependent upon animals their expenditure of energy was wide, for they began to till the land and practice crafts rationally, and they fell into contemplation before their sex: the site of their great energy: THEIR CONVEX MATURITY.

They pulled the sphere lengthways and made the cylinder, this is the VORTEX OF FECUNLITY, and it has left us the masterpieces that are knowns as love charms.

The soil was hard, material difficult to win from nature, storms frequent, as also fevers and other epidemics. They got frightened : This is the VORTEX OF FEAR, its mass is the POINTED CONE, its masterpieces the fetishes.

And WE the moderns : Epstein, Brancusi, Archipenko, Dunikowski, Modigliani, and myself, through the incessant struggle in the complex city, have likewise to spend much energy.

The knowledge of our civilisation embraces the world, we have mastered the elements.

We have been influenced by what we liked most, each according to his own individuality, we have crystallized the sphere into the cube, we have made a combination of all the possible shaped masses—concentrating them to express our abstract thoughts of conscious superiority.

Will and consciousness are our

VORTEX.

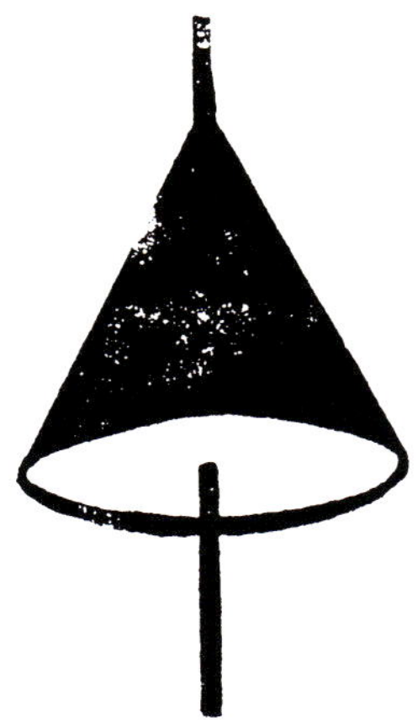

NOTES TO THE TEXT

Introduction

1. F. Marc (1880–1916), A. Macke (1887–1914), G. Apollinaire (1880–1918), R. Duchamp-Villon (1876–1918), U. Boccioni (1882–1916), T. E. Hulme (1883–1917).

2. To Professor Felix E. Schelling, University of Pennsylvania, D. D. Paige (ed.), *Selected Letters 1907–1941 of Ezra Pound*, London, 1971, p. 61.

3. Pound, pp. 20, 106.

4. Christian Roger's photographs for *Henri Gaudier-Brzeska par Ezra Pound*, Editions Tristram, 1992, are of outstanding quality.

1. St Jean de Braye and Orléans

1. One or both families had ancestral links further north than the Loiret. Gaudier gave the destruction of his grandfather's house by the German advance as one of his reasons for returning to France to enlist. *Matka* (CUL), fol. 165.

2. 'Gaudier's ancestors had been masons and stone carvers for generations and had worked on the cathedral of Chartres', Pound, p. 76.

3. *Matka* (Orléans) section 136.

4. Sécretain, pp. 23–24.

5. Kitty Smith interviewed for *Vortex Gaudier-Brzeska*, BBC Radio, 19.5.65. She and her brother visited Orléans in 1913 and spent a day with the Gaudiers, though Henri was then in England and in disgrace with the family for having evaded his military service.

6. *Ibid.*

7. K. Smith to H. Brodzky, 15.9.64 (Tate Gallery Archive).

8. Gaudier to Brzeska, 24.11.1912, Ede, *SM*, pp. 204–5.

9. J. A. Mangeot, *'Benjamin Franklin' Petite Historie d'un Grand Lycée*, n.d.

10. At fourteen, at the end of his third year, he received the Certificat d'Etudes Primaires Supérieures, going on to pass the Brevet Elémentaire which qualified him to enter for the foreign bursary in autumn 1906; B. Fauquembergue, 'Henri Gaudier-Brzeska, vingt-trois ans et demi!' in *Henri Gaudier-Brzeska*, exhibition catalogue, Orléans and Toulouse, 1993, p. 19.

11. Ede, *Life*, colour plate.

12. 'Je les ait [sic] fait, cela me suffit, si je les gardais, je serais tenté de les refaire, et cela me serais plutôt nuisible.' G. Gaudier to Ede(?), 25.11.28 in Cole, p. 9, note 3. Quoted in variant form by Sécretain, p. 24.

13. Ede, *SM*, p. 122.

14. *Matka* (Orléans) fol. 130, section 94.

15. Ede, *SM*, p. 26, asserts that the French idiom Gaudier used – 'je lui ai donné de tels coups de pieds' – was merely a proverb to express his victory in argument. Sécretain, p. 25, suggests they came to blows. Sophie's autobiographical novel dealing with the period of her stay at Combleux, also suggests violence; in response to her praise of Mr Gaudier's courtesy Gaudier replies, 'Il n'est pas méchant maintenant parce que je suis grand mais il me battait affreusement quand j'étais à la maison.' 'Pourquoi?' 'A propos de tout et de rien du tout, il se mettait dans les rages bleus et cela retombait d'habitude sur moi.' *Matka* (Orléans) fol. 130, section 94.

16. See T. Zeldin, *France 1848–1945: Intellect and Pride*, Oxford, 1980, chapter 2 for attitudes to provincial life.

17. *Le Républicain orléanais et du Centre*, 2.8.07.

18. T. Zeldin, *France 1848–1945: Intellect and Pride*, pp. 88–89.

2. Bristol and Cardiff

1. Correspondence now in the Tate Gallery Archive.

2. B. S. Ching to H. S. Ede, 9.1.29 (Kettle's Yard).

3. A. Hazell to H. S. Ede, March 1931, quoted by Cole, p. 10, n. 7 and in *Sixty Drawings by Henri Gaudier-Brzeska*, Mercury Gallery, 1975, n. p.

4. B. S. Ching to H. S. Ede, 7.1.29 (Kettle's Yard). Gaudier worked for Fifoot, Ching & Co. for six months from late September 1908 to March 1909.

5. He wrote his parents on 20.4.09 that he had arrived 'after three days of continual travelling' and that he had sent cards to his sisters from Brussels, Cologne and Frankfurt; Ede, *SM*, p. 30. There are sketches of Antwerp Cathedral, dated 17.4.09, and of Cologne Cathedral, dated 19.4.09, in the Kettle's Yard Sketchbook.

6. Ede, *SM*, p. 30.

7. Gaudier to parents, 31.5.09, from Ede, *SM*, pp. 31–34.

8. Gaudier to K. Smith 18.6.09 (Tate Gallery Archive).

9. Uhlemayr to H. S. Ede, 25.3.29, cit. Cole, p. 12, n. 12.

10. *Baedeker's Guide* of 1914 remarked of Nuremberg 'there is no city in Germany so suggestive of the prosperity and artistic taste of a "city of the empire"'. The Altstadt with its citadel was still enclosed by a wall, tower and dry moat, and there was a profusion of handsome sixteenth- and seventeenth-century townhouses.

11. Sketchbook, Kettle's Yard.

12. Gaudier to K. Smith 18.6.09 (Tate Gallery Archive).

13. There were more than 1,800 resident artists. More than 500 students – both German and foreigners – attended the Munich Academy.

14. Thomas Mann, *Gladius Dei*, cited in 1902, in *Stories of a Lifetime*, London 1961, I, pp. 142–44.

15. The first French Impressionist picture – a Monet – had only entered the Neue Pinakothek collection in 1907 and as it contained no paintings by Cézanne, Gauguin or Van Gogh, its contemporaneity was limited.

16. In practice both the Glaspalast and the Secession Gallery showed Realist, Symbolist and Jugendstil works though the Secession artists tended to be younger and their Gallery showed far fewer historical genre paintings than the popular, fair-like Glaspalast. It did not, however, show work by Cézanne, the Fauves or Picasso and repeatedly rejected the submissions of Kandinsky and Klee and even those of the Jugendstil designers, many of whom resigned and left Munich for other cities like Berlin, Stuttgart and Darmstadt where the arts and crafts received more encouragement. Lively as the city's artistic life may have appeared to an inexperienced newcomer, those like Kandinsky who were already resident and who had experienced at first hand its conservatism took a more jaundiced view. In his 'Letter from Munich' in the newly launched Russian periodical, *Apollon*, in October 1909, Kandinsky reported the disillusioned mood of many of the younger artists at the inertia of artistic life: 'Surrounded by deep moats and fortifications artistic Munich seems to slumber . . . the same iron and glass fortress of the Glaspalast, the same blind facades of the Secession, the same sombre, oppressive pomp of the Künstlerhaus. What is more it appears as if the same thousands of pictures are to hang for all time in the Glaspalast and in the Secession, while the Künstlerhaus is still the same chronic wilderness.' M. Makela, *The Munich Secession*, chapter 5; K. C. Lindsay and P. Vergo (eds.), *W. Kandinsky Complete Writings on Art*, London, 1982, I, pp. 55–59.

17. Gaudier to K. Smith, 31.9.09 (Tate Gallery Archive).

18. Gaudier to K. Smith, 8.9.09 (Tate Gallery Archive).

3. Paris

1. Gaudier to Dr Uhlemayr, 5.3.10, cit. Cole, pp. 12–13.

2. Gaudier to K. Smith, 26.3.10 (Tate Gallery Archive).

3. Gaudier to K. Smith, 2.4.10 (Tate Gallery Archive).

4. Gaudier to K. Smith, 3.5.10 (Tate Gallery Archive).

5. Gaudier to K. Smith, 21.3.11 (Tate Gallery Archive).

6. Notebook called 'Le Chaos', 26.8 × 21.2 cm (private collection).

7. 'Un jeune homme – tout jeune et beau comme un ange – (mais avisé des pèches) assis en face d'elle fait des croquis des assistants et de Pleurette [Sophie]. Il la regarde de ses magnifiques yeux dont étincelle l'intelligence. Il lui sourit d'un sourire engageant et questionneur . . . Le jeune homme est fort sympathique et beau. Ses habits sont très pauvres – sol col presque noir de crasse – ses mains sales – mais Pleurette fait semblant de ne pas voir ces détails, l'homme est intelligent – cela lui suffit.' *Matka*, (Orléans) fols. 124–25.

8. *Matka* (Orléans), sections 114 and 122.

9. *Matka* (Orléans), sections 115–23.

10. 'Voulez vous que je sois votre mère – mère adoptée?' *Matka* (Orléans), section116; 'C'est que j'aime Mamus d'un amour complet. Comme femme, comme soeur, amie et Matka – C'est une passion et une tendresse infini', *Matka* (CUL) fol. 135c, d.

11. Gaudier to Dr Uhlemayr, 24.5.10, from Ede, *SM*, pp. 24–25.

12. Gaudier to Dr Uhlemayr, 18.6.10, from Ede, *SM*, pp. 17–18.

13. Letter, 22.6.10, Ede, *SM*, pp. 35–36.

14. Gaudier to K. Smith, August 1910 (Tate Gallery Archive).

15. In the same letter he speaks of 'forming an anti-parliamentary insurrectional committee' and of the need for 'a radical sweeping away – especially of machines, which must be utterly destroyed.' H. Gaudier to Dr Uhlemayr, 4.10.10, Ede, *SM*, p. 40.

16. Gaudier to Dr Uhlemayr, written from St Jean de Braye, 11.10.10, from Ede, *SM*, p. 44.

17. Brzeska also recorded how Gaudier and his father met her off the train – 'un ouvrier fort simple de toilette et de manières mais assez sympathique' – and that Mr Gaudier spoke of Gaudier as 'sapristi de gamin'; on the other hand she and Gaudier agreed they had both done badly with their mothers: 'elles peuvent rivaliser laquelle aurait le prix de monstruosité'. *Matka* (Orléans) sections 134 and 136.

18. Brzeska quotes him as saying, 'J'ai des amis en Angleterre qui m'aideront à trouver une occupation. Ils m'engagent à venir.' She also relates the fear which, he claimed, had haunted him since he was eight years old: 'cette intuition que je perirai à la guerre.' *Matka* (Orléans), section 145–48, fol. 133b.

4. London

1. 'J'ai cogné un peu à toutes les portes. D'abord chez les sculpteurs pour travaux en marbre et pierre puis chez les sculpteurs en bois. Ensuite dans les ateliers des dessinateurs et de fabriquants d'étoffes. J'ai écrit à tous ceux qui annonçaient soit pour dessins de cartes postales, de sacs à papiers – je me suis presenté avec de caricatures et dessins dans les rédactions de journaux. Enfin il n'y a pas de source à laquelle je n'eusse essayé d'accrocher mon hameçon.' *Matka* (Orléans) section 147, fol. 134.

2. Blue-covered notebook, 25.7 × 21.5, about 60 pages with a further 50–60 missing, private collection.

3. Most of these letters are now in Essex University Library.

4. Ede, *SM*, pp. 48–98.

5. *Matka* (CUL) fol. 10a.

6. Sécretain, pp. 130–31; Ede, *SM*, pp. 158–61.

7. H. Gaudier to R. Gaudier, 28.12.11, Orléans, Musée des Beaux Arts, MO 118, reproduced in Ede, *SM*, pp. 113–17.

8. *Matka* (CUL), fols. 61c, 63c (Autumn 1912), 126b (Autumn 1913), 164a (Summer 1914); 'Five shillin', Lay your money down, sir' drawing accompanying letter from Gaudier to Brzeska, 16.11.12 (Essex University Library).

9. Gaudier to K. Smith, 21.4.11 (Tate Gallery Archive).

5. The Breakthrough

1. Gaudier to H. Macfall, 5.1.12 (National Art Library, Victoria and Albert Museum).

2. H. Macfall, *The Splendid Wayfaring*, London, 1913, p. ix. Published with a few bird and animal illustrations by Gaudier, pp. 30, 90, 167.

3. H. Macfall, 'Lovat Fraser', *Hearth and Home*, 5.12.12, p. 268.

4. Bagnold, p. 69. The sitter told a different story in which she rather than he suffered a nosebleed when interviewed by BBC for *Vortex Gaudier Brzeska* (5.6.65).

5. J. Epstein, *Let There Be Sculpture*, London, 1940, p. 134; E. Silber, *The Sculpture of Epstein*, 1986, no. 39, p. 130.

6. Ede, *SM*, p. 206; Macfall twice describes Lovat Fraser as dandified in an article promoting him as a young talent to be watched for his skill at caricature, illustration, toy and book design in 'Lovat Fraser', *Hearth and Home*, 5.12.12, pp. 268–69. Cf. also 'The Art of Lovat Fraser', *Art Chronicle*, 17.11.11, pp. 24–27. After Fraser's early death in 1921, Macfall's *The Book of Lovat*, London, 1923, described him as 'the last of the dandies'.

7. Gaudier to J. D. Fergusson, 12.6.12, Fergusson Archive item 2419 (Fergusson Gallery, Perth and Kinross District Council). I am indebted to Sheila McGregor for bringing this letter to my attention. See also J. M. Murry, *Between Two Worlds*, 1935, p. 221.

8. *Rhythm*, October 1912, pp. 327–31.

9. A small notebook (Orléans MBA 110) contains pen drawings of a series of bacchante-like figures and medallion designs containing portraits of Murry and Mansfield.

10. *Matka* (CUL), fols. 41a–c; Gaudier to Brzeska, passing references in letters and postcards of September–November 1912, especially 19.10.12 and 14.11.12 (Essex University Library); Ede, *SM*, pp. 146–47; J. M. Murry, *Between Two Worlds*, 1935, pp. 227–31.

11. Murry recalled this visit taking place in early 1913 some months after the break-up of the relationship, J. M. Murry, *Between Two Worlds*, pp. 245–49; 'G' was identified as George Banks by F. A. Lea, *The Life of John Middleton Murry*, p. 35.

12. He mentions Hodler, Klimt and Viennese *art nouveau*, speculates on the Czech modernist movement which he has read about but not seen; letter, June 1912, quoted by Cole, *Gaudier-Brzeska*, 1995, pp. 37–41.

13. Gaudier to Brzeska, 14.11.12 (Essex University Library) connects his imminent removal with his intention to carve in wood.

14. E.g. carving after G. F. Watts' *Clytie* (Manchester City Art Gallery).

15. Brzeska quoting a letter from Gaudier in *Matka* (CUL) fol. 63b, in a passage written 3.1.13.

16. Brodzky, pp. 13–18. Brodzky mistakenly dates the meeting to January 1912 instead of 1913.

17. Gaudier to L. Fraser, 7.3.13 (Mercury Gallery).

18. Brodzky, p. 130.

19. Gaudier to Brzeska, 8.10.13 (Essex University Library), reprinted in Ede, *Life*, pp. 171–72. Gaudier had probably met the young painter Mark Gertler through Sidney Schiff.

20. Gaudier to Brzeska, Ede, *Life*, pp. 171–72, and Fabrucci [sic] account books, cited by R. Cole, p. 34, note 31 and Cole (1995), p. 75, where he states the monthly rent was £1 13s 4d. Fabbrucci is the spelling given in London Directories of 1913–14.

21. Brodzky, pp. 128–30.

22. *Matka* (CUL), fols. 126b–127a. Brzeska refers to 'moi qui suis vièrge à 43 ans', fol. 132d.

23. *Matka* (CUL), section 'A mon fils adoptif', fol. 21b (=117b). Kohnstamm did purchase *Amour*.

24. *Matka* (CUL), section 'A mon fils adoptif', fol. 20d (ii 116d) and 126b.

25. Winifred Gill to Duncan Grant, letter 9, 29.12.66 (Tate Gallery Archive) quoted by J. Collins, *The Omega Workshops*, 1983, p. 70.

26. Gaudier was elected on 7.2.14.; W. Baron, *The Camden Town Group*, 1979, p. 57, fig. 3. There is a reference to Gaudier being proposed to the London Group by Epstein, Lewis and others and to the aspirations of Wolmark, Brodzky and Hamnett to be members in *Matka* (CUL), fol. 139.

27. The Contemporary Art Society lent Epstein's *Bust of Euphemia Lamb*, 1908, and a small nude study, *Nan (the Dreamer)*, 1911; see Silber, *The Sculpture of Epstein*, Oxford, 1986, catalogue nos. 13 and 36. The Modigliani carving and a drawing for sculpture were included in the Jewish Section which also included work by Brodzky, Wolmark, Mark Gertler, Jacob Kramer, David Bomberg and Eli Nadelman.

28. W. Lewis, *Blasting and Bombardiering*, London, 1937, pp. 36–37; Cork, *Vorticism*, I, p. 232.

29. Pound, p. 52. Cole (1995), p. 84, cites a variant account by Kate Lechmere of Gaudier giving Pound the 'darling little fawn'.

30. *Matka* (CUL), fol. 152b.

31. *Matka* (CUL), fols. 132d, 133a, 155b.

32. *Matka* (CUL), fols. 162c–64.

6. War – La Patrie en danger

1. *Matka* (CUL) fol. 164b, c.

2. *Matka* (CUL) fols. 165b, 173. Cole (1995) states that Gaudier made his announcement that he intended to return to France during dinner with Ezra Pound, Dorothy Shakespear and others at Lober's Restaurant in Holland Park Avenue on 4 August 1914 (p. 89).

3. The document giving all his work to Sophie was dated 5.8.14 and has now been reproduced in part by Cole (1995), p. 90. As Cole points out this was not a valid will under English law but an 'inter vivos' gift.

4. Hulme was killed in September 1917. D. L. Murray, unpublished *Memoir of T. E. Hulme*, addressed to A. R. Jones, 1956 (Hull University Library).

5. R. Aldington, *Life for Life's Sake*, p. 152. He adds, 'If this had ever happened, I suspect I should have emerged in stone as a prize-fighter afflicted with microcephaly, elephantiasis and superb appendages.'

6. Gaudier to Mrs Hare, 15.10.14 (Victoria and Albert Museum, National Art Library).

7. Gaudier to Wadsworth, 18.2.15, Pound, p. 74.

8. The passage as quoted here is almost identical to the excerpt used by Hueffer, see note 14; 'Vortex Gaudier-Brzeska', *Blast* 2, July 1915, pp. 33–34. 43, The original, together with the rest of Gaudier's letters to Pound, is in the Beinecke Library, Yale University, Y Cal mss. 53 (Ezra Pound Additional), Box 7, Folder 163.

9. Gaudier to Kitty Smith, 2.2.15 (Tate Gallery Archive).

10. Gaudier to Kitty Smith, 6.4.15 (Tate Gallery Archive).

11. W. Lewis, *Blasting and Bombardiering*, London, 1937, pp. 114–115.

12. J. Cournos, 'Henri Gaudier-Brzeska', *The Egoist*, 2.8.15, p. 121.

13. Epstein to Quinn, 24.10.15 (New York Public Library, John Quinn Collection).

14. F. Madox Hueffer, 'On a notice of "BLAST"', *Outlook*, 31.7.15, pp. 143–44.

15. This is a topic of current research by Christina Biélaszka Du Vernay. See C. Du Vernay, '"And Halo Projects from Incision": Ezra Pound's Deification of Henri Gaudier-Brzeska', *Paideuma*, 22, 1993, pp. 115–27.

16. Pound to Lewis, 25.1.49 (Cornell University Library), cited by T. Materer, *Vortex, Pound, Eliot and Lewis*, 1979, p. 63.

17. It was reissued in 1928, 1939, 1960, 1961 and 1970. The 1960 edition incorporated other pieces on Gaudier – the preface to the 1918 Memorial Exhibition catalogue, 'Gaudier: A Postscript 1934', originally published in *Esquire*, August 1934, and

'Peregrinations', 1960. D. Gallup, *Ezra Pound A Bibliography*, Charlottesville, 1983, pp. 17–20.

18. Brodzky, p. 152.

19. Related by Brzeska (*Journal*, 21.1.18) on hearing of Hulme's death which she greeted as good news, so crushed and degraded had she felt by his offer.

20. *Journal*, 2.4.18.

21. *Journal* entries, 1–6. 1918.

22. Ede, *SM*, pp. 177–78; Brodzky, pp. 155–57.

23. Brodzky, p. 160.

24. Brodzky, pp. 158–89.

25. 15.8.22. Victoria and Albert Museum Registry.

26. Quoted in Cole (1995), p. 183.

27. Cole (1995), pp. 109–84 gives the most detailed account to date of Brzeska's final years and includes translated passages from her journal.

7. Myths and Realities

1. Of the 1,000 sheets printed for the first edition, about 200 were used for the American edition and rather less than 500 sold in Britain, since 100 were bound up in 1927–28, and 250 re-issued in 1939; D. Gallup, *Ezra Pound. A Bibliography*, p. 18.

2. Published in *Famous Plays of 1933–1934*, Gollancz, 1934, pp. 369–472, cit. S. Shalgosky, R. Brookes and J. Beckett, 'Henri Gaudier: art history and the "Savage Messiah"', in *Henri Gaudier-Brzeska, sculptor 1891–1915*, 1983, ed. J. Lewison, p. 21. Daviot was a pseudonym of Elizabeth MacKintosh, who is best known as Josephine Tey, author of *Daughter of Time*, another work in which fictionalized history plays a central role.

3. T. Materer, *Vortex, Pound, Eliot and Lewis*, 1979, p. 63.

4. See T. Materer, *Vortex, Pound, Eliot and Lewis*, 1979, and R. Humphries, 'Demon Pantechnicon Driver: Pound in the London Vortex, 1908–1920', in *Pound's Artists: Ezra Pound and the Visual Arts in London, Paris and Italy*, London, Tate Gallery, 1985, p. 53.

5. Undated letter (Essex University Library), reprinted in Ede, *SM*, pp. 208–9.

6. H. Vollmer, *Allgemeines Lexikon der bildenden Künstler des 20. Jahrhunderts*, 1955 (re-issued 1992), 2, p. 209, states that his father was French and his mother Polish.

7. Brodzky was the probable author; *Colour*, July 1915, p. 226.

8. Macfall to H. Brodzky, 1.9.19 (National Art Library); Gaudier is again described as 'of French and Polish stock' by Macfall in *The Book of Lovat*, 1923, p. 52.

9. 'His mind was intensely French in its crystalline hardness, but all his thought's hardness could not hide the latent temperament of a Pole', J. Cournos, 'Henri Gaudier-Brzeska', *The Egoist*, 2.8.15, p. 121; 'The real genius of the group . . . was Henri Gaudier-Brrzeska, a Franco-Pole', in 'New Tendencies in English Painting and Sculpture', *The Seven Arts*, October, 1917, p. 772.

10. Brodzky, 1933, pp. 11–12.

11. Pound, p. 76.

12. Pound, p. 71.

13. Pound, p. 47.

14. Brodzky, pp. 23–24. See also the obituary in *Colour*, July 1915, p. 226.

15. Ede, *SM*, p. 34; Sécretain, p. 31.

16. *Matka* (CUL) fol. 10a.

17. C. Norman, *The Case of Ezra Pound*, New York, 1948, p. 17.

18. D. Goldring, *Odd Man Out. The Autobiography of a 'Propaganda Novelist'*, London, 1935, p. 100, quoted by Cork, *Vorticism*, p. 23. Posturing of one kind or another was common among those who defined themselves as leaders of the new poetry, painting and sculpture and has been suggested as a defining characteristic by L. Tickner, 'Now and Then: the *Hieratic Head of Ezra Pound*', *Oxford Art Journal*, 16.2.93, p. 59.

19. 'A pallid and thin young man,
A haggard and lank young man,
A greenery-yallery Grosvenor Gallery,
Foot-in-the-grave young man!'
(Gilbert and Sullivan, *Patience*).

The Grosvenor Gallery was the favoured exhibiting gallery of members of the Aesthetic Movement of the 1890s.

20. Paris, Musée National d'Art Moderne.

21. Bristol Sketchbook, Kettle's Yard.

22. See above pp. 22–24.

23. Ede, *SM*, pp. 37–41.

24. Pound, pp. 47, 74.

25. *Matka* (CUL) fol. 1c.

26. R. Aldington, *Life for Life's Sake*, London, 1941, p. 151.

27. Brodzky, pp. 78–79.

28. *Matka* (CUL) fol. 76c.

29. Pound, p. 44.

30. R. Aldington, 'Blast', *The Egoist*, 15.7.14, p. 272.

31. Brodzky, pp. 56–58.

32. *Matka* (CUL) fol. 79d, paraphrased by Ede, *SM*, pp. 233–34. Ede thought the name 'deliciously apropos'.

33. J. Middleton Murry, *Between Two Worlds*, London 1935, p. 223.

34. Pound, p. 45.

35. Brodzky, pp. 15–16.

36. E. Bagnold, *Enid Bagnold's Autobiography (from 1889)*, London, 1969, p. 66.

37. Bagnold, p. 68.

38. Pound, pp. 76–77.

39. J. Epstein, *Let There Be Sculpture*, 1940, p. 58.

40. A. Haskell, *The Sculptor Speaks*, 1931, pp. 133–34.

41. For Pound's belated appreciation of Gaudier's naturalistic works see T. Materer, 'Henri Gaudier's "Three Ninas"', *Paideuma*, 4, 1975, pp. 323–34.

42. R. Fry, 'Gaudier-Brzeska', *Burlington Magazine*, XXIX, 1916, pp. 209–10.

43. H. Macfall to H. Brodzky, 2.10.19 (National Art Library).

44. H. Macfall to H. Brodzky, 1.9, 6.9, 2.10 and 21.10.19 (National Art Library).

45. Brodzky, 'Henri Gaudier', 1919 draft, p. 3, Henry Ransom Humanities Research Center, University of Austin, Texas; Brodzky, p. 88.

46. S. Shalgosky, R. Brookes and J. Beckett usefully discuss the construction of Gaudier as an 'artistic subject' through these texts in 'Henri Gaudier: art history and the "Savage Messiah"', *Henri Gaudier-Brzeska*, Cambridge, 1983, pp. 21–28.

47. For Ede's acquisition of this material see also Cole (1995), pp. 203–27.

48. Ede, *Life*, Preface.

49. Ede, *Life*, p. 2; Sécretain, p. 16; Cole, p. 12; Lewison, p. 31; Beckett, p. 25. Tickner is alone in pointing out their equivocal status, p. 58, n. 40. Cole (1995), pp. 17, 109, refers to Brzeska's planned book as a history of her family and the section after Gaudier's death as both journal and diary.

50. Wade, A. (ed.), *The Letters of W. B. Yeats*, London 1973, p. 782.

51. A description of Brzeska's thwarted attempts at friendship with the artist 'George' Banks, whom she had met at Dan Rider's Bookshop during the summer of 1913, ends with the comment that now, in January 1914, she would know better *Matka* (CUL) fol. 86b(/). Later her account of Pound's offer to place one of her stories, 'Héro', in a journal and a subsequent meeting at which he regrets he can no longer do so, events which she places in December 1913, were actually written when Brzeska was at Littlehampton in May 1914 (fol. 140b).

52. *Matka* (CUL) fol. 137a.

53. Gaudier to Brzeska, 3.6.11 (Essex University Library); Ede, *SM*, pp. 92–93.

54. *Matka* (CUL) fol. 139c.

55. A. Haskell, *The Sculptor Speaks*, p. 134.

56. L. Tickner, 'Now and Then: the *Hieratic Head of Ezra Pound*', *Oxford Art Journal*, 16.2.93, p. 58 citing M. Cousins, 'The Practice of Historical Investigation', in (eds.) D. Attridge, G. Bennington and R. Young, *Post-Structuralism and the Question of History*, Cambridge 1987, pp. 126–36.

57. F. Rutter, *Sunday Times* 3.5.31.

58. *Observer* 19.4.31.

59. My translation. 'C'est impossible que notre histoire ne passe dans la posterité, qu'elle ne produise de réaction sur ceux qui ne connaissent que la sensualité basse – la physique. Notre histoire deviendra une légende – une de ces belles et pures légendes qui élèvent le coeur vers Dieu. Cela m'est une grande consolation. Et même si la malice acharnée des Satans ne me laisse bâtir l'oeuvre que je rêve – et inédite – même alors je ne m'exaspérais pas – ayant la foi que notre légende par elle même est déjà un oeuvre pour édifier du moins les hommes qui sont déjà dans la direction du bon chemin.' *Journal*, 5.6.18.

60. *New Chronicle* 30.4.31.

61. N. D. Vaccaro, 'Gorky's debt to Gaudier-Brzeska', *Art Journal*, XXIII, 1963, pp. 33–34.

8. The Shaping of the Artist

1. Gaudier to Brzeska, 14.11.12, Ede, *SM*, p. 191.

2. This group of studies includes six profiles, five back views and three front views; Orléans, MBA, 847, 865, 871, 889, 914, 930–939.

3. Gaudier to Brzeska, 17.11.12 in Ede, *Life*, p. 138.

4. It is very likely that Gaudier knew at least Rodin's drawings of the famous Cambodian royal dancers who had visited France in 1906 arousing great public interest. *L'Illustration*, the popular weekly, had published an article on Rodin's work from the dancers in Paris and Marseilles, reproducing several of the drawings. The magazine was one of those taken by the Orléans public library; *L'Illustration*, 28.7.06, p. 65.

5. Ink and watercolour, 58 × 28 mm, Orléans, Musée des Beaux-Arts MO 147 and 148; two sheets in a private collection.

6. One sketchbook of 29 pages, 230 × 142 mm, with drawings from December 1908 to May 1909, Musée National d'Art Moderne, Paris; another 141 × 231 mm, covering with drawing from mid-1908 to roughly the same period, Kettle's Yard, Cambridge.

7. Ede, *Life*, pl. VII.

8. Gaudier to Dr Uhlemayr, 18.6.10, Ede, *SM*, p. 18.

9. Orléans, Musée des Beaux-Arts MO 140; also MO 123, 141, 142, see Orléans, 1993, nos. 51, 52.

10. *Matka* (Orléans), fol. 130c.

11. Gaudier to Brzeska, 19.5.11, Ede, *SM*, pp. 69–70.

12. Gaudier to Brzeska, 23.4.11, Ede, *SM*, pp. 51–2, and in square brackets author's translation of omitted passage from original letter (Essex University Library).

13. Gaudier may have been attracted to the tightly interlocked figures and vigorous animality of this scene but he was also amused by it, for he used a quick sketch of the composition to illustrate a letter to Brzeska, anticipating how she would scold him for having broken a jug while taking a bath. Gaudier to Brzeska, 19.5.11, reproduced in Ede, *SM*, p. 65.

14. Series of detached sheets, 16.3 × 7.7 cm, Orléans MO 1308–14.

15. Gaudier to Brzeska, 23.4.11 and 3.6.11 (Essex UL), Ede, *SM*, pp. 51, 89–90.

16. 'Dessiner dans les plans majeurs les masses principales dessiner dans les masses majeures les plans mineurs dessiner dans les plans mineurs les masses mineurs et rendre formes en masses mineurs par l'étude correcte et vraie de tous leurs plans.

'Je crois que cette manière de travailler conduit à un détail magnifiquement véridique mais toujours contenu dans un ensemble imposant – faisant pour ainsi dire cet ensemble même.

'La ligne est une chose purement imaginaire – elle ne vient dans le dessin que pour contenir les plans de la masse – recevant la lumière et créant l'ombre. Ces plans convoient la seule sensation artistique et la ligne ne leur sert que de cadre. L'artiste recherchant la pureté de la ligne et y ajustant les plans erre – il ajuste un tableau à un certain cadre et non un cadre à un certain tableau. C'est pourquoi je haïs Ingres, Flaxman et les préraphaélites – et tous les sculpteurs modernes à l'exception de Dalou, Carpeaux, Rodin, Bourdelle et quelques autres.'

Sketchbook, 1911, fol. 14, private collection, quoted by Pound, p. 42.

17. Gaudier to Brzeska, 19.5.11, Ede, *SM*, p. 71.

18. Gaudier to Brzeska, May 1911; Ede, *SM*, pp. 80–81.

19. Gaudier to Brzeska, May 1911, Ede, *Life*, p. 81.

20. Gaudier to Brzeska 3.6.11, Ede, *SM*, p. 87.

21. Notes in the 1910 'Le Chaos' Sketchbook (private collection), and Ede, *Life*, pl. IV.

22. Ede, *SM*, pp. 37–41.

23. Gustave Hervé, a leading syndicalist and editor of *la guerre sociale*, propounded vehemently anti-militaristic views. Later, in London Gaudier mentioned with approval that Gaylord Wilshire, an American friend of Macfall, was a leading syndicalist; Ede, *SM*, p. 204.

24. Ede, *Life*, pp. 43–44 with Hardie sketch, dated 3 May 1911, reproduced.

25. C. Péguy, *Oeuvres en prose, 1898–1908*, Paris, 1959, p. 483, quoted by M. Antliff, *Inventing Bergson: Cultural Politics and the Parisian Avant-Garde*, Princeton, 1993, p. 4.

26. Gaudier to Dr Uhlemayr, 4.10.10, Ede, *SM*, p. 40.

27. Gaudier to Brzeska, May 1911, Ede, *SM*, p. 83.

28. *Evolution Créatrice*, p. 7.

29. Gaudier to Brzeska, 24.10.12, Ede, *SM*, p. 164.

30. Gaudier to Brzeska, 28.10.12, Ede, *SM*, pp. 170–71.

31. M. Antliff, *Inventing Bergson: Cultural Politics and the Parisian Avant-Garde*, chapter 3.

32. Kandinsky, cit. D. E. Gordon, *Expressionism and After*, New Haven, 1987, p. 34, n. 68.

33. On the idealism and decadence of the neo-Impressionists, Gaudier to Brzeska, 13.5.11 (Essex University Library), Ede, *SM* p. 60.

34. Three recent works by Kandinsky were included in the Allied Artists in March 1914, reviewed by Gaudier in *The Egoist*, 16.3.14, p. 117, reprinted in Pound, p. 32–35.

35. D. E. Gordon, *Expressionism and After*, p. 33.

36. D. E. Gordon, *Modern Art Exhibitions*.

37. D. Karshan states Archipenko established a studio in Montparnasse in 1908 where Modigliani, Gaudier and others studied sculpture with him; *Archipenko: International Visionary*, 1969, p. 110.; K. J. Michaelsen, *Archipenko. A Study of the Early Works 1908–20*, New York, 1977, pp. 24, n. 11; K. J. Michaelsen in *Alexander Archipenko: A Centennial tribute*, 1986, p. 87, note 3, citing Archipenko in interview to E. F. Fry, 1962. No text of the interview has been located but Frances Archipenko Gray confirms that her father spoke of having known Gaudier and Modigliani during his early years in Paris. Archipenko's school was established in 1912 after Gaudier had left Paris but this would not preclude a more casual acquaintance.

38. Gaudier to Uhlemayr, 24.4.10, Ede, *SM*, p. 25. See p. 23 above.

39. *Woman with Cat*, marble, Dusseldorf, Kunstmuseum, inscribed 'Archipenko 11', exhibited Paris, Salon d'Automne, 7.10–2.11.11, 35; plaster, D. Karshan, *Archipenko; Sculpture, Drawings and Prints 1908–1963*, Centre College, Danville, Kentucky and Indiana UP, 1985, no. 5, p. 15, illustrated; *Mother and Child*, marble, private collection, K. J. Michaelsen and N. Guralnik, *Alexander Archipenko: A Centennial Tribute*, Washington and Tel Aviv, 1986, no. 3 and p. 87, note 2.

40. Lewison suggests a knowledge of Archipenko's *Mother and Child*, 1910 in his discussion of *Female Figure*, *Boy with Coney* and *Crouching Figure*; J. Lewison, Cambridge, 1983, nos. 27 and 76.

41. Recorded in Gaudier's *List of Works* for 1910; Ede, *Life*, pp. 192–93.

42. Gertler to Carrington, 24.9.12, N. Carrington (ed.), *Mark Gertler. Selected Letters*, London, 1965, p. 47.

9. Gaudier the Modeller

1. Gaudier to Macfall, 15.1.12 (National Art Library, Victoria and Albert Museum).

2. Sir Anthony Lousada in a letter to the author, February 1993.

3. Sketchbook 'Le Chaos', 26.8 × 20.2 cm, private collection.

4. Maria Carmi (Norma Gilli), born in Florence, made her debut in Vaudeville, Paris 1912, became a pupil of Reinhardt 1915–18 and returned to Italy to make films in 1919. Later she moved to New York.

5. *Daily Telegraph*, 14.2.12.

6. Gaudier to Macfall, 12.2.12 (National Art Library, Victoria and Albert Museum).

7. *Matka* (CUL), fol. 16c.

8. *Observer*, 13.7.13.

9. 'Non, c'est moi qui lui ai proposé. Il faut que je fasse quelques unes de ces gueules pour rien pour me faire la réclame.' *Matka* (CUL), fol. 14d.

10. Bagnold, *Enid Bagnold's Autobiography*, 1969, p. 66.

11. Ede, *SM*, p. 130.

12. 'C'est un homme d'une cinquantaine – un drôle de mélange d'individu. Plutôt petit de taille – assez proportionné. Malgré le corps bien pourtant une face donnant dans les teintes d'écarlate – pleine et ondoyante – il a l'air d'un grandpapa d'un vieillard presque malgré l'aspect d'un homme fort energique et ferme – d'un echter stranner Officier – on le prend pour un individu bonnace [sic] et pantouflard. Un vieux "paterfamilias" dont l'unique préoccupation et seule tache à remplir serait de trainer une digne épouse à son bras – de n'avoir aucun autre souci outre celui de bien marier ses quatre filles. Assez drôle que ce soit ainsi – il n'est – il ne fut jamais marié.' *Matka* (CUL), fols. 14d and 15b.

13. *Matka* (CUL), fol. 15b.

14. Brodzky, pp. 67–69.

15. H. Macfall to H. Brodzky, 1.9.19 (National Art Library, Victoria and Albert Museum), reprinted in part in Brodzky, pp. 169–74.

16. Leeds City Art Gallery. Quoted in Epstein, *Let There Be Sculpture*, London, 1940, pp. 56–57; E. Silber, *The Sculpture of Epstein*, Oxford, 1986, no. 24, p. 19.

17. *Daily Telegraph*, 8.7.12, cit. Brodzky, p. 106–7.

18. *Observer*, 13.7.13.

19. *Matka* (CUL) fol. 127b.

20. *Matka* (CUL) fol. 15b.

21. Reproduced in colour, Brodzky, *Drawings*, pl. 38.

22. G. Konstam in *Alfred Wolmark 1877–1961, Memorial Exhibition of Paintings*, London, Ben Uri Gallery, 1961.

23. Brodzky, p. 109.

24. In a letter to Dr Uhlemayr in 1910. See p. 23.

25. Ede, *SM*, p. 123.

26. Pastel study of 'The Madonna' in blue, green, red, yellow, orange and ochre, reproduced in colour by Brodzky, 1946, frontispiece.

27. Gaudier to Macfall, 26.2.12.

28. Ede, *SM*, p. 185.

10. 'Do you cut . . . direct . . . in stone?'

1. Gaudier to Dr Uhlemayr, 18.6.12, text and sketch reproduced in translation by Cole, pp. 21–22, whereabouts of original unknown.

2. E. Silber, *The Sculpture of Epstein*, 1986, cat. 40, pp. 20–23.

3. Epstein to John Quinn, March 1912, B. L. Reid, *The Man from New York*, 1968, p. 130.

4. Brodzky, pp. 59, 63, 128, 132; D. Hooker, *Nina Hamnett: Queen of Bohemia*, London 1986, p. 36.

5. There is a charcoal drawing almost identical to but much larger than pl. 54, 50.4 × 37.8 cm, Princeton University Art Museum Acc. no. 48–1004; *Record of the Art Museum, Princeton University*, 33, 1974, pp. 22–23.

6. For example Orléans, Musée des Beaux-Arts MO 638–59, all sheets *c.* 20–20.5 × 12.5 cm, probably removed from Chenil Sketchbook 20.5 × 13.8 cm, private collection.

7. See *Torpedo Fish* (*cat.* 80).

8. S. Sitwell, 'Epstein on himself', *Listener*, 19.12.40, p. 873.

9. W. Lewis, 'Relativism and Picasso's Latest Work', *Blast 1*, June 1914, pp. 139–40.

10. Two virtually identical drawings are Orléans, Musée des Beaux-Arts MO 1099 and 1101.

11. Orléans, MBA 820 and, with reversed pose, 792, 799, 800, 818, 841, 843–45.

12. See also the *Study of Legs*, illustrated in Brodzky, opposite p. 119.

13. Gaudier to Brzeska 3.6.11 (Essex University Library); Ede, *SM*, p. 85.

14. In January Epstein exhibited direct carvings at the National Portrait Society while Gill's first one-man show, consisting entirely of carvings, took place at the Chenil Gallery.

15. The Exhibition took place at the Grafton Gallery from 5 October to 31 December 1912. Gill showed *The Golden Calf*, two *Contortionists*, *Poser*, a *Madonna and Child*, *St Simeon Stylites* and the lifesize *Garden Statue*.

16. Note to Brzeska, verso of photography of Epstein, *Euphemia Lamb* (Orléans, MO 52–6–1): 'I went this morning at 8 to see an exhibition of paintings by Augustus John and sculptures by Eric Gill . . .' He made no comment on the Gills, remarked on John's dependance on Puvis de Chavannes and reserved his main comment for the Epstein: 'une tête de pauvre diable un peu idiot à mon avis, les lumières sont riches.'

17. The same basic compositional elements are manipulated in *Sketch for Standing Figure* (*cat.* 54) and *Standing Female Figure* (*cat.* 53).

18. R. Fry, 'An English Sculptor, *The Nation*, 28.1.11, p. 719; C. Lewis Hind, *The Post-Impressionists*, London 1911, p. 68.

19. Kettle's Yard, Cambridge, cat. 45.

20. Compare the high-relief, Cubistic facetting and interplay of convex and concave which was characteristic of Raymond Duchamp-Villon's animal reliefs for the 'Maison Cubiste' in the 1913 Salon d'Automne: G. H. Hamilton, *Raymond Duchamp-Villon*, 1967, pp. 72–75.

21. Pound, p. 49.

22. Brodzky, *Drawings*, pl. 20, 32, 41, 51, 57, 61; Levy, pls. 36, 47; Orléans, Musée des Beaux Arts MO 440, 761.

23. For the female figure in *Man and Woman* see Brodzky, *Drawings*, pl. 92.

24. Cole, p. 83. Lewison, Cambridge 1982, no. 26 also sees the work as Gauguinesque. J. Dubanton has also pointed out the link with Gauguin's *Manao Tupapau*, 'Gaudier-Brzeska et le Primitivisme', Orléans, 1993, p. 63.

25. Pound, p. 20.

26. E. Longford, *Pilgrimage of Passion*, 1979, pp. 393–96.

11. The Fourth Dimension: Movement and Duration

1. Gaudier to Brzeska, 28.11.12 (Essex University Library); Ede, *SM*, p. 213.

2. Brzeska notes his telling her he had destroyed 'the poor imitation of Rodin's', *Matka* (Orléans), fol. 130c.

3. Gaudier to Brzeska, 24.11.12 and 28.11.12 (University of Essex, translated in Ede, *SM*, pp. 209–10.

4. Gaudier to Brzeska, 3–5.12.12, (University of Essex) translated in Ede, *SM*, pp. 217–18.

5. Brodzky, pp. 79–80.

6. H. Moore, *Henry Moore at the British Museum*, 1981, p. 86.

7. Interestingly Fagg has suggested that the *Deity* represents a female dancer and may have been displayed upright as well as upon all fours. Though it was almost certainly on public display in 1912–14, there is no information on how the figure was oriented. W. Fagg, *The Tribal Image*, London, 1970, no. 80 and frontispiece.

8. Gaudier described the statuettes he was to make for Wheeler as 'the height of your little dancer' in a letter to Brzeska, 28.11.12, translated in Ede, *SM*, p. 210. Studies of Nijinsky were shown at Rider's Bookshop and admired by Lord Howard de Walden; Gaudier to Brzeska 24.11.12, in Ede, *SM*, p. 205.

9. S. Casson, *Some Modern Sculptors*, 1928, p. 98.

10. Duncan had performed in Paris over a period of years. In May 1909 *l'Illustration*, pp. 354–58 carried a story and pictures of her performing. Brzeska relates Hamnett's tales of dancing nude while modelling for French artists and of Isadora Duncan asking to meet her; *Matka* (CUL), fol. 154b.

11. The connection is suggested by S. Fauchereau, 'Gaudier-Brzeska: animalist artist' in *Henri Gaudier-Brzeska, sculptor*, 1983–84, pp. 8–9. There remains some doubt about the accessibility of the collection. The Musée Historique was then in the charge of the Societé Archéologique of Orléans and, though some exhibitions of archaeological material did take place in Orléans from time to time, it was not normally open to the public. Mr E. Moinet, current Director of the Orléans Museums, in conversation with the author, has stated categorically that the collection was not open to the public.

12. Gaudier to Brzeska, 24–25.11.12, translated in Ede, *SM*, pp. 206–7.

13. E. Fenollosa, *Epochs of Chinese and Japanese Art*, 1912.

14. Several such drawings were included in an album of Gaudier drawings from various sources, now at the Center for British Art, New Haven. Several, including 46 and 49, carry the initial NH in the lower right hand corner and this has been identified with a Hamnett provenance; M. Antliff (introduction), *Drawings by Henri Gaudier-Brzeska*, Yale Center for British Art 1987.

15. Cork, *Vorticism*, I, p. 176.

16. See also Ede, *Life*, pl. LII.

17. T. E. Hulme, *New Age* 15.1.14, p. 341.

18. Reprinted in Pound, pp. 136–39.

19. Levy, p. 16.

20. Cork, *Vorticism*, I, pp. 172–77.

21. *Matka* (CUL), fols. 133c, 150.

22. A. E. Elsen, *Pioneers of Modern Sculpture*, Arts Council, 1973, p. 19; see also C. Harrison, *English Art and Modernism*, 1981, pp. 105–6, who sees 'an extreme compression of form such as might be found in certain types of primitive Oceanic sculpture.'

23. A. G. Wilkinson sees *Redstone Dancer* as 'having little in common with tribal art', 'Paris and London: Modigliani, Lipchitz, Epstein and Gaudier-Brzeska' *"Primitivism" in 20th Century Art*, Museum of Modern Art, New York, 1984, vol. 2, p. 444; R. Humphries sees it as 'a transitional piece which, perhaps unhappily, brought geometrical emphasis to a sinuous 'organic' work – as if Hulme's vital and geometric styles were locked in a fight', 'Demon Pantechnicon Driver: Pound in the London Vortex, 1908–1920', *Pound's Artists*, 1985, p. 52.

24. Original draft, Tate Gallery Archive. The quoted passage was not included in the edited version, *The Egoist*, 16.3.14, p. 117–18.

25. My translation from *L'Illustration*, 16.6.06, p. 378 reporting the work of a German archaeologist, Louis Pollak; F. Haskell and N. Penny, *Taste and the Antique*, London and New Haven, 1981, pp. 243–47.

26. M. Perloff, *The Futurist Movement: Avant-Garde, Avant-Guerre, and the Language of Rupture*, 1985, chapter 5 on the Vorticists' ambivalent relationship with Futurism, with further bibliography.

27. Cork, *Vorticism*, 2, p. 232.

28. *The Egoist*, 15.6.14, pp. 227–28.

12. 'WE the moderns'

1. Drawing illustrated in *The Egoist*, 16.2.14, p. 80.

2. Bernard Cassat has seen this feature of Gaudier's work primarily as his solution to the problematic placing of the arms in directly carved sculpture, but this is to see one element in isolation. *La Caritas: Une Oeuvre de Gaudier-Brzeska*, Orléans, 1992, pp. 45–49.

3. A. E. Elsen, *Pioneers of Modern Sculpture*, Hayward Gallery, 1968, p. 37.

13. The Omega Workshops

1. *The Egoist*, 15.6.14, p. 227, reprinted in Pound, pp. 30–35.

2. J. Collins, *The Omega Workshops*, 1983, p. 70.

3. *The Athenaeum*, 17.1.14, p. 97.

4. Cole (1995), p. 77, claims that Fry would only include *Redstone Dancer* if other more saleable pieces were also available.

5. R. Cork, *Art Beyond the Gallery*, 1985, chapter 2.

6. Victoria and Albert Museum E.4979–1919, presented by E. Pound.

7. For example D. Grant, *The Blue Sheep: Threefold screen*, 1912–13 and Vanessa Bell, *Bathers in a Landscape Screen*, 1913 (both Victoria and Albert Museum); J. Collins, *The Omega Workshops*, pls. 6, 33.

8. A preparatory drawing for the *Marquetry Tray* is illustrated by J. Collins, *The Omega Workshops*, pl. 26. Another closely related drawing in pencil, 38.1 × 25.4 cm is at Kettle's Yard; illustrated in *Henri Gaudier-Brzeska, sculptor 1891–1915*, Cambridge, Kettle's Yard, 1983, no. 82.

9. Animal ceramic designs, Orléans, Musée des Beaux Arts MO 590, 591, 594, 595. Several illustrated in Orléans, Toulouse, *Henri Gaudier-Brzeska*, 1994, nos. 87–89.

10. Anthony d'Offay Gallery, *The Omega Workshops: Alliance and Enmity in English Art 1911–1920*, 1984, no. 123, colour illustration; Mercury Gallery, *Henri Gaudier-Brzeska 1891–1915*, 1991, no. 3, colour illustration.

14. Gaudier, Epstein and Brancusi

1. E. Silber, *The Sculpture of Epstein*, 1986, nos. 43–56.

2. P. Hulten, N. Dumitresco and A. Istrati, *Brancusi*, 1986, p. 92.

3. 'A Albert Hall il ne faisait que courir après Epstein et Brancusi.' *Matka* (CUL) fol. 133c.

4. Gaudier to Brzeska, 8.10.13 (Essex University Library), reprinted in Ede, *SM*, p. 247.

5. Pound to I. Pound, November 1913, D. D. Paige (ed.), *Selected Letters of Ezra Pound 1907–1941*, London, 1950, 1971 edition, p. 26.

6. Orléans, Musée des Beaux-Arts MO 137B.

7. R. Cork, *Art Beyond the Gallery*, London and New Haven, 1986, p. 84; pls. 11–112.

8. A Baga drum has been suggested as a possible source for *Maquette for Garden Ornament 1*; see J. Dubanton, 'Gaudier-Brzeska et le Primitivisme', Orléans, 1993, pp. 62–69.

9. J. Epstein, *Let There Be Sculpture*, 1940, p. 70.

10. *Matka* (CUL), fol. 150. At the 1914 London Group show Brzeska teases Wolmark, who is complimenting Epstein warmly on his *Doves*, by reminding him that he had criticized them at the Twenty-One Gallery show.

11. *Matka* (CUL), fols. 148–150b.

12. 'Exhibition at the Goupil Gallery', *The Egoist*, 16.3.14, p. 109. Pound considered buying *Bird Pluming Itself* but Dorothy Shakespear did not like it; O. Pound & A. W. Litz (editors), *Ezra Pound and Dorothy Shakespear. Their Letters 1909–1914*, pp. 323, 333.

13. Cork, *Vorticism*, 2, p. 433; J. Lewison, *Henri Gaudier-Brzeska, sculptor 1891–1915*, 1983, no. 83.

14. *Totem*, *c.* 1913, pencil and wash, Tate Gallery, illustrated in Silber et al., *Jacob Epstein Sculpture and Drawings*, 1987, no. 63, p. 164.

15. Gaudier's Vorticism

1. Cork, *Vorticism*, 1, chapter 4.

2. W. Lewis, *Blasting and Bombardiering*, pp. 107–8.

3. D. Sutton (ed.), *Letters of Roger Fry*, London, 1972, 2 pp. 378–79. Lewis is barely mentioned in *Matka* (CUL), unlike Pound, Hulme and Epstein, who make several appearances.

4. Cork sees Gaudier's relationship with Pound as deepened by his contact with the Rebel Art Centre rather than vice versa. His reading depends heavily on agreeing that the making of *Redstone Dancer* marks the moment when Gaudier 'puts eclecticism on one side and embraces the new geometric art propounded by Hulme's Quest Society lecture'. I see *Redstone Dancer* for all its daring as a far more equivocal transitional work and Pound and Epstein bringing Gaudier into the Rebel Art Centre ambiance. Cork, *Vorticism*, 1, p. 175; and, 'Gaudier-Brzeska et le vorticisme', *Henri Gaudier-Brzeska*, Orléans, 1994, pp. 72–76.

5. 'Have just bought two statuettes from *the* coming sculptor, Gaudier-Brzeska. I like him very much. He is the only person with whom I can really be "Altaforte"', Pound to W. C. Williams, 19.12.13, D. D. Paige (ed.), *Selected Letters of Ezra Pound 1907–1941*, p. 27.

6. *Tiger's Head*, 1907, Ede, *Life*, pl. V.

7. Gaudier to Dr Uhlemayr, 4.10.10, Ede, *SM*, pp. 40–41.

8. L. Binyon, *Painting in the Far East*, 1908; *Guide to an Exhibition of Chinese and Japanese Paintings*, 1910; *The Flight of the Dragon*, 1911 (which Pound reviewed). W. Chin Holaday, 'Pound and Binyon: China via the British Museum', *Paideuma*, 6.1.1977, pp. 27–36.

9. Published in London in 1912 and reprinted in October 1913. J. Cayley, 'Ch'eng, or Sincerity', *Paideuma*, 13.1984, pp. 201–10; J. D. Nolde, 'Some observations on Gaudier-Brzeska's bronze drum', *Paideuma*, 15, 1986, pp. 43–46.

10. Pound, p. 46.

11. Pls. 106–7; study for *Caritas* Paris, Orléans, Musée des Beaux-Arts MO 137B.

12. British Museum inventory no. 1947 7–12.

13. 'Exhibition at the Goupil Gallery', *The Egoist*, 16.3.14, p. 109.

14. J. Cayley 'Ch'eng, or Sincerity', *Paideuma*, 13.3.1984, p. 202, suggests Pound's confident references to the Chou (Zhou) 'seem more than just the professional bluff of the art critic' and sees Pound's interest as having been stimulated by Gaudier.

15. *Chinese Art*, 17.10–30.11.13.

16. *Seated Fawn*, pen and ink, 21.6 × 34.4 cm, Orléans, MO 777; the wet ink imprint of this drawing appears on the verso of another pen drawing of a seated deer (Orléans, MO 783/4), together with a pencil sketch for a sculpture, a crouching figure inscribed within a rectangular block.

17. Brodzky, pp. 58–59.

18. Pound, p. 50.

19. Pound, p. 48.

20. Brodzky, p. 59.

21. O. Pound and W. Litz (eds.), *Ezra Pound and Dorothy Shakespear: Their Letters 1909–1914*, London, 1984, pp. 314–15.

22. *Ibid.*, p. 323.

23. Pound, p. 49.

24. For a more complex deconstruction of this work see L. Tickner, 'Now and Then: the *Hieratic Head of Ezra Pound*, *Oxford Art Journal*, 16.2.93, pp. 55–61.

25. Pound, 1916, pl. 21. Cole (1995), p. 79, claims both Gaudier and Pound called it 'Hieratic Head'.

26. R. Aldington, 'Anti-Hellenism', *The Egoist*, 15.1.14, pp. 35–36; H. Gaudier-Brzeska, letter to the Editor, *The Egoist*, 16.3.14, pp. 117–118; Ezra Pound wrote a rebuttal of Auceps in the same issue (p. 117) asserting that 'Greek work was not a uniform and unattainable perfection, but that out of a lot of mediocre work . . . there remain certain masterpieces to be set apart and compared with other masterpieces from Egypt and from India and from China, and possibly from the south seas and other districts equally remote from Victorian or Pateresque culture.'

27. E. Pound, 'The New Sculpture', *The Egoist*, 16.2.14, pp. 67–68.

28. Pound reported Hulme's lecture to the Quest Society in 'The New Sculpture', *The Egoist*, 16.2.14, pp. 67–68, as did Konody, 'The New Geometric Art', *Observer*, 1.2.14, p. 7; T. E. Hulme, 'Modern Art I. The Grafton Group', *New Age*, 14.1.14, pp. 341–2; 'Modern Art II. A Preface Note and Neo-Realism', *New Age*, 14.2.14, pp. 271; 'Modern Art III. The London Group', *New Age*, 26.3.14. His collected writings are published in T. E. Hulme (ed. H. Read, foreword J. Epstein) *Speculations. Essays on Humanism and the Philosophy of Art*, 1924.

29. T. E. Hulme, 'Modern Art', *Speculations*, pp. 80, 91.

30. *Ibid.*, p. 82.

31. For one recent commentator, 'the Vorticists' interest in abstraction seems in historical perspective no more than a brief, exaggerated interlude, encouraged enthusiastically by Hulme for primarily ideological reasons, but never espoused unequivocally by the artists themselves.' A. Robinson, *Poetry, Painting and Ideas, 1885–1914*, 1985, p. 146.

32. W. R. Sickert, *New Age*, 26.3.14, p. 65.

33. Manifesto II, *Blast*, see pp. 279–82; June 1914, p. 33.

34. E. Pound, 'Vortex. Pound', *Blast*, June 1914, pp. 153–54.

35. *Blast*, I, pp. 155–58, see pp. 279–82; republished in Pound, pp. 20–24.

36. 'Vortex. Gaudier Brzeska', *Blast*, June 1914, pp. 155–58; J. Cayley, 'Ch'eng or Sincerity', *Paideuma*, 13.3.84, pp. 201–10; J. J. Nolde, 'Some observations on Gaudier-Brzeska's bronze drum', *Paideuma*, 15.1.86, pp. 43–46.

37. *Observer*, 8.3.1914.

38. *The Athenaeum*, 14.3.14, p. 387.

39. R. Aldington, *The Egoist*, 15.7.14, p. 273.

40. R. Aldington, 'BLAST', *The Egoist*, 15.7.14, p. 273; F. M. Hueffer, 'Literary Portraits – XLIII Mr Wyndham Lewis and "Blast"', *The Outlook*, 4.7.14, p. 16.

41. E. Pound, 'Affirmations', *New Age*, 4.2.15, reprinted in Pound, pp. 102–10.

42. On 7 March 1914, after the London Group private view, Pound wrote, 'Of course Gaudier-Brzeska isn't Epstein – not yet. Epstein's stuff throws him into shadow, but then Epstein is 20 [actually 11] years older.' O. Pound and A. W. Litz (eds.), *Ezra Pound and Dorothy Shakespear. Their Letters 1909–1914*, pp. 314–15.

43. 'Ultimately Gaudier for sculpture, E. P. for poetry, and W. L., the main mover, set down their personal requirements.' E. Pound to G. Hynes, 1956, cited by W. Michel, *Wyndham Lewis. Paintings and Drawings*, London, 1967, p. 67.

44. For two of the abstract pastels see *Signals* and *Composition*, Levy, pls. III and IV.

45. *The Sketch*, 29.10.13.

46. Cork, *Vorticism*, 2, p. 353.

47. Oil on canvas, 1913, Cologne, Wallraf-Richarz Museum.

48. 'Vortex Gaudier-Brzeska', *Blast*, July 1914, p. 158.

Conclusions

1. Pound, pp. 26–28.

2. Gaudier to Pound, 27.1.15, Pound, p. 60.

3. Gaudier to Pound, 15.4.15, Pound, p. 68.

4. F. Marc to R. Piper, 30.4.10, quoted in R. März, *Franz Marc*, Berlin 1987, p. 5.

5. T. E. Hulme, 'Modern Art and Its Philosophy', *Speculations*, p. 96.

6. N. Jason and L. Thompson-Pharoah, *The Sculpture of Frank Dobson*, London, 1994, no. 7, pp. 19, 27–35.

7. L. Taft's 1917 Scammon Lectures published as *Modern Tendencies in Sculpture*, New York, 1921 (reprinted 1970), pp. 27–28, pls. 55–58, reproducing *Seated Woman*, *Singer*, *Caritas* and *Head of Ezra Pound*.

8. E. H. R. Collings, *Modern European Art*, London, 1929, p. 30 and plate opposite p. 28.

9. The private appraisal occurred in his valuation of Brzeska's Estate, see also R. H. Wilenski, *The Modern Movement in Art*, 1927, p. 163.

10. S. Casson, *Some Modern Sculptors*, 1928, pp. 93–100. Casson pairs Gaudier with Gill as carvers.

11. T. Friedman in *Henry Moore Early Carvings 1920–1940*, Leeds, 1982, p. 21.

12. D. Sylvester (ed.), *Henry Moore Sculpture and Drawings 1911–1948*, vol. 1, revised edition, 1957, nos. 2 and 5, 22, 26.

13. *Architectural Association Journal*, May 1930, pp. 408–13, quoted by A. Garrould in *Henry Moore Early Carvings 1920–1940*, Leeds City Art Gallery, 1982, p. 18.

14. H. Moore, in *Unit One*, 1934

(ed. H. Read) reproduced in D. Sylvester (ed.) and H. Read (introduction), *Henry Moore Sculpture & Drawings*, I, 1957, pp. xxx–xxxi.

15. C. Neve, *Leon Underwood*, London 1974, passim, figs. 46–48, 50.

16. P. Curtis and A. G. Wilkinson, *Barbara Hepworth: A Retrospective*, 1994, pp. 15–17.

17. Hepworth's *Carved Figure*, 1929, cf. W. Gibson (L. Browse ed.), *Barbara Hepworth Sculptress*, London 1946, pl. 3; Arthur Ackermann & Son, *John Skeaping 1901–1980. A Retrospective*, 1991.

18. R. H. Wilenski, *The Meaning of Modern Sculpture*, 1932, pp. 91–92, 156–57, pls. 13b, 14b.

19. E. G. Underwood, *A Short History of English Sculpture*, London, 1933, p. 162. Underwood describes the contrast of views on Epstein: 'primarily a modeller . . . practically nothing English . . . with us but not of us . . . wholly exotic' and Gill: 'greatest carver in the world today . . . in the purest English tradition'.

20. Levy, 1965, p. 9.

21. Cole, 1978, p. 45.

22. J. Zilczer, 'The Theory of Direct Carving in Modern Sculpture', *Oxford Art Journal*, 4.2.81, p. 46.

23. My translation, '*Un maçon*' reprinted in E. Pound, *Henri Gaudier-Brzeska par Ezra Pound*, Tristram, Paris, 1992, p. 241.

24. A. Salmon, *La jeune sculpture française*, Paris, 1919, p. 70.

25. L. Gischia and N. Védrès, *La sculpture en France depuis Rodin*, Paris 1945.

26. M. Rowell, *Qu'est-ce que le sculpture moderne?*, Musée National d'Art Moderne, 1986, pp. 138–39. Brancusi could be seen in the same light; M. Rowell, Foreword to 'Brancusi', *Beaux Arts Magazine*, Paris, Centre Georges Pompidou, 1995.

27. Cole (1995), pp. 200–1.

28. Cole (1995), pp. 223–24, 239–42.

29. M. Menier, 'La salle Gaudier-Brzeska au Musée National d'Art Moderne', *La Revue du Louvre*, 3, 1965, pp. 137–48.

30. R. Sécretain, 1979, pp. 14–15.

Catalogue Introduction

1. Leicester Galleries, *A Memorial Exhibition of the Work of Henri Gaudier-Brzeska*, 1918, captioned illustrations; Ede, *Life*, p. 96.

2. Cambridge, Kettle's Yard.

3. Ede, *Life*, pp. 191–201.

4. Discussing the *Watercarrier* Pound noted that before he purchased it from John Quinn's Estate he 'had the carrier only in London for the few months that the whole [sic] contents Gaudier's studio was crammed into my three-room flat.' E. Pound, fragmentary essay on sculpture, Pound Papers, Y Cal Mss. 43, 3497, Beinecke Library, Yale University.

5. Pound, pp. 128–30.

6. Exhibition contents reproduced in Brodzky, pp. 178–82.

7. Brzeska gave reluctant permission for cast to be taken from the *Torso* (*cat.* 60) she had given to the Victoria and Albert Museum, having been approached by Robert Bevan on behalf of the Leicester Galleries; Brzeska *Journal* 16.4.18 (Essex University Library).

8. B. L. Reid, *The Man from New York*, New York, 1968, pp. 251, 374.

9. Public Record Office, Bona Vacantia, J121/7623 contains items related to the search for next-of-kin and the granting of probate. R. H. Wilenski compiled a preliminary report on the Estate (private collection), now published in Cole (1995), pp. 190–98. It includes twenty-five sculptures: *Wrestler*, *Chanteuse Triste*, *Redstone Dancer*, *Imp*, *Mlle Borne* ('woman's head on stand'), *Caritas*, *Bird Swallowing a Fish* (bronze and plaster), 'Adam and Eve' (*Love Scene*), *Wrestlers Relief*, *Monkeys* ('three figures embracing'), a 'toy flenite' identified as 'abstract design of bird' (*Duck*), 'toy cut brass (*Doorknocker*) and '12 other pieces'.

10. O. Brown to C. L. Stocks, 19.10.26, reproduced in Cole (1995), pp. 205–6.

11. Aitken's letter to the Treasury Solicitor, supporting McKnight Kauffer's offer 13.10.27, and other correspondence (Kettle's Yard, Cambridge).

12. A more extensive account of these transactions has recently appeared in Cole (1995), pp. 203–20.

13. H. S. Ede to C. H. Collins Baker, 2.10.31 (Kettle's Yard, Cambridge).

14. C. H. Collins Baker to H. S. Ede, 5.10.31 (Kettle's Yard, Cambridge).

15. *Henri Gaudier-Brzeska, Sculptor 1891–1915*, 1983, pp. 29–31.

16. Cole, p. 22.

17. The works are *Amour* (*cat.* 35), *Weeping Woman* (*cat.* 36), a marble bas-relief and an alabaster statuette of a *Boy* (*cat.* 34, 61), the portland stone *Head of a Young Man* (*cat.* 44), the *Mask of Brodzky* (*cat.* 41) and a *Head of Christ* (*cat.* 42).

18. *Matka* (CUL), fol. 67d.

19. Gaudier to Dr Uhlemayr, 6.1.13, in Ede, *Life*, p. 155.

20. Gaudier to L. Fraser 7.3.13, private collection.

21. *Henri Gaudier-Brzeska, Sculptor 1891–1915*, 1983, p. 31, nos. 10, 52.

22. Smythies to L. Haward, 1930 (Manchester City Art Gallery).

23. For recent new light on this issue, see Cole (1995), pp. 238–48.

24. The only study dedicated exclusively to Gaudier's drawings apart from Brodzky's short book is F. A. Koslow, *The Graphic Work of Henri Gaudier-Brzeska (1891–1915)*, doctoral thesis Boston University, 1981.

BIBLIOGRAPHY

Unpublished sources

Brodzky Papers, Tate Gallery Archive
Brzeska, S., *Journal* (1915–22) and other autobiographical writings, Essex University Library
———, *Matka* (1910–11) Orléans, Musée des Beaux-Arts MO 93.2.1
———, *Matka* (1911–15) Cambridge University Library Add. ms. 8554 (1911–15)
Ede, H. S., Papers, Cambridge, Kettle's Yard
Gaudier-Brzeska, H. to S. Brzeska, correspondence, Essex University Library
——— to L. Fraser, correspondence, Mercury Gallery
——— to H. Macfall, correspondence, National Art Library
——— to E. Marsh, correspondence, Hull University Library
——— to E. Pound, correspondence, Yale University, Beinecke Library Y Cal mss. 53 (E. Pound Additional), Box 7, folder 163
——— to K. Smith correspondence, London, Tate Gallery Archive
Macfall, H. to H. Brodzky, correspondence, National Art Library
Murray, D. L., *Memoir of T. E. Hulme*, Hull University Library
Pound, E., Papers, Yale University, Beinecke Library

Bibliography

Aldington, R., 'Anti-Hellenism', *The Egoist*, 15.1.14, pp. 35–36
———, 'Blast', *The Egoist*, 15.7.14, pp. 272–73
———, *Life for Life's Sake*, London 1941
Anon. (H. Brodzky?), 'Death of Gaudier-Brzeska', *Colour*, 7.15, p. 226
Antliff, M., *Inventing Bergson: Cultural Politics and the Parisian Avant-Garde*, Princeton 1993
——— (introduction), *Gaudier-Brzeska Drawings*, New Haven, Yale Center for British Art 1987
Apollinaire, G., 'Salon d'Automne', *Soirées de Paris*, 18, 1913, pp. 6–10
Arrowsmith's Dictionary of Bristol, 2nd edition, 1906
Auzas-Prevost, J. (introduction) *Henri Gaudier, sculpteur orléanais*, Musée des Beaux Arts, Orléans 1956
Bagnold, E., *Enid Bagnold's Autobiography (from 1889)*, London 1969
Baron, W., *Miss Ethel Sands and Her Circle*, London 1977
———, *The Camden Town Group*, London 1979
Barron, S. (ed.), *German Expressionist Sculpture*, Los Angeles 1984
Battersby, C., *Gender and Genius: Towards a Feminist Aesthetics*, London 1989
Beattie, S., *The New Sculpture*, London and New Haven 1983
Beaumont, C. W. and M. T. H. Sadler (eds.), *New Paths. Verse. Prose. Pictures 1917–18*, London 1918
Beckett, J., 'Cubism and Sculpture in England before the First World War', in S. Nairne and N. Serota (eds.), *British Sculpture in the Twentieth Century*, 1981, pp. 48–61
Binyon, L., *The Flight of the Dragon. An Essay on the Theory and Practice of Art in China and Japan*, London 1911
Blunt, W. S., *My Diaries: Being My Personal Narrative of Events 1888–1914*, London 1919
Bowness, A., 'Gaudier-Brzeska' in *Gaudier-Brzeska Drawings*, Victor Waddington, London 1966
Brettell, R. et al., *The Art of Paul Gauguin*, New York 1988
Brodzky, H., *Henri Gaudier-Brzeska*, London 1932
———, *Gaudier-Brzeska Drawings*, London 1946
Carpenter, H., *A Serious Character. The Life of Ezra Pound*, London 1988
Casson, S., *Some Modern Sculptors*, London 1928
Cayley, J., 'Ch'eng or Sincerity', *Paideuma*, 13.84, pp. 201–10
Cheney, S., *A Primer of Modern Art*, London 1924
Cole, R., *Burning to Speak: The Life and Art of Henri Gaudier-Brzeska*, Oxford 1978
———, 'A Gaudier-Brzeska sculpture rediscovered', *Burlington Magazine*, CXXXII, 1990, p. 874
———, *Gaudier-Brzeska. Artist and Myth*, Bristol 1995
Collins, J., *The Omega Workshops*, London 1983
———, *Eric Gill: Sculpture*, London 1992
———, J., *The Sculpture of Eric Gill*, London, Barbican Art Gallery 1993
Cooper, D., *The Cubist Epoch*, New York 1971
———, and G. Tinterow, *The Essential Cubism 1907–1920*, London 1983
Cork, R., *Vorticism and Its Allies*, London, Arts Council 1973
———, *Vorticism and Abstract Art in the First Machine Age*, 2 vols., London 1976
———, *Henri Gaudier and Ezra Pound: A Friendship*, London, Anthony d'Offay 1982
———, *Art Beyond the Gallery in Early 20th Century England*, New Haven and London 1985

———, 'The Vorticist Circle, Bomberg and the First World War' in *British Art in the 20th Century*, London, Royal Academy, 1987, pp. 139–40
———, *A Bitter Truth: Avant-Garde Art and the Great War*, London 1994
Cournos, J., 'The Battle of the Cubes', *The New Freewoman*, 15.11.13, pp. 214–15
———, 'Henri Gaudier-Brzeska', *The Egoist*, 2.8.15, p. 121
———, 'Gaudier-Brzeska's Art', *The Egoist*, 1.9.15, pp. 137–38
———, 'New Tendencies in English Painting and Sculpture', *The Seven Arts*, October, 1917, p. 772
———, *Autobiography*, New York 1935
Cowan, L., 'Henri Gaudier-Brzeska', *Princeton University Library Chronicle*, XLVI, 1985, pp. 309–16
Cowling, E. and J. Golding, *Picasso: Sculptor/Painter*, London 1994
Cuming, E., S. McGregor, et al., *Colour, Rhythm and Dance. Paintings and Drawings by J. D. Fergusson and his Circle in Paris*, Scottish Arts Council 1985
Daviot, G., *The Laughing Woman. A Play*, London 1934
Deghy, G. and K. Waterhouse, *Café Royal: 90 Years of Bohemia*, London 1955
Drey, O. R., 'The Autumn Salon', *Rhythm*, October 1912, pp. 327–31
Dubanton, J., 'Gaudier-Brzeska et le primitivisme', *Henri Gaudier-Brzeska*, Orléans 1993
Ede, H. S., *A Life of Gaudier-Brzeska*, London 1930
———, *Savage Messiah*, London 1931
———, *Kettle's Yard: a Way of Life*, Cambridge 1984
Eliot, P. D., *Sculpture in France 1918–1939* unpublished PhD, London, Courtauld Institute of Art, 1991
Elsen, A. E., *Pioneers of Modern Sculpture*, London, Arts Council 1973
Epstein, J., *Let There Be Sculpture*, London 1940
Fauchereau, S., 'Gaudier-Brzeska: animalist artist' in *Henri Gaudier-Brzeska, Sculptor* (J. Lewison, ed.), Cambridge 1983
———, 'Gaudier-Brzeska, la caricature, les futurismes', *alfabeta*, 84, 1986, pp. 86–87
Fenollosa, E., *Epochs of Chinese and Japanese Art*, London 1912
Finch, E., *Wilfred Scawen Blunt 1840–1922*, London 1938
Fletcher, J. G., 'Tendencies in Present-Day English Art', in C. W. Beaumont and M. T. H. Sadler (eds.) *New Paths. Verse. Prose. Pictures. 1917–1918*, London 1918
Ford, F. M., see Hueffer, F. M.
Fraser, G. L., *In the Days of my Youth*, London 1970
Fry, R., 'An English Sculptor', *The Nation*, 28.1.11, p. 719
———, 'Gaudier-Brzeska', *Burlington Magazine*, XXIX, 1916, pp. 209–10
Fussell, P., *The Great War and Modern Memory*, Oxford 1975
Gallup, D., *Ezra Pound A Bibliography*, Charlottesville 1983
Gaudier-Brzeska, H., *The Egoist*, 16.2.14, p. 80
———, letter to the Editor, *The Egoist*, 16.3.14, p. 117 (draft, Tate Gallery Archive)
———, *The New Age*, 19.3.14, p. 625
———, 'Allied Artists Association Ltd.', *The Egoist*, 15.6.14, pp. 227–28
———, 'Vortex Gaudier-Brzeska, *Blast 1*, July 1914, pp. 155–58
———, *Colour*, 1.15, p. 235 (illustration)
———, *Colour*, June 1915, p. 195
———, *H. Gaudier-Brzeska, 1891–1915. A Portfolio of Reproductions*, London, Ovid Press 1919
Goldring, D., *Odd Man Out. The Autobiography of a Propaganda Novelist*, London 1935
———, *South Lodge. Reminiscences of Violet Hunt, Ford Madox Ford and the English Review Circle*, London 1943
Goldwater, R., *Primitivism in Modern Art*, 1938, revised edition 1966
Gordon, D. E., *Modern Art Exhibitions 1900–1916*, Munich 1976
———, *Expressionism: Art and Idea*, New Haven and London 1987
Gourmont, R. de (G. S. Burne, trans. and ed.), *Remy de Gourmont Selected Writings*, Ann Arbor 1966
Gray, C., *The Sculpture and Ceramics of Paul Gauguin*, Baltimore 1963
Green, C., *Cubism and Its Enemies*, New Haven and London 1987
Halliday, N. V., *More than a Bookshop: Zwemmer's and Art in the 20th Century*, London 1991
Hamilton, R. H., *Raymond Duchamp-Villon*, New York 1967
Hamnett, N., *Laughing Torso*, New York 1932
Harrison, C., *English Art and Modernism 1900–1939*, Oxford 1981
Haskell, A., *The Sculptor Speaks: Jacob Epstein to Arnold Haskell*, London 1931
Haskell, F. and N. Penny, *Taste and the Antique*, London and New Haven 1981
Hind, C. L., *The English Post-Impressionists*, London 1911
Holaday, W. C., 'Pound and Binyon: China via the British Museum', *Paideuma*, 6, 1, 1977, pp. 27–36
Hooker, D., *Nina Hamnett: Queen of Bohemia*, London 1986

Hueffer, F. M., 'Literary Portraits – XLIII Mr Wyndham Lewis and "Blast"', *The Outlook*, 4.7.14, p. 16

———, 'On a notice of "BLAST"', *Outlook*, 31.7.15, pp. 143–44

———, 'Henri Gaudier: The Story of a Low Tea-shop', *English Review*, 29, 1919, pp. 297–304

Hulme, T. E., 'Modern Art I. The Grafton Group', *The New Age*, 15.1.14, pp. 341–42

———, 'Modern Art II. A Preface Note and Neo-Realism', *The New Age*, 14.2.14

———, 'Contemporary Drawings', *The New Age*, 2.4.14, p. 688

———, 'Modern Art III. The London Group', *The New Age*, 16.3.14

———, (H. Read, ed., J. Epstein, Foreword) *Speculations: Essays on Humanism and the Philosophy of Art*, London 1924

——— (S. L. Hynes, ed.), *Further Speculations by T. E. Hulme*, Minnesota 1955

Hulten, P., N. Dumitresco and A. Istrati, *Brancusi*, Paris 1986

Humphries, R., 'Demon Pantechnicon Driver: Pound in the London Vortex, 1908–1920' in *Pound's Artists: Ezra Pound and the Visual Arts in London, Paris and Italy*, London, Tate Gallery 1985

Hynes, S., *A War Imagined: The First World War and English Culture*, London 1990

James, P. (ed.), *Henry Moore on Sculpture*, London 1966

Jason, N. and L. Thompson-Pharoah, *The Sculpture of Frank Dobson*, London 1994

Jepson, E., *Memories of an Edwardian and Neo-Georgian*, London 1937

Kandinsky, W. (K. C. Lindsay and P. Vergo, eds.), *W. Kandinsky Complete Writings on Art*, 2 vols, London 1982

———, and F. Marc (eds.), *The Blaue Reiter Almanac*, New York 1974

———, (M. T. H. Sadler, introduction) *Concerning the Spiritual in Art*, London, 1977

Karshan, D., *Alexander Archipenko. International Visionary*, Washington 1969

———, *Alexander Archipenko. Fifty Creative Years*, New York 1970

———, *Alexander Archipenko. Sculpture and Graphic Art*, Tübingen 1974

Koslow, F., 'The Evolution of Henri Gaudier-Brzeska's Boston *Wrestlers* Relief', *Bulletin of Boston Museum of Fine Arts*, 1981, pp. 38–49

———, 'Gaudier-Brzeska's Nudes', *The Print Collector's Newsletter*, XVII, 1986, pp. 82–86

Lea, F. A., *The Life of John Middleton Murry*, London 1959

Levy, M., *Henri Gaudier-Brzeska: Drawings and Sculpture*, New York 1965

Lewis, W., *Blasting and Bombardiering*, London 1937

———, (ed.), *Blast*, 1914–15, reprinted Santa Barbara, 1981

Lewison, J. (ed.), *Henri Gaudier-Brzeska, Sculptor 1891–1915*, Cambridge 1983

———, 'Gaudier-Brzeska's "Weeping Woman"', *Burlington Magazine*, CXXIX, 1987, pp. 243–44

MacCarthy, D., 'The Art-Quake of 1910', *Listener*, 1.2.45, pp. 123–24, 129

Macfall, H., 'The Art of Lovat Fraser', *Art Chronicle*, 17.11.11, pp. 24–27

———, 'Lovat Fraser', *Health and Home*, 5.12.12, p. 268

———, *The Splendid Wayfaring*, London 1913

———, *The Book of Lovat*, London 1923

Magid, D. M., 'Notes on Brancusi and the London Salon', *Art Journal*, XXXV, 1975/6, pp. 105–6

Makela, M., *The Munich Secession*, Princeton 1990

Mangeot, J. A., *"Benjamin Franklin": Petite Histoire d'un Grand Lycée*, Orléans n.d.

Maryon, H., *Modern Sculpture: Its Methods and Ideals*, London 1933

Materer, T., 'Henri Gaudier's "Three Ninas"', *Paideuma*, 4, 1975, pp. 323–24

———, *Vortex, Pound, Eliot and Lewis*, Ithaca and London 1979

———, 'From Henry James to Ezra Pound: John Quinn and the Art of patronage', *Paideuma*, 17, 1, 1988, pp. 47–68

McGregor, S., 'J. D. Fergusson and the periodical *Rhythm*', in E. Cuming, et al., *Colour, Rhythm and Dance*, Scottish Arts Council 1985

Ménier, M., 'La Salle Gaudier-Brzeska au Musée National d'Art Moderne', *La Revue du Louvre*, 3, 1965, pp. 1–11

———, R. Cork, G. Dubanton et al., *Henri Gaudier-Brzeska*, Orléans and Toulouse, 1993

Meyers, J., *The Enemy: A Biography of Wyndham Lewis*, London and Henley 1980

Michaelsen, K. J., *Archipenko. A Study of the Early Works 1908–1920*, New York 1977

Michel, W., *Wyndham Lewis. Paintings and Drawings*, London 1967

——— and C. J. Fox, *Wyndham Lewis on Art*, London 1969

Miller, S., *Constantin Brancusi: A Survey of His Work*, Oxford, 1995

Moore, H., *Henry Moore at the British Museum*, London 1981

Murry, J. M., *Between Two Worlds*, London 1935

Nairne, S. and N. Serota (eds.), *British Sculpture in the Twentieth Century*, Whitechapel Art Gallery, London 1981

Nolde, J. D., 'Some observations on Gaudier-Brzeska's bronze drum', *Paideuma*, 15.86, pp. 43–46

Norman, C., *The Case for Ezra Pound*, New York 1948

Paige, D. D. (ed.), *The Selected Letters of Ezra Pound 1907–1941*, London 1971

Palmer, J. W. (introduction), *Henri Gaudier-Brzeska. Sculpture, Pastels and Drawings*, Arts Council, 1955–56

Perloff, M., *The Futurist Moment*, Chicago and London 1986

Pollock, G., 'Artists, Mythologies and Media: Genius, Madness and Art History', *Screen*, 21, 3, 1980, pp. 57–96

Pound, E., 'The New Sculpture', *The Egoist*, 16.2.14, pp. 67–68

———, 'Affirmations. V. Gaudier-Brzeska', *New Age*, 4.2.15

———, *Gaudier-Brzeska. A Memoir*, London and New York 1916

———, introduction to *A Memorial Exhibition of the Work of Henri Gaudier-Brzeska*, London, Leicester Galleries no. 259, 1918

———, *Henri Gaudier-Brzeska con un manifesto vorticista*, Milan 1957

———, R. de Gourmont, M. Ménier, F. Koslow Miller, *Henri Gaudier-Brzeska par Ezra Pound*, Toulouse, 1992

Pound, O. and A. W. Litz, *Ezra Pound and Dorothy Shakespear Their Letters 1909–1914*, London 1984

Raynal, M., *Alexander Archipenko*, Rome 1923

Rewald, J., *Maillol*, London, Paris and New York 1939

Robinson, A., *Poetry, Painting and Ideas 1885–1914*, London and Basingstoke 1985

Rosenblum, R., *Cubism and Twentieth Century Art*, revised edition, New York 1976

Rubin, W. (ed.), *"Primitivism" in 20th Century Art*, 2 vols, New York 1984

Rutter, F., *Evolution in Modern Art*, London 1926

———, *Art in My Time*, London 1933

Sadler, M. H., 'After Gauguin', *Rhythm*, Spring, 1912, pp. 23–29

Schulz, R., 'A Detailed Chronology of Ezra Pound's London Years 1908–20', *Paideuma*, 11, 3, 1982

Sebba, A., *Enid Bagnold: the Authorised Biography*, London 1986

Secrétain, R., *Un sculpteur 'maudit' / Gaudier-Brzeska 1891–1915*, Paris 1979

Selz, P., *German Expressionist Painting*, Berkeley 1957

Shalgosky, S., R. Brookes, and J. Beckett, 'Henri Gaudier: art history and the "Savage Messiah"', in J. Lewison (ed.), *Henri Gaudier-Brzeska, Sculptor, 1891–1915*, Cambridge 1983

Sickert, W., 'On Swiftness', *The New Age*, 26.3.14, pp. 655–56

Silber, E., *The Sculpture of Epstein*, Oxford 1986

———, T. Friedman and others, *Jacob Epstein Sculpture and Drawings*, Leeds City Art Gallery and Whitechapel Art Gallery 1987

Sutton, D. (ed.), *The Letters of Roger Fry*, London 1972

Sylvester, D. (ed.), *Henry Moore, Volume One, Sculpture and Drawings 1921–1948*, London 1957 (revised edition)

Taft, L., *Modern Tendencies in Sculpture*, 1921, reprinted, Freeport, New York, 1970

Taine, H., *Philosophie de l'Art*, 3rd edition, Paris 1879

Thorp, J., *Eric Gill*, London 1929

Tickner, L., 'Now and Then: the Hieratic Head of Ezra Pound', *Oxford Art Journal*, 2, 1993, pp. 55–61

Troy, N. J., *Modernism and the Decorative Arts in France*, New Haven and London 1991

Underwood, E. G., *A Short History of English Sculpture*, London 1933

Vaccaro, N. D., 'Gorky's debt to Gaudier-Brzeska', *Art Journal*, XXIII, 1963, pp. 33–34

Vernay, C. du, '"And Halo projects from Incision": Ezra Pound's Deification of Henri Gaudier-Brzeska', *Paideuma*, 22, 1993, pp. 115–27

Wees, W. C., *Vorticism and the English Avant-Garde*, Toronto and Manchester 1972

Weiss, P., *Kandinsky in Munich: The Formative Jugendstil Years*, Princeton 1979

Wilenski, R. H., *The Modern Movement in Art*, London 1927

———, *The Meaning of Modern Sculpture*, London 1932

Wilkinson, A. G., *Gauguin to Moore: Primitivism in Modern Sculpture*, Toronto 1981

———, 'Paris and London: Modigliani, Lipchitz, Epstein and Gaudier-Brzeska' in W. Rubin (ed.), *"Primitivism" in 20th Century Art*, New York 1984

Worringer, W., *Abstraction and Empathy. A Contribution to the Psychology of Style*, London 1953

Zeldin, T., *France 1848–1945: Intellect and Pride*, Oxford 1980

Zilczer, J., *'The Noble Buyer': John Quinn Patron of the Avant-Garde*, Washington 1978

———, 'The dispersal of John Quinn's Collection', *Connoisseur*, CCII, 1979, pp. 22–27

———, 'The Theory of Direct Carving in Modern Sculpture', *Oxford Art Journal*, 4, 2, 1981, pp. 44–49

Zinnes, H., *Ezra Pound and the Visual Arts*, New York 1980

PRINCIPAL EXHIBITIONS OF GAUDIER-BRZESKA'S WORKS

Unless otherwise stated all exhibition venues are in London.

1913

July *Allied Artists Association*, Royal Albert Hall

October *Royal West of England Academy*, Bath

November *International Society of Sculptors, Painters and Gravers*, Grosvenor Gallery

1914

January *Grafton Group*, Alpine Gallery

March *London Group, 1st Exhibition*, Goupil Gallery, 5 Regent Street

May 8–June 20 *Twentieth Century Art; A Review of Modern Movements*, Whitechapel Art Gallery

June 12–July 7 *Allied Artists Association*, Holland Park Hall

1915

March *London Group 2nd Exhibition*, Goupil Gallery, 5 Regent Street

June *Vorticist Exhibition*, Doré Galleries, 35 New Bond Street

1916

March *Allied Artists Association*, Grafton Galleries

June (?) Dowdeswell Gallery (ref. in Quinn letter)

July–August *Vorticist Exhibition*, Penguin Club, 8 East 15th Street, New York, USA

1917

July–September *The Modern Movement in Art*, Royal Birmingham Society of Artists, New Street, Birmingham

October *The Modern Movement in Art*, Mansard Gallery, Heal's, Tottenham Court Road

1918

May–June *A Memorial Exhibition of the Work of Henri Gaudier-Brzeska*, Leicester Galleries no. 259 (catalogue introduction E. Pound)

1922

March 2–22 *Seven English Modernists*, Sculptors' Gallery, New York, USA

1926

April (?) Brook Street Gallery

1930

November 28–December 13 *Drawings and Sculpture by Some Contemporary Sculptors*, Zwemmer Gallery (catalogue introduction R. H. Wilenski)

1931

April 27–May 23 *Henri Gaudier-Brzeska. An Exhibition of Drawings and Statues*, J. and E. Bumpus, 350 Oxford Street

1933

November 9–25 *Drawings, Paintings and Sculpture by Contemporary Artists*, 36 Bridge Street, Cambridge

1935

An Exhibition of Two Sculptors: Mestrovic and Gaudier-Brzeska, College Art Association, New York

1936

April 25–May 9 *Gaudier-Brzeska: Pen and Ink Drawings*, Zwemmer Gallery

1943

June 26–August 29 *Roy de Maistre Henri Gaudier-Brzeska*, Temple Newsam, Leeds (Foreword P. Hendy)

1952

June 9–28 *Sculpture and Drawings by Henri Gaudier-Brzeska*, Beaux Arts Gallery

1953

July 24–August 8 *Henri Gaudier-Brzeska Sculpture, Painting and Drawings*, The Cardiff Gallery, 62 St Mary Street, Cardiff

1954

October 21–November 24 *Henri Gaudier-Brzeska*, Beaux Arts Gallery

1955

December 7–January 19 1956 *Henri Gaudier-Brzeska. Sculpture, Pastels and Drawings*, Arts Council Gallery, 4 St James's Square, and tour

1956

March 17–April 22 *Henri Gaudier, sculpteur orléanais*,

Musée des Beaux Arts, Orléans (catalogue introduction J. Auzas-Pruvost)

July–August *Wyndham Lewis and Vorticism*, Tate Gallery (catalogue foreword P. James, introduction J. Wood Palmer)

June 26–August 29 *Henri Gaudier-Brzeska. Exhibition of Sculptures and Drawings*, Temple Newsam, Leeds

1957

July *XI Triennale di Milano* (*Head of Ezra Pound* and *Embracers* exhibited), Milan, Italy

December *Omaggio a Gaudier-Brzeska*, Galleria Apollinaire, Milan, Italy (Catalogue, E. Pound, *Henri Gaudier-Brzeska con un manifesto vorticista*)

1958

January *Mostra di Gaudier-Brzeska*, Sala delle Esposizioni, Azienda Autonoma di Soggiorno e Cura, Merano, Italy

1962

March 5–April 13 *Henri Gaudier Brzeska Drawing Exhibition*, Washington Federal Savings and Loan, Miami Beach, Florida, USA (tour includes the Little Gallery, Lewis State Bank, Tallahassee, Florida) Foreword H. S. Ede

October 1–30 *Henri Gaudier-Brzeska*, Leicester Galleries

1964

April 27–May 22 *Gaudier-Brzeska 1891–1915*, Folio Society

1965

October 4–30 *Jacob Epstein. Henri Gaudier-Brzeska*, Tib Lane Gallery, Manchester

Henri Gaudier-Brzeska, Marlborough Gallery

1966

November 22–December 17 *Gaudier-Brzeska Drawings*, Victor Waddington (catalogue introduction A. Bowness)

1967

May 24–June 3 *Sculpture and Drawing by Henri Gaudier-Brzeska*, South Yarra Gallery, South Yarra, New South Wales, Australia

1968

March 12–April 6 *Gaudier-Brzeska Drawings*, Mercury Gallery, 26 Cork Street

1969

Henri Gaudier-Brzeska 1891–1915, Bielefeld Kunsthalle, Germany (catalogue introduction by H. S. Ede and V. Weisner)

1970

July 18–October 2 *Drawings and Sculpture by Henri Gaudier-Brzeska*, Norwich Castle Museum

September–October *Gaudier-Brzeska Drawings*, Mercury Gallery

September 29–October 24 *Henri Gaudier-Brzeska Drawings*, Mercury Gallery

1972

August 12–September 10 *Henri Gaudier-Brzeska Sculptures*, Edinburgh, Scottish National Gallery of Modern Art (Tour: September–October 22 Leeds City Art Gallery; October 27–November 26 Cardiff, National Museum of Wales; catalogue foreword by D. Hale and introduction by R. Cole)

1974

March 27–June 2 *Vorticism and Its Allies*, Hayward Gallery

October *Henri Gaudier-Brzeska Drawings, Pastels and Watercolours*, Maltzahn Gallery

Graphic Gaudier-Brzeska, Princeton Art Museum

1975

October 15–November 15 *Sixty Drawings by Henri Gaudier-Brzeska*, Mercury Gallery

1977

March 15–April 16 *Henri Gaudier-Brzeska Sculpture*, Mercury Gallery (tour to Middlesborough Art Gallery, Towner Art Gallery, Eastbourne, The Scottish Gallery, Edinburgh, Mappin Art Gallery, Sheffield, Bradford Museum and Art Gallery)

September 21–October 29 *Henri Gaudier-Brzeska Sculpture and Drawings*, Gruenebaum Gallery, 38 East 57th Street, New York, USA (catalogue introduction S. Bann)

1978

May 13–June 3 *Henri Gaudier-Brzeska Sculpture and Drawings*, Waddington Galleries, Toronto, Canada

1980

September 19–October 16 *Henri Gaudier-Brzeska Drawings and Pastels from the collection of Ezra Pound*, Anthony d'Offay, 9 and 23 Dering Street (catalogue introduction, R. Cole)

1981

October 7–24 *Henri Gaudier-Brzeska Drawings*, Mercury Gallery

September 7–26 *Drawings and Sculptures by Henri Gaudier-Brzeska*, David Jones Art Gallery, Sydney, Australia (in association with Anthony d'Offay)

1982

February 27–March 25 *Henri Gaudier-Brzeska*, Bohun Gallery, Henley-on-Thames

October 22–November 12 *Henri Gaudier-Brzeska*, Anthony d'Offay, 9 and 23 Dering Street

1983

October 15–November 20 *Henri Gaudier-Brzeska, Sculptor*, Kettle's Yard Gallery, Cambridge (tour: November 26–January 7 1984 Bristol Museum and Art Gallery; January 14–February 19 York City Art Gallery). Catalogue by J. Lewison, S. Fauchereau, S. Shalgosky, R. Brookes and J. Beckett

1984

March 30–April 28 *Gaudier-Brzeska Drawings and Sculpture*, Mercury Gallery, Edinburgh

October–November *Henri Gaudier-Brzeska*, Galleria Peter Coray, Lugano, Italy

1987

February 4–March 29 *Drawings by Henri Gaudier-Brzeska*, Yale Center for British Art, New Haven, USA (catalogue introduction M. Antliff)

May 6–June 6 *Gaudier-Brzeska*, Mercury Gallery

1988

May *Henri Gaudier-Brzeska*, Galerie Centrum, Kraków, Poland

1989

June 14–July 7 *Henri Gaudier-Brzeska Drawings*, Gillian Jason Gallery

1991

September 25–October 26 *Henri Gaudier-Brzeska*, Mercury Gallery (catalogue introduction G. Raffles, R. Cole)

September–October *Gaudier-Brzeska dessins*, Galerie Marwen Hoss, Paris

December–January 1992 *Works by Henri Gaudier-Brzeska*, Princeton Art Museum

1993

June–September *Henri Gaudier-Brzeska*, Musée des Beaux-Arts, Orléans France

October–December, Musée d'Art Moderne, Toulouse France

1994

November 9–26 *Henri Gaudier-Brzeska: Drawings 1913–1915*, Jason and Rhodes, 5 Burlington Place

1995

October *Henri Gaudier-Brzeska. A Sculptor's Drawings*, Peter Nahum, 5 Ryder Street

November 22–December 23 *Henri Gaudier-Brzeska 1891–1915. Sculpture, Watercolours and Drawings*, Mercury Gallery

LIST OF ILLUSTRATIONS

All measurements are given in centimetres, with inches in brackets. Height precedes width.

Figures

1 (half title) *Ex Libris Design with Owl*, 1907–8, pen, ink and wash, 13 × 10.5 (5 × 4). Musée des Beaux-Arts, Orléans

2 (frontispiece) Henri Gaudier-Brzeska. Photograph by Walter Benington

3 *Self-Portrait*, inscribed 'à Mme Hare Noël 1912', pencil, 50.8 × 39.4 (20 × 15½). National Portrait Gallery, London

4 *Study of a Heron*, 20.12.08, pen and ink, 23 × 14.2 (9 × 5½). Sketchbook, Musée National d'Art Moderne, Paris

5 Ornithological displays at the old Cardiff Museum. Early 20th century. National Museum of Wales, Cardiff

6 *View from Bedroom Window, St Jean de Braye*, 1902, 16.7 × 41 (6½ × 16). Musée des Beaux-Arts, Orléans

7 *The Bedroom, St Jean de Braye*, 23.7 × 35.1 (9¼ × 13¾). Musée des Beaux-Arts, Orléans

8 *St Peter's Church, Mary-le-Port, Bristol*, 23 × 14 (9 × 5½). Musée des Beaux-Arts, Orléans

9 *Barn Owl*, 1909, 23 × 14.2 (9 × 5½). Musée National d'Art Moderne, Paris

10 *Drawings after the Parthenon Frieze*, 1909, 23 × 14.2 (9 × 5½). Sketchbook, Musée National d'Art Moderne, Paris

11 *German Street Scene*, 1909, 23 × 14.2 (9 × 5½). Sketchbook, Musée National d'Art Moderne, Paris

12 Peter Vischer, *Self-Portrait* from St Sebald's Shrine, Sebalduskirche, Nuremberg

13 *Peter Vischer, Self-Portrait from St Sebald's Shrine, Sebalduskirche, Nüremberg*, 1909, 16 × 24 (6¼ × 9½). Sketchbook, Kettle's Yard, University of Cambridge

14 *Hüt Harmonie* (Hat Harmony), 1909, 22 × 12 (8½ × 4¾). Copyright British Museum

15 *Studies of Men and Women*, 1910, pen and brown ink on cream wove paper, 22.7 × 35.8 (9 × 14). The Art Institute of Chicago, Gift of Robert Allerton, 1930.333 © 1991 The Art Institute of Chicago. All Rights Reserved

16 Sophie Brzeska (photographer unknown). From H. S. Ede, *Savage Messiah*, London 1931

17 *'Moi je ne suis pas gourmande je n'aime seulement que les petits gâteaux'* ('I'm not really greedy, I only like *small* cakes'), 1910, illustration for magazine, pen and watercolour, 30 × 22.9 (11¾ × 9). Private collection. Courtesy Mercury Gallery, London

18 *A Whitechapel Jewess*, 1912, crayon, 25 × 18.5 (9¾ × 7¼, sight). By courtesy of the Board of the Trustees of the Victoria and Albert Museum, London

19 *Rotten Row*, pen and ink, 25.4 × 38.1 (10 × 15). Courtesy Mercury Gallery, London

20 *Girl with Skirt Blowing*, *c.* 1912, black conté crayon, 25 × 18.7 (9¾ × 7½). Kettle's Yard, University of Cambridge

21 *Self-Portrait*, 1912, pencil, 23.5 × 15.5 (9¼ × 6). National Museum of Wales, Cardiff

22 *Poster Design for Black & White Whisky*, 1911–12, gouache. Kettle's Yard, University of Cambridge

23 King's Road, London, *c.* 1901. Courtesy John Bignell, 381 King's Road, London

24 *Antelope*, ink, 25 × 39 (9¾ × 15¼). By courtesy of the Board of the Trustees of the Victoria and Albert Museum, London

25 *Seated Antelope* (verso of 25), ink, 19.3 × 23.7 (7½ × 9¼). By courtesy of the Board of the Trustees of the Victoria and Albert Museum, London

26 *Profile of Sophie Brzeska and Portrait of Lovat Fraser*, 1912, pencil on beige paper file-divider, height 19.5 (7¾). Musée des Beaux-Arts, Orléans

27 *Lovat Fraser*, March 1912, ink, pastel and wash, 25.5 × 20 (10 × 7¾). Private collection. Photograph courtesy Anthony d'Offay Gallery, London

28 *Katherine Mansfield*, 1912, black crayon on newsprint, 36.3 × 27 (14¼ × 10½). Yale Center for British Art, Paul Mellon Fund, New Haven, CT

29 *Portrait*, 1912, probably of Ewart Wheeler (inscribed 'à mon ami Wheeler'), ink, 25.4 × 20.3 (10 × 8). Courtesy Mercury Gallery, London

30 *The Life Class*, 1912, pencil, 23 × 19.5 (9 × 7¾). Musée des Beaux-Arts, Orléans

31 *Reclining Female Nude*, ink, 25.2 × 37.9 (10 × 15). Courtesy Mercury Gallery, London

32 Drawing accompanying a letter, 31.10.12, present location unknown. From H. S. Ede, *A Life of Gaudier-Brzeska*, London 1930

33 *The Sea Front*, signed 'HGB 1913', pen and watercolour, 25 × 38.5 (9¾ × 15¼). By courtesy of the Board of the Trustees of the Victoria and Albert Museum, London

34 *Stags*, 1913, ink, formerly Eumorfopoulos collection, present location unknown. From Ezra Pound, *Gaudier-Brzeska. A Memoir*, London 1916

35 Excerpt from a letter from Gaudier to Brzeska, 8.10.13. The Albert Sloman Library, University of Essex

36, 37 Horace Brodzky, *Exterior and Interior of Gaudier-Brzeska's Studio, 25 Winthorpe Road, Putney, 29 June, 1915*, pencil, 17.8 × 26 (7 × 10¼). Tate Gallery, London. By kind permission of John Brodzky

38 Roger Fry, *Portrait of Nina Hamnett*, 1917, oil on canvas, 137 × 91.5 (54 × 36). University of Leeds Art Collections

39 *Portrait of Ezra Pound*, *c.* 1913, pen and ink. Courtesy Mercury Gallery, London

40 *Wyndham Lewis*, 1913–14, crayon, 38 × 25 (15 × 9¾). Courtesy Anthony d'Offay Gallery, London

41 *Self-Portrait with Mallet and Chisel*, *c.* 1913, pencil. Musée des Beaux-Arts, Orléans

42 *One of Our Shells Exploding*, 1915, pencil. Musée National d'Art Moderne, Paris

43 Obituary notice from *Blast*, July 1915, p. 34

44 *Self-Portrait* inscribed 'Etude pour un maske de Pik' ('Study for a mask of Pik'), 1911–12, pencil, 28 × 31.8 (11 × 12½), courtesy Gillian Jason. Photograph Miki Slingsby

45 Gaudier carving *Head of Ezra Pound*, spring 1914. Photograph by Walter Benington. Courtauld Institute of Art, London

46 *Horace Brodzky and Sophie Brzeska Seated in the Studio with the Bust of Brodzky*, 1913, pen and ink, 38 × 50.2 (15 × 19¾). Courtesy of the Fogg Art Museum, Harvard University Art Museums, Cambridge, MA. Louise Haskell Daly Fund

47 Design for book jacket for *Matka*, 1912, pen and watercolour on Wulfsberg memo paper, 28.5 × 22.2 (11¼ × 8¾). Courtesy Mercury Gallery, London

Duotone and colour plates

All photographs in duotone and colour are by David Finn, except where alternative sources are given. Details of plates with catalogue numbers will be found in the Catalogue Raisonné, pp. 251–77.

Colour:

ACKNOWLEDGMENTS

The research for this book could not have been completed without the assistance of the British Academy and the Leverhulme Trust in 1992–93. I am deeply grateful to them and to the Henry Moore Foundation who have helped to fund travel and photography. I have received generous support from my colleagues at Birmingham Museums and Art Gallery, especially Michael Diamond and Richard Lockett. My warm thanks to them and to the many people who have in one way or another have helped to sustain this project through all its vicissitudes. Among these are the public and private owners of Gaudier-Brzeska's work who have kindly given me hospitality, access and patiently answered questions, and the late H. S. Ede who gave early encouragement. Museum and library staff have, as always, proved extremely helpful. I particularly wish to thank the staff of the Musée des Beaux-Arts, Orléans for their assistance during my visits, and Gillian Raffles for advice and assistance. Alison Yarrington, Judy Collins and Carolyn Blake have helped with comments on aspects of the text which have been much appreciated. I owe a special debt of thanks to David Finn for his excellent photography, and to Eva Neurath for her enormous commitment and support throughout.

My thanks to: Viscountess Astor; Malcolm Baker, Victoria and Albert Museum; Christine Biélaszky Du Vernay; Sir Alan Bowness; John Brodzky; David Butler, Emerson Gallery, Hamilton College; Andrew Causey; Timothy Clark, Christopher Date and Jessica Harrison-Hall, British Museum; Craig Clunas; Julia Collins, Leicester Museum and Art Gallery; Mrs Pat Denny and Miss Ralph of the Society of Merchant Venturers, Bristol; staff at Doncaster Museum and Art Gallery; members of the Ede family; Mark Evans; Jane Farrington; Serge Fauchereau; Terry Friedman; Dr Oscar Ghez, Musée du Petit Palais, Geneva; Francis Greenacre; Nigel Vaux Halliday; Michael Harrison and staff at Kettle's Yard; Anthony Hepworth; Tessa and Charles King-Farlow; Jeremy Lewison; Professor Walter Litz; Mervyn Levy; the late Sir Anthony Lousada; Lord Lytton; Bernard Meadows; David Ojalvo, Eric Moinet, Katherine Moindreau, Musée des Beaux-Arts, Orléans; Fiona Pearson, Scottish National Gallery of Modern Art; Professor Omar Pound; Mary de Rachewiltz; Gillian Raffles, Mercury Gallery; Lord Rothschild; E. M. Shaw, Bristol Central Library; the late Sir Stephen Spender; Timothy Stevens; David Temperley; Lisa Thompson-Pharoah; Louise Tonkin; Judy Throm, Archives of American Art; Robin Vousden, Anthony d'Offay Gallery; Brian Walkenden; Rowan Watson; Stephen Wildman; Alan Wilkinson, National Gallery of Ontario; David Wynne

Iris and B. Gerald Cantor have most generously supported the publication of the book, thus enabling far more illustration and colour to be used, for which David Finn and I most warmly thank them.

INDEX OF SCULPTURE

INDEX

References to illustrated pages are in *italic*.